P9-BBT-749

MACRO-ECONOMICS

RUDIGER DORNBUSCH
STANLEY FISCHER

Department of Economics
Massachusetts Institute of Technology

SECOND EDITION

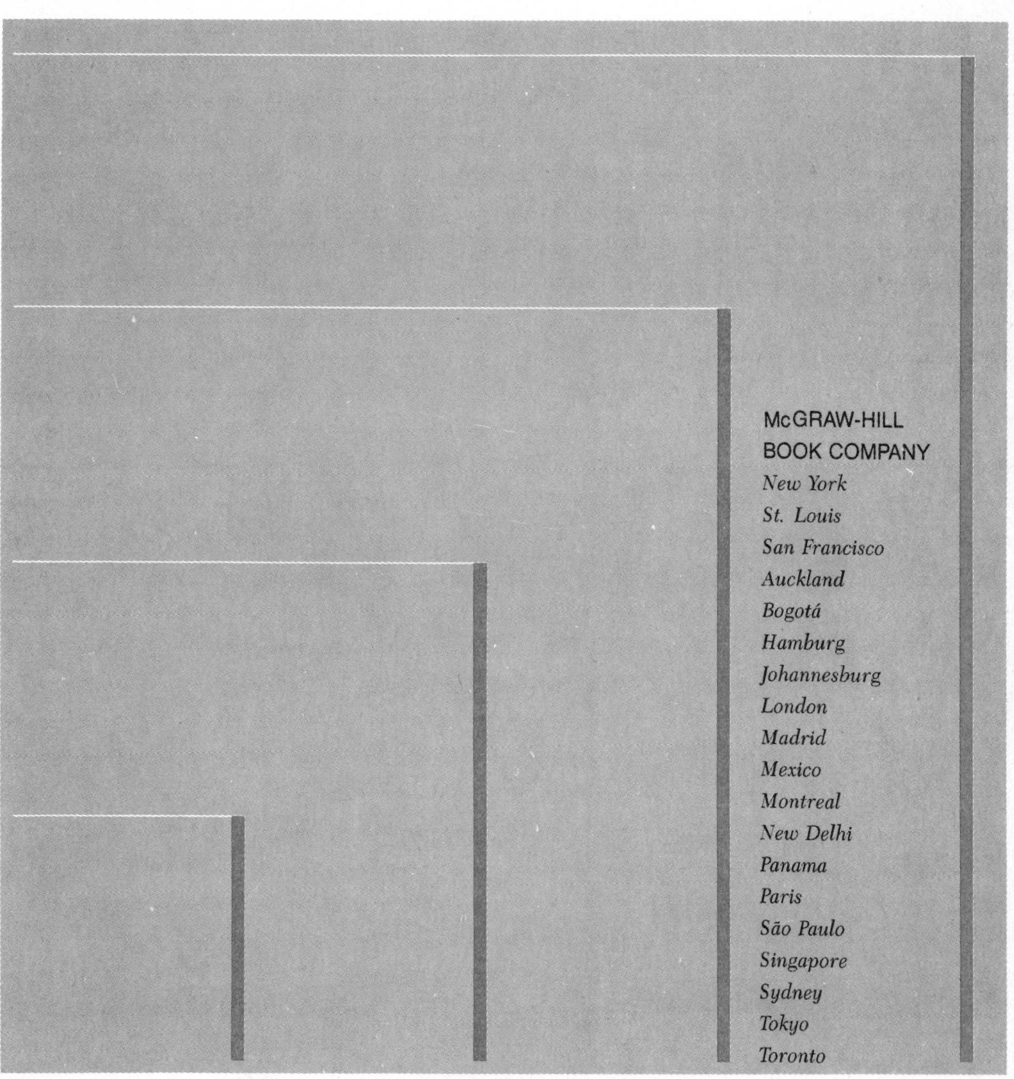

McGRAW-HILL
BOOK COMPANY
New York
St. Louis
San Francisco
Auckland
Bogotá
Hamburg
Johannesburg
London
Madrid
Mexico
Montreal
New Delhi
Panama
Paris
São Paulo
Singapore
Sydney
Tokyo
Toronto

This book was set in Caledonia by Black Dot, Inc.
The editors were Bonnie E. Lieberman and Elisa Adams;
the designer was Joan E. O'Connor;
the production supervisor was Phil Galea.
The drawings were done by J & R Services, Inc.
R. R. Donnelley & Sons Company was printer and binder.

MACROECONOMICS

1 2 3 4 5 6 7 8 9 0 D O D O 8 9 8 7 6 5 4 3 2 1 0

Library of Congress Cataloging in Publication Data

Dornbusch, Rudiger.
Macroeconomics.

Includes index.
1. Macroeconomics. I. Fischer, Stanley, joint
author. II. Title.
HB171.5.D618 1981 339 80-14541
ISBN 0-07-017754-6

To Taeko and Rhoda

CONTENTS

PART IV

PREFACE
TO THE SECOND EDITION

This second edition presents a substantially revised version of our book. All chapters have been revised to reflect the results of new research, new data, readers' comments and suggestions, and our own attempts to improve the text.

There are major changes in the chapters on aggregate supply (Chapter 11) and on the open economy (Chapters 18 and 19). These chapters have been rewritten both to simplify the exposition and to give more space and emphasis to important developments. Thus Chapter 11 deals more extensively with supply shocks, and the open economy section has an expanded discussion of adjustment problems in inflationary economies. The distinction between real and nominal interest rates has been given more emphasis in this edition, particularly in Chapter 13. Chapter 10 has been expanded to include a description and analysis of the Great Depression of the 1930s.

The result of these revisions, we believe, is a text that is substantially improved over the first edition but one that is recognizably the same book. Our overriding objective is still to explain important points of analysis as carefully, thoroughly, and simply as possible, in order to make clear the relevance of macroeconomic theory to the understanding of the behavior of the economy.

We have been delighted with the success of the first edition and are grateful to the many readers who have given us suggestions for improving the text. Since we have been unable to accept all their suggestions, none of them should be held responsible for the deficiencies—we hope they are few—contained in this edition. Among those who have given advice are: Andrew Abel, Elizabeth Allison, Richard Anderson, Francis Bator, Olivier Blanchard, Thomas Bonsor, Cary Brown, Carl Christ, Allan Drazen, Robert Eisner, George Feiwel, Rendigs Fels, Jeffrey Frankel, Benjamin Friedman, Dennis Hanseman, John Kareken, Edi Karni, David Kendrick, David Laidler, Kathleen Langley, Joram Mayshar, Erwin Miller, Frederic Mishkin, Edward Offenbacher, Lucas Papademos, Don Patinkin, Don Richter, Thomas Russell, Walter Salant, Masaki Shinbo, Robert Solow, Michael Spiro, Richard Startz, Houston Stokes, Larry Summers, Peter Temin, and Michael Veall. We benefited, too, from comments and suggestions made by reviewers of the second edition: James Dugan, Michael Edgmand, Hajime Miyazaki, Aris Protopapadakis, and Stephen Van der Ploeg.

A totally revised version of the *Instructor's Manual*, prepared by us, is available on request from McGraw Hill.

A *Study Guide* prepared by Richard Startz of the University of Pennsylvania is now available to accompany this edition. The *Study Guide* contains a wide range of questions, starting from the very easy and progressing in each chapter to material that will challenge the more advanced student. It is a great help in studying, particularly since active learning is so important.

We have once more been fortunate in the assistance we have had. David Modest provided outstanding research assistance and moral support. Carolyn Dedutis did most of the typing.

Rudiger Dornbusch
Stanley Fischer

PREFACE
TO THE FIRST EDITION

Our aim in writing this book has been to explain how modern macroeconomics is used in understanding important economic issues, and to help the reader analyze macroeconomic problems for her or himself. The book provides full coverage of basic macroeconomics, such as national income accounting, aggregate demand, and IS-LM analysis. It goes beyond the standard coverage in presenting also the theory of aggregate supply, the interesting and vitally important topics of inflation and unemployment, and a detailed treatment of basic open-economy macroeconomics. No important topic has been omitted because it is too difficult, but we have taken great pains to make nothing more difficult than it need be.

The book is policy- and issue-oriented, and this orientation is emphasized in a number of ways. Any presentation of macroeconomics and economic policy has to ask why, with all the theory we have at our disposal, recent economic performance has been so poor. We discuss problems of economic policy making directly in Chapters 9 and 15. Then in Chapters 10 and 16 we apply our basic macro theory to study the behavior of the economy in the 1960s and 1970s, respectively. Policy making and its problems are also emphasized by our continual references to economic events, issues, and dilemmas in the postwar United States economy, as we elucidate the relevance of the theoretical material. Finally, policy considerations are emphasized in that a full chapter is devoted to a discussion of the public sector budget and its financing. That chapter discusses not only the facts about government spending, taxes, and the national debt but also considers how the debt is financed, the meaning of the burden of the national debt, and the relationship between government budget deficits and inflation.

Macroeconomics is less cut-and-dried than microeconomics. That makes it unsatisfying if you are looking for definite answers to all economic problems, but should also make it more interesting because you have to think hard and critically about the material being presented. We have not hesitated to indicate where we think theories are incomplete. We unfortunately cannot guarantee that you will not at some future time have to unlearn something you learned from this book, but we hope you will have been warned.

Because the state of macroeconomics is not settled, and because it is so intimately tied up with policy making, the field is often seen as one in which anything goes and in which opposing Monetarist and Keynesian schools contend on almost every point. That is simply untrue. There are substantial areas of agreement among almost all macroeconomists—but it is less interesting to discuss points of agreement once you have understood them than to argue about disagreements. However, we do not emphasize the Keynesian-Monetarist debate in this book, preferring to discuss substantive matters and mentioning alternative views where relevant. Some prepublication reviewers of the book labeled us Keynesians and others called us Monetarists. We are quite happy to be known as neither or both.

HOW TO USE THE BOOK

To the Student:

Because we have not shied away from important topics even if they are difficult, parts of the book require careful reading. There is no mathematics except simple algebra. Some of the analysis, however, involves sustained reasoning. Careful reading should therefore pay off in enhanced understanding. Chapter 1 gives you suggestions on how to learn from this book. The single most important suggestion is that you learn actively. Some of the chapters (such as Chapter 9) are suitable for bedtime reading, but most are not. Use pencil and paper to be sure you are following the argument. See if you can find reasons to disagree with arguments we make. Work the problem sets! Be sure you understand the points contained in the summaries to each chapter. Follow the economic news in the press, and see how that relates to what you are learning. Try to follow the logic of the budget or any economic packages the administration may present. Occasionally, the chairpersons of the Federal Reserve Board or the Council of Economic Advisers testify before the Congress. Read what they have to say, and see if it makes sense to you.

ACKNOWLEDGMENTS

The debts incurred by authors are among the nicest there are, and we are fortunate to have acquired many in a short time. We want first to thank colleagues and present or former students who used the book and/or advised us about it: Richard Anderson, Yves Balcer, Olivier Blanchard, Cary Brown, Robert Bishop, Jacques Cremer, Allan Drazen, Jeffrey Frankel, Paul Joskow, Roger Kaufman, Charles Kindleberger, Mark Kuperberg, Frederic Mishkin, Mary Kay Plantes, Paul Samuelson, Steven Sheffrin, Robert Solow, Charles Steindel, and Hal Varian.

We were fortunate to receive detailed comments on the book from Professors Lloyd Atkinson (American University), Alan Deardorff (University of Michigan), Don Heckerman (University of Arizona), Thomas Mayer (University of California at Davis), William Poole (Brown University), and Steven Shapiro (University of Florida). Their suggestions have led us to make extensive revisions that have clarified, simplified, and sharpened the exposition, and we are very grateful for the encouragement and enthusiasm they have shown. We appreciate also the critical comments on early portions of the manuscript that we received from

Professors Michael Babcock (Kansas State University), Arnold Collery (Amherst College), William Hosek (University of New Hampshire), Timothy Kersten (California Polytechnic State University), Charles Knapp (Department of Labor), Charles Lieberman (University of Maryland), Andrew Policano (University of Iowa), and from some anonymous reviewers.

We have not hesitated to impose on our friends and wish to acknowledge helpful suggestions from Jacob Frenkel (University of Chicago), Ronald Jones (University of Rochester), Edi Karni (Tel Aviv University), David Levhari and Don Patinkin (The Hebrew University), Don Richter (Boston College), and Michael Rothschild (University of Wisconsin).

Stephen Dietrich, McGraw-Hill economics editor, provided us with unfailing support and assistance. It has been a pleasure to work with him and the other members of the McGraw-Hill staff. Carl Shapiro, research assistant extraordinary, Nancy Johnson, and Barbara Ventresco were indispensable in the production of the manuscript(s). Their efficiency, cheerfulness, and willingness to work long hours helped keep us going and are deeply appreciated.

Rudiger Dornbusch
Stanley Fischer

1
PART

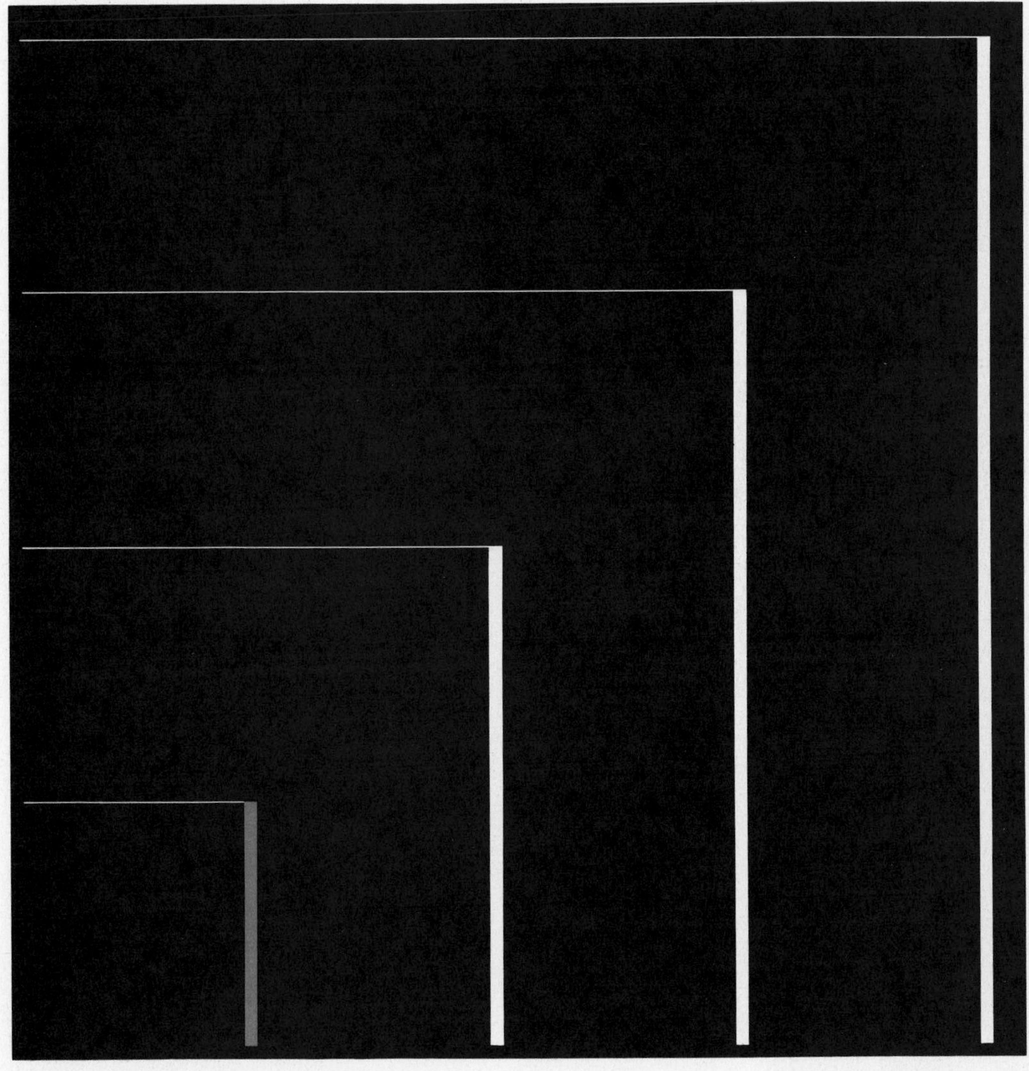

1
INTRODUCTION

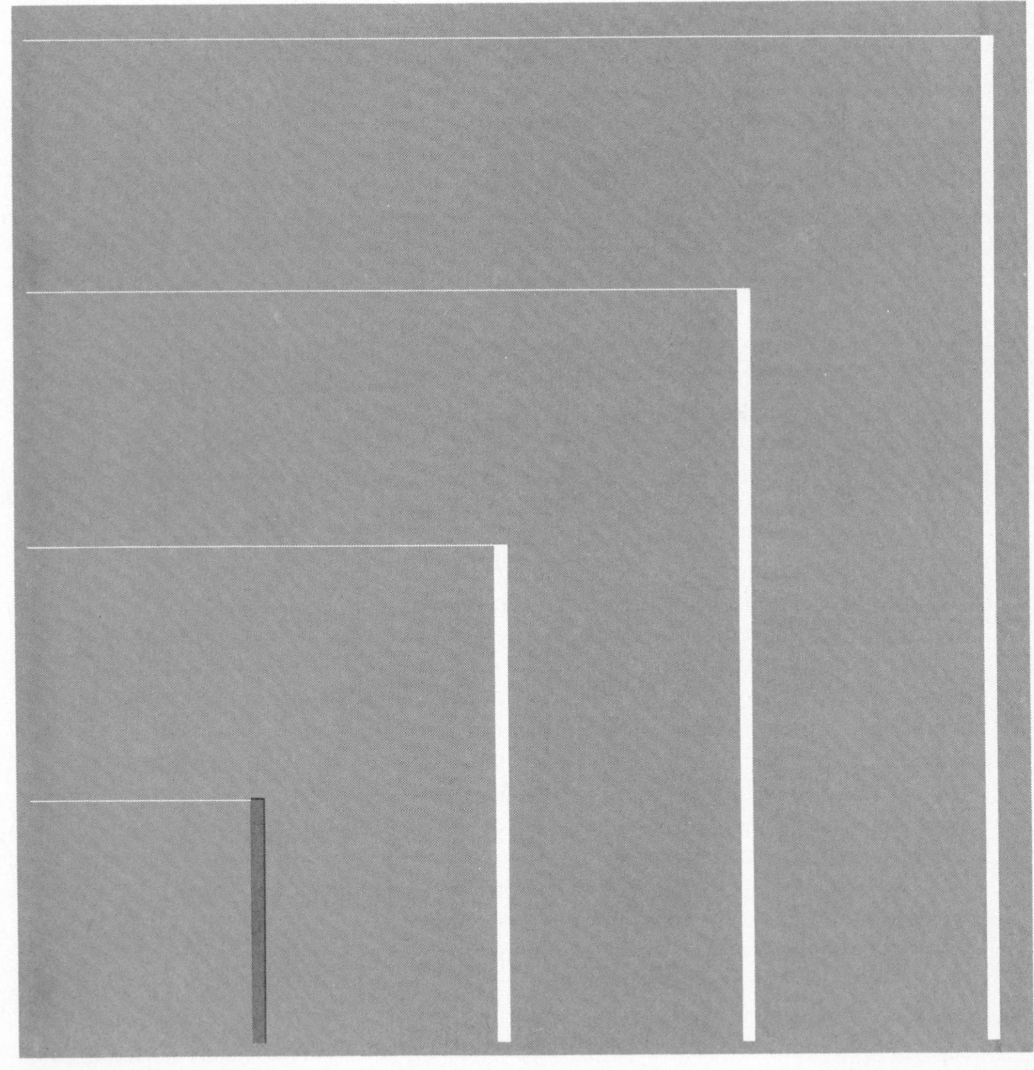

Macroeconomics is concerned with the behavior of the economy as a whole—with booms and recessions, the economy's total output of goods and services and the growth of output, the rates of inflation and unemployment, the balance of payments, and exchange rates. To study the overall performance of the economy, macroeconomics focuses on the economic policies and policy variables that affect that performance—on monetary and fiscal policies, the money stock and interest rates, the public debt, and the federal government budget. In brief, macroeconomics deals with the major economic issues and problems of the day.

Macroeconomics is interesting because it deals with important issues. But it is fascinating and challenging too, because it reduces complicated details of the economy to manageable essentials. *Those essentials lie in the interactions among the goods, labor, and assets markets of the economy.*

In dealing with the essentials, we have to disregard details of the behavior of individual economic units, such as households and firms, or the determination of prices in particular markets, or the effects of monopoly on individual markets. These are the subject matter of microeconomics. In macroeconomics we deal with the market for goods as a whole, treating all the markets for different goods—such as the markets for agricultural products and for medical services—as a single market. Similarly, we deal with the labor market as a whole, abstracting from differences between the markets for, say, migrant labor and doctors. We deal with the assets markets as a whole, abstracting from the differences between the markets for AT&T bonds and Rembrandt paintings. The cost of the abstraction is that omitted details sometimes matter. For example, agricultural price rises in early 1973 had a significant effect on inflation and unemployment, but few macroeconomists had paid attention to the details of agricultural developments before that time. (But they have since!) The benefit of the abstraction is increased understanding of the vital interactions among the goods, labor, and assets markets.

Despite the contrast between macroeconomics and microeconomics, there is no basic conflict between them. After all, the economy in the aggregate is nothing but the sum of its submarkets. The difference between micro- and macroeconomics is therefore primarily one of emphasis and exposition. In studying price determination in a single industry, it is convenient for microeconomists to assume that prices in other industries are given. In macroeconomics, where we study *the* price level, it is for the most part sensible to ignore changes in relative prices of goods among different industries. In microeconomics, it is convenient to assume the total income of all consumers is given and to ask how consumers divide their spending out of that income among different goods. In macroeconomics, by contrast, the aggregate level of income or spending is among the key variables to be studied.

The great macroeconomists, including Keynes, and modern American leaders in the field, like Milton Friedman of the University of Chicago,

Franco Modigliani of MIT, and James Tobin of Yale, have all had a keen interest in the applications of macrotheory to problems of policy making. Developments in macrotheory are closely related to the economic problems of the day. Indeed, the study of macroeconomics does not yield its greatest rewards to those whose primary interest is theoretical. The need for compromise between the comprehensiveness of the theory and its manageability inevitably makes macrotheory a little untidy at the edges. And the emphasis in macro is on the manageability of the theory and on its applications. To demonstrate that emphasis, this book uses the theories we present to illuminate recent economic events from the early 1960s through the end of the 1970s. We also refer continually to recent economic events to elucidate the meaning and the relevance of the theoretical material.

Modern macroeconomics is often seen as the battleground for conflict between two implacably opposed schools of thought—monetarism, represented by its champion, Milton Friedman, and "Keynesianism," or nonmonetarism, or fiscalism, represented by economists such as Franco Modigliani and James Tobin. This view is seriously misleading. There are indeed conflicts of opinion and even theory between monetarists and nonmonetarists, but much more important, there are major areas of agreement: there is far more to macroeconomics than the topics on which monetarists and fiscalists disagree. We do not emphasize the monetarist/fiscalist debate in this book, preferring to discuss substantive matters while mentioning alternative views where relevant.

We shall now in Section 1-1 present an overview of the key concepts with which macroeconomics deals. Section 1-2 presents a diagrammatic introduction to aggregate demand and supply, and their interaction; it gives a very general perspective on the fundamentals of macroeconomics and the organization of this book. Then, in Section 1-3, we outline the approach of the book to the study of macroeconomics and macropolicy making, and present a preview of the order in which topics are taken up. Section 1-4 contains brief remarks on how to use the book.

1-1 KEY CONCEPTS

Gross National Product

Gross national product (GNP) is the value of all goods and services produced in the economy in a given time period. GNP statistics are prepared on a quarterly basis. Chart 1-1 shows two measures of GNP—*nominal*, or *current dollar*, GNP and *real*, or *constant dollar*, GNP.[1] Nominal

[1] Notice that the scale for GNP in Chart 1-1 is not linear. For example, the distance from 600 to 650 is bigger than the distance from 1,450 to 1,500. The scale is logarithmic, which means that equal ratios are represented by equal distances. For instance, the distance from 600 to 1,200 is the same as the distance from 750 to 1,500, since GNP doubles in both cases. On a logarithmic scale, a variable growing at a constant rate (e.g., 4 percent per annum) is represented by a straight line.

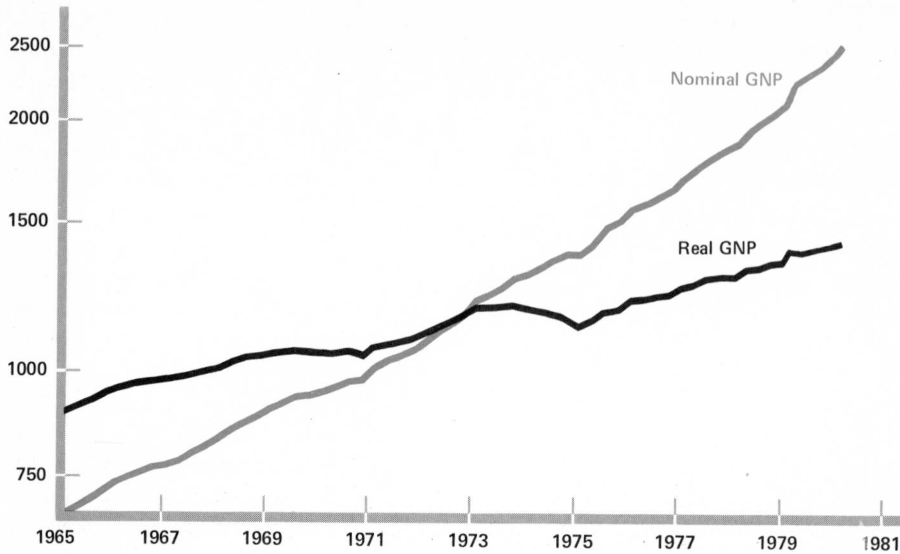

Note: Real GNP is calculated using 1972 prices. The scale is logarithmic. The logarithmic scale is explained in footnote 1.

CHART 1-1 REAL AND NOMINAL GNP, 1965–1980
(Source: Citibank Economic Database)

GNP measures the value of output at the prices prevailing in the period the output is produced, while real GNP measures the output produced in any one period at the prices of some base year. At present, 1972 serves as a base year for real income measurement.

Chart 1-1 shows that *nominal* GNP was equal to $2,369 billion in 1979 and $1,171 billion in 1972. Nominal GNP grew at an average rate of 10.6 percent during that period. If we divide total GNP by population, we obtain *per capita* nominal GNP, which was $10,700 in 1979 and $5,600 in 1972. That is, the average value of output produced in the United States economy in 1979 was $10,700 per member of the population. The chart shows that *real* GNP was $1,432 billion in 1979 and the same $1,171 billion in 1972,[2] implying an average annual growth rate of real GNP of only 2.9 percent over the period.

We will next consider, first, why nominal GNP has grown faster than real GNP, and second, the factors that cause real GNP growth. The difference between the growth rates of nominal and real GNP occurs because the prices of goods produced in the economy change over time.

[2] Why are real and nominal GNP the same for 1972? Because we use 1972 prices to calculate real GNP. You may also want to calculate *real* per capita GNP for 1972 and 1979 from the numbers given in the text.

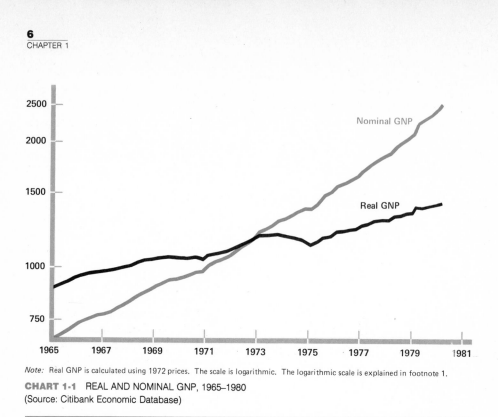

Real GNP calculates the value of goods produced at the prices that prevailed in the base year (1972, in this case), whereas nominal GNP values goods at the prices that prevail when they are produced. Since prices of nearly all goods have been rising, nominal GNP has risen faster—indeed, much faster—than real GNP. Price rises, or *inflation*, at the average rate of 7.7 percent per year for 1972–1979 account for the difference between the growth rates of real and nominal GNP.

With 1972 as the base year for the prices at which output is valued, we observe in Chart 1-1 two implications of the distinction between nominal and real GNP. First, in 1972 the two are equal because, in the base year, current and constant dollars are the same dollars. Second, with inflation, nominal GNP rises faster than real GNP, and therefore, after 1972, nominal GNP exceeds real GNP. The converse is of course true before 1972.

We turn next to reasons for the growth of real GNP. The first reason real GNP changes is that the available amount of resources in the economy may change. The resources are conveniently split into capital and labor. The labor force, consisting of people either working or looking for work, grows over time and thus provides one source of increased production. The capital stock, including buildings and machines, likewise has been rising over time, thereby making increased output possible. Increases in the availability of *factors of production*—the labor and capital used in the production of goods and services—thus account for part of the increase in real GNP.

The second source of change in real GNP is a change in the employment of the given resources available for production. Not all the capital and labor available are actually used at all times. In 1975, for example, a reduction in employment or a rise in *unemployment* showed up as a decline in real GNP. Indeed, in that year unemployment rose to 9 percent, the highest unemployment rate in the post-World War II period. Given factors of production, then, changes in factor utilization change real GNP.

The third reason for real GNP to change is that the *efficiency* with which factors of production work may change.[3] Over time, the same factors of production can produce more output. These increases in the efficiency of production result from changes in knowledge, including *learning by doing*, as people learn through experience to perform familiar tasks better.

Potential Output

One of the key macroeconomic policy concepts is *potential real GNP*, or *potential output*. Potential output is shown along with actual output in Chart 1-2. It is an estimate of the level at which real GNP would be if there

[3] These efficiency improvements are often called *productivity* increases.

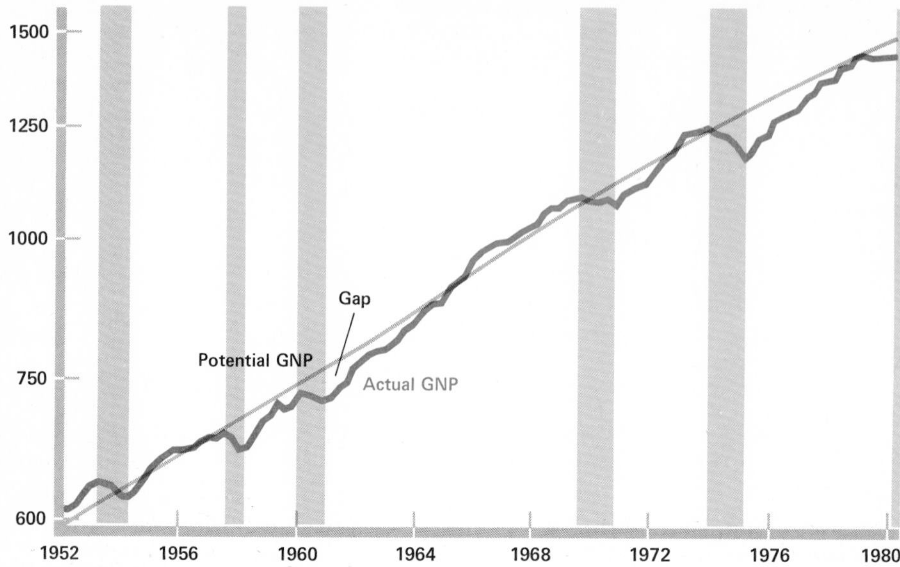

Note: The scale is logarithmic. Actual and potential GNP are in 1972 dollars.

CHART 1-2 ACTUAL AND POTENTIAL GNP (Source: Citibank Economic Database)

were full employment.[4] The difference between potential and actual GNP is called the *GNP gap* and serves as a measure of economic slack or of the waste of productive resources due to insufficiently high levels of employment. As we see from the chart, there are large GNP gaps in the early 1960s and, in particular, during the 1974–1975 recession. More puzzling are the instances of a negative gap—for example, in 1968 and in 1973 when the economy was *overemployed* or in a *boom*.

How do we go about determining the economy's production potential, or potential GNP? The issue is a very important one because potential GNP serves as a guide for macroeconomic policies. The issue is also very controversial because throughout the 1970s, with changes in the composition of the labor force and shocks such as the oil price increases, measures of potential output have repeatedly been reassessed and revised downward. In the 1960s, an unemployment rate of 4 percent of the labor force was thought to constitute full employment. Since the early 1970s, the *bench mark* unemployment rate that is thought to constitute full employment has been revised upward and is now in excess of 5 percent, as shown in Table 1-1.

Potential output increases over time, as seen in Chart 1-2. The growth rate of potential output in the 1960s was around 4 percent per year. In the

[4] For details on the construction of potential output series, see *Economic Report of the President*, in the last few years, particularly 1977.

TABLE 1-1 ACTUAL AND POTENTIAL GNP AND BENCH MARK UNEMPLOYMENT

Year	Potential GNP (billion 1972$)	Actual GNP (billion 1972$)	GNP gap (percent)	Bench mark unemployment (percent)
1960	771.9	736.8	4.5	4.1
1965	925.0	925.9	−0.1	4.4
1970	1,106.2	1,075.3	2.8	4.5
1973	1,227.0	1,235.0	−0.7	4.9
1975	1,302.1	1,202.1	7.7	5.1
1977	1,381.4	1,332.7	3.5	5.1
1979	1,461.1	1,431.6	2.0	5.1

Source: Economic Report of the President, 1978, 1979, and 1980.

seventies, it was successively revised downward and at present is only of the order of 3 percent per year. But what are the sources of potential or full-employment output growth? Potential output, or potential GNP, changes over time because the labor force grows and also because the average output of an employed person grows over time. The typical worker today produces more, in the same amount of time, than the typical worker of 20 years ago. This increase in output per worker is called *productivity increase.* There are two reasons for the increase in productivity. The first is that the typical workers have more capital—machines and factory space—with which to work now than they did then. The second is that there is *technical progress*—workers are better educated and machines are more sophisticated. (Think of pocket calculators!)

Much of the recent history of the economy can be read from Chart 1-2. The economic performance of the Eisenhower years increased the GNP gap as that administration concentrated its attention on fighting inflation. Actual GNP shows clearly the 1957–1958 and 1960–1961 recessions. The Kennedy and Johnson administrations undertook economic policies to increase GNP rapidly, and to reduce the gap, and they were successful in doing so. That success, however, came at the cost of increasing inflation over the period. The Nixon administration inherited the inflation of the last Johnson years and produced the recession of 1970–1971 in fighting that inflation. Then in 1972 and 1973, real GNP grew rapidly under the impetus of expansionary monetary policies of the Federal Reserve. From 1973 to 1975, the economy was in the deepest recession since the thirties. From 1975 to 1979, it recovered from that recession. In 1980 the economy moved into another recession.

Recessions are shown in Chart 1-2 by the vertical shaded lines, as, for instance, from August 1957 to April 1958. Each recession is a period of falling real GNP. The National Bureau of Economic Research, a private research organization, headed by Harvard's Martin Feldstein, provides definitions of periods of recession based on a number of criteria, including the behavior of real GNP. The latest completed recession is indicated by the period November 1973 to March 1975. The recovery started in March 1975 and lasted for nearly 4 years. By early 1979, the GNP gap had declined to only about 2 percent, but the slowdown in the growth of actual GNP set an end to the expansion and made for a widening gap. A recession began in the first quarter of 1980 and worsened substantially in the second quarter.

Growth and Unemployment

Growth in real GNP and the unemployment rate are widely watched as indicators of macroeconomic performance. High growth is viewed as a sign of strength in the economy. High and rising unemployment are seen as signs of weakness. In fact, there is a relationship between real GNP growth and the unemployment rate. Chart 1-3 provides an indication of that link.

We have already noted that changes in the employment of factors provide one of the sources of growth in real GNP. We would then expect

CHART 1-3 THE GROWTH RATE OF REAL OUTPUT AND THE RATE OF UNEMPLOYMENT (Source: Citibank Economic Database)

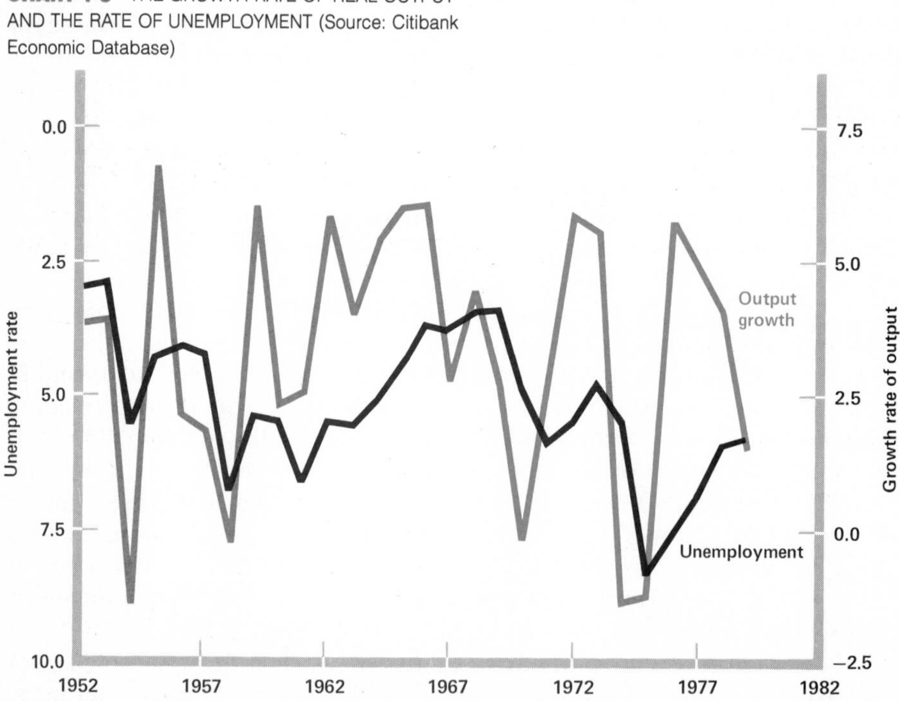

Note: Unemployment rate is on inverted scale.

high GNP growth to be accompanied by declining unemployment. That is indeed the case, as we observe from Chart 1-3. Periods where real GNP rises rapidly, such as the 1960s, 1971–1973, and 1976–1977, are periods where the unemployment rate declines. Conversely, when growth is sluggish and, in particular, when real output actually falls, the unemployment rate increases. This occurred, for example, in 1974–1975, and in 1980.

A relationship between real growth and changes in the unemployment rate is known as *Okun's law*, named after its discoverer, the late Arthur Okun of the Brookings Institution, former chairperson of the Council of Economic Advisers (CEA). Okun's law says that for every two and a half percentage points growth in real GNP above the trend rate that is sustained for a year, the unemployment rate declines by one percentage point. This $2\frac{1}{2}$-to-1 relationship, the status of which is somewhat exaggerated by calling it a law rather than an empirical regularity, provides a rule of thumb for assessing the implications of real growth for unemployment.[5] While the rule is only approximate and will not work very precisely from year to year, it still does give a sensible translation from growth to unemployment.

The relation is a useful guide to policy because it allows us to ask how a particular growth target will affect the unemployment rate over time. Suppose we were in a deep recession with 9 percent unemployment. How many years would it take us to return to, say, 6 percent unemployment? The answer depends, of course, on how fast the economy grows in the recovery. Assume the growth rate of potential output is 3 percent per year. One possible path to return to 6 percent unemployment is for output to grow at $5\frac{1}{2}$ percent per year for 3 years. On this path, each year we are growing $2\frac{1}{2}$ percent above trend and thus each year we take one percentage point off the unemployment rate. An alternative recovery strategy is front-loaded: Growth is high at the beginning and then slows down. Such a path might be one of growth rates equal to $6\frac{1}{2}$, $5\frac{1}{2}$, and $4\frac{1}{2}$ percent, also allowing a return to 6 percent unemployment in 3 years.

Aggregate Demand and Aggregate Supply

The central concerns of macroeconomics are the level of output and the price level or inflation rate. These are determined by the interaction of *aggregate demand* and *aggregate supply*. Under some conditions, employment depends only on total spending or aggregate demand. At other times, supply limitations are an important part of the policy problem and have to receive major attention. From the 1930s to the later 1960s, macroeconomics was very much demand-oriented. But in recent years the emphasis has shifted, and aggregate supply and *supply side economics* have gained in importance. This shift of emphasis and interest was no doubt fostered by

[5] The relation used to be a 3 to 1 law, but changes in the bench mark unemployment rate and revised potential output estimates for the seventies have reduced it to about $2\frac{1}{2}$ to 1 or perhaps even 2 to 1. See *Economic Report of the President*, 1979, p. 74, and the discussion in Chap. 17 below.

the slow growth and high inflation experienced by the industrialized countries in the 1970s.

What are the relationships among aggregate demand and aggregate supply, output or employment, and prices? Aggregate demand is the relationship between spending on goods and services and the level of prices. If output limitations are not operative, increased spending or an increase in aggregate demand will raise output and employment with little effect on prices. In such conditions, such as those of the Great Depression of the thirties, it would certainly be appropriate to use expansionary aggregate demand policies to increase output.

But if the economy is close to full employment, increased aggregate demand will be reflected primarily in higher prices or inflation. The aggregate supply side of the economy has then to be introduced. The aggregate supply curve specifies the relationship between the amount of output firms produce and the price level. The supply side enters the picture not only in telling us how successful demand expansions will be in raising output and employment but also has a role of its own. Supply disturbances or *supply shocks* can reduce output and raise prices, as was the case when increases in the price of oil reduced the productive capacity of the economy. Conversely, policies that increase productivity, and thus the level of aggregate supply at a given price level, can help reduce inflationary pressures.

Inflation

Inflation is the rate of increase of prices. Expansionary aggregate demand policies tend to produce inflation, unless they occur when the economy is at high levels of unemployment. Protracted periods of low aggregate demand tend to reduce the inflation rate. Chart 1-4 shows one measure of inflation for the United States economy for the period since 1952. The inflation measure in the chart is the rate of change of the *consumer price index*, the cost of a given basket of goods, representing the purchases of a typical urban consumer.[6]

The rate of inflation shown in Chart 1-4 fluctuates considerably. Just as we could tell much about the recent history of the economy from looking at Chart 1-2's picture of the course of actual and potential GNP, we can likewise see much of recent economic history in Chart 1-4. In particular, there is the long period of steady inflation from 1960 through 1964 when the inflation rate hovered around the 2 percent level. Then there is a slow climb in the inflation rate from 1965 to 1970, followed by a slowing down till mid-1972. And finally there are the inflationary bursts from 1972 through 1974 and 1978 to 1980 as the inflation rate rose to 12 percent and above.

Chart 1-4 presents the percentage *rate of change* of the consumer price

[6] Data for years prior to 1979 refer to typical urban wage earners rather than consumers.

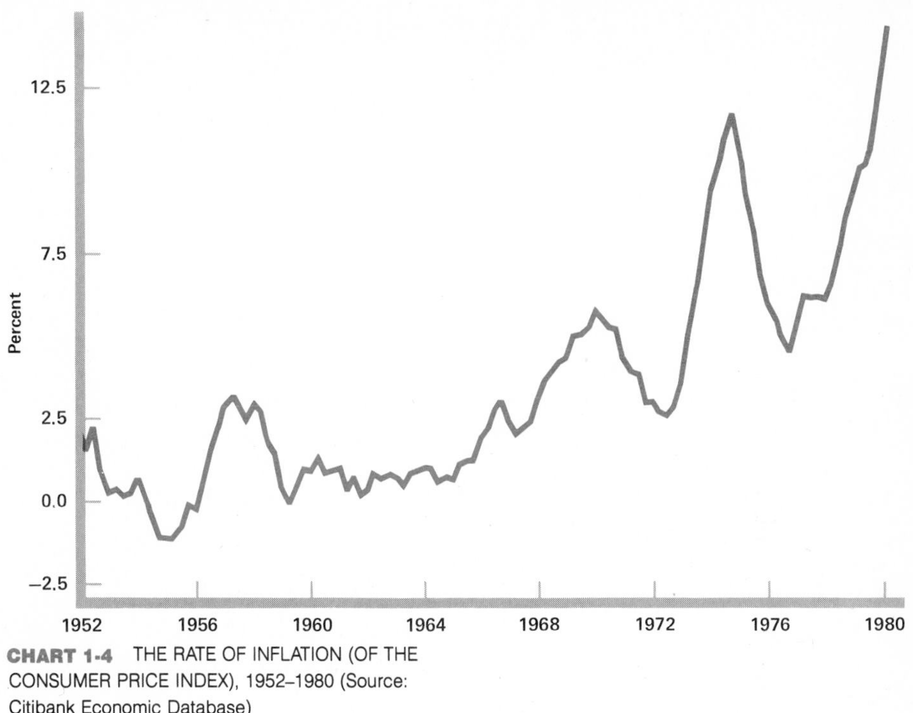

CHART 1-4 THE RATE OF INFLATION (OF THE CONSUMER PRICE INDEX), 1952–1980 (Source: Citibank Economic Database)

index. It is interesting to ask how all those changes add up. Since 1952, consumer prices have more than tripled; in other words, the total increase in the price index since 1952 is over 200 percent. Much of that increase took place in the past few years.

Inflation, like unemployment, is a major macroeconomic problem. However, the costs of inflation are much less obvious than those of unemployment. In the case of unemployment, it is clear that potential output is going to waste, and therefore it is clear why the reduction of unemployment is desirable. In the case of inflation, there is no obvious loss of output. Nonetheless, policy makers have been willing to increase unemployment in an effort to reduce inflation—that is, to *trade off* some unemployment for less inflation.

Inflation-Unemployment Tradeoffs

The *Phillips curve* is a relationship between the rates of inflation and unemployment that has played a key role in macroeconomic policy discussions since its publication in 1958. Figure 1-1 presents a typical Phillips curve, showing that high rates of inflation are accompanied by low

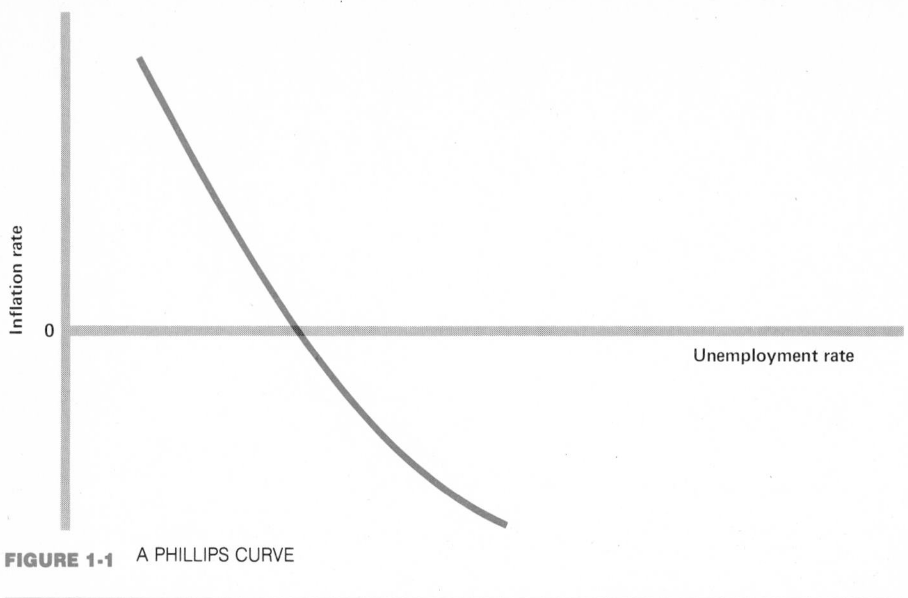

FIGURE 1-1 A PHILLIPS CURVE

rates of unemployment and vice versa. The curve suggests that less unemployment can always be attained by incurring more inflation and that the inflation rate can always be reduced by incurring the costs of more unemployment. In other words, the curve suggests there is a *tradeoff* between inflation and unemployment.

Economic events of the past decade, particularly the combination of high inflation *and* high unemployment in 1974, have led to considerable skepticism about the unemployment-inflation relation shown in Figure 1-1. Chart 1-5 presents the inflation and unemployment rate combinations for the years 1963 to 1979. There is clearly no simple relationship of the form shown in Figure 1-1.

Nonetheless, there remains a tradeoff between inflation and unemployment which is more sophisticated than a glance at Figure 1-1 would suggest, and which will enable us to make sense of Chart 1-5. In the short run, of say 2 years, there is a relation between inflation and unemployment of the type shown in Figure 1-1. That *short-run Phillips curve*, however, does not remain stable. It shifts as expectations of inflation change. In the long run, there is no tradeoff worth speaking about between inflation and unemployment. In the long run, the unemployment rate is basically independent of the long-run inflation rate.

The short- and long-run tradeoffs between inflation and unemployment are obviously a major concern of policy making and are the basic determinants of the potential success of stabilization policies.

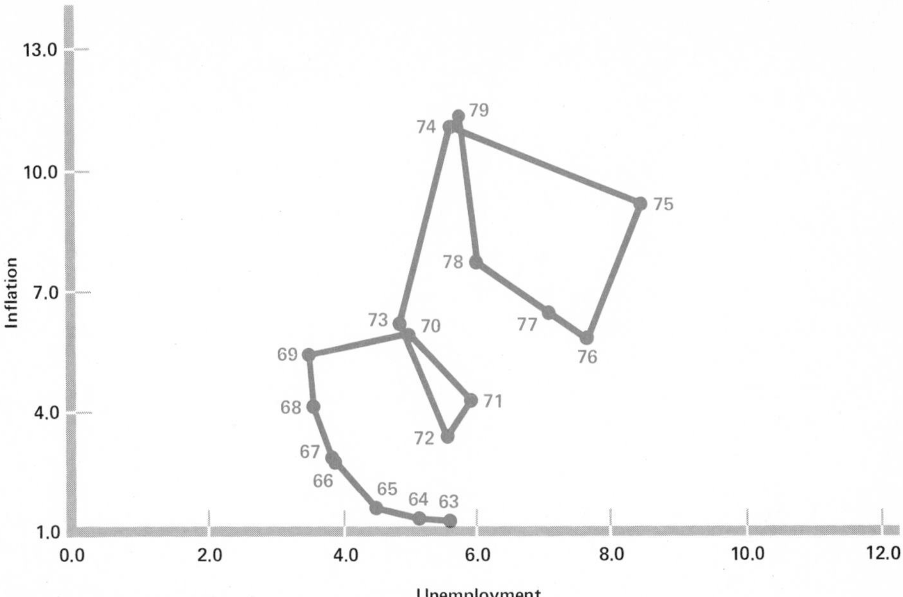

CHART 1-5 INFLATION AND UNEMPLOYMENT, 1963–1979 (Source: Citibank Economic Database)

Stabilization Policy

Policy makers have at their command two broad classes of policies with which to affect the economy. The first is *monetary policy*, which is controlled by the Federal Reserve System (the Fed). The instruments of monetary policy are changes in the stock of money, changes in the interest rate—the discount rate—at which the Fed lends money to banks, and some controls over the banking system. The second class of policies is *fiscal policy* under the control of the Congress, usually initiated by the executive branch of the government. The instruments of fiscal policy are tax rates and government spending.

Monetary and fiscal policies affect the economy mainly through their effects on aggregate demand—these are *demand management* policies. Fiscal policy can also be used to some extent to affect aggregate supply through policies known as *supply management*.

One of the central facts of policy is that the effects of monetary and fiscal policy on the economy are not fully predictable, both in their *timing* and in the *extent* to which they affect demand. These two uncertainties are at the heart of the problems of *stabilization policy*—policies designed to moderate the fluctuations of the economy, and particularly the fluctuations of the rates of inflation, output, and unemployment. Chart 1-5 shows the recent fluctuations of the rates of inflation and unemployment, and suggests strongly that stabilization policy has not been fully successful in keeping them within narrow bounds. The failures of stabilization policy are due mostly to uncertainty about the way it works.

However, there are also questions of political economy involved in the way stabilization policy has been operated. The speed at which to proceed in trying to eliminate unemployment, at the risk of increasing inflation, is a matter of judgment about both the economy and the costs of mistakes. Those who regard the costs of unemployment as high, relative to the costs of inflation, will run greater risks of inflation to reduce unemployment than will those who regard the costs of inflation as primary and unemployment as a relatively minor misfortune.

Political economy affects stabilization policy in more ways than through the costs which policy makers of different political persuasions attach to inflation and unemployment, and the risks they are willing to undertake in trying to improve the economic situation. There is also the so-called *political business cycle*, which is based on the observation that election results are affected by economic conditions. When the economic situation is improving and the unemployment rate is falling, incumbent presidents tend to be reelected. There is thus the incentive to policy makers running for reelection, or who wish to affect the election results, to use stabilization policy to produce booming economic conditions before elections. There is no question, for example, that economic policy in 1971 was shaped by the upcoming election.

Stabilization policy is also known as *countercyclical* policy, that is, policy to moderate the trade cycle or *business cycle*, consisting of fairly regular cycles of booms, declines, recessions, and recoveries.[7] Chart 1-2 shows that cycles in the past 15 years have been far from regular. The behavior, and even the existence, of the trade cycle is substantially affected by the conduct of stabilization policy. Successful stabilization policy smooths out the cycle, while unsuccessful stabilization policy may worsen the fluctuations of the economy. Indeed, one of the tenets of monetarism is that the major fluctuations of the economy are a result of government actions rather than the inherent instability of the economy's private sector.

Monetarism, Nonmonetarism, and Activism

We noted above that there is some controversy over the existence of the tradeoff between inflation and unemployment. That controversy arose around 1967–1968 in the context of the debate in macroeconomics between monetarists and nonmonetarists, or fiscalists. We have already identified some of the major participants in the debate as Milton Friedman on the

[7] See, for instance, Paul A. Samuelson, *Economics*, 11th ed. (New York; McGraw-Hill, 1980), chap. 14.

monetarist side and Franco Modigliani and James Tobin on the nonmonetarist side. But macroeconomists cannot be neatly classified into one camp or the other. Instead, there is a spectrum of views. There are monetarists who make Friedman look like a fiscalist or Keynesian, and Keynesians who make Modigliani look like a monetarist. Not only that; there is no compelling unity in the views that are identified with monetarism, and the balanced economist is likely to accept some monetarist arguments and reject others. Nor is the debate one in which there is no progress. For example, both theory and empirical evidence have been brought to bear on the issue of the inflation-unemployment tradeoff, and it is no longer central to the monetarist/fiscalist debate.

Another major point of contention is the relation between *money* and *inflation*. *Monetarists* tend to argue that the quantity of money is the prime determinant of the level of prices and economic activity, and that excessive monetary growth is responsible for inflation and unstable monetary growth for economic fluctuations. Since they contend that variability in the growth rate of money accounts for variability of real growth, they are naturally led to argue for a monetary policy of low and constant growth in the money supply—a monetary growth rule. *Activists*, by contrast, point out that there is no close relationship between monetary growth and inflation in the short run and that monetary growth is only one of the factors affecting aggregate demand. They maintain that policy makers are—or at least can be—sufficiently careful and skillful to be able to use monetary and fiscal policy to control the economy effectively.

The skill and care of the policy makers are important because monetarists raise the issue of whether aggregate demand policies might not worsen the performance of the economy. Monetarists point to episodes, such as the overexpansionary policies followed by the Fed in 1972, to argue that policy makers cannot and do not exercise sufficient caution to justify using activist policy. Here the activists are optimists, suggesting that we can learn from our past mistakes.

A further issue that divides the two camps concerns the proper role of government in the economy. This is not really an issue that can be analyzed using macroeconomic theory, but it is difficult to follow some of the debate without being aware that the issue exists. Monetarists tend to be conservatives who favor small government and abhor budget deficits and a large public debt. They would favor tax cuts during recessions and cuts in public spending during booms with the net effect of winding up with a smaller share of government in the economy. Activists, by contrast, tend to favor an important and large role for government and are therefore not disinclined to use increased government spending and transfers as tools of stabilization policy. Differences between monetarists and activists must, therefore, be seen in a much broader perspective than their particular disagreements about the exact role of money in the short run.

1-2 AGGREGATE DEMAND AND SUPPLY

We have sketched the major issues and concepts we shall be discussing and using in the book. The key overall concepts are aggregate demand and aggregate supply. In this section we provide a brief preview of those concepts and of their interaction, with the aims of showing where we are heading and of keeping the material of Chapters 3 through 10 in perspective.

Figure 1-2 shows aggregate demand and supply curves. The vertical axis P is the price level, and the horizontal axis Y is the level of real output or income. Although the curves look like the ordinary supply and demand curves of microeconomics, a full understanding of them will not be reached until Chapter 12.

Aggregate demand is the total demand for goods and services in the economy. It depends on the aggregate price level, as shown in Figure 1-2. It can be shifted through monetary and fiscal policy. The aggregate supply curve shows the price level associated with each level of output. It can, to some extent, be shifted by fiscal policy. Aggregate supply and demand interact to determine the price level and output level. In Figure 1-2, P_0 is the equilibrium price level and Y_0 the equilibrium level of output. If the Y^d curve in this figure shifts up to the right, then the extent to which output and prices, respectively, are changed depends on the steepness of the aggregate supply curve.[8] If the Y^s is very steep, then a given change

[8] Experiment with graphs like Fig. 1-2 to be sure you understand this fact.

FIGURE 1-2 AGGREGATE DEMAND AND SUPPLY

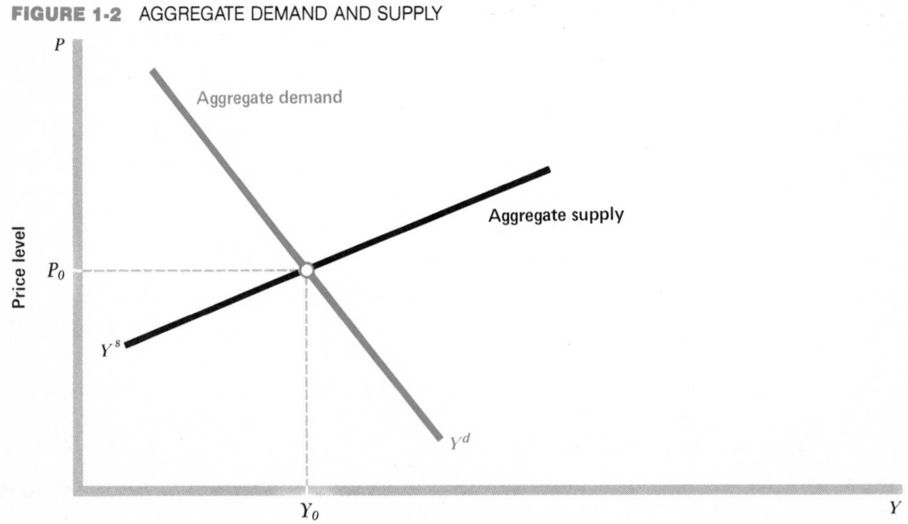

in aggregate demand mainly causes prices to rise and has very little effect on the level of output. If the Y^s curve is flat, a given change in aggregate demand will be translated mainly into an increase in output and very little into an increase in the price level.

One of the crucial points about macroeconomic adjustment is that the aggregate supply curve is not a straight line. Figure 1-3 shows that at low levels of output, below potential output Y_p, the aggregate supply curve is quite flat. When output is below potential, there is very little tendency for prices of goods and factors (wages) to fall. Conversely, for output above potential, the aggregate supply curve is steep and prices tend to rise continuously. The effects of changes in aggregate demand on output and prices therefore depend on the level of output relative to potential.

All these observations are by way of a very important warning. In Chapters 3 through 10 we focus on aggregate demand as the determinant of the level of output. We shall assume that prices are given and constant, and that output is determined by the level of demand—that there are no supply limitations. We are thus talking about the very flat part of the aggregate supply curve, at levels of output below potential.

The suggestion that output rises to meet the level of demand without a rise in prices leads to a very activist conception of policy. Under these circumstances, without any obvious tradeoffs, policy makers would favor very expansionary policies to raise demand and thereby cause the economy

FIGURE 1-3 AGGREGATE DEMAND AND NONLINEAR AGGREGATE SUPPLY

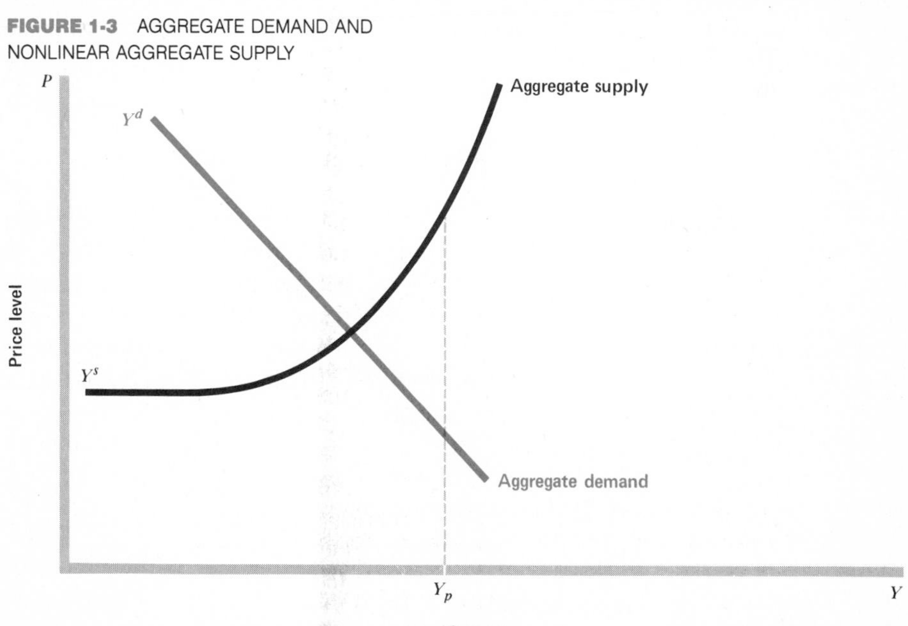

to move to a high level of employment and output. There are circumstances where such a policy view is altogether correct. The early 1960s are a case in point. Chart 1-2 shows that in those years output was substantially below potential. There were unused resources and the problem was a deficiency of demand. By contrast, in the late 1960s and early 1970s the economy was operating at full employment. There was no significant GNP gap. An attempt to expand output or real GNP further would run into supply limitations and force up prices rather than the production of goods. In these circumstances, a model that assumes that output is demand-determined and that increased demand raises output and *not* prices is simply inappropriate.

Should we think that the model with fixed prices and demand-determined output is very restricted and perhaps artificial? The answer is no. There are two reasons for this. First, the circumstances under which the model is appropriate—those of high unemployment—are neither unknown nor unimportant. Unemployment and downward price rigidity are continuing features of the United States economy. Second, even when we come to study the interactions of aggregate supply and demand in Chapter 12 and later, we need to know how given policy actions *shift* the aggregate demand curve at a given level of prices. Thus all the material of Chapters 3 through 10 on aggregate demand retains a vital part in the understanding of the effects of monetary and fiscal policy on the price level as well as output in circumstances where the aggregate supply curve is upward-sloping.

What, then, is the warning of this section? It is simply that the very activist spirit of macroeconomic policy under conditions of unemployment must not cause us to overlook the existence of supply limitations and price adjustment when the economy is near full employment.

1-3 OUTLINE AND PREVIEW OF THIS TEXT

We have sketched the major issues we shall be discussing in the book. We can now outline our approach to macroeconomics and the order in which the material will be presented. The key overall concepts, as already noted, are aggregate demand and aggregate supply. Aggregate demand is influenced by monetary policy, primarily via interest rates and expectations, and by fiscal policy. Aggregate supply is affected by fiscal policy and also by disturbances such as changes in the supply of oil.

Figure 1-4 presents a schematic view of the approach of the book to macroeconomics. Being schematic, the diagram is not comprehensive, but it does show the most important relationships we shall examine.

In broad outline, Chapters 3 and 4 are concerned with aggregate demand, Chapter 11 with aggregate supply, and Chapters 12 and 13 with the interactions between aggregate supply and demand. Chapters 5 through 10 present material which clarifies and deepens understanding of

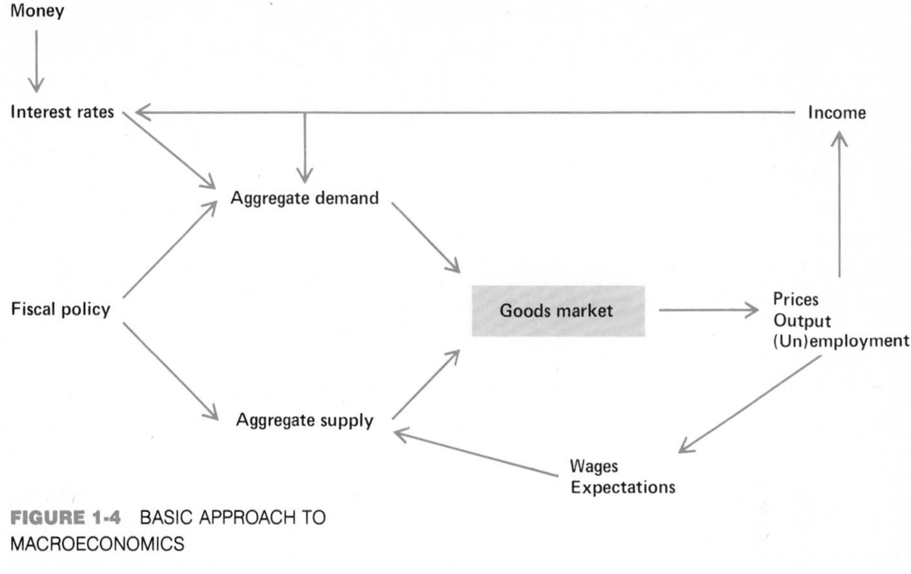

FIGURE 1-4 BASIC APPROACH TO MACROECONOMICS

aggregate demand and of the ways in which monetary and fiscal policies affect the economy. Chapters 14 through 17 perform a similar service for aggregate supply and the interactions of aggregate supply and demand. Chapters 18 and 19 examine effects of international trade in goods and assets on the economy.

We now proceed to a chapter-by-chapter outline of the book. Chapter 2 is concerned with some definitions and relationships that arise in national income accounting. Many of these relationships, such as that between savings and investment, are used repeatedly in the rest of the book. Chapter 3 is the first, rudimentary model of aggregate demand and the determination of real output. This simple model shows how aggregate demand determines the level of output. While it is decidedly simple, it nevertheless contains some of the essential elements of modern macroeconomics, and it is the backbone for some of the subsequent and more developed models. This rudimentary model enables us to give preliminary answers to questions about fiscal policy, such as: What is the effect on output of a 10 percent cut in taxes? What is the effect on output of an increase in government spending matched by an equal increase in taxes?

Chapter 3 abstracts entirely from monetary considerations in discussing income determination. Chapter 4 introduces those considerations. In that chapter, the simultaneous determination of output and interest rates is studied and emphasis is given to the interaction between the goods market—the market for goods and services—and assets or financial markets. A main point of that chapter is to study the role of money in the economy and to show how variations in the quantity of money, by changing interest rates, exert an effect on aggregate demand and thereby on the level of output.

Chapters 5 through 8 put flesh on the skeleton model which is used in Chapter 4 to study output determination and the channels through which monetary and fiscal policies affect the economy. Chapter 5 examines the determinants of consumption spending, which is the major component of aggregate demand. Chapter 6 discusses investment spending, which is important because it fluctuates a good deal and is significantly affected by monetary and fiscal policies. Chapter 7 examines the determinants of the demand for money, and Chapter 8 discusses the money supply process. Chapter 8 clarifies the role of the Federal Reserve System in affecting and controlling the money supply and explains the mechanics of the way in which the Fed conducts monetary policy.

Chapters 9 and 10 are the first chapters discussing stabilization policy. Chapter 9 examines the problems of stabilization policy. It asks why it is not easier to apply the lessons of Chapters 3 through 8 to the control of the economy than the performance of the economy in recent years suggests it is. Chapter 10 briefly describes economic events of the Great Depression of the thirties, which still influence the structure of the United States economy and macroeconomic theories, and then reviews the Keynesian economic policies of the Kennedy and Johnson years. This chapter illustrates the use of the tools acquired in earlier chapters. There is, for example, a detailed examination of the effects of the successful 1964 tax cut.

Chapter 11 begins the move over from the aggregate demand approach of the earlier chapters, which are of major relevance when the economy is operating at less than full capacity and prices can be taken to be more or less constant, to examine aggregate supply. Chapter 12 then combines the aggregate supply relationship with the aggregate demand apparatus, developed in Chapter 4, to study the joint determination of the levels of real output, interest rates, and prices.

Chapter 13 moves on from the determination of the price level and level of output to discuss inflation, output, and unemployment. The apparatus of Chapter 12 is useful in examining the effects of one-time changes in the money supply and fiscal policy on the economy, but quite unwieldy for the study of ongoing processes of inflation and changes in output over time. The model of Chapter 13 is well suited to discuss ongoing inflation along with output and unemployment.

Recent experience has made it quite obvious that interest rates and the inflation rate are related: interest rates are high when the inflation rate is high. This relationship was studied by Irving Fisher of Yale in the early part of the century. He concluded that interest rates rise with inflation to compensate lenders for the loss of purchasing power of money they lend that is implied by rising prices. The *Fisher relationship* between interest rates and inflation is also examined with the aid of the model of Chapter 13.

Chapter 14 returns to fiscal policy and the role of government spending in the economy. We are particularly concerned in that chapter with the financing of government spending and the effects of budget deficits on inflation. The chapter discusses, too, the components of government spending and the way in which taxes are raised.

Chapter 15 returns to the inflation-unemployment tradeoff and the costs of inflation and unemployment. It examines the anatomy of unemployment in detail and draws the important distinction between anticipated and unanticipated inflation in discussing the costs of inflation. Chapter 16 then examines the record of the economy over the 1969–1979 period, using the apparatus of Chapter 13 to illuminate recent economic developments. It also draws on the discussion of Chapter 15 in trying to understand why policy makers made the policy choices they did.

Chapter 17 turns aside from the primarily short- and intermediate-run orientation of the book to examine long-term economic growth and the explanations for United States growth over the past century. In so doing, it essentially provides a detailed accounting of the development of potential output and the determinants of productivity growth that have, up to that point, not been carefully examined. In Chapter 17 we also examine the severe slowdown in productivity growth that has hit the United States and other industrialized economies in the past decade and ask what supply side policies can be used to offset this adverse change.

Chapters 18 and 19 are devoted to international trade in goods and in assets. Although international trade is less important for the American economy than for most others, trade has been increasing as a fraction of GNP since World War II, and the major economic shocks of the seventies—oil price increases—were trade-connected. Chapter 18 examines the ways in which trade affects GNP determination and the roles of monetary and fiscal policy under a system of fixed exchange rates. The fixed exchange rate system of the post-World War II world economy came under increasing pressure in the late sixties and early seventies and finally dissolved in 1973. From 1973, exchange rates have been *flexible* in that they change from day to day. Chapter 19 discusses trade and capital flows under flexible exchange rates, as well as the appropriate uses of monetary and fiscal policy in stabilizing an open economy.

1-4 PREREQUISITES AND RECIPES

In concluding this introductory chapter, a few words on how to use this book will be helpful. First, we note that there is no mathematical prerequisite beyond high school algebra. We do use equations whenever they appear helpful, but they are not an indispensable part of the exposition. Nevertheless, they can and should be mastered by any serious student of macroeconomics.

The technically harder chapters or sections are marked by an asterisk (*). They can be skipped or dipped into. Either we present them as supplementary material or we provide with them sufficient nontechnical coverage to help the reader get on without them later in the book. The reason we do present more advanced material or treatment is to afford a complete and up-to-date coverage of the main ideas and techniques in macroeconomics. Even though you may not be able to grasp every point of a section marked by an asterisk on first reading—and should not even try to—these sections should certainly be read to get the main message and an intuitive appreciation of the issues that are raised.

The main problem you will encounter comes from the interaction of several markets and many variables. As Figure 1-4 already suggests, the direct and feedback effects in the economy constitute a quite formidable system. How can you be certain to progress efficiently and with some ease? The most important thing is to ask questions. Ask yourself, as you follow the argument: Why is it that this or that variable should affect, say, aggregate demand? What would happen if it did not? What is the critical link?

There is no substitute whatsoever for an *active form of learning.* Reading sticks at best for 7 weeks. Are there simple rules for active study? The best way to study is to use pencil and paper and work the argument by drawing diagrams, experimenting with flowcharts, writing out the logic of an argument, working out the problems at the end of each chapter, and underlining key ideas. The *Study Guide* by Richard Startz of the University of Pennsylvania contains both much useful material and problems that will help in your studies. Another valuable exercise is to take issue with an argument or position, or to spell out the defense for a particular view on policy questions. Beyond that, if you get stuck, read on for half a page. If you are still stuck, go back five pages.

You should also learn to use the Index. Several concepts are discussed at different levels in different chapters. If you come across an unfamiliar term or concept, check the Index to see whether and where it was discussed earlier in the book.

As a final word, this chapter is designed for reference purposes. You should return to it whenever you want to check where a particular problem fits or where a particular subject matter is relevant. The best way to see the forest is from Chapter 1.

2

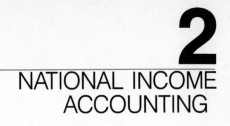

NATIONAL INCOME ACCOUNTING

2
NATIONAL INCOME ACCOUNTING

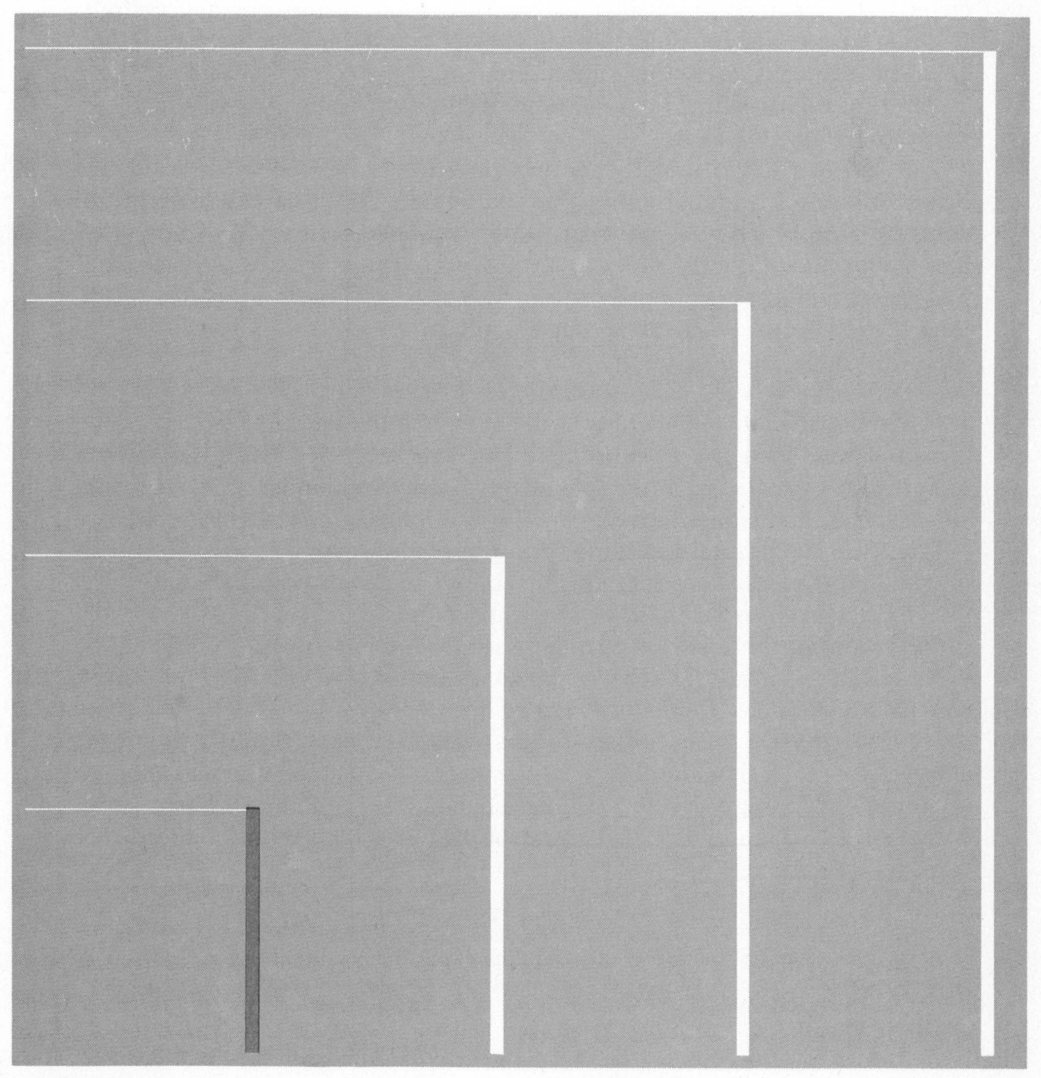

Macroeconomics is ultimately concerned with the determination of the economy's total output, the price level, the level of employment, interest rates, and other variables discussed in Chapter 1. A necessary step in understanding how these variables are determined is *national income accounting*. The national income accounts provide both the actual measures of such macroeconomic variables as output and income and a conceptual framework for relating the various measures to one another.

We study national income accounting not only because it provides us with our basic measure of the performance of the economy in producing goods and services, but also because it highlights the relationships among three key macroeconomic variables: output, income, and spending. This chapter will introduce a few accounting relationships among output, income, spending, and components of spending, and in so doing, will advance us right into the subject of macroeconomics—because those accounting relationships involve some of the chief concepts with which we deal throughout the book.

Before we delve into the details of national income accounting, we briefly indicate the main relationships among the key variables. The central concept is gross national product (GNP), which measures the value of all final goods and services currently produced in the economy and valued at market prices. GNP is thus a measure, indeed the basic measure, of the total output produced in the economy in a given year.[1] GNP includes the value of goods, such as automobiles and eggs, produced, along with the value of services, such as haircuts or medical services.

Starting from the concept of GNP, it will be shown, first, that the value of output produced gives rise to the total income received by wage earners and the recipients of interest, profits, and dividends. Second, total spending on goods and services in the economy is equal to the value of output. And third, total spending is therefore also related to the value of all incomes received. The relationship between total spending and total income suggests, correctly, that spending on goods and services plays a role in determining the levels of income and production in the economy. The economics of the interactions between spending and the level of output constitutes the main theme of Chapter 3.

Although the three relationships we have just described appear simple, there is considerable complexity in the actual national income accounts in relating GNP to national income and to total spending. Those complexities arise in large part from the way in which indirect and direct taxes affect national income relative to GNP, but also involve the role of

[1] GNP suffers from some defects as a measure of the performance of the economy because it does not value certain economic activities that are hard to measure, such as the value of housespouses services or the work of volunteers, and also because it does not deduct the cost of nuisance outputs, such as pollution, from the value of output. For a discussion of a measure that attempts to remedy those defects, Net Economic Welfare (NEW), see Paul A. Samuelson, *Economics*, 11th ed., (New York: McGraw-Hill, 1980).

foreign trade. We investigate the details of the relationships among output, income, and spending in Sections 2-1 through 2-3, starting in Section 2-1 with a description of GNP.

In Section 2-4, we further expand on the distinction between *nominal* GNP, or output measured in current prices, and *real* GNP. The discussion is followed in Section 2-5 with a brief look at different price indexes. Here we distinguish the consumer price index from producer prices and the GNP deflator. In Section 2-6, we set out the national income relations formally, as a prelude to the economic analysis that begins in Chapter 3.

2-1 GROSS NATIONAL PRODUCT AND NET NATIONAL PRODUCT

Our aim in this section is to describe some important aspects of the measurement of GNP. This will set the scene for the discussion of the relationships among GNP, income, and spending, which were emphasized in the introduction and which will be examined in Sections 2-2 and 2-3.

As we noted earlier, GNP measures the value of all final goods and services produced in the economy during a given period. It includes the value of such goods produced as houses and bourbon, and the value of services, like brokers' services and economists' lectures. Each of these is valued at its market price and the values are added together to give GNP. In a simple economy that produces twenty bananas, each of which is valued at 30 cents, and sixty oranges, each of which is valued at 25 cents, GNP is equal to \$21 [= (30 cents × 20) + (25 cents × 60)]. In the United States economy in 1979, the value of GNP was \$2,369 billion.

There are a number of subtleties in the calculation of GNP that are important to keep in mind. First, we are talking about *final* goods and services. The insistence on final goods and services is simply to make sure that we do not double-count. For example, we would not want to include the full price of an automobile in GNP, and then also include the value of the tires that were sold to the automobile producer as part of GNP. The components of the car, sold to the manufacturers, are called *intermediate* goods, and their value is not included in GNP. Similarly, the wheat that goes into bread is an intermediate good, and we do not count the value of the wheat sold the miller and the value of the flour sold the baker, as well as the value of the bread, as part of GNP.

In practice, double-counting is avoided by working with *value added*. At each stage of the manufacture of a good, only the value added to the good at that stage of manufacture is counted as part of GNP. The value of the wheat produced by the farmer is counted as part of GNP. Then the value of the flour sold by the miller *minus* the cost of the wheat is the miller's value added. If we follow this process along, we will see that the sum of value added at each stage of processing will be equal to the final value of the bread sold.[2]

The second point is that GNP consists of the value of output *currently* produced. It thus excludes transactions in existing commodities such as old masters or existing houses. We count the construction of new houses as part of GNP, but we do not add trade in existing houses. We do, however, count the value of realtors' fees in the sale of existing houses as part of GNP. The realtor provides a current service in bringing buyer and seller together, and that is appropriately part of current output.

Third, GNP values goods at *market prices*. It is important to recognize that the market price of many goods includes indirect taxes such as the sales tax and various excise taxes, and thus the market price of goods is not the same as the price the seller of the good receives or the cost of production. The price net of indirect taxes is the *factor cost*, which is the amount received by the factors of production that manufactured the good. GNP is valued at market prices, and not at factor cost. This point becomes important when we relate GNP to the incomes received by the factors of production.

Valuation at market prices is a principle that is not uniformly applied because there are some components of GNP that are difficult to value. There is no very good way of valuing the services of housepersons, or a self-administered haircut, or, for that matter, the services of the police force or the government bureaucracy. Some of these activities are simply omitted from currently measured GNP, as, for instance, housepersons' services. Government services are valued at cost, so that the wages of government employees are taken to represent their contribution to GNP. There is no unifying principle in the treatment of these awkward cases, but rather a host of conventions is used, which we will not detail here.

Net national product (NNP) as distinct from GNP deducts from GNP the *depreciation* of the existing capital stock over the course of the period. The production of GNP causes wear and tear on the existing capital stock; for example, a house depreciates over the course of time, or machines wear out as they are used. If resources were not used to maintain or replace the existing capital, GNP could not be kept at the current level. Accordingly, we use NNP as a better measure of the rate of economic activity that could be maintained over long periods, given the existing capital stock and labor force. Depreciation is a measure of the part of GNP that has to be set aside to maintain the productive capacity of the economy, and we deduct that from GNP to obtain NNP. In 1979, depreciation was $243 billion, or about 10 percent of GNP. We tend to work with the GNP rather than the NNP data because depreciation estimates are quite inaccurate, and also are not quickly available, whereas the GNP estimate for each calendar quarter is

[2] How about the flour that is directly purchased by households for baking in the home? It is counted as a contribution toward GNP since it represents a final sale.

available in preliminary form about a month and a half after the end of the quarter.[3]

Now that we have defined the basic concept of the value of output or GNP in the economy, we will proceed to develop the relationships described earlier, which center around GNP. In particular, we will focus on the following three areas:

1 The production of GNP has as its counterpart the income of the factors of production. We will want to know what the breakdown of income is among wages and salaries, rents, interest, and profits.
2 Cutting across the categories of income described in point 1, we will want to examine what part of GNP accrues to households, whether in the form of wages, or interest, or rental income, or profits. We are led to the concept of *personal disposable income*, the amount of income households have available for spending or saving. We will want to see how that is related to GNP.
3 The production of GNP gives rise to a supply of goods and services that is sold. We will want to know how GNP is divided among the types of goods sold and what sectors of the economy buy the output. Here we will examine the breakdown of GNP into consumption, investment, government purchases of goods and services, and net exports as components of the aggregate demand for output.

Points 1 and 2 are taken up in Section 2-2, and point 3 is analyzed in Section 2-3.

2-2 GNP AND INCOME

We now consider the relation between the value of output or GNP and the incomes that are generated in the production process. In this section we show that *income is equal to the value of output* because the receipts from the sale of output must accrue to someone as income. The purchaser of bread is indirectly paying the farmer, the miller, the baker, and the supermarket operator for the labor and capital used in production and is also contributing to their profits.

GNP and National Income

Our statement above equating the value of output and income is correct with two qualifications:

[3] National income accounts are regularly reported in the *Survey of Current Business*. Historical data are available in *Business Statistics*, a biennial edition, and the *Economic Report of the President*. Recently the Commerce Department has begun to issue preliminary estimates of GNP for a given quarter before the end of the quarter.

TABLE 2-1 GNP AND NATIONAL INCOME, 1979 *(in billions of dollars)*

Gross national product (GNP)		$2,369
Less:		
Capital consumption allowance	$243	
Equals:		
Net national product (NNP)		$2,126
Less:		
Indirect taxes	$186	
Other (net)	$ 15	
Equals:		
National income		$1,925

Note: Numbers may not add because of rounding.
Source: Citibank Economic Database.

1 The first correction arises from depreciation. As already noted, part of GNP has to be set aside to mantain the productive capacity of the economy. Depreciation should not be counted as part of income, since it is a cost of production. As a rule, depreciation amounts to about 10 percent of GNP. Depreciation is usually referred to in the national income accounts as the *capital consumption allowance*. After subtracting depreciation from GNP, we have NNP.
2 The second adjustment arises from indirect taxes, in particular, sales taxes, that introduce a discrepancy between market price and prices received by producers. GNP is valued at market price, but the income accruing to producers does not include the sales taxes that are part of market price, and thus falls short of GNP. Indirect taxes, along with some other items of the same nature, account for about 10 percent of GNP.

With these two deductions we can derive *national income* from GNP, as shown in Table 2-1, which gives the dollar figures for 1979.[4] National income gives us the value of output at *factor cost* rather than market prices, which is GNP. It tells us what factors of production actually receive as income before direct taxes and transfers.

Factor Shares in National Income

We next ask how national income is split among different types of incomes, as shown in Table 2-2.

[4] The item "Other (net)" in Table 2-1 includes a statistical discrepancy. In addition, it subtracts from NNP business transfer payments but adds subsidies to, less current surpluses of, government enterprises. The adjustment for government enterprises is required because, in the case of subsidies, market price understates the factor cost. In the case of deficits, similarly, the value of output measured at market prices falls short of the factor cost.

TABLE 2-2 NATIONAL INCOME AND ITS DISTRIBUTION, 1979 *(in billions of dollars)*

National income	$1,925	100%
Compensation of employees	$1,459	76%
Proprietors' income	$ 131	7%
Rental income of persons	$ 27	1%
Corporate profits	$ 178	9%
Net interest	$ 130	7%

Note: Numbers may not add because of rounding.
Source: Citibank Economic Database.

The most striking fact of Table 2-2 is the very large share of wages and salaries—compensation of employees—in national income. This accounts for 76 percent of national income. Proprietors' income is income from unincorporated businesses. Rental income of persons includes the *imputed* income of owner-occupied housing[5] and income from ownership of patents, royalties, and so on. The net interest category includes interest payments by domestic businesses and the rest of the world to individuals and firms who have lent to them.

The division of national income into various classes is not too important for our macroeconomic purposes. It reflects, in part, such questions as whether corporations are financed by debt or equity, whether a business is or is not incorporated, and whether the housing stock is owned by persons or corporations—which, in turn, are owned by persons.[6]

National Income and Personal Income

A considerably more important question from the macroeconomic viewpoint is how much the personal sector—households and unincorporated businesses—actually receives as income, inclusive of transfers. This quantity is measured by *personal income*. *Transfers* are those payments that do *not* arise out of current productive activity. Thus, welfare payments and unemployment benefits are examples of transfer payments. The level of personal income is important because it is a prime determinant of household consumption and saving behavior.

To go from national income to personal income, we have to remove those parts of national income that are earned by the corporate sector and add net transfer payments to the personal sector. Table 2-3 shows the steps needed to make the transition from national income to personal income.

[5] GNP includes an estimate of the services homeowners receive by living in their homes. This is estimated by calculating the rent on an equivalent house. Thus the homeowner is treated as if she pays herself rent for living in her house.

[6] You might want to work out how Table 2-2 would be modified for each of the possibilities described in this sentence.

Three items are deducted from national income:

1 Corporate profits (pretax), which clearly are not directly part of personal income.[7]
2 Net interest. This is the interest paid by domestic business, less the interest received by it, plus the net interest received from abroad. Interest paid by consumers and the government is not included in this measure, which is the amount of interest counted in national income.
3 Contributions for social insurance. These are contributions by both corporations and the personal sector, which are essentially taxes paid to the government sector and thus not part of personal income.

We then add back four items:

1 Government transfer payments to persons, consisting of various Social Security benefits, state unemployment insurance benefits, and veterans' benefits.
2 Personal interest income, which is the interest income of persons from all sources. This item, along with the net interest subtracted above, ensures that the interest left in personal income consists only of interest received by households.
3 Dividends (distributed after-tax corporate profits).
4 Business transfer payments, such as write-offs for bad debts and contributions to charities and nonprofit institutions.

After making these adjustments, we have a measure of the income received by persons and unincorporated businesses. Personal income is a useful measure particularly because it is available monthly, as opposed to most national income measures, which are published only quarterly. The Commerce Department publishes the monthly personal income data, which are used as a guide to the behavior of GNP by those who follow economic events closely.

Although we have derived personal income in Table 2-3 by starting with national income and making adjustments, we should recognize that it is also possible to build up to an estimate of personal income by looking at its components in a way similar to that shown in Table 2-2. In particular, personal income consists of labor income, plus proprietors' income, plus persons' rental, dividend, and interest income, plus transfer payments, minus personal contributions for social insurance.

[7] Corporate profits in the national income accounts are adjusted by correcting firms' estimates of (*a*) depreciation (the capital consumption adjustment) and (*b*) the costs of inventories used up in production (the inventory valuation adjustment). The second adjustment occurs because computed profits are affected by the value firms place on the goods they use up in production. In inflationary times, typical ways of valuing inventories *understate* the cost of goods sold and thus *overstate* profits. The inventory valuation adjustment is an attempt to correct that error. The corporate profits deducted from national income in Table 2-3 include the two adjustments mentioned in this footnote.

TABLE 2-3 NATIONAL INCOME AND PERSONAL INCOME, IN 1979 *(in billions of dollars)*

National income		$1,925
Less:		
Corporate profits	$178	
Net interest	$130	
Social insurance contributions	$190	
Plus:		
Government transfers to persons	$242	
Personal interest income	$192	
Dividends	$ 53	
Business transfer payments	$ 10	
Equals:		
Personal income		$1,924

Source: Citibank Economic Database.

Disposable Personal Income and Its Allocation

Not all personal income is available for spending by households. The amount available for spending, ***disposable personal income***, deducts from personal income the personal tax and certain nontax payments made by the household sector. The nontax payments include such items as license fees and traffic tickets.

Disposable personal income is then available for personal consumption expenditures, interest payments by consumers, transfers to foreigners, and savings. By far the largest outlay is for personal consumption, as shown in Table 2-4.

TABLE 2-4 PERSONAL INCOME, DISPOSABLE PERSONAL INCOME, AND ITS DISPOSITION IN 1979 *(in billions of dollars)*

Personal income		$1,924		
Less:				
Personal tax and nontax payments	$ 300			
Equals:				
Disposable personal income		$1,624		100%
Personal outlays:		$1,551		95%
Personal consumption expenditures	$1,510		93%	
Interest paid by consumers	$ 40		2%	
Transfers to foreigners	$ 1		0%	
Personal saving		$ 74		5%

Note: Third and fourth columns show the breakdown of disposable personal income as a percentage of disposable personal income. Numbers may not add because of rounding.
Source: Citibank Economic Database.

In summary, this section has shown the relation between GNP, which is a measure of productive activity in the economy, and income receipts that accrue to the household sector. The main steps in the long chain we have followed arise from taxes, transfers between sectors, depreciation, and profits, including the valuation adjustments.

These intermediate steps remind us that there is an important difference between GNP as the value of output at market prices and the spendable receipts of the household sector. We could have a positive disposable personal income even if GNP were zero, provided there was someone to make the necessary transfer payments. Likewise, GNP could be large and disposable income small if the government sector took in a lot of taxes. The larger taxes are relative to government transfers, the smaller is disposable income relative to GNP.

Summary

We summarize here in a few identities (and in the accompanying Chart 2-1) the relationships reviewed in each table:

GNP − capital consumption allowance ≡ NNP (Table 2-1) (1)

NNP − indirect taxes ≡ national income (Table 2-1) (2)

National income ≡ wages and salaries + proprietors' income + rental income of persons + corporate profits + net interest (Table 2-2) (3)

National income − corporate profits − social insurance contributions − net interest + personal interest + dividends + transfer receipts ≡ personal income (Table 2-3) (4)

Personal income − personal tax and nontax payments ≡ disposable personal income (Table 2-4) (5)

Disposable personal income ≡ personal outlays + personal savings (Table 2-4) (6)

2-3 OUTPUT AND COMPONENTS OF DEMAND

In the previous section, we started with GNP and asked how much of the value of goods and services produced actually gets into the hands of households. In this section we present a different perspective on GNP by asking who buys the output, rather than who receives the income. More technically, we look at the demand for output and speak of the *components* of the aggregate demand for goods and services. Total demand for domestic output is made up of four components: (1) consumption spending by households; (2) investment spending by businesses or households; (3)

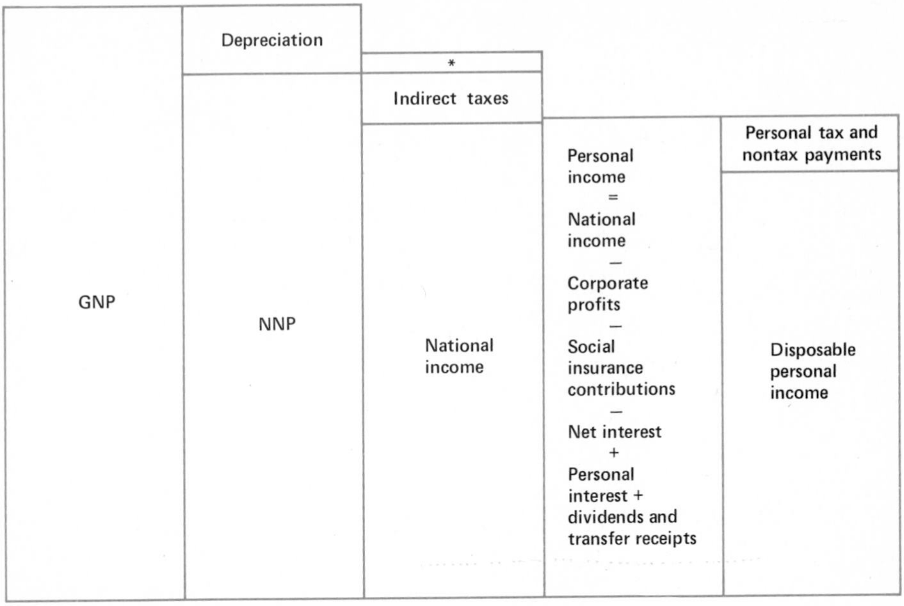

*Statistical discrepancy plus subsidies less current surplus of government enterprises.

CHART 2-1 THE RELATION BETWEEN GNP AND DISPOSABLE PERSONAL INCOME

government (federal, state, and local) purchases of goods and services; and (4) foreign demand. We shall now look more closely at each of these components.

Table 2-5 presents a breakdown of the demand for goods and services in 1979 by components of demand. The table illustrates that the chief component of demand is consumption spending by the personal sector. This includes anything from food to golf lessons but involves also, as we shall see in discussing investment, consumer spending on durable goods

TABLE 2-5 GNP AND COMPONENTS OF DEMAND, 1979 *(in billions of dollars)*

Personal consumption expenditures	$1,510	64%
Gross private domestic investment	$ 387	16%
Government purchases of goods and services	$ 476	20%
Net exports of goods and services	$− 5	− 0%
Gross national product (GNP)	$2,369	100%

Note: Numbers do not add because of rounding.
Source: Citibank Economic Database.

such as automobiles—spending which might be regarded as investment rather than consumption.

Next in importance we have government purchases of goods and services. Here we have such items as national defense expenditures, road paving by state and local governments, and salaries of government employees.

We should draw attention here to the use of certain words in connection with government spending. We refer to government spending on goods and services as *purchases* of goods and services, and we speak of *transfers plus purchases* as *government expenditure*. The federal government budget, of the order of $650 billion, refers to federal government expenditure. Less than half that sum is for federal government purchases of goods and services.

Gross private domestic investment is an item that requires some definitions. First, throughout this book, we will mean by investment additions to the physical stock of capital. As we use the term, investment does *not* include buying a bond or purchasing stock in General Motors. Practically, investment includes housing construction, building of machinery, business construction, and additions to a firm's or store's inventories of goods. Recently, additions to the stock of mobile homes made the transition from consumption spending to inclusion in investment. This illustrates that the classification of spending as consumption or investment remains to a significant extent a matter of convention. From the economic point of view, there is little difference between a household building up an inventory of peanut butter and a grocery store doing the same. Nevertheless, in the national income accounts, the individual's purchase is treated as a personal consumption expenditure, whereas the store's purchase is treated as investment in the form of inventory investment. Although these borderline cases clearly exist, we can retain as a simple rule of thumb that investment is associated with the business sector's adding to the physical stock of capital, including inventories.

Similar issues arise in the treatment of household sector expenditures. For instance, how should we treat purchases of automobiles by households? Since automobiles usually last for several years, it would seem sensible to classify household purchases of automobiles as investment. We would then treat the *use* of automobiles as providing consumption services. (We could think of imputing a rental income to owner-occupied automobiles.) However, the convention is to treat all household expenditures as consumption spending. This is not quite so bad as it might seem, since the accounts do separate out households' purchases of durable goods like cars and refrigerators from their other purchases. There is thus information in the accounts on those parts of household spending that, with considerable justification, could be categorized as investment spending. When consumer spending decisions are studied in detail, expenditures on consumer durables are usually treated separately.

The convention that is adopted with respect to the household sector's purchases of houses also deserves comment. The accounts treat the building of a house as investment by the business sector. When the house is sold to a private individual, the transaction is treated as the transfer of an asset, and not then an act of investment. Even if a house is custom-built by the owner, the accounts treat the builder who is employed by the owner as undertaking the act of investment in building the house. The investment is thus attributed to the business sector.

In passing, we note that in Table 2-5, investment is defined as "gross" and "domestic." It is gross in the sense that depreciation is not deducted. Net investment is gross investment minus depreciation. Thus NNP is equal to net investment plus the other categories of spending in Table 2-5.

The term *domestic* means that this is investment spending by domestic residents but is not necessarily spending on goods produced within this country. It may well be an expenditure that falls on foreign goods. Similarly, consumption and government spending may also be partly for imported goods. On the other hand, some of domestic output is sold to foreigners.

The item "Net exports" appears in Table 2-5 to show the effects of domestic spending on foreign goods and foreign spending on domestic goods on the aggregate demand for domestic output. The total demand for the goods we produce includes exports, the demand from foreigners for our goods. It excludes imports, the part of our domestic spending that is not for our own goods. Accordingly, the difference between exports and imports, called *net exports*, is a component of the total demand for our goods.

The point can be illustrated with an example. Assume that instead of having spent $1,510 billion, the personal sector had spent $20 billion more. What would GNP have been? If we assume that government and investment spending had been the same as in Table 2-5, we might be tempted to say that GNP would have been $20 billion higher. That is correct if all the additional spending had fallen on our goods. The other extreme, however, is the case where all the additional spending falls on imports. In that event, consumption would be up $20 billion *and* net exports would be down $20 billion, with no net effect on GNP.

2-4 REAL AND NOMINAL GNP

Nominal GNP measures the value of output in a given period in the prices of that period or, as it is sometimes put, in *current dollars*. Thus 1980 nominal GNP measures the value of the goods produced in 1980 at the market prices that prevailed in 1980, and 1976 GNP measures the value of goods produced in 1976, at the market prices that prevailed in 1976. Nominal GNP changes from year to year for two reasons. The first is that the physical output of goods changes. The second is that market prices change. As an extreme and unrealistic example, one could imagine the economy producing exactly the same output in 2 years, between which all prices have doubled. Nominal GNP in the second year would be double nominal GNP in the first year, even though the physical output of the economy has not changed at all.

Real GNP is a measure that attempts to isolate changes in physical output in the economy between different time periods by valuing all goods produced in the two periods *at the same prices*, or in *constant dollars*. Real GNP is now measured in the national income accounts in the prices of 1972. That means that, in calculating real GNP, today's physical output is multiplied by the prices that prevailed in 1972 to obtain a measure of what today's output would have been worth had it been sold at the prices of 1972. We can return to the extremely simple example we used at the beginning of the chapter of an economy that produces only bananas and oranges to illustrate the calculation of real GNP. The hypothetical outputs and prices of bananas and oranges in the 2 years are shown in the first two columns of Table 2-6. Nominal GNP in 1972 was $11.25 and nominal GNP in 1980 was $21.00, or an increase in nominal GNP of 87 percent. However, much of the increase in nominal GNP is purely a result of the increase in prices between the 2 years and does not reflect an increase in physical output. When we calculate real GNP in 1980 by valuing 1980 output in the prices of 1972, we find real GNP equal to $13.80, which is an increase of 23 percent rather than 87 percent. The 23 percent increase is a better measure of the increase in physical output of the economy than the 87 percent increase.

We see from the table that the output of bananas rose by 33 percent, while the output of oranges increased by 20 percent from 1972 to 1980. We should thus expect our measure of the increase in real output to be somewhere between 20 percent and 33 percent, as it is. You will realize that the increase in real GNP that is calculated depends on the prices that are used in the calculation. If you have a calculator you might want to compare the increase in real GNP between 1972 and 1980 if the prices of 1980 are used to make the comparison. The ambiguities that arise in comparisons using different prices to calculate real GNP are an inevitable result of the attempt to use a single number to capture the increase in output of both bananas and oranges when those two components did not

TABLE 2-6 REAL AND NOMINAL GNP, AN ILLUSTRATION

1972 nominal GNP		1980 nominal GNP		1980 real GNP*	
15 bananas @ 15c	$ 2.25	20 bananas @ 30c	$ 6.00	20 bananas @ 15c	$ 3.00
50 oranges @ 18c	$ 9.00	60 oranges @ 25c	$15.00	60 oranges @ 18c	$10.80
	$11.25		$21.00		$13.80

*Measured in 1972 prices.

increase in the same proportion. However, the ambiguity is not a major concern when there is inflation at any substantial rate, and that is precisely when we most want to use real (rather than nominal) GNP to study the performance of the economy.

Chart 2-2 shows the behavior of real and nominal GNP over the past few years. It is particularly noteworthy that nominal GNP fell only once (from 1974/IV to 1975/I) during the period, even while real GNP fell in 2 consecutive years from 1973 to 1975. It would clearly be a mistake to regard the increases in nominal GNP as indicating that the performance of the economy was improving from 1973 to 1975, despite the fall in physical output. Real GNP is the better measure of the performance of the economy in producing goods and services, and it is the measure we should and do use in comparing output in different years.

2-5 PRICE INDEXES

The calculation of real GNP gives us a useful measure of inflation known as the GNP *deflator*. Returning to the hypothetical example of Table 2-6, we can get a measure of inflation between 1972 and 1980 by comparing the value of 1980 GNP in 1980 prices and 1972 prices. The ratio of nominal to

CHART 2-2 REAL AND NOMINAL GNP (Source: Citibank Economic Database)

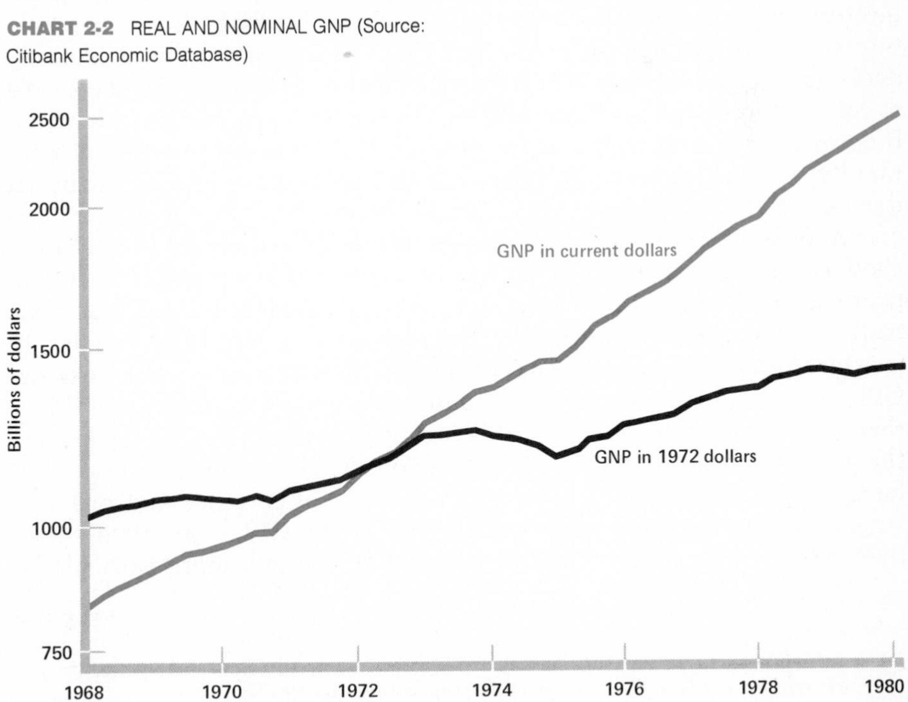

real GNP in 1980 is 1.52(=21 ÷ 13.80). In other words, output is 52 percent higher in 1980 when it is valued using the higher prices of 1980 than when it is valued in the lower 1972 prices. We ascribe, accordingly, the 52 percent increase to price changes, or inflation, over the period 1972–1980. The GNP deflator is the ratio of nominal GNP in a given year to real GNP, and it is a measure of inflation from the period from which the base prices for calculating real GNP are taken to the current period.

Since the GNP deflator is based on a calculation involving all the goods produced in the economy, it is a very widely based price index that is frequently used to measure inflation. It differs in four main ways from the other major index, the *consumer price index* (CPI), or cost of living index. First, it measures the prices of a much wider group of goods than the CPI, which is based on the market basket of goods consumed by an urban consumer. Second, the CPI measures the cost of a given basket of goods, which is the same from year to year. The basket of goods included in the GNP deflator, however, differs from year to year, depending on what is produced in the economy in each year. The goods valued in the deflator in a given year are the goods that are produced in the economy in that year. When corn crops are high, corn receives a relatively large weight in the computation of the GNP deflator. By contrast, the CPI measures the cost of a fixed bundle of goods that does not vary over time.[8] Third, the CPI directly includes prices of imports, whereas the deflator includes only prices of goods *produced* in the United States. Fourth, there is a significant interest cost component in the CPI, representing housing costs. Changes in interest rates through this channel have an important, and probably overstated, effect on the CPI. The behaviors of the two main indexes used to compute inflation, the GNP deflator and the CPI, accordingly differ from time to time. For example, at times when the price of imported oil rises rapidly, or when interest rates rise, the CPI is likely to rise faster than the deflator.

A third important price index is the *producer price index* (PPI).[9] Like the CPI, this is a measure of the cost of a given basket of goods. It differs from the CPI partly in its coverage, which includes, for example, raw materials and semifinished goods. It differs, too, in that it is designed to measure prices at an early stage of the distribution system. Whereas the CPI measures prices where urban households actually do their spending—that is, at the retail level—the PPI is constructed from prices at the level of the first significant commercial transaction. This difference is important because it makes the PPI a relatively flexible price index and one that signals changes in the general price level, or the CPI, some time before they actually materialize. For this reason the PPI and, more particularly,

[8] Price indexes are, however, occasionally revised to change weights to reflect current expenditure patterns.

[9] The PPI is the successor to the *Wholesale Price Index*, or WPI. It was introduced in 1978. The new name was selected to reflect the coverage of the data more accurately.

some of its subindexes, such as the index of "sensitive materials," serves as one of the business cycle indicators that are closely watched by policy makers.

Table 2-7 shows the CPI, the PPI, and the GNP deflator for the past 29 years. Both the CPI and PPI use 1967 as their base. This means that the weights in the standard basket that is priced are those of 1967. The GNP deflator expresses prices in the current year relative to 1972 prices, using quantities of the current year as weights. We note from the table that all three indexes have been increasing throughout the period. This is a reflection of the fact that the average price of goods has been rising, whatever basket we look at. We note, too, that the cumulative increase (price 1979/price 1950) differs across indexes. This difference occurs because the indexes represent the prices of different commodity baskets.

The mechanics of price indexes are illustrated with the help of the price index formula.[10] Both the PPI and CPI are price indexes which compare the current and base year cost of a basket of goods of *fixed* composition. If we denote the base year quantities of the various goods by q_0^i and their base year prices by p_0^i, the cost of the basket in the base year is $\Sigma p_0^i q_0^i$, where the summation (Σ) is over all the goods in the basket. The cost of a basket of the *same* quantities but at today's prices is $\Sigma p_t^i q_0^i$, where p_t^i is today's price. The CPI or PPI is the ratio of today's cost to the base year cost, or

$$\text{Price index} = \frac{\Sigma p_t^i q_0^i}{\Sigma p_0^i q_0^i} \times 100$$

[10] Detailed discussion of the various price indexes can be found in the Bureau of Labor statistics, *Handbook of Methods*, and in the Commerce Department biennial edition of *Business Statistics*. See, too, problem 7 at the end of this chapter.

TABLE 2-7 IMPORTANT PRICE INDEXES

	CPI (1967 = 100)	PPI (1967 = 100)	GNP deflator (1972 = 100)
1950	72.1	81.8	53.6
1960	88.7	94.9	68.7
1967	100.0	100.0	79.0
1972	125.3	119.1	100.0
1976	170.5	182.9	133.8
1979	217.4	235.4	165.5
Increase:			
Price 1979/price 1950	201.5%	187.8%	208.8%

Source: Citibank Economic Database.

multiplied, as a matter of convention, by 100.[11] Table 2-7 thus shows that in 1979 the cost of the standard (1967) consumer basket had increased relative to 1967 by 117 percent. Similarly, the PPI had risen relative to the base year by 135 percent.

2-6 SOME IMPORTANT IDENTITIES

In this section we formalize the discussion of Sections 2-1 through 2-3 by writing down a set of relationships which will be used extensively in Chapter 3. We introduce here some notation and conventions that we will follow throughout the book.

For analytical work in the following chapters, we will not use all the detail that comes up in national income accounting. Specifically, we will simplify our analysis by omitting the distinction between GNP and national income. For the most part we will disregard depreciation and thus the difference between GNP and NNP, as well as the difference between gross and net investment. We shall refer simply to investment spending. We will also disregard indirect taxes and business transfer payments. With these conventions in mind *we refer to national income and GNP interchangeably as income or output*. These simplifications have no serious consequence and are made only for expositional convenience. Finally, and only for a brief while, we omit both the government and the foreign sector.

A Simple Economy

We denote the value of output in our simple economy, which has neither a government nor foreign trade, by Y. Consumption is denoted by C and investment spending by I. The first key identity we want to establish is that between output produced and output sold. Output produced is Y, which can be written in terms of the components of demand as the sum of consumption and investment spending. (Remember, we have assumed away the government and foreign sectors.) Accordingly, we can write the identity of output sold and output produced as[12]

$$Y \equiv C + I \tag{7}$$

[11] The price index defined here is called a Laspeyres index. A Laspeyres index uses base year weights and in that respect differs from a Paasche index, which uses current year quantities as weights. The GNP deflator is a Paasche index. See problem 7.

[12] Throughout the book we will be careful to distinguish identities from equations. Identities are statements that are *always* true because they are directly implied by definitions of variables or accounting relationships. They do not reflect any economic behavior but are extremely useful in organizing our thinking. Identities, or definitions, will be shown with the sign $\equiv$, and equations with the usual equality sign $=$.

Now the question is whether Equation (7) is really an identity. Is it inevitably true that all output produced is either consumed or invested? After all, do not firms sometimes make goods that they are unable to sell? The answer to each of the questions is yes. Firms do sometimes make output that they cannot sell and that accumulates on their shelves. However, we count that accumulation of inventories as part of investment (as if the firms sold it to themselves), and, therefore, all output is either consumed or invested. Note that we are talking here about *actual* investment, which includes investment in inventories that firms might be very unhappy to make. Because of the way investment is defined, output produced is identically equal to output sold.

Identity (7) formalizes the basis of Table 2-5 (we are still assuming away the government and external sectors). The next step is to draw up a corresponding identity for Table 2-4 and identity (6), which examined the disposition of personal income. For that purpose, it is convenient to ignore the existence of corporations and consolidate or add together the entire private sector. Using this convention, we know that private sector income is Y, since the private sector receives as income the value of goods and services produced. Why? Because who else would get it?—there is no government or external sector yet. Now the private sector receives, as disposable personal income, the whole of income Y. How will that income be allocated? Part will be spent on consumption and part will be saved. Thus we can write[13]

$$Y \equiv S + C \tag{8}$$

where S denotes private sector saving. Identity (8) tells us that the whole of income is allocated to either consumption or saving.

Next, identities (7) and (8) can be combined to read:

$$C + I \equiv Y \equiv C + S \tag{9}$$

The left-hand side of Equation (9) shows the components of demand, and the right-hand side shows the allocation of income. The identity emphasizes that output produced is equal to output sold. The value of output produced is equal to income received, and income received, in turn, is spent on goods or saved.

The identity in Equation (9) can be slightly reformulated to look at the relation between saving and investment. Subtracting consumption from each part of Equation (9), we have

$$I \equiv Y - C \equiv S \tag{10}$$

[13] Again ask yourself why Eq. (8) should be identically true. What could you do with your income other than consume or save it? There is no alternative.

Identity (10) is an important result. It shows first that in this simple economy, saving is identically equal to income less consumption. This result is not new, since we have already seen it in Equation (8). The new part concerns the identity of the left and right sides: Investment is identically equal to saving. One can think of what lies behind this relationship in a variety of ways. In a very simple economy, the only way the individual can save is by undertaking an act of physical investment—by storing grain or building an irrigation channel. In a slightly more sophisticated economy, one could think of investors financing their investing by borrowing from individuals who save. However, it is important to recognize that Equation (10) expresses the identity between investment and saving, and that some of the investment might well be undesired inventory investment, occurring as a result of mistakes by producers who expected to sell more than they actually do. The identity is really only a reflection of our definitions—output less consumption is investment, output is income, and income less consumption is saving. Even so, we will find that identity (10) will play a key role in Chapter 3.

Reintroducing the Government and Foreign Trade

We can now reintroduce the government sector and the external sector. First, for the government we shall denote purchases of goods and services by G and all taxes by T. Transfers to the private sector (including interest) are denoted by R. Net exports (exports minus imports) are denoted by NX.

We return to the identity between output produced and sold, taking account now of the additional components of demand, G, and NX. Accordingly, we restate the content of Table 2-5 by writing

$$Y \equiv C + I + G + NX \tag{11}$$

Once more we emphasize that in Equation (11) we use actual investment in the identity and thus do not preclude the possibility that firms might not at all be content with the investment. Still, as an accounting identity, Equation (11) will hold.

Next we turn to the derivation of the very important relation between output and disposable income. Now we have to recognize that part of income is spent on taxes, and that the private sector receives net transfers R in addition to national income. Disposable income is thus equal to income plus transfers less taxes:

$$Y_d \equiv Y + R - T \tag{12}$$

We have written Y_d to denote disposable income. Disposable income, in turn, is allocated to consumption and saving, so that we can write

$$Y_d \equiv C + S \tag{13}$$

Combining Equations (12) and (13) allows us to write consumption as the difference between income, plus transfers minus taxes, and saving:

$$C + S \equiv Y_d \equiv Y + R - T \tag{14}$$

or

$$C \equiv Y_d - S \equiv Y + R - T - S \tag{14a}$$

Identity (14*a*) states that consumption is disposable income less saving, or alternatively, that consumption is equal to income plus transfers less taxes and saving. Now we use the right-hand side of Equation (14*a*) to substitute for C in identity (11). With some rearrangement we obtain

$$S - I \equiv (G + R - T) + NX \tag{15}$$

Identity (15) cannot be overemphasized. What it states is that the excess of saving over investment of the private sector $(S - I)$ is equal to the *budget deficit* $(G + R - T)$ plus the *trade surplus* (NX). On the right-hand side of Equation (15), the first term is the budget deficit of the government—government spending plus transfers (including interest payments) less tax collection. The second term on the right-hand side of Equation (15) shows net exports. Even without any behavioral content, Equation (15) is already useful because it suggests that there are important relations between the accounts of the domestic private sector $S - I$, the government budget $G + R - T$, and the external sector. Identity (15) states that if the private sector is in balance in the sense that saving equals investment, then any government budget deficit (surplus) is reflected in an equal external deficit (surplus).

Another perspective on this key identity is gained by singling out the government budget:[14]

$$T - R - G \equiv (I - S) + NX \tag{15a}$$

If the government has a budget surplus because purchases and transfers are

[14] *Government* throughout this chapter means the federal government plus state and local governments. A breakdown between these entities can be found in the *Economic Report of the President.* There one would see, for example, that state and local governments run surpluses in their public enterprises and are net recipients of interest payments.

smaller than tax collection, then the counterpart is either an external surplus or an excess of private investment over saving. The principle can be generalized by noting that any imbalance in the budget or the balance between saving and investment must be reflected in a matching external deficit. If the domestic economy absorbs more resources than it produces—if investment exceeds savings and/or the budget is in deficit—then there is an external deficit. Conversely, if a country spends less than its income, there will be an external surplus. Individuals spending less than their income will each build up assets or claims on other people. For example, these assets could be money, or bonds, or stocks. A sector that spends less than its income accumulates claims on other sectors. Thus, if we have an excess of saving over investment, then the domestic private sector will be accumulating claims on either the government—if there is a budget deficit—or on the rest of the world—if there is an external surplus. One sector's deficit is always equal to another's surplus simply because one person's receipts are another person's expenditures.

2-7 SUMMARY

We conclude with a brief summary of the major points of this chapter.

1 Nominal GNP is the value of the economy's output of final goods and services measured at market prices.
2 Real GNP is the value of the economy's output measured in the prices of some base year. Real GNP comparisons, based on the same set of prices for valuing output, provide a better measure of the change in the economy's physical output than nominal GNP comparisons, which also reflect inflation.
3 National income is equal to GNP minus depreciation and indirect taxes.
4 National income is equal to the incomes received in the economy, valued at factor cost.
5 Spending on GNP is conveniently divided into consumption, investment, government purchases of goods and services, and net exports. The division between consumption and investment in the national income accounts is somewhat arbitrary at the edges.
6 One sector's surplus is another sector's deficit. For example, the excess of the private sector's savings over investment is equal to the sum of the budget deficit and the foreign trade surplus.
7 For the remainder of the book we use a simplified model for expositional convenience. We assume away depreciation, indirect taxes, business transfer payments, and the difference between households and corporations. For this simplified model, Chart 2-3 and Equation (16) review the *basic macroeconomic identity:*

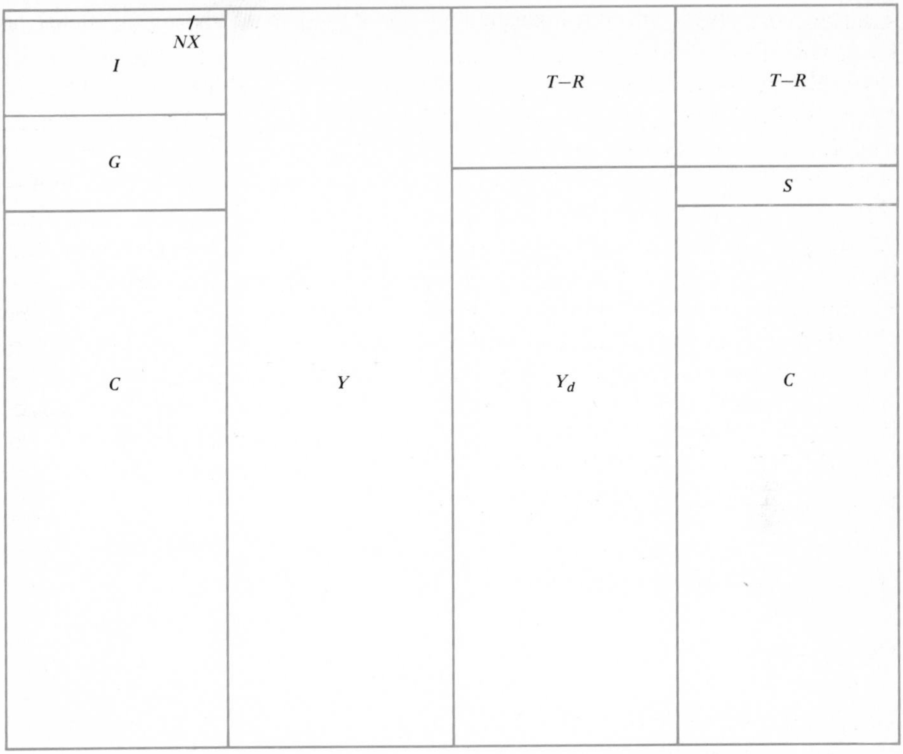

CHART 2-3 THE BASIC MACROECONOMIC IDENTITY

$$C + G + I + NX \equiv Y \equiv Y_d + (T - R) \equiv (T - R) + S + C \quad (16)$$

The left-hand side is the demand for output by components which is identically equal to output supplied. Output supplied is equal to income. Disposable income is equal to income plus transfers less taxes. Disposable income is allocated to saving and consumption.

PROBLEMS

1 Show from national income accounting that:
  (*a*) An increase in taxes (while transfers remain constant) must imply a change in the trade balance, government purchases, or the saving-investment balance.
  (*b*) An increase in disposable income must imply an increase in consumption or an increase in saving.

(c) An increase in both consumption and saving must imply an increase in disposable income.

2 The following is information from the national income accounts for a hypothetical country:

GNP	2,400
Gross investment	400
Net investment	150
Consumption	1,500
Government purchases of goods and services	480
National income	1,925
Wages and salaries	1,460
Proprietors' income + rental income of persons	160
Dividends	50
Net interest	130
Government budget surplus	15
Social insurance contributions	190
Personal interest income	190
Government transfers to persons	250
Business transfer payments	10
Personal tax and nontax payments	300

What is:

(a) NNP?
(b) Net exports?
(c) Indirect taxes?
(d) Corporate profits?
(e) Taxes—transfers?
(f) Personal income?
(g) Disposable personal income?
(h) Personal saving?
(i) Corporate saving?

3 What would happen to GNP if the government hired unemployed workers, who had been getting R in unemployment benefits, as government employees to do nothing, still giving them R? Explain.

4 What is the difference in the national income accounts between:

(a) A firm's buying an auto for an executive and the firm's paying the executive additional income to buy himself a car?
(b) Your hiring your spouse (who takes care of the house) rather than just having him or her do the work without pay?
(c) Your deciding to buy an American car rather than a German car?

5 Explain the following terms:

(a) Value added
(b) Factor cost
(c) Inventory investment
(d) GNP deflator

6 Use the information in the various tables to construct a table showing government receipts and outlays as well as the government budget deficit for 1979. (Corporate profit taxes were \$93 billion, subsidies less surpluses of government enterprises were \$2 billion, and net government interest was \$34 billion in 1979.)

7 This question deals with price index numbers. Consider a simple economy where there are only three items in the CPI: food, housing, and entertainment (fun).

Assume in the base period, say 1967, the household consumed the following quantities at the then prevailing prices:

	Quantities	Prices per unit, dollars	Expenditure, dollars
Food	5	14	70
Housing	3	10	30
Fun	4	5	20
Total			120

(*a*) Consider what the CPI will be in 1980 if the prevailing prices have changed as follows: food, $30 per unit; housing, $20 per unit; and fun, $6 per unit. In making your calculations, use the formula for the CPI given in the text.

*(*b*) Show that the change in the CPI relative to the base year is a weighted average of the individual price changes where the weights are given by the base year expenditure shares of the various goods.

(*c*) Price indexes that use base year quantities are called Laspeyres indexes. By contrast, an index that uses current year quantities is called a Paasche index. A Paasche index, therefore, is defined by the formula:

$$\text{Price index} = \frac{\Sigma q_t^i p_t^i}{\Sigma q_t^i p_0^i} \times 100$$

You are asked to calculate both the Laspeyres and Paasche indexes for the information provided in Table 2-6. In addition, find the GNP deflator (base year 1972) appropriate for that table. How do the three indexes compare?

8 This question is a national income accounting puzzle. Consider an economy where disposable personal income is $1,000. Corporate profits are $120. Gross investment is $180, and net investment is $140. There are no valuation adjustments. The government makes transfer payments to persons of $100. Indirect business taxes are $190. The government collects $150 in personal income taxes and Social Security contributions. Government enterprises make a deficit of $4. Business transfer payments are $9. Dividends are $20. Personal interest income is $400. Net interest is $25. Given this information, what is GNP?

9 Discuss the implications of the following events for national income and disposable personal income:

(*a*) The government increases the corporate income tax rate from 46 percent to 60 percent.

(*b*) Pennsylvania's state liquor stores (part of "government enterprises") increase the profits on their operation.

(*c*) Social Security taxes are increased.

(*d*) There is an increase in veterans' benefits payments.

In all these questions, assume that GNP remains unchanged.

10 Assume that GNP is $1,200, personal disposable income is $1,000, and the government budget deficit is $70. Consumption is $850, the trade surplus is $20. Corporate savings is zero.

(*a*) How large is saving S?

(*b*) What is the size of investment I?

(*c*) How large is government spending?

3

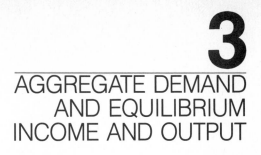

AGGREGATE DEMAND AND EQUILIBRIUM INCOME AND OUTPUT

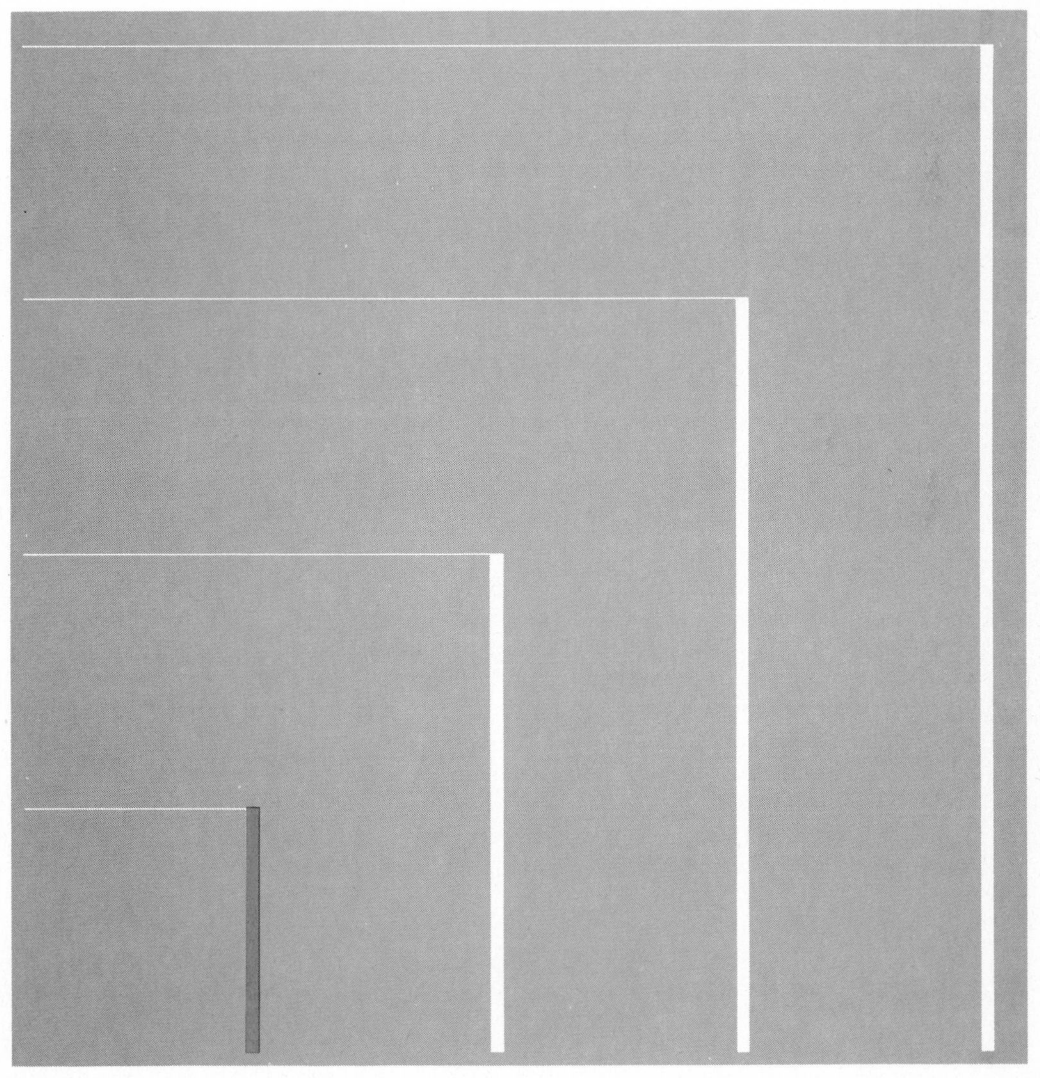

In Chapter 2 we studied the measurement of national income and output (GNP). With these fundamental concepts, we are now able to begin our study of the factors that determine the level of national income and product. Ultimately, we want to know why national income sometimes falls (and the rate of unemployment rises), as it did in 1974–1975 and 1980, and why at other times income rises very rapidly (and unemployment falls), as it did in 1976–1978. We also want to know what determines the rate of inflation. Why was it so high in 1974? Why did it rise from 1976 to 1979? We want to know whether public policies, such as changes in government spending and tax rates, or changes in the growth rate of the money supply, or changes in interest rates, can affect the level of income and the rates of inflation and unemployment, and if they can, we want to know how.

The study of those questions occupies the rest of the book. But we will proceed slowly. We begin in this chapter with a simplified model of the economy that isolates the crucial concept of *aggregate demand,* while still omitting both some factors that affect aggregate demand and considerations of aggregate supply. In later chapters we gradually introduce those other factors. By the time we have completed Chapter 13, we will be able to understand the behavior of the key macroeconomic variables—the rates of unemployment and inflation, and the level of GNP.

Our discussion of the determination of the level of output in this chapter starts from the basic macroeconomic identities in Equation (16) of Chapter 2 and in Chart 2-3: First, net national product (NNP) is equal to total spending on goods and services, consisting of consumption C, net investment I, government purchases of goods and services G, and net exports NX. Second, net national product is also equal to net income received in the economy.[1] Income, in turn, increased by transfers R and reduced by taxes T, is allocated to consumption C and saving S. Thus:

$$C + I + G + NX \equiv Y \equiv S + (T - R) + C$$

In this chapter we go beyond that *accounting identity* to begin our study of the factors that determine the level of national product or output. In particular, we focus on the interactions between the level of output and aggregate demand. We shall see that there is a single level of *equilibrium* output at which the aggregate (total) demand for goods and services is equal to the level of output. To begin with, we simplify our task by discussing a hypothetical world without a government ($G \equiv T \equiv R \equiv 0$) and without foreign trade ($NX \equiv 0$). In such a world, the accounting identity simplifies to

$$C + I \equiv Y \equiv S + C \tag{1}$$

[1] Because net national product (or output) is equal to net income received in the economy, economists tend to use the terms *income* and *output* interchangeably when discussing the level of economic activity.

where Y denotes the real value of output and income. Further, we will remember that throughout this chapter a change in a macroeconomic aggregate is a change in its *real* value at constant prices. Thus, when we speak of a change in income or a change in consumption spending, we mean a change in real income or a change in real consumption spending.

We shall study in Section 3-1 the important concepts of *goods market equilibrium* and *equilibrium output*. In that section we assume, for expositional purposes, that aggregate demand is *autonomous*—that is, independent of the level of income. In fact, however, consumption spending is related to the level of income—that is, changes in consumption spending are *induced* by changes in income.[2] Accordingly, in Section 3-2 we recognize this point and discuss the factors that affect the level of consumption by introducing the *consumption function*. We derive an explicit formula for the equilibrium level of income and output. Section 3-3 studies the effects of changes in autonomous spending on equilibrium output. The effects of those changes are summarized by the *multiplier*, which is examined in detail in Section 3-3. The government sector is introduced in Section 3-4, which includes the first discussion of fiscal policy. The discussion of fiscal policy is extended to the government budget in Section 3-5.

We do not in this chapter extend the analysis to include foreign trade, despite its importance. Instead, issues of the open economy are left for an integrated treatment in Chapters 18 and 19. For the impatient reader, we have set a tough problem that deals with trade at the end of this chapter.

3-1 EQUILIBRIUM OUTPUT

In this chapter and the next we shall assume a world where all prices are given and constant. Such a world would exist if a sufficient level of unemployment of resources allowed firms, within the relevant range, to supply any amount of output without significantly affecting their unit costs.[3] In terms of Figure 1-1, we are dealing with a situation in which the aggregate supply curve is horizontal.

If firms could supply any amount of output at the prevailing level of prices, what would determine the level of output actually produced? Demand must enter the picture. We would expect firms to produce at a level just sufficient to meet demand. If output produced was in excess of demand, firms would find their inventories piling up, and conversely, if

[2] The terms *autonomous* and *induced* are traditionally used to indicate spending that is independent of the level of income and dependent on the level of income, respectively. More generally, autonomous spending is spending that is independent of the other variables explained in a given theory.

[3] It is important to note that the assumption that prices are constant is made to simplify the exposition of Chaps. 3 and 4. In later chapters, we use the theories developed in Chaps. 3 and 4 to study the factors that determine the price level and cause it to change over time.

production fell short of demand, inventories would be running down or households would be unable to make the consumption purchases they had planned.

The preceding paragraph suggests a notion of equilibrium output as that level where demand equals supply, so that unintended changes in inventories are zero and households' actual consumption is equal to their planned consumption. Before exploring that notion further, we have to dispose of an unsettling issue that arises from the accounting identity in Equation (1), derived from our study of national income accounting. The identity in Equation (1) states that demand, $C + I$, is *identically* equal to supply Y, *whatever* the level of output. That seems to mean that demand equals supply at *any* level of output, so that any level of output could be the equilibrium level.

The issue is resolved by remembering that in Equation (1), investment is *actual* investment and consumption is *actual* consumption. The investment measured in Equation (1) includes involuntary, or unintended, inventory changes, which occur when firms find themselves selling more or less goods than they had planned to sell. Similarly, if households cannot buy all the goods they want, the consumption measured in Equation (1) will be different from planned consumption. By contrast, our concept of equilibrium output suggests a situation where unintended inventory changes are zero and consumption is equal to planned consumption. We clearly have to make a distinction between the *actual* aggregate demand that is measured in an accounting context and the relevant economic concept of *planned* (desired, intended) aggregate demand.

Actual aggregate demand $(C + I)$ is, by the accounting identity in Equation (1), equal to the level of output (Y). The output level is determined by firms. In deciding how much to produce, firms calculate how much investment, including inventory investment, they want to undertake. They also produce to meet the demand for consumption they forecast will be forthcoming from households. *Planned* aggregate demand consists of the amount of consumption households plan to carry out plus the amount of investment planned by firms.[4] If firms miscalculate households' consumption demands, planned aggregate demand does not equal actual aggregate demand. Suppose first that firms overestimate consumption demand. The firms find their inventories increasing by more than they had planned, because some of the goods they had planned to sell are not bought by consumers and have instead to be added to inventories. In that case, actual aggregate demand or output exceeds planned aggregate demand, and firms have unanticipated or unintended inventory investment. Similarly, if firms underestimate households' consumption demand, there is unintended

[4] From now on we shall assume that actual consumption is equal to planned consumption, so that all differences between actual and planned aggregate demand are reflected in unintended inventory changes. In practical terms, this means we are not considering situations where firms put "Sold Out" signs in their windows and customers cannot buy what they want.

inventory decumulation, and actual aggregate demand is less than planned aggregate demand. If we denote aggregate demand by A, the above discussion implies

$$I_{\text{unintended}} \equiv A_{\text{actual}} - A_{\text{planned}} \tag{2}$$

Now actual aggregate demand (A_{actual}) is equal to the level of output Y, and planned aggregate demand (A_{planned}) is the sum of consumption and intended investment $C + I_{\text{int}}$.[5] Thus, using Equation (2), we find

$$\begin{aligned} I_{\text{unintended}} &\equiv A_{\text{actual}} - A_{\text{planned}} \\ &\equiv Y - (C + I_{\text{int}}) \end{aligned} \tag{3}$$

The identity in Equation (3) can now be linked with the discussion of equilibrium output. We defined equilibrium output as the level of production such that actual aggregate demand is equal to planned aggregate demand. By Equation (3), this implies that unintended inventory accumulation is zero when output is at its equilibrium level.

We shall adopt the convention of using the term *aggregate demand* only in the sense of "planned" and reserve for it the notation A. Similarly, we shall use the term *investment demand* exclusively for planned investment spending—the amount firms plan to spend for investment and denote it by I. Unintended inventory changes will be denoted by I_u. With these conventions, we can rewrite Equation (3) as

$$I_u \equiv Y - A \equiv Y - C - I \tag{3a}$$

where we have used the fact that $A \equiv C + I$ (aggregate demand is the sum of consumption and investment demands).

So far, we have isolated a *concept* of equilibrium output. We have said that there is equilibrium when output supplied is equal to aggregate demand. We define that situation as equilibrium because then households find themselves consuming at the rate they planned, and firms find themselves investing at the rate they planned. We have also defined aggregate demand in terms of planned spending. To repeat, aggregate demand is the sum of the amounts households plan to spend on consumption goods and firms plan to spend on investment.

Now we want to go beyond the mere concept of equilibrium output and find out what the equilibrium level of output actually is. For that purpose we need to make an assumption about aggregate demand. The simplest assumption we can make is that aggregate demand is some constant level $\bar{A}$. Our simplest assumption thus makes the demands for consumption and investment independent of the level of income (or autonomous). With this

[5] Recall that we are assuming actual consumption is equal to planned consumption.

aggregate demand function, it is easy to determine the equilibrium level of output. Recalling that the equilibrium condition is that output supplied equals aggregate demand, we have

$$Y = \bar{A} \tag{4}$$

There are some insights to be gained even from this simple model. Turn to Figure 3-1, where we have plotted on the horizontal axis output Y and, on the vertical axis, aggregate demand A. The aggregate demand function $A = \bar{A}$ is shown as the horizontal line with intercept $\bar{A}$. We show, too, a 45° line that serves as a reference line in that it translates any horizontal distance into an equal vertical distance. For any given level of Y on the horizontal axis, the 45° line gives the level of A on the vertical axis such that $Y = A$. Clearly, from Equation (4) and Figure 3-1, the equilibrium level of output is $Y_0 = \bar{A}$.

Consider now a level of output below Y_0, corresponding to a situation in which firms produce less than the equilibrium level of output. At any level of output below Y_0, aggregate demand $\bar{A}$ exceeds the level of output so that there is an *excess demand*—aggregate demand exceeds output. Consequently, inventories are run down, or unintended inventory reductions take place. The magnitude of unintended inventory changes is given by the vertical distance between the aggregate demand schedule $\bar{A}$ and the 45°

FIGURE 3-1 EQUILIBRIUM WITH CONSTANT AGGREGATE DEMAND

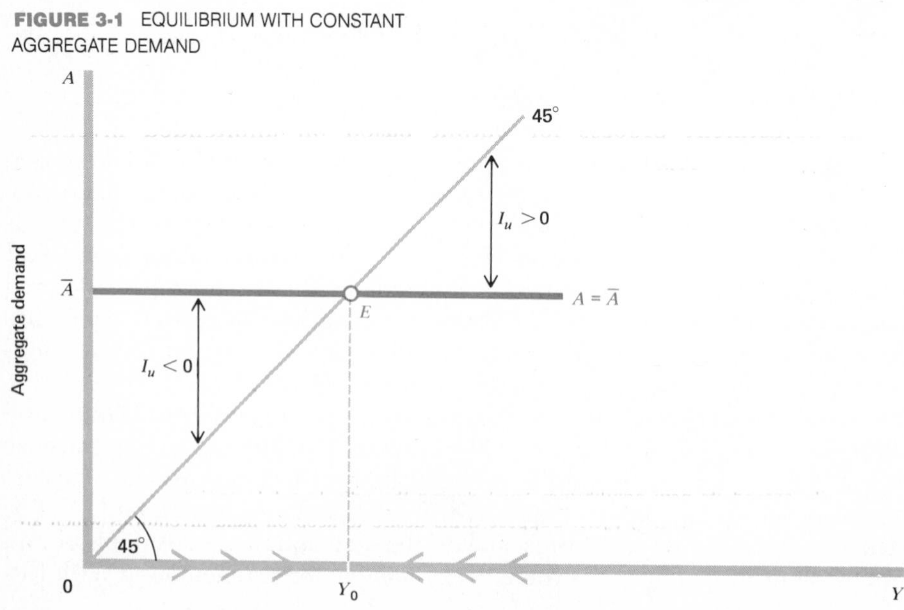

line at each level of income, since, using (3*a*), $I_u \equiv Y - \overline{A}$. At a level of income above Y_0, by contrast, output exceeds aggregate demand, and inventories consequently pile up at a rate equal to the difference between the 45° line and the aggregate demand schedule. At Y_0, output exactly equals aggregate demand, and correspondingly there are no unintended inventory changes.

Will the economy actually reach the equilibrium output level, Y_0? It is reasonable to assume that firms cut production whenever an excess of output over aggregate demand causes inventories to pile up. Suppose now that output initially exceeds the equilibrium level, Y_0. Then firms are unable to sell all the goods they produce and find themselves with increasing inventories. As they find their inventories increasing, they reduce the level of production so as to prevent a further buildup of inventories. Conversely, suppose that the level of output is below the equilibrium level, Y_0. Then firms find their inventories decreasing because demand exceeds their production.[6] Under those circumstances, they will increase output to meet the demand for goods. The arrows on the horizontal axis in Figure 3-1 are a convenient way of describing the behavior of firms that we have discussed. The arrows show that the level of output is decreasing whenever output is above Y_0 and increasing whenever Y is less than Y_0. Accordingly, Y will move to the equilibrium level Y_0, which is precisely what our verbal discussion leads us to believe.[7]

We have now mastered both the concept and the mechanics of the determination of equilibrium output. There are three essential notions:

- Aggregate demand determines the equilibrium level of output.
- At equilibrium, unintended changes in inventories are zero, and households consume the amount they have planned to consume.
- An adjustment process for output based on unintended inventory changes will actually move output to its equilibrium level.

Note, too, that the definition of equilibrium implies that actual spending on consumption and investment equals planned spending. In equilibrium, aggregate demand, which is planned spending, equals output. Since output identically equals income, we see also that in equilibrium, planned spending equals income.

[6] Alternatively, if inventories are zero, firms find themselves having to turn away customers because goods are out of stock. This too would lead firms to increase their output.

[7] You may have noticed that the adjustment process we describe raises the possibility that output will temporarily exceed its new equilibrium level during the adjustment to an increase in aggregate demand. This is the *inventory cycle*. Suppose firms desire to keep on hand inventories which are proportional to the level of demand. When demand unexpectedly rises, inventories are depleted. In subsequent periods, the firms have to produce not only to meet the new higher level of aggregate demand, but also to restore their depleted inventories and to raise them to a higher level. While they are rebuilding their inventories and also producing to meet the higher level of demand, their total production will exceed the new level of aggregate demand.

3-2 THE CONSUMPTION FUNCTION AND AGGREGATE DEMAND

The preceding section studied the equilibrium level of output (and income) on the assumption that aggregate demand was simply a constant $\overline{A}$. In this section, we extend the discussion to a more realistic specification of aggregate demand and begin to examine the economic variables that determine it. We separate aggregate demand into its components, consumption and investment demand, and assume an explicit *consumption function*. The assumed consumption function relates consumption spending by households to the level of income. Planned investment is treated as constant at the level $\overline{I}$. Because consumption demand depends on the level of income, so too does aggregate demand. Aggregate demand is no longer constant, as in Section 3-1, and we shall have to modify Figure 3-1 accordingly. First, though, we examine the consumption function.

The Consumption Function

We assume that consumption spending is a linear function of income:[8]

$$C = \overline{C} + cY \tag{5}$$

where

$$\overline{C} > 0 \qquad \text{and} \qquad 0 < c < 1$$

This consumption function is shown in Figure 3-2*a*. The *intercept* is $\overline{C}$ and the *slope* is c.

The fundamental notion underlying this consumption function is that an individual's level of consumption is primarily determined by her income. The higher the income, the higher the level of consumption.

The consumption function [Equation (5)] implies that at low levels of income, consumption exceeds income, while at high levels of income, consumption falls short of income. This feature can be seen in Figure 3-2*a*, which includes a 45° line along which income is equal to consumption. At low levels of income, the consumption function lies above the 45° line, and consumption therefore exceeds income. As we shall see, that means that at low levels of income, the individual or household is dissaving. At high levels of income, the household saves, since consumption is less than income.

These relationships between income and consumption arise from the

[8] Note that because income is equal to output, we use the same symbol, Y, for both income and output.

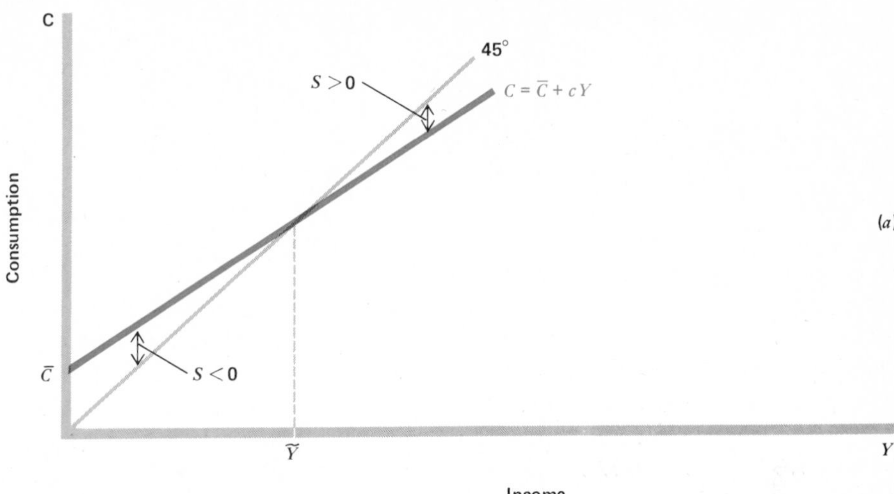

FIGURE 3-2a THE CONSUMPTION FUNCTION

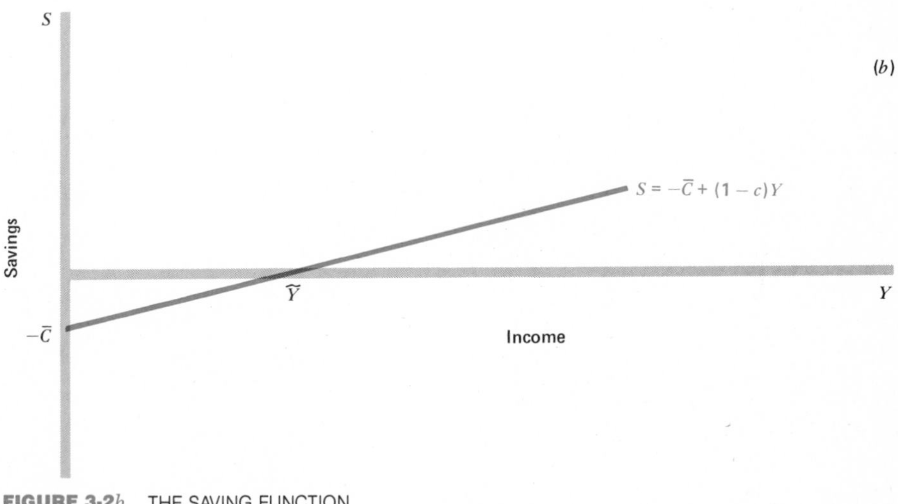

FIGURE 3-2b THE SAVING FUNCTION

positive intercept, $\overline{C}$, in Equation (5), and the fact that the coefficient c is less than unity. The coefficient c is sufficiently important for us to have a special name for it. The coefficient c is called the ***marginal propensity to consume***: it is the increase in consumption per unit increase in income. In our case, the marginal propensity to consume is less than unity, which implies that out of a dollar increase in income, only a fraction c is spent on consumption. For example, if c is 0.9, then, when income rises by \$1, consumption increases by 90 cents.

Consumption and Saving

What happens to the rest, the fraction $(1 - c)$ that is not spent on consumption? Looking at the right-hand side of Equation (1) above (namely, $Y \equiv S + C$), we recognize that there is a relationship among income, consumption, and saving. Specifically, Equation (1) says that income that is not spent on consumption is saved, or

$$S \equiv Y - C \tag{6}$$

What Equation (6) tells us is that by definition, *saving is equal to income minus consumption*. This means that we cannot postulate, in addition to the consumption function, an independent saving function and still expect consumption and saving to add up to income.

The consumption function in Equation (5), together with Equation (6), which we call the *budget constraint*, implies a saving function. The saving function is the function that relates the level of saving to the level of income. Substituting the consumption function in Equation (5) into the budget constraint in Equation (6) yields the saving function

$$\begin{aligned} S &\equiv Y - C \\ &= Y - (\overline{C} + cY) \\ &= -\overline{C} + (1 - c)Y \end{aligned} \tag{7}$$

From Equation (7), saving is an increasing function of the level of income because the *marginal propensity to save*, $s = 1 - c$, is positive. Furthermore, the saving function is the mirror image of the consumption function. At low levels of income, saving is negative, thus reflecting the fact that consumption exceeds income. Conversely, at sufficiently high levels of income, saving becomes positive and thus reflects the fact that not all income is spent on consumption.

The interrelationship between the consumption and saving functions examined in Equation (7) can also be seen graphically in Figure 3-2, where the vertical distance between the consumption function and the 45° line at each level of income measures saving. Figure 3-2*b* shows the saving function that is derived from the consumption function in Figure 3-2*a* by plotting the vertical distance between income and consumption spending at each level of income. Of course, Figure 3-2*b* is merely a representation of Equation (7). Note that the slope of the saving function in Figure 3-2*b* is the marginal propensity to save, $s = 1 - c$, as defined above.

Planned Investment and Aggregate Demand

We have now specified one component of aggregate demand, consumption spending. To complete the specification of aggregate demand, we must also consider the determinants of investment spending, or an *investment function*. We shall cut short the discussion for the present by simply assuming that planned investment spending is at a constant level $\bar{I}$.[9] Having specified each of the components of aggregate demand, we can now write the aggregate demand function as their sum:

$$A \equiv C + I \text{ intended}$$

$$\equiv \bar{C} + cY + \bar{I} \tag{8}$$

Equilibrium Income and Output

The next step is to use this aggregate demand function to determine the equilibrium level of income and output. We therefore return to the *equilibrium condition* in the goods market:

$$Y = A \tag{9}$$

which states that in equilibrium, output supplied, or income, equals output demanded, or planned aggregate spending. The level of aggregate demand is specified in Equation (8), so that substituting for A in Equation (9), we have the equilibrium condition as

$$Y = \bar{C} + cY + \bar{I} \tag{10}$$

Since we have Y on both sides of the equilibrium condition in Equation (10), we can solve for the equilibrium level of income and output, denoted by Y_0, in terms of the parameters of the aggregate demand function $(\bar{C}, \bar{I}, c)$. From Equation (10), we can write

$$Y - cY = \bar{C} + \bar{I}$$

or

$$Y(1 - c) = \bar{C} + \bar{I}$$

Thus the equilibrium level of income, at which aggregate demand equals output, is[10]

$$Y_0 = \frac{1}{1 - c}(\bar{C} + \bar{I}) \tag{11}$$

[9] In Chaps. 4 and 6, investment spending will become a function of the rate of interest and will gain an important place in the transmission of monetary policy.

[10] As a convention, we use the subscript $_0$ to denote the equilibrium level of a variable.

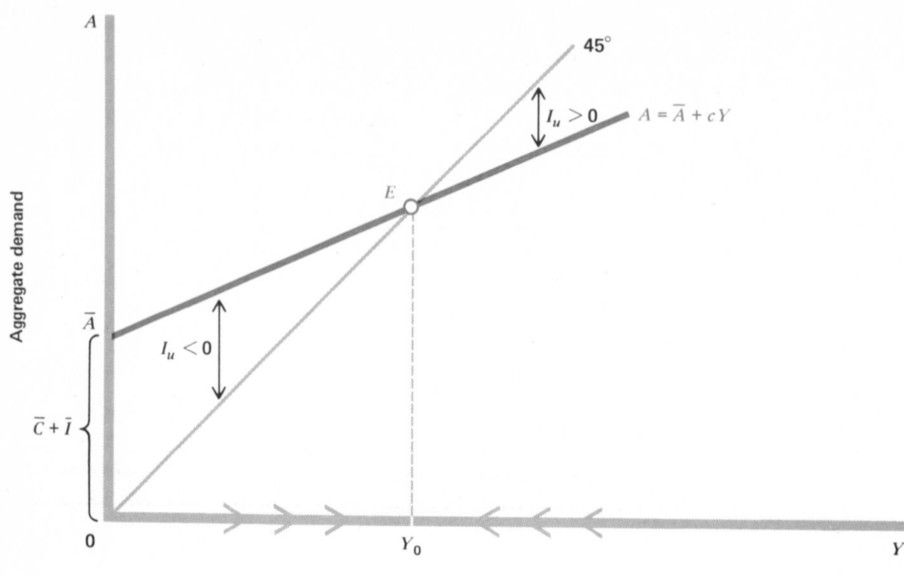

FIGURE 3-3 DETERMINATION OF EQUILIBRIUM INCOME

We have arrived rather quickly at Equation (11) for the equilibrium level of income and output. It is therefore worthwhile to retrace our steps and use Figure 3-3 to gain understanding of what is involved in the derivation. We plot the aggregate demand function shown in Equation (8). The intercept $\overline{A}$—autonomous spending—is equal to $\overline{C} + \overline{I}$, and the slope is given by the marginal propensity to consume, c. This aggregate demand schedule shows the planned level of spending in the economy (consumption plus investment spending) that is associated with each level of income. As is apparent from the figure, aggregate demand increases as the level of income rises. In fact, Figure 3-3 differs from Figure 3-1 only in that the aggregate demand function of Figure 3-3 is upward-sloping rather than horizontal. This relation arises because consumption spending, a component of aggregate demand, increases as income increases.

Consider now the determination of the equilibrium level of income. Remember that the equilibrium level of income is such that aggregate demand equals output (which in turn equals income). The 45° line in Figure 3-3 shows points at which output and aggregate demand are equal. The aggregate demand schedule in Figure 3-3 cuts the 45° line at E, and it is accordingly at E that aggregate demand is equal to output (equals income). Only at E, and at the corresponding equilibrium level of income and output, Y_0, does aggregate demand exactly equal output. At that level of output and income, planned spending precisely matches production.

We also showed in Section 3-1 that at the equilibrium level of output, unintended inventory changes are zero. In Figure 3-3, unintended changes in inventories associated with each level of output are equal to the vertical distance between the aggregate demand function and the 45° line. At levels of income below Y_0, unintended inventory changes are therefore negative because aggregate demand exceeds output. Conversely, at levels of output above Y_0, involuntary inventory changes are positive because aggregate demand falls short of output. Only at the equilibrium level of income, Y_0, are unintended inventory changes equal to zero.

The arrows in Figure 3-3 indicate once again how we reach equilibrium. If firms expand production whenever they face unintended decreases in their inventory holdings, then they increase output at any level below Y_0, because, below Y_0, aggregate demand exceeds output and inventories are declining. Conversely, for output levels above Y_0, firms find inventories piling up and therefore cut production. This process will lead us to the output level Y_0, where current production exactly matches planned aggregate spending. Again, the arrows in Figure 3-3 represent the dynamic process by which the economy moves to the equilibrium level of output Y_0.[11]

Figure 3-3 sheds light, too, on the determinants of the equilibrium level of income calculated in Equation (11). The position of the aggregate demand schedule is characterized by its slope c and intercept $\bar{A}$. The intercept $\bar{A}$ is the level of autonomous spending, that is, spending that is independent of the level of income. For our aggregate demand function, Equation (8), autonomous spending is equal to $\bar{C} + \bar{I}$. The other determinant of the equilibrium level of income is the marginal propensity to consume, c, which is the slope of the aggregate demand schedule. Given the intercept, a steeper aggregate demand function—as would be implied by a higher marginal propensity to consume—implies a higher level of equilibrium income. Similarly, for a given marginal propensity to consume, a higher level of autonomous spending—in terms of Figure 3-3, a larger intercept—implies a higher equilibrium level of income. These results, suggested by Figure 3-3, are easily verified from Equation (11), which gives the formula for the equilibrium level of income.

Saving and Investment

A further perspective on equilibrium income can be gained from Figure 3-4. Here we have shown separately the consumption schedule and the aggregate demand function. The vertical distance between the two

[11] Do you see that there is once more the possibility of an inventory cycle? Refer back to footnote 7.

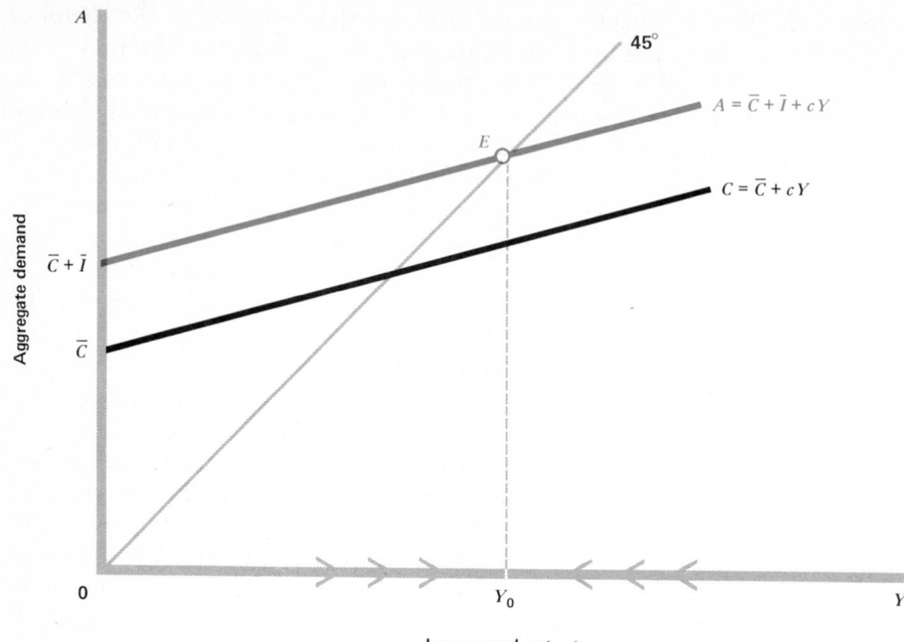

FIGURE 3-4 CONSUMPTION AND INVESTMENT AS COMPONENTS OF AGGREGATE DEMAND

schedules represents the constant level of planned investment spending, $\overline{I}$. As we saw earlier, the equilibrium level of income is Y_0, because only at that level of output does aggregate planned spending equal income. The breakdown of aggregate spending into its consumption and investment components is useful to bring out an important relationship that holds in equilibrium in this simple economy without a government and foreign trade. Specifically, *in equilibrium, planned investment equals saving.*

We recall from Figure 3-2 that the vertical distance between the consumption schedule and the 45° line measures saving at each level of income. The vertical distance between the aggregate demand schedule and the consumption schedule measures planned investment spending. At the equilibrium level of income, these two distances coincide, and accordingly, saving equals (planned) investment.[12] By contrast, above the equilibrium level of income Y_0, saving (the distance between the 45° line and the consumption schedule) exceeds investment, while below Y_0, investment exceeds saving.

[12] Recall that we have agreed to mean "planned investment" when we use the term *investment*.

Now, is the equality between saving and investment at equilibrium an essential characteristic of the equilibrium level of income, or is it a mere curiosity? It is an essential characteristic of equilibrium. We can see that by starting with the basic equilibrium condition Equation (9), which states that in equilibrium, $Y = A$. If we subtract consumption from both Y and A, we realize that $Y - C$ is saving and $A - C$ is planned investment. In symbols,

$$\begin{aligned} Y &= A \\ Y - C &= A - C \\ S &= \bar{I} \end{aligned} \tag{12}$$

Thus, the definition of equilibrium, "aggregate demand is equal to output," is equivalent to the condition that saving equals investment. The condition $S = \bar{I}$ is merely another way of stating the basic equilibrium condition.[13]

Recall also that in equilibrium, unintended inventory accumulation is zero. The "saving equals investment" definition of equilibrium also implies that in equilibrium there is no unintended inventory investment. Saving is income less consumption. Given the equality of income and output, saving is therefore the excess of output over consumption. That excess must exactly equal planned investment spending for there to be no unintended inventory changes. But that says that saving has to be equal to planned investment if there are to be no unintended inventory changes.

There is also a diagrammatic derivation of the equilibrium level of income that corresponds to the statement of the equilibrium condition in Equation (12) as the balance between saving and investment. In Figure 3-5,

[13] In the problem set, we ask you to derive Eq. (11) for Y_0 by starting from $S = \bar{I}$ and substituting for S from Eq. (7).

FIGURE 3-5 SAVING AND INVESTMENT

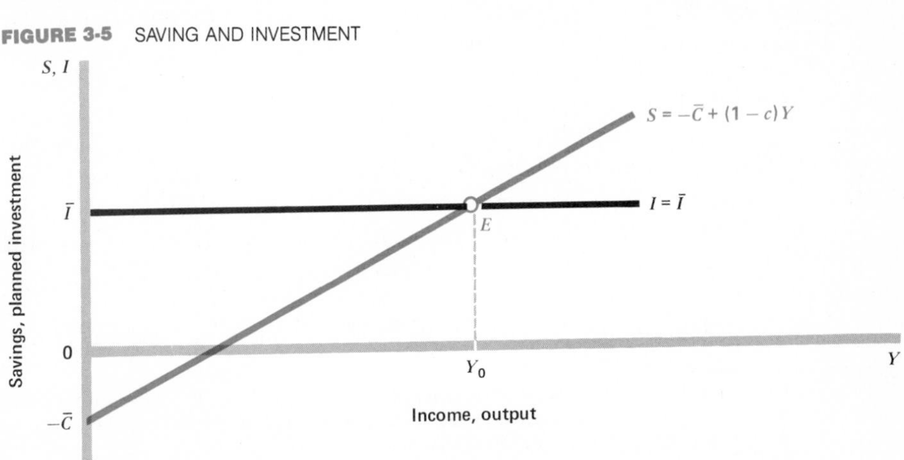

we show the saving function that was derived in Figure 3-2. We have drawn, too, planned investment spending indicated by the horizontal line with intercept $\overline{I}$. Equilibrium income is shown as the level Y_0. To complete the argument, remember that from Equation (3*a*) unintended inventory changes are defined as:

$$I_u = Y - C - \overline{I} \qquad (3a)$$

Substituting the definition of saving $S \equiv Y - C$, we have

$$I_u = S - \overline{I} \qquad (13)$$

Equation (13) shows us that when saving equals investment, the unintended inventory changes are zero, and thus serves as a check on Equation (12) as a statement of the equilibrium condition.

3-3 THE MULTIPLIER

In this section we develop an answer to the following question: By how much does a $1 increase in *autonomous* spending raise the equilibrium level of income?[14] There would appear to be a simple answer. Since, in equilibrium, income equals aggregate demand, it would seem that a $1 increase in (autonomous) demand or spending should raise equilibrium income by $1. That answer is wrong. Let us now see why.

Suppose first that output increased by $1 to match the increased level of autonomous spending. This output and income increase would in turn give rise to further *induced* spending as consumption rises because the level of income has risen. How much of the initial $1 increase in income would be spent on consumption? The answer to that question is given by the marginal propensity to consume, c. Out of an additional dollar of income, a fraction c is consumed. Assume then that production increases further to meet this induced expenditure, that is, that output and so income increase by $1 + c$. That will still leave us with an excess demand because the very fact of an expansion in production and income by $1 + c$ will give rise to further induced spending. This story could clearly take a long time to tell. We seem to have arrived at an impasse where expansion in output to meet excess demand leads to a further expansion in demand without an obvious end to that process.

It helps to lay out the various steps in this chain more carefully. We

[14] Recall that autonomous spending $\overline{A}$ is spending that is independent of the level of income. Note also that the answer to this question is contained in Eq. (11). Can you deduce the answer directly from Eq. (11)? This section provides an explanation of that answer.

start off in the first round with an increase in autonomous spending $\Delta\overline{A}$. Next we allow an expansion in production to exactly meet that increase in demand. Production accordingly expands by $\Delta\overline{A}$. This increase in production gives rise to an equal increase in income and, therefore, via the consumption function, $C = \overline{C} + cY$, gives rise in the second round to induced expenditures of size $c\,(\Delta\overline{A})$. Assume again that production expands to meet the increase in spending. The production adjustment this time is $c\,(\Delta\overline{A})$ and so is the increase in income. This gives rise to a third round of induced spending equal to the marginal propensity to consume times the increase in income $c(c\,\Delta\overline{A}) = c^2\,\Delta\overline{A}$. Careful inspection of the last term shows that induced expenditures in the third round are smaller than those in the second round. Since the marginal propensity to consume, c, is less than 1, the term c^2 is less than c.

If we write out the successive rounds of increased spending, starting with the initial increase in autonomous demand, we obtain

$$\begin{aligned}\Delta A &= \Delta\overline{A} + c\,(\Delta\overline{A}) + c^2\,\Delta\overline{A} + c^3\,\Delta\overline{A} + \cdots \\ &= \Delta\overline{A}(1 + c + c^2 + c^3 + \cdots)\end{aligned} \tag{14}$$

It is obvious that for $c<1$, the successive terms in the series become progressively smaller. In fact, we are dealing with a geometric series the sum of which is calculated as

$$\Delta A = \frac{1}{1-c}\,\Delta\overline{A} = \Delta Y_0 \tag{15}$$

From Equation (15), therefore, the cumulative change in aggregate spending is equal to a multiple of the increase in autonomous spending. This could also have been deduced from Equation (11).[15] The multiple $1/(1 - c)$ is called the *multiplier*. It tells us by how much we have to multiply a given change in autonomous spending to obtain the corresponding change in equilibrium income and aggregate demand. Because the multiplier exceeds unity, we know that a \$1 change in autonomous spending increases equilibrium income and output by more than \$1.[16] The concept of the

[15] If you are familiar with the calculus, you will realize that the multiplier is nothing other than the derivative of the equilibrium level of income, Y_0, in Eq. (11) with respect to autonomous spending. Use the calculus on Eq. (11) above and Eq. (26) below to check the statements of the text.

[16] *Two warnings*: (1) The multiplier is necessarily greater than 1 in this very simplified model of the determination of income, but as we shall see in the discussion of "crowding out" in Chap. 4, there may be circumstances under which it is less than 1. (2) The term *multiplier* is used more generally in economics to mean the effect on some endogenous variable (a variable whose level is explained by the theory being studied) of a unit change in an exogenous variable (a variable whose level is not determined within the theory being examined). For instance, one can talk of the multiplier of a change in the income tax rate on the level of unemployment. However, the classic use of the term is as we are using it here—the effects of a change in autonomous spending on equilibrium output.

multiplier is sufficiently important to create a new notation. Defining the multiplier as α, we have

$$\alpha \equiv \frac{1}{1 - c} \tag{16}$$

Inspection of the multiplier in Equation (16) shows that the larger the marginal propensity to consume, the larger the multiplier. With a marginal propensity to consume of 0.75, the multiplier is 4; for a marginal propensity to consume of 0.8, the multiplier is 5. The reason is simply that a high marginal propensity to consume implies that a large fraction of an additional dollar income will be consumed. Accordingly, expenditures induced by an increase in autonomous spending are high and, therefore, so is the expansion in output and income that is needed to restore balance between income and demand (or spending).

Before proceeding further, we note that the relationship between the marginal propensity to consume, c, and the marginal propensity to save, s, allows us to write Equation (16) in a somewhat different form. Remembering from the budget constraint that saving plus consumption adds up to income, we realize that the fraction of an additional dollar of income consumed plus the fraction saved must add up to a dollar or

$$1 \equiv s + c$$

We can use the relation $s \equiv 1 - c$ and substitute in Equation (16) to obtain an equivalent formula for the multiplier in terms of the marginal propensity to save:

$$\alpha \equiv \frac{1}{s} \tag{16a}$$

Figure 3-6 provides a graphic interpretation of the effects of an increase in autonomous spending on the equilibrium level of income. The initial equilibrium is at point E with an income level Y_0. Consider next an increase in autonomous spending from $\bar{A}$ to $\bar{A}'$. This is represented by a parallel upward shift of the aggregate demand schedule where the shift is exactly equal to the increase in autonomous spending. The upward shift means that now, at each level of income, aggregate demand is higher by an amount $\Delta\bar{A} \equiv \bar{A}' - \bar{A}$.

At the initial level of income, Y_0, aggregate demand now exceeds income or output. Consequently, unintended inventory decumulation is taking place at a rate equal to the increase in autonomous spending, equal to the vertical distance $\Delta\bar{A}$. Firms will respond to that excess demand by expanding production, say, to income level Y'. This expansion in production

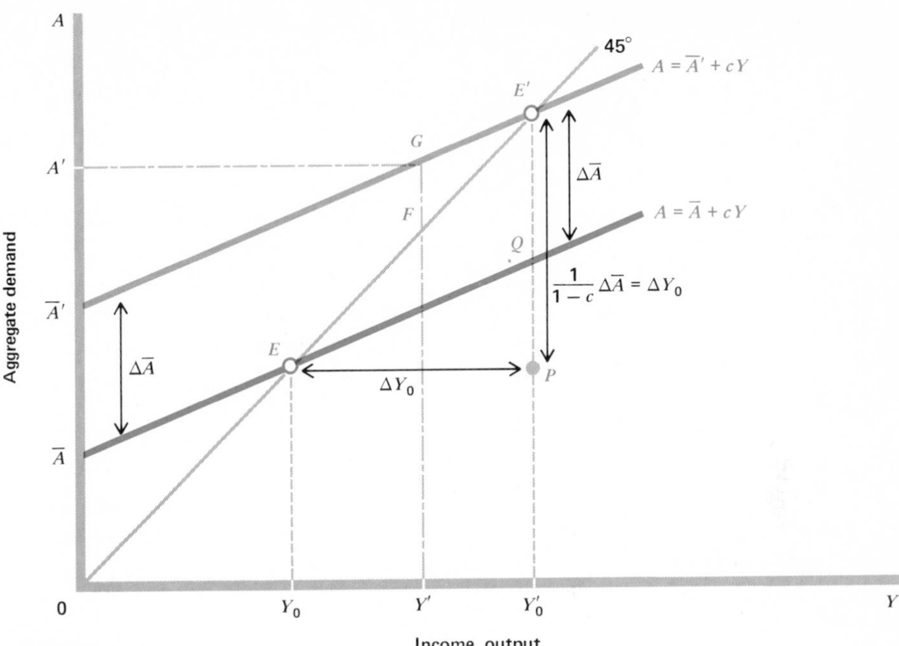

FIGURE 3-6 GRAPHICAL DERIVATION OF THE MULTIPLIER

has two effects. First, it gives rise to induced expenditure, increasing aggregate demand to the level A'. Second, at the same time, it reduces the gap between aggregate demand and output to the vertical distance FG. Additional spending is induced because the marginal propensity to consume out of additional income is positive, while the gap between aggregate demand and output narrows because the marginal propensity to consume is less than 1. Thus, a marginal propensity to consume that is positive but less than unity implies that a sufficient expansion in output will restore the balance between aggregate demand and output. In Figure 3-6 the new equilibrium is indicated by point E' and the corresponding level of income is Y'_0. The change in income required is therefore, $\Delta Y_0 = Y'_0 - Y_0$.

The magnitude of the income change required to restore equilibrium depends on two factors. The larger the increase in autonomous spending, represented in Figure 3-6 by the parallel shift in the aggregate demand schedule, the larger the income change. Furthermore, the larger the marginal propensity to consume—that is, the steeper the aggregate demand schedule—the larger the income change.

As a further check on our results, we want to verify from Figure 3-6 that the change in equilibrium income in fact exceeds the change in autonomous spending. For that purpose, we simply use the 45° line to compare the change in income ΔY_0 ($= EP = PE'$) with the change in autonomous spending that is equal to the vertical distance between the new and old aggregate demand schedule (QE'). It is clear from Figure 3-6 that the change in income PE' exceeds the change in autonomous spending QE'.

Finally, there is yet another way of deriving the multiplier. The relationship between the change in equilibrium income and a change in autonomous spending can be directly derived from the concept of equilibrium. We remember that in equilibrium, aggregate demand equals income or output. From one equilibrium to another, it must therefore be true that the change in income ΔY_0 is equal to the change in aggregate demand ΔA:

$$\Delta Y_0 = \Delta A \tag{17}$$

Next we split up the change in aggregate demand into the change in autonomous spending, $\Delta \bar{A}$, and the change in expenditure induced by the consequent change in income—that is, $c\,\Delta Y_0$.

$$\Delta A = \Delta \bar{A} + c\,\Delta Y_0 \tag{18}$$

Combining Equations (17) and (18), we obtain the change in income as

$$\Delta Y_0 = \Delta \bar{A} + c\,\Delta Y_0$$

or

$$\Delta Y_0(1 - c) = \Delta \bar{A}$$

or

$$\Delta Y_0 = \frac{1}{1 - c}\,\Delta \bar{A} = \alpha\,\Delta \bar{A} \tag{19}$$

There are three important points to remember from this discussion:

- An increase in autonomous spending raises the equilibrium level of income.
- The increase in income is a multiple of the increase in autonomous spending.
- The larger the marginal propensity to consume, the larger the multiplier, arising from the relation between consumption and income.

As a check on your understanding of the material of this section, you should develop the same analysis, and the same answers, in terms of Figure 3-5.

3-4 THE GOVERNMENT SECTOR

So far, we have ignored the role of the government sector in the determination of equilibrium income. The government affects the level of equilibrium income in two separate ways. First, government purchases of goods and services, G, is a component of aggregate demand. Second, taxes and transfers affect the relation between output and income, Y, and the *disposable income*—income that is available for consumption or saving—that accrues to the private sector, Y_d. In this section, we will be concerned with the way in which government purchases, taxes, and transfers affect the equilibrium level of income.

We start again from the basic national income accounting identities. The introduction of the government restores government purchases (G) on the expenditure side of Equation (1) of this chapter, and taxes (T) less transfers (R) on the allocation of income side. We can, accordingly, rewrite the identity in Equation (1) as

$$C + I + G \equiv S + (T - R) + C \qquad (1a)$$

The definition of aggregate demand has to be augmented to include government purchases of goods and services—the purchases of military equipment and services of bureaucrats, for instance. Thus we have

$$A \equiv C + \overline{I} + G \qquad (5a)$$

Consumption will no longer depend on income but rather on *disposable* income, Y_d. Disposable income, Y_d, is the net income available for spending by households after paying taxes to, and receiving transfers from, the government. It thus consists of income less taxes plus transfers, $Y + R - T$. The consumption function is now

$$C = \overline{C} + cY_d = \overline{C} + c(Y + R - T) \qquad (6a)$$

A final step is a specification of *fiscal policy*. Fiscal policy is the policy of the government with regard to the level of government purchases, the level of transfers, and the tax structure. We assume that the government purchases a constant amount $\overline{G}$, that it makes a constant amount of transfers $\overline{R}$, and that it collects a fraction t of income in the form of taxes. For example, if t equals 0.2, there is an income tax equal to 20 percent of income.

$$G = \overline{G} \qquad R = \overline{R} \qquad T = tY \tag{20}$$

With this specification of fiscal policy we can rewrite the consumption function, after substitution from Equation (20) for R and T in Equation (6a), as

$$C = \overline{C} + c(Y + \overline{R} - tY)$$

$$= (\overline{C} + c\overline{R}) + c(1 - t)Y \tag{21}$$

We note from Equation (21) that the presence of transfers raises autonomous consumption spending by the marginal propensity to consume out of disposable income c times the amount of transfers.[17] The presence of income taxes, by contrast, lowers consumption spending at each level of income. That reduction arises because households' consumption is related to disposable income rather than income itself, and income taxes reduce disposable income relative to the level of income. While the marginal propensity to consume out of disposable income remains c, the marginal propensity to consume out of income now is $c(1 - t)$, where $1 - t$ is the fraction of income left after taxes.

Equilibrium Income

We are now set to study income determination when the government's role is included. We return to the equilibrium condition for the goods market, $Y = A$, and after substituting from Equations (21) and (5a), we can write the equilibrium condition as

$$Y = (\overline{C} + c\overline{R}) + c(1 - t)Y + \overline{I} + \overline{G}$$

$$= (\overline{C} + c\overline{R} + \overline{I} + \overline{G}) + c(1 - t)Y$$

$$= \overline{A} + c(1 - t)Y$$

We can solve this equation for Y_0, the equilibrium level of income, by collecting terms in Y:

$$Y[1 - c(1 - t)] = \overline{A}$$

$$Y_0 = \frac{1}{1 - c(1 - t)}\overline{A} \tag{22}$$

[17] Note that we are assuming no taxes are paid on transfers from the government. As a matter of fact, taxes are paid on some transfers, such as interest payments on the government debt, and not paid on other transfers, such as welfare and unemployment benefits.

In comparing Equation (22) with Equation (11), we see that the government sector makes a substantial difference. It raises autonomous spending by the amount of government purchases, $\overline{G}$, and by the amount of induced spending out of net transfers, $c\overline{R}$. At the same time, income taxes lower the multiplier. As can be seen from Equation (22), if the marginal propensity to consume is 0.8 and taxes are zero, the multiplier is 5; with the same marginal propensity to consume and a tax rate of 0.25, the multiplier is cut in half to $1/[1 - 0.8(0.75)] = 2.5$. Income taxes reduce the multiplier because they reduce the induced increase of consumption out of changes in income. When there are no taxes, a dollar increase in income raises disposable income by exactly a dollar and induced consumption increases by c times the increase in disposable income. If there are taxes, however, a dollar increase in income raises disposable income by only $(1 - t)$ dollars. Induced consumption rises, therefore, only by $c(1 - t)$. In terms of Figure 3-2, the presence of transfers shifts the intercept of the aggregate demand schedule up by $c\overline{R}$. The slope, which is the marginal propensity to consume out of income, declines because of the presence of income taxes.

Effects of a Change in Government Purchases

We want now to consider the effects of changes in fiscal policy on the equilibrium level of income. We can distinguish three possible changes in fiscal variables: changes in government purchases, changes in transfers, and income tax changes. The simplest illustration is that of a change in government purchases. This case is shown in Figure 3-7, where the initial level of income is Y_0. An increase in government purchases represents a change in autonomous spending and therefore shifts the aggregate demand schedule upward in a parallel fashion by an amount equal to the increased government expenditure. At the initial level of output and income, the demand for goods exceeds output and, accordingly, firms expand production until the new equilibrium at point E' is reached. By how much does income expand? We remember that the change in equilibrium income will equal the change in aggregate demand, or

$$\Delta Y_0 = \Delta\overline{G} + c(1 - t)\Delta Y_0$$

where the remaining terms ($\overline{C}$, $\overline{R}$, and $\overline{I}$) are constant by assumption. Thus, the change in equilibrium income is

$$\Delta Y_0 = \frac{1}{1 - c(1 - t)} \Delta\overline{G} = \overline{\alpha}\Delta\overline{G} \tag{23}$$

where we have introduced the notation $\overline{\alpha}$ to denote the multiplier in the presence of income taxes:

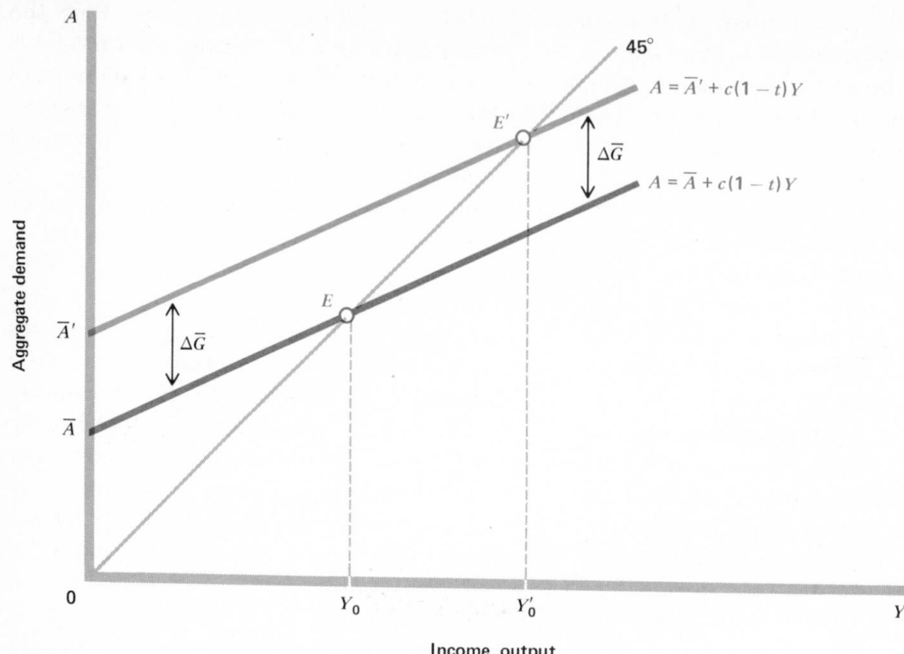

FIGURE 3-7 THE EFFECTS OF AN INCREASE IN GOVERNMENT PURCHASES

$$\overline{\alpha} \equiv \frac{1}{1 - c(1 - t)} \tag{24}$$

From Equation (23) it is apparent that a \$1 increase in government purchases will lead to an increase in income in excess of a dollar. Thus, as we have already seen, with a marginal propensity to consume of $c = 0.8$ and an income tax rate of $t = 0.25$, we would have a multiplier of 2.5: a \$1 increase in government spending raises equilibrium income by \$2.50.

Effects of Increased Transfer Payments

Consider next an increase in transfer payments. In terms of Figure 3-7, we again have an increase in autonomous spending, so that aggregate demand increases at each level of income. The parallel shift in the aggregate demand schedule will be equal to the marginal propensity to spend out of disposable income, c, times the increase in transfers, or $c\,\Delta\overline{R}$. Again, the demand for goods will exceed production at the initial level of income and output, and an expansion in output will take place to eliminate the excess demand. To calculate the change in equilibrium income, we again use the condition that the change in aggregate demand will equal the change in income. The change in aggregate demand in this case is the change in autonomous spending, $c\Delta\overline{R}$, plus induced spending $c(1 - t)\Delta Y$, so that we can write

$$\Delta Y_0 = c\,\Delta\overline{R} + c(1 - t)\Delta Y_0$$

or

$$\Delta Y_0 = \frac{1}{1 - c(1 - t)}(c\Delta\overline{R}) = \overline{\alpha}\, c\Delta\overline{R} \tag{25}$$

Equation (25) shows that an increase in transfer payments will raise the equilibrium level of income. For plausible values of c and t, it furthermore remains true that we have a multiplier effect—that a dollar increase in transfers raises equilibrium income by more than a dollar. Thus, for $c = 0.8$ and $t = 0.25$, the multiplier for transfer payments is 2.0.

The multiplier for government purchases is higher than the multiplier for transfers because a dollar increase in government purchases translates into a dollar increase in autonomous spending, whereas a dollar increase in transfers results in an increase of only c (less than 1) dollars in autonomous spending.

The Effects of an Income Tax Change

The final exercise in fiscal policy is a reduction in the income tax rate. This is illustrated in Figure 3-8 by an increase in the slope of the aggregate demand function because that slope is equal to the marginal propensity to spend out of income, $c(1 - t)$. The figure shows that at the initial level of income, the aggregate demand for goods now exceeds output because the tax reduction gives rise to increased consumption. The new higher equilibrium level of income is indicated by Y_0'.

To calculate the change in equilibrium income, we equate the change in income to the change in aggregate demand. The change in aggregate demand has two components. First, we have the change in spending at the initial level of income that arises from the tax cut. This part is equal to the marginal propensity to consume out of disposable income times the change in disposable income due to the tax cut, $cY_0\Delta t$, where the term $Y_0\Delta t$ is the initial level of income times the change in the tax rate. The second component of the change in aggregate demand is the induced spending due to higher income. This is now evaluated at the new tax rate t' and has the value $c(1 - t')\Delta Y_0$. We can therefore write [18]

[18] You should check Eq. (27) by using Eq. (22) to write out Y_0 corresponding to a tax rate of t, and Y_0' corresponding to t'. Then subtract Y_0 from Y_0' to obtain ΔY_0 as given in Eq. (27).

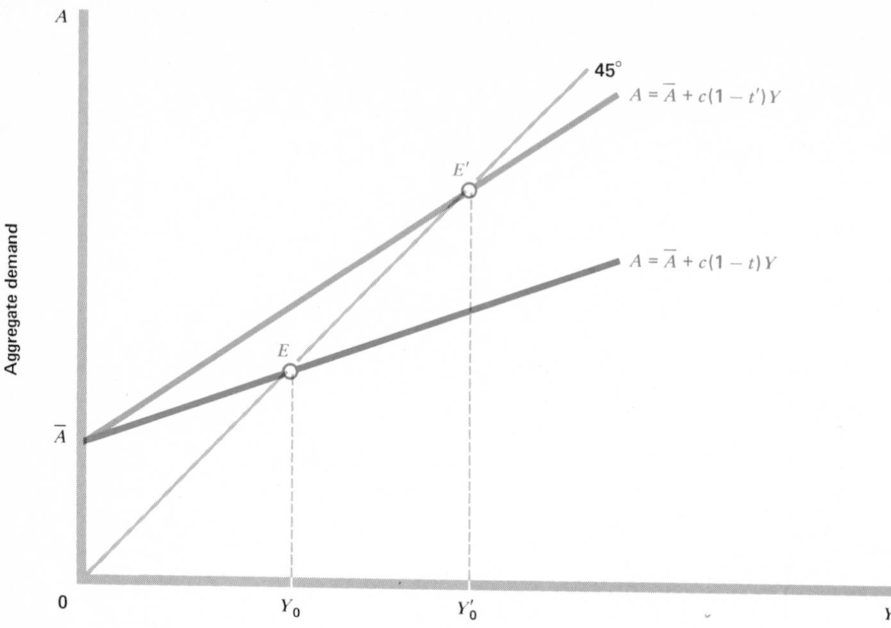

FIGURE 3-8 THE EFFECTS OF A DECREASE IN THE TAX RATE

$$\Delta Y_0 = -cY_0\Delta t + c(1 - t')\,\Delta Y_0 \tag{26}$$

or

$$\Delta Y_0 = -\frac{1}{1 - c(1 - t')}\,cY_0\Delta t \tag{27}$$

An exercise will clarify the effects of an income tax cut. Assume initially a level of income equal to $Y_0 = 100$, a marginal propensity to consume $c = 0.8$, and a tax rate $t = 0.2$. Assume next a tax cut that reduces the income tax rate to $t' = 0.1$. At the initial level of income, disposable income therefore rises by $100(t - t') = \$10$. Out of the increase in disposable income of \$10, a fraction $c = 0.8$ is spent on consumption so that aggregate demand, at the initial level of income, increases by \$8. This corresponds to the first term on the right-hand side of Equation (26). The increase in aggregate demand gives rise to an expansion in output and income. Per dollar increase in income, disposable income rises by a fraction $(1 - t')$ of the increase in income. Furthermore, of the increase in disposable income, only a fraction, c, is spent. Accordingly, induced consumption spending is equal to $c(1 - t')\Delta Y_0$, which is the second term in Equation (26). How much does the income tax cut achieve in terms of output expansion? Substituting our parameters in Equation (27), we have

$$\Delta Y_0 = -\frac{1}{1 - 0.8(1 - 0.1)}(0.8)(100)(0.1 - 0.2) = (3.57)(8)$$

$$= 28.56 \tag{27a}$$

In our example, a cut in the tax rate, such that taxes fall by \$10 at the initial level of income, raises equilibrium income by \$28.56.

Note, however, that although taxes are initially cut by \$10, the government's total taxes received fall by less than \$10. Why? The reason is that the government receives 10 percent of the induced increase in income, or \$2.856, as taxes. Thus the final reduction in tax receipts by the government is not the initial \$10, but rather \$7.144.[19]

Summary

1 Government purchases and transfer payments act like increases in autonomous spending in their effects on equilibrium income.
2 Income taxes reduce disposable income relative to the level of income and their effects on equilibrium income and output are thus the same as those resulting from a reduction in the propensity to consume.

As a final comment on the material of this section, we note that all the results we have derived can be obtained in a straightforward manner by taking the change in aggregate demand at the initial level of income times the multiplier. (Check this proposition for each of the fiscal policy changes we have considered.) You will want to consider, too, the effect on equilibrium income of an increase in government purchases combined with an equal reduction in transfer payments, $\Delta\overline{G} = -\Delta\overline{R}$.[20]

3-5 THE BUDGET

In this section we deal with the government budget. We start by defining the concept of the *budget surplus*, denoted by BuS. The surplus is the excess of the government's revenues, consisting of taxes, over its total expenditures, consisting of purchases of goods and services and transfer payments:

[19] We leave it to you to calculate the multiplier relating the change in equilibrium income to the total change in taxes received by the government. How does it compare with the multiplier for transfer payments at the new tax rate t'? Check Eqs. (27) and (25) to make sure your answer is correct.

[20] See problem 9 at the end of the chapter.

$$\text{BuS} \equiv T - G - R \tag{28}$$

A negative budget surplus—an excess of government expenditure over revenues—is a *budget deficit.*

Since the budget surplus (and especially the deficit) receives much attention from politicians, economists, and the press, we want now to study the budget surplus in relation to the level of income. Substituting in Equation (28) the assumption of a proportional income tax that yields a tax revenue $T = tY$ gives us

$$\text{BuS} = tY - G - R \tag{28a}$$

In Figure 3-9 we plot the budget surplus as a function of the level of income for given $G = \overline{G}$, $R = \overline{R}$, and income tax rate t. At low levels of income, the budget is in deficit (the surplus is negative) because payments $\overline{G} + \overline{R}$ exceed income tax collection. For high levels of income, by contrast, the budget shows a surplus, since income tax collection outweighs expenditures in the form of government purchases and transfers.

Figure 3-9 shows immediately that the budget surplus can be changed by changes in income that derive from sources other than a change in fiscal policy. Thus, for example, an increase in income that arises because of increased autonomous investment spending will give rise to an increase in the budget surplus or a reduction in the budget deficit. Why? Because the increase in income raises income tax collection and, therefore, for a given level of government outlays, lowers the deficit. To make the same point in a somewhat different manner, a reduction in economic activity, given fiscal policy as summarized by the parameters $\overline{G}$, $\overline{R}$, and t, must lead to a reduction in the budget surplus, or an increase in the deficit.

This feature of the budget, or of fiscal policy, whereby taxes are

FIGURE 3-9 THE BUDGET SURPLUS

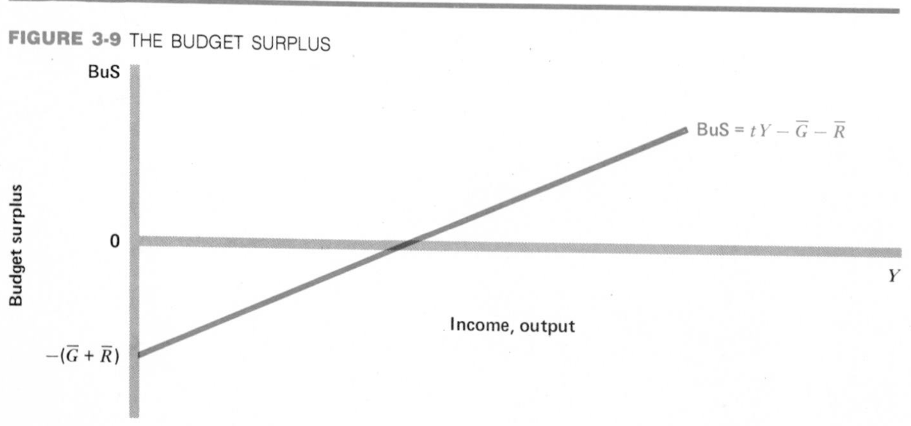

automatically reduced when income falls, is called *automatic stabilization*. Its effects were described in Section 3-4 as a reduction in the multiplier due to income taxes. The presence of income taxation ensures that a given reduction in autonomous spending will lead to less of a decline in income than would occur in the absence of income taxes because the multiplier $\bar{\alpha}$ is smaller than the multiplier α. In general, *automatic stabilizers* are those elements in the economy that reduce the impact of changes in autonomous spending on the equilibrium level of income. Unemployment benefits, for example, are also an automatic stabilizer.

The Effects of Government Purchases and Tax Changes on the Budget Surplus

Next we want to inquire how various changes in fiscal policy affect the budget. In particular, we want to find out whether an increase in government purchases must reduce the budget surplus. At first sight, this would appear obvious because increased government purchases, from Equation (28), are reflected in a reduced surplus, or increased deficit. At further thought, it becomes apparent, however, that the increased government purchases will give rise to a (multiplied) increase in income and, therefore, to increased income tax collection. This raises the interesting possibility that tax collection might increase by more than government purchases.

A brief calculation will show that the first guess is right—increased government purchases reduce the budget surplus. From Equation (23) the change in income due to increased government purchases is equal to $\Delta Y_0 = \bar{\alpha}\Delta\bar{G}$. A fraction of that increase in income is collected in the form of taxes so that tax revenue increases by $t\bar{\alpha}\Delta\bar{G}$. The change in the budget surplus is therefore[21]

$$\begin{aligned}\Delta \text{BuS} &= \Delta T - \Delta\bar{G} \\ &= t\bar{\alpha}\,\Delta\bar{G} - \Delta\bar{G} \\ &= \left[\frac{t}{1 - c\,(1-t)} - 1\right]\Delta\bar{G} \\ &= -\frac{(1-c)\,(1-t)}{1 - c\,(1-t)}\,\Delta\bar{G} \qquad (29)\end{aligned}$$

which is unambiguously negative. We have, therefore, shown that an increase in government purchases will reduce the budget surplus, although by considerably less than the increase in purchases. For instance, for $c = 0.8$ and $t = 0.2$, a dollar increase in government purchases will create a 44-cent reduction in the surplus.[22]

[21] We use Eq. (24) to substitute for $\bar{\alpha}$ in Eq. (29).

[22] In this case, $\bar{\alpha} = 1/[1 - 0.8(0.8)] = 2.78$. So $\Delta\text{BuS} = -2.78\,(0.2)(0.8) = -0.44$.

In the same way, we can consider the effects of an increase in the tax rate on the budget surplus. We know that the increase in the tax rate will reduce the level of income. It might thus appear that an increase in the tax rate, keeping the level of government spending constant, could reduce the budget surplus. In fact, an increase in the tax rate increases the budget surplus, despite the reduction in income that it causes.[23]

Finally, we can investigate the budgetary effects of simultaneous changes in income tax rates and goverment purchases. We will work through these cases by using a simple example. We assume that a fiscal policy is implemented that reduces the income tax rate from $t = 0.2$ to $t' = 0.1$. At an initial level of income of $100, such a tax cut results in a loss of tax revenue of $10. In combination with the tax cut, we implement a reduction of government purchases in the amount of $10. What is the net effect on equilibrium income and the budget of the fiscal policy package, assuming a marginal propensity to consume of $c = 0.8$? With an income tax rate of $t' = 0.1$, the multiplier will be a $\overline{\alpha} = 3.57$. A $10 decrease in government purchases accordingly lowers income by $35.70. The tax cut, in turn, will raise income by $28.56 = (0.8)(0.1)(100)(3.7). The net effect of the package on income is therefore a reduction in income of the order of $7.14. What is the effect on the budget? Government purchases decline by $10; tax revenue declines at the initial level of income by $10, owing to the tax cut, and suffers a further reduction, due to the decline in income, of $(0.1)(7.14) = 0.71$. The net effect of this cut in government purchases, combined with a decrease in taxes that is equal, *at the initial level of income*, to the cut in government purchases, is therefore a slight increase in the budget deficit. The budget deficit changes because the level of income falls and taxes therefore fall more than they were reduced initially.

In this example, the combined tax decrease and government purchases decrease raised the budget deficit. What would happen to the level of income if government purchases and taxes changed by exactly the same amount, so that the budget surplus remained unchanged between the initial and final level of income? The answer to this question is contained in the famous *balanced budget multiplier* result. The result is that the balanced budget multiplier is exactly 1. That is, an increase in government purchases, accompanied by an equal increase in taxes, increases the level of income by exactly the amount of the increase in purchases.[24] This interesting result is derived in the appendix to this chapter.

The major points of the preceding discussion are that a balanced budget cut in government purchases lowers equilibrium income and that a

[23] The effects of an increase in the tax rate on the budget surplus are examined in detail in problem 7 at the end of this chapter.

[24] Note that the balanced budget multiplier may well be less than 1 in the more sophisticated models of Chap. 4, in which investment spending depends on the interest rate.

dollar increase in government purchases has a stronger impact on equilibrium income than a dollar cut in taxes. A dollar cut in taxes leads only to a fraction of a dollar's increase in consumption spending, the rest being saved, while government purchases are reflected dollar for dollar in a change in aggregate demand.[25]

The Full-Employment Budget Surplus

A final topic to be treated here is the concept of the *full-employment budget surplus*.[26] Recall that increases in taxes add to the surplus and that increases in government expenditures reduce the surplus. Increases in taxes have been shown to reduce the level of income, and increases in government purchases and transfers to increase the level of income. It thus seems that the budget surplus is a convenient, simple measure of the overall effects of fiscal policy on the economy. When government expenditure increases, the level of income rises and the budget surplus falls. When taxes increase the level of income falls and the budget surplus rises.

However, the budget surplus by itself suffers from a serious defect as a measure of the direction of fiscal policy. The defect is that the surplus can change *passively* because of changes in autonomous private spending, as we have seen. Thus, if the economy moves into a recession, tax revenue automatically declines and the budget moves into a deficit (or reduced surplus). Conversely, an increase in economic activity causes the budget to move into a surplus (or reduced deficit). These changes in the budget take place automatically for a given tax structure. This implies that we cannot simply look at the budget deficit as a measure of whether government fiscal policy is expansionary or deflationary. A given fiscal policy may imply a deficit if private spending is low and a surplus if private spending is high. Thus, it is important to note that increases in the budget deficit do not necessarily mean that the government has changed its policy in an expansionary direction in an attempt to increase the level of income.

Since we frequently want to measure the way in which fiscal policy is being *actively*, rather than *passively*, used to affect the level of income, we require some measure of policy that is independent of the particular position of the business cycle—boom or recession—in which we may find ourselves. Such a measure is provided by the *full-employment budget surplus*, which we shall denote by BuS^*. BuS^* measures the budget, not at the actual level of income, but rather at the full-employment level of income or at potential output. Thus, a given fiscal policy summarized by $\overline{G}$,

[25] Rather than go through the analysis of changes in transfer payments, we will leave it to you to work through an example of the effects on the budget of a change in transfer payments in the problems at the end of the chapter.

[26] The concept of the full-employment surplus was first used by E. Cary Brown, "Fiscal Policy in the Thirties: A Reappraisal," *American Economic Review*, December 1956.

$\overline{R}$, and t is assessed by the level of the surplus, or deficit, that is generated at full employment. Using Y_p to denote the full-employment level of income, we can write

$$\text{BuS}^* = tY_p - \overline{G} - \overline{R} \tag{30}$$

In Figure 3-10 we replicate the budget surplus schedule from Figure 3-9 but add the full-employment level of income Y_p. The full-employment budget surplus is indicated by the corresponding point on the budget surplus schedule. To see the difference between the actual and the full-employment budget, we subtract the actual budget in Equation (28*a*) from Equation (30) to obtain

$$\text{BuS}^* - \text{BuS} = t(Y_p - Y) \tag{31}$$

It is apparent that the only difference arises from income tax collection.[27] Specifically, if output is below full employment, the full-employment surplus exceeds the actual surplus. Conversely, if actual output exceeds full-employment (or potential) output, the full-employment surplus is less than the actual surplus.

Chart 3-1 shows the actual and full-employment budget surplus as a fraction of GNP for the years 1950 to 1979. It is apparent that in a recession like the 1974–1976 one, the actual deficit by far exceeds the full-employment (or high-employment) deficit. The change in the full-employment budget from near balance in 1974 to a deficit in 1975 reflects

[27] In practice, transfer payments, such as welfare and unemployment benefits, are also partly affected by the state of the economy, so that R also depends on the level of income. But the major cause of differences between the actual surplus and the full-employment surplus is the income tax.

FIGURE 3-10 THE ACTUAL AND FULL-EMPLOYMENT BUDGET SURPLUSES

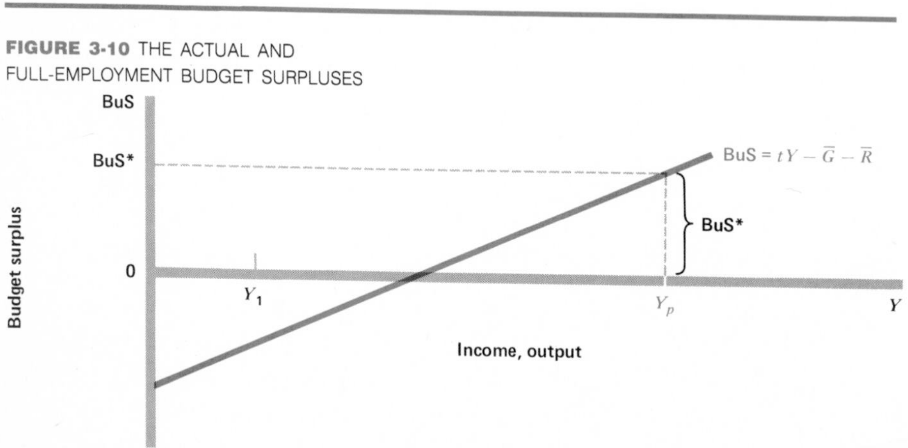

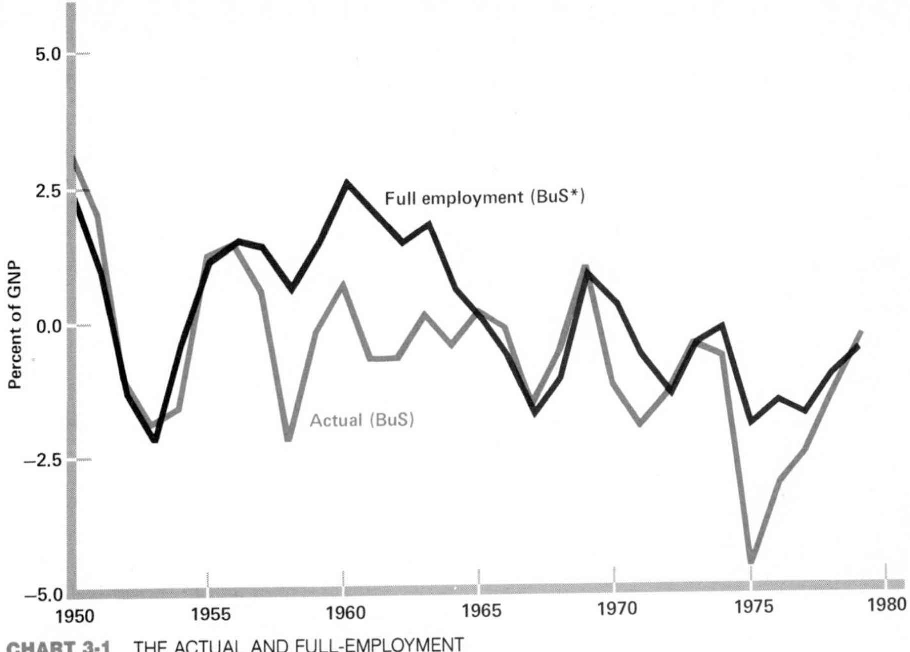

CHART 3-1 THE ACTUAL AND FULL-EMPLOYMENT BUDGET SURPLUS AS A FRACTION OF GNP (Source: Citibank Economic Database)

the active use of fiscal policy to combat the recession—there was a substantial decrease in tax rates in early 1975. The drop in the actual budget surplus in that period is due in part to this active stimulus and in part to the drop in revenues resulting from the recession. By contrast, in the years 1965 to 1969, the actual and full-employment budgets were very close. This, by Equation (31), is a reflection of the fact that the economy was near full employment in that period. Note that the actual budget surplus has been continuously less than the full-employment surplus since 1973. This reflects the persistence of economic slack or a situation where actual output is below potential, $Y < Y_p$.

One final word of warning: The high-employment surplus is a better measure of the direction of active fiscal policy than the actual budget surplus. But it is not a perfect measure of the thrust of fiscal policy. The reason is that balanced budget increases in government purchases are themselves expansionary, so that an increase in government purchases matched by a tax increase that keeps the surplus constant leads to an increase in the level of income. Because fiscal policy involves the setting of a number of variables—the tax rate, transfers, and government purchases—it is difficult to describe the thrust of fiscal policy perfectly in a single number.[28] But the high-employment surplus is nevertheless a useful guide to the direction of fiscal policy.

3-6 SUMMARY

1 Output is at its equilibrium level when the aggregate demand for goods is equal to the level of output.
2 Aggregate demand consists of planned spending by households on consumption, firms on investment goods, and government on its purchases of goods and services.
3 When output is at its equilibrium level, there are no unintended changes in inventories and all economic units are making precisely the purchases they had planned to. An adjustment process for the level of output based on the accumulation or decumulation of inventories leads the economy to the equilibrium output level.
4 The level of aggregate demand is itself affected by the level of output (equal to the level of income) because consumption demand depends on the level of income.
5 The consumption function relates consumption spending to income. Income that is not consumed is saved, so that the saving function can be derived from the consumption function.
6 The multiplier is the amount by which a one-dollar change in autonomous spending changes the equilibrium level of output. The greater the propensity to consume the higher the multiplier.
7 Government purchases and government transfer payments act like increases in autonomous spending in their effects on the equilibrium level of income. A proportional income tax has the same effects on the equilibrium level of income as a reduction in the propensity to consume. A proportional income tax thus reduces the multiplier.
8 The budget surplus is the excess of government receipts over its expenditure. When the government is spending more than it receives, the budget is in deficit. The size of the budget surplus (deficit) is affected by the government's fiscal policy variables—government purchases, transfer payments, and tax rates.
9 The budget surplus is also affected by changes in taxes and transfers resulting from changes in the level of income occurring as a result of changes in private autonomous spending. The *full-employment* (high-employment) budget surplus is accordingly frequently used as a measure of the active use of fiscal policy. The full-employment surplus

[28] A very lucid discussion of the full-employment surplus and other measures—such as the weighted full-employment surplus—that attempt to adjust for the imperfections of the full-employment surplus measure is contained in Alan S. Blinder and Robert M. Solow, "Analytical Foundations of Fiscal Policy," in Alan S. Blinder et al., *The Economics of Public Finance* (Washington, D.C.: The Brookings Institution, 1974).

measures the budget surplus that would exist if output were at its potential (full-employment) level.

APPENDIX

This appendix considers the ***balanced budget multiplier*** result mentioned in the text. The balanced budget multiplier refers to the effects of an increase in government purchases accompanied by an increase in taxes such that, in the new equilibrium, the budget surplus is exactly the same as in the original equilibrium. The result is that the multiplier of such a policy change is unity. In other words, the balanced budget multiplier is 1. A multiplier of unity obviously implies that output expands by precisely the amount of the increased government purchases with no induced consumption spending. It is apparent that what must be at work is the effect of higher taxes that exactly offset the effect of the income expansion. and that thus maintain disposable income, and hence consumption, constant. With no induced consumption spending, output expands simply to match the increased government purchases.

We can derive this result formally by noting that the change in aggregate demand ΔA is equal to the change in government purchases plus the change in consumption spending. The latter is equal to the marginal propensity to consume out of disposable income, c, times the change in disposable income, ΔY_d, that is, $\Delta Y_d = \Delta Y_0 - \Delta T$, where ΔY_0 is the change in output. Thus:

$$\Delta A = \Delta \overline{G} + c(\Delta Y_0 - \Delta T) \tag{A1}$$

Since from one equilibrium to another the change in aggregate demand has to equal the change in output, we have

$$\Delta Y_0 = \Delta \overline{G} + c(\Delta Y_0 - \Delta T)$$

or

$$\Delta Y_0 = \frac{1}{1-c}(\Delta \overline{G} - c\,\Delta T) \tag{A2}$$

Next we note that by assumption the change in government purchases between the new equilibrium and the old one is exactly matched by a change in tax collection so that $\Delta \overline{G} = \Delta T$. It follows from this last equality, after substitution in Equation (A2), that with this particular restriction on fiscal policy we have

$$\Delta Y_0 = \frac{1}{1-c}(\Delta \overline{G} - c\,\Delta \overline{G}) = \Delta \overline{G} = \Delta T \tag{A3}$$

so that the multiplier is precisely unity.

Another way of deriving the balanced budget multiplier result is by considering the successive rounds of spending changes caused by the government policy changes.

TABLE A3-1 THE BALANCED BUDGET MULTIPLIER

	Change in spending resulting from			
Spending round	$\Delta \overline{G} = 1$	$\Delta T = 1$	Net this round	Total
1	1	$-\bar{c}$	$1 - \bar{c}$	$1 - \bar{c}$
2	$\bar{c}$	$-\bar{c}^2$	$\bar{c} - \bar{c}^2$	$1 - \bar{c}^2$
3	$\bar{c}^2$	$-\bar{c}^3$	$\bar{c}^2 - \bar{c}^3$	$1 - \bar{c}^3$
4	$\bar{c}^3$	$-\bar{c}^4$	$\bar{c}^3 - \bar{c}^4$	$1 - \bar{c}^4$
⋮				
n	$\bar{c}^{n-1}$	$-\bar{c}^n$	$\bar{c}^{n-1} - \bar{c}^n$	$1 - \bar{c}^n$

Suppose each of government purchases and taxes increased by $1. Let $c(1 - t)$, the induced increase in aggregate demand caused by a $1 increase in income in the presence of taxes, be denoted by $\bar{c}$. Now Table A3-1 shows the spending induced by the two policy changes. The first column shows the changes in spending resulting from the change in government purchases and its later repercussions. The second column similarly gives the spending effects in successive rounds of the tax increase. The third column sums the two effects for each spending round, while the final column adds all the changes in spending induced so far. Since $\bar{c}$ is less than 1, $\bar{c}^n$ becomes very small as the number of spending rounds, n, increases, and the final change in aggregate spending caused by the balanced budget increase in governmental spending is just equal to $1.

Finally, the balanced budget multiplier can also be thought of from a somewhat different perspective. Consider the goods market equilibrium condition in terms of saving, taxes, investment, transfers, and government purchases

$$S + T - R = \overline{I} + G \tag{A4}$$

Now, using the definition of the budget surplus, BuS $\equiv T - R - G$,

$$\text{BuS} = \overline{I} - S \tag{A5}$$

If there is no change in the budget deficit, nor a change in investment, then the equilibrium change in saving is zero. For saving not to change, disposable income must remain unchanged. This says that $\Delta Y_d = \Delta Y - \Delta T = 0$, and hence shows once more that the change in income equals the change in taxes. This in turn equals the change in government purchases. Hence, the balanced budget multiplier, or more precisely the multiplier associated with an unchanging budget surplus or deficit, is equal to unity. This perspective on the income determination process is very useful because it emphasizes the fact that a change in the surplus or deficit of one sector is matched by a corresponding change in the deficit or surplus of the remaining sectors. If the government surplus is constrained by fiscal policy to be unchanged, so too must be the private sector's surplus, $S - \overline{I}$.

PROBLEMS

1 Here we investigate a particular example of the model studied in Sections 3-2 and 3-3 with no government. Suppose the consumption function is given by $C = 100 + 0.8Y$ while investment is given by $\bar{I} = 50$.

(*a*) What is the equilibrium level of income in this case?

(*b*) What is the level of saving in equilibrium?

(*c*) If for some reason output was at the level of 800, what would the level of involuntary inventory accumulation be?

(*d*) If $\bar{I}$ were to rise to 100 (we will discuss what determines $\bar{I}$ in later chapters), what would be the effect on equilibrium income?

(*e*) What is the multiplier, α, here?

(*f*) Draw a diagram indicating the equilibria in both 1(*a*) and 1(*d*).

2 Suppose consumption behavior were to change in problem 1 so that $C = 100 + 0.9Y$ while $\bar{I}$ remained at 50.

(*a*) Would you expect the equilibrium level of income to be higher or lower than in 1(*a*)? Calculate the new Y_0' to verify this.

(*b*) Now suppose investment increases to $\bar{I} = 100$ just as in 1(*d*). What is the new equilibrium income?

(*c*) Does this change in investment spending have more or less of an effect on Y_0 than in problem 1? Why?

(*d*) Draw a diagram indicating the change in equilibrium income in this case.

3 We showed in the text that the equilibrium condition $Y = A$ is equivalent to the $S = \bar{I}$, or saving = investment, condition. Starting from $S = \bar{I}$ and the saving function, derive the equilibrium level of income.

4 This problem relates to the so-called *paradox of thrift*. Suppose $I = \bar{I}$ is fixed, and that $C = \bar{C} + cY$.

(*a*) What is the savings function, that is, the function that shows how savings is related to income?

(*b*) Suppose individuals want to save more at every level of income. Show, using a figure like Figure 3-5, how the savings function is shifted.

(*c*) What effect does the increased desire to save have on the new equilibrium level of savings? Explain the paradox.

5 Now let us look at a model which is an example of the one presented in Sections 3-4 and 3-5; that is, it includes government purchases, taxes, and transfers. It has the same features as the one in problems 1 and 2, except that it also has a government. Thus, suppose consumption is given by $C = 100 + 0.8Y_d$ and $\bar{I} = 50$, while fiscal policy is summarized by $\bar{G} = 200$, $\bar{R} = 62.5$, $t = 0.25$.

(*a*) What is the equilibrium level of income in this more complete model?

(*b*) What is the new multiplier $\bar{\alpha}$? Why is this less than the multiplier in problem 1(*e*)?

6 Using the same model as in problem 5 above:

(*a*) What is the value of the budget surplus BuS when $\bar{I} = 50$?

(*b*) What is BuS when $\bar{I}$ increases to 100?

(*c*) What accounts for the change in BuS from 5(*a*) to 5(*b*)?

(*d*) Assuming that the full-employment level of income Y_p is 1,200, what is the full-employment budget surplus BuS* when $\bar{I} = 50$? 100? (Be careful.)

(*e*) What is BuS* if $\bar{I} = 50$ and $\bar{G} = 250$, with Y_p still equal to 1,200?

(f) Explain why we use BuS* rather than simply BuS to measure the direction of fiscal policy.

7 Suppose we expand our model to take account of the fact that transfer payments R do depend on the level of income Y. When income is high, transfer payments like unemployment benefits will fall. Conversely, when income is low, unemployment is high and so are unemployment benefits. We can incorporate this into our model by writing transfers as $R = \overline{R} - bY$, $b > 0$. Remembering that our equilibrium income is derived as the solution to $Y_0 = C + \overline{I} + \overline{G} = \overline{C} + cY_d + \overline{I} + \overline{G}$, where $Y_d = Y + R - T$ is disposable income,

(a) Derive the expression for Y_0 in this case, just as Equation (22) was derived in the text.

(b) What is the new multiplier now?

(c) Why is the new multiplier less than the standard one, $\overline{\alpha}$?

8 Now we look at the role taxes play in determining equilibrium income. Suppose we have an economy of the type in Sections 3-4 and 3-5 described by the following functions:

$$\begin{aligned} C &= 50 + 0.8Y_d \\ \overline{I} &= 70 \\ \overline{G} &= 200 \\ \overline{R} &= 100 \\ t &= 0.20 \end{aligned}$$

(a) Calculate the equilibrium level of income and the multiplier in this model.

(b) Calculate also the budget surplus, BuS.

(c) Suppose now t is increased to 0.25. What is the new equilibrium income? The new multiplier?

(d) Calculate the change in the budget surplus. Would you expect the change in the surplus to be more or less if $c = 0.9$ rather than 0.8?

(e) Can you explain why the multiplier is 1 when $t = 1$?

9 Suppose the economy is operating at equilibrium with $Y_0 = 1{,}000$. If the government undertakes a fiscal change so that the tax rate t increases by 0.05 and government spending increases by 50, will the budget surplus go up or down? Why?

10 Suppose Congress decides to reduce transfer payments (such as welfare), but to increase government purchases of goods and services by an equal amount. That is, it undertakes a change in fiscal policy such that $\Delta\overline{G} = -\Delta\overline{R} > 0$.

(a) Would you expect equilibrium income to rise or fall as a result of this change? Why? Check out your answer with the following example: Suppose initially $c = 0.8$, $t = 0.25$, and $Y_0 = 600$. Now let $\Delta\overline{G} = 10$, $\Delta\overline{R} = -10$.

(b) Find the change in equilibrium income, ΔY_0.

(c) What is the change in the budget surplus, ΔBuS? Why has BuS changed?

*11 We have seen in problem 10 that an increase in G accompanied by an equal decrease in R does not leave the budget unchanged. What would the effect on equilibrium income be if R and G change to leave the budget surplus BuS fixed?

Notice that BuS $= T - R - G$. We want ΔBuS $= \Delta T - \Delta R - \Delta G = 0(*)$ so $\Delta\overline{R} = T - \Delta\overline{G}$. Since t is constant, $\Delta T = t\,\Delta Y_0(**)$. We also know that $Y_0 = \overline{\alpha}(\overline{C} + \overline{I} + \overline{G} + c\overline{R})$ and $\Delta Y_{0a} = \overline{\alpha}(\Delta\overline{G} + c\,\Delta\overline{R})$.

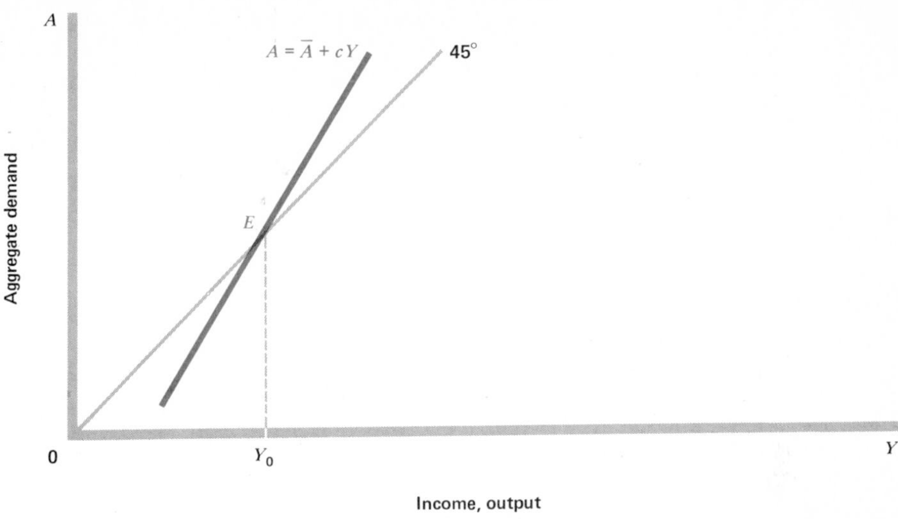

Substituting (*) and (**) into this last equation, derive an expression for ΔY in terms of ΔG. Simplify that expression, using the fact that $\overline{\alpha} = \{1/[1 - c(1 - t)]\}$, to obtain the balanced budget result in the case of changes in transfers and government spending.

*12 In the preceding problem and in the appendix we derived the balanced budget multiplier result. It states that if $\Delta G = \Delta T$ from the initial to final equilibrium, then $\Delta Y = \Delta G$. Let us look at an example of this balanced budget multiplier in action. Consider the economy described by the following functions:

$$C = 85 + 0.75Y_d$$
$$\overline{I} = 50$$
$$\overline{G} = 150$$
$$\overline{R} = 100$$
$$t = 0.20$$

(*a*) Derive the multiplier $\overline{\alpha}$ and the level of autonomous spending $\overline{A}$.
(*b*) From 12(*a*) calculate the equilibrium level of income and the budget surplus.
(*c*) Now suppose G rises to 250 while t increases to 0.28. Repeat step 12(*a*) for the new fiscal policy.
(*d*) Calculate Y_0' and BuS′, the new income and budget surplus.
(*e*) What are ΔT, ΔG, ΔY, ΔBuS?
(*f*) In view of this result and that of problem 10, what do you think the effect on income would be if we had a balanced budget change where $\Delta R = \Delta T$?

*13 Suppose the aggregate demand function is as in the above figure. Notice that at Y_0 the slope of the aggregate demand curve is *greater* than 1. (This would happen if $c > 1$.) Complete this picture as is done in Figure 3-1 to include the arrows indicating adjustment when $Y \neq Y_0$ and show what I_u is for $Y < Y_0$ and $Y > Y_0$.

What is happening in this example, and how does it differ fundamentally from Figure 3-1?

*14 This problem anticipates our discussion of the open economy in Chapter 18. It is hard and only the advanced student can expect to cope with it. You are asked to derive some of the results that will be shown there. We start with the assumption that foreign demand for our goods is given and equal to $\overline{X}$. Our demand for foreign goods or imports, denoted Q, is a linear function of income:

$$\text{Exports} = \overline{X}, \text{ Imports} = Q = \overline{Q} + mY$$

where m is the ***marginal propensity to import.***

(*a*) The trade balance or net exports, NX, is defined as the excess of exports over imports. Write an algebraic expression for the trade balance and show in a diagram net exports as a function of the level of income. (Put Y on the horizontal axis.)

(*b*) Show the effect of a change in income on the trade balance, using your diagram. Show also the effect on the trade balance of a change in exports, given income.

(*c*) The equilibrium condition in the goods market is that aggregate demand for *our* goods is equal to supply. Aggregate demand for our goods includes exports but excludes imports. Thus we have

$$Y = C + \bar{I} + NX$$

where we have added net exports (exports less imports) to investment and consumption. Using the expression for net exports developed in 14(*a*) and the consumption function $C = \overline{C} + cY$, derive the equilibrium level of income, Y_0.

(*d*) Using your expression for the equilibrium level of income in 14(*c*), what is the effect of a change in exports, $\overline{X}$, on equilibrium income? Interpret your result and discuss the multiplier in an open economy.

(*e*) Using your results in 14(*a*) and 14(*d*), show the effect of an increase in exports on the trade balance.

4

MONEY, INTEREST, AND INCOME

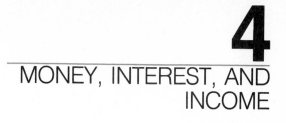

4
MONEY, INTEREST, AND INCOME

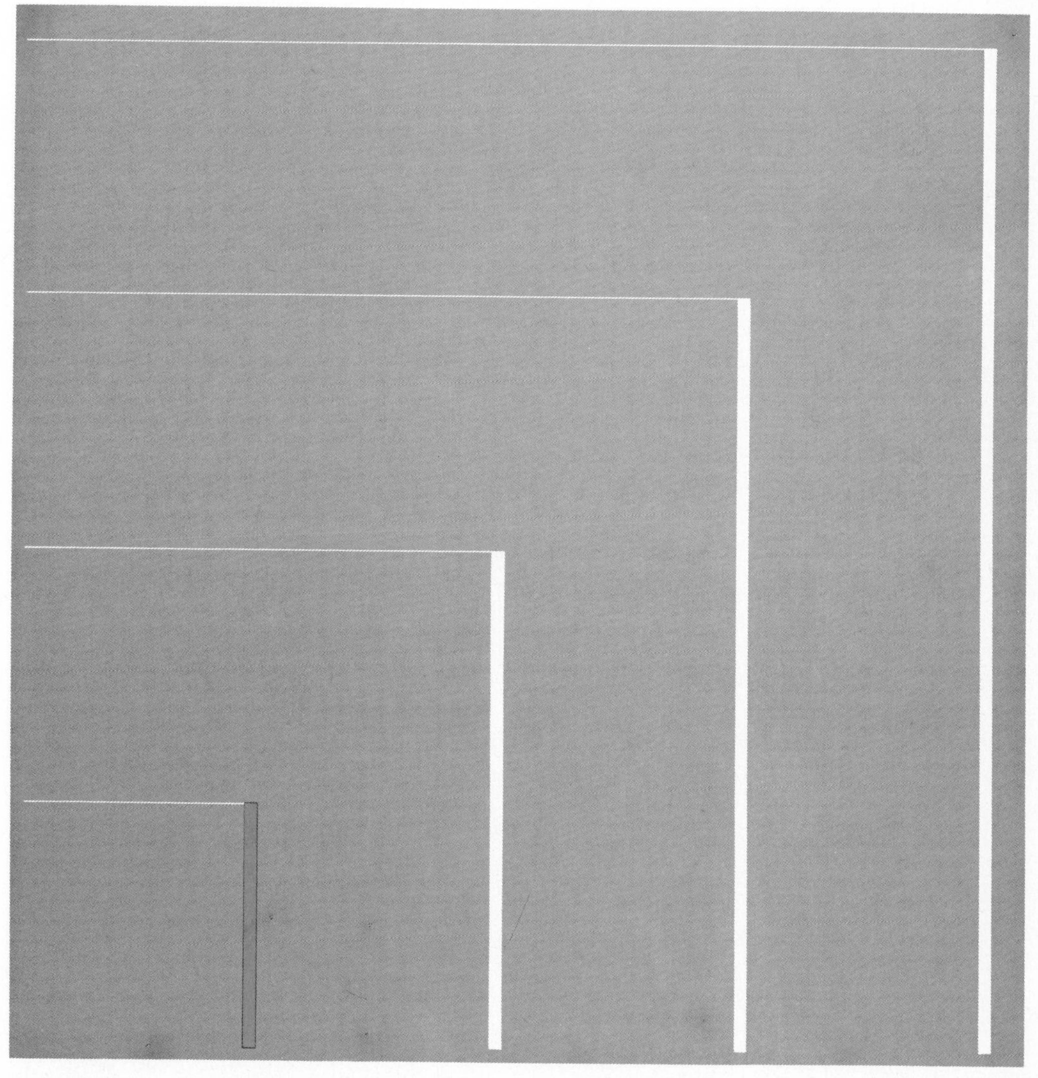

The stock of money, interest rates, and the Federal Reserve seemingly had no place in the model of income determination developed in Chapter 3. Clearly, though, we know that money has an important role to play in the determination of income and employment. Interest rates are frequently mentioned as an important determinant of aggregate spending, and the Federal Reserve and monetary policy receive at least as much public attention as fiscal policy. This chapter introduces money and monetary policy, and builds an explicit framework of analysis in which the interaction of goods and assets markets can be studied.

The model we will study here, called the IS-LM model, is the core of modern macroeconomics. It maintains the spirit and, indeed, many details of the previous chapter. In particular, it remains true that aggregate demand determines the equilibrium level of output.

The model is broadened, though, by introducing the interest rate as an additional determinant of aggregate demand. In Chapter 3, autonomous spending and fiscal policy were the chief determinants of aggregate spending. Now we add the interest rate and argue that a reduction in the rate of interest raises aggregate demand. This seems a minor extension, which can readily be handled in the context of Chapter 3. This is not entirely correct, because we have to ask what determines the rate of interest. That question extends our model to include the markets for financial assets and forces us to study the interaction of goods and assets markets. Interest rates and income are jointly determined by equilibrium in goods and assets markets.

What is the payoff for that complication? The introduction of assets markets and interest rates serves three important purposes. First, we need the extension to understand how monetary policy works. Second, the analysis qualifies the conclusions of Chapter 3. To appreciate the latter point, consider Figure 4-1, which lays out the logical structure of the model. In Chapter 3, we looked at the submodel of autonomous spending and fiscal policy as determinants of aggregate demand and equilibrium income. Here the inclusion of assets markets—money demand and supply, as we shall see—introduces an additional channel. Thus, an expansionary fiscal policy, for example, would in the first place raise spending and income. That increase in income, though, would affect the assets markets by raising money demand and thereby raising interest rates. The higher interest rates in turn reduce aggregate spending and thus, as we will show, dampen the expansionary impact of fiscal policy. Indeed, under certain conditions, the increase in interest rates may be sufficiently important to *fully* offset the expansionary effects of fiscal policy. Clearly, such an extreme possibility is an important qualification to our study of fiscal policy in Chapter 3.

Third, even if the interest rate changes just mentioned only dampen (rather than fully offset) the expansionary effects of fiscal policy, they nevertheless have an important side effect. The composition of aggregate demand between investment and consumption spending will depend on the rate of interest. Higher interest rates dampen aggregate demand mainly by reducing investment. Thus, an expansionary fiscal policy would tend to raise consumption through the multiplier, but it would tend to reduce investment through the induced increase in interest rates. The side effects of fiscal expansion on interest rates and investment continue to be a sensitive and important issue in policy making. An influential view is that fiscal expansion should not be used as a tool for demand management because the increase in government spending takes place at the expense of private investment. Government spending *crowds out*, or displaces, private investment because it tends to raise interest rates.

These three reasons justify the more complicated model we study in this chapter. There is the further advantage that the extended model helps us to understand the functioning of financial markets.

We can use Figure 4-1 once more to lay out the structure of this chapter. We start in Section 4-1 with a discussion of the link between interest rates and aggregate demand. Here we use the model of Chapter 3 directly, augmented to include an interest rate as a determinant of aggregate demand. We will derive a key relationship—the IS curve—that shows combinations of interest rates and levels of income for which the goods markets clear. In Section 4-2, we turn to assets markets and, in particular, to the money market. We show that the demand for money depends on interest rates and income and that there is a combination of interest rates and income levels—the LM curve—for which the money market clears.[1] In Section 4-3, we combine the two schedules to study the

[1] The term IS and LM are shorthand representations, respectively, of investment equals saving (goods market equilibrium) and money demand (L) equals money supply (M), or money market equilibrium. The classic article that introduced this model is J. R. Hicks, "Mr. Keynes and the Classics: A Suggested Interpretation," *Econometrica*, 1937, pp. 147–159. The article remains worth reading.

FIGURE 4-1 THE LOGICAL STRUCTURE OF THE IS-LM MODEL

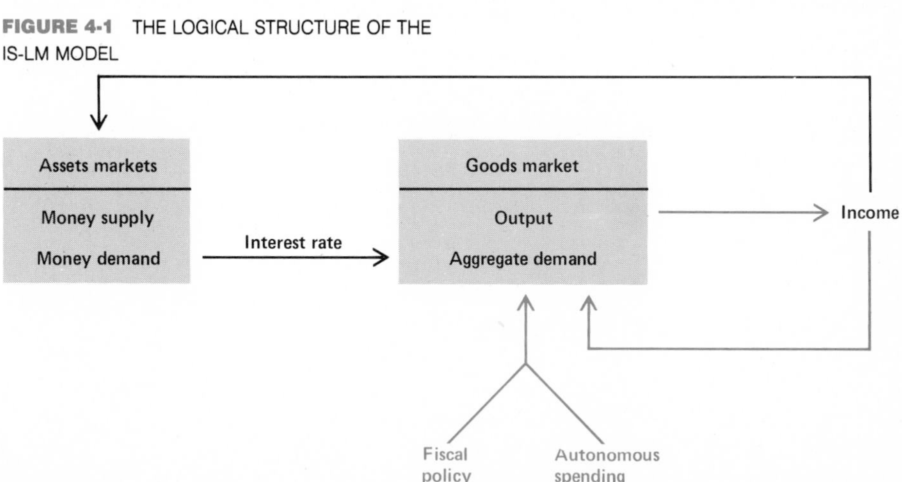

joint determination of interest rates and income, as a brief glance ahead at Figure 4-10 will show. Section 4–4 lays out the adjustment process toward equilibrium. Monetary and fiscal policy are discussed in Sections 4-5 and 4-6. The political economy of monetary and fiscal policy is taken up in Section 4-7. We conclude the chapter with a formal statement of the model. An appendix discusses the relationship between interest rates, asset prices, and asset yields.

4-1 THE GOODS MARKET AND THE IS CURVE

In this section, we will derive a "goods market equilibrium schedule"—a combination of interest rates and levels of income such that the goods market is in equilibrium. That is the IS schedule, which is shown in Figure 4-2*b*. To derive the IS schedule, we start with the analysis of goods market equilibrium of Chapter 3, and modify it to take account of the relationship between investment spending and the interest rate.

In Chapter 3, we relied on an aggregate demand function of the form

$$A = \overline{A} + \overline{c}Y \tag{1}$$

where $\overline{A}$ denotes autonomous spending and is equal to

$$\overline{A} \equiv \overline{C} + \overline{I} + \overline{G} + \overline{c}\overline{R} \tag{2}$$

and where we have introduced the shorthand notation $\overline{c} \equiv c(1 - t)$ to denote the marginal propensity to spend out of income.

Equilibrium in the goods market requires that output equals aggregate demand:

$$Y = A \tag{3}$$

and leads, by substitution from Equation (1), to the equation

$$Y = \overline{A} + \overline{c}Y \tag{3a}$$

This can be solved for the equilibrium level of income:[2]

$$Y_0 = \frac{\overline{A}}{1 - \overline{c}} = \overline{\alpha}\overline{A} \tag{3b}$$

In Equation (3*b*) we have used the shorthand notation for the multiplier with taxes, $\overline{\alpha} \equiv 1/(1 - \overline{c})$.

The level of planned investment $\overline{I}$ in Equation (2) was treated as constant in Chapter 3. However, planned investment spending is influ-

[2] To move from Eq. (3*a*) to Eq. (3*b*), we collect terms in Y to obtain $Y(1 - \overline{c}) = \overline{A}$. Then we divide both sides by $(1 - \overline{c})$ to yield Eq. (3*b*).

enced by the rate of interest, being inversely related to it. We explore the determinants of investment spending in depth in Chapter 6, but a simple argument will show why planned investment spending is negatively related to the interest rate. Investment is spending on additions to the capital stock. Such investment is undertaken with an eye to the profits that can be obtained in the future by operating machines and factories. Now, suppose firms borrow to buy the capital, in the form of machines and factories, that they use. Then the higher the interest rate, the more firms have to pay out in interest each year from the earnings they receive from their investment. Thus, the higher the interest rate, the less the profits to the firm after paying interest, and the less it will want to invest. Conversely, a low rate of interest makes investment spending profitable and is, therefore, reflected in a high level of planned investment.

Accordingly, we modify the assumption that investment spending is constant by specifying an investment spending function of the form[3]

$$I = \bar{I} - bi \qquad b > 0 \tag{4}$$

where i is the rate of interest and b measures the interest response of investment. $\bar{I}$ now denotes autonomous investment spending, that is, investment spending that is independent of both income *and* the rate of Interest.[4] Equation (4) states that the lower the interest rate, the higher the planned investment, with the coefficient b measuring the responsiveness of investment spending to the interest rate.

We now modify the aggregate demand function Equation (1) to reflect the new planned investment spending schedule Equation (4). Aggregate demand still consists of the demand for consumption goods, investment, and government spending on goods and services. Only now investment spending depends on the interest rate. We have

$$\begin{aligned} A &\equiv C + I + G \\ &= \bar{C} + c\bar{R} + c(1 - t)Y + \bar{I} - bi + \bar{G} \\ &= \bar{A} + \bar{c}Y - bi \end{aligned} \tag{1a}$$

where

$$\bar{A} \equiv \bar{C} + c\bar{R} + \bar{I} + \bar{G} \tag{2a}$$

[3] Here and in other places in the book, we specify linear (straight-line) versions of behavioral functions. We use the linear specifications to simplify both the algebra and the diagrams. The linearity assumption does not lead to any great difficulties so long as we confine ourselves to talking about small changes in the economy. You should often draw nonlinear versions of our diagrams to be sure you can work with them. This would be particularly useful where, as in Fig. 4-2, the position and shape of one curve (in this case, the IS curve) depend on the position and shape of another curve (the aggregate demand schedules in the upper panel, in this case).

[4] In Chap. 3, investment spending was defined as autonomous with respect to income. Now that the interest rate appears in the model, we have to extend the definition of autonomous to mean independent of both the interest rate and income. To conserve notation, we continue to use $\bar{I}$ to denote autonomous investment, but recognize that the definition is broadened.

From Equation (1a) it is clear that an increase in the interest rate reduces aggregate demand at a given level of income because an interest rate increase reduces investment spending. Note that the term $\bar{A}$, which is the part of aggregate demand unaffected by either the level of income or the interest rate, does include part of investment spending, namely, $\bar{I}$. As noted earlier, $\bar{I}$ is the *autonomous* component of investment spending, which is independent of the interest rate (and income).

At any given level of the interest rate, we can still proceed as in Chapter 3 to determine the equilibrium level of income and output. As the interest rate changes, the equilibrium level of income changes. The relationship we shall now derive between the interest rate and the equilibrium level of income in the goods market is the *IS curve*.

Figure 4-2 is used to derive the IS curve. For a given level of the interest rate, say i_1, the last term of Equation (1a) is a constant (bi_1), and we can in Figure 4-2a draw the aggregate demand function of Chapter 3, this time with an intercept $\bar{A} - bi_1$. The equilibrium level of income obtained in the usual manner is Y_1 at point E_1. Since that equilibrium level of income was derived for a given level of the interest rate i_1, we can plot that pair (namely, i_1, Y_1) in the bottom panel as point E_1. We now have one point, E_1, on the IS curve.

Consider next a lower interest rate, i_2. At a lower interest rate, aggregate demand would be higher at each level of income because investment spending is higher. In terms of Figure 4-2a, that implies an upward shift of the aggregate demand schedule. The entire aggregate demand schedule shifts upward by $-b\,\Delta i$, where Δi, the assumed change in the interest rate, is negative. The curve shifts upward because the intercept $\bar{A} - bi$ has been increased. Given the increase in aggregate demand, we note that the equilibrium level of income rises to point E_2, with an associated income level Y_2. At point E_2, in the bottom panel, we record the fact that an interest rate i_2 implies an equilibrium level of income, Y_2—equilibrium in the sense that the goods market is in equilibrium (or that the goods market *clears*). Point E_2 is another point on the IS curve.

We can apply the same procedure to all conceivable levels of the interest rate and thereby generate all the points which make up the IS curve. They have in common the property that they constitute combinations of interest rates and income (output) such that the goods market clears. We therefore refer to the IS curve as the *goods market equilibrium schedule*.

Figure 4-2 shows that the IS curve is negatively sloped, reflecting the increase in aggregate demand associated with a reduction in the interest rate. We can alternatively derive the IS curve by using the goods market equilibrium condition:

$$Y = A \tag{5}$$

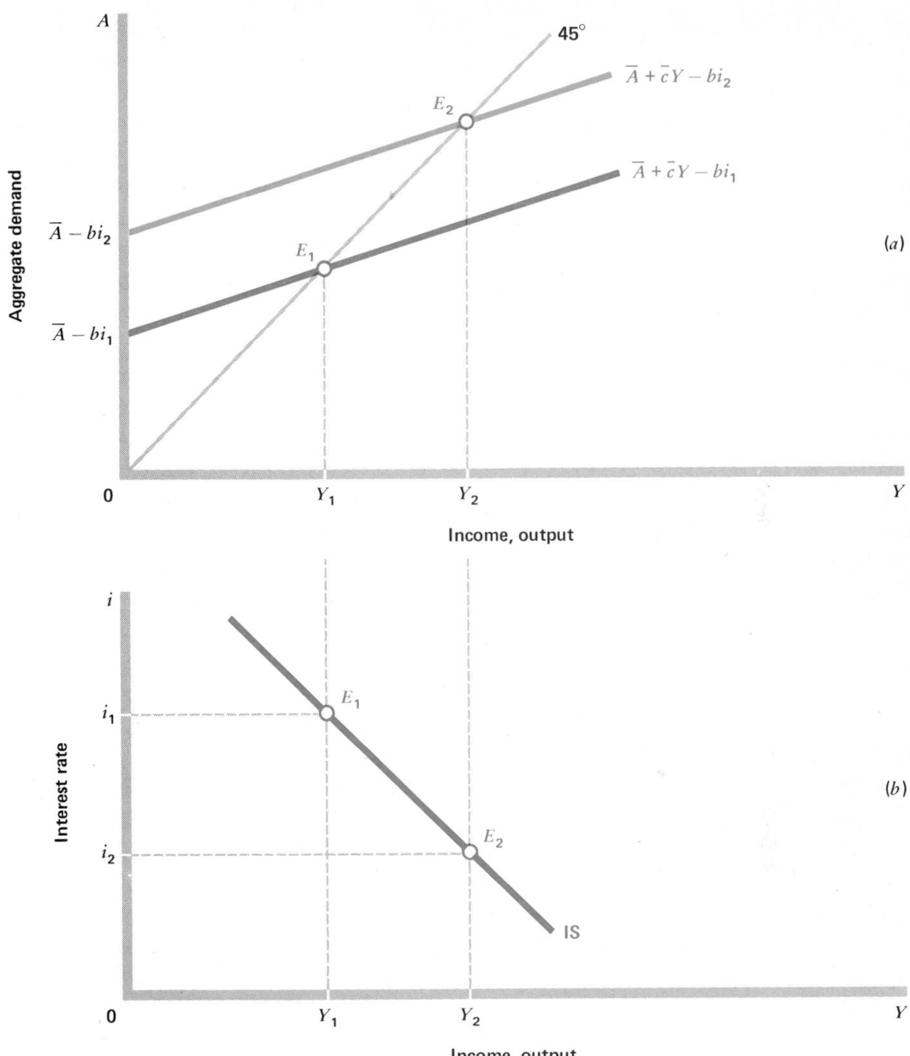

FIGURE 4-2 DERIVATION OF THE IS CURVE

Substituting from Equation (1*a*) for aggregate demand in Equation (5), we obtain

$$Y = \overline{A} + \bar{c}Y - bi \tag{6}$$

which can be simplified to

$$Y = \bar{\alpha}(\overline{A} - bi) \qquad \bar{\alpha} \equiv \frac{1}{1 - \bar{c}} \tag{6a}$$

From Equation (6*a*), we note that a higher interest rate implies a lower level of equilibrium income for a given $\bar{A}$, as Figure 4-2 shows. (Recall that $\bar{\alpha}$ is the multiplier of Chapter 3.)

The construction of the IS curve is quite straightforward and may even be deceptively simple. We can gain further understanding of the economics of the IS curve by asking and answering the following questions:

- What determines the slope of the IS curve?
- What determines the position of the IS curve, given its slope, and what causes the curve to shift?
- What happens when the interest rate and income are at levels such that we are not on the IS curve?

The Slope of the IS Curve

We have already noted that the IS curve is negatively sloped because a higher level of the interest rate reduces investment spending, therefore reduces aggregate demand, and therefore reduces the equilibrium level of income. The steepness of the curve depends on how sensitive investment spending is to changes in the interest rate, and also on the multiplier $\bar{\alpha}$ in Equation (6*a*).

Suppose that investment spending is very sensitive to the interest rate, so that b in Equation (6*a*) is large. Then, in terms of Figure 4-2, a given change in the interest rate produces a large change in aggregate demand, and thus shifts the aggregate demand curve in Figure 4-2*a* up by a large distance. A large shift in the aggregate demand schedule produces a correspondingly large change in the equilibrium level of income. If a given change in the interest rate produces a large change in income, the IS curve is very flat. Thus the IS curve is flat if investment is very sensitive to the interest rate, that is, if b is large. Correspondingly, with b small and investment spending not very sensitive to the interest rate, the IS curve is relatively steep.

Consider next the effects of the multiplier $\bar{\alpha}$ on the steepness of the IS curve. Figure 4-3 shows aggregate demand curves corresponding to different multipliers. The coefficient $\bar{c}$ on the darker aggregate demand curves is smaller than the corresponding coefficient $\bar{c}'$ on the lighter aggregate demand curves. The multiplier is accordingly larger on the lighter aggregate demand curves. The initial levels of income, Y_1 and Y_1', correspond to the interest rate i_1 on the lower of each of the darker and lighter aggregate demand curves, respectively. A given reduction in the interest rate, to i_2, raises the intercept of the aggregate demand curves by the same vertical distance, as shown in the top panel. However, the implied change in income is very different. For the lighter curve, income rises to Y_2', while it rises only to Y_2 on the darker line. The change in

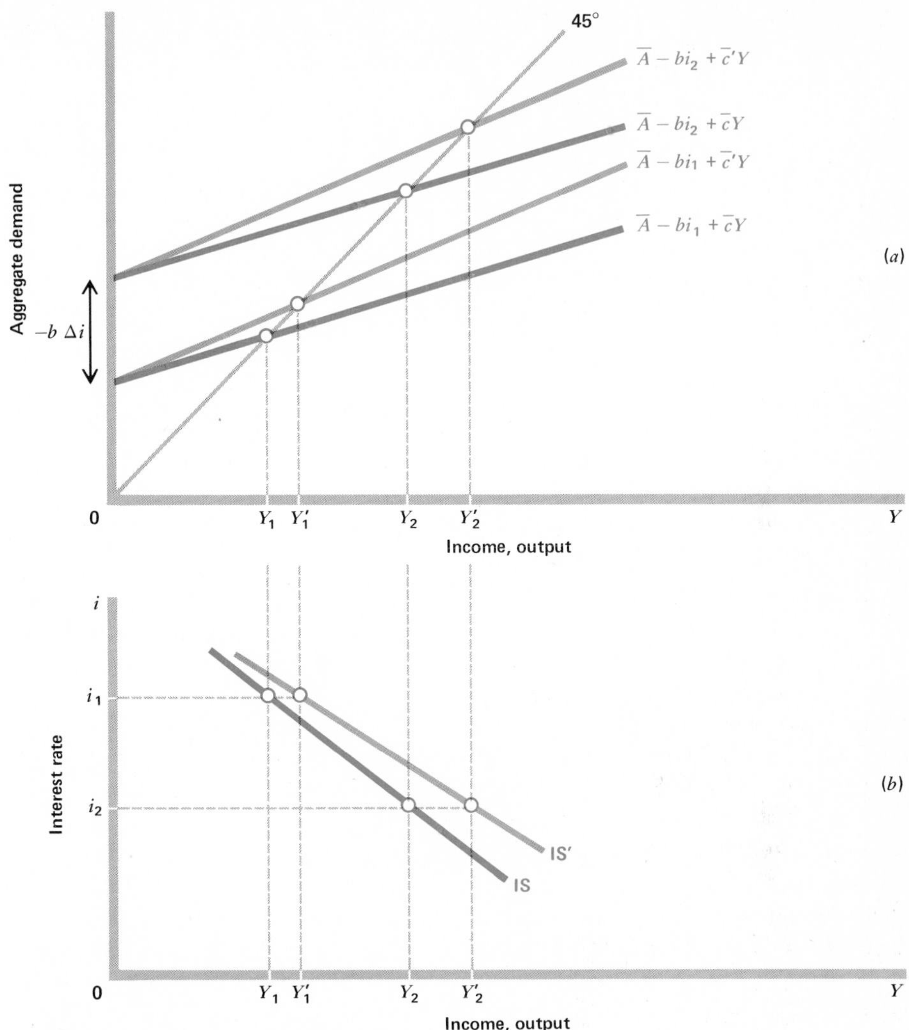

FIGURE 4-3 EFFECTS OF THE MULTIPLIER ON THE STEEPNESS OF THE IS CURVE

equilibrium income corresponding to a given change in the interest rate is accordingly larger as the aggregate demand curve is steeper; that is, the larger the multiplier, the greater the rise in income. That should not be surprising since effectively the change in the interest rate and induced change in investment acts in the same way on the aggregate demand curves as a change in autonomous spending $\bar{A}$. As we see from Figure 4-3*b*, the smaller the multiplier, the steeper the IS curve. Equivalently, the larger the multiplier, the larger the change in income produced by a given change in the interest rate.

We have thus seen that the smaller the sensitivity of investment spending to the interest rate and the smaller the multiplier, the steeper the IS curve. This conclusion can be confirmed by using Equation (6*a*). We can turn Equation (6*a*) around to express the interest rate as a function of the level of income:

$$i = \frac{\bar{A}}{b} - \frac{Y}{\bar{\alpha} b} \tag{6b}$$

Thus, for a given change in Y, the associated change in i will be larger in size as b is smaller and $\bar{\alpha}$ is smaller.

Given that the slope of the IS curve depends on the multiplier, fiscal policy can affect that slope. The multiplier $\bar{\alpha}$ is affected by the tax rate:

$$\bar{\alpha} = \frac{1}{1 - c(1 - t)} \tag{7}$$

An increase in the tax rate reduces the multiplier. Accordingly, the higher the tax rate, the steeper the IS curve.

The Position of the IS Curve

We now want to answer the question of what determines the position of the IS curve, and what causes it to shift that position. Figure 4-4 shows two different IS curves, the lighter one of which lies to the right and above the darker IS curve. What might cause the IS curve to be at IS′ rather than at IS in Figure 4-4? The answer is an increase in the level of autonomous spending.

In Figure 4-4*a* we show an initial aggregate demand curve drawn for a level of autonomous spending $\bar{A}$ and for an arbitrary interest rate i_1. Corresponding to the initial aggregate demand curve is the point E_1 on the IS curve in Figure 4-4*b*. Now, at the same interest rate, let the level of autonomous spending increase to $\bar{A}'$. The increase in autonomous spending increases the equilibrium level of income at the interest rate i_1. The point E_2 in Figure 4-4*b* is thus a point on the new goods market equilibrium schedule IS′. Since E_1 was an arbitrary point on the initial IS curve, we can perform the exercise for all levels of the interest rate and thereby generate our new curve IS′. We see that an increase in autonomous spending shifts the curve out to the right.

By how much does the curve shift? The change in income, as a result of

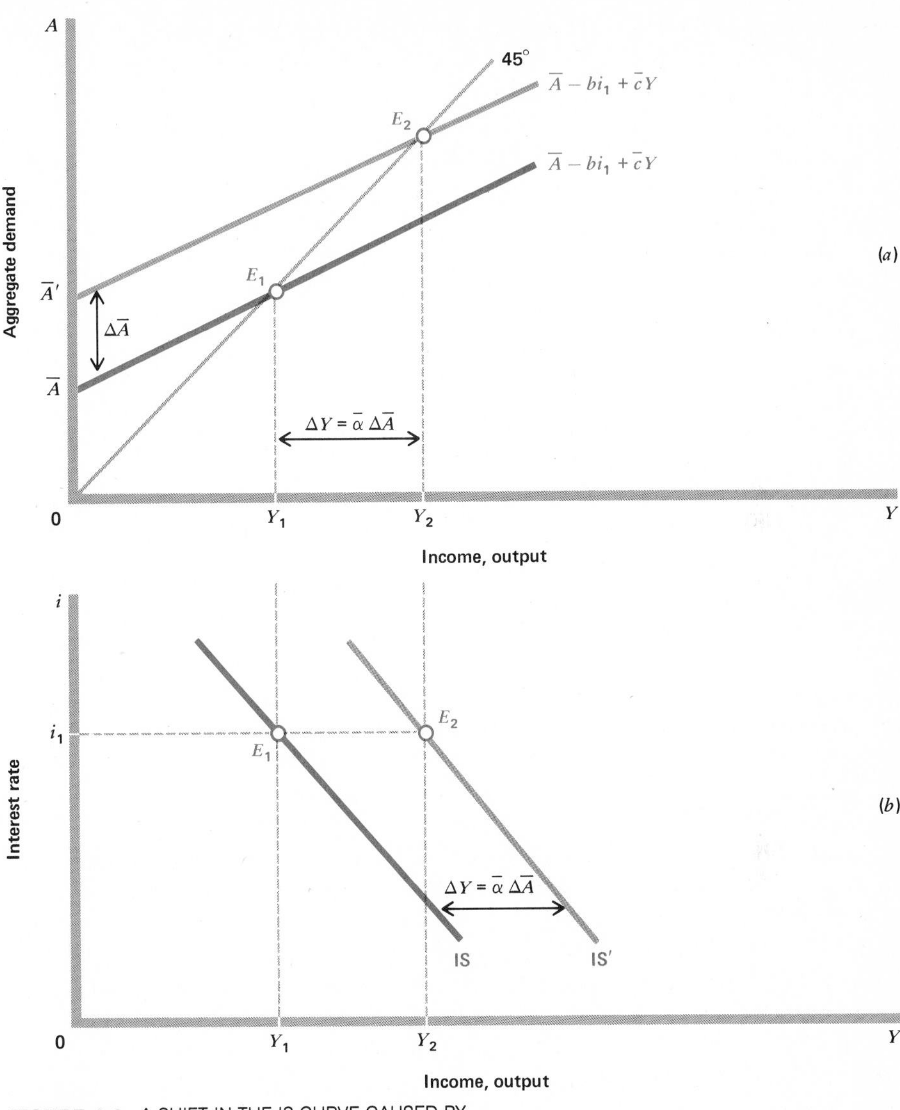

FIGURE 4-4 A SHIFT IN THE IS CURVE CAUSED BY A CHANGE IN AUTONOMOUS SPENDING

the change in autonomous spending, can be seen from the top panel to be just the multiplier times the change in autonomous spending. That means that the IS curve is shifted horizontally by a distance equal to the multiplier times the change in autonomous spending, as can be seen from the fact that the distance between E_1 and E_2, in the lower panel, is the distance between Y_1 and Y_2 in the upper panel.

Now the level of autonomous spending is

$$\bar{A} \equiv \bar{C} + \bar{I} + \bar{G} + c\bar{R} \tag{2}$$

Accordingly, an increase in government purchases or transfer payments will shift the IS curve out to the right, the extent of the shift depending on the size of the multiplier. A reduction in transfer payments or in government purchases shifts the IS curve to the left.

Positions off the IS Curve

We gain understanding of the meaning of the IS curve by considering points off the curve. Figure 4-5 reproduces Figure 4-2, along with two additional points—the *dis*equilibrium points E_3 and E_4. Consider first the question of what is true for points off the schedule, points such as E_3 and E_4. In Figure 4-5*b*, at point E_3 we have the same interest rate i_2 as at point E_2, but the level of income is lower than at E_2. Since the interest rate i_2 at E_3 is the same as at E_2 in Figure 4-5*b*, we must have the same aggregate demand function corresponding to the two points. Accordingly, looking now at Figure 4-5*a*, we find both points are on the same aggregate demand schedule. At E_3 on that schedule, aggregate demand exceeds the level of output. Point E_3 is therefore a point of *excess demand for goods*: the interest rate is too low or output is too low for the goods market to be in equilibrium. Demand for goods exceeds output.

Consider, next, point E_4 in Figure 4-5*b*. Here we have the same rate of interest i_1 as at E_1, but the level of income is higher. Given the interest rate i_1, the corresponding point in Figure 4-5*a* is at E_4 where we have an *excess supply of goods*, since output is larger than aggregate demand—that is, aggregate demand given the interest rate i_1 and the income level Y_2.

The preceding discussion can be generalized by saying that points above and to the right of the IS curve—points like E_4—are points of excess supply of goods. This is indicated by ESG (excess supply of goods) in Figure 4-5*b*. Points below and to the left of the IS curve are points of excess demand for goods. At a point like E_3, the interest rate is too low and aggregate demand is therefore too high, relative to output. EDG (excess demand for goods) shows the region of excess demand in Figure 4-5.

Summary

The major points about the IS curve are:

1 The IS curve is the schedule of combinations of the interest rate and level of income such that the goods market is in equilibrium.

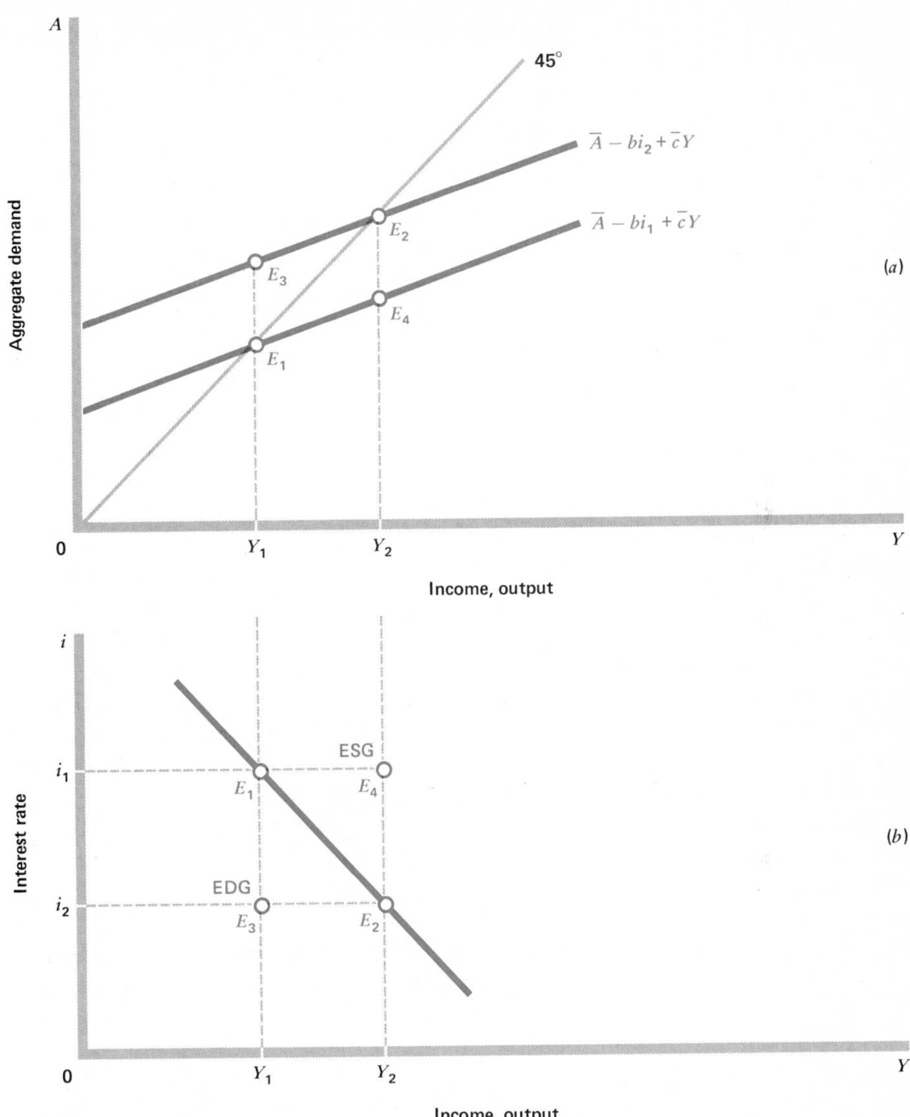

FIGURE 4-5 EXCESS SUPPLY (ESG) AND DEMAND (EDG) IN THE GOODS MARKET TO THE RIGHT AND LEFT, RESPECTIVELY, OF THE IS CURVE

2 The IS curve is negatively sloped because an increase in the interest rate reduces planned investment spending and therefore reduces aggregate demand, thus reducing the equilibrium level of income.

3 The smaller the multiplier and the less sensitive investment spending is to changes in the interest rate, the steeper the curve.
4 The IS curve is shifted by changes in autonomous spending. An increase in autonomous spending, including an increase in government purchases, shifts the IS curve out to the right.
5 At points to the right of the curve, there is excess supply in the goods market, and at points to the left of the curve, there is excess demand for goods.

We turn now to examine behavior in the assets markets.

4-2 THE ASSETS MARKETS AND THE LM CURVE

In the preceding section, we discussed aggregate demand and the goods market. In the present section, we turn to assets markets. The assets markets are the markets in which money, bonds, stocks, houses, and other forms of wealth are traded. Up to this point in the book, we have ignored the role of those markets in affecting the level of income, and it is now time to remedy the omission.

There is a large variety of assets, and a tremendous volume of trading occurs every day in the assets markets, but we shall simplify matters by grouping all available financial assets into two groups, *money* and *interest-bearing assets.*[5] By analogy with our treatment of the goods market, where we proceeded as if there were a single commodity called output, we will proceed in the assets markets as if there are only two assets, money and all others. It will be useful to think of the other assets as marketable claims to future income such as *bonds.*

A bond is a promise to pay to its holder certain agreed-upon amounts of money at specified dates in the future. For example, a borrower sells a bond in exchange for a given amount of money today, say $100, and promises to pay a fixed amount, say $6, each year to the person who owns the bond, and to repay the full $100 (the principal) after some fixed period of time, such as 3 years, or perhaps longer. In this example, the interest rate is 6 percent, for that is the percentage of the amount borrowed that the borrower pays each year.

[5] We shall be assuming in this section that certain assets, such as the capital that firms use in production, are not traded. That too is a simplification. A more complex treatment of the assets markets would allow for the trading of capital and would introduce a relative price for the capital operated by firms. This treatment is usually reserved for advanced graduate courses. For such a treatment of the assets markets, see James Tobin, "A General Equilibrium Approach to Monetary Theory," *Journal of Money, Credit and Banking*, February 1969, pp. 15–29, and, by the same author, "Money, Capital, and Other Stores of Value," *American Economic Review*, May 1961, pp. 26–37.

The Wealth Constraint

At any given time, an individual has to decide how to allocate her financial wealth between alternative assets. The more bonds held, the more interest received on total financial wealth. The more money held the less likely the individual is not to have money available when she wants to make a purchase. The person who has \$1,000 in financial wealth has to decide whether to hold, say, \$900 in bonds and \$100 in money, or rather, \$500 in each type of asset, or even \$1,000 in money and none in bonds. We refer to decisions on the form in which to hold assets as *portfolio decisions.*

The example makes it clear that the portfolio decision on how much money to hold and the decision on how many bonds to hold are really the same decision. Given the level of financial wealth, the individual who has decided how many bonds to hold has implicitly also decided how much money to hold. There is thus a *wealth budget constraint* which implies that the sum of the individual's demands for money and bonds has to add up to that person's total financial wealth.

At this stage we have to reintroduce the crucial distinction between *real* and *nominal* variables. The nominal demand for money is the individual's demand for a given number of dollars, and similarly, the nominal demand for bonds is the demand for a given number of dollars' worth of bonds. By contrast, the real demand for money is the demand for money expressed in terms of the number of units of goods that money will buy: it is equal to the nominal demand for money divided by the price level. If the nominal demand for money is \$100 and the price level is \$2 per good—meaning that the representative basket of goods cost \$2—then the real demand for money is fifty goods. If the price level later doubles to \$4 per good and the demand for nominal money likewise doubles to \$200, the real demand for money is unchanged at fifty goods. Real money balances—real balances, for short—are the quantity of nominal money divided by the price level, and the real demand for money is often called *the demand for real balances.* Similarly, real bond holdings are the nominal quantity of bonds divided by the price level.

The wealth budget constraint in the assets markets states that the demand for real balances, which we shall denote L, plus the demand for real bond holdings, which we denote V, must add up to the real financial wealth of the individual. Real financial wealth is, of course, simply nominal wealth W divided by the price level P:

$$L + V = \frac{W}{P} \tag{8}$$

Note, again, that the wealth budget constraint implies, given an individual's real wealth, that a decision to hold more real balances is also a decision to hold less real wealth in the form of bonds. This implication turns out to be both important and convenient. It will allow us to discuss assets markets entirely in terms of the money market. Why? Because, given real wealth, when the money market is in equilibrium, the bond market will turn out also to be in equilibrium. We shall now show why that should be.

The total amount of real financial wealth in the economy consists of real money balances and real bonds in existence. Thus, total real financial wealth is equal to

$$\frac{W}{P} \equiv \frac{M}{P} + V^s \tag{9}$$

where M is the stock of nominal money balances and V^s is the real value of the supply of bonds. Total real financial wealth consists of real balances and real bonds. The distinction between Equations (8) and (9) is that Equation (8) is a constraint on the amount of assets individuals *wish* to hold, whereas Equation (9) is merely an accounting relationship which tells us how much financial wealth there is in the economy. There is no implication in the accounting relationship in Equation (9) that individuals are necessarily happy to hold the amounts of money and bonds that actually exist in the economy.

Now we substitute Equation (8) into Equation (9) and rearrange terms to obtain

$$\left(L - \frac{M}{P}\right) + (V - V^s) = 0 \tag{10}$$

Let us see what Equation (10) implies. Suppose first that the demand for real balances L is equal to the existing stock of real balances M/P. Then, the first term in parentheses in Equation (10) is equal to zero, and therefore the second term in parentheses must also be zero. Thus, if the demand for real balances L is equal to the supply of real balances M/P, the demand for real bonds V must be equal to the supply of real bonds V^s.

Stating the same proposition in terms of "markets," we can say that the asset budget constraint implies that when the money market is in equilibrium so that $L = M/P$, so too is the bond market in equilibrium and therefore $V = V^s$. Similarly, when there is excess demand in the money market so that $L > M/P$, Equation (10) implies that there is an excess supply of bonds, $V < V^s$. We can therefore fully discuss the assets markets by concentrating our attention on the money market.

The Demand for Money

We can now proceed by concentrating on the money market, and initially on the demand for real balances.[6] The demand for money is a demand for

[6] The demand for money is studied in depth in Chap. 7; here we only briefly present the arguments underlying the demand for money.

real balances because the public holds money for what it will buy. The higher the price level, the more nominal balances a person has to hold to be able to purchase a given quantity of goods. If the price level doubles, then an individual has to hold twice as many nominal balances in order to be able to buy the same amount of goods.

The demand for real balances depends on the level of real income and the interest rate. It depends on the level of real income because individuals hold money to finance their expenditures, which, in turn, depend on income. This demand for money to finance regular spending on goods is known as the transactions demand for money. The demand for money depends also on the interest rate. The cost of holding money is the interest that is forgone by holding it rather than interest-bearing assets. The higher the interest rate, the more costly it is to hold money, rather than other assets, and accordingly, the less cash will be held at each level of income. Individuals can economize on their holdings of cash, when the interest rate rises, by being more careful in managing their money, by making transfers from money to bonds whenever their money holdings reach any appreciable magnitude. If the interest rate is 1 percent, then there is very little benefit from holding bonds rather than money. However, when the interest rate is 10 percent, one would probably go to some effort not to hold more money than needed to finance day-to-day transactions.

On these simple grounds, then, the demand for real balances increases with the level of real income and decreases with the interest rate.[7] The demand for real balances is accordingly written[8]

$$L = kY - hi \qquad k > 0 \qquad h > 0 \tag{11}$$

The parameters k and h reflect the sensitivity of the demand for real balances to the level of income and the interest rate, respectively. A \$5 increase in real income raises money demand by $5k$ real dollars. An increase in the interest rate by one percentage point reduces real money demand by h real dollars.

The demand function for real balances, Equation (11), implies that for a given level of income, the demand is a decreasing function of the rate of interest. Such a demand curve is shown in Figure 4-6 for a level of income Y_1. The higher the level of income, the larger the demand for real balances, and therefore the further to the right the demand curve. The demand curve for a higher level of real income Y_2 is also shown in Figure 4-6.

[7] As we shall see in Chap. 7, there are motives other than transactions motives for holding money, and they too point to a negative relationship between the demand for money and the interest rate.

[8] Once again, we write the demand for real balances as a linear function of real income and the interest rate, though that cannot be true for all levels of the interest rate. The demand for real balances cannot be negative. The linear form of the demand function applies only over a limited range of values of income and the interest rate. You should experiment with a nonlinear form of the demand function in some of the diagrams below.

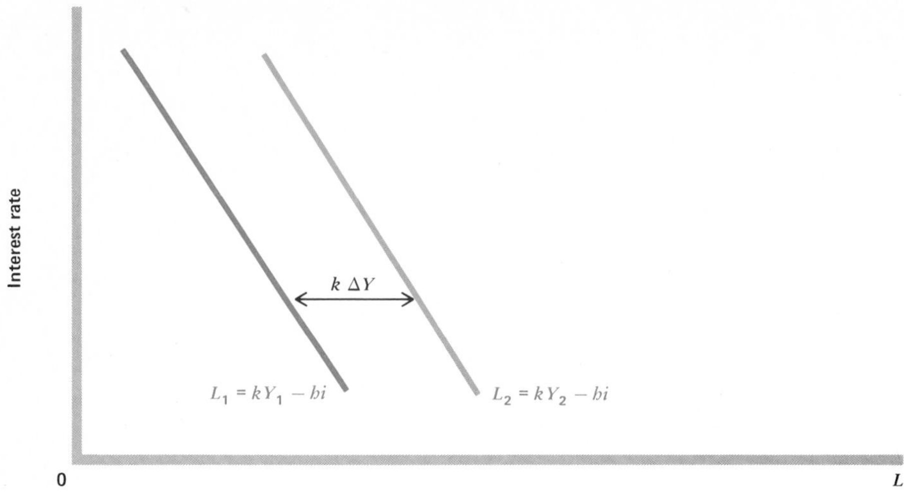

FIGURE 4-6 THE DEMAND FOR REAL BALANCES AS A FUNCTION OF THE INTEREST RATE AND REAL INCOME

The Supply of Money, Money Market Equilibrium, and the LM Curve

Now that we have specified a demand function for money, we can study the equilibrium in the money market. For that purpose we have to say how the supply of money is determined. The nominal quantity of money M is controlled by the Federal Reserve System, and we shall take it as given at the level $\overline{M}$. We are assuming the price level is constant at the level $\overline{P}$, so that the real money supply can be taken to be fixed at the level $\overline{M}/\overline{P}$.[9]

In Figure 4-7, we show combinations of interest rates and income levels such that the demand for real balances exactly matches the available supply. Starting with the level of income Y_1, we have the associated demand curve for real balances L_1, in Figure 4-7*b*. It is drawn, as in Figure 4-6, as a decreasing function of the interest rate. The existing supply of real balances $\overline{M}/\overline{P}$ is shown by the vertical line, since it is given and therefore independent of the interest rate. The interest rate i_1 has the property that it clears the money market. At that interest rate, the demand for real balances equals the supply. Therefore, point E_1 is an equilibrium point in the money market. That point is recorded in Figure 4-7*a* as a point on what we shall be calling the *money market equilibrium schedule*, or the *LM curve*.

[9] Since for the present we are holding constant the money supply and price level, we refer to them as exogenous and denote that fact by a bar.

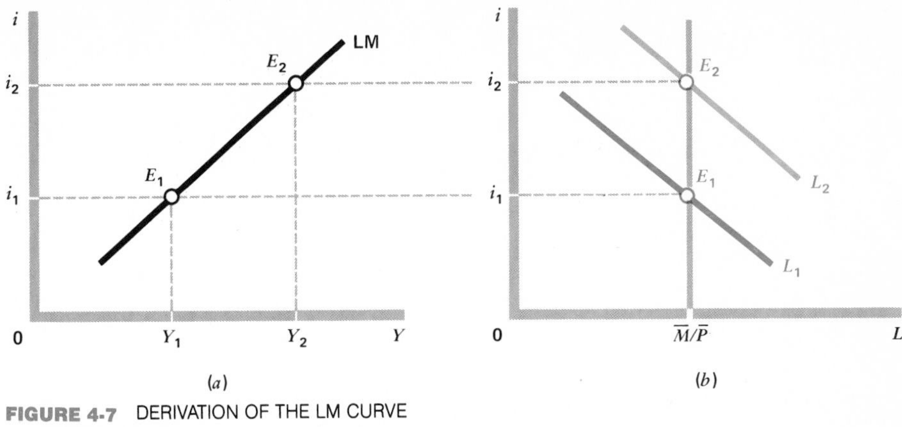

FIGURE 4-7 DERIVATION OF THE LM CURVE

Consider next the effect of an increase in income to Y_2. In Figure 4-7*b*, the higher level of income causes the demand for real balances to be higher at each level of the interest rate, so the demand curve for real balances shifts up and to the right to L_2. At the initial interest rate i_1, there is an excess demand for money. Therefore, we require an increase in the interest rate to i_2 to maintain equilibrium in the money market at that higher level of income. Accordingly, our new equilibrium point is E_2. In Figure 4-7*a*, we record point E_2 as a point of equilibrium in the money market. Performing the same exercise for all income levels, we generate a series of points that can be linked up to give us the LM schedule, or the money market equilibrium schedule. Along the LM schedule, the demand for real balances is equal to the given real money supply.

Given the fixed supply of real balances, the LM curve is positively sloped. An increase in the interest rate reduces the demand for real balances. To maintain the demand for real balances equal to the fixed supply, the level of income has, therefore, to rise. Accordingly, money market equilibrium implies that an increase in the interest rate is accompanied by an increase in the level of income.

The LM curve can be obtained directly by combining the demand curve for real balances, Equation (11), and the fixed supply of real balances. For the money market to be in equilibrium, we require that demand equals supply, or that

$$\frac{\overline{M}}{\overline{P}} = kY - hi \tag{12}$$

Solving for the interest rate, we have

$$i = \frac{1}{h}\left(kY - \frac{\overline{M}}{\overline{P}}\right) \tag{12a}$$

The relationship (12*a*) is the LM curve.

Next we ask the same questions about the properties of the LM schedule that we asked about the IS curve.

The Slope of the LM Curve

The larger the responsiveness of the demand for money to income, as measured by k, and the lower the responsiveness of the demand for money to the interest rate h, the steeper will be the LM curve. This point can be established by experimenting with Figure 4-7. It can also be confirmed by examining Equation (12*a*), where a given change in income ΔY has a larger effect on the interest rate i, the larger is k and the smaller is h. If the demand for money is relatively insensitive to the interest rate, so that h is close to zero, the LM curve is nearly vertical. If the demand for money is very sensitive to the interest rate, so that h is large, then the LM curve is close to horizontal. In that case, a small change in the interest rate is accompanied by a large change in the level of income to maintain money market equilibrium.

The Position of the LM Curve

The real money supply is held constant along the LM curve. It follows that a change in the real money supply will shift the LM curve. In Figure 4-8, we show the effect of an increase in the real money supply In Figure 4-8*b*, we have drawn the demand for real money balances for a level of income Y_1.

FIGURE 4-8 AN INCREASE IN THE SUPPLY OF MONEY FROM $\overline{M}$ TO $\overline{M}'$ SHIFTS THE LM CURVE TO THE RIGHT

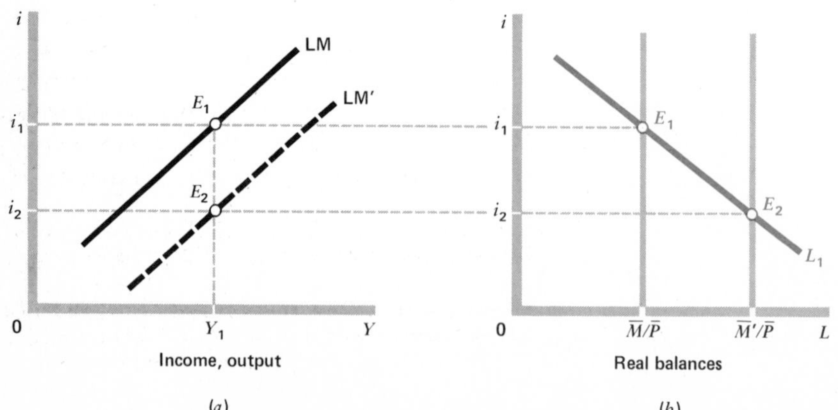

With the initial real money supply $\overline{M}/\overline{P}$, the equilibrium is at point E_1, with an interest rate i_1. The corresponding point on the LM schedule is E_1. Consider next the effect of an increase in the real money supply to $\overline{M}'/\overline{P}$, which is represented by a rightward shift of the money supply schedule. At the initial level of income and, hence, on the demand schedule L_1, we now have an excess supply of real balances. To restore money market equilibrium at the income level Y_1, the interest rate has to decline to i_2. The new equilibrium is, therefore, at point E_2. This implies that in Figure 4-8*a*, the LM schedule *shifts* to the right and down to LM′. At each level of income the equilibrium interest rate has to be lower to induce people to hold the larger real quantity of money. Alternatively at each level of the interest rate, the level of income has to be higher so as to raise the transactions demand for money and thereby absorb the higher real money supply. These points can be noted, too, from inspection of the money market equilibrium condition in Equation (12*a*).

Positions off the LM Curve

Next we consider points off the LM schedule, to characterize them as points of excess demand or supply of money. For that purpose, we look at Figure 4-9, which reproduces Figure 4-7 but adds the disequilibrium points E_3 and E_4.

Consider first point E_1, where the money market is in equilibrium. Next assume an increase in the level of income to Y_2. This will raise the demand for real balances and shift the demand curve to L_2. At the initial interest rate, the demand for real balances would be indicated by point E_4

FIGURE 4-9 EXCESS DEMAND (EDM) AND SUPPLY (ESM) OF MONEY TO THE RIGHT AND LEFT OF THE LM CURVE, RESPECTIVELY

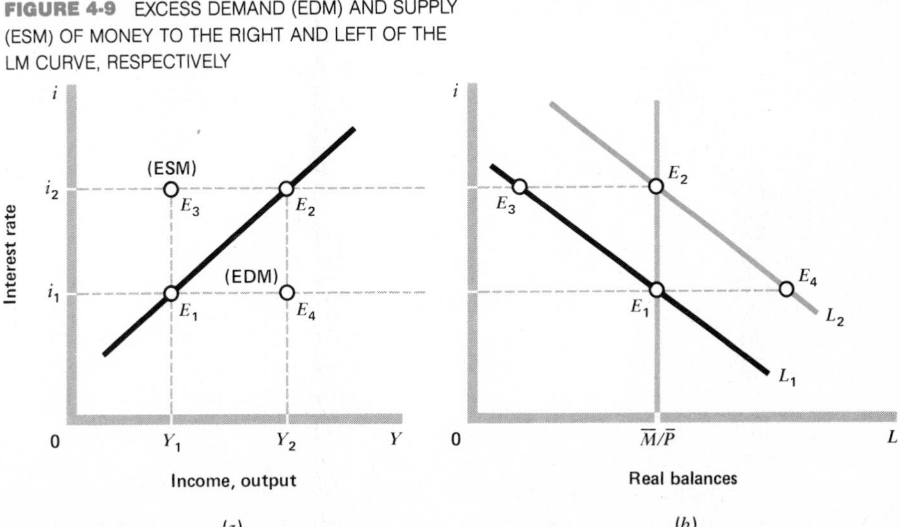

in Figure 4-9*b*, and we would have an excess demand for money—an excess of demand over supply—equal to the distance E_1E_4. Accordingly, point E_4, in Figure 4-9*a*, is a point of excess demand for money: the interest rate is too low and/or the level of income too high for the money market to clear. Consider next point E_3, in Figure 4-9*b*. Here we have the initial level of income Y_1, but an interest rate that is too high to yield money market equilibrium. Accordingly, we have an excess supply of money equal to the distance E_3E_2. Point E_3 in Figure 4-9*a* therefore corresponds to an excess supply of money.

More generally, any point to the right and below the LM schedule is a point of excess demand for money, and any point to the left and above the LM curve is a point of excess supply. This is shown by the EDM and ESM notations in Figure 4-9*a*.

Summary

The following are the major points about the LM curve.

1 The LM curve is the schedule of combinations of the interest rate and level of income such that the money market is in equilibrium.
2 When the money market is in equilibrium, so too is the bond market. The LM curve is, therefore, also the schedule of combinations of the level of income and the interest rate such that the bond market is in equilibrium.
3 The LM curve is positively sloped. Given the fixed money supply, an increase in the level of income, which increases the demand for money, has to be accompanied by an increase in the interest rate. This reduces the demand for money and thereby keeps the demand for money equal to the supply.
4 The LM curve is shifted by changes in the money supply. An increase in the money supply shifts the LM curve out to the right.
5 At points to the right of the LM curve, there is an excess demand for money, and at points to its left, there is an excess supply of money.

We are now ready to discuss the joint equilibrium of the goods and assets markets.

4-3 EQUILIBRIUM IN THE GOODS AND ASSETS MARKETS

We have so far studied the conditions that have to be satisfied for the goods and money markets, respectively, to be in equilibrium. These conditions are summarized by the IS and LM schedules. The task now is to determine how these markets are brought into *simultaneous* equilibrium. For simultaneous equilibrium, interest rates and income have to be such that *both* the goods market *and* the money market are in equilibrium. That condition is satisfied at point E in Figure 4-10. The equilibrium interest rate is therefore i_0, and the equilibrium level of income is Y_0, *given* the exogenous variables,[10] in particular, the real money supply and fiscal policy. At point E, *both* the goods market and the assets markets are in equilibrium.

Now that we have moved rather quickly from the derivation of the IS and LM curves to the equilibrium of the economy that is implied by their intersection, it is worth stepping back to review our assumptions and the meaning of the equilibrium at E. The major assumption that we are making is that the price level is constant and that firms are willing to supply whatever amount of output is demanded at that price level. Thus, we assume the level of output Y_0, in Figure 4-10, will be willingly supplied by firms at the price level $\overline{P}$. We repeat again that this assumption is one that is needed for the development of our analysis; it will be dropped in Chapter 11 when we begin to study the determinants of the price level.

At the point E, in Figure 4-10, the economy we are studying is in equilibrium, given the price level, because both the goods and money markets are in equilibrium. The demand for goods is equal to the level of output on the IS curve. And on the LM curve, the demand for money is equal to the supply of money. That also means the supply of bonds is equal to the demand for bonds, as our discussion of the wealth budget constraint showed. Accordingly, at point E, firms are producing the amount of output

[10]Recall from Chap. 3 that exogenous variables are those whose values are not determined within the system being studied.

FIGURE 4-10 GOODS AND ASSETS MARKET EQUILIBRIUM

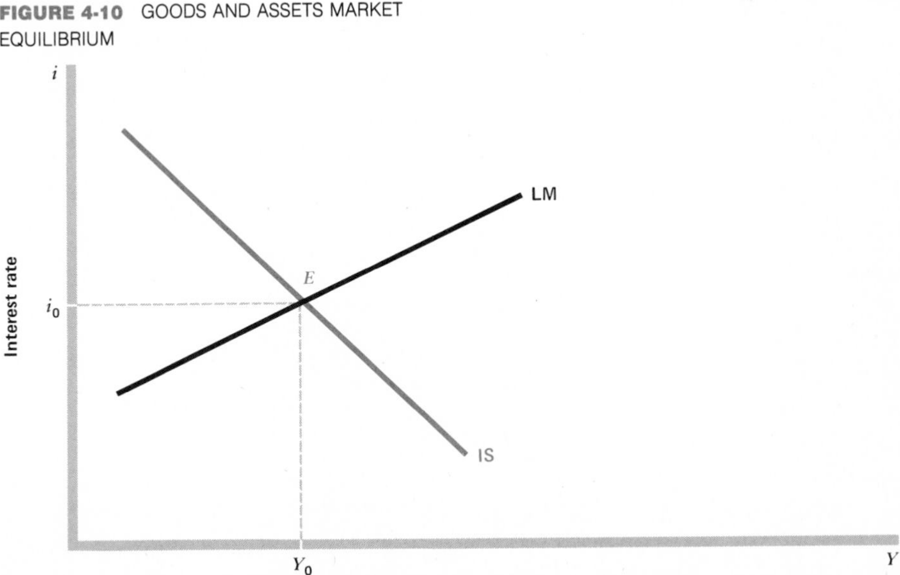

they plan to (there is no unintended inventory accumulation or decumulation), and individuals have the portfolio compositions they desire.

Changes in the Equilibrium Levels of Income and the Interest Rate

The equilibrium levels of income and the interest rate will change when either the IS or the LM curve shifts. Figure 4-11, for example, shows the effects on the equilibrium levels of income and the interest rate of an increase in the rate of autonomous consumption $\overline{C}$. Such an increase raises autonomous spending $\overline{A}$, and therefore shifts the IS curve out to the right. That results in a rise in the level of income and an increase in the interest rate.

We recall from Section 4-2 that a change in autonomous spending, equal in this case to $\Delta\overline{C}$, shifts the IS curve to the right by the amount $\overline{\alpha}\,\Delta\overline{C}$, as we show in Figure 4-11. In Chapter 3, where we dealt only with the goods market, we would have argued that $\overline{\alpha}\,\Delta\overline{C}$ would be the change in the level of income resulting from the change of $\Delta\overline{C}$ in autonomous spending. But it can be seen in Figure 4-11 that the change in income here is only ΔY_0, which is clearly less than the shift in the IS curve $\overline{\alpha}\,\Delta\overline{C}$.

What explains the fact that the increase in income is smaller than the increase in autonomous spending, $\Delta\overline{C}$, times the simple multiplier, $\overline{\alpha}$?

FIGURE 4-11 EFFECTS OF AN INCREASE IN AUTONOMOUS SPENDING ON INCOME AND THE INTEREST RATE

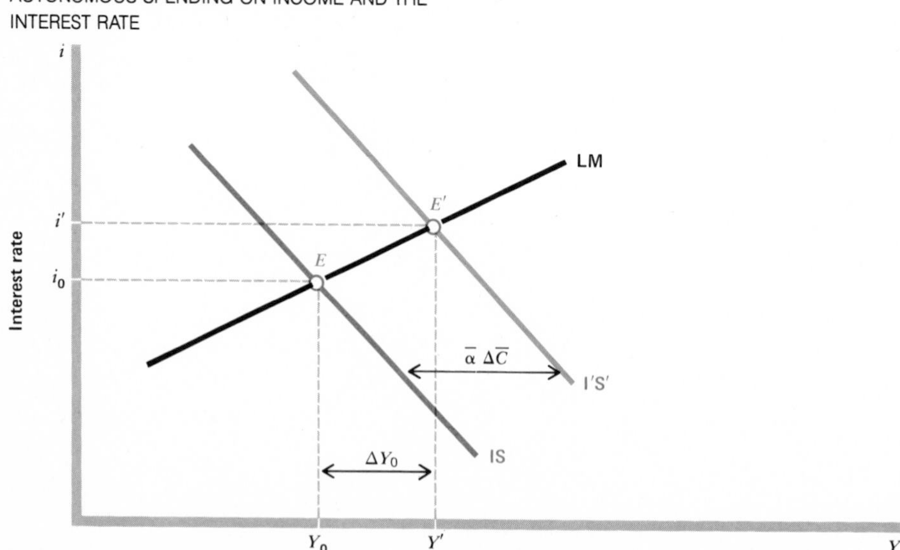

Diagrammatically, it is clear that it is the slope of the LM curve. If the LM curve were horizontal, there would be no difference between the extent of the horizontal shift of the IS curve and the change in income. If the LM curve were horizontal, then the interest rate would not change when the IS curve shifts. It will be recalled that we stated in Chapter 3 that we were assuming a fixed interest rate, so that the results of that chapter correspond to this case.

What is the economics of what is happening? The increase in autonomous spending does tend to increase the level of income. But an increase in income increases the transactions demand for money. With the supply of money fixed, the interest rate has to rise to ensure that the demand for money stays equal to the fixed supply. When the interest rate rises, investment spending is reduced because investment is negatively related to the interest rate. That means the total change in aggregate demand is less than $\overline{\alpha}\,\Delta\overline{C}$. Accordingly, the equilibrium change in income is less than the horizontal shift of the IS curve.

We have now provided an example of the uses of the IS-LM apparatus. That apparatus is most useful for studying the effects of monetary and fiscal policy on income and the interest rate, and we shall so use it in Sections 4-5 and 4-6. Before we do that, however, we want to ask how the economy moves from one equilibrium, like E, to another, like E'.

4-4 ADJUSTMENT TOWARD EQUILIBRIUM

Suppose the economy were initially at a point like E in Figure 4-11, and that one of the curves then shifted, so that the new equilibrium was at a point like E'. How would that new equilibrium actually be reached? The adjustment will involve changes in both the interest rate and the level of income. To study how they move over time, we make two assumptions:

1 Output increases whenever there is an excess demand for goods (EDG) and contracts whenever there is an excess supply of goods (ESG). This assumption reflects the adjustment of firms to undesired decumulation and accumulation of inventories, as in Chapter 3.
2 The interest rate rises whenever there is an excess demand for money (EDM) and falls whenever there is an excess supply of money (ESM). This adjustment occurs because an excess demand for money implies an excess supply of other assets (bonds). In attempting to satisfy an excess demand for money, people sell off bonds and thereby cause their prices to fall or their yields (interest rates) to rise.

A detailed discussion of the relationship between the price of a bond and its yield is presented in the appendix to this chapter. Here we give only a brief explanation. For simplicity, consider a bond which promises to pay the holder of the bond \$5 per year forever. The \$5 is known as the bond *coupon*, and a bond which promises to pay a given amount to the holder of the bond forever is known as a *perpetuity*. If the yield available on other assets is 5 percent, the perpetuity will sell for \$100 because at that price it too yields 5 percent (= \$5/\$100). Now suppose that the yield on other assets rises to 10 percent. Then the price of the perpetuity will drop to \$50, because only at that price does the perpetuity yield 10 percent, that is, the \$5 per year interest on a bond costing \$50 gives its owners a 10 percent yield on their \$50. This example makes it clear that the *price* of a bond and its *yield* are inversely related, given the coupon.

We discussed the way in which an excess demand for money causes asset holders to attempt to sell off their bonds, thereby causing their prices to fall and their yields to rise. Conversely, when there is an excess supply of money, people attempt to use their money to buy up other assets, raising their prices and lowering their yields.[11]

In Figure 4-12 we use the analysis underlying Figures 4-5 and 4-9 to study the adjustment of the economy. Four regions are represented in Figure 4-12, and they are characterized in Table 4-1. We know from Figure 4-9 that there is an excess supply of money above the LM curve, and hence we show ESM in regions I and II in Table 4-1. Similarly, we know from Figure 4-5 that there is an excess demand for goods below the IS curve.

[11] We assume that the rate of adjustment in each market is proportional to the excess demand in that market.

FIGURE 4-12 DISEQUILIBRIUM AND DYNAMICS IN THE GOODS AND MONEY MARKETS

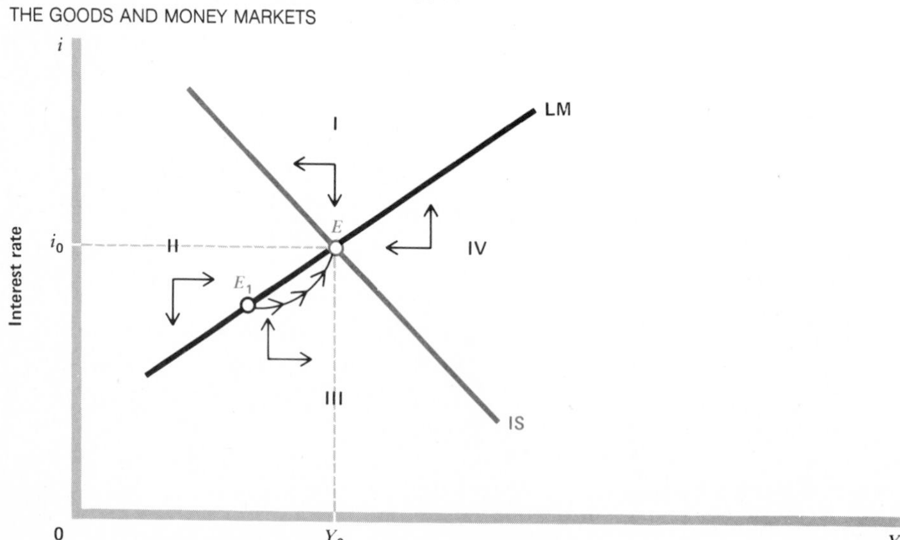

TABLE 4-1 DISEQUILIBRIUM REGIONS IN FIGURE 4-12

	Goods market	Money market
I	ESG ($Y>A$)	ESM ($L<M/P$)
II	EDG ($Y<A$)	ESM ($L<M/P$)
III	EDG ($Y<A$)	EDM ($L>M/P$)
IV	ESG ($Y>A$)	EDM ($L>M/P$)

Hence, we show EDG for regions II and III in Table 4-1. You should be able to fill in the remaining details of Table 4-1.

The adjustment directions specified in assumptions 1 and 2 above are represented by arrows. Thus, for example, in region IV we have an excess demand for money that causes interest rates to rise as other assets are sold off for money and their prices decline. The rising interest rates are represented by the upward-pointing arrow. There is, too, an excess supply of goods in region IV, and, accordingly, involuntary inventory accumulation to which firms respond by reducing output. Declining output is indicated by the leftward-pointing arrow. The adjustments shown by the arrows will lead ultimately, perhaps in a cyclical manner, to the equilibrium point E. For example, starting at E_1 we show the economy moving to E, with income and the interest rate increasing along the *adjustment path* indicated.

For many purposes it is useful to restrict the dynamics by the reasonable assumption that the money market adjusts very fast and the goods market adjusts relatively slowly. Since the money market can adjust merely through the buying and selling of bonds, it is reasonable to think of the interest rate as adjusting rapidly and the money market effectively being always in equilibrium. Such an assumption will imply that we are always on the LM curve: any departure from the equilibrium in the money market is almost instantaneously eliminated by an appropriate change in the interest rate. In disequilibrium, we therefore move along the LM curve, as is shown in Figure 4-13. The goods market adjusts relatively slowly because firms have to change their production schedules, which takes time. For points below the IS curve, we move up along the LM schedule with rising income and interest rates, and for points above the IS schedule, we move down along the LM schedule with falling output and interest rates until point E is reached. The adjustment process is *stable* in that the economy does move to the equilibrium position at E.

The adjustment process shown in Figure 4-13 is very similar to that of Chapter 3. To the right of the IS curve, there is an excess supply of goods, and firms are therefore accumulating inventories. They cut production in response to their inventory buildup, and the economy moves down the LM curve. The difference between the adjustment process here and in Chapter

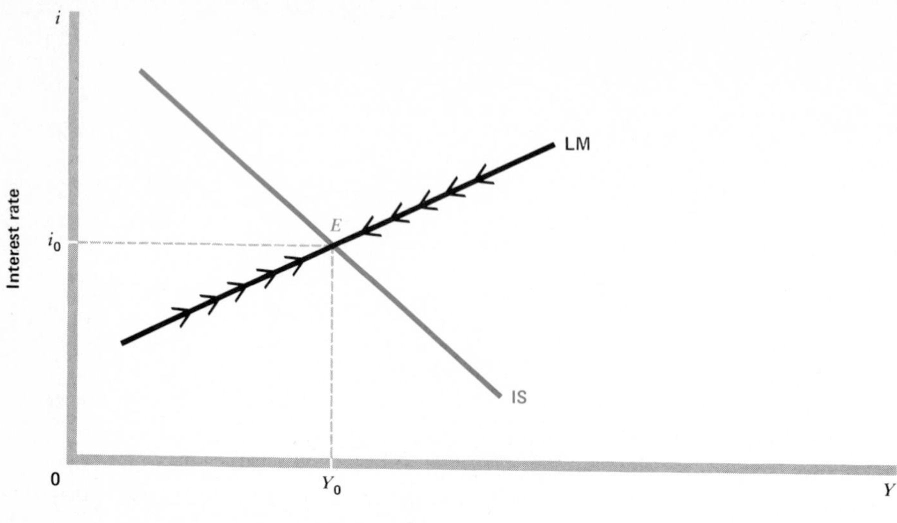

FIGURE 4-13 ADJUSTMENT TO EQUILIBRIUM WHEN THE MONEY MARKET ADJUSTS QUICKLY

3 is that as the economy moves toward the equilibrium level of income here, with a falling interest rate, desired investment spending is actually rising as the interest rate falls.[12]

Now that we have established that the economy does adjust toward its equilibrium position, we turn to examine the effects of monetary and fiscal policy on the equilibrium interest rate and level of income.

4-5 MONETARY POLICY

In this section we are concerned with the effect of an increase in the real quantity of money on the interest rate and level of income. We will break up that inquiry into two separate questions. First, what is the ultimate effect of the increase in the money supply when the new equilibrium is reached? Second, how is that new equilibrium reached, or what is the *transmission mechanism*?

Through monetary policy, the Federal Reserve System manipulates the quantity of money to affect interest rates and income. We shall here take the case of an *open market purchase*. That is a government purchase of bonds and (equal) sale of money. The purchase is made by the Federal Reserve System (Fed), which pays for its purchase with money that it can

[12] In a more detailed analysis, one would want to allow for the possibility that desired investment would be cut back in response to excess inventories. This again raises the possibility of the *inventory cycle*, referred to in Chap. 3.

create. One can usefully think of the Fed printing money with which to buy bonds, even though that is not strictly accurate, as we shall see in Chapter 8. The purpose of an open market operation is to change the available *relative* supplies of money and bonds and thereby change the interest rate or yield at which the public is willing to hold this modified composition of assets. When the Fed buys bonds, it reduces the supply of bonds available in the market and thereby tends to increase their price, or lower their yield. Only at a lower interest rate will the public be prepared to hold a larger fraction of their given wealth in the form of money, and a lower fraction in the form of bonds.

In Figure 4-14 we show graphically how the open market purchase works. The initial equilibrium at point E is on the initial LM schedule that corresponds to a real money supply, $\overline{M}/\overline{P}$. Consider next an open market operation that increases the nominal quantity of money, and given the price level, the real quantity of money. We showed in Section 4-2 that, as a consequence, the LM schedule will shift to LM′. Therefore our new equilibrium will be at point E' with a lower interest rate and a higher level of income. The equilibrium level of income rises because the open market purchase reduces the interest rate and thereby increases investment.

As can be seen from Figure 4-14, the flatter the IS schedule, the larger

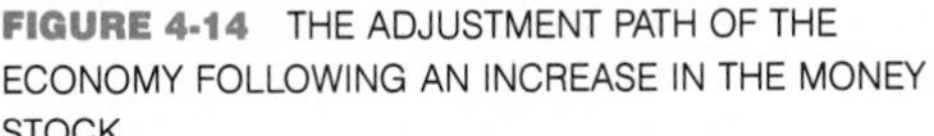

FIGURE 4-14 THE ADJUSTMENT PATH OF THE ECONOMY FOLLOWING AN INCREASE IN THE MONEY STOCK

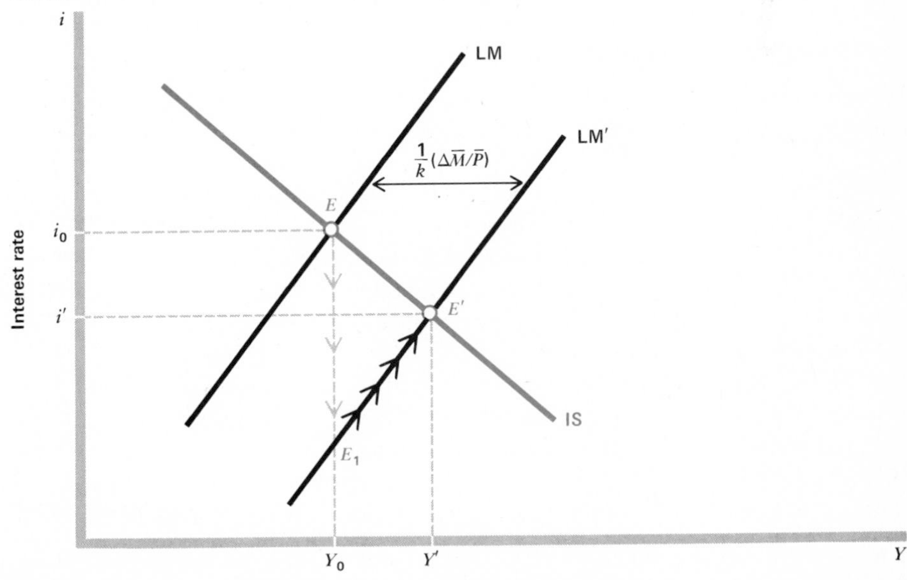

will be the change in income. If money demand is very sensitive to the interest rate, then a given change in the money stock can be absorbed in the assets markets with only a small change in the interest rate. The effects of an open market purchase on investment spending would then be small. By contrast, if the demand for money is not very sensitive to the interest rate, a given change in the money supply will cause a large change in the interest rate and have a big effect on investment demand.[13] Similarly, if the demand for money is very sensitive to income, a given increase in the money stock can be absorbed with a relatively small change in income.

Consider next the adjustment process to the monetary expansion. At the initial equilibrium point E, the increase in the money supply creates an excess supply of money to which the public adjusts by attempting to reduce its money holdings by buying other assets. In the process, asset prices increase and yields decline. By our assumption that the assets markets adjust rapidly, we move immediately to point E_1, where the money market clears, and where the public is willing to hold the larger real quantity of money because the interest rate has declined sufficiently. (The lower the responsiveness of the demand for money to the interest rate, the larger the change in the interest rate that is required.) At point E_1, however, there is an excess demand for goods. The decline in the interest rate, given the initial income level Y_0, has raised aggregate demand and is causing inventories to run down. In response, output expands and we start moving up the LM schedule. Why does the interest rate rise in the adjustment process? Because the increase in output raises the demand for money and that increase has to be checked by higher interest rates.

The Transmission Mechanism

Two steps in the transmission mechanism—the process by which changes in monetary policy affect aggregate demand—are essential. The first is that an increase in real balances generates a *portfolio disequilibrium*—at the prevailing interest rate and level of income, people are holding more money than they want. This causes portfolio holders to attempt to reduce their money holdings by buying other assets, thereby changing asset yields. In other words, the change in the money supply changes interest rates. The second stage of the transmission process occurs when the change in interest rates affects aggregate demand.

These two stages of the transmission process are essential in that they appear in almost every analysis of the effects of changes in the money supply on the economy. The details of the analysis will often differ—some analyses will have more than two assets and more than one interest rate, some will include an influence of interest rates on categories of demand

[13] In the problem set, we ask you to provide a similar explanation of the role of the slope of the IS curve—which is determined by the multiplier and the interest sensitivity of investment demand—in determining the effect of monetary policy on income.

other than investment, and so on—but these two stages will be present.[14] For example here is a description of the process provided by Warren L. Smith:[15]

> The way in which monetary policy induces portfolio adjustments which will, in due course, affect income and employment may be described briefly as follows: A purchase of, say, Treasury bills by the Federal Reserve will directly lower the yield on bills and, by a process of arbitrage involving a chain of portfolio substitutions will exert downward pressure on interest rates on financial assets generally. . . .
>
> With the expected yield on a unit of real capital initially unchanged, the decline in the yields on financial assets, and the more favorable terms on which new debt can be issued, the balance sheets of households and businesses will be thrown out of equilibrium. The adjustment toward a new equilibrium will take the form of a sale of existing financial assets and the issuance of new debt to acquire real capital and claims thereto. . . . This stock adjustment approach is readily applicable, with some variations to suit the circumstances, to the demands for a wide variety of both business and consumer capital—including plant and equipment, inventories, residential construction, and consumer durable goods.

In studying the details of the transmission process, it is important to see how much influence money has at each stage. For instance, if the demand for money is very sensitive to changes in the interest rate, or if interest rate changes have only a small effect on aggregate demand,[16] then monetary policy tends to be relatively ineffective. Conversely, to obtain a large increase in income from a monetary increase, we require a low responsiveness of money demand to the interest rate and a high responsiveness of aggregate demand to a change in the interest rate.

The Liquidity Trap

In discussing the effects on monetary policy on the economy, two extreme cases have received much attention. The first is the *liquidity trap*, a situation in which the public is prepared, at a given interest rate, to hold whatever amount of money is supplied. This implies that the LM curve is horizontal and that changes in the quantity of money do not shift it. In that

[14] Some analyses also include a mechanism by which change in real balances have a direct effect on aggregate demand through the *real balance effect*. Essentially, the argument is that wealth affects consumption demand (as we shall see in Chap. 5) and that an increase in real balances increases wealth and therefore consumption demand.. This effect would not apply in the case of an open market purchase, which merely exchanges one asset for another (bonds for money) without changing wealth. The real balance effect is not very important empirically because the relevant real balances are only a small part of wealth.

[15] Warren L. Smith, "A Neo-Keynesian View of Monetary Policy," *Controlling Monetary Aggregates* (Boston: Federal Reserve Bank of Boston, 1969), pp. 105–117.

[16] We refer to the responsiveness of aggregate demand—rather than investment demand—to the interest rate because consumption demand may also respond to the interest rate. Higher interest rates may lead to more saving and less consumption at a given level of income. Empirically, it has been difficult to isolate such an interest rate effect on consumption.

case, monetary policy carried out through open market operations[17] has no effect on either the interest rate or level of income. In the liquidity trap, monetary policy is powerless to affect the interest rate.

There is a liquidity trap at a zero interest rate. At a zero interest rate, the public would not want to hold any bonds, since money, which also pays zero interest, has the advantage over bonds of being usable in transactions. Accordingly, if the interest rate ever, for some reason, got down to zero, increases in the quantity of money could not induce anyone to shift into bonds and thereby reduce the interest rate on bonds even below zero. An increase in the money supply in that case would have no effect on the interest rate and income, and the economy would be in a liquidity trap.

The belief that there was a liquidity trap at low positive (rather than zero) interest rates was quite prevalent during the forties and fifties. It was a notion associated with the Keynesian followers and developers of the theories of the great English economist John Maynard Keynes—although Keynes himself did state that he was not aware of there ever having been such a situation.[18] The importance of the liquidity trap stems from its presenting a circumstance under which monetary policy has no effect on the interest rate and thus on the level of real income. Belief in the trap, or at least the strong sensitivity of the demand for money to the interest rate, was the basis of the Keynesian belief that monetary policy has no effects on the economy. There is no strong evidence that there ever was a liquidity trap, and there certainly is not one now.

The Classical Case

The polar opposite of the horizontal LM curve—which implies that monetary policy cannot affect the level of income—is the vertical LM curve. The LM curve is vertical when the demand for money is unaffected by the interest rate. Under those circumstances, any shift in the LM curve has a maximal effect on the level of income. Check this by moving a vertical LM curve to the right and comparing the resultant change in income with the change produced by a similar horizontal shift of a nonvertical LM curve.

The vertical LM curve is called *classical*. It implies that the demand for money depends only on the level of income and not at all on the interest rate. This view was associated with the classical *quantity theory of money* which argued that the level of nominal income was determined solely by the quantity of money. We return to this view in Section 4-8. As we shall see, a vertical LM curve implies not only that monetary policy has a

[17] We say "through open market operations" because an increase in the quantity of money carried out simply by giving the money away increases individuals' wealth and, through the real balance effect, has some effect on aggregate demand. An open market purchase, however, increases the quantity of money and reduces the quantity of bonds by the same amount, leaving wealth unchanged.

[18] J. M. Keynes, *The General Theory of Employment, Interest and Money* (New York: Macmillan, 1936), p. 207.

maximal effect on the level of income, but also that fiscal policy has no effect on income. The vertical LM curve, implying the comparative effectiveness of monetary policy over fiscal policy, is sometimes associated with the view that "only money matters" for the determination of output. Since the LM curve is vertical only when the demand for money does not depend on the interest rate, the interest sensitivity of the demand for money turns out to be an important issue in determining the effectiveness of alternative policies.

4-6 FISCAL POLICY

In this section we are concerned with the effects of fiscal policy on the economy. Specifically, we examine the effect of an increase in government spending, given the tax structure and the real quantity of money.

The effects of an increase in government spending can be determined from Figure 4-15. We start off at point E, where both markets clear. The increase in government spending creates an excess demand for goods at the initial point and therefore shifts the IS schedule to IS$'$. For goods market equilibrium we require at the initial interest rate a higher level of income, namely, the level indicated by point E_1, where the distance EE_1 is equal to the multiplier $\bar{\alpha}$ times the increase in government spending.

At the ultimate equilibrium position E', we have a higher interest rate

FIGURE 4-15 EFFECTS OF AN INCREASE IN GOVERNMENT SPENDING

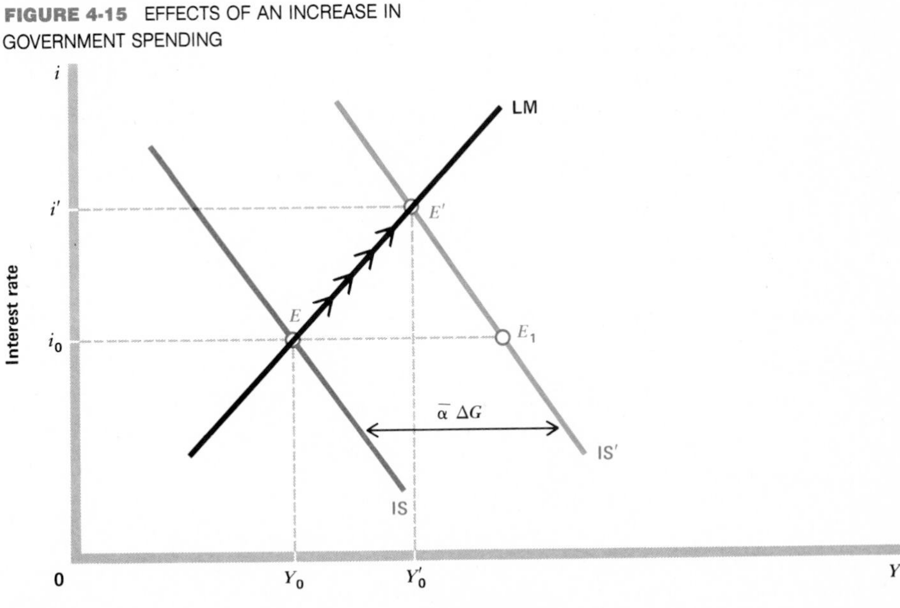

and a higher level of income than at E. Therefore, an increase in government spending is expansionary with respect to income. The expansion of income is, however, less than that indicated by the simple multiplier and point E_1. This is because the interest rate rises, reduces investment, and thereby somewhat offsets the multiplier effect on private aggregate demand. The higher interest rate is required in order to maintain monetary equilibrium at the higher level of income, as we discussed in Section 4-3.

The flatter the LM schedule, the larger the increase in income that is generated by the increased government spending, as you can show by using the diagram. The increase in income is also larger, the bigger the multiplier, $\bar{\alpha}$, as one would expect. Finally, the increase in income is smaller, the more responsive is aggregate demand to the interest rate—for the larger the response of aggregate demand to the induced increase in the interest rate, the more the initial expansionary multiplier effect is offset.

Consider next the adjustment process starting from the initial equilibrium at point E. We continue to assume that the money market clears fast and continuously, while output adjusts only slowly. This implies that as government spending increases, we stay initially at point E, since there is no disturbance in the money market. The excess demand for goods, however, causes output to be increased and that increase in output and income raises the demand for money. The resulting excess demand for money, in turn, causes interest rates to be bid up and we proceed up along the LM curve with rising output and rising interest rates until the new equilibrium at point E' is reached.

The fact that we do not have an increase in output to the full extent of the simple multiplier $\bar{\alpha}$ times the increase in government spending is entirely due to our now taking account of the assets markets. As income rises, the demand for money increases and people try to sell off other assets to acquire cash balances and, in doing so, cause asset prices to decline and interest rates to rise. This increase in interest rates, in turn, reduces investment spending and dampens the expansionary effect of increased government spending by reducing aggregate private demand relative to what it would have been at a constant interest rate.

The Liquidity Trap Again

In the analysis of fiscal policy, there has also been consideration of the two extreme cases we discussed in connection with monetary policy. If the economy is in the liquidity trap so that the LM curve is horizontal, then an increase in government spending has its full multiplier effect on the equilibrium level of income. There is no change in the interest rate associated with the change in government spending, and thus no investment spending is cut off. There is therefore no dampening of the effects of the increased government spending on income.

You should draw your own IS-LM diagrams to confirm that if the LM curve is horizontal, monetary policy has no impact on the equilibrium of the economy and fiscal policy has a maximal effect on the economy. Less dramatically, if the demand for money is very sensitive to the interest rate, so that the LM curve is almost horizontal, fiscal policy changes have a relatively large effect on output, while monetary policy changes have little effect on the equilibrium level of output.

As a preview of our later discussion of monetary and fiscal policy in the 1960s in Chapter 10, we point out one other circumstance in which fiscal policy has its full multiplier effect on the level of income. So far, we have taken the money supply to be constant at the level $\overline{M}$. It is possible that the Fed might instead manipulate the money supply so as to keep the interest rate constant. In that case, we could talk of a money supply *function* which is very elastic with respect to the interest rate. More simply, the Fed increases the money supply whenever there are signs of an increase in the interest rate, and reduces the money supply whenever the interest rate seems about to fall. If the money supply function is very elastic with respect to the interest rate, the LM curve again becomes very flat and fiscal policy has large impacts on the level of output.

The Classical Case Again and Crowding Out

If the LM curve is vertical, then an increase in government spending has no effect on the equilibrium level of income. It only increases the interest rate. This case is shown in Figure 4-16, where an increase in government spending shifts the IS curve to IS′ but has no effect on income. If the demand for money is not related to the interest rate, as a vertical LM curve implies, then there is a unique level of income at which the money market is in equilibrium, and fiscal policy cannot affect the level of income.

Given that an increase in government spending does not change the level of income when the LM curve is vertical, we know also that aggregate demand must be unchanged. Therefore, we have to ask what component of spending (investment or consumption) is reduced when government spending is increased but total aggregate demand remains unchanged. The answer is that investment spending is reduced by an amount exactly equal to the increase in government spending. Consumption spending does not change because the level of income is unchanged and autonomous demand is unchanged. Thus we are assured that the increase in government spending is precisely offset by reduced investment spending. This phenomenon is known as *crowding out*—the government spending crowds out some other component of spending and has no effect on total spending. The crowding out argument is one which is frequently made in the press to suggest that government spending has no effects on output and employment.[19]

[19] Note again that, in principle, consumption spending could be reduced by increases in the interest rate, and then both investment and consumption would be crowded out.

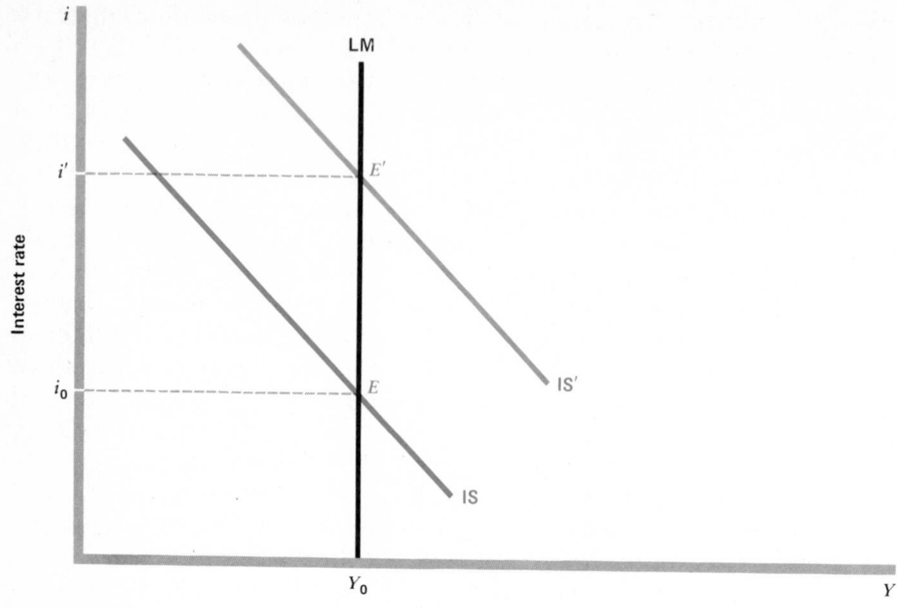

FIGURE 4-16 THE VERTICAL LM CURVE AND CROWDING OUT

The view that government spending merely crowds out private spending is widely held by monetarist economists, such as Milton Friedman, who place primary emphasis on the role of the money stock in determining the level of income.[20] The monetarist emphasis on the stock of money is also implied by the LM curve's being vertical, so that in the IS-LM context, monetarism is consistent with the view that the LM curve is vertical, or that the demand for money does not depend on the interest rate. However, there are other circumstances, such as a situation of full employment, in which there is crowding out. If output is at the full-employment level, any increase in government spending has to take place at the expense of another component of aggregate demand, and crowding out will occur.[21]

In brief, in the IS-LM context in which we are now working, with the price level given and the level of output responding to aggregate demand,

[20] We discuss monetarism in Chap. 16.

[21] Friedman has argued that his views do not depend on the demand for money not being a function of the interest rate, making essentially the second argument above for crowding out. See Milton Friedman, "Interest Rates and the Demand for Money," in his *Optimum Quantity of Money* (Chicago: Aldine, 1969).

monetarist views on crowding out and the major importance of money are fully consistent with the LM curve's being vertical. Equivalently, they depend on the assumption that the demand for money does not depend on the interest rate. But there are also other conditions in which there is crowding out.

The extreme cases of a vertical LM curve or a flat LM curve represent boundaries that are useful for reference purposes. Beyond that, their use is quite limited, since any reasonable description for policy purposes will want to assume the intermediate case of an upward-sloping LM curve, so that both monetary and fiscal policy work. As we show in Chapter 7, the demand for real balances is definitely negatively related to the interest rate

4-7 THE COMPOSITION OF OUTPUT

We have now seen that both monetary and fiscal policy can be used to expand aggregate demand and thus raise the equilibrium level of output. Since the liquidity trap and the classical case represent at best extremes useful for expositional purposes, it is apparent that policy makers can use either monetary or fiscal policy to affect the level of income.

In Figure 4-17 we address the policy problem of an economy that is in

FIGURE 4-17 EXPANSIONARY POLICIES AND THE COMPOSITION OF OUTPUT

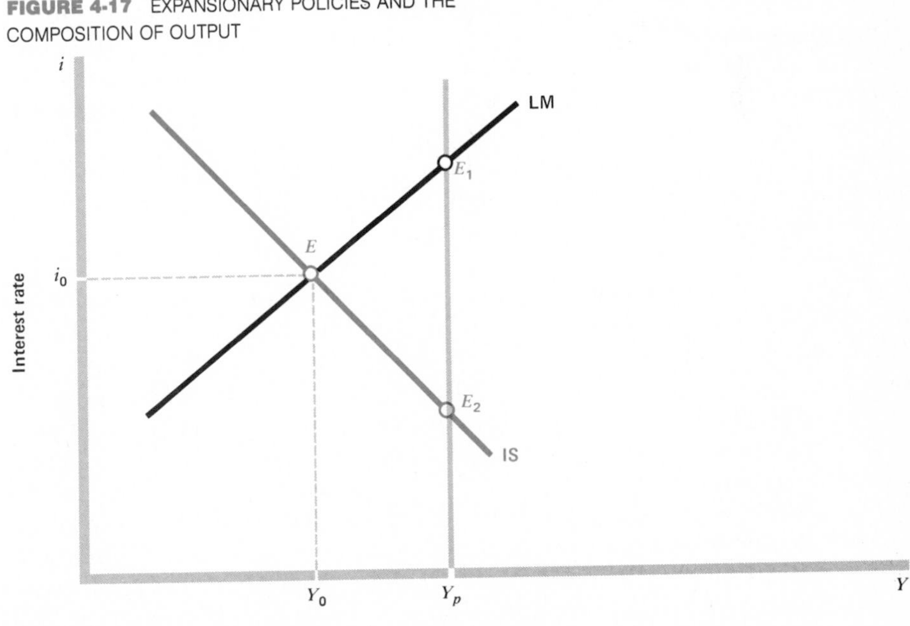

equilibrium at point E with an output level Y_0, below the full-employment level Y_p. What policy choices does that economy have? From the preceding analysis, it is obvious that we could use an expansionary monetary policy. By increasing the money supply, we could shift the LM curve down and to the right, lower interest rates, and raise aggregate demand until we reach E_2. Alternatively, we can use an expansionary fiscal policy to shift the IS curve up and to the right until we reach E_1. Finally, we can use a combination of monetary and fiscal policy. What package should we choose?

The choice of monetary and fiscal policy as tools of stabilization policy is an important and quite controversial topic. In Chapter 9 we will address some technical issues that deal with the flexibility and speed with which these policies can be implemented and can take effect. Here we do not discuss speed and flexibility, but rather look at what these policies do to the composition of aggregate demand.

Now, in that respect, there is a sharp difference between monetary and fiscal policy. Monetary policy operates by stimulating interest-responsive components of aggregate demand (primarily investment spending and, in particular, residential construction). There is strong evidence that the immediate and strongest effect of monetary policy is on residential construction. Fiscal policy, by contrast, operates in a manner that depends on precisely what goods the government buys or what taxes and transfers it changes. Here we might be talking of government purchases of goods and services such as road paving, or a reduction in the corporate profits tax, or in sales taxes, or Social Security contributions. Each policy affects the level of aggregate demand and will cause an expansion in output, except that the type of output and the beneficiaries of the fiscal measures differ. A corporate tax cut, as we shall see in Chapter 10 (where we review the 1964 tax cut), affects both investment spending and, through distributed profits, personal consumption. An income tax cut has a direct effect on consumption spending. Given the quantity of money, all expansionary fiscal policies have in common that they will raise the interest rate.

Once we recognize that all the policies raise output but differ significantly in their impact on different sectors of the economy, we open up a problem of political economy. Given the decision of expanding aggregate demand, who should get the primary benefit? Should the expansion take place through a decline in interest rates and increased investment spending, or should it take place through a cut in taxes and increased personal spending, or should it take the form of an increase in the size of government?

Questions of speed and predictability of policies apart—these are taken up in Chapter 9—the issues raised above have been settled by political preferences. Conservatives will argue for a tax cut anytime. They will favor stabilization policies that in a recession cut taxes and in a boom cut government spending. Over time, given enough cycles, you wind up with a government sector that becomes very small, just as a conservative would want it to be. The counterpart view belongs to those who feel that there is much scope for government spending in education, environment, job training and rehabilitation, and the like, and who, accordingly, favor expansionary policies in the form of increased government spending. Growth-minded people and the construction lobby finally argue for expansionary policies that operate through low interest rates.

What is the historical record? We study that question in more detail in Chapter 10, but we can already note that expansionary fiscal policies in the sixties, such as the 1964 tax cut, were accompanied by expansionary monetary policies so as to achieve a balanced expansion. We shall also see, though, that there were a number of episodes in which very tight monetary policy was used to restrain aggregate demand. In those episodes, the major impact of the restrictive policies on aggregate demand occurred through reduced investment, particularly in housing.

The recognition that monetary and fiscal policy changes have different effects on the composition of output is important. It suggests that policy makers can choose a *policy mix* that will both get the economy to full employment and also make a contribution to solving some other policy problem. We anticipate here several subsequent discussions in which we point out two other targets of policy which have been taken into account in setting monetary and fiscal policy—growth and balance of payments equilibrium.

In the sixties, policy makers were growth- and investment-oriented. The argument was that today's investment provides tomorrow's jobs. Moreover, investment in raising productivity would reduce costs and thus reduce the rate of inflation. This line of argument would suggest that expansionary policies should take the route of low interest rates so as to ensure that a significant part of the required increase in aggregate demand would take the form of investment. The counterargument came from the international side of the economy. Here it was argued that low interest rates would lead to outflows of funds and balance of payments problems. If United States interest rates declined relative to those in the rest of the world, people would get out of United States assets and into foreign assets. The United States would suffer a balance of payments deficit. With that line of argument, high interest rates were called for and an expansion in aggregate demand would preferably be achieved through fiscal expansion, rather than monetary expansion. Similar arguments were prominent in 1979.

As we shall see in Chapters 16 and 17, policy discussion is now returning to the importance of growth and investment, and concern with the composition of output can be expected to be a live issue in the eighties.

*4-8 A FORMAL TREATMENT

So far, we have relied on a verbal and graphical treatment of the model, and we round off the discussion now by using the equilibrium conditions in Equations (6*a*) and (12*a*). To determine the equilibrium level of income, we want both the goods and money markets to clear. Repeating these equilibrium conditions here for convenience, we have

Goods market: $$Y = \bar{\alpha}(\bar{A} - bi) \tag{6a}$$

Money market: $$i = \frac{1}{h}\left(kY - \frac{\overline{M}}{\overline{P}}\right) \tag{12a}$$

Since we wish to have equilibrium simultaneously in both markets, we may solve these two equations simultaneously for the equilibrium interest rate and income level as functions of the exogenous variables. We proceed by substitution. Substituting Equation (12*a*) in Equation (6*a*) yields

$$Y = \bar{\alpha}\left[\bar{A} - \frac{b}{h}\left(kY - \frac{\overline{M}}{\overline{P}}\right)\right] \tag{13}$$

or after collecting terms in Y,

$$Y_0 = \frac{h\bar{\alpha}}{h + kb\bar{\alpha}}\bar{A} + \frac{b\bar{\alpha}}{h + kb\bar{\alpha}}\frac{\overline{M}}{\overline{P}} \tag{13a}$$

where Y_0 is now the equilibrium level of income. The terms that multiply the exogenous variables $\bar{A}$ and $\overline{M}/\overline{P}$ can be thought of as more complicated multipliers that reflect the monetary repercussions that characterize this model and differentiate it from the simple Keynesian model. It is useful to rewrite Equation (13*a*) in a somewhat simplified form as

$$Y_0 = \beta\bar{A} + \gamma\frac{\overline{M}}{\overline{P}} \tag{14}$$

where

$$\beta \equiv \frac{h\bar{\alpha}}{h + bk\bar{\alpha}} \tag{15}$$

and

$$\gamma \equiv \frac{b\bar{\alpha}}{h + bk\bar{\alpha}} \tag{16}$$

Here β and γ will be referred to as the *fiscal* and *money multipliers*, respectively.

The fiscal multiplier β tells us by how much an increase in government spending affects the equilibrium level of income, holding the real money supply constant. Examine Equation (13a) and consider the effect of an increase in government spending on income. The increase in government spending $\Delta \overline{G}$ is a change in autonomous spending, so that $\Delta \overline{A} = \Delta \overline{G}$. The effect of the change in $\overline{G}$ is given by

$$\frac{\Delta Y_0}{\Delta \overline{G}} = \frac{h\overline{\alpha}}{h + bk\overline{\alpha}} \equiv \beta \tag{17}$$

We note that the expression in Equation (17) is zero if h becomes very small and will be equal to $\overline{\alpha}$ if h approaches infinity. This corresponds, respectively, to a vertical and horizontal LM schedule. Similarly, a large value of either b or k serves to reduce the effect on income of government spending. Why? A high value of k implies a large increase in money demand as income rises and hence a large increase in interest rates in order to maintain money market equilibrium. In combination with a high b, this implies a large reduction in private aggregate demand. Equation (17) thus presents the algebraic analysis that corresponds to the graphical analysis of Figures 4-11 and 4-15.

Similarly, the money multiplier γ tells us by how much an increase in the real money supply affects the equilibrium level of income, keeping fiscal policy unchanged. Using Equation (13a) to examine the effects of an increase in the real money supply on income, we have

$$\frac{\Delta Y_0}{\Delta(\overline{M}/\overline{P})} = \frac{b\overline{\alpha}}{h + bk\overline{\alpha}} \equiv \gamma \tag{18}$$

The smaller h and k and the larger b and $\overline{\alpha}$, the more expansionary, the effect of an increase in real balances on the equilibrium level of income. Large b and $\overline{\alpha}$ correspond to a very flat IS schedule. Equation (18) thus corresponds to the graphical analysis presented in Figure 4-14.

The Classical Case and the Liquidity Trap

We return now to Equation (13a) to consider two extreme possibilities. One is the world of constant velocity. We define the *income velocity of money* as the ratio of income to money:

$$V \equiv \frac{Y}{M/P} \equiv \frac{PY}{M} \tag{19}$$

where PY is the level of nominal income. Income velocity V is thus the ratio of the level of nominal income to the nominal money stock. If the demand for money is unresponsive to the interest rate, then $h = 0$ and Equation (13a) reduces to

$$Y = \frac{1}{k}\frac{\overline{M}}{\overline{P}} = \frac{V}{\overline{M}/\overline{P}} \tag{20}$$

where

$$V \equiv \frac{1}{k}$$

or

$$PY = VM \tag{20a}$$

This is the world of the *quantity theory of money* where nominal income PY is proportional to the nominal quantity of money, and changes in the nominal quantity of money are reflected in equiproportionate changes in nominal income. This is what we previously called the classical case. From Equation (20a) we see that given the price level (say $\overline{P}$), and for fixed velocity, real income can change only if the nominal money supply changes. Fiscal policy is totally ineffective in this case.

The other extreme is represented by a world where h is infinite, so that money and other assets are effectively perfect substitutes. In such a world, Equation (13a) reduces to

$$Y = \overline{\alpha}\overline{A} \tag{21}$$

This is a "multiplier world" where autonomous spending entirely determines the level of real income. It occurs if the economy is in a liquidity trap.

4-9 SUMMARY

The IS-LM model presented in this chapter is a simplified, but useful, model of the economy that lays particular stress on the channels through which monetary and fiscal policy affect the economy. The analysis proceeds by first studying equilibrium in the goods and money markets, respectively. The overall equilibrium of the model is achieved when the level of income and the interest rate are such that both markets are in equilibrium. If the money market is in equilibrium, then the other assets markets, represented here by the catch-all "bond market," are also in equilibrium.

We have shown how the economy adjusts to changes and that under the reasonable dynamic assumptions made, the economy does move toward the equilibrium.

In Section 4-5, we saw how monetary policy affects the economy, in the first instance by disturbing the equilibrium in the assets markets and thus changing the interest rate, and then through the effects of the interest rate on aggregate demand. Fiscal policy continues to affect the level of income as in Chapter 3, but the multiplier effects of fiscal changes on income are dampened by the effects of rising income on interest rates and thus on aggregate demand.

We also examined two extreme cases. In the liquidity trap, in which increases in the money supply affect neither the interest rate nor the level of income, only fiscal policy changes the level of income. Further, because the interest rate is unchanged by the fiscal policy action, there is no induced reduction in investment spending and no dampening effect on output arising from falling investment. In the classical case, in which the demand for money does not depend on the interest rate, the level of income cannot change unless the supply of money changes. Fiscal policy changes affect only interest rates and the rate of investment while leaving total spending unchanged.

The extreme cases are of interest from a historical perspective, and useful for understanding the model, but neither is very helpful for understanding the current American economy. There is much evidence that the demand for real balances is significantly related to the interest rate but not so strongly that we are in a liquidity trap.

And a final warning, which has already been mentioned: We are assuming here that any level of output that is demanded can be produced by firms at the constant price level. Price level behavior, including inflation, will be discussed in substantially more detail in Chapters 11 to 13. Those chapters build on the analysis of the IS-LM model.

*APPENDIX: INTEREST RATES, PRESENT VALUES, AND DISCOUNTING

In this appendix we deal with the relationships among bond coupons, interest rates and yields, and the prices of bonds. In doing so, we shall introduce the very useful concept of present discounted value (PDV).

Section 1

We start with the case of a perpetual bond, or perpetuity. Such bonds have been issued in a number of countries, including the United Kingdom, where they are called Consols.

The Consol is a promise by the British government to pay a fixed amount to the holder of the bond every year and forever. Let us denote the promised payment per Consol by Q_c, the *coupon.*[22]

The *yield* on a bond is the return per dollar that the holder of the bond receives. The yield on a savings account paying 5 percent interest per year is obviously just 5 percent. Someone paying $25 for a Consol that has a coupon of $2.5 obtains a yield of 10 percent [($2.5/25) × 100].

The yield on a Consol and its price are related in a simple way. Let us denote the price of the Consol by P_c and the coupon by Q_c. Then, as the above example suggests, the yield i is just

$$i = \frac{Q_c}{P_c} \tag{A1}$$

which says that the yield on a perpetuity is the coupon divided by the price. Alternatively, we can switch Equation (A1) around to

$$P_c = \frac{Q_c}{i} \tag{A2}$$

which says that price is the coupon divided by the yield. So, given the coupon and the yield, we can derive the price, or given the coupon and the price, we can derive the yield.

None of this is a theory of the determination of the yield or the price of a perpetuity. It merely points out the relationship between price and yield. Our theory of the determination of the yield on bonds is, of course, presented in this chapter. The interest rate in this chapter corresponds to the yield on bonds, and we tend to talk interchangeably of interest rates and yields.

We shall return to the Consol at the end of this appendix.

Section 2

Now we move to a short-term bond. Let us consider a bond which was sold by a borrower for $100, on which the borrower promises to pay back $108 after one year. This is a one-year bond. The yield on the bond to the person who bought it for $100 is 8 percent. For every $1 lent, the lender obtains both the $1 principal and 8 cents extra at the end of the year.

Next we ask a slightly different question. How much would a promise to pay $1 at the end of the year be worth? If $108 at the end of the year is worth $100 today, then $1 at the end of the year must be worth $100/108, or 92.6 cents. That is the value today of $1 in one year's time. In other words, it is the *present discounted value* of $1 in one year's time. It is the present value because it is what would be paid today for the promise of

[22] The *coupon rate* is the coupon divided by the face value of the bond, which is literally the value printed on the face of the bond. Bonds do not necessarily sell for their face value, though customarily the face value is close to the value at which the bonds are sold when they first come on the market.

money in one year's time, and it is discounted because the value today is less than the promised payment in a year's time.

Denoting the one-year yield or interest rate by i, we can write that the present discounted value of a promised payment Q_1, one year from now, is

$$\text{PDV} = \frac{Q_1}{1+i} \tag{A3}$$

Let us return to our one-year bond and suppose that the day after the original borrower obtained the money, the yield on one-year bonds rises. How much would anyone *now* be willing to pay for the promise to receive $108 after one year? The answer must be given by the general formula (A3). The bond is just a promise to pay $108 in one year's time, and if the yield on one-year bonds is i, then the present value of the promise is given by Equation (A3). That means that the price of the one-year bond will fall when the interest rate or yield on such bonds rises. Once again, we see that the price of the bond and the yield are inversely related, given the promised payments to be made on the bond.

As before, we can reverse the formula for the price in order to find the yield on the bond, given its price and the promised payment Q_1. Note that the price P is equal to the present discounted value (PDV), so that we can write

$$1 + i = \frac{Q_1}{P} \tag{A4}$$

Thus, given the price of the bond and the promised payment, we can find the yield.

Section 3

Next we consider a 2-year bond. Such a bond would typically promise to make a payment, which we shall denote Q_1, of interest at the end of the first year, and then a payment of interest and principal (usually the amount borrowed) Q_2, at the end of the second year. Given the yield i on the bond, how do we compute its PDV, which will be equal to its price?

We start by asking first what the bond will be worth one year from now. At that stage, it will be a one-year bond, promising to pay the amount Q_2 in one year's time, and yielding i. Its value one year from now will accordingly be given by Equation (A3) except that Q_1 in Equation (A3) is replaced by Q_2. Let us denote the value of the bond one year from now by PDV_1, and note that

$$\text{PDV}_1 = \frac{Q_2}{1+i} \tag{A5}$$

To complete computing the PDV of the 2-year bond, we can now treat it as a one-year bond, which promises to pay Q_1 in interest one year from now, and also to pay PDV_1 one year from now, since it can be sold at that stage for that amount. Hence, the PDV of the bond, equal to its price, is

$$\text{PDV} = \frac{Q_1}{1+i} + \frac{\text{PDV}_1}{1+i} \tag{A6}$$

or

$$\text{PDV} = \frac{Q_1}{1+i} + \frac{Q_2}{(1+i)^2} \tag{A6a}$$

As previously, given the promised payments Q_1 and Q_2, the price of the bond will fall if the yield rises, and vice versa.

It is now less simple to reverse the equation for the price of the bond to find the yield than it was before: that is because from Equation (A6), we obtain a quadratic equation for the yield, which has two solutions.

Section 4

We have now provided the outline of the argument whereby the present discounted value of *any* promised stream of payments for any number of years can be computed. Suppose that a bond, or any other asset, promises to pay amounts $Q_1, Q_2, Q_3, \ldots, Q_n$ in future years, 1, 2, 3, . . . , n years away. By pursuing the type of argument given in Section 4-3, it is possible to show that the PDV of such a payments stream will be

$$\text{PDV} = \frac{Q_1}{1+i} + \frac{Q_2}{(1+i)^2} + \frac{Q_3}{(1+i)^3} + \cdots + \frac{Q^n}{(1+i)^n} \tag{A7}$$

As usual, the price of a bond with a specified payments stream will be inversely related to its yield.

Section 5

Finally, we return to the Consol. The Consol promises to pay the amount Q_c forever. Applying the formula, we can compute the present value of the Consol by

$$\text{PDV} = Q_c\left[\frac{1}{(1+i)} + \frac{1}{(1+i)^2} + \frac{1}{(1+i)^3} + \cdots + \frac{1}{(1+i)^n} + \cdots\right] \tag{A8}$$

The contents of the parentheses on the right-hand side are an infinite series, the sum of which can be calculated as $1/i$. Thus,

$$\text{PDV} = \frac{Q_c}{i} \tag{A9}$$

This section casts a slightly different light on the commonsense discussion of Section 1 of this appendix. Equations (A8) and (A9) show that the Consol's price is equal to the PDV of the future coupon payments.

PROBLEMS

1 The following equations describe an economy. (Think of C, I, G, etc., as being measured in billions and i as percent; a 5 percent interest rate implies $i = 5$.)

$$C = 0.8(1 - t)Y \tag{1}$$
$$t = 0.25 \tag{2}$$
$$I = 400 - 20i \tag{3}$$
$$\overline{G} = 500 \tag{4}$$
$$L = 0.25Y - 30i \tag{5}$$
$$\frac{\overline{M}}{\overline{P}} = 350 \tag{6}$$

(*a*) What is the equation that describes the IS curve?
(*b*) What is the general definition of the IS curve?
(*c*) What is the equation that describes the LM curve?
(*d*) What is the general definition of the LM curve?
(*e*) What are the equilibrium levels of income and the interest rate?
(*f*) Describe in words the conditions that are satisifed at the intersection of the IS and LM curves, and why this is an equilibrium.

2 Continue with the same equations.

(*a*) What is the value of $\overline{\alpha}$, which corresponds to the simple multiplier (with taxes) of Chapter 3?
(*b*) By how much does an increase in government spending of $\Delta\overline{G}$ increase the level of income in this model, which includes the assets markets?
(*c*) By how much does a change in government spending of $\Delta\overline{G}$ affect the equilibrium interest rate?
(*d*) Explain the difference between your answers to 2(*a*) and 2(*b*).
(*e*) Relate your answer to 2(*d*) to the question of *crowding out*.
(*f*) What is the money multiplier in this system? (In other words, by how much does a change in the real money stock of $\Delta\overline{M}/P$ affect the equilibrium level of income?)

3 (*a*) Explain in words how and why the multiplier $\overline{\alpha}$ and the interest sensitivity of aggregate demand affect the slope of the IS curve.
(*b*) Explain why the slope of the IS curve is a factor in determining the working of monetary policy.

4 Explain in words how and why the income and interest sensitivities of the demand for real balances affect the slope of the LM curve.

5 (*a*) Why does a horizontal LM curve imply that fiscal policy has the same effects on the economy as we derived in Chapter 3?
(*b*) What is happening in this case in terms of Figure 4-1?
(*c*) Under what circumstances might the LM curve be horizontal?

6 We mentioned in the text the possibility that the interest rate might affect

consumption spending. An increase in the interest rate could in principle lead to increases in saving and therefore a reduction in consumption given the level of income. Suppose that consumption were in fact reduced by an increase in the interest rate. How would the IS curve be affected?

7 Suppose that the money supply, instead of being constant, increased (slightly) with the interest rate.
 (*a*) How would this change affect the construction of the LM curve?
 (*b*) Could you see any reason why the Fed might follow a policy of increasing the money supply along with the interest rate?

8 (*a*) How does an increase in the tax rate affect the IS curve?
 (*b*) How does it affect the equilibrium level of income?
 (*c*) How does it affect the equilibrium interest rate?

9 Draw a graph of how i and Y respond over time (i.e., use time as the horizontal axis) to:
 (*a*) An expansion in the money supply
 (*b*) An increase in taxes
 You may assume that the money market adjusts much more rapidly than the goods market.

10 In Figure 4-17, the economy can move to full employment by an expansion in either money or the full-employment deficit. Which policy leads to E_1 and which to E_2? How would you expect the choice to be made? Who would most strongly favor moving to E_1? E_2? What policy would correspond to "balanced growth"?

11 "We can have the GNP path we want equally well with a tight fiscal policy and an easier monetary policy, or the reverse, within fairly broad limits. The real basis for choice lies in many subsidiary targets, besides real GNP and inflation, that are differentially affected by fiscal and monetary policies." What are some of the subsidiary targets referred to in the quote? How would they be affected by alternative policy combinations?

*12 (*a*) Nominal GNP in 1978 was about $2,100 billion, and the money supply was about $350 billion. What then was the income velocity of money? What was it last year?
 (*b*) We noted that if the demand for money is totally interest-insensitive, velocity V is just the inverse of the coefficient k of our money demand function, where k represents the income sensitivity of the demand for money. We can interpret k as the fraction of a year's income that people hold in the form of money. Using the numbers of (12*a*), what fraction of the year's income do people hold as money? How many weeks' income on average are people holding in the form of money?

*13 A bond promises to pay the holder $6 at the end of the first year and $106 at the end of the second year.
 (*a*) If the interest rate or yield is 6 percent, what is the value of the bond?
 (*b*) Without necessarily solving the arithmetic, write out an expression for how much the bond will be worth if the interest rate drops to 5 percent. Is this more or less than in 13(*a*)? Why?

2

PART

2 PART

5

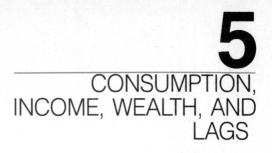

CONSUMPTION, INCOME, WEALTH, AND LAGS

The IS-LM model developed in Chapter 4 provides a framework which enables us to understand the interaction of some of the main macroeconomic variables. Now we retrace our steps to present a more detailed and more sophisticated treatment of the key equations in the IS-LM model. The present chapter deals with the consumption function. The following three chapters deal with investment, money demand, and money supply. As a unit, these chapters flesh out the behavioral equations of the IS-LM model and thus move us toward a more realistic and reliable understanding of the working of the economy.

Our starting point in examining consumption behavior is the consumption function we have been using in the previous chapters. Thus far, we have been assuming that consumption is a linear function of disposable income:

$$C = \overline{C} + cY_d \qquad \overline{C} > 0, \quad 1 > c > 0 \tag{1}$$

Now what does the empirical evidence show? Do the data for the post-World War II period bear out the hypothesis of a consumption function such as Equation (1)? We plot consumption and disposable income (both in 1972 dollars) for each of the years from 1953 through 1979 in Chart 5-1. The diagram clearly reveals a close positive relationship between consumption and disposable income. To find numerical estimates of the intercept ($\overline{C}$) and the marginal propensity to consume (c) we "fit" a regression line to the observations. The regression line is fitted to the data using the method of least squares, which produces the linear equation that best characterizes the relation between consumption and disposable income contained in the data.[1]

The estimated regression line is shown in Chart 5-1 as the solid line and is reported in Equation (2). The estimate of the intercept is $\overline{C} = 6.71$ (6.71 billion 1972 dollars) and the estimate of the marginal propensity to consume is 0.90.

$$C = 6.71 + 0.90Y_d \qquad \text{(annual data, 1953–1978)} \tag{2}$$

Two characteristics of a consumption function such as Equation (1) are borne out by the empirical Equation (2). There is a positive intercept

[1] It is frequently useful to summarize a relationship, such as that of Chart 5-1, between consumption expenditures and disposable income by writing an equation such as Eq. (2), which has specific numerical values in it, rather than the more general form of Eq. (1), which does not specify numerical values of the coefficients $\overline{C}$ and c. The line drawn in Chart 5-1 is the line represented by Eq. (2). That line is calculated by minimizing the sum of the squares of the vertical distances of the points in Chart 5-1 from the line, and it provides a good description of the general relationship between the two variables. For further details on the fitting of such lines, called least-squares regression lines, see Robert S. Pindyck and Daniel L. Rubinfeld, *Econometric Models and Economic Forecasts*, 2d ed. (New York: McGraw-Hill, 1980).

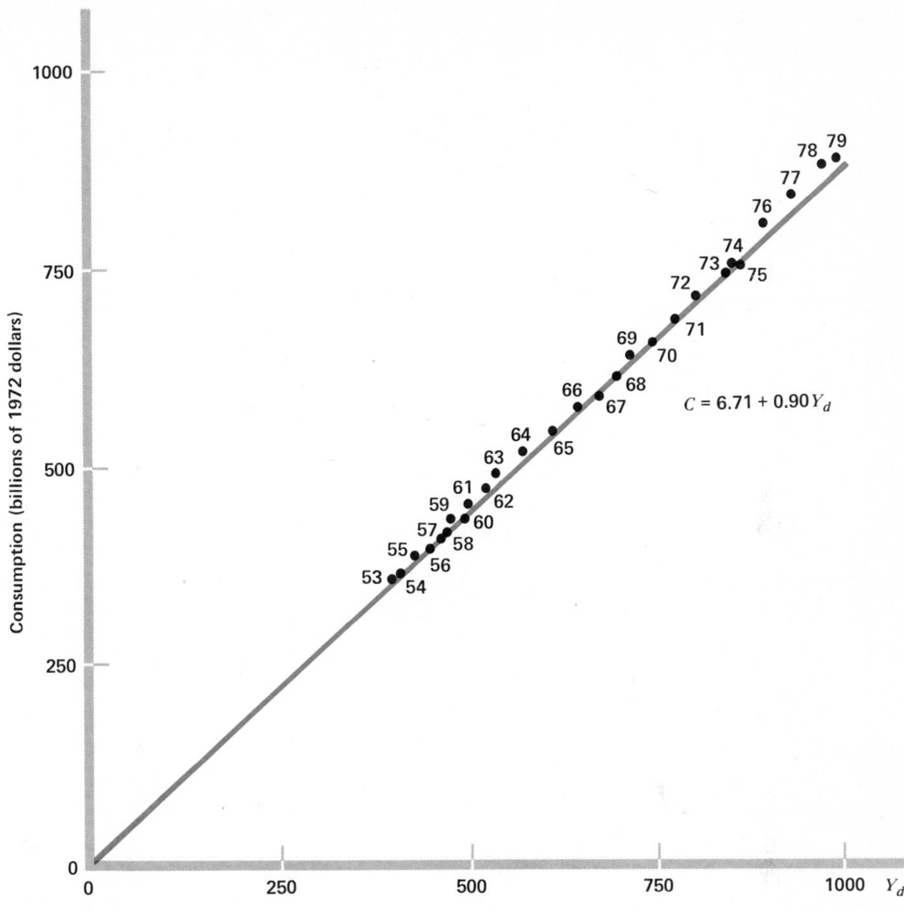

CHART 5-1 THE CONSUMPTION-INCOME RELATION 1953–1979

($\overline{C} = 6.71$), and the marginal propensity to consume ($c = 0.90$) is positive and less than unity.

If we divide through by Y_d in Equation (2), we obtain an equation that gives the average propensity to consume (C/Y_d) as a function of disposable income:

$$\frac{C}{Y_d} = \frac{6.71}{Y_d} + 0.90 \tag{3}$$

Equation (3) indicates that the average propensity to consume declines as disposable income rises.[2] However, although the intercept, 6.71, is positive, it is very small relative to disposable income, which was $965.5 billion in 1978.[3] If the intercept were actually zero, then we see from Equations (1) and (3) that consumption would be proportional to disposable income, with $C/Y_d = c$. The marginal and average propensities to consume would be equal. The relationship shown by Chart 5-1 and Equation (2) is essentially one of proportionality, with the average and marginal propensities to consume out of disposable income equal to each other, at about 0.91.

Inspection of the regression line in Chart 5-1 suggests that the estimated equation fits well. There are no points far off the fitted line. As a first approximation, then, Equation (2) provides a reasonable summary of consumption behavior. The next step is to ask whether there is reason to believe Equation (2) can be improved upon, and if so, to determine how.

Chart 5-2 shows the average propensity to consume, as calculated from Equation (3), the smooth line, and the actual propensity to consume in each year. The smooth line, the predicted average propensity to consume,

[2] You should check a data source, such as the *Economic Report of the President*, to see how well the predicted average propensity to consume from Eq. (3) matches the actual propensity for 1979 and 1980.

[3] Technically, the intercept is statistically not significantly different from zero. See Pindyck and Rubinfeld, op. cit., for the meaning of tests of significance.

CHART 5-2 THE ACTUAL AND PREDICTED AVERAGE PROPENSITY TO CONSUME, 1953–1979

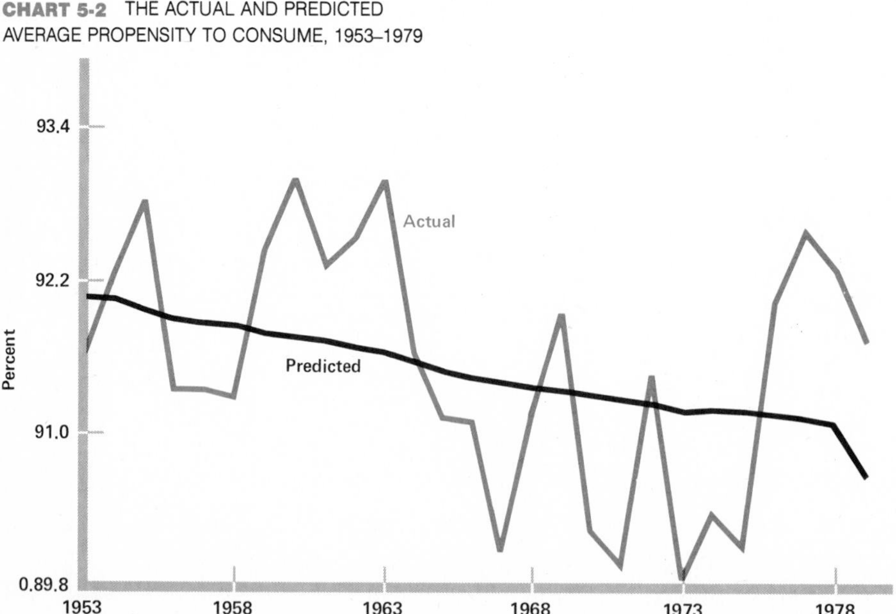

declines slightly over time as Y_d rises. The actual propensity to consume jumps around a good deal, and it seems to be above or below the predicted line for some years at a time, for example, from 1959 to 1964, or 1973 to 1975.

The deviations of the actual ratio from the predicted one raise the question of how well the equation predicts consumption behavior. For example, in 1973 the actual propensity to consume was 0.898, whereas the predicted propensity was 0.911. The error of 0.013 translates into an error in predicting consumption of almost $11 billion, nearly 1 percent of GNP.[4] The differences between actual and predicted C/Y_d shown in Chart 5-2 suggest that the simple consumption function Equation (2) can be improved upon.

In this chapter, we shall explore three more sophisticated formulations of the consumption function than Equation (1). These are the *life-cycle* theory of consumption, the *permanent-income hypothesis*, and the *relative-income* formulation, described in Sections 5-2 through 5-4. Before we examine those theories, though, we outline in Section 5-1 an empirical puzzle about the consumption function that was historically important in leading to the new theories of the consumption function.

5-1 A CONSUMPTION FUNCTION PUZZLE

The puzzle we describe consists of two types of evidence that made their appearance in the late 1940s and that were apparently in conflict. The first type of evidence came from estimates of the standard consumption function, Equation (1), using annual data for the 1929–1941 period. (No earlier data were available then.) The estimated equation (in 1972 dollars) is

$$C = 47.6 + 0.73Y_d \qquad \text{(annual data, 1929–1941)} \tag{4}$$

This equation clearly implies that the average propensity to consume falls as the level of income rises. It also has a low marginal propensity to consume. If we used Equation (4) to predict today's average propensity to consume, the estimate would be around 0.8, which of course is far off the actual ratio of about 0.9.

The second piece of evidence was the finding by Simon Kuznets, using averages of data over long periods—10 and 30 years—that there was near proportionality between consumption and income.[5] This is consistent with the intercept term in Equation (1) being zero. The average propensity to consume that he found for three overlapping 30-year periods is shown in

[4] Disposable income in 1973 was $854.7 billion, measured in 1972 dollars.

[5] Simon Kuznets, *National Product Since 1869*, and *National Income, A Summary of Findings* (New York: National Bureau of Economic Research, 1946).

TABLE 5-1 THE KUZNETS FINDING

	1869–1898	1884–1913	1904–1933
Average propensity	.867	.867	.879

Source: Simon Kuznets, *National Income, A Summary of Findings*, (New York: National Bureau of Economic Research, 1946), table 16.

Table 5-1. The Kuznets results suggest, using long-term averages, that there is little variation in the ratio of consumption to income and, in particular, that there is no tendency for the average propensity to decline.

There is clearly a conflict between the implications of the consumption function in Equation (4) and Kuznets' findings. The Kuznets results suggest that the average propensity to consume is constant over long periods, whereas Equation (4) suggests it falls as income rises. It is also clear that the consumption function estimated in Equation (4) on the basis of the prewar data is inconsistent with the same function estimated on the basis of postwar data, that is, Equation (2).

The puzzle of the discrepancy between Kuznets' findings and Equation (4) was well known by the time the three alternative theories we outline below were developed. In resolving the puzzle, all three theories draw on the notion that consumption is related to a broader income measure than just current income. As already noted, the broader measures go under the names of *lifetime income*, *permanent income*, and *relative income*. These concepts have in common the recognition that consumption spending is maintained relatively constant in the face of fluctuations of current income. Consumption spending is not geared to what we earn today, but to what we earn on average. The important question obviously is what "average" means in this context.

The theories we present all imply that there is a difference between the marginal propensity to consume in the short run and the marginal propensity to consume in the long run. The short-run consumption function—the relationship between consumption spending and *current* disposable income—is indeed quite flat. However, this consumption function shifts upward over time. These shifts in the relationship between consumption and current disposable income bring into the discussion the roles of *wealth* and *permanent income* in affecting consumer spending.[6] These considerations are taken up in the next two sections.

[6] The theories of the consumption function developed hereafter are also useful for explaining another empirical puzzle that we shall not go into in detail. In *cross-sectional* studies of the relationship between consumption and income—studies in which the consumption of a sample of families is related to their income—the marginal propensity to consume out of disposable income also appears to be lower than the average propensity to consume, with the average propensity to consume falling as the level of income rises. If you are interested in the reconciliation of this evidence with the long-run evidence of Kuznets, you should look at the ingenious explanation advanced by Milton Friedman through the permanent-income hypothesis. Follow up the reference given in footnote 12.

5-2 THE LIFE-CYCLE THEORY OF CONSUMPTION AND SAVING

The consumption function (1) is based on the simple notion that individuals' consumption behavior in a given period is related to their income in that period. The life-cycle hypothesis views individuals, instead, as planning their consumption and saving behavior over long periods, with the intention of allocating their consumption in a satisfactory way over their entire lifetimes. The life-cycle hypothesis views savings as resulting mainly from individuals' desires to provide for consumption in old age. As we shall see, the theory points to a number of unexpected factors affecting the savings rate of the economy; for instance, the age structure of the population is, in principle, an important determinant of consumption and savings behavior.

To anticipate the main results of this section, we can already state here that we will derive a consumption function of the form

$$C = a\frac{W}{P} + cY_d \tag{5}$$

where W/P is real wealth, a is the marginal propensity to consume out of wealth, and c is the marginal propensity to consume out of disposable income. We will show what determines the marginal propensities, why wealth should be an argument in the consumption function, and what the life-cycle consumption theory implies about the ratio of consumption to income, C/Y_d.

Consider now a woman who expects to live for L years, work and earn income for N years, and be in retirement for $(L - N)$ years. The individual's consumption planning is assumed to start when she begins work, so that year 1 is the first year of work. We shall, in what follows, ignore any uncertainty about either life expectancy or the length of working life. We shall assume, too, that no interest is earned on savings, so that current saving translates dollar for dollar into future consumption possibilities. With these assumptions, we can approach the saving or consumption decision with two questions. First we ask, What are the individual's lifetime consumption possibilities? Second, we are interested in the way this woman will choose to distribute her consumption over her lifetime. We shall now consider the consumption possibilities.

For the moment we ignore property income (income from assets) and focus attention on labor income. We denote the annual real labor income by Z. Given N years of working, *lifetime income* (from labor) is ZN, income per working year times the number of working years. Consumption over the individual's lifetime cannot exceed this lifetime income unless she is born with wealth, which we initially assume is not the case. Accordingly, we have determined the first part of the consumer's problem in finding the limit of lifetime consumption.

We assume the individual will want to distribute consumption over her lifetime so that she has a flat or even flow of consumption. Rather than consume a lot in one period and very little in another, the preferred profile is to consume exactly equal amounts in each period.[7] Clearly, this assumption implies that consumption is not geared to *current* income (which is zero during retirement) but rather to *lifetime income*.

Lifetime consumption equals lifetime income. This means that the planned level of consumption C, which is the same in every period, times the number of years in life L equals lifetime income:

$$CL = ZN \tag{6}$$

Lifetime income is equal to ZN. Dividing through by L, we have planned consumption per year, C, that is proportional to labor income:

$$C = \frac{N}{L}Z \tag{7}$$

The factor of proportionality in Equation (7) is N/L, the fraction of lifetime spent working. Accordingly Equation (7) states that in each year of life a fraction of labor income is consumed, where that fraction is equal to the proportion of working life in total life.

The counterpart of Equation (7) is the saving function. Remembering that saving is equal to income less consumption we have

$$S \equiv Z - C = \frac{Z(L - N)}{L} \tag{8}$$

Equation (8) states that saving during the period in which the individual works is equal to a fraction of labor income, with that fraction being equal to the proportion of life spent in retirement.

Figure 5-1 shows the pattern of consumption, saving, and dissaving.[8] Over the whole lifetime, there is an even flow of consumption at the rate C,

[7] Why? The basic reason is the notion of diminishing marginal utility of consumption. Consider two alternative consumption plans. One involves an equal amount of consumption in each of two periods; the other involves consuming all in one period and none in the other. The principle of diminishing marginal utility of income implies that in the latter case, we would be better off by transferring some consumption from the period of plenty toward that of starvation. The loss in utility in the period of plenty is *more* than compensated by the gain in utility in the period of scarcity. And there is a gain to be made by transferring consumption so long as there is any difference in consumption between the two periods. The principle of diminishing marginal utility of consumption conforms well with the observation that most people choose stable life-styles—not, in general, saving furiously in one period to have a big bust in the next, but rather, consuming at about the same level from period to period.

[8] Figure 5-1 was developed by Franco Modigliani in "The Life Cycle Hypothesis of Saving, the Demand for Wealth and the Supply of Capital," *Social Research*, vol. 33, no. 2, 1966. Modigliani, together with Richard Brumberg and Albert Ando, formulated the life-cycle theory.

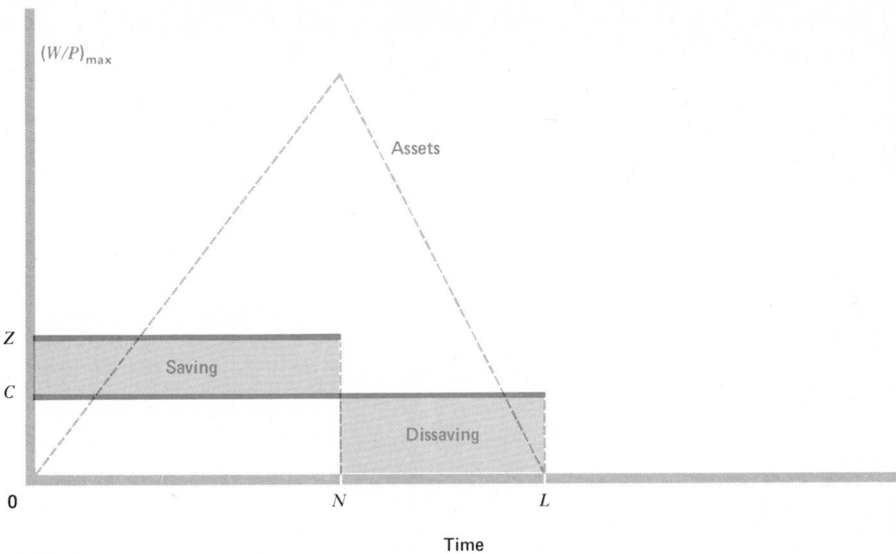

FIGURE 5-1 LIFETIME INCOME, CONSUMPTION, SAVINGS, AND WEALTH IN THE LIFE-CYCLE MODE

amounting in total to CL. That consumption spending is financed during working life out of current income. During retirement the consumption is financed by drawing down the savings that have been accumulated during working life. Therefore the shaded areas $(Z - C)N$ and $C(L - N)$ are equal, or equivalently saving during working years finances dissaving during retirement. The important idea of lifetime consumption theory is apparent from Figure 5-1. It is that consumption plans are made so as to achieve a smooth or even level of consumption by saving during periods of high income and dissaving during periods of low income. This is, therefore, an important departure from consumption based on current income. It is an important difference because, in addition to current income, the whole future profile of income enters into the calculation of lifetime consumption. Before developing that aspect further, however, we return to Figure 5-1 to consider the role of assets.

During the working years, the individual saves to finance consumption during retirement. The savings build up assets, and we accordingly show in Figure 5-1 how the individual's wealth or assets increase over working life and reach a maximum at retirement age. From that time on, assets decline because the individual sells assets to pay for current consumption. We can briefly ask, What is the maximum level that assets reach? We remember that assets are built up to finance consumption during retirement. Total consumption during retirement is equal to $C(L - N)$. Furthermore since annual consumption is equal to $C \equiv ZN/L$, the maximum stock of assets is $(W/P)_{max} = ZN(L - N)/L$, which is reached exactly at the point of retirement. From then on, assets decline until they reach precisely zero at the end of life.

Introducing Wealth

The next step is to extend this model and allow for initial assets or wealth, that is, assuming the individual is born to wealth.[9] We can simply draw on the previous insight that the individual consumer will spread any existing resources to achieve an even lifetime consumption profile. The individual who has assets in addition to labor income will plan to use these assets to add to lifetime consumption. An individual who is at some point T in life, with a stock of wealth W/P and labor income accruing for another $(N - T)$ years at the rate of Z, and with a life expectancy of $(L - T)$ years to go, will behave as follows. The person's lifetime consumption possibilities are

$$C(L - T) = \frac{W}{P} + (N - T)Z \tag{9}$$

where we have included wealth W/P along with lifetime labor income as a source of finance for lifetime consumption. From Equation (9), consumption in each period is equal to

$$C = a\frac{W}{P} + cZ \qquad a \equiv \frac{1}{L - T} \qquad c \equiv \frac{N - T}{L - T} \qquad N \geq T \tag{10}$$

where the coefficients a and c are, respectively, the marginal propensities to consume out of wealth and labor income.

It is important to recognize from Equation (10) that the marginal propensities are related to the individual's position in the life cycle. The closer a person is to the end of lifetime, the higher the marginal propensity to consume out of wealth. Thus, a man with 2 more years of life will consume half his wealth in each of the remaining 2 years. The marginal propensity to consume out of labor income is related both to the number of years during which further income will be earned, $N - T$, and to the number of years over which these earnings are spread, $L - T$. It is quite clear from Equation (10) that an increase in either wealth or labor income will raise consumption expenditures. It is apparent, too, that lengthening

[9] The individual may receive wealth early in life through gifts or bequests. In the fully developed life-cycle theory, the individual, in calculating lifetime consumption, has also to take account of any bequests he or she may want to leave.

working life relative to retirement will raise consumption simply because it increases lifetime income. The most basic point, however, is that Equation (10) shows both (lifetime) income and wealth as determinants of consumption spending.

To summarize where we have come so far, we note that in this form of the life-cycle model:

1 Consumption is constant over the consumer's lifetime.
2 Consumption spending is financed by lifetime income plus initial wealth.
3 During each year a fraction $1/(L - T)$ of wealth plus expected earnings will be consumed.
4 Current consumption spending depends on current wealth and lifetime income.

Extensions

The model as so far outlined makes very strong simplifying assumptions. It can be extended to remove most of the strong assumptions without affecting the underlying properties of Equation (10), that consumption is related to both income and wealth.

First, it is necessary to take account of the possibility that saving earns interest, so that a dollar not consumed today will provide more than a dollar's consumption tomorrow. Second, the analysis is little affected when it is extended to allow for the facts that individuals are uncertain of the length of their lifetimes, and also that they sometimes want to leave bequests to their heirs. In this latter case, they would not plan to consume all their resources over their own lifetimes. Similarly, the model has to be extended to take account of the composition of the family over time, so that some consumption is provided for children before they begin to work. But, to repeat, these extensions do not change the basic results contained in Equation (10).

A final extension is very important. In practice, one never knows exactly what one's lifetime labor income will be, and lifetime consumption plans have to be made on the basis of predictions of future labor income. This, of course, raises the issue of how income is to be predicted. We will not pursue this important issue here, but will leave it to the next section on permanent income, which is an estimate of lifetime income. However, expected lifetime labor income would be related to current disposable income, leading to a form of the consumption function like Equation (5), perhaps with other variables also included. Indeed, it is useful to think of the life-cycle and permanent-income theories as being fundamentally the same, with the life-cycle theory developing most carefully the implications of the model for the role of wealth and other variables in the consumption function,[10] and the permanent-income theory concentrating on the best way of predicting lifetime income.

Aggregate Consumption and Saving

The theory as so far outlined is strictly a theory about consumption and saving by single individuals over the course of their lifetimes. How does it relate to aggregate consumption, which is, after all, the focus of macroeconomic interest in consumption? Imagine an economy in which population and GNP were constant through time. Each individual in that economy would go through the life cycle of saving and dissaving outlined in Figure 5-1. The economy as a whole, though, would not be saving. At any one time, the saving of working people would be exactly matched by the dissaving of retired people. However, if population were growing, there would be more young people than old, thus more saving in total than dissaving, and there would be net saving in the economy. Thus, aggregate consumption depends in part on the age composition of the population. It also depends on such characteristics of the economy as the average age of retirement and the presence or absence of Social Security. These surprising implications of the theory indicate the richness of the approach.

Implications

We want to return to Equation (5) to emphasize again the role of wealth. Note from (5) that if there were an increase in wealth, the ratio of consumption to disposable income would rise. This has a bearing on the puzzle described in Section 5-1, where the average propensity to consume seems, on the basis of Equation (4), to decline with income, and on the basis of Kuznets' findings, to remain constant on average over long periods.

If we divide through in Equation (5) by Y_d, we obtain

$$\frac{C}{Y_d} = a\,\frac{W/P}{Y_d} + b \tag{11}$$

Now, if the ratio of wealth to disposable income is constant, then Equation (11) shows that the ratio of consumption to disposable income will be constant. However, if the ratio of wealth to disposable income is changing, the average propensity to consume will be changing.

This suggests, as an explanation of the Kuznets puzzle, the possibility that the ratio of wealth to disposable income is roughly constant over long periods, and that it varied considerably during the 1930s to which period the consumption function, Equation (4), applies. Similarly, Equation (11)

[10] The other variables indicated here will be discussed in the next paragraph.

suggests that the variability of the average propensity to consume in the short run, as seen in Chart 5-2, is explained in part by fluctuations in the ratio of wealth to disposable income. And indeed, the ratio of wealth to disposable income is reasonably constant in the long run, but fluctuates considerably in the short run in a way that helps explain the fluctuations in the average propensity to consume shown in Chart 5-2.[11]

One further interesting implication of the life-cycle hypothesis is that it provides a route for the stock market to affect consumption behavior. The value of stocks held by the public is part of wealth and should be—and is—included in W/P in Equation (5). When the value of stocks is high—when the stock market is booming—W/P is high and tends to increase consumption, and the reverse occurs when the stock market is depressed.

We continue now to the permanent-income theory of consumption, bearing in mind that we have not yet discussed the determinants of expected lifetime labor income in Equation (10) in any detail, and recalling that the two theories should be thought of as complementary rather than competing.

5-3 PERMANENT-INCOME THEORY OF CONSUMPTION

In the long run, the consumption-income ratio is very stable, but in the short run it fluctuates. The behavior of the propensity to consume implied by the standard consumption function, Equation (1), appears to differ when the equation is fitted over different periods. The life-cycle approach explains these observations by pointing out that people want to maintain a smooth profile of consumption even if their lifetime income profile is uneven, and thus emphasizes the role of wealth in the consumption function. Another explanation, which differs in details but entirely shares the spirit of the life-cycle approach, is the permanent-income theory of consumption.

The theory, which is the work of Milton Friedman,[12] argues that people gear their consumption behavior to their permanent or long-term consumption opportunities, not to their current level of income. A suggestive

[11] The life-cycle theory also suggests why the simple consumption function of Eq. (2) would look different when estimated over different time periods, for example, 1953–1978 and 1929–1941. Equation (2) omits a variable, wealth, that should be in the consumption function. This means that the estimates we get for the intercept and the marginal propensity to consume will depend on how wealth changes in the period for which we are fitting the line. As a difficult problem, see whether you can show that the estimated average propensity to consume will be constant if the ratio of wealth to disposable income is constant, but is omitted from the equation when it is fitted. Similarly, show that when wealth is constant and is omitted when fitting Eq. (2), the estimated average propensity to consume will decline with income.

[12] Milton Friedman, *A Theory of the Consumption Function* (Princeton, N.J.: Princeton University Press, 1957).

example provided by Friedman involves someone who is paid or receives her income only once a week on Fridays. But we clearly do not expect that individual to concentrate her entire consumption on that one day on which income is received, with zero consumption on every other day. Again we are persuaded by the argument that individuals prefer a smooth consumption flow rather than plenty today and scarcity tomorrow or yesterday. On that argument, consumption on any one day of the week would be unrelated to income on that particular day but would rather be geared to average daily income—that is, income per week divided by the number of days per week. It is clear that in this extreme example, income for a period longer than a day is relevant to the consumption decision. Similarly, Friedman argues, there is nothing special about a period of the length of one quarter or one year that requires the individual to plan consumption within the period solely on the basis of income within the period; rather, consumption is planned in relation to income over a longer period.

The idea of consumption spending that is geared to long-term or average or permanent income is appealing and essentially the same as the life-cycle theory. It leaves two further questions. The first concerns the precise relationship between current consumption and permanent income. The second question is how to make the concept of permanent income operational, that is, how to measure it.

In its simplest form the permanent-income hypothesis of consumption behavior argues that consumption is proportional to permanent income:

$$C = cY^P \tag{12}$$

where Y^P is permanent (disposable) income. From Equation (12), consumption varies in the same proportion as permanent income. A 5 percent increase in permanent income raises consumption by 5 percent. Since permanent income should be related to long-run average income, this feature of the consumption function is clearly in line with the observed long-run constancy of the consumption-income ratio.

The next problem is how to think of, and measure, permanent income. Think of a person whose income has risen this year. She has to decide whether that income increase represents a permanent increase, or merely a *transitory* change, one that will not persist. In any particular case, the individual may know whether the increase is permanent or transitory. A government official who is promoted one grade will know that the increase in income is likely to be maintained. Or the worker who has exceptionally high overtime in a given year will likely regard that year's increased income as transitory. But in general, a person is not so certain about what part of any change in income is likely to be maintained, and is therefore permanent, and what part is not likely to be maintained, and is therefore transitory. Since the individual assumes that transitory income on average cancels out over the life span, being positive in some periods and negative in others, transitory income is assumed not to have any substantial effect on consumption.

The question of how to infer what part of an increase in income is permanent is resolved in a pragmatic way by assuming that permanent income is related to the behavior of current and past incomes. To give a simple example, we might estimate permanent income as being equal to last year's income plus some fraction of the change in income from last year to this year:

$$\begin{aligned} Y^P &= Y_{-1} + \theta (Y - Y_{-1}) \qquad 0 < \theta < 1 \\ &= \theta Y + (1 - \theta) Y_{-1} \end{aligned} \tag{13}$$

where θ is a fraction and Y_{-1} is last year's income. The second line in Equation (13) writes permanent income as a *weighted average* of current and past income. The second formulation is of course equivalent to that in the first line. To understand Equation (13), assume we had a value of $\theta = 0.6$ and that this year's income was $Y = \$12{,}000$ and last year's income was $Y_{-1} = \$11{,}000$. The value of permanent income would be $Y^P = \$11{,}600$ $(= 0.6 \times \$12{,}000 + 0.4 \times \$11{,}000)$. Thus, permanent income is an average of the two income levels. Whether it is closer to this year's or last year's income depends on the weight θ given to current income. Clearly, in the extreme with $\theta = 1$, permanent income is equal to current income.

An estimate of permanent income that uses only current and last year's income is an oversimplification. Friedman forms the estimate by looking at incomes in many earlier periods, as well as current income, but with weights that are larger for the more recent, as compared with the more distant, incomes.[13] There is no simple theory which would tell us what the relative magnitude of the weights on different incomes should be, except for two considerations. First, income in the distant past—say more than 3 years ago—should have less influence on permanent income than more recent incomes. Second, current income should have a weight that is less than 1, so that we look at both current and past incomes in forming our estimate. We should also repeat that we cannot expect a formula like Equation (13), based on the behavior of income in the past, to include all the factors that influence a person's beliefs about future income. The discovery of a vast amount of oil in a country, for instance, would raise the permanent incomes of the inhabitants of the country as soon as it was announced, even though a (mechanical) formula like Equation (13) based on past levels of income would not reflect such a change.

There are some special features of Equation (13) which deserve comment. First, if $Y = Y_{-1}$, that is, if this year's income is equal to last year's, then permanent income is equal to the income earned this year and

[13] Friedman also adjusts permanent income by taking into account the growth of income over time.

last year. This guarantees that an individual who had always earned the same income would expect to earn that income in the future. Second, note that if income rises this year compared with last year, then permanent income rises by *less* than current income. The reason is that the individual does not know whether the rise in income this year is permanent. Not knowing whether the increase in income will be maintained or not, the individual does not immediately increase the expected or permanent income measure by the full amount of the actual or current increase in income.

Using Equations (12) and (13), we can now rewrite the consumption function:

$$C = cY^P = c\theta Y + c(1 - \theta)Y_{-1} \tag{14}$$

The marginal propensity to consume out of *current* income is then just $c\theta$, which is clearly less than the long-run average propensity to consume, c. Hence, the permanent-income hypothesis implies that there is a difference between the short-run marginal propensity to consume and the long-run marginal (equal to the average) propensity to consume.

We shall see shortly that this implication is supported by the data. But first we explore it in more detail. The reason for the lower short-run marginal propensity to consume is that when current income rises, the individual is not sure that the increase in income will be maintained over the longer period on which she bases consumption plans. Accordingly, the person does not fully adjust consumption spending to the higher level that would be appropriate if the increase in income were permanent. However, if the increase turns out to be permanent, that is, if next period's income is the same as this period's, then the person will (next year) fully adjust consumption spending to the higher level of income. Note, though, that the adjustment here is completed in 2 years only because we have assumed, in Equation (13), that permanent income is an average of 2 years' income. Depending on how expectations of permanent income are formed, the adjustment could be much slower.

The argument is illustrated in Figure 5-2. Here we show the long-run consumption function as a straight line through the origin with slope c, which is the constant average and marginal propensity to consume out of permanent income. The lower flat consumption function is a short-run consumption function drawn for a given history of income which is reflected in the intercept $c(1 - \theta)Y_0$. The consumption function is therefore appropriate if last year's income was Y_0. Assume, in fact, that we start out in long-run equilibrium with actual and permanent income equal to Y_0 and consumption therefore equal to cY_0, as is shown at the intersection of long-run and short-run consumption functions at point E. Assume next that income increases to the level Y'. In the short run, which means during the

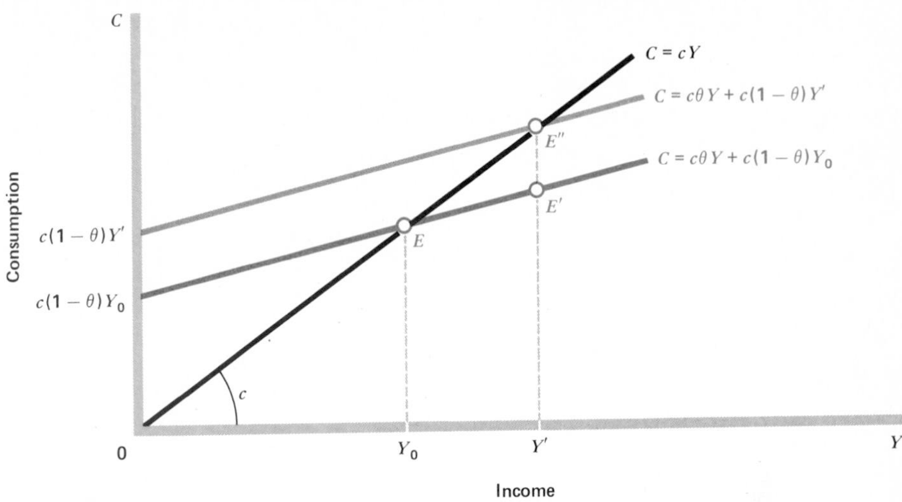

FIGURE 5-2 THE EFFECT ON CONSUMPTION OF A SUSTAINED INCREASE IN INCOME

current period, we revise our estimate of permanent income upward by θ times the increase in income and consume a fraction c of that increase in permanent income. Accordingly, consumption moves up along the short-run consumption function to point E'.

Note immediately that in the short run the ratio of consumption to income declines as we move from point E to E'. Going one period ahead and assuming that the increase in income persists so that income remains at Y', we get a shift in the consumption function. The consumption function shifts upward because, as of the given higher level of income, the estimate of permanent income is now revised upward to Y'. Accordingly, consumers want to spend a fraction of c of their new estimate of permanent income Y'. The new consumption point is E'', where the ratio of consumption to income is back to the long-run level. The example makes clear the point that in the short run, an increase in income causes a decline in the average propensity to consume because people do not anticipate that the increase in income will persist or be permanent. Once they do observe that the increase in income does persist, however, they fully adjust consumption to match their higher permanent income.

We show that the data bear out this implication of permanent-income theory by providing another estimate of the parameters in Equation (1). Equation (2) was estimated using annual data. But there are quarterly data available for the period 1953–1978 over which Equation (2) was fitted. If we fit consumption function (1) using quarterly data, we obtain

$$C = 203.4 + 0.53Y_d \qquad \text{(quarterly data, 1953–1978)} \qquad (2a)$$
$$C = 6.71 + 0.90Y_d \qquad \text{(annual data, 1953–1978)} \qquad (2b)$$

Equation (2) is reproduced to facilitate comparison of the results. They are strikingly different. The equation using annual data suggests that an additional dollar of income leads to 90 cents of additional consumption, while the equation using quarterly data suggests that a dollar of additional income increases consumption by only 53 cents.

These results reinforce the lesson of the permanent-income hypothesis. Consumption behavior is geared to permanent income, not income in any given day, or month, or quarter. Quarterly data contain a lot of "noise" or transitory components in the sense that income fluctuates around its trend; in some quarters it is low and in others it is high. But these fluctuations do not affect permanent income and thus consumption substantially. Therefore a change in income in the current quarter, viewed largely as transitory, has less effect on consumption than a change in income that lasts for a year: the regression coefficient (c) is therefore smaller in the quarterly regression than in the annual regression. In annual data, a good part of the short-term fluctuations average out, and more of the changes in income represent permanent rather than transitory changes. Hence there is a difference between Equations (2a) and (2b).

Like the life-cycle hypothesis, the permanent-income hypothesis has some other unexpected and interesting implications. Consider, for instance, the weight that should be given to current income in forming an estimate of permanent income as a function of the extent to which current income varies for a given individual. An individual whose income has been extremely unstable in the past will not give a large amount of weight to a change in income in any one year. The weight θ in Equation (14) for such an individual will be relatively small, and the marginal propensity to consume out of current income will accordingly be relatively small. On the other hand, an individual whose income has been very stable in the past will put a lot of weight on changes in current income and have a relatively large θ in Equation (14).[14] His marginal propensity to consume out of current income will therefore be relatively large. Friedman shows that this implication is borne out by the facts. Farmers, for instance, have very variable incomes and a low marginal propensity to consume out of current income.

To conclude this section, it is worth considering again the relationship between the life-cycle and permanent-income hypothesis briefly. The two hypotheses are not mutually exclusive. The life-cycle hypothesis pays rather more attention to the motives for saving than the permanent-income

[14] Recall that, although we restricted our measure of permanent income to a 2-year average, there is no reason why the average should not be taken over longer periods. If current income is unstable, an appropriate measure of permanent income may well be an average over 5 or more years.

hypothesis does, and provides convincing reasons to include wealth as well as income in the consumption function. The permanent-income hypothesis, on the other hand, pays more careful attention to the way in which individuals form their expectations about their future incomes than the original life-cycle hypothesis does. Recall that current labor income entered the life-cycle consumption function to reflect expectations of future income. The more detailed analysis of the determinants of expected future income that is provided by the permanent-income hypothesis can be, and has been, included in the life-cycle consumption function.

Indeed, modern theories of the consumption function combine the expectations formation emphasized by the permanent-income approach with the emphasis on wealth and demographic variables suggested by the life-cycle approach. A simplified version of a modern consumption function would be

$$C = a\frac{W}{P} + b\theta Y_d + b(1 - \theta)\, Y_{d-1} \qquad (15)$$

where Y_d in Equation (15) would be disposable labor income. Equation (15) combines the main features that are emphasized by modern consumption theory.[15] It has a short-run marginal propensity to consume out of disposable labor income ($b\theta$) that is lower than the long-run marginal propensity (b). It also shows the role of wealth, which is an important influence on consumption spending.

Recent research on consumption has combined the two theories and has been aimed particularly at checking the implications of the permanent-income—and life-cycle—theory that transitory changes in income have little effect on consumption.[16]

We end this section by repeating a warning that is important enough for us to risk overstating. An equation like (15) performs quite well on average in predicting consumption. But it is always important to remember the underlying theory when using it. Equation (15) embodies the estimate of permanent income implied by Equation (13). If we have knowledge about some particular change in income—for example, that it is transitory—then we should use that knowledge in predicting consumption. For instance, a temporary one-year tax increase that reduced current

[15] To fix ideas, you should draw a graph of Eq. (15) with consumption on the vertical axis and current disposable labor income on the horizontal axis. What is the intercept? How does the diagram differ from Fig. 5-2? Show now the effects of (1) a transitory increase in income, (2) a sustained increase in income, and (3) an increase in wealth.

[16] See, for example, Robert E. Hall, "Stochastic Implications of the Life Cycle–Permanent Income Hypothesis: Theory and Evidence," *Journal of Political Economy*, December 1978. We should warn you that this is difficult reading.

disposable income would reduce current consumption by much less than a tax increase of the same size that was known to be permanent, even though Equation (15) does not show that.

5-4 THE RELATIVE-INCOME HYPOTHESIS

Modern theories of the consumption function have in common the objective of explaining short-run fluctuations in the ratio of consumption to disposable income combined with virtual constancy of the ratio of consumption to disposable income in the long run. Life-cycle and permanent-income theories explain this behavior as an attempt to maintain a smooth flow of consumption that is geared to long-run consumption opportunities, as measured by lifetime income and wealth or by permanent income.

An earlier and influential theory along much the same lines is the relative-income hypothesis that was advanced by James Duesenberry.[17] The theory argues that current consumption depends not only on current income but also on the history of income. Individuals build up consumption standards that are geared to their *peak* income levels. If income declines relative to past income, then individuals will not immediately sacrifice the consumption standard they have adopted. There is a *ratchet effect*, and they will only adjust to a small extent to the decline in current income. However, there is an asymmetry because an increase in income relative to past peaks immediately raises the consumption level.

Figure 5-3 shows consumption behavior according to the relative-income hypothesis. The dark line is the consumption function if current income is the peak level of income. Thus, if current income is Y_d^0 *and* exceeds previous levels of income, then consumption would be at point E on the consumption function $C = cY_d$. If income declined from the level Y_d^0 to Y_d', then consumption would adjust along the light schedule to E'. The peak level of income Y_d^0 would continue to influence consumption because it determines the consumption standard that individuals seek to maintain. In the short run, therefore, saving adjusts so as to allow consumption to be maintained close to the habitual level. Assume next that income rose to the level Y_d''. This would be a new peak level of income, and consumption accordingly would rise to E''. If income were to decline back to Y_d^0, the new peak level Y'' would continue to influence consumption, so that we would find ourselves at point E'''.

The theory is very suggestive again of the attempt to smooth consumption in the face of income fluctuations. It has an intuitive appeal in its emphasis on consumption standards geared to peak income. It lacks,

[17] See James Duesenberry, *Income, Savings and the Theory of Consumer Behavior* (Cambridge, Mass.: Harvard University Press, 1952).

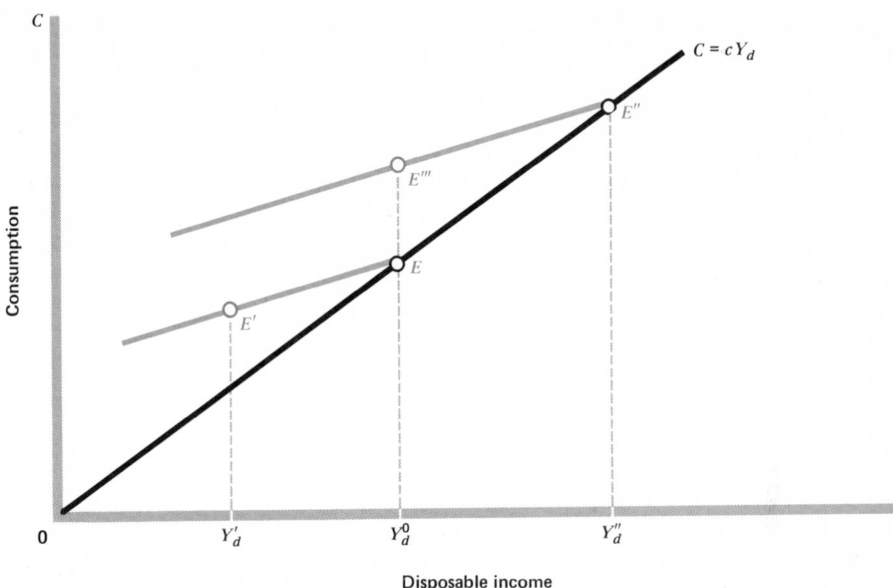

FIGURE 5-3 THE RELATIVE-INCOME HYPOTHESIS

perhaps, the economic richness that the later theories of the life cycle and permanent income added. Its main shortcoming is the asymmetry that suggests that a current increase in income, if it exceeds a previous peak, immediately induces a new consumption standard. Here the alternative theories are more persuasive in that they suggest a partial adjustment for both an increase and a decrease in income. But the theory does suggest that as the level of income rises over time, consumption will rise roughly in proportion, along the line $C = cY_d$.

*5-5 LAGS AND DYNAMICS

In this section we explore the implications of the permanent-income hypothesis for the adjustment of equilibrium output to changes in autonomous spending. Our theory of the consumption function implies that households only gradually adjust their consumption spending to a sustained change in income. What is the implication of such gradual adjustment of consumption, once we place the consumption function in the broader context of the determination of *equilibrium* income?

For example, suppose autonomous investment spending increases and that firms raise output to meet the increased demand. This, of course, raises income and evokes an increase in consumer spending which in turn induces a further rise in income. But the story does not stop here, because consumption only gradually rises to the full extent implied by the long-run consumption-income relation. Therefore the manner in which households form expectations about permanent income will affect the time path of consumption-income relation. Therefore, the manner in which households form expectations about permanent income will affect the time path of and, at the same time, use the opportunity to show the implications of permanent-income theory for saving behavior. We assume throughout that individuals have no special knowledge about the permanence of changes in income, and thus use Equation (13) to form their estimates.

Permanent Income and Saving

Our permanent-income theory of consumption gave us in Equation (14) a consumption function with current and lagged income as determinants of current consumption spending. The consumption function of course implies a saving function which is derived using the definition of saving and substituting from (14) to obtain

$$S = Y - C = (1 - c\theta)Y - c(1 - \theta)Y_{-1} \qquad (16)$$

The saving function has two important properties. First, if income is constant ($Y = Y_{-1}$), then saving is proportional to income. This is the long-run saving function shown in Equation (16*a*)

$$S = (1 - c)Y \qquad (16a)$$

Second, the short-run propensity to save, given Y_{-1}, is equal to $s = 1 - c\theta$ and thus is larger than the long-run propensity.[18] This reflects the fact that consumers interpret a current change in income partly as transitory and do not adjust consumption fully; accordingly, a transitory increase in income leads to a relatively large increase in saving. If the increase in income is sustained, then, over time, consumption adjusts and savings decline to the long-run level implied by Equation (16*a*). In Figure 5-4, we show the long-run saving function that makes saving proportional to income. We also show the short-run saving function, drawn for a given level of past income, Y_{-1}. The two schedules intersect at the level of income $Y = Y_{-1}$ since, as argued above, if income is constant, we are on our long-run saving function. If current income, Y, exceeds last period's income, saving is above the long-run level, and if income is below the level of last period, the converse will be true. The figure clearly reflects the fact that the short-run propensity to save is higher than the long-run propensity.

[18] Remember θ is a fraction—say $\theta = .6$—and hence $1 - c\theta$ is larger than $1 - c$.

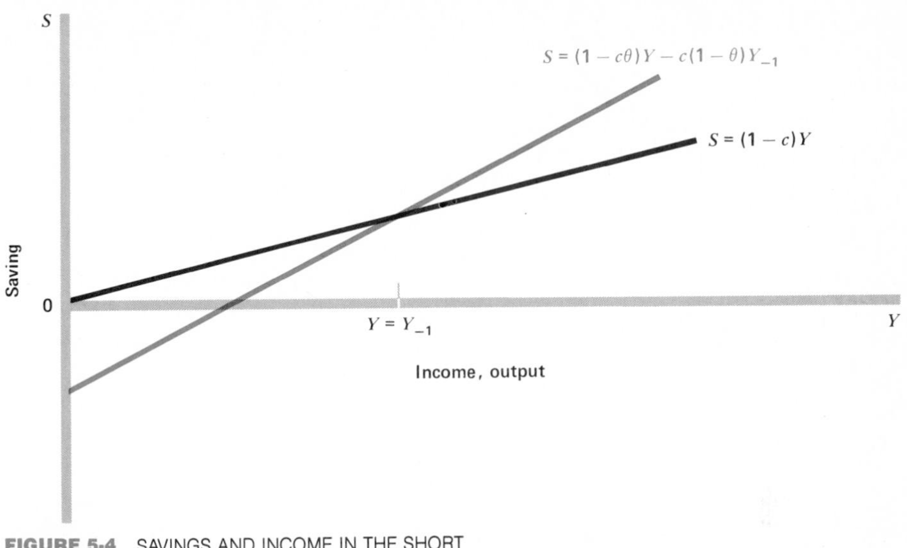

FIGURE 5-4 SAVINGS AND INCOME IN THE SHORT AND LONG RUNS

Consider now using permanent-income saving behavior in a more complete macroeconomic setting. Assume we look at the models of income determination in Chapter 3, where assets markets were disregarded. In that setting, the equilibrium output level is determined by the equality of income and aggregate demand, or equivalently, by the equality of saving and investment. (We disregard the government sector here.) Using our saving function and treating investment as exogeneous, we can write the equilibrium condition, $I = S$, as

$$\bar{I} = (1 - c\theta)Y - c(1 - \theta)Y_{-1} \tag{17}$$

In Figure 5-5, we add the level of investment, $\bar{I}$, to the diagram. The initial equilibrium is at point E. At point E, saving—as given by the short-term saving function—is equal to investment, and thus the equilibrium condition in Equation (17) is satisfied. We also assume that we have reached a *full* equilibrium in that saving has fully adjusted to the level of income and we are saving according to permanent income. Hence, we are also on the long-run saving function.

The Adjustment Process

Suppose now that there is a permanent increase in investment to the level $\bar{I}'$. The investment schedule shifts upward. At the initial income level, Y_0, investment exceeds saving, there is an excess demand for goods, and

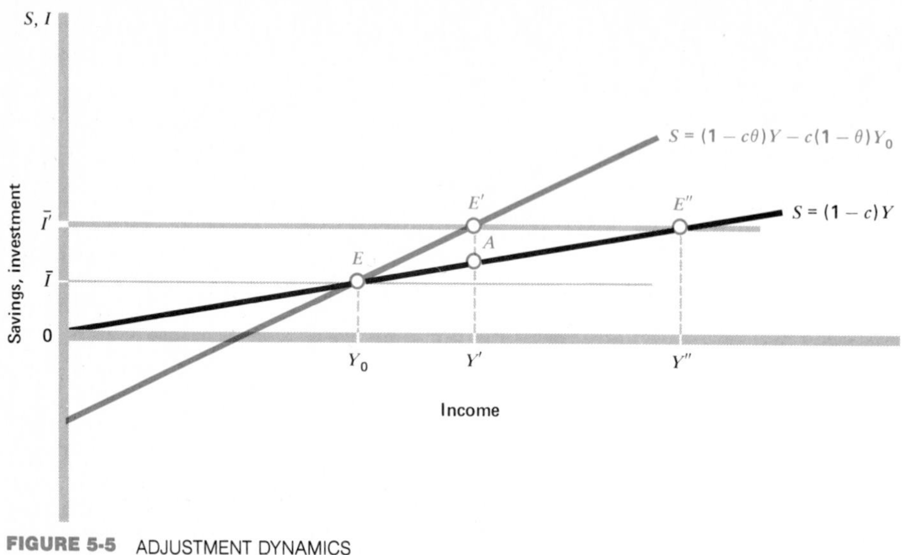

FIGURE 5-5 ADJUSTMENT DYNAMICS

accordingly, income expands until we reach a level Y'. At Y', short run saving is equal to investment. Much of the increased income is saved, therefore freeing resources to meet the increased level of investment. But the equilibrium is only a short-run one because, as it persists, households recognize that the increase in income is not transitory. They adjust their permanent-income forecast and accordingly revise upward their consumption plans. The short-run saving schedule in the next period would shift downward (not drawn) through point A. The increased consumption would create excess demand for goods and thus lead to a further income expansion. The process of income expansion and revision of permanent income will continue over time until we reach point E''. Point E'' marks the new, long-run equilibrium or full equilibrium. Here, long-run saving is equal to investment. When we have reached that level of income, saving has fully adjusted and no more income changes take place.

There are two important implications of our analysis. The first is the distinction between short-run and long-run multipliers. In the short run, an increase in investment leads to an income expansion to point E'. In the long run, we have a much larger expansion to point E''. The difference arises because the short-run propensity to consume is small—because income changes are taken as transitory rather than permanent—and hence there is relatively little induced spending. The second implication is that the adjustment process to a change in autonomous spending is a *dynamic* one. It is a process that occurs over time, rather than instantaneously, because only over time do households adjust their forecasts of permanent income and hence of planned saving and consumption. These adjustments in turn feed back to the equilibrium level of income and imply that output adjustment occurs over time.

The dynamic adjustment of output to a change in autonomous spending can be represented in terms of Figure 5-5 as the movement from E to E' to E''. Over time, income increases from period to period and we can plot, as in Figure 5-6, each period's level of income. The initial disturbance immediately raises income from Y_0 to Y', or gives us a first-period increase in income of ΔY_1. In the second period, as households recognize the persistence of higher income, they raise their spending and thus induce a further rise in income to the level Y_2. The second-period rise in income, ΔY_2, is thus entirely due to the adjustment of consumption to the revision in permanent-income estimates. The same is true for the subsequent income adjustments. The time pattern of changes in income caused by the increases in $\bar{I}$ is called the *dynamic multiplier* of $\bar{I}$.

An exercise at the end of this chapter asks you to show that the period-to-period changes in income following the increase in autonomous investment get smaller and smaller, as is shown by the shaded areas in Figure 5-6. The fact that these changes occur over time and that the

FIGURE 5-6 THE INCOME ADJUSTMENT PROCESS

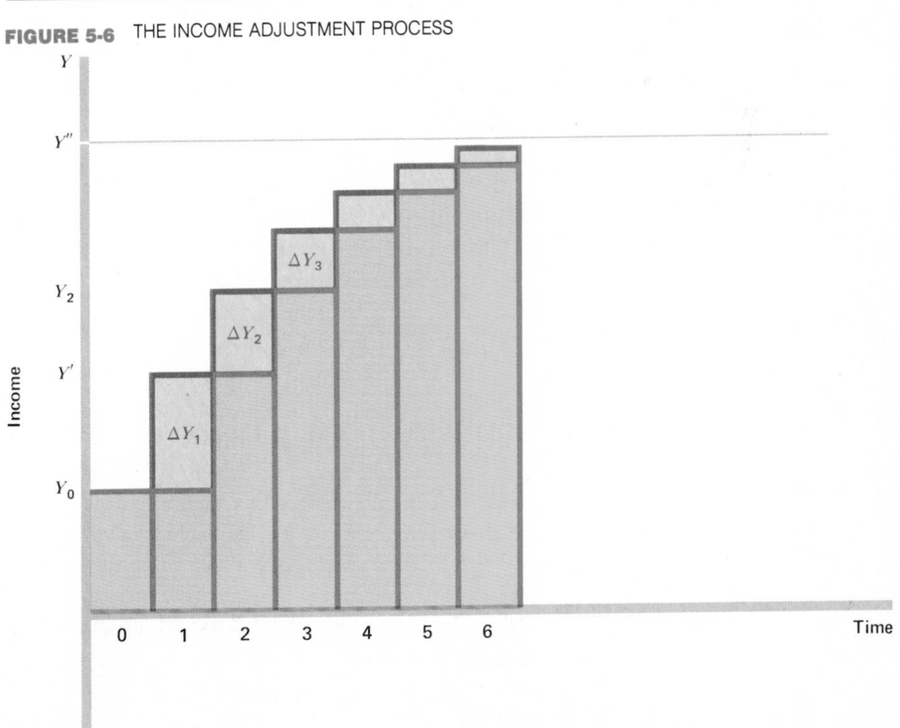

second, third, and subsequent period income changes may be quite sizable has important implications for policy, to which we turn now.

Policy Implications

Suppose we have a permanent decline in investment expenditure. With output demand determined, the decline in spending would of course lead to a fall in output and employment, occurring over a period of time.

Suppose the government wants to offset the reduction in aggregate demand by using tax cuts to keep income at the full-employment level. Since consumption adjusts only gradually to changes in income resulting from both the initial fall in investment and tax cuts, the policy maker who wants to stabilize output *over time* will have to know about the adjustment pattern of consumption so as not to overreact. The problems may be further complicated, as we discuss in Chapter 9, by the fact that frequently the policy maker too reacts only with a lag to changed circumstances.

In the short run, consumption does not respond fully to changes in income. Therefore it takes a relatively large tax cut to obtain a given change in consumption with which to offset the decline in investment. Over time, though, consumption adjusts to the change in disposable income and the tax cut that was initially just sufficient to offset reduced investment now turns out to be too generous. The compensating policy must therefore be one of a tax cut that is *front-loaded* and gradually phased down to the long-run level. The difference between the short-run and long-run tax cuts is determined by the relative size of the short-run and long-run tax multipliers.

In Chapters 9 and 10 we shall return to the question of lags in behavior and the implications for policy. We simply note here that the question has indeed been critical in an important policy context. The policy error involved the tax increase in 1968 which the public recognized as not permanent. The tax increase was needed to reduce aggregate demand. Given that the tax increase was not considered permanent, it had very little impact on aggregate demand and certainly a smaller impact than the policy makers had predicted. By contrast, a permanent tax increase, if it is perceived as such, may well have a strong immediate impact on demand as people immediately make the full adjustment in their calculation of permanent income.

Indeed, the observant reader will recall that we assumed consumers had no special knowledge about the nature of the changes in income they experienced as a result both of the initial change in investment and of subsequent tax adjustments. Remarkably enough, if consumers knew that the investment shift was permanent, and if they could be persuaded that the change in government policy was permanent, a one-time reduction in taxes, calculated using the long-run multiplier implied by the consumption function, would precisely stabilize income. For, in that case, the response to the fall in investment would recognize the permanent nature of the change, implying the long-run multiplier is relevant, and the response to the tax change would also recognize the permanent nature of the change. Consumption would adjust immediately, rather than gradually over the course of time.

The alternative theories of consumption we have presented in this chapter all include current disposable income among the factors that explain consumption behavior. Each, however, points to other factors that also affect consumption. These other factors—wealth and lagged income—have to be taken into account when consumption spending is predicted for policy purposes. Large-scale econometric models do indeed embody more sophisticated consumption theories than the simple consumption function (1) of this and earlier chapters.

5-6 SUMMARY

This chapter has studied the consumption function in great detail.

1 The chapter starts out with the simple Keynesian consumption function:

$$C = 6.71 + 0.90Y_d \tag{2}$$

and finds that such a consumption function accounts well for observed consumption behavior. The equation suggests that out of an additional dollar of disposable income, 90 cents is spent on consumption. The consumption function implies, too, that the ratio of consumption to income, C/Y_d, declines somewhat with the level of income.

2 Early empirical work on short-run consumption behavior showed that the marginal propensity to consume was lower than that found in longer-period studies. The evidence revealed also that the average propensity to consume declined with the level of income. Postwar studies, by contrast, find a relatively constant average propensity to consume of about 0.9.

3 The evidence is reconciled by a reconsideration of consumption theory. Individuals will want to maintain relatively smooth consumption profiles over their lifetime. Their consumption behavior is geared to their long-term consumption opportunities—permanent income or lifetime income plus wealth. With such a view, current income is only one of the determinants of consumption spending. Wealth and expected income play a role, too. A consumption function that represents this idea is

$$C = a\frac{W}{P} + b\theta Y_d + b(1-\theta)Y_{d-1} \qquad (15)$$

which allows for the role of real wealth, W/P, current disposable income, Y_d, and lagged disposable income, Y_{d-1}.

4 The relative-income hypothesis argues that current consumption is related not only to current income but also to previous peak income. The argument for this is that individuals find it difficult to reduce rates of consumption to which they have become accustomed.

5 Lagged adjustment of consumption to income results in a gradual adjustment of the level of income in the economy to changes in autonomous spending and other economic changes. An increase in autonomous spending raises income. But the adjustment process is spread out over time because the rising level of income raises consumption only gradually. This adjustment process is described by dynamic multipliers that show by how much income changes in each period following a change in autonomous spending (or other exogenous variables).

6 The dynamic adjustment of the economy to changes in policy variables, such as a change in government spending or transfers, creates a problem for policy making. The analysis of Section 5-4 shows that the policy maker needs detailed information about the dynamic responses of the economy, if policy is not to result in income levels that differ from the target levels. In a dynamic setting, the making of policy requires the policy maker to consider how much any particular policy action will affect income in each time period and to calculate *time paths* for policy variables that will bring about the desired performance.

PROBLEMS

1 What is the significance of the ratio of consumption to GNP in terms of the level of economic activity? Would you expect it to be higher or lower than normal during a recession (or depression)? Do you think the ratio would be higher in developed or underdeveloped countries? Why?

The Life-Cycle Hypothesis

2 The text implies that the ratio of consumption to accumulated savings declines over time until retirement.
(*a*) Why? What assumption about consumption behavior leads to this result?
(*b*) What happens to this ratio after retirement?

3 (*a*) Suppose you earn just as much as your neighbor but are in much better health and expect to live longer than she does. Would you consume more or

less than she does? Why? Derive your answer from Equation (7).

(*b*) According to the life-cycle hypothesis, what would the effect of the Social Security system be on your average propensity to consume out of (disposable) income?

(*c*) How would Equation (10) be modified for an individual who expects to receive $\$X$ per year of retirement benefits? Verify your result in 3*b*.

4 Give an intuitive interpretation of the marginal propensities to consume out of wealth and income at time T in the individual's lifetime in Equation (10).

*5 In Equation (7), consumption in each year of working life is given by

$$C = \left[\frac{N}{L}\right] Z \qquad (7)$$

In Equation (10), consumption is given as

$$C = a\frac{W}{P} + cZ \qquad a \equiv \frac{1}{L-T} \qquad c \equiv \frac{N-T}{L-T} \qquad (10)$$

Show that Equations (7) and (10) are consistent for an individual who started life with zero wealth and has been saving for T years. [*Hint*: First, calculate the individual's wealth after T years of saving at rate $Z - C$. Then calculate the level of consumption implied by Equation (10) when wealth is at the level you have computed.]

Permanent-Income Hypothesis

6 In terms of permanent-income hypothesis, would you consume more of your Christmas bonus if:

(*a*) You knew there was a bonus every year.

(*b*) This was the only year such bonuses were given out.

7 Suppose that permanent income is calculated as the average of income over the past 5 years; that is,

$$Y^P = \tfrac{1}{5}(Y + Y_{-1} + Y_{-2} + Y_{-3} + Y_{-4})$$

Suppose, further, that consumption is given by $C = 0.9Y^P$.

(*a*) If you have earned \$10,000 per year for the past 10 years, what is your permanent income?

(*b*) Suppose next year (period $t + 1$) you earn \$15,000. What is your new Y^P?

(*c*) What is your consumption this year and next year?

(*d*) What is your short-run MPC? Long-run?

(*e*) Assuming you continue to earn \$15,000 starting in period $t + 1$, graph the value of your permanent income in each period using the equation above.

8 Explain why good gamblers (and thieves) might be expected to live very well even in years when they don't do well at all.

*9 The graph (bottom of page) shows the lifetime earnings profile of a person who lives for four periods and earns incomes of \$30, \$60, and \$90 in the first three periods of the life cycle. There are no earnings during retirement.

(*a*) You are asked to determine the level of consumption, compatible with the budget constraint, for someone who wants an even consumption profile throughout the life cycle. Indicate in which periods the person saves and dissaves and in what amounts.

(*b*) Assume now that contrary to 9(*a*), there is no possibility for borrowing. The credit markets are closed to the individual. Under this assumption, what is the flow of consumption the individual will pick over the life cycle? In providing an answer, continue to assume that if possible, an even flow of consumption is preferred.

(*c*) Assume next that the person described in 9(*b*) receives an increase in wealth or nonlabor income. The increase in wealth is equal to \$13. How will that wealth be allocated over the life cycle with and without access to the credit market? How would your answer differ if the increase in wealth were \$23?

*10 Consider the consumption function in Equation (15). Assume autonomous investment spending is constant, as is government spending. The economy is close to full employment and the government wishes to maintain aggregate demand precisely constant. In these circumstances, assume there is an increase in real wealth of \$10 billion. What change in income taxes will maintain constant the equilibrium level of income in the present period? What change is required to maintain income constant in the long run?

*11 Assume the income tax rate is $t = 0.2$. Using Equation (15) and the information from Section 5-5, determine the size of the short-run and long-run multipliers.

12 Equation (15) shows consumption as a function of wealth, current and lagged disposable income. To reconcile that consumption function with permanent income expectations formation, you are asked to use Equation (13) and the consumption function

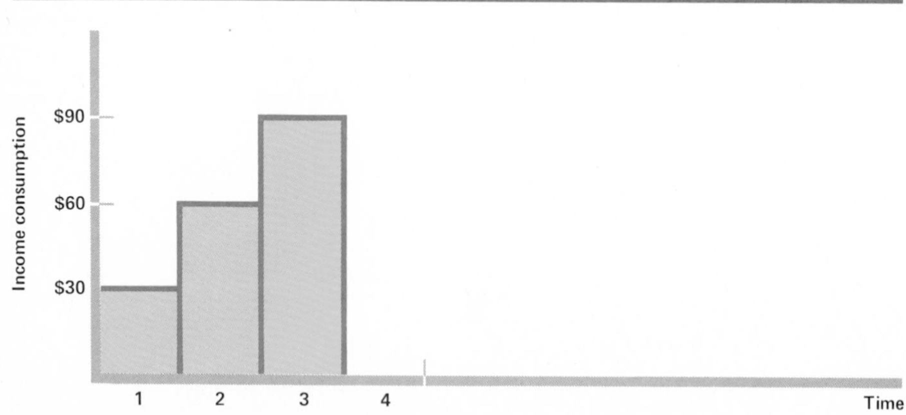

$$C = .045 \frac{W}{P} + .55\, Y_d + .17\, Y_{d_{-1}}$$

to determine the magnitude of θ and $(1 - \theta)$ that is implied by Equation (15).

*Adjustment and Dynamics

*13 Consider the equilibrium condition in Equation (17).

(*a*) Given the past level of income, Y_{-1}, what is equilibrium current income? Give the answer both algebraically, solving for Y, and geometrically.

(*b*) Define the change in income $\Delta Y = Y - Y_1$ and use this definition to rewrite Equation (17) as

$$\bar{I} = (1 - c\theta)\Delta Y + (1 - c)Y_{-1}$$

or

$$\Delta Y = \frac{1}{1 - c\theta}[\bar{I} - (1 - c)Y_{-1}]$$

Show this equation in a diagram with ΔY and Y on the axes.

(*c*) Using your diagram developed in 13(*b*), what is the long-run level of income ($\Delta Y = 0$)?

(*d*) Consider now a permanent increase in investment to $\bar{I}'$. Use your diagram to show the change in income in the first period and in the long run.

(*e*) Assume $\bar{I} = 50$, $c = 0.8$, and $\theta = 0.75$. Calculate the initial full equilibrium value of income ($Y = Y_{-1}$). Next, consider an increase in investment to $\bar{I}' = 100$. Given Y_{-1} calculated before, what is the new level of income? What happens in the second period? What is the change in long-run income?

*14 Here is a challenge to your ability to develop diagrams. You are asked to show short-run and long-run income determination in the 45° diagram.

Draw the short-run and long-run consumption functions and the aggregate demand schedule with $I = \bar{I}$.

(*b*) Show the initial full equilibrium.

(*c*) Show the short-run and long-run effects of increased investment on equilibrium income.

6

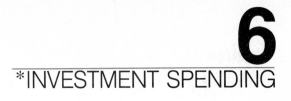

*INVESTMENT SPENDING

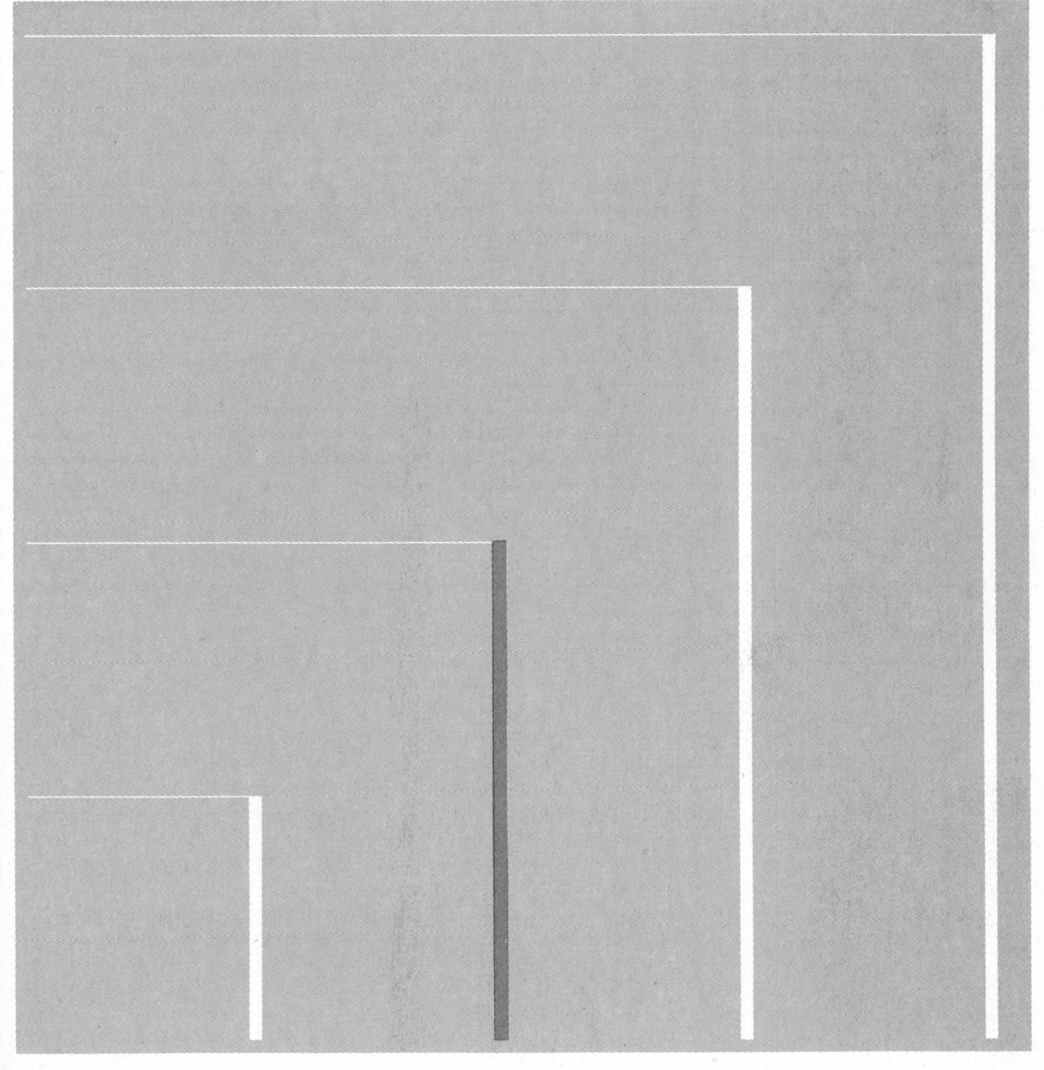

In this chapter we continue our in-depth analysis of the macroeconomic relationships of the IS-LM model studied in Chapter 4. Chapter 5 moved beyond the simple consumption function of Chapter 3, paying particular attention to the role of lags and the precise way in which income enters the consumption function. Similarly, this chapter moves beyond the simple investment function of Chapter 4, in which investment was treated as a function of the interest rate. It provides a theoretical foundation for understanding how interest rates affect the level of investment. In addition, we will see how lags and variables other than interest rates—including tax rates—also affect the rate of investment.

Why study investment spending? In the first place, investment is a significant component of aggregate demand. The share of investment spending in GNP is shown in Chart 6-1. In 1979, it accounted for 16 percent of aggregate demand, and it was as high as 19 percent of aggregate demand in 1950. Clearly, investment spending constitutes a much smaller part of aggregate demand than consumption spending. Nonetheless, it plays an

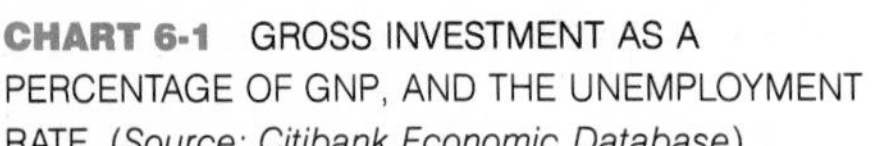

CHART 6-1 GROSS INVESTMENT AS A PERCENTAGE OF GNP, AND THE UNEMPLOYMENT RATE (*Source: Citibank Economic Database*)

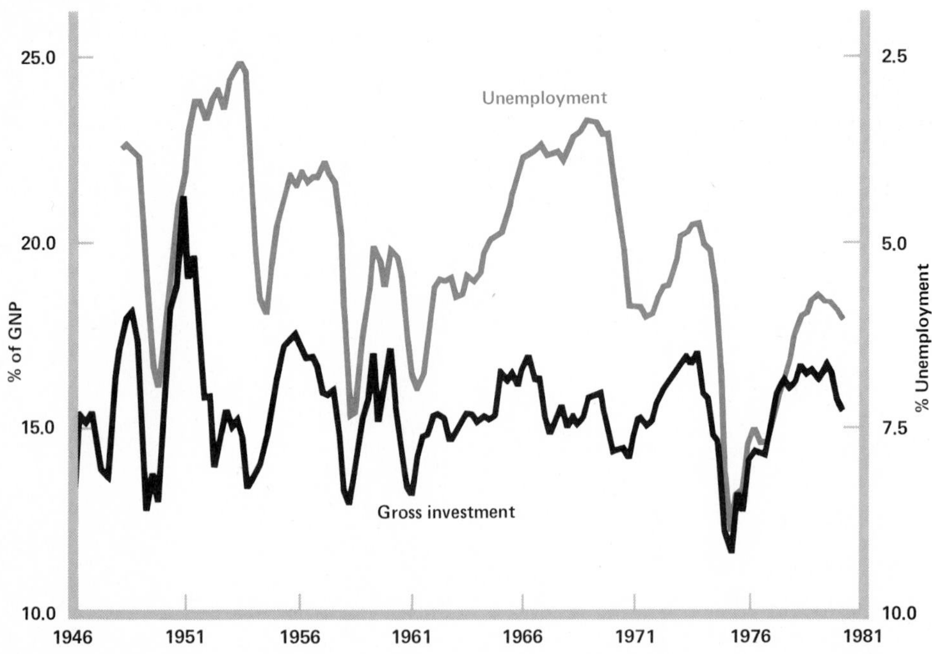

Note: The unemployment rate is on an inverted scale.

important role in the fluctuations of GNP over the course of the business cycle because it varies proportionately much more than consumption spending. Chart 6-1 also highlights the role of investment in relation to the business cycle. Gross investment as a percentage of GNP is plotted along with the unemployment rate (note that the scale for the unemployment rate is reversed). There is quite clearly a relationship between fluctuations in the level of economic activity, as indicated by the unemployment rate, and the share of investment spending in income. When unemployment is high, investment spending as a fraction of income is low, and vice versa. Indeed, this relationship goes back a long way. During the Great Depression, investment spending was under 4 percent of GNP in both 1932 and 1933.

Second, investment is important because it is significantly affected by both monetary and fiscal policy. For instance, changes in the investment tax credit (to be described later) are a standard tool of fiscal policy, designed to affect investment spending. Monetary policy, too, has an important effect on investment, particularly on residential construction. Thus, changes in investment spending constitute one of the major channels by which monetary and fiscal policy affect aggregate demand.

One simple relationship is vital to the understanding of investment. *Investment is spending devoted to increasing or maintaining the stock of capital.* The stock of capital consists of the factories, machines, offices, and other durable products used in the process of production. The capital stock also includes residential housing as well as inventories. Investment is spending that adds to these components of capital stock. Recall the distinction drawn in Chapter 2 between *gross* and *net investment*. Gross investment represents total additions to the capital stock. Net investment subtracts depreciation—the reduction in the capital stock that occurs each period through wear and tear and the simple ravages of time—from gross investment. Net investment thus measures the increase in the capital stock in a given period of time.

In this chapter we disaggregate investment spending into three categories. The first is *business fixed investment*, consisting of business firms' spending on durable machinery, equipment and structures, such as factories and machines. The second is *residential investment*, consisting largely of investment in housing. And the third is *inventory investment*, some elements of which were discussed in Chapter 3.

In 1979, investment spending in the three categories was as shown in Table 6-1. Chart 6-2 shows the components of investment spending in the post-World War II period. Inventory investment and residential investment fluctuate more, as a share of GNP, than business fixed investment does. Business fixed investment is, however, the largest component of investment spending. Note that the negative inventory investment in 1975

TABLE 6-1 GROSS DOMESTIC PRIVATE INVESTMENT IN 1978 *(in billions of dollars)*

1. Business fixed investment	$254.9
2. Residential investment	114.1
Total fixed investment	369.0
3. Change in inventories	18.2
Gross private domestic investment	$387.2

Source: Citibank Economic Database.

seen in Chart 6-2 is unusual, and that over most of the postwar period, inventory investment has been positive.[1]

In the remainder of this chapter, we develop theories and discuss evidence about the determinants of the rate of investment in each of the three major categories shown in Chart 6-2. We will develop what look like

[1] How can inventory investment be negative? Recall that investment is spending on *increases* in capital. In some years, inventories are actually reduced rather than increased, and it is in those years that inventory investment is negative.

CHART 6-2 COMPONENTS OF INVESTMENT SPENDING AS A PERCENTAGE OF GNP *(Source: Citibank Economic Database)*

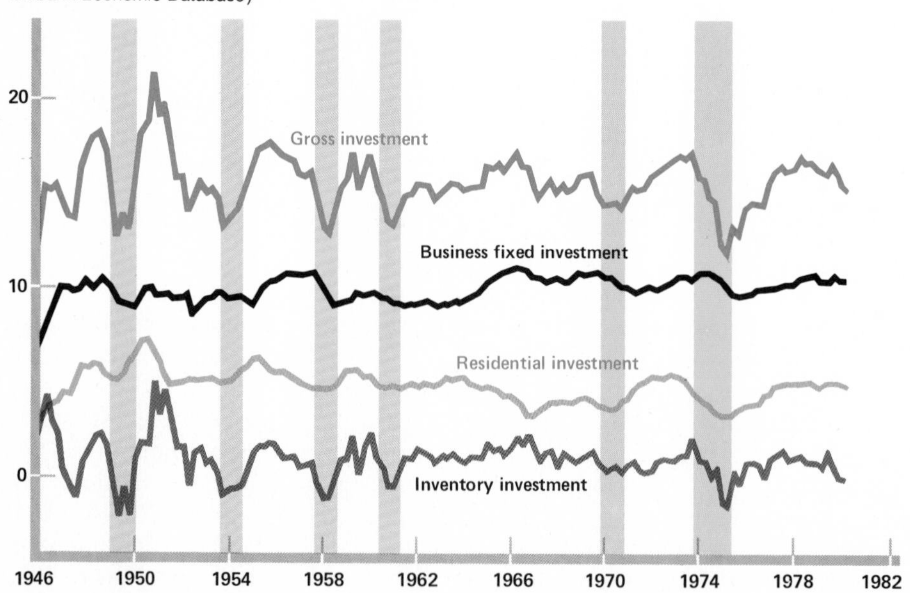

Note: Shaded regions indicate recessions.

different models to explain each of the categories of investment spending. However, as we discuss in Section 6-4, the theories are essentially very similar, sharing a common view of the interaction between a desired capital stock and the rate at which the economy adjusts toward that desired stock.

6-1 BUSINESS FIXED INVESTMENT

The machinery, equipment, and structures used in the production of goods and services constitute the *stock* of business fixed capital. Our analysis of business fixed investment proceeds in two stages. First, we ask how much capital firms would like to use, given the costs and returns of using capital and the level of output they expect to produce. That is, we ask what determines the *desired capital stock*. The desired capital stock is the capital stock that firms would like to have in the long run, abstracting from the delays they face in adjusting their use of capital. However, because it takes time to order new machines, build factories, and install the machines, firms cannot instantly adjust the stock of capital used in production. Second, therefore, we discuss the rate at which firms adjust from their existing capital stock toward the desired level over the course of time. The rate of adjustment determines how much firms spend on adding to the capital stock in each period; that is, it determines the rate of investment.

The Desired Capital Stock: Overview

Firms use capital, along with labor, to produce goods and services for sale. In deciding how much capital to use in production, they have to balance the contribution that more capital makes to their profits against the cost of using more capital. The contribution that an extra unit of capital makes to profits is determined by the *marginal product of capital*, the extra amount of output that can be produced by using that unit of capital. The cost of using more capital is known as the *rental cost of capital*, or the *user cost of capital*.

To derive the rental cost of capital, we think of the firm as financing the purchase of the capital (whether the firm produces the capital itself or buys it from some other firm) by borrowing, at an interest cost i. In order to obtain the services of an extra unit of capital, in each period the firm must pay the interest cost i for each dollar of capital that it buys.[2] Thus the basic measure of the rental cost of capital is the interest rate. Later we shall go into more detail about the rental cost of capital, but for the meantime we shall think of the interest rate as determining the rental cost.

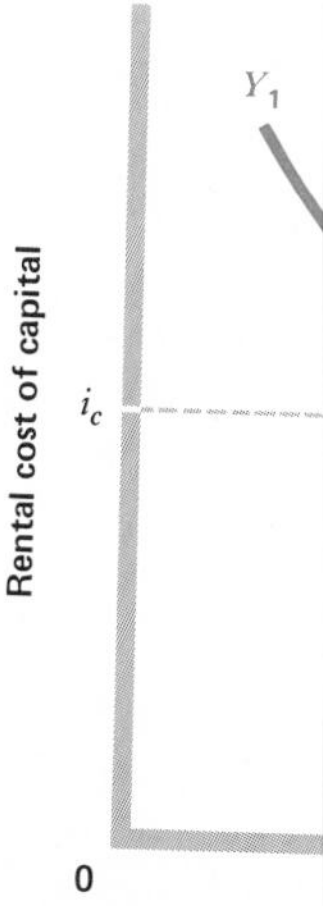

[2] Even if the firm finances the investment out of profits it has made in the past—retained earnings—it should still think of the interest rate as the cost of using the new capital, since it could otherwise have lent out those funds and earned interest on them, or paid them out as dividends to shareholders.

capital even when its marginal productivity is quite low. If the rental cost of capital is high, the firm will be willing to use capital only if its marginal productivity is high—which means that the firm will not want to use very much capital. In producing a higher level of output, say Y_2, the firm will use both more capital and more labor, given the rental cost of capital.[3] Therefore, at higher levels of output, the desired capital stock is higher.

The Cobb-Douglas Production Function

While Equation (1) provides the general relationship determining the desired capital stock, a particular form of the equation, based on the Cobb-Douglas production function,[4] is frequently used in studies of investment behavior. The particular equation that is used is[5]

$$K^* = \frac{aY}{i_c} \tag{2}$$

where a is a constant. In this case, the desired capital stock varies in proportion to output. Given output, the desired capital stock varies inversely with the rental cost of capital.

Expected Output

In determining the desired capital stock, the relevant time period for which the decision on the capital stock applies is obviously an important issue. In

[3] Throughout this discussion, we have implicitly been assuming that the real wage paid to labor is given and does not change as the rental cost of capital changes.

[4] The Cobb-Douglas production function is written in the form

$$Y = N^{1-a}K^{a} \qquad 1 > a > 0$$

where N is the amount of labor used. This production function is particularly popular because it is easy to handle, and also because it appears to fit the facts of United States economic experience quite well. The coefficient a appearing in Eq. (2) is the same as the a of the production function. The reader trained in calculus will want to show that a is the share of capital in total income.

[5] We draw attention here to a very subtle point. Equation (2) gives the marginal product of capital (*MPK*) when the *input of labor* is held fixed, while in Figs. 6-1 and 6-2 we work with the *MPK* when labor is being adjusted so that *output* is kept fixed. The desired capital stock that corresponds to Figs. 6-1 and 6-2 is

$$K^* = \left[\frac{aw}{(1-a)\,i_c}\right]^{1-a} Y \tag{2a}$$

where w is the real wage.
Equation (2′), like Equation (2), implies that desired capital is proportional to Y and varies inversely with the rental cost of capital. We use (2) rather than (2′) in the text because it is the form that has been used in empirical studies.

this section we are discussing the capital stock that the firm desires to hold at some future time. Accordingly, the level of output in Equations (1) and (2) should be the level of output which firms expect to be producing at that time. For some investments—such as that in machinery to produce hula hoops—the future time at which the output will be produced is a matter of months or only weeks. For other investments—such as that in airplane factories—the future time at which the output will be produced is years away.

This suggests that the notion of permanent income (in this case, permanent output) is relevant to investment as well as consumption. For longer-lived investments, the firm's capital demand is governed primarily by its views on the level of output it will be producing on average in the future. The firm's long-run demand for business fixed capital, depending on the normal or permanent level of output, is thus relatively independent of the current level of output, and depends on *expectations* of future output levels. However, it is affected by current output to the extent that current output affects expectations of permanent output.[6]

Summary on the Desired Capital Stock

It is worthwhile stepping back for a moment to summarize the main results so far.

1 The firm's demand for capital—the desired capital stock K^*—depends on the rental cost of capital i_c and the expected level of output.
2 Firms balance the costs and benefits of using capital. The lower the rental cost of capital, the larger the optimal level of capital relative to output. This relation reflects the lower marginal productivity of capital when it is used relatively intensively. The intensive use of capital will be profitable only if the rental cost of capital is low.
3 The higher the level of output, the larger the desired capital stock.
4 The firm plans its capital stock in relation to expected future or permanent output.
5 Current output affects capital demand to the extent that it affects expectations about future output.

The Rental Cost of Capital Again

We have already introduced the notion of the rental or user cost of capital in determining the firm's desired capital stock. As a first approximation, we identified the rental cost of capital with the interest rate, on the argument that firms would have to borrow to finance their use of capital. Now we go into more detail on the costs per period of using capital.

[6] The role of permanent income in investment has been emphasized by Robert Eisner. Much of his work is summarized in his book *Factors in Business Investment* (Cambridge, Mass.: Ballinger, 1978).

To use capital for a single period, say a year, the firm can be thought of as buying the capital with borrowed funds and paying the interest on the borrowing. At the end of the year, the firm will still have some of the capital left. But the capital is likely to have depreciated over the course of the year. We shall assume that the firm intends to continue using the remaining capital in production in future years, and that its depreciation simply represents the using up of the capital in the process of production—physical wear and tear. We shall now examine the rental cost, taking into account interest costs and depreciation. Although taxes affect the cost to the firm of using capital, we shall for the meantime ignore taxes and return to them later.

Leaving aside taxes, we want now to examine the two elements in the rental cost of capital in more detail. For the moment, let us write the interest cost as i. Insofar as depreciation is concerned, we assume that a fixed proportion d of the capital is used up per period. The depreciation cost, per dollar of capital, is d.[7] The rental cost, or user cost, of capital, per dollar's worth of capital, which we denote by i_c, is therefore

$$i_c \equiv i + d \tag{3}$$

A simple numerical example should help in understanding Equation (3). Suppose the interest rate is 10 percent per year and the rate of depreciation is 15 percent. That means that by the end of the year, the firm will have had to spend 15 cents per dollar of capital to maintain capital's production efficiency in the face of depreciation. The costs to the firm of using the capital for the year are then the interest cost, 10 cents per dollar of capital, and the depreciation cost, 15 cents per dollar of capital. The cost of using capital for a year is thus 25 cents per dollar's worth of capital.

The Real Rate of Interest

It is time now to examine the interest component of the rental cost of capital in more detail. We have not, so far, distinguished between the *real* and the *nominal* rates of interest. The real rate of interest is the nominal rate of interest minus the rate of inflation. In general, someone borrowing at a stated nominal rate of interest, say 10 percent, does not know what the rate of inflation over the period of the borrowing will be. Accordingly, the real rate of interest relevant when a loan transaction is entered into is the *expected* real rate of interest—the stated nominal interest rate minus the rate of inflation expected over the period of the loan.

The notion of the real rate of interest is extremely important. Suppose

[7] Why is depreciation considered as a cost? We want to remind ourselves that the firm continues using the capital and therefore has to devote expenditures to maintaining the productive efficiency of capital and thus wear and tear. We are assuming that per dollar of capital, d dollars per period are required to maintain productive efficiency.

that the nominal interest rate, the rate stated in the loan agreement, is 10 percent. Then suppose also that prices are rising at 10 percent. Someone borrowing \$100 at the beginning of the year pays back \$110 at the end of the year. But those dollars in which repayment is made buy less goods than the dollars lent at the beginning of the year when the loan was made. If the inflation rate is 10 percent, then the \$110 paid at the end of the year buys the same amount of goods that could have been bought with the original \$100 at the beginning of the year. In *real* terms, in terms of the goods which the money can buy, the lender has no more at the end than at the beginning of the year. Thus the *real* interest rate actually received was zero, even though the *nominal* interest rate was 10 percent. Putting things slightly differently, given the *nominal* interest rate, the higher the rate of inflation, the lower the *real* interest rate. In practice, nominal interest rates tend to be higher when inflation is higher.

Now, it is the *expected real* rate of interest that should enter the calculation of the rental cost of capital. Why? The firm is borrowing in order to produce goods for sale. On average, across all firms, it is reasonable to believe that the prices of the goods the firms sell will be rising along with the general price level. Thus the value of what the firm will be producing in the future will be rising with the price level, but the nominal amount of interest it has to pay back on account of its borrowings does not rise with the price level. The real value of the debt it has incurred by borrowing will be falling over time, as a result of inflation, and it should take that reduction in the real value of its outstanding debts into account in deciding how much capital to employ. To put it differently, the firm will be paying off its debts with dollars of lower real value than the dollars it borrowed.

Accordingly, we can be more precise in the way we write Equation (3) for the rental cost of capital. We write the rental cost of capital, taking account of expected inflation at the rate π^*, as

$$i_c \equiv i_r + d \equiv i - \pi^* + d \tag{4}$$

where i_r is the real interest rate, i the nominal interest rate, and

$$i_r \equiv i - \pi^* \tag{5}$$

Equation (5) states that the real rate of interest is the nominal interest rate minus the expected rate of inflation. Implicitly, Equation (5) refers to the expected real rate of interest. At the end of the period, when the rate of inflation is known, we can also state what the *actual* or realized real rate of interest for the period was—namely, the nominal interest rate i minus the actual rate of inflation.

To reiterate, it is important to note that the interest rate relevant to the firms's demand for capital is the *real* rate, and not the nominal rate. This makes it clear that the nominal rate of interest is not a good guide to the

credit, will each increase the rate of investment. We thus have derived a quite complete theory of business fixed investment that includes many of the factors we should expect to affect the rate of investment. And the theory of investment embodied in Equation (7) also contains aspects of *dynamic behavior*—that is, of behavior that depends on values of economic variables in periods other than the current period.

There are two sources of dynamic behavior in Equation (7). The first arises from expectations. The K^* term depends on the firm's estimate of future or permanent output. To the extent that the firm forms its estimates of permanent output as a weighted average of past output levels, there will be lags in the adjustment of the level of permanent output to the actual level of output. Accordingly, the desired capital stock will adjust only slowly over time to a change in the level of output. And in turn, investment will therefore also adjust slowly to a change in the level of output. The second source of dynamic behavior arises from adjustment lags, in the specification that firms plan to close only a proportion of the gap between

FIGURE 6-3 ADJUSTMENT OF THE CAPITAL STOCK

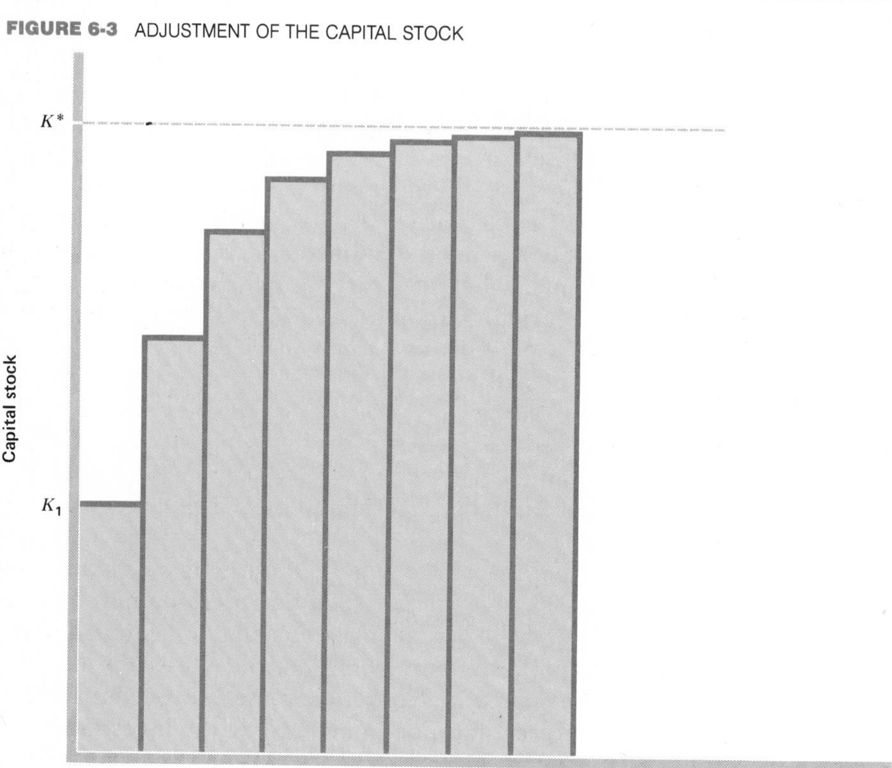

the actual and desired capital stocks each period, as shown in Figure 6-3. The adjustment lags produce lagged response of investment to changes in the variables that affect the desired capital stock.

Empirical Results

At this point it is useful to ask how the investment model we have developed in Equation (7) performs empirically. To use Equation (7), it is necessary to substitute some specific equation for K^*, the desired capital stock. Frequently the much-used Cobb-Douglas form, Equation (2), is chosen. Using Equation (2) in Equation (7) yields a (net) investment function of the form

$$I = \lambda \left(\frac{aY}{i_c} - K_{-1} \right) \tag{8}$$

The rental cost of capital, i_c in Equation (8), is as in Equation (4), but also adjusted for taxes.

Empirical work, in particular that of Dale Jorgenson and his associates, shows that an investment function including the variables in Equation (8) provides a reasonable explanation of the behavior of business fixed investment. However, the form shown in Equation (8) can be improved upon by allowing more scope for lagged or slow adjustment.[14] As it stands, Equation (8), with the output variable not being explicitly permanent output, shows an immediate impact from a change in current output to investment spending. Moreover, Equation (8) implies that if the output increase were maintained, the first-period adjustment to the increase would be larger than the second-period adjustment, and so forth, as suggested by Figure 6-3. However, the empirical evidence suggests that the adjustment instead takes the bell-shaped form shown in Figure 6-4. The major impact of a change in output on actual investment occurs with a two-period (year) lag. The short-run impact on investment is less than the impact 2 years later. Investment spending, like consumption spending, adjusts only slowly over time.

There are two, not mutually exclusive, explanations for the behavior shown in Figure 6-4, corresponding to the two sources of dynamic behavior in Equation (7) that we discussed above. The first possibility is that the lag pattern of Figure 6-4 reflects the way in which expectations about future output, and thus the long-run desired capital stock, are formed. In that view, only a sustained increase in output will persuade firms that the capital

[14] See Dale W. Jorgenson, "Econometric Studies of Investment Behavior: A Survey," *Journal of Economic Literature*, December 1971, and Peter K. Clark, "Investment in the 1970's: Theory, Performance, and Prediction," *Brookings Papers on Economic Activity*, 1979: 1 (Washington, D.C.: The Brookings Institution, 1979).

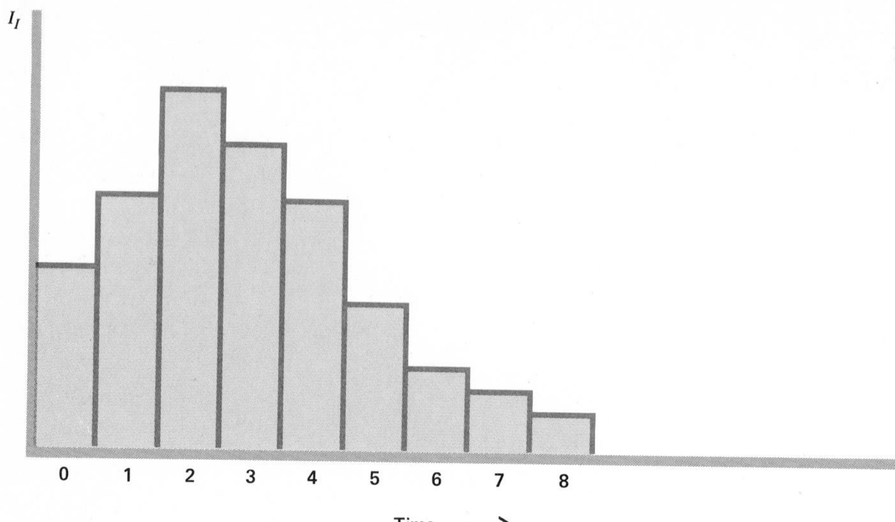

FIGURE 6-4 EFFECTS OF AN INCREASE IN OUTPUT IN PERIOD ZERO ON NET INVESTMENT IN SUBSEQUENT PERIODS

stock should be increased in the long run. Figure 6-4 would then imply that it takes about 2 years for changes in the variables that determine the desired capital stock to have their major impact on expectations.

The second explanation relies less on expectations and more on the physical delays in the investment process. That interpretation would be that Figure 6-4 reflects the long time it takes for a change in the desired capital stock to be translated into investment spending. In industries in which investment can be undertaken quickly, there may be some response within a year. But in the economy as a whole, the maximum impact on investment of a change in the desired capital stock happens only 2 years after the change in the desired stock.

In brief, the first explanation is that Figure 6-4 represents the slow adjustment of the desired capital stock to changes in the variables that, in the long run, determine that desired stock. The second explanation is that Figure 6-4 represents the long adjustment lags of investment in response to changes in the desired capital stock.

For many purposes, it does not matter which explanation of the form of Figure 6-4 is correct, and it is difficult to tell the explanations apart empirically. It is undoubtedly true that both explanations are relevant. The important point is that lags in the determination of the level of business fixed investment are long.

Sales and Profits as Determinants of Investment

Some studies of investment find either the level of sales or total profits to be factors explaining the level of investment. The level of sales could be interpreted as affecting expectations of future output and thus affecting the desired capital stock. Note that output and sales differ by the amount of inventory accumulation.

The role of profits can be interpreted similarly. High profits may provide an indication of future demand for the firm's product, and thus of future output. Alternatively, it is often argued that firms prefer to use retained profits to finance investment, rather than borrow. The preference might result from the expense of having to raise outside funds relative to using inside funds. However, it has to be remembered that in using its retained profits to finance investment rather than borrow. The preference might result from the expense of having to raise outside funds relative to them to the firm's owners.

The Timing of Investment and the Investment Tax Credit

The flexible accelerator model provides a useful summary of the dynamics of investment. But it does not sufficiently emphasize the *timing* of investment. Because investment is undertaken for the long run and often requires several years to complete, there is some flexibility in the dates on which the actual investment is undertaken. For example, suppose a firm wanted to have some machinery in place within 3 years. Suppose that it knew the investment tax credit would be raised substantially a year from now. Then the firm might be wise to delay the investment for a year and to make the machinery at a faster rate during the next 2 years, receiving the higher investment tax credit as the reward for waiting the extra year. Similarly, if a firm somehow knew that the cost of borrowing next year would be much lower than this year, it might wait a year to undertake its investment project.

The flexibility in the timing of investment leads to an interesting contrast between the effects of the investment tax credit and the income tax on investment and consumption, respectively. We saw in Chapter 5 that a permanent change in the income tax has a much larger effect on consumption than a transitory change. However, the rate of investment *during the period* that a temporary investment tax credit is in effect would be higher than the rate of investment that would occur over the same period during which a permanent credit of the same magnitude was in effect. Why? If firms knew the investment tax credit was temporary, they would advance the timing of their planned investments in order to take advantage of the higher credit during the current period. If there were a permanent change in the investment tax credit, then the desired capital stock would rise, and there would on that account be more investment. But there would not also be a bunching of investment.

It is for this reason that temporary changes in the investment tax credit have been suggested as a highly effective countercyclical policy measure. However, this is not a simple policy tool, as expectations about the timing and duration of the credit might worsen the instability of investment.

Summary on Business Fixed Investment

The main conclusions of the theory of business fixed investment as developed here are:

1 Over time, net investment spending is governed by the discrepancy between actual and desired capital.
2 Desired capital depends on the rental (user) cost of capital and the expected level of output. Capital demand rises with expected output and the investment tax credit, and declines with an increase in *real* interest rates.
3 There is strong evidence that adjustment of actual to desired capital is a slow process. A sustained change in the profitability of capital or the level of income will not exert its maximum effect on investment for 2 years.
4 Although the adjustment of actual to desired capital is a slow process, what matters for aggregate demand management is the level of investment. From this perspective, monetary and fiscal policy do exert an effect on investment via the desired capital stock, although the short-run impact is likely to be minor. The longer-run effects are larger. The lags with which these investment effects occur are important to bear in mind in shaping stabilization policy.
5 Investment theory, like consumption theory, emphasizes the role of expected or permanent income or output and other permanent variables as determinants of capital demand.

6-2 RESIDENTIAL INVESTMENT

We study residential investment separately from business fixed investment both because somewhat different theoretical considerations are relevant[15] and because institutional features of the United States economy make residential investment especially sensitive to changes in interest rates.

[15] In the concluding section of this chapter, we explain why slightly different theoretical models are used in explaining business fixed investment and residential investment.

Chart 6-3 shows residential investment spending in constant (1972) dollars for the period 1953–1979. Residential investment declines in all recessions. Thus in 1953–1954, 1957–1958, 1960–1961, and 1970, there is a dip in residential investment. The same is true for the minirecession in 1966–1967 and certainly during the 1974–1976 recession and in 1980. The 1966 minirecession is of particular interest in this context because, as we shall see in Chapter 10, the very tight monetary policy of that year fell particularly hard on residential construction. This is shown as a major dip in Chart 6-3.

Theory

Residential investment consists of the building of single-family and multifamily dwellings which we shall call housing. Housing is distinguished as an asset by its long life. Consequently, investment in housing in any one year tends to be a very small proportion of the existing stock of housing—about 3 percent. The theory of residential investment starts by considering the demand for the existing stock of housing. Housing is viewed as one among the many assets that a wealth holder can own.

In Figure 6-5*a* we show the demand for the stock of housing in the downward-sloping D_0D_0 curve. The lower the price of housing (P_H), the

CHART 6-3 FIXED RESIDENTIAL INVESTMENT SPENDING (*Source: Citibank Economic Database*)

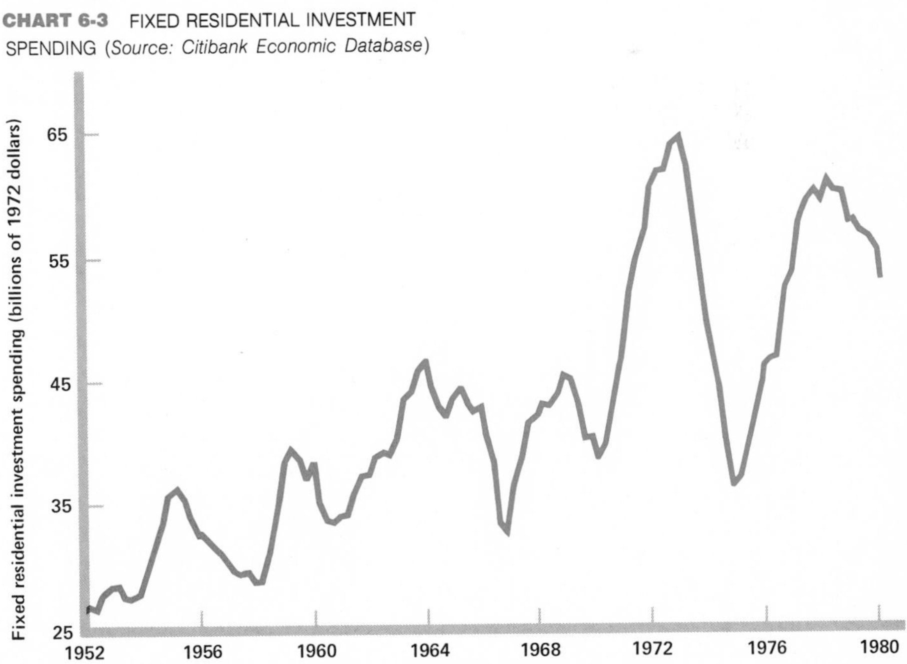

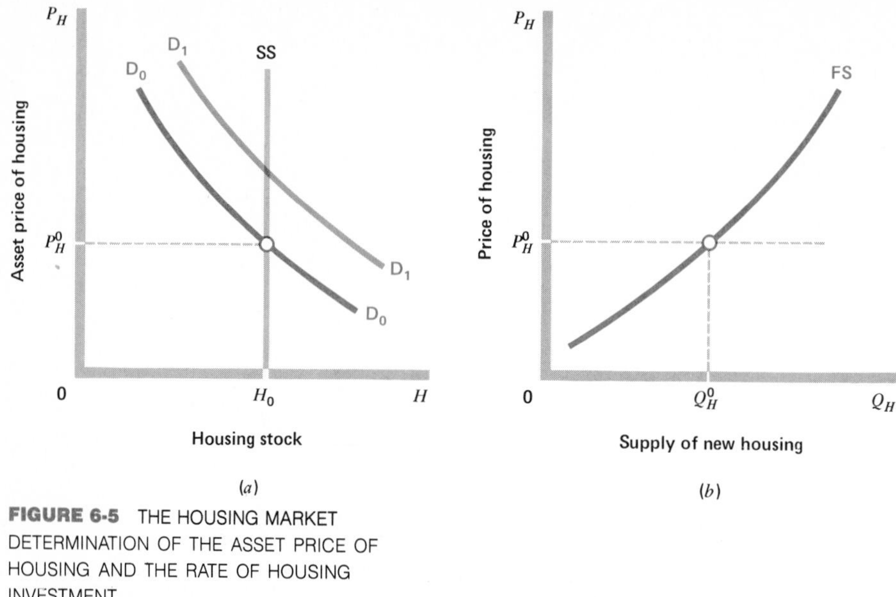

FIGURE 6-5 THE HOUSING MARKET
DETERMINATION OF THE ASSET PRICE OF HOUSING AND THE RATE OF HOUSING INVESTMENT

greater the demand. The position of the demand curve itself depends on a number of economic variables: First, the greater the wealth, the greater the demand for housing. The more wealthy individuals are, the more housing they desire to own. Thus an increase in wealth would shift the demand curve from D_0D_0 to D_1D_1. Second, the demand for housing as an asset depends on the real return available on other assets. If returns on other forms of holding wealth—such as bonds—are low, then housing looks like a relatively attractive form in which to hold wealth. The lower the return on other assets, the greater the demand for housing. A reduction in the return on other assets, such as bonds or common stock, shifts the demand curve from D_0D_0 to D_1D_1.

Third, the demand for the housing stock depends on the net real return obtained by owning housing. The gross return—before taking costs into account—consists of rent, if the housing is rented out, or the implicit return that the homeowner receives by living in the home, plus capital gains arising from increases in the value of the housing. In turn, the costs of owning the housing consist of interest cost, typically the mortgage interest rate, plus any real estate taxes, and depreciation. These costs are deducted from the gross return and, after tax adjustments, constitute the net return. An increase in the net return on housing caused, for example, by a reduction in the mortgage interest rate, makes housing a more attractive form in which to hold wealth and shifts up the demand curve for housing from D_0D_0 to D_1D_1.

The price of housing is determined by the interaction of this demand with the stock supply of housing. At any one time the stock supply is fixed—there is a given stock of housing that cannot be adjusted quickly in response to price changes. The supply curve of the stock of housing is the SS curve of Figure 6-5*a*. The equilibrium *asset price of housing*, P_H^0, is determined by the intersection of the supply and demand curves. The asset price of housing is simply the price of a typical house or apartment. At any one time, the market for the stock of housing determines the asset price of housing.

We now consider the determinants of the rate of investment in housing, and for that purpose turn to Figure 6-5*b*. The curve FS represents the supply of new housing as a function of the price of housing. This curve should be thought of in the same way as the regular supply curve of any industry. The supply curve, it will be recalled, represents the amount of a good that suppliers want to sell at the specified price. In this case, the good being supplied is new housing. The position of the FS curve is affected by the costs of factors of production used in the construction industry and by technological factors affecting the cost of building.

The curve FS is sometimes called the flow supply curve, since it represents the *flow* of new housing into the market in a given time period. In contrast, the *stock* supply curve SS represents the total amount of housing in the market at a moment of time.

Given the price of housing established in the asset market, P_H^0, building contractors supply the amount of new housing, Q_H^0, for sale at that price. The higher the asset price, the greater the supply of new housing. Now the supply of new housing is nothing other than gross investment in housing—total additions to the housing stock. Figure 6-5 thus represents our basic theory of the determinants of housing investment.

Any factor affecting the demand for the existing stock of housing will affect the asset price of housing, P_H, and thus the rate of investment in housing. Similarly, any factor shifting the flow supply curve FS will affect the rate of investment. We have already investigated the major factors shifting the DD demand curve for housing, but will briefly repeat that analysis.

Suppose the interest rate rises. Then the asset demand for housing falls and the price of housing falls; that in turn induces a decline in the rate of production of new housing, or a decline in housing investment. Or, suppose that the mortgage interest rate rises: once again there is a fall in the asset price of housing and a reduction in the rate of construction. Or let there be an increase in wealth that increases the demand for housing. The asset price of housing and the rate of construction—the rate of housing investment—both rise.

Because the existing stock of housing is so large relative to the rate of investment in housing, we can ignore the effects of the current supply of new housing on the price of housing in the short run. However, over time, the new construction shifts the SS curve of the left-hand panel to the right as it increases the housing stock. The long-run equilibrium in the housing industry would be reached, in an economy in which there was no increase in population or wealth over time, when the housing stock was constant. Constancy of the housing stock requires gross investment equal to depreciation, or net investment equal to zero. The asset price of housing would have to be at the level such that the rate of construction was just equal to the rate of depreciation of the existing stock of housing in long-run equilibrium. If population or income and wealth were growing at a constant rate, the long-run equilibrium would be one in which the rate of construction was just sufficient to cover depreciation and the steadily growing stock demand. In an economy subjected to continual nonsteady changes, that long-run equilibrium is not necessarily ever reached.

Minor qualifications to the basic theoretical structure arise chiefly because new housing cannot be constructed immediately in response to changes in P_H; rather, it takes a short time for that response to occur. Thus, the supply of new housing responds, not to the actual price of housing today, but to the price expected to prevail when the construction is completed. However, the lags are quite short; it takes less than a year to build a typical house. Another qualification stems from that same construction delay. Since builders have to incur expenses before they sell their output, they need financing over the construction period. They are frequently financed at the mortgage interest rate by the thrift institutions, that is, savings and loan associations and mutual savings banks. Hence, the position of the flow supply curve is affected by the mortgage interest rate as well as the amount of lending undertaken by the thrift institutions.[16] We next discuss the reason that the amount of lending undertaken by the thrift institutions has an effect over and above that of the mortgage interest rate on the flow supply of housing.

Housing, Mortgages, and Regulation Q

The mortgage interest rate and the availability of mortgages play a special role in the housing market and in fluctuations in housing investment. The reason is that most houses are purchased with the aid of mortgage financing. Since the 1930s, a mortgage has typically been a debt instrument of very long maturity, 20 to 30 years, with a fixed rate and with monthly nominal repayments to the lending institution which remain fixed for the term to maturity.

Mortgages are the chief assets of the thrift institutions that specialize in housing finance. Many of the liabilities of the thrift institutions, however,

[16] The theory of housing investment of this section is the basis of the study of the housing market undertaken by Brigham Young University's James Kearl in his 1975 MIT Ph.D. dissertation, "Inflation-Induced Distortions of the Real Economy: An Econometric and Simulation Study of Housing and Mortgage Innovation."

are relatively short-term instruments. These liabilities are essentially deposits at savings and loan associations and mutual savings banks, most of which can be withdrawn on demand by the depositors. Recently, savings and loans have been issuing new types of securities. Some are longer-term liabilities, of up to 4 years' maturity. Others are 6-month deposits, which pay a slightly higher interest rate to depositors than the Treasury bill rate. These so-called money market certificates, which we shall discuss again, are an important innovation introduced in the thrift industry in June 1978.

Until recently, the thrift institutions were very vulnerable to the phenomenon of *disintermediation.* The interest rates the thrifts could pay on their liabilities were, in effect, controlled by the Fed's Regulation Q.[17] In the past, when market interest rates on assets such as commercial paper have risen above the Regulation Q ceiling, depositors in the thrifts have removed their deposits and moved to higher-yielding assets. Acordingly, the thrifts did not have any funds with which to make loans, so that mortgages became unavailable even at the quoted mortgage interest rates. These episodes of disintermediation—the outflow of funds from the thrifts and the drying up of mortgage lending—happened in the *credit crunches* of 1966, 1969–1970, and 1974–1975.

The impact of the unavailability of mortgages on housing investment is strong, as can be observed by the fluctuations in residential investment shown in Charts 6-2 and 6-3. These impacts would be expected on the basis of the theory summarized in Figure 6-5. The general increase in interest rates increases the attractiveness of assets other than housing. The increase in mortgage rates and the unavailability of mortgages make housing more costly or difficult to hold. Each of these factors thus shifts the DD curve downward, reducing the asset price of housing. Then the unavailability of mortgages and the increased mortgage rate shift up the FS curve. Each of these shifts reduces the rate of housing investment.

Why did the Fed keep the Regulation Q ceiling low during the previous periods of disintermediation, rather than allow the interest rates paid by the thrifts to rise sufficiently to prevent the outflow of deposits? The reason was that the thrifts had a large stock of mortgage loans outstanding that they had made at low interest rates. If the rate they had to pay on deposits went up, they might well have found themselves paying out more in interest than they were taking in from their outstanding loans. In each period, there was fear for the solvency of many of them. Of course, the alternative of the credit crunch was not apparently very attractive either.

However, it was true that a significant part of the influence of monetary policy on aggregate demand during those episodes came from the impact of high interest rates and the unavailability of mortgages on housing

[17] Formally, the interest ceilings for the savings and loan associations (SLAs) are set by the Federal Home Loan Bank Board, an organization whose role in relation to the SLAs is similar to that of the Fed in relation to banks. In practice, the FHLBB sets the ceiling one-quarter percentage point above Regulation Q levels set by the Fed for the commercial banks.

investment. If restrictive monetary policy is to be used to affect the economy, it has been argued that the housing sector is a desirable target. The reason is that major changes in the rate of housing investment have very little impact in the short run on the overall availability of housing (since the housing stock is so large relative to the rate of investment) and thus cause relatively little distress to consumers. The Fed may accordingly not have been totally unhappy to use Regulation Q to affect the availability of mortgages, despite the dislocation caused to the thrift institutions and the construction industry.[18]

In the 1978–1979 period of high interest rates, there was no credit crunch. This was a result of the introduction of the money market certificates mentioned earlier, which essentially meant that the thrifts were allowed to pay market interest rates on their deposits, provided the deposits were held for 6 months.[19] New mortgages were made at interest rates well above those paid on the money market certificates, and the thrifts were not under any major financial strain. This was in part due also to the fact that there had been several recent periods of high interest rates, so that the interest being received on outstanding mortgages was not very far below the rates being paid on the money market certificates.

There was no serious disintermediation, and construction activity remained strong through 1979. The only problem was that high interest rates seemed to be having less effect on the economy than before. Some economists argued that interest rates would have to go to unprecedently high levels if monetary policy was to exert any restraining influence on the economy. And indeed, in late 1979 and early 1980, interest rates did rise well above historical highs as the Fed forcefully restrained demand, thereby sharply reducing construction activity.

6-3 INVENTORY INVESTMENT

Inventories consist of goods in the process of production and completed goods held by firms in anticipation of their sale. The ratio of inventories to final sales, at an annual rate, in the United States has been in the range of 25 to 35 percent over the past 20 years. That is, on average, firms hold inventories that constitute 3 to 5 months' worth of their final sales.

The inventories of interest to us are those held to meet future demands for goods. Firms hold such inventories because goods cannot be instantly manufactured or obtained from the manufacturer to meet demand. Some inventories are held as an unavoidable part of the production process; there

[18] One way for the thrifts to reduce their vulnerability to high short-term interest rates, suggested in 1974, was to introduce variable rate mortgages, on which the interest payment varies with the general level of interest rates. This, and other forms of flexible interest rate mortgages, is becoming increasingly common under the influence of high and varying inflation and short-term interest rates.

[19] For a discussion of the importance of this factor, see Dwight M. Jaffee and Kenneth T. Rosen, "Mortgage Credit Availability and Residential Construction," *Brookings Papers on Economic Activity*, 1979, 2.

is an inventory of meat and sawdust inside the sausage machine during the manufacture of sausage, for example. Inventories are also held because it is less costly for a firm to order goods less frequently in large quantities than to order small quantities frequently—just as the average household finds it useful to keep several days' supplies on hand in the house so as not to have to visit the supermarket daily.

Firms have a desired ratio of inventories to final sales that depends on economic variables. The smaller the cost of ordering new goods and the greater the speed with which such goods arrive, the smaller the inventory-sales ratio. The more uncertainty about the demand for the firm's goods, given the expected level of sales, the higher the inventory-sales ratio. The inventory-sales ratio may also depend on the level of sales, with the ratio falling with sales because there is relatively less uncertainty about sales as sales increase. Finally, there is the interest rate. Since firms carry inventories over time, they must tie up money to buy and hold them. There is an interest cost involved in such inventory holding, and the desired inventory-sales ratio should be expected to fall with increases in the interest rate. However, such a link has been difficult to establish empirically.

The most interesting aspect of inventory investment lies in the distinction between anticipated and unanticipated investment. Inventory investment could be high in two circumstances. First, if sales are unexpectedly low, firms would find unsold inventories accumulating on their shelves; that constitutes unanticipated inventory investment. This is the type of inventory investment discussed in Chapter 3. Second, inventory investment could be high because firms plan to restore depleted inventories. The two circumstances obviously have very different implications for the behavior of aggregate demand. Unanticipated inventory investment is a result of unexpectedly low aggregate demand. On the other hand, planned inventory investment can be a response to recent, unexpectedly high aggregate demand. That is, rapid accumulation of inventories could be associated with either rapidly declining aggregate demand or rapidly increasing aggregate demand.

The behavior of inventory investment in the period since 1946 is shown in Chart 6-2. On the whole, inventory investment over the one-year periods of the chart has been closely tied to the behavior of the business cycle as represented by the unemployment rate. Inventory investment has been low when unemployment has been high, and vice versa.

However, inventory behavior over shorter time periods is more interesting and illuminating. Inventory behavior over the business cycle is well illustrated in the 1973–1975 recession. In Chart 6-4, we show real output (in 1972 dollars) as well as final sales other than for inventory. The discrepancy between GNP and final sales is equal to changes in inventories. Thus, when output exceeds final sales, inventories are increasing. Now we observe that we move into the recession with final sales declining in the fourth quarter of 1973 while output is still increasing. Throughout 1974,

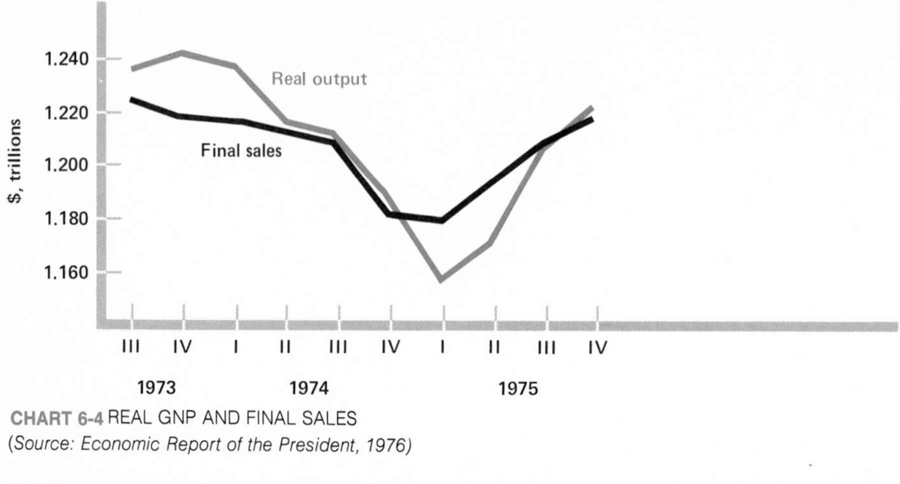

CHART 6-4 REAL GNP AND FINAL SALES
(*Source: Economic Report of the President, 1976*)

final sales and output decline but, throughout, output exceeds sales so that inventories keep accumulating. Firms are not yet fully adjusting production to the lower and declining level of demand. Finally, at the end of 1974 and in the first quarter of 1975, there is a dramatic reduction in output and production, and output falls below the level of final sales. Up to the third quarter of 1975, firms are decumulating inventories and meeting the excess of demand over production in that manner. Finally, in the last quarter with both sales and output back on the upswing, production roughly matches sales.

The implied behavior of the ratio of inventories to final sales is shown in Chart 6-5. It is clear that this ratio is significantly affected by the business cycle. In the early phase of a decline in aggregate demand, there is relatively little production adjustment, and accordingly, inventories are built up. The inventory-sales ratio increases as the economy heads into a recession. Once the recession is fully under way, production is cut more severely because firms find themselves with excessive inventories and attempt to unload them. Finally, in the recovery phase, demand moves ahead of production, thus allowing inventories to further decline absolutely and relative to output or sales. The inventory-sales ratio decreases as the economy moves out of the recession. The behavior of inventories thus matches rather precisely the story of the adjustment process that we told in discussing the simple Keynesian model. In the initial phase of the downswing, inventories (passively) adjust to absorb the excess of production over demand. Subsequently, as involuntary inventory accumulation shows up in a high ratio of inventories to sales, firms cut production and thus actively restore the preferred ratio of inventories to sales.

As we noted in Chapter 3, the behavior of inventories not only reflects

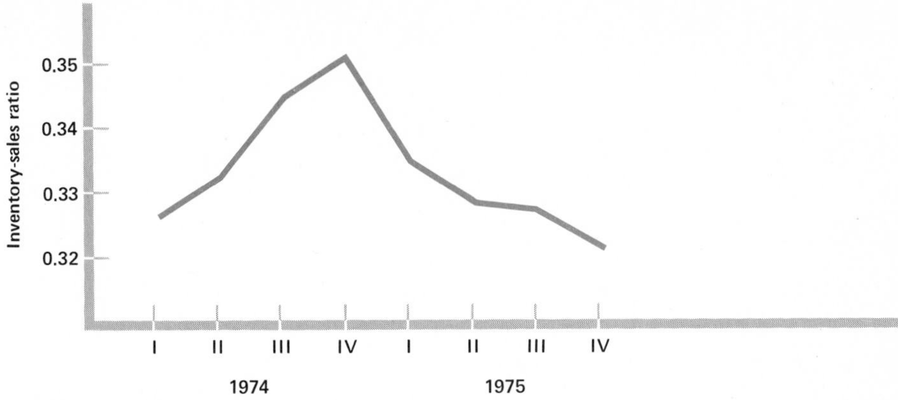

CHART 6-5 INVENTORY–FINAL SALES RATIO, 1974–1975 (*Source: Economic Report of the President, 1976*)

fluctuations in the economy, but also contributes to those fluctuations through the so-called *inventory cycle*. When there is a fall in demand, inventories initially begin to increase, as can be seen at the beginning of the period shown in Chart 6-4, for example. When firms decide to reduce their inventories, they have to cut back their orders or reduce their own production for inventory, thus reducing demand by more than the initial fall in aggregate demand. This stage worsens the decline, as can be seen in the first quarter of 1975 in Chart 6-4. When the inventories are back to their desired level, firms will restore their inventory investment to a higher level again.

To make the point in a different way, we can consider the case of a hypothetical automobile dealer who sells, say, thirty cars per month, and holds an average of one month's sales—namely, thirty cars—in inventory. As long as sales stay steady at thirty cars per month, she will be ordering thirty cars per month from the factory. Now suppose sales drop to twenty-five cars per month, and it takes the dealer 2 months to respond to the change. During those 2 months her inventory will have climbed to forty cars. In future she will want an inventory of only twenty-five cars on hand. Thus when she does respond to the fall in demand, she cuts her order from the factory from thirty to fifteen in the third month, to get the inventory back to one month's sales. After the desired inventory-sales ratio has been restored, she will then order twenty-five cars per month from the factory. We see in this extreme case how the drop in demand of five cars, instead of leading to a simple drop in car output of five cars per month, causes a drop in output of fifteen cars in one month, followed by the longer-run drop in output of five cars per month.

6-4 CONCLUSIONS

In this chapter we have seen how investment fluctuates over the business cycle. We have broken investment spending down into the three categories of business fixed investment, residential investment, and inventory investment, and we have presented theories to explain the behavior of each type of investment.

Slightly different theoretical considerations are relevant to the determination of each of the three categories of investment we have discussed. Nonetheless, there is a basic common element. That is the interaction, in each of the theories, of the demand for the stock of capital with the determinants of the rate of investment. The theory of business fixed investment started by examining the determinants of the desired capital stock, whereas the theory of residential investment looked at the demand for the stock of housing. The discussion of inventory investment started by examining the determinants of the desired inventory-sales ratio. Then, in each case, we went on to analyze or describe the determinants of the rate of that type of investment.

We come now to the question of why there is a difference between the theoretical models used to explain the level of business fixed investment and residential investment. The fundamental difference arises from the degree of standardization of the capital and the associated question of the existence of a good market for the used capital goods. Much of business fixed investment is in capital that is specifically designed for a given firm and is not of much use to other firms. It is, accordingly, difficult to establish a market price for the stock of that type of capital, and the theory used in discussing residential investment would be difficult to apply in that case. Although housing too varies a good deal, it is nonetheless possible to talk of a price of housing. Further, used housing is a very good substitute for new housing, whereas that is less often true for many capital goods.[20] If we disaggregated business fixed investment further than we have, we might well find that the model used to study housing investment is readily applicable for certain categories of business fixed investment, for which the capital good in question is relatively standard and has a good secondhand market.

Of the factors affecting the rate of investment, the real rate of interest is important because it affects both business fixed investment and housing investment. It does not appear to have strong effects on inventory

[20] The two models look very different. However, you may be able to see a way of casting the analysis of the housing market in terms of the theory used in discussing business fixed investment. You can define the desired capital stock of housing as that stock which the economy will eventually reach when the price of housing reaches a constant level. Then the level of investment will be an increasing function of the difference between that stock and the existing stock. Similarly, the model we have used for housing investment can be transformed into a model of business fixed investment. This is the so-called *Tobin's q* theory of investment. See James Tobin, "A General Equilibrium Approach to Monetary Theory," *Journal of Money, Credit and Banking,*" February 1969.

spending. Fiscal policy affects the rate of business fixed investment by affecting the rental cost of capital and can also affect residential investment by its treatment of the tax deductibility of interest payments used to finance home ownership.

Different variables affect the scale of each type of investment. The expected level of output is the major determinant of the overall scale of business fixed investment. Wealth is the major scale variable affecting the demand for housing and thus, ultimately, the rate of housing investment. The desired stock of inventory capital is related to the level of sales, but there is no simple relationship between the rate of inventory investment and changes in the level of output. A high rate of inventory investment may either be an addition to aggregate demand (if the investment is planned) or a reflection of a low level of aggregate demand (if the investment is unanticipated).

There are differences, too, in the stress placed on other factors affecting each category of investment. Lags in adjustment and lags arising from expectations that depend on past history are extremely important determinants of the rate of business fixed investment. Institutional arrangements, particularly those relating to the thrift institutions, play an important role in affecting the rate of residential investment. These arrangements are largely responsible for past severe fluctuations in residential construction in the United States economy.

Total investment in the economy is simply the sum of investment spending in each of the three categories that we have studied separately in this chapter. Thus, each of the factors that affects the components of investment spending also affects the level of total investment. The real interest rate is thus one of the major factors that has an unambiguous effect on investment spending. Similarly, the level of permanent output affects investment spending, as do the fiscal variables that influence the rental cost of capital. Monetary policy influences the level of investment by affecting the real rate of interest and also through use of Regulation Q.

In brief, this chapter provides the theory that explains the role of the interest rate in the investment function of Chapter 4 while pointing out that the interest rate used there should be a *real* interest rate. It also showed that other variables, such as the level of output and the level of wealth, affect the rate of investment. Finally, it clarified the ways in which monetary and fiscal policy variables affect the rate of investment.

APPENDIX: THE ACCELERATOR MODEL OF INVESTMENT

The flexible accelerator model described in Section 6-1 is a substantial generalization of the original accelerator model of investment, which argued that the rate of investment is proportional to the *change* in GNP. To derive the accelerator model of investment, assume that there is complete adjustment of the capital stock to its desired level within one period (i.e., that $\lambda = 1$), so that $K = K^*$, that there is no depreciation so that $d = 0$, and that the desired capital output ratio is a constant, independent of the rental cost of capital:

$$K^* = \beta Y \tag{A1}$$

In Equation (A1), β is a constant which should not be confused with the β in any other chapter. Substituting Equation (A1) into Equation (9), setting $\lambda = 1$, and noting that $K_{-1} = K^*_{-1}$, we obtain

$$I = \beta(Y - Y_{-1}) \tag{A2}$$

which is precisely the original accelerator model of investment.

While the flexible accelerator model Equation (9) is indeed a considerable generalization of the simple accelerator model, the simpler model drives home the point that the rate of investment depends on the lagged, as well as the current, value of GNP. This means that any action taken this period to affect current investment and thus current GNP will also affect investment—and thus GNP—in subsequent periods. As we saw in our discussion of the permanent-income hypothesis, such a relationship presents considerable difficulties to policy makers.

PROBLEMS

1 We have seen in Chapters 5 and 6 that *permanent* income and output, rather than current income and output, determine consumption and investment.
 (*a*) How does this affect the IS-LM model built in Chapter 4?
 (*b*) What are the policy implications of the use of the "permanent" measures?
2 In Chapter 4 it was assumed that investment rises during periods of low interest rates. That, however, was not the case during the 1930s, when investment and interest rates were both very low. Explain how this can occur. What would have been appropriate fiscal policy in such a case?
3 According to the description of business fixed investment in this chapter, how would you expect a firm's investment decisions to be affected by a sudden increase in demand for its product? What factors would determine the speed of its reaction?
4 It is often suggested that investment spending is dominated by "animal spirits"—the optimism or pessimism of investors. Is this argument at all consistent with the analysis of Section 6-2?
5 Explain how the two panels of Figure 6-5 react together over time. What would happen if the demand for housing stock (DD) shifts up and to the right over time?
6 Trace carefully the step-by-step effects on the housing market (using Figure 6-5) of an increase in interest rates. Explain each shift and its long-run and short-run effects.
7 (*a*) Explain why the housing market usually prospers when (real) mortgage rates are low.
 (*b*) In some states, usury laws prohibit (nominal) mortgage rates in excess of a

legal maximum. Explain how this could lead to an exception to the conclusion in 7(*a*).

(*c*) Could this happen in the absence of inflation? Explain.

8 In the past, restrictive monetary policy seriously hurt the housing industry in an effort to avoid excess aggregate demand.

(*a*) What is the mechanism by which this happened?

(*b*) Can you suggest ways in which this heavy burden can be spread out rather than be concentrated on the housing industry?

(*c*) Should the burden be spread?

9 (*a*) Explain how final sales and output can differ.

(*b*) Point out from Chart 6-4 the periods of planned and unplanned inventory investment and decumulation.

(*c*) During a period of slow but steady growth, how would you expect final sales and output to be related? Explain. Draw a hypothetical figure like Chart 6-4 for such a period.

(*d*) Do the same as in 9(*c*) for Chart 6-5.

10 Suppose that an explicitly temporary tax credit is enacted. The tax credit is at the rate of 10 percent and lasts only one year.

(*a*) What is the effect of this tax measure on investment in the long run (say after 4 or 5 years)?

(*b*) What is the effect in the current year and the following year?

(*c*) How will your answers under 10(*a*) and 10(*b*) differ if the tax credit is permanent?

11 In Chart 6-4 we discuss the pattern of inventory adjustment during the 1973–1975 recession. Is this pattern typical of all the postwar recessions?

(*a*) Use Chart 1-1, which shows the major recessions, and data on inventory investment from the *Economic Report of the President*, to study this issue.

(*b*) What was the pattern of inventory investment during the 1980 recession?

12 For this question use the Cobb-Douglas production function, and the corresponding desired capital stock given by Equation (2). Assume that $a = 0.3$, $Y =$ 2.5 trillion, and $i_c = 0.15$.

(*a*) Calculate the desired capital stock K^*.

(*b*) Now suppose that Y is expected to rise to 3 trillion. What is the corresponding desired capital stock?

(*c*) Suppose that the capital stock was at its desired level before the change in income was expected. Suppose further that $\lambda = 0.4$ in the flexible accelerator model of investment. What will be the rate of investment in the first year after expected income changes? In the second year?

(*d*) Does your answer in (*c*) refer to gross or net investment?

7

THE DEMAND FOR MONEY

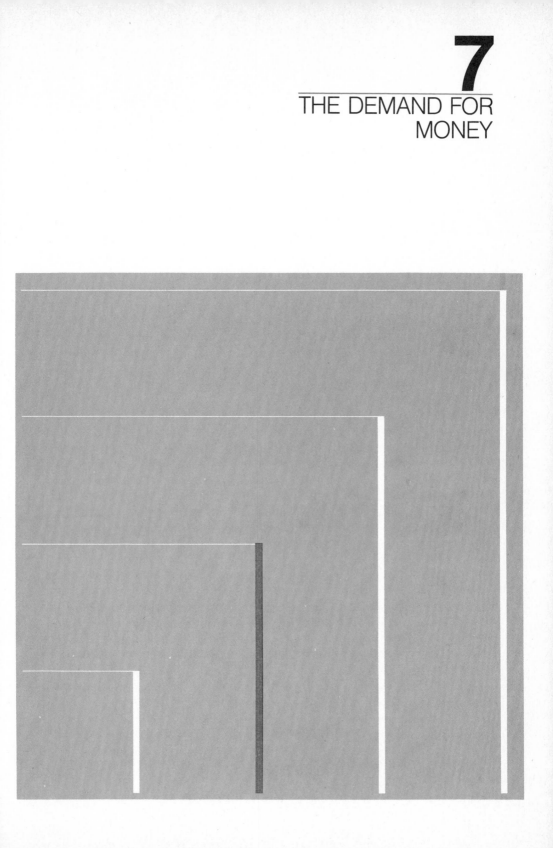

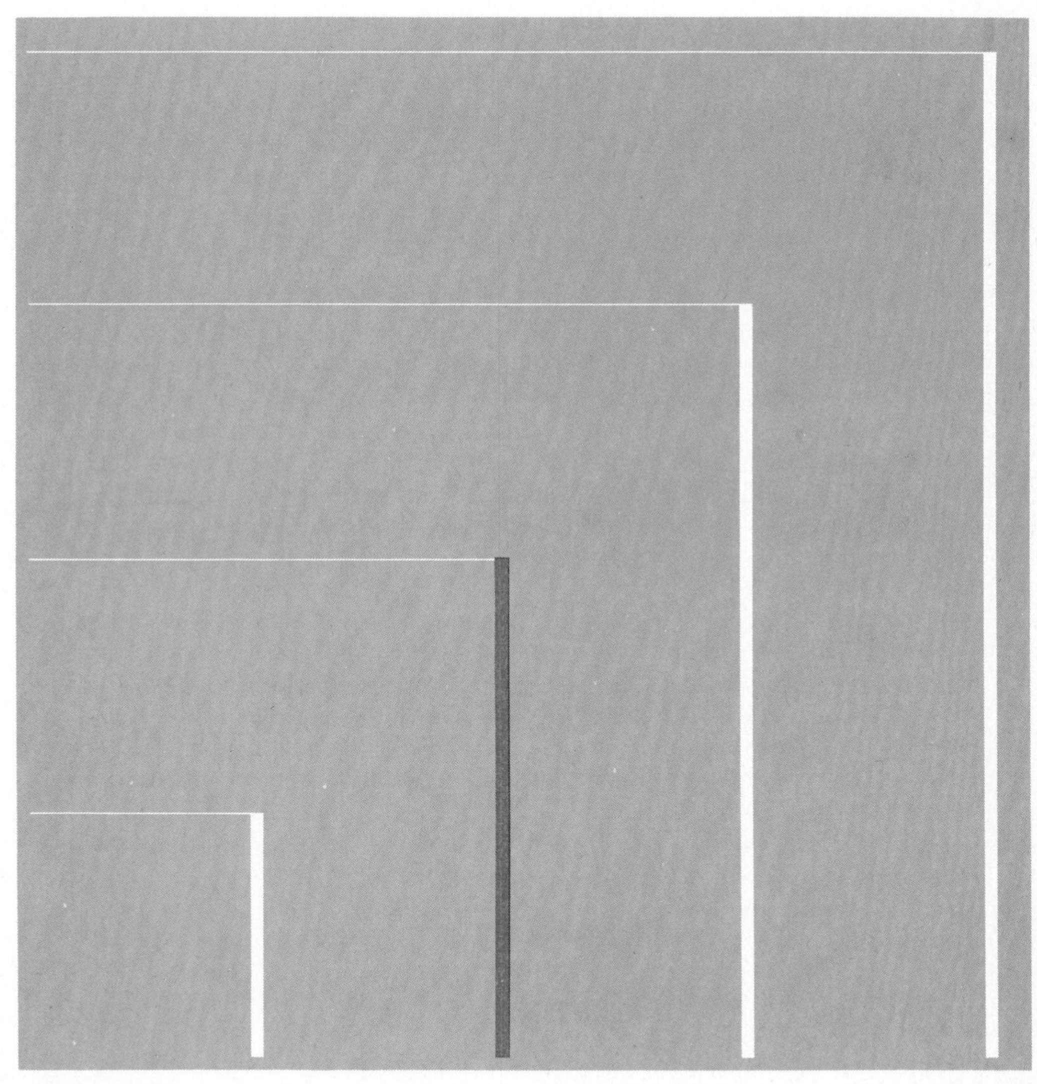

This chapter continues the process of filling in the details of the IS-LM model that we studied in Chapter 4. In Chapters 5 and 6, we took a closer look at theoretical and empirical aspects of the major private sector components of demand in the goods market—consumption and investment spending. In this chapter, we analyze the demand for money, and thus move from the goods market to the assets markets. In Chapter 8, we complete our discussion of the assets markets in the IS-LM framework by examining the determinants of the supply of money and the role of the Federal Reserve System in the money markets.

We start discussing the topic of money demand with the concept of the demand for *real balances*, introduced in Chapter 4. One of the essentials of money demand is that individuals are interested in the purchasing power of their money holdings—the value of their cash balances in terms of the goods the cash will buy. They are not concerned with their *nominal* money holdings, that is, the number of dollar bills they hold. What this means in practice is that (1) *real* money demand is unchanged when the price level increases, but *all* real variables, such as the interest rate, real income, and real wealth, remain unchanged; and (2) *nominal* money demand increases in proportion to the increase in the price level, given the constancy of the real variables just specified.[1]

We have a special name for behavior that is not affected by changes in the price level itself, all real variables remaining unchanged. We say that an individual is free from *money illusion* if a change in the level of prices, holding all real variables constant, leaves real behavior, including real money demand, unchanged. By contrast, an individual whose real behavior is affected by a change in the price level, all real variables remaining unchanged, is said to suffer from money illusion.

We shall see that empirical evidence supports the theoretical argument that the demand for money is a demand for real balances—or that the demand for nominal balances, holding real variables constant, is proportional to the price level. In Chapter 4, we also assumed that the demand for money increases with the level of real income and decreases with the nominal interest rate. We shall see that, in this chapter, both theory and evidence support the type of demand for money function used in Chapter 4.

You will also recall that the demand for money is important in determining the effectiveness of fiscal policy in changing the level of income. Changes in fiscal variables, such as tax rates or government spending, affect the level of income if the demand for money changes when the interest rate changes—if the demand for money is interest-elastic. If the demand for money is totally interest-inelastic—if it does not react at all to changes in the interest rate—increases in government spending totally *crowd out* private spending and leave the level of income unaffected.

The demand for money has been studied very intensively at both the

[1] Be sure you understand that (1) and (2) say the same thing in slightly different ways.

theoretical and empirical levels. There is by now almost total agreement that the demand should, as a theoretical matter, increase as the level of real income rises and decrease as the nominal interest rate rises. Empirical work bears out these two properties of the demand for money function. However, a demand for money function based on data from the 1950s and 1960s does not well explain present money demand. Since about 1974, the money demand function appears to have been shifting in that the demand for money at given levels of income and the interest rate is less than past experience would predict. This instability in the demand for money function has occurred at the same time as, and is undoubtedly partially explained by, a series of changes in the financial system that we shall discuss below.

We start in Section 7-1 by examining the components of the stock of money in the United States. Then, in Section 7-2, we briefly review the traditional reasons for the use of money. Section 7-3, the longest of the chapter, presents the basic theory of the demand for money. Section 7-4 examines the evidence supporting the theoretical conclusions. Sections 7-5 and 7-6 discuss the *velocity* of money—a concept related to the demand for money—and the effects of anticipated inflation on the demand for money, respectively.

7-1 COMPONENTS OF THE MONEY STOCK

Money supply definitions for the United States were changed early in 1980. The money supply concept we shall be using in most of this chapter is M1-B, which consists of currency plus demand deposits. Table 7-1 shows that M1-B in March 1980 was equal to $392.3 billion, of which $108.9 billion was currency and the remaining $283.4 billion demand deposits.

Currency consists of notes and coin in circulation, most of it in the form of notes (dollar bills). Demand deposits are "checkable" deposits—deposits against which checks can be written—in commercial banks and thrift

TABLE 7-1 COMPONENTS OF THE MONEY STOCK, MARCH 1980 *(In billions of dollars; seasonally adjusted)*

(1) Currency	(2) Demand deposits	(3) M1-B = (1) + (2)	(4) Time and savings deposits, etc. (excluding large time deposits and term RPs)	(5) M2 = M2 + (4)
108.9	283.4	392.3	1,158.0	1,550.3

Note: Details may not add to totals owing to rounding. Monthly figures are an average of daily figures.
Source: Citibank Economic Database.

institutions.[2] The financial institutions referred to as thrifts are savings and loan associations, mutual savings banks, and credit unions. Prior to the 1980 changes in money supply definitions, only demand deposits at commercial banks were included in what was *then* called M1. However, because there was no obvious difference in economic function served by demand deposits at commercial banks and other thrift institutions, the definition of M1 was replaced by two money supply measures. M1-B, as already noted, includes other checkable deposits, such as NOW and POW accounts, as well as ATS deposits.[3] M1-A corresponds closely, but not exactly, to the old M1, and excludes NOW, POW, and ATS accounts.[4]

We concentrate on M1-B because it is the definition of the money supply that corresponds most closely to the role of money as a *medium of exchange* or as the means of making payments. Payments can be made directly with coin and notes and also, for most transactions, with a check. To make a payment using a passbook savings account, it is generally necessary first to transfer money out of the savings account into a checking account, and only then to write the check. That is why savings and similar accounts are not included in the basic definition of the money supply.

Information on the distribution of the ownership of demand deposits is available, but there are no records of the ownership of currency.[5] About a third of demand deposits are held by consumers, with businesses holding most of the rest. There is no very good information on the distribution of the ownership of currency because individuals are reluctant to discuss how much currency they hold when they are asked. The question sounds like the prelude to a robbery or a visit from the Internal Revenue Service.

Although the money supply concepts have recently been revised, the present definition of M1-B still does not correspond exactly to the role of money as a means of making payments. In particular, many individuals hold accounts with *money market funds* against which checks can be written. A money market fund is a fund that invests its assets in short-term

[2] Not all demand deposits held at United States banks are part of M1-B. Demand deposits held by foreign official institutions and foreign commercial banks are excluded.

[3] A NOW is a negotiable order of withdrawal, and POW is a payment order of withdrawal. These essentially relate to interest-bearing checking accounts. For legal reasons, the checks are not called checks, but rather NOWs, POWs, etc. ATS deposits are savings deposits that banks are allowed to transfer automatically into demand deposit accounts if there is a shortage of cash in the demand deposit account. They are therefore essentially accounts against which checks can be written.

[4] For details of the financial innovations in the seventies which led to the need to redefine the money supply concepts, see "A Proposal for Redefining the Monetary Aggregates," *Federal Reserve Bulletin*, January 1979. The new definitions are in "The Redefined Monetary Aggregates," *Federal Reserve Bulletin*, February 1980.

[5] The data, available each quarter, are published in the *Federal Reserve Bulletin*.

interest-bearing securities, such as certificates of deposit (CDs)[6] and Treasury bills. Although checks can be written against accounts in money market funds, they are not presently counted as part of M1-B, though they are part of M2.

Similarly, there is a question as to whether credit cards should not be regarded as a means of making payment. If so—and the argument is certainly compelling—we should probably count the amount that people are allowed to charge by using their credit cards as part of the money stock. Another definitional issue arises in the case of travellers' checks, which will eventually be included in M1-B when the Fed obtains adequate data.

Historically, there have often been changes in the type of assets which can be used as means of payment, and simultaneous disagreements about what constitutes money in those circumstances. When checks first began to be widely used in England early in the nineteenth century, there was a disagreement over whether demand deposits should be regarded as part of the money stock. Now that point is not disputed. We can expect there to be continuing changes in the financial structure over the years, with consequent changes in the definitions of the various money supply concepts.

Table 7-1 also shows a broader definition of the money supply, M2. M2 adds a variety of interest bearing time and savings deposits at banks and thrifts, as well as money market mutual funds, to M1-B. The largest part of M2 is made up of savings deposits and small time deposits at banking and thrift institutions, with some specialized assets constituting the rest. Certain large denominations of time deposits are excluded from M2. The components of M2 that are not part of M1-B are in general less *liquid* than M1-B in that they cannot immediately and conveniently be used for making payments. However, they are assets that are close to being money in the sense that they are available with only a little difficulty for making payments.

It is worth discussing briefly the reasons for the recent changes in money supply definitions. The definitional changes followed financial innovations that changed the nature of the assets that banks and thrifts issued. For instance, thrifts, which pay interest on deposits and had been forbidden to have checkable accounts, invented NOW accounts as a way of getting around the prohibition. A NOW, a negotiable order of withdrawal, looks and smells like a check, but is not, legally speaking, a check. Banks were trying to compete with one another and thrifts by finding ways of paying interest on demand deposits, again something they were forbidden

[6] Certificates of deposit are liabilities of banks that can be bought and sold in the open market like other securities. Typically, they come in large denominations of $100,000 or more. The stock of CDs in December 1979 was $94 billion.

from doing. As ways around the prohibitions were found, deposits formerly called savings deposits, such as NOW accounts, became in fact demand deposits, and eventually the definitions changed.

In summary, there is no unique set of assets which will always constitute the money supply. At present, there are arguments for using a broader definition of the money stock than M1-B, and even arguments for using a less broad definition—should $1,000 bills be included, for example? And over the course of time, the particular assets that serve as a medium of exchange, or means of payment, will certainly change further.

Definitions notwithstanding, we shall from now on use M1 to denote M1-B, unless there is risk of confusion.

7-2 THE FUNCTIONS OF MONEY

Money is so widely used that we rarely step back to think how remarkable a device it is. It is impossible to imagine a modern economy operating without the use of money or something very much like it. The essential role of money is to separate the acts of buying and selling goods. In a mythical barter economy in which there is no money, every transaction has to involve an exchange of goods (and/or services) on both sides of the transaction. The examples of the difficulties of barter are endless. The economist wanting a haircut would have to find a barber wanting to listen to a lecture on economics; the peanut farmer wanting a suit would have to find a tailor wanting peanuts, and so on. Without money, modern economies could not operate. In this context, money is a *medium of exchange*, and that is its essential function.

Money, as a medium of exchange, makes it unnecessary for there to be a "double coincidence of wants" in exchanges. By the double coincidence, we have in mind the above examples. The wants of two individuals would have to be identically matched for the exchange to take place. For instance, the man selling peanuts would have to find a buyer whose goods he wanted to buy (the suit) while, at the same time, the woman selling suits would have to find a buyer whose goods she wanted to buy (the peanuts).

There are four traditional functions of money, of which the medium of exchange is the first.[7] The other three are store of value, unit of account, and standard of deferred payment. These stand on a different footing from the medium of exchange function.

A *store of value* is an asset that maintains value over time. Thus, an individual holding a store of value can use that asset to make purchases at a future date. If an asset were not a store of value, then it would not be used as a medium of exchange. Imagine trying to use ice cream as money, in the

[7] See W. S. Jevons, *Money and the Mechanism of Exchange* (London: Routledge, Kegan, Paul, 1910.)

absence of refrigerators. There would hardly ever be a good reason for anyone to give up goods for money (ice cream) if the money were sure to melt within the next few minutes. And if the seller were unwilling to accept the ice cream in exchange for his or her goods, then the ice cream would not be a medium of exchange. But there are many stores of value other than money—such as bonds, stocks, and houses.

The *unit of account* is the unit in which prices are quoted and books kept. Prices are quoted in dollars and cents, and dollars and cents are the units in which the money stock is measured. Usually, the money unit is also the unit of account, but that is not essential. In the German hyperinflation of 1922–1923, dollars were the unit of account for some firms, whereas the mark was the medium of exchange.

Finally, as a *standard of deferred payment*, money units are used in long-term transactions, such as loans. The amount that has to be paid back in 5 or 10 years is specified in dollars and cents. Dollars and cents are acting as the standard of deferred payment. Once again, though, it is not essential that the standard of deferred payment be the money unit. For example, the final payment of a loan may be related to the behavior of the price level, rather than being fixed in dollars and cents. This is known as an indexed loan.

The last two of the four functions of money are, accordingly, functions which money *usually* performs, but not functions that it *necessarily* performs. And the store of value function is one that many assets perform.

There are fascinating descriptions of different types of money that have existed in the past that we do not have room to review here.[8] But there is one final point we want to emphasize. *Money is whatever is generally accepted in exchange.* However magnificently a piece of paper may be engraved, it will not be money if it is not accepted in payment. And, however unusual the material of which it is made, anything that is generally accepted in payment is money. The only reason money is accepted in payment is that the recipient believes that it can be spent at a later time. There is thus an inherent circularity in the acceptance of money. Money is accepted in payment because it is believed that it will also be accepted in payment by others.

7-3 THE DEMAND FOR MONEY: THEORY

In this section we review the three major motives underlying the demand for money. In doing so, we will concentrate on the effects of changes in income and changes in the interest rate on money demand.

The three theories we are about to review correspond to Keynes's

[8] See Paul Einzig, *Primitive Money* (New York: Pergamon, 1966).

famous three motives for holding money:[9] (1) the transactions motive, which is the demand for money arising from the use of money in making regular payments; (2) the precautionary motive, which is the demand for money to meet unforeseen contingencies; and (3) the speculative motive, which arises from the uncertainties about the money value of other assets that an individual can hold. In discussing the transactions and precautionary motives, we are mainly discussing M1, whereas the speculative motive refers more to M2, as we shall see.

Although we examine the demand for money by looking at the three motives for holding it, we cannot separate out a particular person's money holdings, say $500, into three neat piles of, say, $200, $200, and $100, that are being held from each motive. Money being held to satisfy one motive is always available for another use. The person holding unusually large balances for speculative reasons also has those balances available to meet an unexpected emergency, so that they also serve as precautionary balances. All three motives influence an individual's holdings of money, and, as we shall see, each leads to the prediction that the demand for money should fall as the interest rate on other assets increases.

This final point is worth emphasizing. Money (M1) generally earns no interest or less interest than other assets. Anyone holding money is giving up interest that could be earned by holding some other asset, such as a savings deposit or a bond. The higher the interest loss from holding a dollar of money, the less money we expect the individual to hold. The demand for money will thus be higher, the greater the interest rate on money itself if interest is paid on demand deposits, and will be lower, the higher the interest rate on alternative assets. In practice, we can measure the cost of holding money as the difference between the interest rate paid on money (perhaps zero) and the interest rate paid on the most nearly comparable other asset, such as a savings deposit or, for corporations, a certificate of deposit or commercial paper.

For most of the remainder of the chapter, we shall assume that money earns no interest. This is in fact true of most of the M1 stock. Further, it is easy to modify the analysis to take account of the payment of interest on money. All that is necessary is to substitute the difference between the interest rate on the alternative asset and the interest rate on money in places we mention only the interest rate on the alternative asset.

The Transactions Demand

The transactions demand for money arises from the use of money in making regular payment for goods and services. In the course of each month, an individual makes a variety of payments for such items as rent or mortgage,

[9] J. M. Keynes, *The General Theory of Employment, Interest and Money* (New York: Macmillan, 1936), chap. 13.

groceries, the newspaper, and other purchases. In this section we examine how much money an individual would hold for such purchases.

In analyzing the transactions demand, we are concerned with a tradeoff between the amount of interest an individual forgoes by holding money and the costs and inconveniences of holding a small amount of money. To make the problem concrete, consider a man who is paid, say, $1,200 each month. Assume that he spends the $1,200 evenly over the course of the month, at the rate of $40 per day. Now at one extreme, the individual could simply leave his $1,200 in cash (whether currency or demand deposits) and spend it at the rate of $40 per day. Alternatively, on the first day of the month the individual could take his $40 to spend that day and put the remaining $1,160 in a daily-interest savings accounts. Then every morning he could go to the bank to withdraw that day's $40 from the savings account. By the end of the month he would have earned interest on the money he had each day in the savings account. This would be the *benefit* of keeping his money holdings down as low as $40 at the beginning of each day. The *cost* of keeping money holdings down is simply the cost and inconvenience of the trips to the bank to withdraw the daily $40. To decide on how much money to hold for transactions purposes, the individual has to weigh the costs of holding small balances against the interest advantage of doing so.

We now study the tradeoff in more detail and derive a formula for the demand for money. Suppose the nominal monthly income[10] of the individual is Y_N. We make the simplifying assumption that Y_N is paid in to his savings account, rather than his checking account, each month. The money is spent at a steady rate over the course of the month. To spend it, the individual has to get it out of the savings account and into cash, which may be currency or a checking account. If left in the savings accounts, the deposit earns interest at a rate of i per month. It earns zero interest as cash. The cost to the individual of making a transfer between cash and the savings account (which we henceforth call bonds for convenience) is $\$b$.[11] That cost may be the individual's time, or it may be a cost that he explicitly pays someone else to make the transfer. For convenience we refer to it as a broker's fee.

Although we are describing an individual's transactions demand, similar considerations are relevant for firms deciding how to manage their money. You should think of this model as applying equally well, with small changes in terminology and assumptions, to firms and households.

The analysis of the demand for money we are now outlining is known as an *inventory-theoretic approach*. Originally, the approach was developed to determine the inventories of goods a firm should have on hand. In that context, the amount Y_N would be the monthly sales of the good, b, the cost

[10] As a reminder, nominal income Y_N is defined as real income Y times the price level P: $Y_N \equiv PY$.

[11] This b should not be confused with the b in earlier chapters; there are not sufficient letters of the alphabet for us to use each letter for only one concept.

of ordering the good, and i the interest cost of carrying the inventory. The analogy between money as an inventory of purchasing power, standing ready to buy goods, and an inventory of goods, standing ready to be bought by customers, is quite close. The inventory-theoretic approach to the demand for money is associated with the names of William Baumol and James Tobin.[12] The most famous result of Baumol and Tobin's work is the *square-root law* of the demand for money, which is presented later in Equation (4).

The individual has to decide how many transactions to make between bonds and cash each month. If he makes just one transaction, transferring Y_N into cash at the beginning of the month, his cash balance over the course of the month will be as shown in Figure 7-1*a*. It starts at Y_N, is spent evenly over the month, and is down to zero by the end of the month, at which time a new payment is received by the individual and transferred into his checking account. If he makes two withdrawals from the savings account, he first transfers $Y_N/2$ into cash at the beginning of the month, resulting in a cash balance that is run down to zero in the middle of the month, at which time another $Y_N/2$ is transferred into cash and spent evenly over the rest of the month.[13] Figure 7-1*b* shows the individual's cash holdings in that case.

We shall denote the size of a cash withdrawal from the bond portfolio

[12] William Baumol, "The Transactions Demand for Cash: An Inventory Theoretic Approach," *Quarterly Journal of Economics*, November 1952; and James Tobin, "The Interest-Elasticity of Transactions Demand for Cash," *Review of Economics and Statistics*, August 1956.

[13] With simple interest being paid on the savings account, it is true that the individual's transactions between bonds and cash should be evenly spaced over the month. We leave the proof of that for the case where there are two transactions to the problem set.

FIGURE 7-1 THE AMOUNT OF CASH HELD DURING THE MONTH RELATED TO THE NUMBER OF WITHDRAWALS

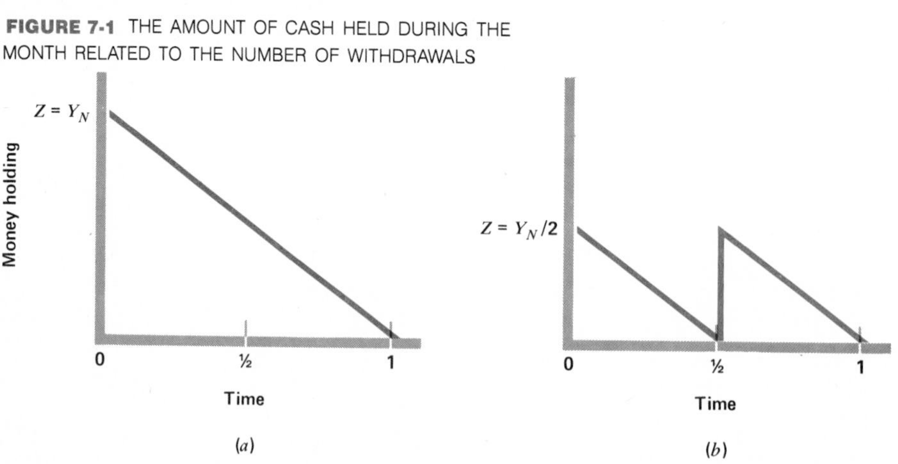

(savings account) by Z,[14] and the number of withdrawals from the bond portfolio by n. Thus, n is the number of times the individual adds to his cash balance during the month. If he makes n equal-sized withdrawals during the month, transferring funds from his savings account to his checking account, then the size of each transfer is Y_N/n, since a total of Y_N has to be transferred from the savings account into cash. For example, if Y_N is $1,200, and n, the number of transactions, is 3, then Z, the amount transferred to cash each time, is $400. Accordingly, we can write

$$nZ = Y_N \tag{1}$$

Suppose that the amount Z is transferred from bonds to cash at each withdrawal. What then is the *average* cash balance over the course of the month? We want to find the size of the average cash balance in order to measure the interest that is lost as a result of holding cash; if that amount were not held as cash, it could be held as interest-earning bonds. In Figure 7-1*a*, the average cash balance held during the month is $Y_N/2 = Z/2$, since the cash balance starts at Y_N and runs down in a straight line to zero.[15] In the case of Figure 7-1*b*, the average cash balance for the first half of the month is $Y_N/4 = Z/2$, and the average cash balance for the second half of the month is also $Z/2$. Thus, the average cash balance for the entire month is $Y_N/4 = Z/2$. Similarly, if three withdrawals were made, the average cash balance would be $Y_N/6 = Z/2$. In general, the average cash balance is $Z/2$, as you might want to confirm by drawing diagrams similar to Figure 7-1 for $n = 3$ or other values of n.

The interest cost of holding money is the interest rate times the average cash balance, or $iZ/2$. From Equation (1), that means the total interest cost is $iY_N/2n$. The other component of the cost of managing the portfolio is the brokerage cost, or the cost in terms of the individual's time and inconvenience in managing his money. That cost is just the number of withdrawals made, n, times the cost of each withdrawal, b, and is thus equal to nb. The total cost of managing the portfolio is the interest cost plus the total brokerage cost:

$$\text{Total cost} = nb + \frac{iY_N}{2n} \tag{2}$$

Equation (2) shows formally that the brokerage cost nb increases as the

[14] Please do not confuse Z in this chapter with Z in Chap. 5.

[15] The average cash balance is the average of the amount of cash the individual holds at each moment during the month. For instance, if he held $400 for 3 days and zero for the rest of the month, the average cash balance would be $40, or one-tenth (3 days divided by 30 days) of the month times $400.

number of withdrawals (transactions between bonds and money) rises, and that the interest cost decreases as the number of withdrawals increases. It thus emphasizes the tradeoff faced in managing money, and suggests that there is an optimal number of withdrawals the individual should make to minimize the total cost of holding money to meet transactions requirements for buying goods.

To derive that optimal point, we want to find the point at which the benefit of carrying out another withdrawal is less than, or just equal to, the cost of making another transaction between bonds and money. If the benefit of making another transaction were greater than the cost, then another withdrawal should be made, and the original point could not have been optimal. The cost of making another transaction is always equal to b. In Figure 7-2, we show the costs of making a further transaction by the marginal cost curve MC, which is horizontal at the level b. The financial benefit from making another transaction is represented by the MB (marginal benefit) curve in Figure 7-2, which represents the interest *saved* by making another withdrawal and thus having a smaller cash balance on average during the month.

The more transactions between money and bonds an individual makes, the lower the total interest cost is. But the reduction of the interest cost that is obtained by making more transactions falls off rapidly as the number of withdrawals increases. There is a substantial saving in interest costs by making two withdrawals rather than one, but very little saving in interest costs by making thirty-one transactions rather than thirty.

FIGURE 7-2 OPTIMAL CASH MANAGEMENT: DETERMINING THE OPTIMAL NUMBER OF WITHDRAWALS

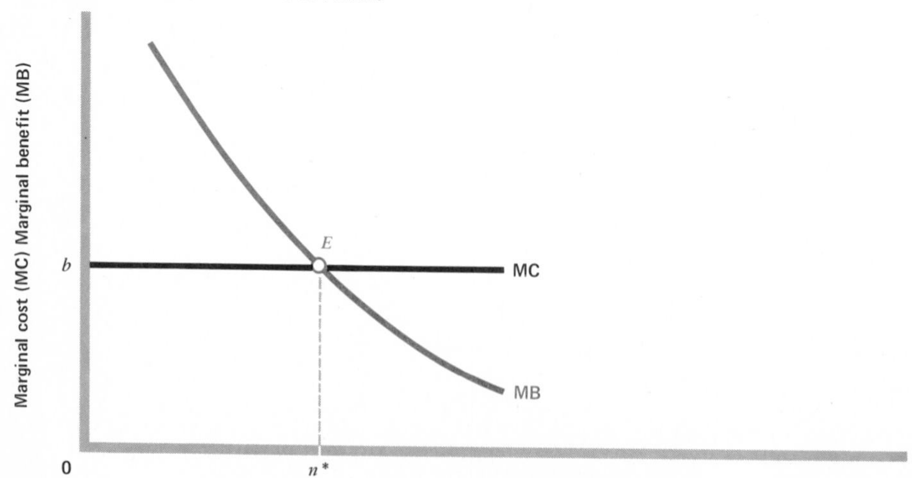

This suggests that the marginal benefit of making more withdrawals decreases as the number of withdrawals becomes large. The MB curve in Figure 7-2 is, accordingly, downward-sloping.[16]

In Figure 7-2, the optimal number of transactions is given by n^*, the number at which the marginal benefit in terms of interest saved is equal to the marginal cost of making a transaction. Given the number of transactions and the individual's income, we also know the average cash balance M, using the relationship between average money holdings and the size of each transfer which we derived earlier:

$$M = \frac{Z}{2} = \frac{Y_N}{2n} \tag{3}$$

From Figure 7-2 we can see two of the important results of the inventory theory of the transactions demand for money. First, suppose the brokerage cost rises. That shifts the MC curve up, decreases the number of withdrawals n, and therefore [from Equation (3), where M is inversely related to n] increases the average holding of money. Second, an increase in the interest rate shifts up the MB curve, therefore increases n, and thus [again, from Equation (3)] reduces the holding of money: when the interest rate is higher, the individual is willing to make more trips to the bank to earn the higher interest now available. Figure 7-2 thus shows one of the key results we wanted to establish—that the demand for money is inversely related to the interest rate.

In the case of an increase in income, Figure 7-2 is unfortunately less useful. An increase in income shifts up the MB curve and thus increases the number of transactions. But from Equation (3), we see that an increase in the number of transactions accompanying an increase in income does not necessarily imply that the demand for money rises. If the number of transactions increases less than in proportion to the increase in income, then the income increase raises the demand for money. However, if the number of transactions increases more than in proportion to the increase in income, the increase in income could lower the demand for money. This second eventuality sounds strange; fortunately, as a more complete algebraic analysis of the individual's optimal behavior would show, it is not possible under the assumptions we have made so far.

The famous square-root formula to which we referred earlier both makes the results of the graphical analysis of Figure 7-2 more precise and resolves the ambiguity about the effects of income on the demand for

[16] Two points about Fig. 7-2: First, note that we have, for convenience, drawn the curves as continuous, even though you will recognize that it is only possible to make an integral number of transactions, and not, for example, 1.6 or 7.24 transactions. Second, if you can use the calculus, try to derive the equation of the marginal benefit curve from the component of costs in Eq. (2) that is due to interest lost.

money. The formula gives the demand for money that is obtained as a result of minimizing the total costs in Equation (2) with respect to the number of withdrawals, and then using Equation (3) to derive the cash balance.[17] The formula is

$$M^* = \sqrt{\frac{bY_N}{2i}} \tag{4}$$

Equation (4) shows that the transactions demand for money increases with the brokerage fee, or the cost of transacting, and with the level of income. The demand for money decreases with the interest rate.

Equation (4) also shows that an increase in income raises the demand for money proportionately less than the increase in income itself. To put the same point somewhat differently, the ratio of income to money, Y_N/M, rises with the level of income. A person with a higher level of income than another holds proportionately less money than the other person. This point is sometimes put in different words by saying that there are *economies of scale* in cash management.

Yet another way of saying the same thing is that the income elasticity of the demand for money is less than 1 [it is equal to ½ in Equation (4)]. The income elasticity measures the percentage change in the demand for money due to a 1 percent change in income.[18]

Similarly, Equation (4) implies that the elasticity of the demand for money with respect to the brokerage fee is ½, and the elasticity with respect to the interest rate is − ½.

What accounts for the fact that people can somehow manage with less cash per dollar of spending as income increases? The reason is that cash management is more effective at high levels of income because the average cost per dollar of transaction is lower with large-size transactions. In turn, the lower average cost of transactions results from the fixed brokerage fee per transaction; it costs as much to transfer $10 as $10 million, so that the average cost per dollar transferred is lower for large transfers.

However, in the case of households, we should recognize that the "brokerage cost" b, the cost of making withdrawals from a savings account, is in part the cost of time and the nuisance of having to go to the bank. Since the cost of time to individuals is likely to be higher the higher their income,

[17] If you can handle calculus, try to derive Eq. (4).

[18] The income elasticity of demand is $\frac{\Delta(M/P)}{M/P} \Big/ \frac{\Delta Y}{Y}$.

Similarly, the interest elasticity is $\frac{\Delta(M/P)}{M/P} \Big/ \frac{\Delta i}{i}$.

b may rise with Y_N. In that case, an increase in income would result in an increase in the demand for money by more than the income elasticity of ½ indicates because b goes up together with Y_N.

The Demand for Real Balances

We started this chapter by emphasizing that the demand for money is a demand for real balances. It is worth confirming that the inventory theory of the demand for money implies that the demand for real balances does not change when all prices double (or increase in any other proportion). When all prices double, both Y_N and b in Equation (4) double—that is, both nominal income and the nominal brokerage fee double. Accordingly, the demand for nominal balances doubles, so that the demand for real balances is unchanged. The square-root formula does not imply any money illusion in the demand for money. Thus we should be careful when saying the income elasticity of demand for money implied by Equation (4) is ½. The elasticity of the demand for *real* balances with respect to *real* income is ½. But if income rises only because all prices (including b) rise, then the demand for *nominal* balances rises proportionately.

*Integer Constraints

So far we have, in the text, ignored the important constraint that it is possible to make only an integral number of transactions, such as 1, 2, 3, etc., and that it is not possible to make 1.25 or 3.57 transactions. However, when we take account of this constraint, we shall see that it implies that many people do not make more than the essential one transaction between money and bonds within the period in which they are paid.[19] Consider our previous example of the person who received $1,200 per month. Suppose, realistically, that the interest rate per month on savings deposits is ½ percent. The individual cannot avoid making one initial transaction, since income initially arrives in the savings account. The next question is whether it pays to make a second transaction. That is, does it pay to keep half the monthly income for half a month in the savings account and make a second withdrawal after half a month? With an interest rate of ½ percent per month, interest for half a month would be ¼ percent. Half the income would amount to $600 and the interest earnings would, therefore, be $600 × ¼ percent = $1.50.

Now if the brokerage fee exceeds $1.50, the individual will not bother to make more than one transaction. And $1.50 is not an outrageous cost in terms of the time and nuisance of making a transfer from the savings to the checking account. Thus, for many individuals whose monthly net pay is

[19] If we had assumed that individuals were paid in cash, it would turn out that many people would not make any transactions between money and bonds in managing their transactions balances.

below \$1,200, we do not expect formula (4) to hold exactly. Their cash balance would instead simply be half their income. They would make one transfer into cash at the beginning of the month; Figure 7-1*a* would describe this cash balance. For such individuals, the income elasticity of the demand for money is 1, since their demand for money goes up precisely in proportion with their income. The interest elasticity is zero, so long as they make only one transaction, because they transfer all their income into cash immediately as they receive it.

The very strong restrictions on the income and interest elasticities of the demand for money of Equation (4) are not valid when the integer constraints are taken into account. Instead, the income elasticity is an average of the elasticities of different people, some of whom make only one transaction from bonds to money, and the elasticity is therefore between ½ and 1. Similarly, the interest elasticity is also an average of the elasticities across different individuals, being between −½ and zero.[20] Because firms deal with larger amounts of money, they are likely to make a large number of transactions between money and bonds, and their income and interest elasticities of the demand for money are therefore likely to be close to the ½ and −½ predicted by Equation (4).

*The Payment Period

Once the integer constraints are taken into account, it can also be seen that the transactions demand for money depends on the frequency with which individuals are paid (the payment period). If one examines the square-root formula (4), the demand for money does not seem to depend on how often a person is paid, since an increase in the payments period increases both Y_N and i in the same proportion. Thus the demand for money appears unaffected by the length of the period. However, consider a person who makes only one transaction from bonds to money at the beginning of each month. Her money demand is $Y_N/2$. If such a person were paid weekly, her demand for money would be only one-quarter of the demand with monthly payments. Thus we should expect the demand for money to increase with the length of the payments period.

Summary

The inventory-theoretic approach to the demand for money gives a precise formula for the transactions demand for money: The income elasticity of the demand for money is ½ and the interest elasticity is −½. When integer constraints are taken into account, the limits on the income elasticity of demand are between ½ and 1, and the limits on the interest elasticity are

[20] See Robert J. Barro, "Integer Constraints and Aggregation in an Inventory Model of Money Demand," *Journal of Finance*, March 1976.

between −½ and zero. We have outlined the approach in terms of an individual's demand for money, but a similar approach is relevant for firms.

Some of the assumptions made in deriving the square-root formula are very restrictive. People do not spend their money evenly over the course of the month, and they do not know exactly what their payments will be. Their checks are not paid into savings accounts, and so on. It turns out, though, that the major results we have derived are not greatly affected by the use of more realistic assumptions. There is thus good reason to expect the demand for money to increase with the level of income and to decrease as the interest rate (or generally, the cost of holding money) increases.

The Precautionary Motive

In discussing the transactions demand for money, we focused on transactions costs and ignored uncertainty. In this section, we concentrate on the demand for money that arises because people are uncertain about the payments they might want to, or have to, make.[21] Suppose, realistically, that an individual did not know precisely what payments he would be receiving in the next few weeks and what payments he would have to make. He might decide to have a hot fudge sundae, or need to take a cab in the rain, or have to pay for a prescription. If he did not have money with which to pay, he would incur a loss. The loss could be missing a fine meal, or missing an appointment, or having to come back the next day to pay for the prescription. For concreteness, we shall denote the loss incurred as a result of being short of cash by $\$c$.[22] The loss clearly varies from situation to situation, but as usual we simplify.

The more money the individual holds, the less likely he is to incur the costs of illiquidity (that is, not having money immediately available). But the more money he holds, the more interest he is giving up. We are back to a tradeoff situation similar to that examined in relation to the transactions demand. Somewhere between holding so little money for precautionary purposes that it will almost certainly be necessary to forgo some purchase (or to borrow in a hurry) and so much money that there is little chance of not being able to make any payment that might be necessary, there must be an optimal amount of precautionary balances to hold. That optimal amount will involve the balancing of interest costs against the advantages of not being caught illiquid.

Once more, we write down the total costs of holding an amount of money M.[23] This time we are dealing with expected costs, since it is not certain what the need for money will be. We denote the probability that the

[21] See Edward H. Whalen, "A Rationalization of the Precautionary Demand for Cash," *Quarterly Journal of Economics*, May 1966.

[22] This c should not be confused with the marginal propensity to consume.

[23] This paragraph contains technical material that is optional and can easily be skipped.

individual is illiquid during the month by $p(M,\sigma)$. The function $p(M,\sigma)$ indicates that the probability of the person's being illiquid at some time during the month depends on the level of money balances M being held and the degree of uncertainty σ about the net payments that will be made during the month. The probability of illiquidity is lower, the higher is M, and higher, the higher is the degree of uncertainty σ. The *expected cost* of illiquidity is $p(M,\sigma)c$—the probability of illiquidity times the cost of being illiquid. The interest cost associated with holding a cash balance of M is just iM. Thus, we have

$$\text{Expected costs} = iM + p(M,\sigma)c \tag{5}$$

To determine the optimal amount of money to hold, we compare the marginal costs of increasing money holding by \$1 with the expected marginal benefit of doing so. The marginal cost is again the interest forgone, or i. That is shown by the MC curve in Figure 7-3. The marginal benefit of increasing money holding arises from the lower expected costs of illiquidity. Increasing precautionary balances from zero has a large marginal benefit, since that takes care of small, unexpected disbursements that are quite likely. As we increase cash balances further, we continue to reduce the probability of illiquidity, but at a decreasing rate. We start to hold cash to insure against quite unlikely events. Thus, the marginal benefit of additional cash is a decreasing function of the level of cash holdings—more cash on hand is better than less, but at a diminishing rate. The marginal benefit of increasing cash holdings is shown by the MB curve in Figure 7-3.

FIGURE 7-3 THE PRECAUTIONARY DEMAND FOR MONEY

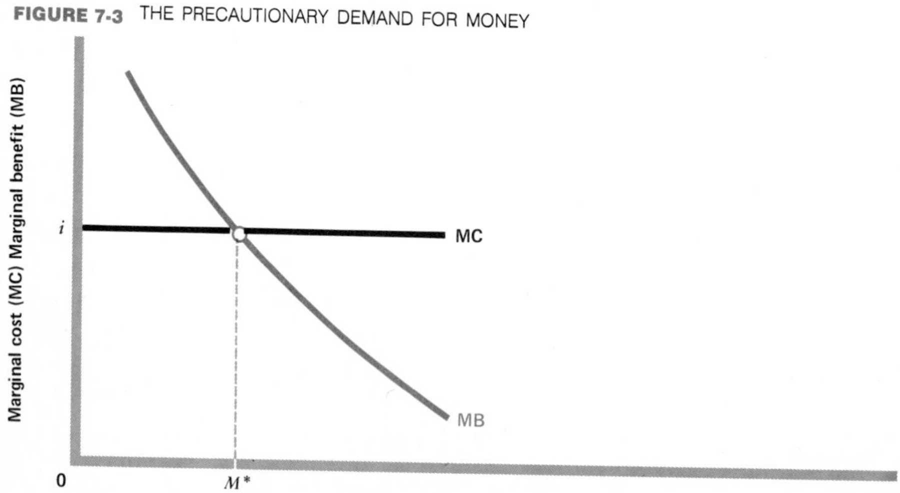

The optimal level of the precautionary demand for money is reached where the two curves intersect. That level of money is shown as M^* in Figure 7-3. Now we can use Figure 7-3 to examine the determinants of the optimal level of the precautionary demand. It is, first, apparent that precautionary balances will be larger when the interest rate is lower. A reduction in the interest rate shifts the MC curve down and increases M^*. The lower costs of holding money makes it profitable to insure more heavily against the costs of illiquidity. An increase in uncertainty leads to increased money holdings because it shifts up the MB curve. With more uncertainty about the flow of spending, there is more scope for unforeseen payments and thus a greater danger of illiquidity. It therefore pays to insure more heavily by holding larger cash balances. Finally, the lower the costs of illiquidity, c, the lower the money demand. A reduction in c moves the MB curve down. Indeed, if there were no cost to illiquidity, no one would bother to hold money. There would be no penalty for not having it, while at the same time, holding it would mean a loss of interest.

The model of precautionary demand can be applied to goods other than money. It is a broad theory that applies to any commodity inventory that is held as insurance against contingencies. For instance, cars carry spare tires. You can work out circumstances under which one would want to have more than one spare tire in a car, and even circumstances in which zero would be the optimal number. The idea of the precautionary demand for money or for goods is quite general. So, too, are the determinants of the precautionary demand; the alternative cost in terms of interest forgone, the cost of illiquidity, and the degree of uncertainty that determines the probability of illiquidity.

The Speculative Demand for Money

The transactions demand and the precautionary demand for money emphasize the medium of exchange function of money, for each refers to the need to have money on hand to make payments. Each theory is more relevant to the M1 definition of money than any other, though the precautionary demand could certainly explain part of the holding of savings accounts and other relatively liquid assets which are part of M2. Now we move over to the store of value function of money and concentrate on the role of money in the investment portfolio of an individual.

An individual who has wealth has to hold that wealth in specific assets. Those assets make up a *portfolio*. One would think an investor would want to hold the asset which provides the highest returns. However, given that the return on most assets is uncertain, it is unwise to hold the entire portfolio in a single *risky asset*. You may have the hottest tip that a certain stock will surely double within the next 2 years, but you would be wise to recognize that hot tips are far from infallible, and that you could lose a lot of money in that stock as well as make money. A prudent, risk-averse investor does not put all her eggs in one basket. Uncertainty about the returns on risky assets leads to a diversified portfolio strategy.

As part of that diversified portfolio, the typical investor will want to hold some amount of a safe asset as insurance against capital losses on assets whose prices change in an uncertain manner. The safe asset would be held precisely because it is safe, even though it pays a lower expected return than risky assets. Money is a safe asset in that its nominal value is known with certainty.[24] In a famous article, James Tobin argued that money would be held as the safe asset in the portfolios of investors.[25] The title of the article, "Liquidity Preference as Behavior towards Risk," explains the essential notion. In this framework, the demand for money—the safest asset—depends on the expected yields, as well as on the riskiness of the yields, on other assets. The riskiness of the return on other assets is measured by the variability of the return. Using reasonable assumptions, Tobin shows that an increase in the expected return on other assets—an increase in the opportunity cost of holding money (that is, the return lost by holding money)—lowers money demand. By contrast, an increase in the riskiness of the returns on other assets increases money demand.

An investor's aversion to risk certainly generates a demand for a safe asset. The question we want to consider is whether that safe asset is money. That is, we want to ask whether considerations of portfolio behavior do generate a demand for money. The relevant considerations in the portfolio are the returns and the risks on assets. From the viewpoint of the yield and risks of holding money, it is clear that time or savings deposits have the same risks as currency or demand deposits. However, they generally pay a higher yield. The risks in both cases are the risks arising from uncertainty about inflation. Given that the risks are the same, and with the yields on time and savings deposits higher than on currency and demand deposits, portfolio diversification explains the demand for assets such as time and savings deposits better than the demand for M1. We therefore regard the speculative demand as applying primarily to M2.

The implications of the speculative, or risk-diversifying, demand for money are similar to those of the transactions and precautionary demands. An increase in the interest rate on nonmoney assets, such as long-term bond yields or equity yields, will reduce the demand for M2. An increase in the rate paid on time deposits will increase the demand for time deposits, perhaps even at the cost of the demand for M1, as people take advantage of the higher yields they can earn on their investment portfolios to increase the size of those portfolios. One important difference between the

[24] Of course, when the rate of inflation is uncertain, the real value of money is also uncertain, and money is no longer a safe asset. Even so, the uncertainties about the values of equity are so much larger than the uncertainties about the rate of inflation that money can be treated as a relatively safe asset.

[25] James Tobin, "Liquidity Preference as Behavior towards Risk," *Review of Economic Studies*, February 1958.

speculative and the other two categories of demand is that here the level of wealth is clearly relevant to the demand for M2. The level of wealth determines the size of the total portfolio, and we expect that increases in wealth lead to increases in the demand for the safe asset, and thus in M2 demand.

One final point on the speculative demand. Many individuals with relatively small amounts of wealth will indeed hold part of that wealth in savings accounts in order to diversify their portfolios. But bigger investors are sometimes able to purchase other securities which pay higher interest and also have fixed (i.e., risk-free) nominal values. Large CDs (in excess of $100,000) are sometimes an example of such assets, as are Treasury bills on occasion. For such individuals or groups, the demand for a safe asset is not a demand for money.

7-4 EMPIRICAL EVIDENCE

This section examines the empirical evidence—the studies made using actual data—on the demand for money. We noted in Chapter 4, and again at the beginning of Section 7-3, that the *interest elasticity* of the demand for money plays an important role in determining the effectiveness of monetary and fiscal policies. We then showed in Section 7-3 that there are good theoretical reasons for believing the demand for real balances should depend on the interest rate. The empirical evidence supports that view very strongly. Empirical studies have established that the demand for money is responsive to the interest rate. An increase in the interest rate reduces the demand for money.

The theory of money demand also predicts that the demand for money should depend on the level of income. The response of the demand for money to the level of income, as measured by the *income elasticity* of money demand, is also important from a policy viewpoint. The income elasticity of money demand provides a guide to the Fed as to how fast to increase the money supply to support a given rate of growth of GNP without changing the interest rate.

Suppose that the aim is for GNP growth of 10 percent, 6 percent real growth and 4 percent inflation. If the Fed wants to provide a sufficient growth rate of money to prevent interest rates from rising, it has to know the income elasticity of the demand for real balances. Suppose the real income elasticity is ½. Then the Fed would have to produce monetary growth of 7 percent to prevent an increase in interest rates. Why? First, the demand for nominal money increases in proportion to the price level, since money demand is a demand for real balances. Thus 4 percent growth in money is needed to meet the increased demand from the 4 percent increase in the price level. The 6 percent growth in real income would increase the demand for real balances by 3 percent (= 6 percent × ½), given the real income elasticity of ½. Hence, the needed 7 percent (= 4 + 3) growth in the nominal money supply to meet the increased demand arising from the increase in income.

The empirical work on the demand for money has introduced one complication that we did not study in the theoretical section—that the demand for money adjusts to changes in income and interest rates *with a lag*. When the level of income or the interest rate changes, there is first only a small change in the demand for money. Then, over the course of time, the change in the demand for money increases, slowly building up to its full long-run change. Reasons for this lag are not yet certain. The two usual possibilities exist in this case too. The lags may arise because there are costs of adjusting money holdings, or they may arise because money holders' expectations are slow to adjust. If people believe that a given change in the interest rate is temporary, they may be unwilling to make a major change in their money holdings. As time passes and it becomes clearer that the change is not transitory, they are more willing to make a larger adjustment.

Empirical evidence on the demand for money in the United States up to 1973 has been reworked and summarized in a comprehensive study by Stephen Goldfeld of Princeton University.[26] Goldfeld studied the demand for M1 using quarterly postwar data and, of course, the pre-1980 definition of M1. Table 7-2 summarizes the major conclusions from that earlier empirical work. The table shows the elasticities of the demand for real balances with respect to real income Y (real GNP) and interest rates. The rate on time deposits, i_{TD}, and the rate on commercial paper, i_{CP}, are the interest rates used by Goldfeld. Commercial paper represents short-term borrowing by corporations. That interest rate is relevant to the demand for money because commercial paper is an asset which is very liquid for corporations that hold it instead of money for short periods of time.

[26] Stephen M. Goldfeld, "The Demand for Money Revisited," *Brookings Papers on Economic Activity*, 1973:3 (Washington, D.C.: The Brookings Institution, 1973). A review of other work on the demand for money is contained in the very readable book by David Laidler, *The Demand for Money: Theories and Evidence*, 2d ed. (New York: Dun-Donnelley, 1977).

TABLE 7-2 ELASTICITIES OF REAL MONEY DEMAND

	Y	i_{TD}	i_{CP}
Short run	0.19	−0.045	−0.019
Long run	0.68	−0.16	−0.067

Source: S Goldfeld, "The Demand for Money Revisited," *Brookings Papers on Economic Activity* 1973:3 (Washington, D.C.: The Brookings Institution, 1973), p. 602, Regression A.

In the short run (one quarter), the elasticity of demand with respect to real income is 0.19. This means that a 1 percent increase in real income raises money demand by 0.19 percent, which is considerably less than proportionately. The table shows that the interest elasticity of money demand with respect to interest rates is negative: an increase in interest rates reduces money demand. The short-run interest elasticities are quite small. An increase in the rate on time deposits from 4 percent to 5 percent, that is, a 25 percent increase ($\frac{5}{4} = 1.25$), reduces the demand for money by only 1.12 percent (= 0.045 × 25 percent). An increase in the rate on commercial paper from 4 to 5 percent would reduce money demand by only 0.47 percent.

The long-run elasticities exceed the short-run elasticities by a factor of more than 3, as Table 7-2 shows. The long-run real income elasticity is 0.68, meaning that in the long run the increase in real money demand occurring as a result of a given increase in real income is only 68 percent as large as the proportional increase in income. Real money demand thus rises less than proportionately to the rise in real income. The long-run interest elasticities sum to a little over 0.2, meaning that an increase in *both* i_{TD} and i_{CP} from 4 percent to 5 percent would reduce the demand for money by a little over 5 percent.

How long is the long run? That is, how long does it take the demand for money to adjust from the short-run elasticities of Table 7-2 to the long-run elasticities shown in the table? Actually, it takes forever for the full long-run position to be reached. Table 7-3, however, shows the elasticities of the demand for real balances in response to changes in the level of income and interest rates after one, two, three, four, and eight quarters. Three-fourths of the adjustment is complete within the first year, and over 90 percent of the adjustment is complete within the first 2 years.

In summary, we have so far described three essential properties of money demand:

TABLE 7-3 DYNAMIC PATTERNS OF ELASTICITIES OF MONEY DEMAND WITH RESPECT TO REAL INCOME AND INTEREST RATES

Quarters elapsed	Y	i_{TD}	i_{CP}
1	0.19	−0.045	−0.019
2	0.33	−0.077	−0.033
3	0.43	−0.100	−0.042
4	0.50	−0.117	−0.049
8	0.63	−0.148	−0.062
Long run	0.68	−0.160	−0.067

Source: S. Goldfeld, "The Demand for Money Revisited," *Brookings Papers on Economic Activity* 1973:3 (Washington, D.C.: The Brookings Institution, 1973).

1 The demand for real money balances responds negatively to the rate of interest. An increase in interest rates reduces the demand for money.
2 The demand for money increases with the level of real income. However, the income elasticity of money demand is less than 1 so that money demand increases less than proportionately with income.
3 The short-run responsiveness of money demand to changes in interest rates and income is considerably less than the long-run response. The long-run elasticities are estimated to be over three times the size of the short-run elasticities.

There is one more important question Goldfeld considered. This is the question of how money responds to an increase in the level of prices. Here Goldfeld, like other researchers before him, finds strong evidence that an increase in prices raises nominal money demand in the same proportion. We can add, therefore, a fourth conclusion:

4 The demand for nominal money balances is proportional to the price level. There is no money illusion; in other words, the demand for money is a demand for *real* balances.

Since 1973, when Goldfeld estimated the demand function for money whose properties are summarized in Table 7-2, there has been a shift in the money demand function. If an equation similar to Goldfeld's is used to predict money demand, starting in 1973, then by the beginning of 1979 the demand for money predicted by the equation turns out to be over 15 percent higher than the actual money stock.[27] This extraordinary shift has naturally been the focus of much research, which has centered on two possibilities.

The first is that the financial innovations mentioned earlier led to changes in money demand.[28] For example, in 1975 it became possible to make transfers between accounts by telephone instruction rather than by actually going to the bank. This reduces the brokerage cost, b, and reduces the demand for M1. Similarly, during this period corporations were for the first time allowed to own savings deposits, leading them to reduce holdings of M1. In addition, the invention of money market funds (see Section 7-1) would reduce the demand for money. Such explanations do appear to account for part of the shift in money demand.

An associated explanation argues that there have been permanent shifts in money demand associated with the very high interest rates of 1973–1974 and 1978–1980. The argument here is that when interest rates

[27] These calculations are presented in Richard Porter, Thomas Simpson, and Eileen Mauskopf, "Financial Innovation and the Monetary Aggregates," *Brookings Papers on Economic Activity*, 1979:1 (Washington, D.C.: The Brookings Institution, 1979).

[28] Ibid.

became very high, firms undertook studies of how to economize on money, developing new methods of *cash management*. These are sophisticated methods for firms to reduce the amount of money held in the normal course of business.[29] Among these methods are "bank-managed checking accounts" where the bank undertakes to monitor the account and automatically invests any excess balances in short-term financial assets.

Adoption of the new methods leads to a permanent reduction in the demand for money even after interest rates have fallen from their record levels. This is because once the firm has figured out the new methods of managing its cash, it continues to use them.[30] It is clear that firms have increasingly used sophisticated methods of cash management. The explanation that centers on cash management obtains further support from two facts: First, the shift in money demand since 1973 can be traced entirely to a shift in the demand for demand deposits rather than currency; and second, a substantial role in the shift can be traced to reduced demand for money by corporations.

The second main possibility is that the Goldfeld demand function omits some relevant variables. Here the leading candidate has been the long-term interest rate. It has been argued that since all assets are potentially substitutes for money in the portfolios of money holders, there is no reason why only short-term interest rates should enter the demand function for money. Inclusion of the long-term interest rate and an estimate of the return on equity does improve the fit of the money demand function.[31]

Given the institutional changes in the financial markets during the seventies, it should be no surprise that there have been shifts in the money demand function. We thus put considerable weight on the roles of financial innovation and cash management in producing the shift in the money demand function.

Finally, amid all the excitement we should remember that despite the recent shifts in money demand, empirical work still finds that the demand for money is positively related to income and negatively related to interest rates.

*7-5 THE INCOME VELOCITY OF MONEY

The *income velocity of money* is the number of times the stock of money is turned over per year in financing the annual flow of income. Thus in 1979 GNP was about $2,369 billion, the money stock (M1) was $360 billion, and

[29] A variety of these methods are described in Porter, Simpson, and Mauskopf, cited in footnote 27.

[30] Note, though, that the demand for money would still be higher at low interest rates than it would be at high interest rates, once the new methods have been adopted.

[31] This is shown by Michael Hamburger, "Behavior of the Money Stock: Is There a Puzzle?" *Journal of Monetary Economics*, July 1977.

velocity was therefore about 6.6. The average dollar of money balances financed \$6.60 of spending on final goods and services, or the public held on average just over 15 cents of M1 per dollar of income.[32] While we usually calculate velocity for the economy as a whole, we can also calculate it for an individual. For instance, for someone earning \$12,000 per year, who has average money balances during the year of \$1,000, the income velocity of money holdings is 12.

Income velocity (from now on we shall refer to velocity rather than income velocity) is defined, as in Section 4-8, as

$$V \equiv \frac{Y_N}{M} \tag{6}$$

the ratio of nominal income to nominal money stock. If we rewrite (6) as

$$Y_N \equiv VM \tag{6a}$$

we see one of the major reasons economists have examined the behavior of velocity. Given the nominal money stock and the velocity, we know the level of nominal income. Thus, if we can predict the level of velocity, we can predict the level of nominal income, given the money stock.

Further, *if* velocity were constant, changing the money supply would result in proportionate changes in nominal income. Any policies, including fiscal policies, that did not affect the money stock would not affect the level of income. You will probably now recognize that we have previously discussed a case of constant velocity. In Chapter 4, we discussed the effectiveness of fiscal policy when the demand for money is not a function of the interest rate and the LM curve is therefore vertical. That vertical LM curve is the same as the assumption of constant velocity.

The discussion of constant velocity suggests that the behavior of velocity is closely related to the behavior of the demand for money. Indeed, the notion of velocity is important because it is a convenient way of talking about money demand. For that reason, the term is frequently used in policy discussions. Discussions about monetary policy would be difficult to follow (or even more difficult to follow than they now are) without knowledge of the meaning of velocity.

We now examine the relationship between velocity and the demand for

[32] Why do we say income velocity and not plain velocity? There is another concept, transactions velocity, that is, the ratio of total transactions to money balances. Total transactions far exceed GNP for two reasons. First, there are many transactions involving the sale and purchase of assets that do not contribute to GNP. Second, a particular item in final output typically generates total spending on it that exceeds the contribution of that item to GNP. For instance, one dollar's worth of wheat generates transactions as it leaves the farm, as it is sold by the miller, as it leaves the baker for the supermarket, and then as it is sold to the household. One dollar's worth of wheat may involve several dollars of transactions before it is sold for the last time. Transactions velocity is thus higher than income velocity.

money. Let the demand for real balances be written $L(i,Y)$ consistent with Chapter 4. Recall that Y is real income. Then, when the supply of money is equal to the demand for money, we have

$$\frac{M}{P} = L(i,Y) \tag{7}$$

or $M = PL(i,Y)$. Now we can substitute for the nominal money supply into Equation (6) to obtain

$$V = \frac{Y_N}{PL(i,Y)} = \frac{Y}{L(i,Y)} \tag{6b}$$

where we have recognized that Y_N/P is the level of real income. Income velocity is the ratio of the level of real income to the demand for real balances.

From Equation (6*b*) we note that velocity is a function of real income and the interest rate. Consider first the effects of a change in the interest rate on velocity. An increase in the interest rate reduces the demand for real balances and therefore increases velocity: when the cost of holding money increases, money holders make their money do more work, and thus turn it over more often.

The way in which changes in real income affect velocity depends on the income elasticity of the demand for money. If the income elasticity of the demand for real balances were 1, then the demand for real balances would change in the same proportion as income. In that case, changes in real income would not affect velocity. For, suppose that real income Y increased by 10 percent. The numerator Y in Equation (6*b*) would increase by 10 percent as would the denominator, and velocity would be unchanged. However, we have seen that the income elasticity of the demand for money is less than 1. That means that velocity *increases* with increases in real income. For example, suppose that real income rose 10 percent, and the demand for real balances increased only by 6.8 percent (= 0.68 × 10 percent), as Goldfeld's results suggest. Then the numerator of Equation (6*b*) would increase by more than the denominator, and velocity would rise.

The empirical work reviewed in Section 7-4 makes it clear that the demand for money and, therefore, also velocity do react systematically to changes in interest rates and the level of real income. The empirical evidence therefore decisively refutes the view that velocity is unaffected by changes in interest rates and that fiscal policy is, accordingly, incapable of affecting the level of nominal income. In terms of Equation (6*b*), and using the analysis of Chapter 4, expansionary fiscal policy can be thought of as working by increasing interest rates, thereby increasing velocity, and thus making it possible for a given stock of money to support a higher level of nominal GNP.

The empirical evidence we reviewed in Section 7-4 is useful in interpreting the long-run or *trend* behavior in velocity shown in Chart 7-1. The chart shows a striking and steady increase in velocity. The velocity of M1 has doubled from about 3 in the mid-fifties to over 6 in 1980. The average dollar finances twice the income flow now than it did in the mid-fifties.

This increase in velocity can of course be explained by the same factors that explain the demand for money. Velocity has risen because income has risen (since the income elasticity of demand is less than 1) and because interest rates have risen. In addition, the financial innovations that reduced money demand in the seventies increased velocity. A look at Equation (6*b*) shows that anything which reduces the demand for money, in the denominator, for a given level of Y, in the numerator, increases velocity.

In contrast to the longer-term trends, the importance of the behavior of velocity (or money demand) in the short run and the way in which the behavior of velocity is discussed in policy making are brought out by events at the end of 1975. Chart 7-2 shows a rapid rise in velocity from

CHART 7-1 THE INCOME VELOCITY OF MONEY (M1): THE TREND *(Source: Citibank Economic Database)*

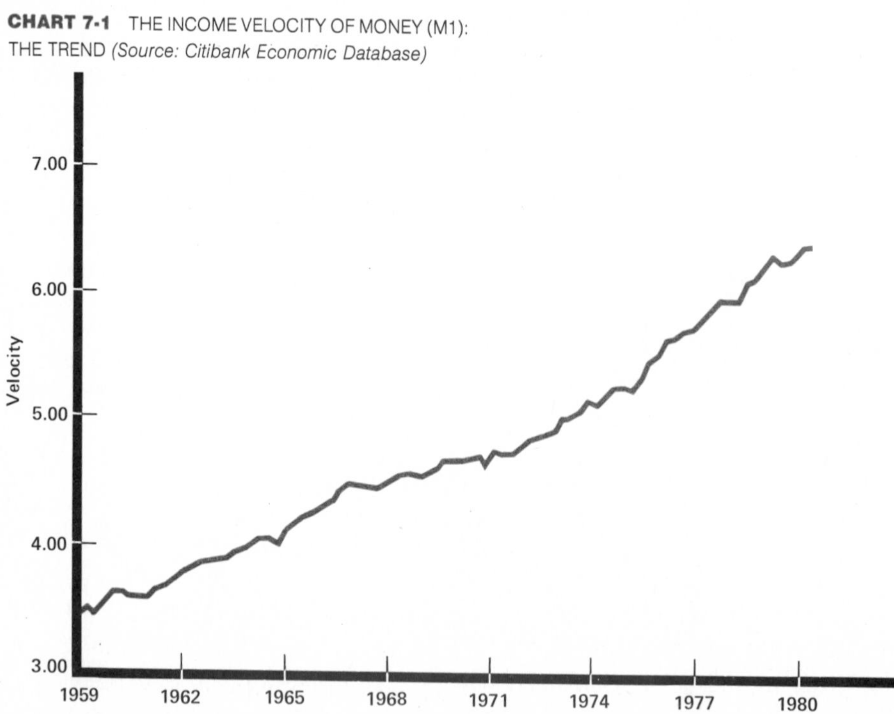

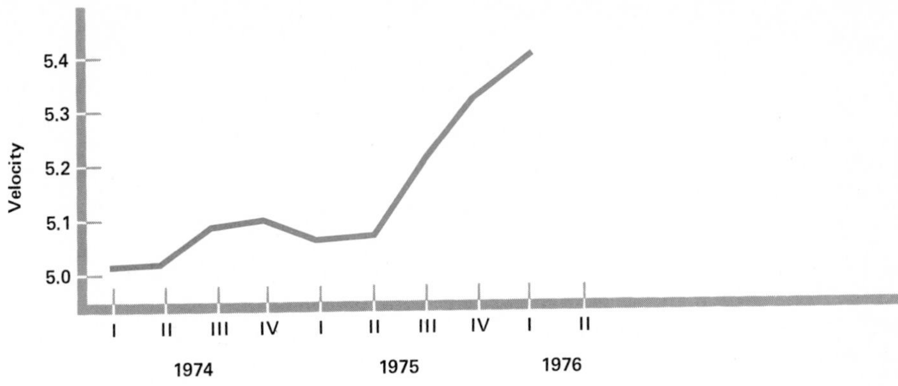

CHART 7-2 THE INCOME VELOCITY OF MONEY IN THE SHORT RUN. *(Source: Economic Report of the President 1977)*

the second quarter of 1975. This rise in velocity played an important role in the recovery from the recession. Monetary growth was quite slow in those quarters, and the Fed set itself a goal of increasing the M1 money stock at a rate of only 5 to 7 percent. Since the inflation rate that was expected for the period was in the 7 to 8 percent range, the Fed was implicitly setting a target for the growth rate of real balances of zero or less.[33] Many outside economists feared that low growth of real balances would result in an increase in interest rates that would choke off the recovery. However, the Fed stuck to its guns, arguing that velocity typically increases during business-cycle recoveries.

Commenting later, Arthur Burns, then chairperson of the Fed, testified to Congress:[34]

> We knew from a careful reading of history that the turnover of money balances tends to rise rapidly in the early stages of an economic upswing. Consequently, we resisted the advice of those who wanted to open the tap and let money flow out in greater abundance. Subsequent events have borne out our judgments . . . increases in the turnover of money balances have been larger than we at the Federal Reserve had anticipated.

We shall make two brief comments on Burns's statement. First, "turnover" of money balances is nothing other than velocity. Second, note that the very small short-run income elasticity of demand for real balances

[33] Be sure you understand why planned monetary growth of, say, 6½ percent and expected inflation of 7½ percent implies that real balances are expected to fall.

[34] Statement by Arthur F. Burns before the Committee on Banking, Currency, and Housing, U.S. House of Representatives, Feb. 3, 1976. Reprinted in the *Federal Reserve Bulletin*, February 1976, pp. 119–125.

shown in Section 7-4 implies that velocity should rise rapidly when income increases. In the short run, increases in income during a recovery do not increase the demand for money by very much, and velocity thus tends to increase much more rapidly than it would given the same increase in income maintained for a longer period. Nonetheless, it remains true that velocity in the last part of 1975 increased even more rapidly than the results of Section 7-4 predicted, and, as Burns noted, also more rapidly than the Fed had predicted. Without that increase in velocity, and given the slow growth of money (2.7 percent in the second half of 1975) at the time, the recovery could not have taken place as quickly as it did. Of course, if velocity had not increased as it did, the Fed could have increased the growth rate of money.

7-6 VELOCITY AND INFLATION

We begin to discuss inflation systematically only in Chapter 13, but we can take up here an important and fascinating aspect of inflation. The question is: How does inflation affect the demand for money? It is especially important to distinguish here between the demand for *nominal* and *real* money balances. Earlier in the chapter we have seen that (1) an increase in the price level, all real variables remaining unchanged, leaves the demand for real balances unchanged and increases the demand for nominal balances in proportion to the increase in the price level, and (2) an increase in the rate of interest increases the cost of holding money and reduces the demand for real balances.

These two points are relevant in discussing the effects of expected inflation—expected continuing increases in prices—on the demand for real balances. We have seen that a one-time increase in the price level, all real variables remaining unchanged after this increase, leaves the demand for real balances unaffected. But now assume that prices increase and that the public interprets the price increases as merely the prelude to further continuing price increases. That is, the public anticipates inflation. Inflation reduces the purchasing power of money. Thus, inflation at the rate of 5 percent reduces the real value of a nominal dollar that is held for a period of one year by 5 percent. Inflation acts as a tax on real balances.[35] Someone holding \$100 for a year during which inflation is 5 percent in effect pays \$5 for holding that money during the year. If she held less money, she would pay a smaller tax; if she reduced her cash holdings to \$50, the tax would be only \$2.50. There is thus an incentive, when increased

[35] We explore the notion of inflation as a tax on real balances in more detail in Chap. 14, which deals with the budget.

inflation is expected, to try to reduce holdings of real balances and, instead, hold assets whose value is not as adversely affected by inflation. It is precisely this consideration that causes the public to reduce the demand for real balances when inflation is expected.

The effects of expected inflation on the demand for real balances have a strong influence on the behavior of the price level when money supply growth increases. Suppose the money supply has been growing at 5 percent, that real income was constant, and the inflation rate had been a steady 5 percent. Then let the money supply start growing more rapidly, say at 10 percent. Ultimately, prices will increase at a 10 percent rate as well. But with 10 percent inflation expected, the demand for real balances is lower than when the expected inflation rate is only 5 percent. This means that at some stage during the process by which the economy adapts from an inflation rate of 5 percent to a rate of 10 percent, real balances have to be reduced. The only way real balances can fall is for prices to increase more rapidly than the money supply. Accordingly, at some point during the adjustment process, prices have to increase more rapidly than at 10 percent, which is the rate at which the nominal money supply is growing, which means that an increase in the growth rate of money to a new higher level produces, at some point, a rate of inflation higher than the rate of growth of money. The adjustment of real balances during an inflationary period will imply that prices increase more rapidly than the nominal money stock.

How does this observation link up with evidence on money demand during inflationary periods? Phillip Cagan of Columbia University studied the demand for real balances during *hyperinflations*—extremely rapid inflations—in an interesting and famous article.[36] His evidence shows that the demand for real balances declines dramatically as inflation reaches very high levels. As we noted earlier, expected inflation reduces the demand for money because it is a cost of holding money. For instance, during the Austrian hyperinflation in 1922–1923, the *monthly* rate of inflation rose from roughly zero to more than 80 percent. This extraordinary increase in inflation brought about a decline in real money demand to *one-fifth* the level that had been held at zero inflation. Velocity increased by a factor of 5. The evidence for other countries is, if anything, even more striking.

Cagan's evidence raises the question of how real money demand, or velocity, can be so flexible. How do people manage to reduce their money holdings per dollar, or crown, of income by so much? As inflation increases, the public takes more care in how it manages its cash balances. Money is spent more rapidly after it is received. Firms begin to pay their workers

[36] Phillip Cagan, "The Monetary Dynamics of Hyperinflation," in Milton Friedman (ed.), *Studies in the Quantity Theory of Money* (Chicago: The University of Chicago Press, 1956).

more frequently. Money becomes like a hot potato, with people anxious to pass it on rapidly. One can almost see the velocity of circulation increasing as people scurry to get rid of cash. These changes in payments patterns and shopping habits do impose costs on money holders that are the major cost of expected inflation, as we shall see in Chapter 15.

The adjustment of the demand for money to expected inflation is, in principle, no different from the adjustment to changes in the interest rate, which also increase the cost of holding money. Indeed, in countries with sufficiently well-developed capital markets, expected inflation is reflected in nominal interest rates. When inflation is expected, borrowers know that they will repay their debts in money that has lower purchasing power than the money they originally borrowed, and lenders know that too. Lenders, accordingly, become more reluctant to lend at any given level of the nominal interest rate, and borrowers become more anxious to borrow at a given nominal interest rate. The result is that the *nominal* interest rate rises when inflation is expected, thus compensating lenders for the loss of purchasing power of money.

The rise in the nominal interest rate that we are talking about reminds us of the distinction between *real* and *nominal* interest rates made in Chapter 6. When the expected rate of inflation rises, nominal interest rates—interest rates which specify how many dollars have to be repaid—increase. The real interest rate—the nominal interest rate minus the expected rate of inflation—need not rise and may even fall. Undoubtedly, one of the major reasons for the increase in nominal interest rates in the United States since the fifties is the increase in the expected rate of inflation. This relationship will be investigated in more detail in Chapter 13. In some Latin American countries where inflation rates have reached 100 percent per year or more, no one is surprised by bank loan rates of, say, 80 percent.

In talking about both the expected rate of inflation itself and nominal interest rates, we raise the question of whether each is a separate influence on the demand for money. In well-developed capital markets, in which interest rates are free to move to reflect expected inflation, the nominal interest rate is the relevant opportunity cost of holding money. That is because individuals could make investments at that interest rate. In markets where interest rates are controlled and rates do not rise to reflect expected inflation, individuals begin to think of the alternative of buying goods rather than holding money when the expected rate of inflation rises. The expected inflation rate itself then becomes a separate influence on the demand for money. Franco Modigliani has offered the following useful rule of thumb to decide whether the nominal interest rate or the expected rate of inflation should be included as determining the demand for money: If the nominal interest rate exceeds the expected rate of inflation, the nominal interest rate should be thought of as the cost of holding money. If the expected inflation rate exceeds the nominal interest rate, think of the expected inflation rate as the cost of holding money.

7-7 SUMMARY

1 The demand for money is a demand for real balances. It is the purchasing power, not the number, of their dollar bills that matters to holders of money.
2 The money supply M1-B is made up of currency and checkable deposits. A broader measure, M2, includes savings and time deposits at depositary institutions as well as some other interest-bearing assets.
3 The chief characteristic of money is that it serves as a means of payment.
4 There are two broad reasons why people hold money and thus forgo interest that they could earn by holding alternative assets. These reasons are transactions costs and uncertainty.
5 Transactions costs are an essential aspect of money demand. If it were costless to move (instantaneously) in and out of interest-bearing assets, nobody would hold money. Optimal cash management would involve transfers from other assets (bonds or saving deposits) just prior to outlays, and it would involve immediate conversion into interest-bearing form of any cash receipts. The existence of transactions costs—brokerage costs, fees, and time costs—makes it optimal to hold some money.
6 The inventory-theoretic approach shows that an individual will hold a stock of real balances that varies inversely with the interest rate but increases with the level of real income and the cost of transactions. The income elasticity of money demand is less than unity, so that there are economies of scale.
7 Transactions costs, in combination with uncertainty about payments and receipts, give rise to a precautionary demand for money. Money holdings provide insurance against illiquidity. Optimal money holdings are higher, the higher the variability of net disbursements and the higher the cost of illiquidity. Since money holdings involve forgoing interest, the optimal money holding will vary inversely with the rate of interest.
8 Portfolio diversification involves the tradeoff between risk and return. Saving deposits form part of an optimal portfolio because they are not risky—their nominal value is constant. Saving deposits dominate currency or demand deposits, which are also safe nominal assets, because they bear interest. Thus the speculative portfolio demand for money is a demand for saving or time deposits.
9 The empirical evidence provides strong support for a negative interest

elasticity of money demand and a positive income elasticity. Because of lags, short-run elasticities are much smaller than long-run elasticities. The long-run income elasticity is about 0.7, and the long-run interest elasticity is about −0.2.

10 The income velocity of money is defined as the ratio of income to money or the rate of turnover of money. Since the fifties, velocity has doubled to a level in excess of 6.

11 The empirical evidence implies that an increase in real income raises velocity, as does an increase in the rate of interest. At higher levels of income or at higher interest rates, there is a lower demand for money in relation to income. Higher interest rates lead people to economize on cash balances.

12 Inflation implies that money loses purchasing power, and inflation thus creates a cost of holding money. The higher the rate of inflation, the lower the amount of real balances that will be held. Hyperinflations provide striking support for this prediction. Under conditions of very high expected inflation, money demand falls dramatically relative to income. Velocity rises as people use less money in relation to income.

PROBLEMS

1 To what extent would it be possible to design a society in which there was no money? What would the problems be? Could currency at least be eliminated? How? (Lest all this seems too unworldly, you should know that some people are beginning to talk of a "cashless economy" in the next century.)

2 Evaluate the effects of the following changes on the demand for M1 and M2. Which of the functions of money do they relate to?

(*a*) "Instant cash" machines which allow 24-hour withdrawals from savings accounts at banks

(*b*) The employment of more tellers at your bank

(*c*) An increase in inflationary expectations

(*d*) Widespread acceptance of credit cards

(*e*) Fear of an imminent collapse of the government

(*f*) A rise in the interest rate on time deposits

*3 The assumption was made in the text that in the transactions demand for cash model, it is optimal to space transactions evenly throughout the month. Prove this as follows in the case where $n = 2$. Since one transaction must be made immediately, the only question is when to make the second one. For simplicity, call the beginning of the month $t = 0$, and the end of the month $t = 1$. Then consider a transaction strategy which performs the second transaction at time t_0. If income is Y_N, then this will require moving $t_0 Y_N$ into cash now, and $(1 - t_0)Y_N$ at time t_0. Calculate the total cost incurred under this strategy, and try various values of t_0 to see which is optimal. (If you are familiar with calculus, prove that $t_0 = ½$ minimizes total cost.)

*4 For those students familiar with calculus, derive Equation (4) from Equation (2) by minimizing total costs with respect to n.

5 (*a*) Determine the optimal strategy for cash management for the person who earns $1,600 per month, can earn 0.5 percent interest per month in the savings account, and has a transaction cost of $1.
  (*b*) What is the individual's average cash balance?
  (*c*) Suppose her income rises to $1,800. By what percentage does her demand for money rise? (Pay attention to the integer constraints.)

6 Discuss the various factors that go into an individual's decision regarding how many traveler's checks to take on a vacation.

7 In the text, we said that the transactions demand-for-money model can also be applied to firms. Suppose a firm sells steadily during the month and has to pay its workers at the end of the month. Explain then how it would determine its money holdings.

8 In the text we argued that the demand for money fell when corporations received permission to hold savings accounts.
  (*a*) For which money demand concept is this true? False?
  (*b*) Explain why this change would have been more important for small firms than for large ones.

9 (*a*) Is V high or low relative to trend during recessions? Why?
  (*b*) How can the Fed influence velocity?

10 This chapter emphasizes that the demand for money is a demand for real balances. At the same time, inflation causes the real demand to fall. Explain how these two assertions can both be correct.

11 "Muggers favor deflation." Comment.

8

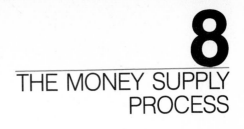

THE MONEY SUPPLY PROCESS

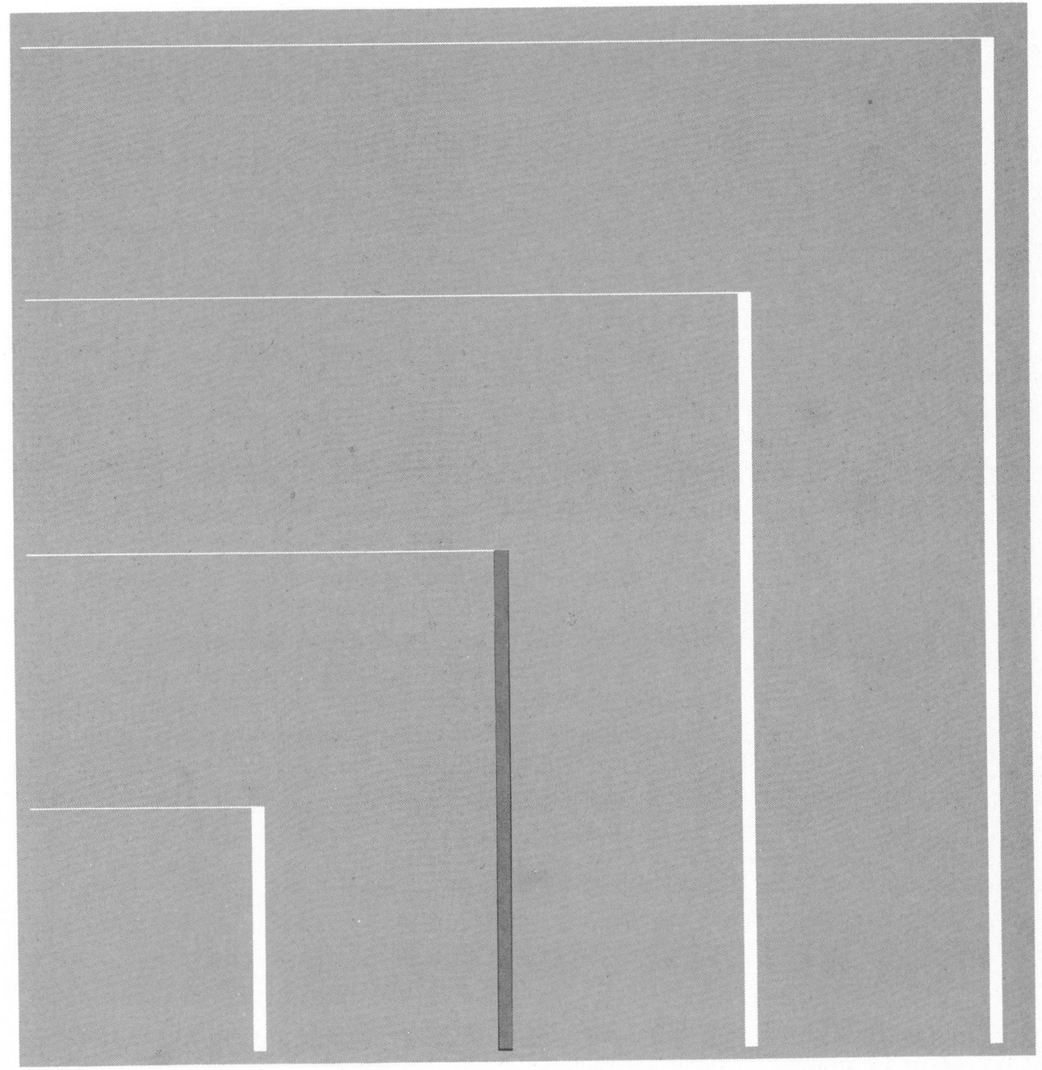

We have so far taken the money supply to be given and determined by the Federal Reserve System. By and large, the Fed is indeed able to determine the money supply quite accurately, but it does not set it directly. In this chapter we study the way in which the actions of the Fed, the banks, and the public interact in determining the stock of money.

In conducting monetary policy, the Fed pays attention to the behavior of both interest rates and the money supply. We will show that the Fed cannot simultaneously set both the money supply and the interest rate at whatever levels it wants, though it can set either the money supply or the interest rate. In addition, we shall introduce the notion of a money supply function—the supply of money as a function of the interest rate.

8-1 DEFINITIONS

We noted in Chapter 7 that the money supply measure M1 is the sum of demand deposits, *DD*, plus currency held by the public, *CU*.

$$\mathrm{M1} = DD + CU \tag{1}$$

A broader measure of the money supply is M2, which adds time, savings, and other deposits, *TD*, to M1:

$$\mathrm{M2} = \mathrm{M1} + TD \tag{2}$$

We shall henceforth refer to the difference between M2 and M1 as consisting of time deposits, though the total in fact includes savings and other deposits.

Chart 8-1 shows the history of these aggregates and their components. (Currency is not shown but is the difference between M1 and demand deposits.) Time deposits have been growing more rapidly than the other components of the money supply, and M2 has accordingly been growing more rapidly than M1. Over the 1970–1979 period, M1 grew at 6.4 percent per annum and M2 at 9.6 percent. The 6.4 percent growth rate of M1 from 1970 to 1979 is well above the average rate of growth of M1 of 3.8 percent from 1960 to 1969.

Table 8-1 reproduces Table 7-1 and shows the March 1980 components of the money stock. M1 (recall that we mean M1-B) is about $392 billion, a little over a quarter of that consisting of currency. The difference between M2 and M1 of $1,158 billion is composed chiefly of time and savings deposits.

For simplicity, we shall now ignore the distinction between demand

portfolios. Ba
deposits of $2
The Fed
money, or the
(notes and coi
by the publi
remaining cu
notes that con
the Fed[2] and
liability of th

8-2 THE MC

In this sectio
determinatio
supply of, hi
currency and
by the Fed, i
We start
base (the te
money, H^d, a
demand by m

The righ
demand for h
the money s
which can be
deposit ratio

or

In Equation
supply M and
CU. In mov

[2] Coins are minte
bookkeeping but i

TABLE 8-1 COMPONENTS OF THE MONEY STOCK, MARCH 1980 *(in billions of dollars; seasonally adjusted)*

(1) Currency	(2) Demand deposits	(3) M1-B =(1) + (2)	(4) Time and savings deposits, etc. (excluding large time deposits and term RPs)	(5) M2 = M1 + (4)
108.9	283.4	392.3	1,158.0	1,550.3

Note: Individual items may not add to totals owing to rounding. Monthly figures are an average of daily figures.
Source: Citibank Economic Database.

and time deposits and consider the money supply process as if there were only a uniform class of deposits D. Using that simplification, we define money as deposits plus currency:

$$M \equiv CU + D \tag{3}$$

Starting from Equation (3), we now begin to develop the details of the

CHART 8-1 MONETARY AGGREGATES. *(Source: Citibank Economic Database)*

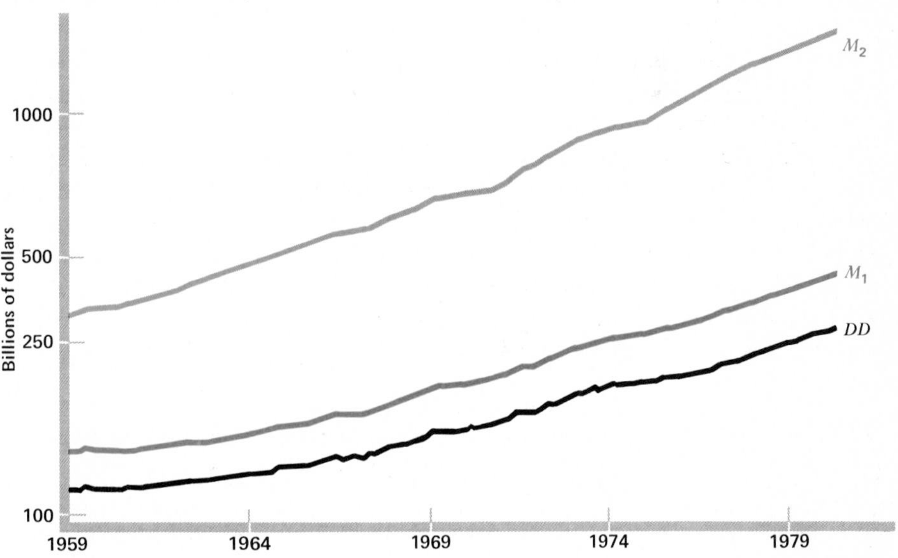

Note: The scale is logarithmic.

view" to contrast it with an earlier and mechanical approach that viewed the money multiplier m as constant. Robert Rasche, in reviewing the empirical literature on the interest-responsiveness of money supply, concludes:[17]

> The available evidence suggests quite conclusively that the short-run feedbacks through interest rate changes which would be generated by policy changes in reserve aggregates, are very weak and should cause little, if any, difficulty for the implementation of policy actions aimed at controlling the money stock through the control of reserve aggregates.

The conclusion, then, is that induced interest rate movements will dampen the money supply expansion brought about by an increase in high-powered money, but that this dampening effect is not very important.

We can similarly analyze the effects of an increase in the discount rate on the money stock and the LM curve. An increase in the discount rate causes banks to want to hold more reserves, since the costs of running short of reserves are raised when the discount rate rises. Accordingly, the supply schedule shifts to the left and equilibrium interest rates increase, while the money supply declines. Similarly, an increase in reserve requirements causes an increase in the reserve-deposit ratio, a decline in the money multiplier, and a leftward shift of the money supply schedule. The resulting effect is again an increase in equilibrium interest rates and a reduction in the money supply.

8-9 CONTROL OF THE MONEY STOCK AND CONTROL OF THE INTEREST RATE

We make a simple but important point in this section: The Fed cannot simultaneously set both the interest rate and the stock of money at any given target levels that it may choose. If the Fed wants to achieve a given interest rate target, such as 5 percent, it has to supply the amount of money that is demanded at that interest rate. If it wants to set the money supply at a given level, say \$450 billion in the month of June 1982, it has to allow the interest rate to adjust to equate the demand for money to that supply of money.

Figure 8-6 illustrates the point. Suppose that the Fed, for some reason, decides that it wants to set the interest rate at a level i^* and the money stock at the level M^*, but that the demand for money function is as shown in $L(i, Y_0)$. The Fed is able to move the money supply function around, as in Figure 8-4, but it is not able to move the money demand function around. It therefore has to accept that it can set only the combinations of the interest rate and the money supply that lie along the money demand function. At

[17] Robert Rasche, "A Review of Empirical Studies of the Money Supply Mechanism," Federal Reserve Bank of St. Louis, *Review*, July 1972, p. 19.

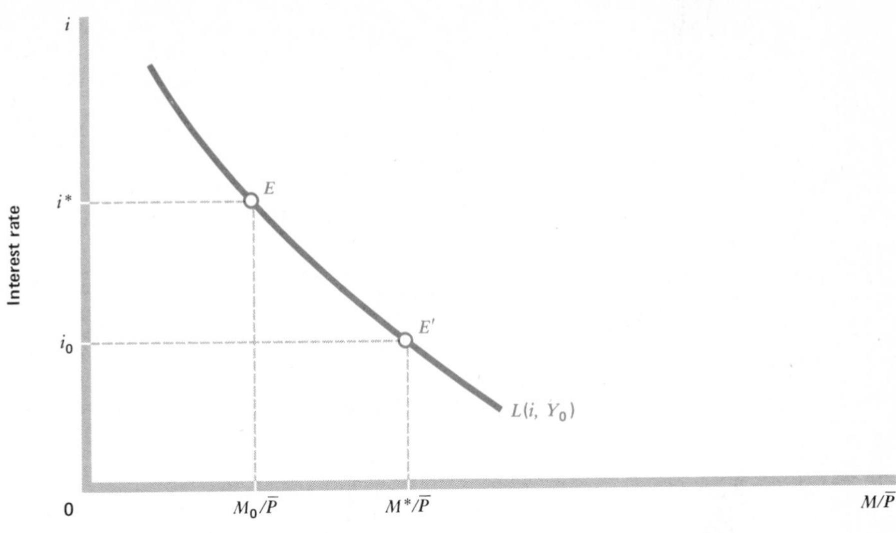

FIGURE 8-6 Controlling the Money Stock and Interest Rates

the interest rate i^*, it can have the money supply $M_0/\overline{P}$. At the target money supply $M^*/\overline{P}$, it can have the interest rate i_0. But it cannot have both $M^*/\overline{P}$ and i^*.

The point is sometimes put more dramatically as follows. When the Fed decides to set the interest rate at some given level and keep it fixed—a policy known as *pegging* the interest rate—it loses control over the money supply. It has to supply whatever amount of money is demanded at that interest rate. If the money demand curve were to shift, because of income growth, say, the Fed would have to increase the stock of high-powered money to increase the money supply.

As an operational matter, the Fed, in its day-to-day operations can more easily control interest rates exactly than it can control the money stock exactly. The Fed buys and sells government securities—primarily Treasury bills—from its *open market desk* in the New York Fed every day. If the Fed wanted to raise the price of government securities (lower the interest rate), it would have to buy the securities at the price it wanted. If it wanted to reduce prices of government securities (raise the interest rate), it would have to sell a sufficient amount of securities from its large portfolio. Thus, on a day-to-day basis, the Fed can determine interest rates quite accurately.[18]

[18] For a discussion of techniques of monetary control, see the papers by William Poole, "The Making of Monetary Policy: Description and Analysis," and Paul Meek, "Nonborrowed Reserves or the Federal Funds Rate as Desk Targets—Is There a Difference," in *New England Economic Review*, March/April 1975.

However, the Fed cannot determine the money supply precisely on a day-to-day basis. For one thing, there is a lag in obtaining data on the money stock. Some time must pass before reasonably good money supply data for a given date become available. That would not affect the Fed's ability to control the money stock if the money multiplier were constant, for then it would be able to deduce, from the behavior of the monetary base, what the money stock was. But the multiplier is not constant. It varies as a result of changes in the currency-deposit and reserve-deposit ratios.

Thus the Fed's inability to control the money supply exactly, to which we referred in Section 8-1, is caused by the unpredictability of the reserve and currency-deposit ratios. The reserve ratio varies as deposits shift among banks with reserve ratios that differ. Similarly, the currency-deposit ratio changes as shifts in demands for currency and deposits take place.

These are *technical* reasons the Fed cannot control the money supply exactly in the sense that the Fed cannot hit the target stock of money exactly even if it wants to. But, over a slightly longer period, the Fed can determine the money supply fairly accurately. As data on the behavior of the money stock and the money multiplier become available, the Fed can make mid-course corrections to its setting of the base. For example, if the Fed were aiming for monetary growth of 5 percent over a given period, it might start the base growing at 5 percent. If it found halfway into the period that the multiplier had been falling and the money stock therefore growing less than 5 percent, it could step up the growth rate of the base to compensate.

The main reason the Fed does not hit its money growth targets are not technical, but rather have to do with its having both interest and *and* money stock targets, and as we have seen in this section, it cannot hit them both at the same time.

8-10 MONEY STOCK TARGETS

In March 1975 the Fed, at the direction of the Congress, began to announce target rates of growth of the money stock for the coming 12 months. Each quarter the Fed announces what growth rate of the various money stock measures it is aiming for over the next year. For example, Table 8-7 shows some target growth rates announced one year earlier for the quarter ending as shown.[19] Thus, 4½ to 7½ percent was the target range announced at the end of the fourth quarter of 1975 for the growth rate of M1 over the next year. Although the Fed usually achieved most of its targets, in some years it did not achieve all. For instance, in the year ending in the fourth quarter of 1977, money growth exceeded the target range for M1 although the M2 target was achieved.

[19] The money stock measures in Table 8-7 refer to the pre-1980 measures of money. The precise definitions do not matter for purposes of this section.

TABLE 8-7 TARGET AND ACTUAL GROWTH RATES OF MONEY

Period (percent change from a year earlier)	M1	M2
1976/IV		
Projected range	4½–7½	7½–10½
Actual	5.8	10.9
1977/IV		
Projected range	4½–6½	7–10
Actual	7.9	9.8
1978/IV		
Projected range	4–6½	6½–9
Actual	7.2	8.7
1979/IV		
Projected range	1½–4½	5–8
Actual	5.5	8.3

Note: Old definitions.
Source: Citibank Economic Database and various issues of the *Federal Reserve Bulletin.*

Why does the Fed not hit all its targets? The main reason is that it has too many of them. The Fed cannot control the rates of growth of the different monetary aggregates sufficiently finely to hit target growth rates for each. If the public decides to move out of demand deposits and into other deposits that are part of M2, the growth rate of M1 will tend to be low at the expense of a high growth rate of M2. There is not much the Fed can do about that. It can change the interest rate that banks are allowed to pay on other deposits (through Regulation Q), but it still cannot control the growth rates of the different aggregates precisely.

The Fed also has interest rate targets which are not stated in Table 8-7. As one instance, it did not want short-term interest rates to rise much in the year ending in 1977/IV, at the same time as it wanted M1 and M2 to grow at the indicated rates. Interest rates did begin to rise during that period, and the Fed therefore had to decide whether it preferred to stick to the money targets or to let interest rates rise. As it typically does, it compromised, allowing interest rates to rise and money growth (of M1) to go above the target range. You can show this compromise in terms of Figure 8-7 by allowing the money demand curve to shift up.

8-11 SUMMARY

There are four major points in this chapter.

1 The nominal money supply is determined by the actions of the public through the currency-deposit ratio, the banks through the reserve-deposit ratio, and by the Fed.

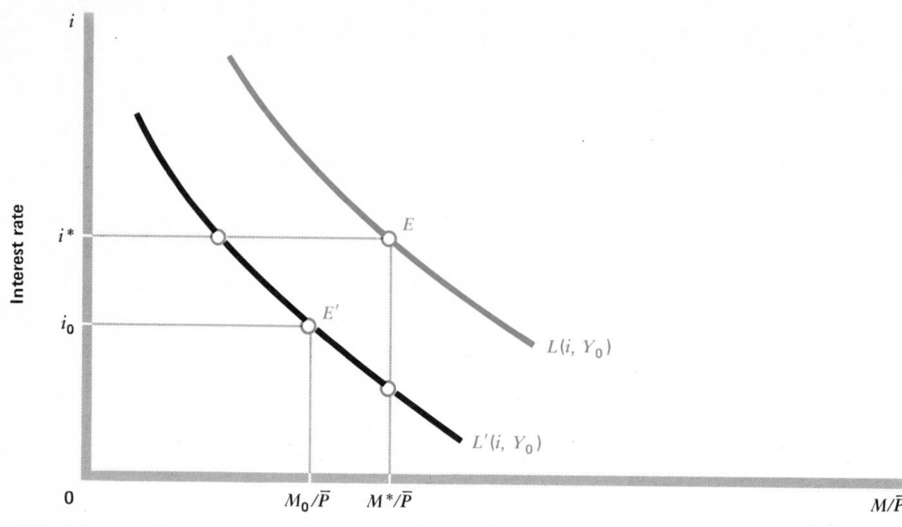

FIGURE 8-7 TARGETS AND COMPROMISES IN MONETARY POLICY

2 The Fed affects the money supply primarily through open market operations which control the monetary base, or high-powered money. The Fed can also affect the money supply indirectly through the effects of the discount rate and required reserve ratios on the banks' reserve-deposit ratio, and through Regulation Q.
3 Given the stock of high-powered money, the supply of money is a function of the interest rate.
4 The Fed cannot set both the interest rate and the stock of money at whatever target levels it chooses. If it controls the interest rate, it gives up control over the money supply, and vice versa.

PROBLEMS

1 Use Figure 8-3 to show the equilibrium amounts of currency and deposits.
2 In the 1930s the stock of money fell despite a substantial increase in high-powered money. How do you explain this fact?
3 When the Fed buys or sells gold or foreign exchange, it automatically offsets or sterilizes the impact of these operations on the monetary base by compensating open market operations. Show the effects on the Fed balance sheet of a purchase of gold and a corresponding sterilization through an open market operation.
4 Table 8-3 shows the initial impact on the Fed's balance sheet of an open market purchase. As noted in the text, at the end of the process both currency and

member bank deposits rise. What is the final increase in currency? Use the ratios *cu* and *r* in arriving at your answer.

5 Explain how the Fed's balance sheet would be affected if it valued gold at the market price.

6 "All money is credit." Discuss.

7 "All credit is money." Discuss.

8 A proposal for "100 percent banking" involves a reserve-deposit ratio of unity. Such a scheme has been proposed for the United States in order to enhance the Fed's control over the money supply. Indicate (*a*) why such a scheme would help monetary control and (*b*) what bank balance sheets would look like under this scheme. (*c*) How would banking remain profitable, under 100 percent money?

9 Suppose a bank has excess reserves and makes a loan to someone who immediately withdraws the deposit the bank gives him and holds it as currency. Why does the bank's granting of the loan increase the money supply?

10 Discuss the impact of credit cards on the money multiplier.

11 This problem extends the analysis of the chapter by distinguishing between M1 and M2. Assume a currency-demand deposit ratio *cu* and a desired ratio of demand to time deposits of the public, $d = DD/TD$. Assume, too, that banks have reserve preferences, described by r_D and r_T, with respect to demand and time deposits, where the reserve ratio for time deposits r_T is lower than that for demand deposits r_D.

(*a*) Use the definition of M1 and the ratios d, r_T, and r_D to derive an expression for the equilibrium stock of M1.

(*b*) Use the definition of M2 and the ratios to derive an expression for the equilibrium stock of M2.

(*c*) Show the effects of an increase in the demand-time deposit ratio on credit.

12 By using Figures 8-1, 8-4, and 8-5, show the effect of an increase in required reserves on:

(*a*) The equilibrium money supply

(*b*) Interest rates

(*c*) The equilibrium level of income

13 The Federal Deposit Insurance Corporation (FDIC) insures commercial bank deposits against bank default. Discuss the implications of that deposit scheme for the money multiplier.

14 Until 1933 the Fed bought and sold gold in transactions with private residents at \$20 an ounce. Discuss the implications of a hypothetical gold discovery in Illinois for the money supply, interest rates, and income, under the assumption that the Fed would buy or sell any amount of gold at \$20 an ounce.

15 Assume required reserves were zero. Would banks hold any reserves?

16 Use a *Federal Reserve Bulletin* of about a year ago and find the announced monetary targets for the coming year. Using the most recent issue of the *Bulletin*, check whether these targets were fulfilled. If not, present an analytical argument for the failure.

9

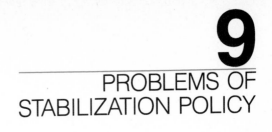

PROBLEMS OF STABILIZATION POLICY

This is the first of two chapters that discuss the problems of macroeconomic policy making. An understanding of the general difficulties of carrying out successful stabilization policies—policies to reduce the fluctuations of the economy—helps explain economic performance over the past 30 years. Chart 9-1, which shows the unemployment rate over the past 50 years, gives the clear impression that stabilization policy has left something to be desired. Even before the recessions of 1974–1975 and 1980, unemployment was frequently high in the post-World War II period.

The reason for discussing the problems of stabilization policy here is that the preceding chapters have laid out a clear body of theory that seems to show exactly the policy measures that can be used to maintain full employment. We saw that high unemployment, or a large GNP gap, can be reduced by an expansion in aggregate demand. An increase in aggregate demand in turn can be achieved by expansionary monetary or fiscal policies: an increase in the money supply, a reduction in taxes, an increase in government spending, or an increase in transfers. Similarly, a boom can be contained by restrictive monetary or fiscal policies.

The policies needed to prevent the fluctuations in unemployment shown in Chart 9-1 accordingly appear to be simple and obvious. How, then, did the fluctuations occur? The answer obviously is that policy making is far from simple. Part of the difficulty of policy making arises from the

CHART 9-1 UNEMPLOYMENT RATE IN THE UNITED STATES, 1926-1979 *(Source: Citibank Economic Database)*

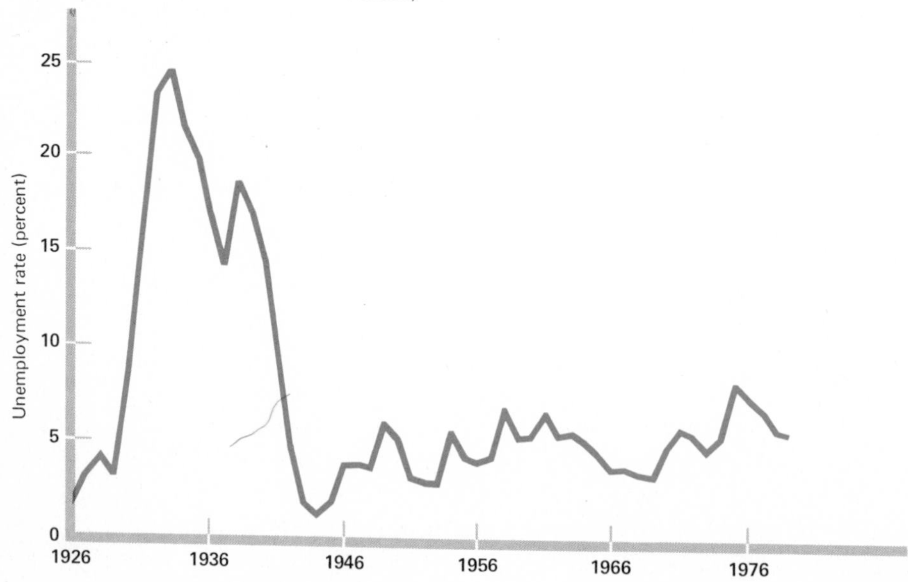

possible *conflict between the maintenance of full employment and the target of low inflation.* That important issue is discussed in the second of the two general chapters on the problems of policy making, Chapter 15. Chapters 10 and 16 apply some of the lessons of the two policy chapters to examine policy making in the United States economy in the sixties and seventies, respectively.

In this chapter we discuss in detail three problems that suggest why policy should not be expected to achieve its targets, such as full employment, at all times. The three *handicaps of policy making* are:

1 *Lags* in the effects of policy
2 The role of *expectations* in determining private sector responses to policy
3 *Uncertainty* about the effects of policy

In a nutshell, we are going to argue that a policy maker who (1) observes a disturbance, (2) does not know whether it is permanent or not, (3) takes time to develop a policy which (4) takes still more time to affect behavior, and (5) has uncertain effects on aggregate demand is very poorly equipped to do a perfect job of stabilizing the economy.

9-1 ECONOMIC DISTURBANCES

Before identifying in detail the obstacles in the way of successful policy making, we discuss *economic disturbances* in terms of their sources, persistence, and importance for policy. Disturbances are shifts in aggregate demand or aggregate supply, or shifts in money demand or supply, that cause output, interest rates, or prices to diverge from the target path.

We return to the IS-LM model as the framework for the discussion of economic disturbances in this chapter. In Figure 9-1 we show the IS and LM schedules and also the full-employment level of output, Y_p. The economy is initially at full employment at point E. Now what disturbances might cause the economy to move away from full employment? Obviously, anything that shifts the IS and/or LM curves would disturb the economy and move it away from E.

In terms of overall economic impact, the major disturbances to the economy—the forces moving the IS and LM curves—have been wars. The effects of the increases in government spending associated with World War II, the Korean War, and the Vietnam war can be seen in Chart 9-1 in the very low unemployment rates in those periods. Of these, World War II had the largest impact on the economy. At the height of the war, in 1944, federal government spending exceeded 45 percent of GNP.

As shown in Figure 9-1, an increase in government spending would shift the IS schedule upward and therefore lead to an excess demand for

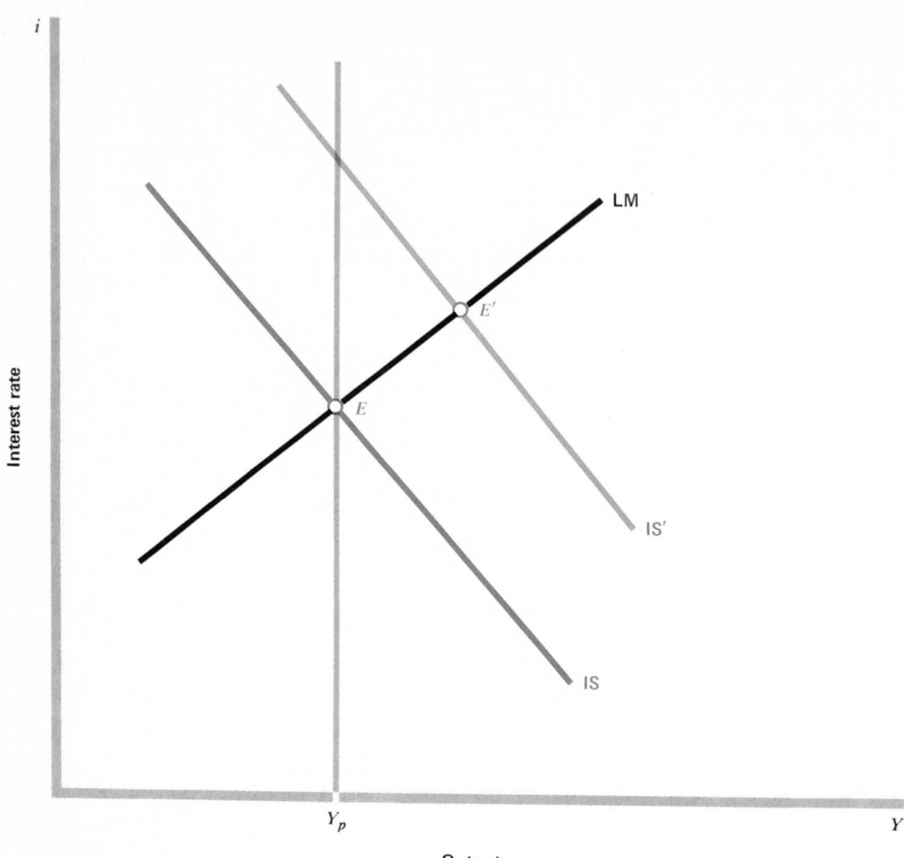

FIGURE 9-1 An Aggregate Demand Disturbance

goods. To contain aggregate spending to the full-employment level of output, increased government spending would have to be offset by a reduction in private demand, that is, a reduction in investment and/or consumption spending. Investment spending can be reduced by allowing the interest rate to rise, and consumption spending can be reduced by increasing income taxes. These conventional economic policies may not be sufficient in wartime, however. In World War II more direct methods of reducing investment and consumption were used. A system was set up in which investment projects had to be licensed. That system served to reduce the overall rate of private investment and also to direct investment toward areas helpful for the war effort. There was also some rationing of consumption goods, which reduced consumption expenditure as some of the rationed demand spilled over into increased saving rather than being diverted toward other goods. Thus, the aggregate level of consumption spending was reduced by using rationing to reduce the consumption of various goods essential for the war effort (gasoline, tires, meat, shoes, etc.).[1]

Changes in government spending or tax policies not connected with wars may also constitute economic disturbances. Government spending or taxes may be increased or reduced for reasons which have to do with the government's view of desirable social policies. Those changes too may affect the level of aggregate demand if not accompanied by appropriate monetary and fiscal policies.

Other economic disturbances that lead to changes in aggregate demand, which originate in the private sector, are shifts in the consumption or investment function. If consumers decide to consume more out of their disposable income at any given level of income, the IS curve of Figure 9-1 shifts upward, tending to increase the level of income. If there is no economic explanation for the shift in the consumption function, then it is attributed to a change in the tastes of consumers between consumption and saving. In such a case, we describe the shift as a disturbance.

Similarly, if investment spending increases for no apparent economic reason, then we attribute the increase to an unexplained change in the optimism of investors about the returns from investment. Again, we regard that change in investment behavior as a disturbance to the system. Changes in the optimism of investors are sometimes described as changes in their *animal spirits*—a term that suggests that there may be little rational basis for those spirits.[2] Some shifts in the investment function are caused by new inventions that require large amounts of investment for their successful marketing, such as the development of the railroads in the nineteenth century and the spread of the automobile in the 1920s.

Shifts in the demand for money may affect the interest rate, and thus indirectly affect the rate of investment; they, too, constitute a possible source of private sector economic disturbances.

Disturbances that we have not yet incorporated in our basic theoretical framework also affect the level of income. These include increases in exports, caused by changes in foreigners' demand for our goods, which tend to increase the level of income. Changes in supply conditions, such as the

[1] In passing, it is worth considering for a moment why partial rationing might work as a macroeconomic policy, that is, as a policy reducing aggregate demand. The reason must be that part of the expenditure that is precluded by rationing does not shift to other goods but, instead, increases saving, that is, future consumption.

[2] Keynes, in particular, argued that shifts in the investment function were a major cause of fluctuations in the economy. See J. M. Keynes, *The General Theory of Employment, Interest and Money* (New York: Macmillan, 1936), chap. 22.

oil embargo of 1973–1974, will affect the level of income and are discussed in Chapter 11. In Chapter 13, we also discuss the possibility that the behavior of wages may constitute a source of economic disturbances.

Finally, there is the interesting possibility that disturbances may be caused by the policy makers themselves. There are two different arguments concerning this possibility. First, since policy making is difficult, it is entirely possible that the attempts of policy makers to stabilize the economy could be counterproductive. Indeed, a forcefully stated and influential view of the causes of the Great Depression[3] argues that an inept monetary policy by the Federal Reserve System was chiefly responsible for the severity of the depression. The argument of Friedman and Schwartz is basically that the officials in charge of the Federal Reserve System in the early 1930s did not understand the workings of monetary policy and therefore carried out a policy that made the depression worse rather than better.

The second argument that policy makers themselves may be responsible for economic disturbances arises from the relationship between election results and economic conditions in the period before the election.[4] It appears that incumbents tend to be reelected when economic conditions, primarily the unemployment rate, are improving in the year before the election. Accordingly, it is tempting for incumbents to try to *improve* economic conditions in the period before the election; their efforts may involve tax reductions or increases in government spending. It is now quite common to talk of the *political business cycle*, meaning that business fluctuations are significantly affected by government economic policies undertaken for political reasons.

It has been argued that election results are significantly affected by the growth rate, rather than the level, of income, in the year leading up to an election. If that is so, then it is tempting indeed for governments to start an expansion in an election year. Despite the difficulties of policy making, it is always easy to start an economic expansion in the short run—though not to control it later when its inflationary consequences appear. While there is some evidence to support the notion of a political business cycle, the argument should be regarded as tentative because the link between economic conditions and election results is not yet firmly established.

We proceed next to discuss the three factors that make the task of policy makers far more difficult than an overliteral interpretation of the simple IS-LM model in Figure 9-1 might suggest.

[3] See Milton Friedman and Anna J. Schwartz, *The Great Contraction* (Princeton, N.J.: Princeton University Press, 1965). We review the argument in Chap. 10.

[4] See, for example, Edward R. Tufte, *Political Control of the Economy* (Princeton, N.J.: Princeton University Press, 1978).

9-2 LAGS IN THE EFFECTS OF POLICY

Suppose that the economy was at full employment and has been affected by an aggregate demand disturbance that raises the equilibrium level of income above full employment in Figure 9-1 toward point E'. Suppose further that there was no advance warning of this disturbance and that, consequently, no policy actions were taken in anticipation of its occurrence. Policy makers now have to decide *whether at all* and *how* to respond to the disturbance.

The first concern—and the first difficulty—should be over the permanence of the disturbance and its subsequent effects. Suppose the disturbance is only transitory, such as a one-period reduction in consumption spending. When the disturbance is transitory so that consumption rapidly reverts back to its initial level, the best policy may be to do nothing at all. Provided suppliers or producers do not mistakenly interpret the increase in demand as permanent but, rather, perceive it as transitory, they will absorb it by production and inventory changes rather than capacity adjustments. The disturbance will affect income in this period but will have very little permanent effect. Policy actions generally do not affect the economy immediately. Any policy actions taken to offset the disturbance this period, for example, a tax increase, will have their impact on spending and income only over time. In later periods, however, the effects of the initial rise in demand on the level of income will be very small, and without the policy action the economy would tend to be very close to full employment. The effects of a tax increase, therefore, would be to lower income in later periods and move it away from the full-employment level. Thus, if the disturbance is temporary and it has no long-lived effects and policy operates with a lag, then the best policy is to do nothing.

Figure 9-2 illustrates the main issue. Assume an aggregate demand disturbance reduces output below potential, starting at time t_0. Without active policy intervention output declines for a while but then recovers and reaches the full-employment level again at time t_2. Consider next the path of GNP under an active stabilization policy, but one that works with the disadvantage of lags. Thus, expansionary policy might be initiated at time t_1 and start taking effect some time after. Output now tends to recover faster as a consequence of the expansion and, because of poor dosage and/or timing, actually overshoots the full-employment level. By time t_3, restrictive policy is initiated, and some time after, output starts turning down toward full employment and may well continue cycling for a while. If this is an accurate description of the potency or scope of stabilization policy, then the question must seriously arise whether it is worth trying to stabilize output or whether the effect of stabilization policy is, in fact, to make things worse. Stabilization policy may actually *destabilize* the economy.

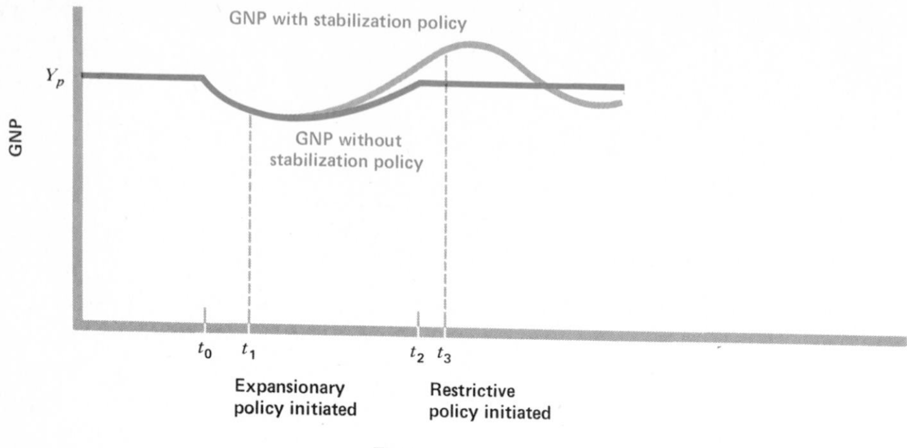

FIGURE 9-2 Lags and Destabilizing Policy

One of the main difficulties of policy making is in establishing whether or not a disturbance is temporary. It was clear enough in the case of World War II that a high level of defense expenditures would be required for some years. However, in the case of the Arab oil embargo of 1973–1974, it was not clear at all how long the embargo would last or whether the high prices for oil that were established in late 1973 would persist. At the time, there were many who argued that the oil cartel would not survive and that oil prices would soon fall—that is, that the disturbance was temporary. That did not turn out to be true. Let us suppose, however, that it is known that the disturbance will have effects that will last for several quarters, and that the level of income will, without policy, be below the full-employment level for some time. What lags do policy makers encounter?

We now consider the steps required before a policy action can be taken after a disturbance has occurred, and then the process by which that policy action affects the economy. There are delays, or lags, at every stage. It is customary and useful to divide the lags into an *inside* lag, which is the time period it takes to undertake a policy action—such as a tax cut, or an increase in the money supply—and the *outside* lag, which describes the timing of the effects of the policy action on the economy. The inside lag in turn is divided into *recognition*, *decision*, and *action* lags.

The Recognition Lag

The recognition lag is the period that elapses between the time a disturbance occurs and the time the policy makers recognize that action is required. This lag could in principle be *negative* if the disturbance could be predicted and appropriate policy actions considered *before* it even occurs.

For example, we know that seasonal factors affect behavior. Thus it is known that at Christmas the demand for currency is high. Rather than allow this to exert a restrictive effect on the money supply, the Fed will accommodate this seasonal demand by an expansion in high-powered money.

In other cases the recognition lag has been positive, so that some time has elapsed between the disturbance and the recognition that active policy was required. This was true, for example, of the 1974–1975 recession. The unemployment rate started increasing very rapidly in the third, and particularly in the fourth, quarter of 1974. It is now clear that expansionary action was required no later than September 1974. Yet, in October 1974, the administration was still calling for a tax *increase* to reduce aggregate demand and inflation. By December, a sharp increase in the unemployment rate led forcefully to the recognition by most economists that there was need for expansionary action. Only in January, in his State of the Union address, did the President call for a tax reduction, which was implemented in the Tax Reduction Act of 1975. Solow and Kareken have studied the history of policy making and have found that on average the recognition lag is about 5 months.[5] That lag was found to be somewhat shorter when the required policy was expansionary and somewhat longer when restrictive policy was required. The speed with which tax cuts follow sharp increases in unemployment was clearly evident in both 1975 and 1980.

The major reason that there is any recognition lag at all, apart from the delay in collecting statistical data, is that it is never certain what the consequences of a disturbance will be. That uncertainty in turn is a result of economists' lack of knowledge of the workings of the economy (which is discussed in Section 9-4 below) as well as political uncertainties.

The Decision and Action Lags

The recognition lag is the same for monetary and fiscal policy. The Federal Reserve Board, the Treasury, and the Council of Economic Advisers are in constant contact with one another and share their predictions about the future course of the economy. For the decision lag—the delay between the recognition of the need for action and a policy decision—by contrast there is a difference between monetary and fiscal policy. The Federal Reserve System's Open Market Committee meets at least monthly to discuss and decide on policy. Thus, once the need for a policy action has been recognized, the decision lag for monetary policy is short. Further, the

[5] See John Kareken and Robert Solow "Lags in Monetary Policy," in *Stabilization Policies*, prepared for the Commission on Money and Credit (Englewood Cliffs, N.J.: Prentice-Hall, 1963). See, too, the review of the evidence in Thomas Mayer, *Monetary Policy in the United States* (Random House, 1968), chap. 6, and Michael J. Hamburger, "The Lag in the Effect of Monetary Policy: A Survey of the Recent Literature," Federal Reserve Bank of New York, *Monthly Review*, December 1971.

action lag—the lag between the policy decision and its implementation—for monetary policy is also short. The major monetary policy actions, we have seen, are open market operations, changes in the discount rate, and changes in interest rate ceilings through regulation Q. Each of these policy actions can be undertaken almost as soon as it has been decided. Thus, under the existing arrangements for the Federal Reserve System, the decision lag for monetary policy is short and the action lag practically zero.

However, fiscal policy actions are less rapid. Once the need for a fiscal policy action has been recognized, the administration has to prepare legislation for that action. Next, the legislation has to be considered and approved by both houses of Congress before the policy change can be made. Depending on the degree of agreement between the administration and the Congress, that may be a lengthy process. Even after the legislation has been approved, the policy change has still to be put into effect. If the fiscal policy takes the form of a change in tax rates, it may be some time before the changes in tax rates begin to be reflected in paychecks—that is, there may be an action lag. On occasion, though, as in early 1975 when taxes were reduced, the fiscal decision lag may be short; in 1975 it was about 2 months.

The lengthy legislative process for fiscal policy in the United States has led to repeated suggestions that the President be granted the authority to undertake certain fiscal actions without legislation. One proposal is that the President should be allowed to vary tax rates by limited amounts in either direction without first obtaining specific authorization from Congress but subject to congressional veto.[6] This proposal would reduce the decision lag. Whether such a change is desirable from the economic viewpoint depends obviously on whether the President would on average make changes in tax rates that tend to offset disturbances to the economy. Do remember, though, the political business cycle.

The existence of the inside lag of policy making focuses attention on the *built-in* or *automatic stabilizers* that we discussed in Chapter 3. One of the major benefits of automatic stabilizers is that their inside lag is zero. Recall from Chapter 3 that the most important automatic stabilizer is the income tax. It stabilizes the economy by reducing the multiplier effects of any disturbance to aggregate demand. The multiplier for the effects of changes in autonomous spending on GNP is inversely related to the income tax rate. The higher the tax rate, the smaller the effects of any given change in autonomous demand on GNP. Similarly, unemployment compensation is another automatic stabilizer. When workers become unemployed and reduce their consumption, that reduction in consumption demand tends to have multiplier effects on output. Those multiplier effects are reduced

[6] Report of the Commission on Money and Credit, *Money and Credit—Their Influence on Jobs, Prices and Growth* (Englewood Cliffs, N.J.: Prentice-Hall, 1961), pp. 133–137.

when a worker receives unemployment compensation because her disposable income is reduced by less than the loss in earnings.

Chart 9-2 shows the practical importance of automatic stabilizers (and active fiscal policy) in the United States economy. The chart shows personal disposable income as a fraction of national income. Personal disposable income, as you will remember from Chapter 2, is the income that actually accrues to households after all taxes but inclusive of all transfers. The chart brings out the fact that during periods of a high GNP gap—the early sixties, the 1969–1971 period, and most particularly 1974–1975—personal disposable income rises relative to national income. In these periods, transfer payments rise and the growth in income tax collection slows down. For the whole period 1960–1979, the ratio of personal disposable income to national income was on average 85 percent. In a recession such as 1974–1975, however, the ratio increases sharply, whereas, during a period of high aggregate demand and expansion such as in 1965–1969, the ratio declines below average.[7] In passing, we leave you with these questions: What is the

[7] To be precise, the chart reflects both automatic stabilizers and discretionary changes in taxes and transfers. Thus the increase in the ratio in 1975 reflects not only automatic transfers but also the tax rebate of early 1975. The data that would separate out the automatic stabilizers are not conveniently available.

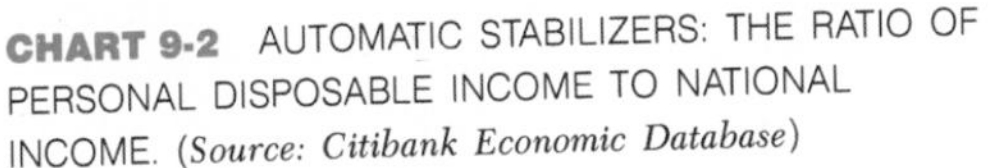
CHART 9-2 AUTOMATIC STABILIZERS: THE RATIO OF PERSONAL DISPOSABLE INCOME TO NATIONAL INCOME. (*Source: Citibank Economic Database*)

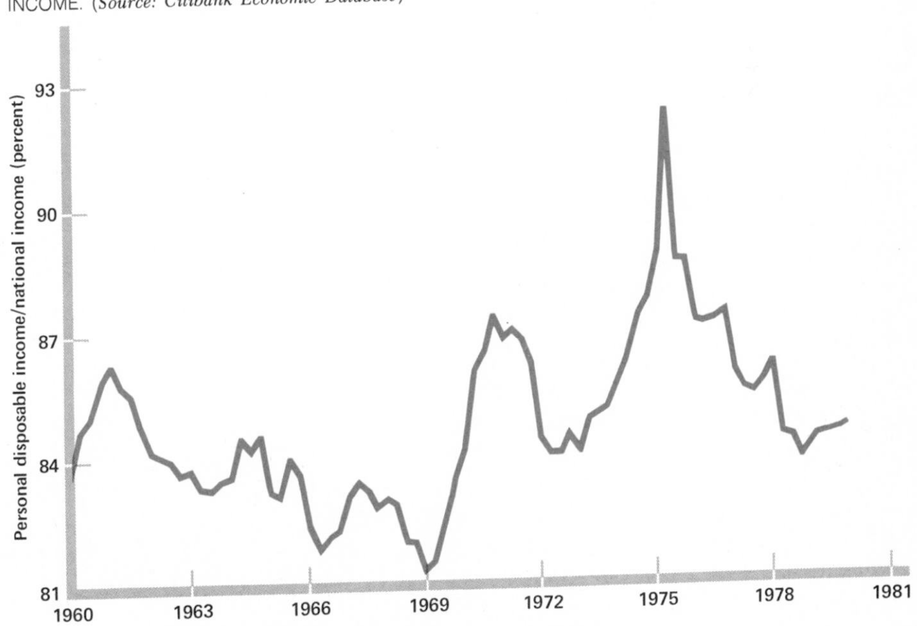

counterpart of the increase in the ratio of personal disposable income to national income in a recession? What ratio would you expect to decline sharply?

Although built-in stabilizers have desirable effects, they cannot be carried too far without also affecting the overall performance of the economy. The multiplier could be reduced to 1 by increasing the tax rate to 100 percent, and that would appear to be a stabilizing influence on the economy. But with 100 percent marginal tax rates, the desire to work, and consequently the level of GNP, would be reduced. Thus there are limits on the extent to which automatic stabilizers are desirable.[8] Nonetheless, automatic stabilizers play an important role in the economy; it has been argued that the absence of significant unemployment compensation in the 1930s was one of the major factors making the Great Depression so severe, and that the existence of the stabilizers alone makes the recurrence of such a deep depression unlikely.

The Outside Lag

The inside lag of policy is a *discrete* lag in which policy can have no effect on the economy until it is implemented. The outside lag is generally a *distributed* lag: once the policy action has been taken, its effects on the economy are spread over time. There is usually a small immediate effect of a policy action, but other effects occur later.

The idea that policy operates on aggregate demand and income with a distributed lag is shown in Figure 9-3*a* and *b*. Suppose that we are considering a once-and-for-all increase in high-powered money at time t_0, as shown in Figure 9-3*a*. This increase in high-powered money, by affecting interest rates and therefore aggregate spending, changes the level of income in subsequent quarters by the amounts indicated in Figure 9-3*b*. The height of the bars shows the amount by which GNP exceeds the level that it would have had in the absence of the policy change. Figure 9-3*b* is thus a *dynamic multiplier*, as discussed in Chapter 5. The main point to be made is that monetary or fiscal policies taken now affect the economy over time, with most of the effects typically not occurring in the first quarter. Thus, in Figure 9-3, a given increase in high-powered money in the short run raises GNP by only a small amount, although over the full adjustment period, the increase in GNP is substantial.

Figure 9-3 makes it clear that the impact of an increase in high-powered money (corresponding to an open market purchase by the Federal Reserve) is initially very small, and that it continues to increase over a long period of time. Thus, if it were necessary to increase the level of employment rapidly to offset a demand disturbance, a large open market

[8] For a discussion of the history of automatic stabilizers, see Herbert Stein, *The Fiscal Revolution in America* (Chicago: The University of Chicago Press, 1969).

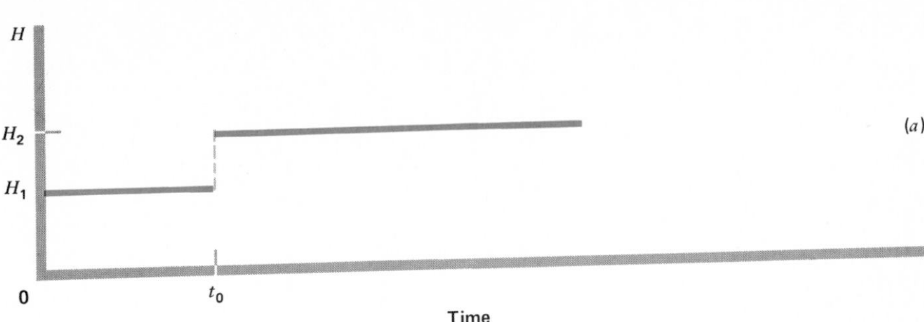

FIGURE 9-3*a* Time Path of High-Powered Money

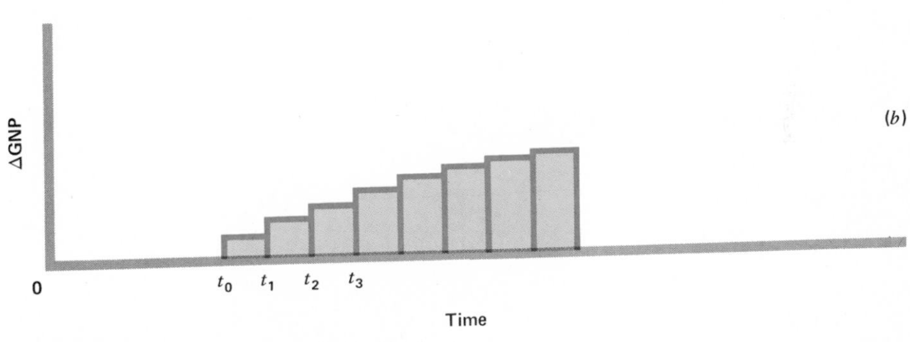

FIGURE 9-3*b* Dynamic Multipliers for the Effects of the Change in High-Powered Money on GNP

purchase would be necessary. But in later quarters, the larger initial open market purchase would build up large effects on GNP, and those effects would probably overcorrect the unemployment, leading to inflationary pressures. It would then be necessary to reverse the open market purchase and conduct open market sales to avoid the inflationary consequences of the initial open market purchase.

It should thus be clear that when policy acts slowly, with the impacts of policy building up over time, considerable skill is required of policy makers if their own attempts to correct an initially undesirable situation are not to lead to problems that themselves need correcting. Recall also that we have been talking here about the *outside* lag, and that the policy action we are considering would be taken only 6 months after the initial disturbance if the inside lag is 6 months long.

Why are there such long outside lags? We have already discussed some of the reasons for these lags in Chapter 5 on the consumption function, where current consumption depends on lagged income, and also in Chapter 6 on investment, where the accelerator models imply that investment depends on lagged and current income. Similar lags are also present in the financial sector of the economy, where the demand for money depends on lagged income. Each of these sources of lags creates an outside lag, and their interaction generally produces longer lags than each of the underlying lags.

Because the point is so important, let us describe in more detail how the lags of monetary policy arise. Suppose the Fed conducts an open market purchase. Because aggregate demand depends heavily on lagged values of income, interest rates, and other economic variables, the open market purchase initially has effects mainly on short-term interest rates and not on income. Short-term interest rates, such as the Treasury bill rate, affect long-term interest rates with a lag. The long-term interest rates in turn affect investment with a lag, and also affect consumption by affecting the value of wealth.[9] Then when aggregate demand is affected by the initial open market purchase, the increase in aggregate demand itself produces lagged effects on subsequent aggregate demand through the fact that both consumption and investment depend on past values of income. So the effects of an initial open market purchase will be spread through time, as in Figure 9-3.

Monetary and Fiscal Policy Lags

The discussion of the previous paragraph suggests that fiscal policy and certainly changes in government spending, which act directly on aggregate demand, may affect income more rapidly than monetary policy. This is indeed the case. However, the fact that fiscal policy acts faster on aggregate demand than monetary policy must not lead us to overlook the fact that fiscal policy has a considerably longer inside lag. Moreover, the inside lag for government spending is longer than that for taxes because when the government purchases goods and services, it has to decide what goods to buy, have bids for the sale of those goods submitted by the private sector, and then decide on the award of the contracts. In summary, therefore, fiscal policy is attractive because of the short outside lag, but that advantage is more than offset by a potentially long inside lag.

Our analysis of lags indicates clearly one difficulty in undertaking stabilizing short-term policy actions: it takes time to set the policies in action, and then the policies themselves take time to affect the economy. But that is not the only difficulty. Further difficulties considered in Sections 9-3 and 9-4 arise from uncertainty about the exact timing and magnitude of the effects of policy. The dynamic multiplier of Figure 9-3 itself is not

[9] Recall that in Chap. 5 we discussed the life-cycle model of consumption demand, in which consumption is affected by the level of wealth. Part of wealth is the value of stock market assets; the value of stock market assets rises when the long-term interest rate falls. Thus, interest rates affect consumption through a wealth effect.

unchanging, and we do not know for sure how a particular policy will affect income in subsequent periods.

9-3 THE ROLE OF EXPECTATIONS

We have discussed the two basic sources of lags in economic behavior in earlier chapters. The first source is the costs of rapid adjustment. For example, in Chapter 6 we showed how the costs of adjusting the actual capital stock to the desired capital stock led to lags in the investment function. The second source of lags is expectations. In this section we focus on expectations, their formation, and the effects they have on policy and its effectiveness.

While it is undoubtedly true that the past behavior of a variable influences expectations about its future behavior, it is also true that consumers and investors will sometimes use more information than is contained in the past behavior of a variable when trying to predict its future behavior. Consider, in particular, forecasts of permanent income—long-run average income. In Chapter 5, as in Friedman's original work on the consumption function, permanent income is estimated as an average of income in the recent past. Suppose, however, that you were a resident of a small country that had just discovered vast gold deposits. You would then take the information about the gold discovery into account in forming an estimate of your permanent income. You would *immediately* estimate a permanent income substantially higher than your historical average income. Or, suppose that you have been estimating the expected rate of inflation as an average of past rates of inflation at a time when the inflation rate is high and a new government is elected on a strictly anti-inflationary platform. Then you would lower your estimate of the inflation rate; that is, you would use more information in predicting it than is contained solely in its past behavior. It should be clear that it is in general very difficult to incorporate *all* relevant information that is used by economic agents within a simple economic model. That means there will inevitably be errors in what the models predict for the consequences of various policy actions, meaning in turn that it is difficult to control the economy precisely.

Reliance on models in which expectations are based on past behavior can easily lead to policy mistakes, as was the case with the 1968 tax increase. With low unemployment but inflation that was thought to be excessively high and accelerating, a contraction in aggregate demand was called for. The administration decided to ask for a tax increase in the form of a 10 percent surcharge on personal and corporate income taxes. Every taxpayer would have to pay 10 percent more tax on the same income than in the past year.

To predict the effects of the policy, it was obviously necessary to consider the effects of the tax surcharge on consumer spending and thus on the level of income. This was done using a consumption function that related the level of consumption to current and past levels of disposable income, as in our formulation of the permanent-income consumption function. Predictions were that the tax increase would have a substantial direct and induced effect on the level of aggregate demand and income—so much of an impact that the Federal Reserve System decided to undertake an expansionary monetary policy to offset part of the contractionary effects of the tax increase. However, the combined contractionary fiscal policy and expansionary monetary policy did not reduce the rate of inflation.

What went wrong? The major clue is that the tax increase was explicitly stated to be a *temporary* tax surcharge that was supposed to last only one year. But that meant that the tax increase would have a much smaller effect on consumers' estimates of their permanent income than would a similar *permanent* tax increase. A 10 percent increase in taxes in one year has a much smaller effect on lifetime income than a permanent 10 percent tax increase. Thus, if a tax increase is expected to be temporary, as was the 1968 tax increase, its effects on consumption will be smaller than if the increase is expected to be permanent.

It is now clear that calculation of the effects of the tax surcharge should have taken account of its temporary nature. Does the lesson that economists learned from the 1968 experience guarantee that similar mistakes will not be made in the future? Unfortunately, there is no such guarantee. Expectations enter economic models in many places, and in order to estimate the models using actual data, it is necessary to include some method of calculating the expectations, such as permanent income, or the expected rate of inflation. A careful user of an economic model will no doubt try to check for the reasonableness of the expectations that it includes, but because there are so many places in which expectations matter, it is unlikely that they will always be treated appropriately.

It is particularly important to consider the effects of a given policy action itself on expectations, since it is possible that a new type of policy will affect the way in which expectations are formed.[10] Suppose that the Federal Reserve System announced a new monetary policy designed to stabilize the average level of income and avoid booms and recessions. The new policy would be to reduce the money supply whenever the income level rose and to increase the money supply whenever the income level fell. Such a *countercyclical rule* has implications for expectations. Clearly, it would be entirely inappropriate in the presence of such monetary policy to use an expectations mechanism that implies that an increase in income will persist. The monetary policy rule implies that the money supply would be reduced following an increase in income, and one expects the reduction in

[10] The role of expectations in economics and the interaction between policy and expectations in particular have been the subject of much recent research. See, for example, Thomas J. Sargent and Neil Wallace, "Rational Expectations and the Theory of Economic Policy," *Journal of Monetary Economics*, April 1976. See also our discussion in Chap. 16.

money to exert at least a dampening effect on income. While correct expectations mechanisms must therefore use information about policy responses to disturbances, such care is difficult to apply in practice. Most expectations mechanisms embodied in econometric models of the United States economy and used for the assessment of policies assume that expectations affecting consumption and investment spending are based entirely on past values.

This section has made two important points about the role of expectations in explaining the difficulties of policy making. First, the general point is that the difficulties of modeling the way in which expectations are formed will inevitably lead to errors in economists' forecasts of the effects of particular policy actions on the economy. The second point, a particular one, is that expectations themselves are likely to be affected by policy measures, and that failure to take account of the effects of policy on expectations will lead to mistaken predictions of the effects of those policies.

9-4 UNCERTAINTY

In Sections 9-2 and 9-3 we discussed the difficulties created for stabilization policy by uncertainty about lags and the nature of private sector expectations. In Section 9-1 we described uncertainty about the nature and permanence of the disturbances affecting the economy. These sources of uncertainty make it impossible to predict the effects of any given policy action exactly. In this section we point to other uncertainties complicating the task of policy making.

First, though, we want to extend the discussion of economic disturbances of Section 9-1. In that section we considered major disturbances to the economy. However, there are countless minor disturbances, of the same general nature as the major disturbances outlined in Section 9-1, that continually affect the economy. The weather and other natural phenomena affect the level of output and employment. Consumption and investment are subject to changes resulting from changes in tastes and animal spirits. Strikes—which have important economic causes, but probably also some noneconomic causes—take place, and affect the level of output temporarily. Political events affect the economy. New inventions lead to economic changes. Disturbances of these sorts occur all the time, and need not be major, but they do mean that there will always be uncertainty about the future behavior of the economy.

In addition, there remain major uncertainties about the structure of the economy. It is convenient to distinguish between uncertainty about the correct model of the economy and uncertainty about the precise values of the parameters or coefficients within a given model of the economy, even though the distinction is not watertight. First, there is considerable uncertainty about the correct model of the economy. There is disagreement among economists on some of the behavioral functions of the economy. For example, we discussed a number of models of consumption. As yet, there has not been decisive evidence clearly demonstrating that one and only one of those models is correct. Accordingly, different economists use different models of consumption. Of course, the models have much in common, but they are not identical. There are also minor disagreements, for example, on the demand-for-money function, and those disagreements in turn lead to different predictions about the effects of policy.

Reasonable economists can and do differ about what theory and empirical evidence suggest are the correct behavioral functions of the economy. Generally, each economist will have reasons for favoring one particular form, and will use that form. But, being reasonable, the economist will recognize that the particular formulation being used may not be the correct one, and will thus regard its predictions as subject to a margin of error. Policy makers in turn will know that there are different predictions about the effects of a given policy, and will want to consider the range of predictions that are being made in deciding on policy.

Second, even within the context of a given model, there is uncertainty about the numerical values of the parameters of the model. Suppose for a moment that all economists agree that the life-cycle model of consumption, precisely as specified in Chapter 5, is the only correct model of consumption behavior. On the basis of the historical evidence that we have, it is still not possible to measure the values of the marginal propensities to consume out of labor income and wealth in that consumption function without error. We stated in Chapter 5 that the propensity to consume out of income is about 0.90. However, we cannot be certain that the number is 0.9 and not 0.95, say, because the statistical evidence is not strong enough to enable us to specify the number exactly. The statistical evidence does enable us to say something about the likely range of the parameters,[11] so that we could be relatively certain that the true coefficient is between, say, 0.85 and 0.95, but at present, and for the forseeable future, we would not know it exactly. That uncertainty about the exact values of parameters in our models again means that the effects of policy cannot be predicted with accuracy.

This type of uncertainty has been called *multiplier uncertainty* to emphasize the fact that policy makers will not know the correct magnitude of policy actions, such as tax cuts, because they do not know what the multiplier is. Thus, with a marginal propensity to consume of 0.7, the multiplier would be 3.3 [= 1/(1 − 0.7)], while a marginal propensity to consume of 0.6 would imply a multiplier of 2.5. If the GNP gap were estimated at, say, $30 billion, a multiplier of 3.3 would call for a $9 billion

[11] We are discussing here *confidence intervals* about estimates of parameters; see Robert S. Pindyck and Daniel L. Rubinfeld, *Econometric Models and Economic Forecasts*, 2d ed. (New York: McGraw-Hill, 1980), for further discussion.

increase in spending while a multiplier of 2.5 would require $12 billion. If 3.3 was the true multiplier but policy makers erroneously picked 2.5, they would find themsleves overshooting their target by $6 billion.

What is optimal behavior in the face of such multiplier uncertainty? The more precisely policy makers are informed about the relevant parameters, the more activist the policy can afford to be. Conversely, if there is a considerable range of error in the estimate of the relevant parameters—in our example, the multiplier—then policy should be more modest. With poor information, very active policy runs a large danger of introducing unnecessary fluctuations in the economy.

9-5 ACTIVIST POLICY

We started this chapter asking why there are any fluctuations in the American economy when the policy measures needed to iron out those fluctuations seem to be so simple. The list of difficulties in the way of successful policy making that we have outlined may have raised a different question: Why should one believe that policy can do anything to reduce fluctuations in the economy?

Indeed, considerations of the sort spelled out in the previous three sections have led Milton Friedman and others to argue that there should be no use of active countercyclical monetary policy,[12] and that monetary policy should be confined to making the money supply grow at a constant rate. The precise value of the constant rate of growth of money, Friedman suggests, is less important than the fact that monetary growth be constant and that policy should *not* respond to disturbances. At various times, he has suggested growth rates for money of 2 percent or 4 percent or 5 percent. As Friedman has expressed it, "By setting itself a steady course and keeping to it, the monetary authority could make a major contribution to promoting economic stability. By making that course one of steady but moderate growth in the quantity of money, it would make a major contribution to avoidance of either inflation or deflation of prices."[13]

In discussing the desirability of active monetary and fiscal policy, we want to distinguish between policy actions taken in response to major disturbances to the economy and *fine tuning* in which policy variables are continually adjusted in response to small disturbances to the economy. We see no case for arguing that monetary and fiscal policy should not be used actively in the face of major disturbances to the economy. Most of the considerations of the previous three sections of this chapter indicate some uncertainty about the effects of policy, but there are still clearly definable

[12] See Milton Friedman, *A Program for Monetary Stability* (New York: Fordham University Press, 1959).

[13] Milton Friedman, "The Role of Monetary Policy," *American Economic Review*, March 1968.

circumstances in which there can be no doubt that the appropriate policy is expansionary or contractionary. An administration coming to power in 1933 should not have worried about the uncertainties associated with expansionary policy that we have outlined. The economy does not move from 25 percent unemployment to full employment in a short time (precisely because of those same lags that make policy difficult). Thus, expansionary measures, such as a rapid growth of the money supply, or increased government expenditures, or tax reductions, or all three, would have been appropriate policy since there was no chance they would have an impact only after the economy was at full employment. Similarly, contractionary policies for private demand are called for in wartime. Early in 1975, with unemployment at 8.2 percent and rising rapidly and forecasts of unemployment for the next 2 years being very high, policies designed to reduce unemployment were appropriate.[14] In the event of large disturbances in the future, active monetary and/or fiscal policy should once again be used.[15]

Fine tuning presents more complicated issues. The basic question is whether policy variables should be adjusted at frequent intervals to attempt to smooth out minor disturbances to the economy. For example, should an increase of 0.5 percent in the unemployment rate lead to a small tax reduction, or a small increase in the rate of growth of the money supply, or should policy simply not respond to such disturbances? One possibility is that the initial increase in the unemployment rate is transitory and that policy action is therefore inappropriate; the other is that the initial disturbance is permanent and perhaps even the first sign of a major disturbance, in which case a policy reaction is suitable. If the disturbance is permanent, the appropriate policy response to a small disturbance is a small change in the course of policy. Thus, even if it turned out that the policy action was inappropriate because the disturbance was transitory, the (undesirable) consequences of the policy action would be limited because only a small adjustment had been made. Accordingly, we believe that fine tuning is appropriate provided so that policy responses are always kept small in response to small disturbances.

However, we should emphasize that the argument for fine tuning is a controversial one. The major argument against it is that in practice policy makers cannot behave as suggested—making only small adjustments to small disturbances. Rather, it is argued they tend to try to do too much, if allowed to do anything. Instead of merely trying to offset disturbances, they attempt to keep the economy always at full employment and therefore

[14] Because the inflation rate was high in early 1975, policy making then required some judgment about the costs of inflation compared with those of unemployment, a topic discussed in Chap. 15. Policy in early 1975 was thus more difficult than policy in 1933. Policy decisions in early 1980 with rising unemployment and very high inflation were also very tough.

[15] Interestingly, in the article cited in footnote 13, Friedman argues for the use of active policy in the face of major disturbances.

undertake inappropriately large policy actions in response to small disturbances.

The major lesson of the previous three sections of this chapter is not that policy is impossible, but that policy that is too ambitious in trying to keep the economy always at full employment (with zero inflation) is impossible. The lesson is to proceed with extreme caution, always bearing in mind the possiblity that policy itself may be destabilizing. We see no reason why the Federal Reserve System should try to keep the money supply always growing at the same rate; we believe, on the contrary, that the stability of the economy would be improved by its following a careful countercyclical policy. Similarly, if fiscal policy were not subject to a long inside lag, we would believe it possible for cautiously used fiscal policy to be stabilizing.

Rules versus Discretion

Finally, in this chapter, we want to discuss an issue that has perhaps had more attention in the economics literature than it deserves. This is the issue of "rules versus discretion." The issue is whether the monetary authority and also the fiscal authority should conduct policy in accordance with a preannounced rule that describes precisely how their policy variables will be determined in all future situations, or whether they should be allowed to use their discretion in determining the values of the policy variables at different times. One example is the rule establishing the constant growth rate—say, at 4 percent—for monetary policy. The rule is that *no matter what happens*, the money supply will be kept growing at 4 percent.[16] Another example would be a rule that the money supply growth rate will be increased by 2 percent per year for every 1 percent unemployment in excess of, say, 5 percent. Algebraically, such a rule would be expressed as

$$\frac{\Delta M}{M} = 4.0 + 2(u - 5.0) \tag{1}$$

where the growth rate of money $\Delta M/M$ is at an annual percentage rate, and u is the percentage unemployment rate.

The activist monetary rule of Equation (1) is shown in Figure 9-4. On the horizontal axis, we show the unemployment rate, and on the vertical axis, the growth rate of the money stock. At 5 percent unemployment, monetary growth is 4 percent. If unemployment rises above 5 percent, monetary growth is *automatically* increased. Thus, with 7 percent unemployment, monetary growth would be 8 percent. Conversely, if unemploy-

[16] Recall from Chap. 8 that although the monetary authority cannot control the money supply and its growth rate exactly, it is able to control the money stock with considerable accuracy.

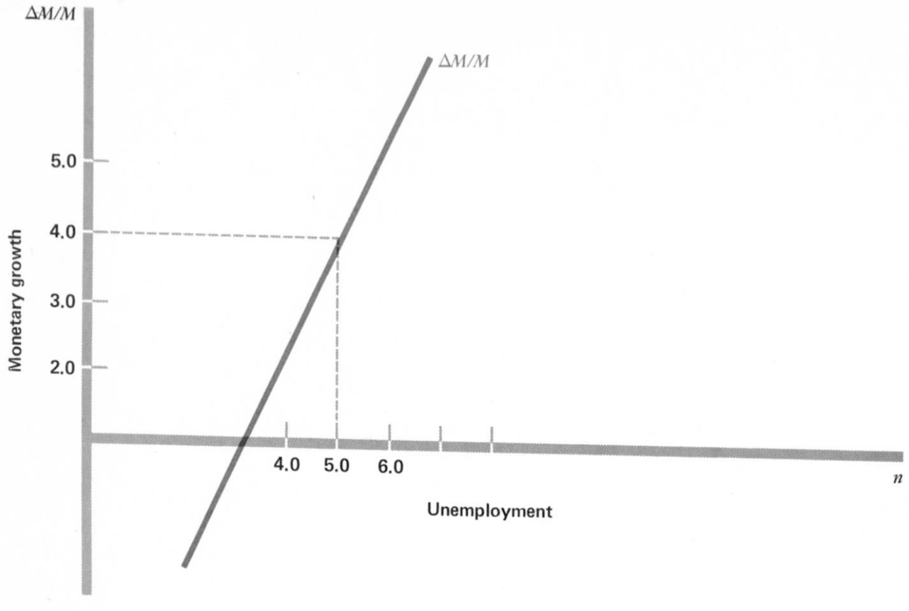

FIGURE 9-4 An Activist Monetary Rule

ment dropped below 5 percent, monetary growth would be lowered below 4 percent. The rule therefore gears the amount of monetary stimulus to an indicator of the business cycle. By linking monetary growth to the unemployment rate, an activist, anticyclical monetary policy is achieved, but this is done without any discretion.

The issue of rules versus discretion has been clouded by the fact that most proponents of rules have been nonactivists, whose preferred monetary rule is a constant growth rate rule.[17] Consequently, the argument has tended to center on whether activist policy is desirable or not. The fundamental point to recognize is that we can design *activist rules*. We can design rules that have countercyclical features without at the same time leaving any discretion in their actions to policy makers. The point is made by Equation (1), which is an activist rule because it expands money when unemployment is high and reduces it when unemployment is low. It leaves no room for policy discretion and in this respect is a rule.

Given that the economy and our knowledge of it are both changing over time, there is no economic case for stating permanent policy rules that would tie the hands of the monetary and fiscal authorities permanently. The practical issue in rules versus discretion then becomes that of whether the

[17] An assessment of the issues is provided in Arthur Okun, "Monetary-Fiscal Activism: Some Analytical Issues," *Brookings Papers on Economic Activity*, 1972:1 (Washington, D.C.: The Brookings Institution, 1972).

policy makers should announce in advance what policies they will be following for the foreseeable future. This would seem to be a desirable development in that it would aid private individuals in forecasting the future course of the economy. In fact, since 1975 the chairperson of the Federal Reserve Board has been required to announce to Congress the Fed's forecasts of its policies over the next year.[18]

9-6 SUMMARY

1 Despite the apparent simplicity of policies needed to maintain continuous full employment, the historical record of the behavior of unemployment, shown in Chart 9-1, implies that successful stabilization policy is difficult to carry out.
2 Many of the complications in the execution of stabilization policy are a result of the tradeoff between inflation and unemployment in the short run. This important topic is deferred to Chapter 15. The present chapter concentrates on other sources of difficulty for stabilization policy.
3 The potential need for stabilizing policy actions arises from economic disturbances. Some of these disturbances, such as changes in money demand, consumption spending, or investment demand, arise from within the private sector. Others, such as wars, may arise for noneconomic reasons.
4 Inappropriate economic policy may also tend to move the economy away from full employment. Policy may be inappropriate because policy makers make mistakes or because policy is manipulated for political reasons, leading to the political business cycle.
5 The first difficulty of carrying out successful stabilization policy is that policy works with lags. The *inside* lag—divided into recognition, decision, and action lags—is the period between which an action becomes necessary and when it is taken. The *outside* lag is the period between which a policy action is taken and when it affects the economy. The outside lag is generally a distributed lag: the effects of a policy action build up over the course of time.
6 The behavior of expectations is a further source of difficulty for policy making. First, it is difficult to know exactly what determines expectations and to capture those factors in a simple formula. Second, policy actions themselves are likely to affect expectations.
7 More generally, there is always uncertainty about the effects of a given policy action on the economy. Economists are not agreed on the "correct" model of the economy, and evidence is not likely to be at

[18] See Chap. 8 for recent monetary growth targets.

hand soon to settle decisively disagreements over some behavioral functions—such as the consumption function. And even if we did know the form of the behavioral functions, the statistical evidence would be insufficient to pinpoint the values of the relevant parameters.

8 There are clearly occasions on which active monetary and fiscal policy actions should be taken to stabilize the economy. These are situations in which the economy has been affected by major disturbances.

9 Fine tuning—continuous attempts to stabilize the economy in the face of small disturbances—is more controversial. If fine tuning is undertaken, it calls for small policy responses in an attempt to moderate the economy's fluctuations, rather than to remove them entirely. A very active policy in response to small disturbances is likely to destabilize the economy.

10 The real issue in rules versus discretion is whether policy actions should be announced as far in advance as possible. Such announcements are desirable in that they aid private individuals in forecasting the future behavior of the economy.

10

THE THIRTIES AND THE SIXTIES: CREATING THE MODERN ECONOMY AND ITS PROBLEMS

10

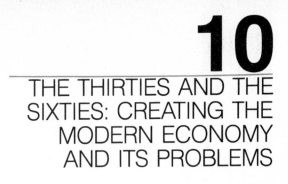

THE THIRTIES AND THE SIXTIES: CREATING THE MODERN ECONOMY AND ITS PROBLEMS

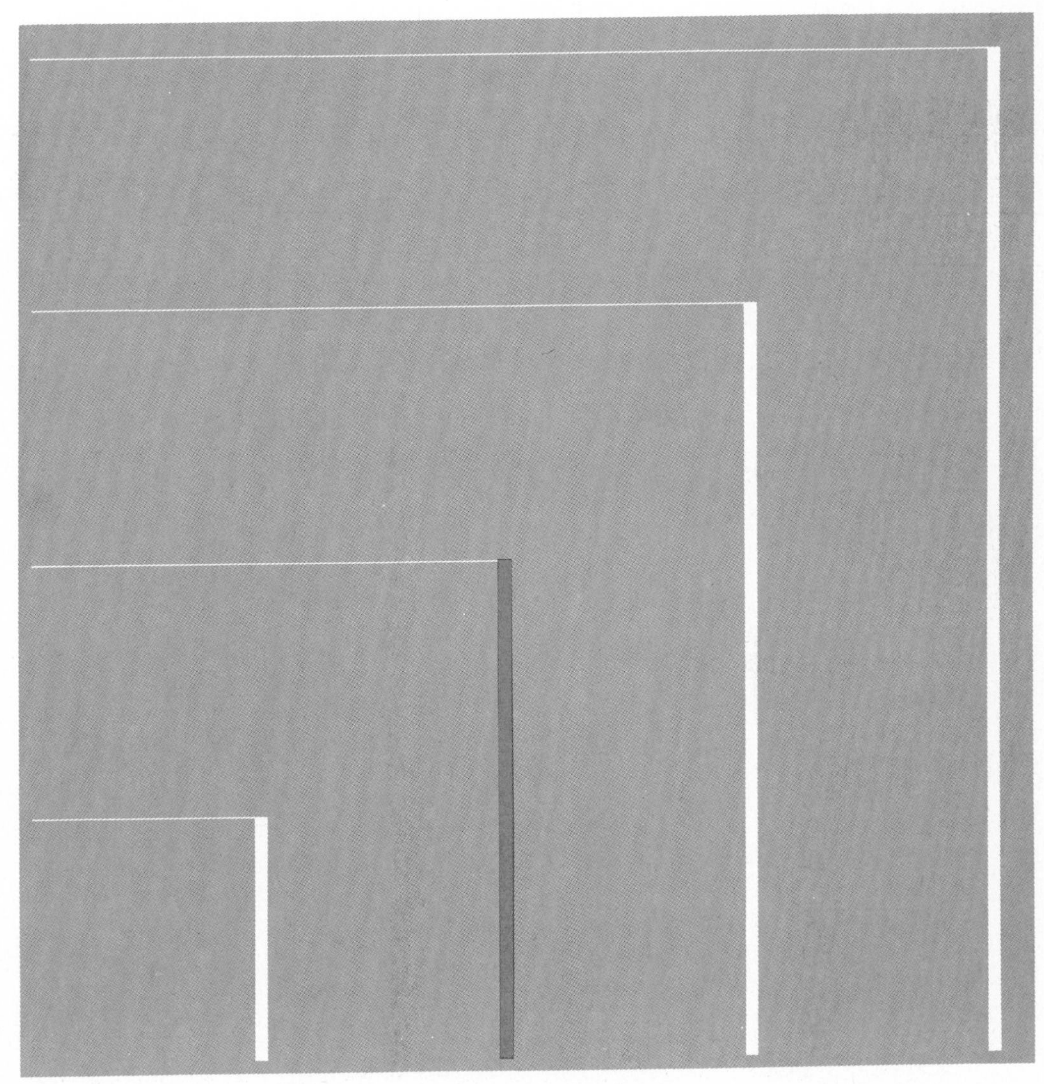

In this chapter we study economic developments and policy in the United States in the thirties and the sixties, two periods important in creating the economy of the eighties and modern economics. We use the analytical tools developed in earlier chapters to interpret and understand the behavior of the economy in those periods.

The Great Depression of the 1930s is worth studying in the first place purely for historical interest: As shown in Chart 10-1, GNP fell below its 1929 level in 1930, not to reach it again until 1939, and prices fell by 25 percent from 1929 to 1933. The unemployment rate reached 25 percent in 1933 and was above 14 percent from 1931 to 1939. The money supply fell more than 25 percent from 1929 to 1933; stock prices in 1932 were one-third their 1929 level. These extraordinary facts are set out in Table 10-1.

Second, and equally important, the thirties and the war that followed molded many of the institutions and views of the modern economy. The role of government expanded markedly, and it was the experience of the

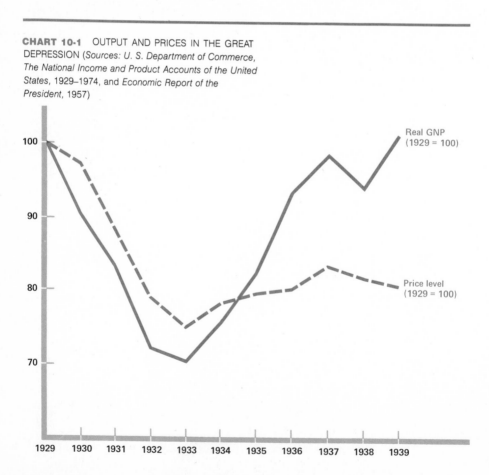

CHART 10-1 OUTPUT AND PRICES IN THE GREAT DEPRESSION (*Sources: U. S. Department of Commerce, The National Income and Product Accounts of the United States*, 1929–1974, and *Economic Report of the President*, 1957)

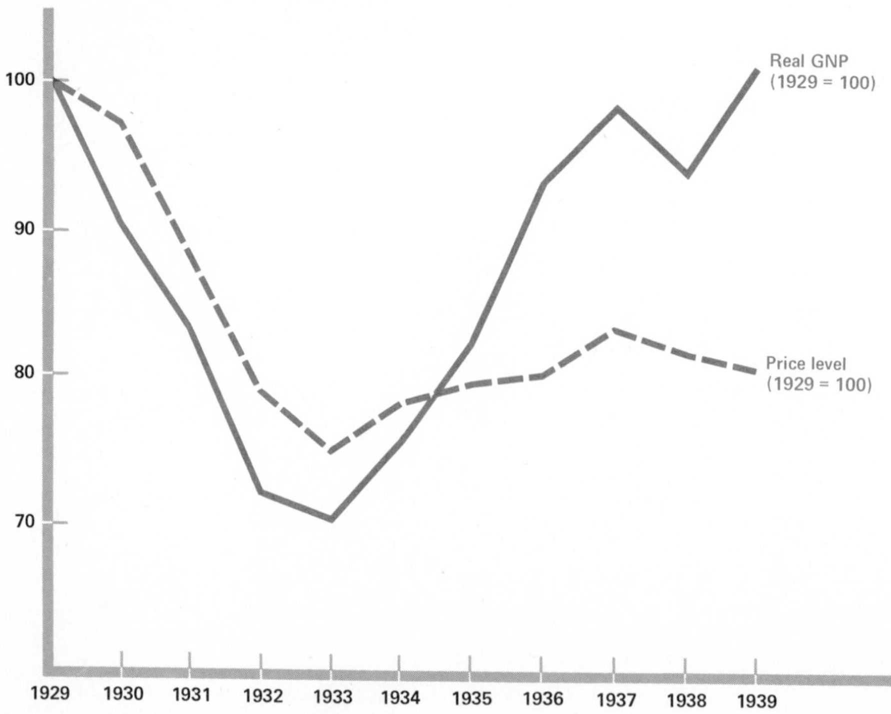

TABLE 10-1 ECONOMIC STATISTICS OF THE GREAT DEPRESSION

Year	GNP (billion 1972 $)	Gross I / GNP (%)	G (billion 1972 $)	Unemployment rate (%)	CPI (1929=100)	Commercial paper rate (%)	Aaa rate (%)	Stock market index	$M1$ (1929=100)	Full-employment surplus/Y_p (%)
1929	314.7	17.8	40.9	3.2	100	5.9	4.7	83.1	100	−0.8
1930	285.2	13.5	44.6	8.7	97.4	3.6	4.6	67.2	96.2	−1.4
1931	263.3	9.0	46.2	15.9	88.7	2.6	4.6	43.6	89.4	−3.1
1932	226.8	3.5	44.0	23.6	79.7	2.7	5.0	22.1	78.0	−0.9
1933	222.1	3.8	42.8	24.9	75.4	1.7	4.5	28.6	73.5	1.6
1934	239.4	5.5	48.7	21.7	78.0	1.0	4.0	31.4	81.4	0.2
1935	260.8	9.2	49.8	20.1	80.1	0.8	3.6	33.9	96.6	−0.1
1936	296.1	10.9	58.5	16.9	80.9	0.8	3.2	49.4	110.6	−1.1
1937	309.8	12.8	56.3	14.3	83.8	0.9	3.3	49.2	114.8	1.8
1938	297.1	8.1	61.3	19.0	82.3	0.8	3.2	36.7	115.9	0.6
1939	319.7	10.5	63.8	17.2	81.0	0.6	3.0	38.5	127.3	−0.1

Note: Stock market index is the Standard & Poor's composite index, which includes 500 stocks. September 1929 set equal to 100. Y_p denotes full employment output.

Sources:

Cols. 1, 2, 3: ***The National Income and Product Accounts of the United States, 1929–1974***, U.S. Department of Commerce.

Col. 4: Revised Bureau of Labor Statistics data taken from Michael Darby, "Three-and-a-Half Million Employees Have Been Mislaid: Or an Explanation of Unemployment, 1934–1941," ***Journal of Political Economy***, February 1976.

Cols. 5, 6, and 7: ***Economic Report of the President, 1957***.

Col. 8: ***Security Price Index Record***, 1978, Standard & Poor's Statistical Service.

Col. 9: Milton Friedman and Anna J. Schwartz, ***A Monetary History of the United States, 1867–1960*** (Princeton, N.J.: Princeton University Press, 1963), table A1, col. 7.

Col. 10: E. Cary Brown, "Fiscal Policy in the Thirties: A Reappraisal," ***American Economic Review***, December 1956, table I, cols. 3, 5, and 19.

thirties, embodied in the Employment Act of 1946, that led to the view, now taken for granted in practice, that the government has primary responsibility for satisfactory economic performance. The Social Security system and the present structure of the Federal Reserve System are products of the thirties. So too is Keynesian economics. And third, the thirties are a major battleground on which alternative macroeconomic theories compete to explain history, and in so doing, find support from the 1930s experience.

We describe the economic history of the thirties in Section 10-1 and review the controversy over the causes of the Depression in Section 10-2.

In the United States, the sixties were the first period in which Keynesian analysis was applied systematically in an attempt to reduce the unemployment rate and increase the growth rate of the economy. By the mid-sixties, the unemployment rate, which was 6.7 percent in 1961, had fallen to 4.5 percent, close to full employment, and it continued to fall, reaching 3.5 percent in 1969. The second half of the sixties was a period of full employment and high aggregate demand of the kind progressive democracies are committed to achieve. Essentially full employment was attained even before the Vietnam war increase in government spending.

Perspectives on economic policy in the sixties appear to differ widely. In one view, the period was one of high employment and prosperity, thanks to the activist stance of policy. An alternative view is that overexpansionist policies in that period were responsible for the inflation that was to prove to be the economic policy problem of the seventies. Actually, both views are correct. Policy in the early sixties was indeed successful. And economic policy in the second half of the period was overexpansionary or, equivalently, not sufficiently contractionary, in the face of increases in government spending related to the Vietnam war.

Both the major achievement and the major cost of economic policy in the sixties can be seen in Chart 10-2. The main achievement is the decline in the unemployment rate from 1961 to 1969. The main cost is the increase in the inflation rate over the period, from 1.0 percent in 1961 to 5.4 percent in 1969. The lowering of unemployment was accompanied by a growth rate of real GNP at an average annual rate from 1961 to 1969 of 4.8 percent, substantially greater than the average growth rate of real GNP of 2.2 percent over the 5 years from 1956 to 1961, or the 2.2 percent since 1969.

Macroeconomic policy in the sixties is reviewed in Sections 10-3 through 10-7. In Section 10-3, we outline the main tenets of the New Economics which the economic advisers of the Kennedy and Johnson years brought to bear on policy. In Section 10-4, we look at the 1964 tax cut, which remains the textbook example of successful expansionary fiscal policy. The *credit crunch* of 1966 is examined in Section 10-5. In Section 10-6, we look at the 1968 tax surcharge and use it to discuss the role of transitory taxes and the importance of the coordination of monetary and fiscal policies. Finally, Section 10-7 briefly considers the end of the sixties

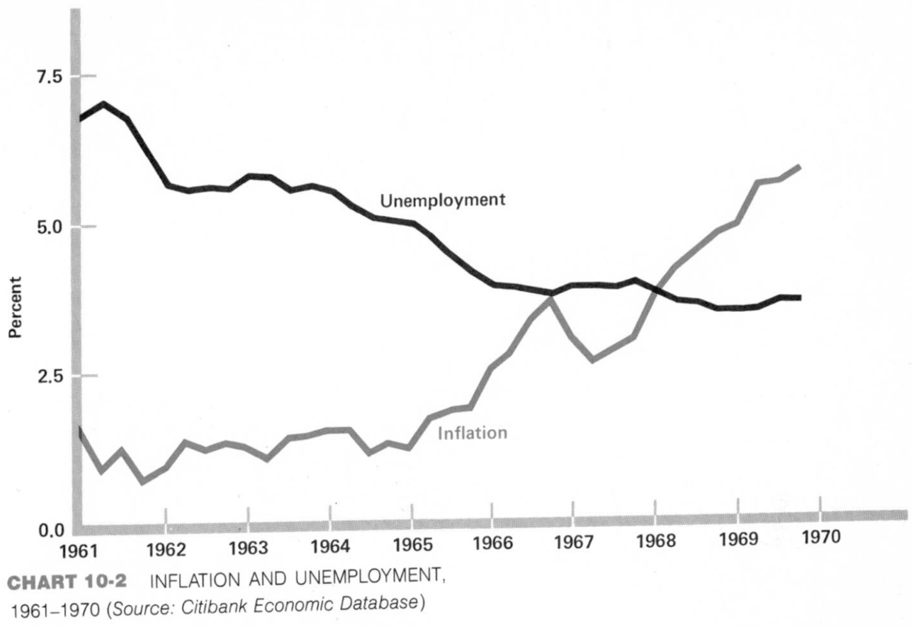

CHART 10-2 INFLATION AND UNEMPLOYMENT, 1961–1970 (*Source: Citibank Economic Database*)

and the onset of restrictive policies in 1969 to fight inflation. The appendix to the chapter contains a chronological review of the fiscal policy actions undertaken from 1961 to 1969. It can be used as a reference for details of policies discussed in the text.

The chapter is intended to serve two purposes. One is to use the theoretical tools of the previous chapters to show how they are useful, and indeed essential, to an understanding of macroeconomic policy problems. In so doing, we also illustrate some of the problems of policy making that were discussed in Chapter 9. The second purpose of the chapter is to show how the experience of the 1930s and the 1960s shaped much of the thinking that now goes into current economic policy making, and how policy in the sixties led to many of the economic problems faced in the seventies and early eighties.

10-1 THE THIRTIES: THE FACTS

Table 10-1 presents data describing the performance of the economy in the 1930s. Between 1929 and 1933, GNP fell by nearly 30 percent and unemployment rose from 3 to 25 percent. Investment collapsed; indeed, *net* investment was negative from 1931 to 1935. The consumer price index fell nearly 25 percent from 1929 to 1933; the stock market fell 80 percent between September 1929 and March 1933. From 1933 to 1937, real GNP grew fast, at an annual rate of nearly 9 percent, but even that did not get the unemployment rate down to normal levels. Then, in 1937–1938 there was a major recession within the depression, pushing the unemployment rate back up to nearly 20 percent. In the second half of the decade, short-term interest rates, such as the commercial paper rate, were near zero.

Facts such as those in Table 10-1 raise a host of questions. The two most important are, "*Why did this happen?*" and, "*Could it have been prevented?*" Underlying these questions is one that many economists are asked whenever the economy is in recession, and that they ask themselves in their bad moments: "*Could it happen again?*"

The Depression and the stock market crash of October 1929 are popularly thought of as almost the same thing. In fact, the economy started turning down before the stock market crash. The peak of the business cycle is estimated to have been in August 1929, and the stock market itself peaked in September 1929. Using September 1929 as the base period, Standard & Poor's composite stock price index fell from 100 in September to 66 in November. It rose again through March 1930, but then the collapse continued until the index fell to 15 in June 1932. We ask, in Section 10-2, what role the stock market crash played in the Depression.

By early 1931, the economy was suffering from a very severe depression, but not one that was out of the range of the experience of the previous century.[1] It was in the period from early 1931 until Franklin Roosevelt became President in March 1933 that the Depression became "Great."

What was economic policy doing during this period? The money stock fell from 1929 to 1930, and then fell rapidly in 1931 and 1932 and continued falling through March 1933. At the same time, the composition of the money stock changed. In March 1931 the currency-demand deposit ratio was 18.5 percent; 2 years later, it was 40.7 percent. The fall in the money stock was accompanied by three waves of bank failures, in which banks closed because they were unable to pay cash to their depositors. The bank failures culminated in the bank holiday of March 1933, a measure imposed by the new president's closing all banks in the country for a week. Many of the closed banks never reopened. It was the bank failures that reduced depositors' confidence and led them to increase the currency-demand deposit ratio. The Fed took very few steps to offset the fall in the money supply; for a few months in 1932 it did undertake a program of open market

[1] Milton Friedman and Anna J. Schwartz, in *A Monetary History of the United States 1867–1960* (Princeton, N.J.: Princeton University Press, 1963), give a very detailed account of the Great Depression, comparing it with other recessions and emphasizing the role of the Fed. For a more general economic history of the period, see Robert A. Gordon, *Economic Instability: The American Record* (New York: Harper & Row, 1974), chap. 3.

purchases, but otherwise seemed to acquiesce in bank closings and certainly failed to understand that the central bank should act vigorously in a crisis to prevent the collapse of the financial system.[2]

Fiscal policy too was not vigorous. The natural impulse of politicians then was to balance the budget in times of trouble, and much rhetoric was devoted to that proposition. The presidental candidates in 1932 campaigned on balanced budget platforms. In fact, as Table 10-2 shows, the federal government ran enormous deficits, particularly for that time, averaging 2.5 percent of GNP from 1931 to 1933, and even more later. The belief in budget balancing was more than rhetoric, however, for state and local governments raised taxes to match their expenditures,[3] as did the federal government, particularly in 1932 and 1933. President Roosevelt tried seriously to balance the budget—he was no Keynesian. The full-employment surplus which we introduced in Chapter 3 shows fiscal policy (combined state, local, and federal) as most expansionary in 1931, and moving to a more contractionary level from 1932 to 1934. In fact, the

[2] Friedman and Schwartz speculate on the reasons for the Fed's inaction; the whodunit or "who didn't do it" on pp. 407–419 of their book (cited in footnote 1) is fascinating.

[3] You can calculate the surplus of state and local governments as a percentage of GNP by subtracting column 4 in Table 10-2 from column 2.

TABLE 10-2 GOVERNMENT SPENDING AND REVENUE, 1929–1939 *(in percent)*

	Total government		Federal government		Total government
Year	Expenditure / GNP	Actual surplus / GNP	Expenditure / GNP	Actual surplus / GNP	Full employment surplus/Y_p*
1929	10.0	1.0	2.5	1.2	−0.8
1930	12.3	−0.3	3.1	0.3	−1.4
1931	16.4	−3.8	5.5	−2.8	−3.1
1932	18.3	−3.1	5.5	−2.6	−0.9
1933	19.2	−2.5	7.2	−2.3	1.6
1934	19.8	−3.7	9.8	−4.4	0.2
1935	18.6	−2.8	9.0	−3.6	−0.1
1936	19.5	−3.8	10.5	−4.4	−1.1
1937	16.6	0.3	8.2	0.4	1.8
1938	19.8	−2.1	10.2	−2.5	0.6
1939	19.4	−2.4	9.8	−2.4	−0.1

*Y_p = potential output.
Sources:
Cols. 1, 2, 3, 4: *Economic Report of the President, 1972*, tables B1 and B70.
Col. 5: E. Cary Brown, "Fiscal Policy in the Thirties: A Reappraisal," *American Economic Review*, December 1956, table 1, cols. 3, 5, and 19.

full-employment surplus was positive in 1933 and 1934, despite the actual deficits.[4] Of course, the full-employment surplus concept had not been invented in the 1930s.

Economic activity recovered in the period from 1933 to 1937, with fiscal policy becoming more expansionary and the money stock growing rapidly. The growth of the money stock was based on an inflow of gold from Europe. This provided high-powered money for the monetary system. It was in the thirties that the Fed acquired most of its current holdings of gold.[5]

The period from 1933 to 1937 also saw substantial legislative and administrative action—the *New Deal*—from the Roosevelt administration. The Fed was reorganized and the Federal Deposit Insurance Corporation (FDIC) was established, as were a variety of regulatory agencies and the Social Security Administration.

The FDIC insures deposits in participating banks, thus assuring depositors that their funds (up to a maximum that is raised periodically) can be obtained even if the bank fails. Deposit insurance both reduces the likelihood that depositors will cause a run on a bank and ensures that depositors do not lose wealth if banks do fail. Regulation Q, forbidding the payment of interest on demand deposits, was instituted, based on the belief that excessive competition among banks in the late twenties had caused them to offer depositors higher interest rates than were wise, and thus had caused bank failures.

A number of regulatory agencies were also created, most notably the Securities and Exchange Commission, which regulates the securities industry. Its purpose was to prevent speculative excesses that were thought largely responsible for the stock market crash. The Social Security Administration was set up, so that the elderly would not in the future have to rely on their own savings to ensure themselves a minimally adequate standard of living in retirement. The Roosevelt administration also believed that the route to recovery lay in increasing wages and prices, so it encouraged trade unionization, and price-raising and price-fixing schemes by business, through the National Recovery Administration.

The 1937–1938 recession was very sharp, and it followed the tightening of *both* monetary and fiscal policy. Table 10-2 shows the full-employment surplus rising rapidly from 1936 to 1937. The increase in the full-employment surplus was equal to 2.9 percent of GNP, the biggest change in the decade. On the monetary side, the Fed acted in 1936 and 1937 to reduce the excess reserves held by the banking system. From 1929 to 1937, banks had been increasing their holdings of reserves over and above those required by the Fed. In 1936, member banks of the Federal Reserve

[4] Note that in this chapter, unlike Chap. 3 and elsewhere in the book, the full-employment deficit includes federal, state, and local governments.

[5] For details of the way in which the Fed acquired the gold, see Friedman and Schwartz, op. cit., p. 506.

System held over 20 percent of their assets as excess reserves (required reserves were only 6.2 percent of assets). The Fed feared that if it ever wanted to control the money supply by an open market sale, the banks would have excess reserves sufficiently large that they would not have to reduce their total assets, but would instead merely reduce their reserve ratio.[6] Since the reserves were excess, the Fed decided to eliminate them merely by increasing required reserves.

When the Fed increased required reserves, the banks reacted by reducing their outstanding credit and maintaining the excess reserves. That is, it became clear that the excess reserves were assets the banks really wanted to hold. The reasons are fairly obvious. First, many banks had collapsed for lack of readily realizable assets just a few years before, and it was wise to be able to avoid that problem. And second, interest rates were so low at the time that it was cheap to hold excess reserves. The effect of the Fed's actions was to reduce the money supply by nearly 3 percent from early 1937 to mid-1938. Thereafter, the money supply resumed growth, fiscal policy became less contractionary, and the recovery proceeded.

Another important aspect of the Depression deserves mention: it was virtually worldwide. To some extent, this was the result of the collapse of the international financial system.[7] It resulted too from the mutual adoption of high tariff policies by many countries (including the United States), keeping out foreign goods to protect domestic producers. And, of course, if each country keeps out foreign goods, the volume of world trade declines, providing a contractionary influence on the world economy.

The experience of the thirties varied internationally. Sweden suffered its depression in the twenties and benefited from expansionary policies in the thirties. Britain's economy too suffered more in the twenties than in the thirties. Germany grew rapidly after Hitler came to power and expanded government spending. China escaped the recession until after 1931, essentially because it had a floating exchange rate. As always, there is much to be learned from the exceptions.

In 1939, the United States real GNP rose above its 1929 level for the first time in the decade. But it was not until 1942, after the United States formally entered World War II, that the unemployment rate finally fell below 5 percent.

10-2 THE GREAT DEPRESSION: THE ISSUES

In Section 10-1 we asked four questions about the Great Depression. What caused it? Could it have been avoided? Can it happen again? What was the

[6] Check back to Chap. 8 to see how a reduction in the reserve ratio can offset the effects of a change in the monetary base (H) on the money stock.

[7] This aspect of the Depression is emphasized by Charles Kindleberger, *The World in Depression, 1929–1939* (Berkeley: University of California Press, 1973).

role of the stock market crash? The first question is still hotly debated, and we shall review the arguments below. The verdict on the second and third questions is favorable: It is generally agreed that the Depression could have been avoided, and that it is unlikely to happen again. There is some disagreement about the fourth question.

Before we enter the debate on the causes of the Great Depression, it is important to bear in mind that there need not have been a single cause. Theories that are presented as competing may well be complementary. We also want to note the distinction in the controversy between, first, what started the initial downturn and, second, what moved the economy into an unprecedented depression. With these points in mind, there are essentially two *hypotheses* about the causes of the initial downturn and the deepening of the decline in activity. These are, respectively, (1) an autonomous decline in aggregate demand and (2) a monetary contraction. Within the "autonomous demand" camp (1), most claim that investment demand declined,[8] while some view consumption demand as having decreased autonomously. We now review these hypotheses.

We start with the autonomous demand reduction hypotheses. Growth in the twenties, in this view, was based on the mass production of the automobile and radio, and was fueled by a housing boom. The collapse of growth in the thirties resulted from the drying up of investment opportunities and a downward shift in investment demand. The collapse of investment, shown in Table 10-1, fits in with this picture. Poor fiscal policy, as reflected in the perverse behavior of the full-employment surplus from 1931 to 1933, shares the blame, particularly for making the Depression worse.

What does the autonomous demand view have to say about the monetary collapse? The Fed argued in the thirties that there was little it could have done to prevent the Depression, because interest rates were already as low as they could possibly go. A variety of sayings of the type, "You can lead a horse to the water but you can't make it drink," were used to explain that further reductions in interest rates would have had no effect if there was no demand for investment. Investment demand was thought to be very unresponsive to the rate of interest—implying a very steep IS curve. At the same time, the LM curve was believed to be quite flat, though not necessarily reaching the extreme of a liquidity trap. In this situation, as we saw in Chapter 4, monetary expansion would be relatively ineffective in stimulating demand and output.

It was also widely believed that the experience of the Depression showed that the private economy was inherently unstable in that it could self-depress with no difficulty if left alone. The experience of the thirties,

[8] This view is argued, for example, in Robert A. Gordon, *Economic Instability and Growth: The American Record* (New York: Harper & Row, 1974), chap. 3.

implicitly or explicitly, was the basis for the belief that an active stabilization policy was needed to maintain good economic performance.

The view that monetary policy in the thirties had been impotent was sharply challenged in 1963 by Friedman and Schwartz in their *Monetary History*. They argued that the Depression, far from showing that money does not matter, "is in fact a tragic testimonial to the importance of monetary factors."[9] They argued, with skill and style, that the failure of the Fed to prevent bank failures and the decline of the money stock from the end of 1930 to 1933 was largely responsible for the recession being as serious as it was. This monetary view in turn came close to being accepted as the orthodox explanation of the Depression.

A challenge to the monetary view has recently been issued by Peter Temin,[10] who focuses on the comparatively narrow question of what actually caused the Depression, rather than on whether it could have been avoided. Temin argues that the decline in the money stock was a *result* of the decline in economic activity, not a cause. The cause, he contends, was a fall in consumption (rather than investment) spending that set off a fall in income, which then in turn affected the monetary sector. Reinforced by the Fed's incompetence, this led to a dramatic reduction in money that aggravated the Depression. In terms of IS-LM schedules, Temin sees an initial, moderate leftward shift of the IS schedule in Figure 10-1.

But what about the reduction in the money stock? Should that not have caused the LM curve to move to the left simultaneously? Here we have to recognize that the IS and LM curves in Figure 10-1 are drawn for a given price level. But the aggregate price level was falling through this period, so that the LM curve would not necessarily have shifted to the left. The fall in the money supply was tending to make it move left, but the fall in the price level was offsetting that leftward shift. What, then, was the role of the bank failures? Temin argues that they were *caused* by the decline in income and the shift in the IS curve, since with a falling price level, low interest rates, and declining output, the *nominal* stock of money had to fall if the demand for real balances was to stay equal to supply. Bank failures were merely the mechanism that reduced the money supply.

How would one choose between the monetary and autonomous demand hypotheses? Temin focuses on the behavior of interest rates. A leftward shift of the LM curve would have caused interest rates to rise, (point E_1), whereas a downward shift of the IS curve would have caused them to fall (point E_2). In fact, interest rates fell, suggesting the IS curve shifted down. Proponents of the monetary view criticize this test for failing to distinguish between real and nominal interest rates. We shall have to wait till Chapter 13 to obtain a full understanding of this point, but the

[9] Friedman and Schwartz, op. cit., p. 300.

[10] Peter Temin, *Did Monetary Forces Cause the Great Depression?* (New York: Norton, 1976).

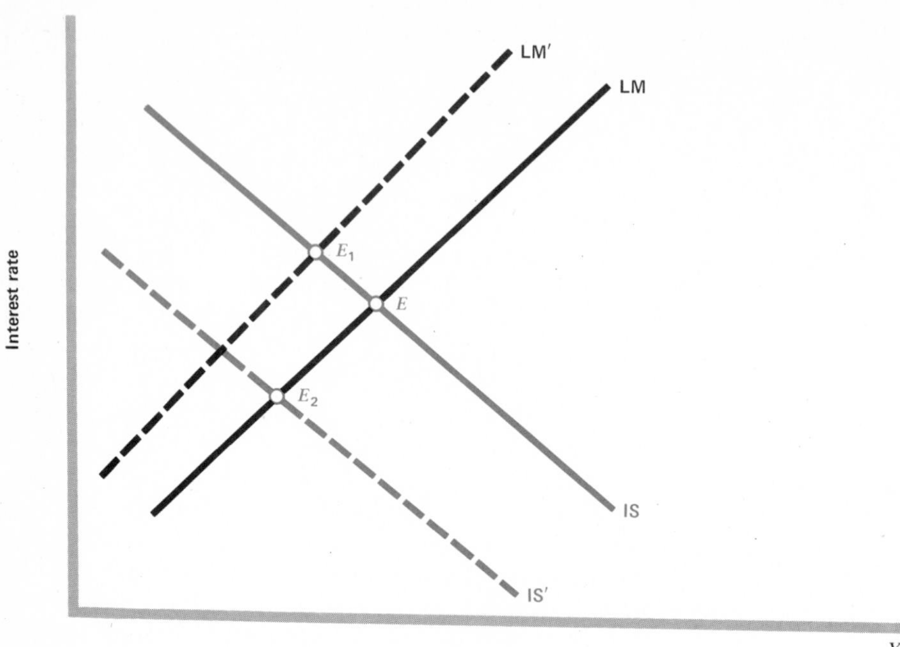

FIGURE 10-1 COMPETING EXPLANATIONS OF THE GREAT DEPRESSION

argument is that although the nominal interest rate in the thirties seems low, the *real* rate, the nominal rate minus the expected rate of inflation, could have been high. How? Because prices were falling at the time, supporters of the monetary view maintain that people must have been expecting deflation. Hence, despite the low nominal rate, the real interest rate was high. And that, they argue, is consistent with the Friedman-Schwartz view. The controversy will continue for some time.

As is often the case, there is more agreement here among economists than there seems to be. A careful reading of the Friedman-Schwartz book will show that they are really quite agnostic about what started the Depression in 1929. The main thrust of their argument relates to the second question we asked: Could the Depression have been avoided? And here they argue vigorously that expansive monetary policy, particularly in 1930 but also in the following years, would have prevented the Depression from being more than a serious recession. Temin is chiefly interested in what started the recession—which, on the basis of econometric evidence, he blames mainly on a downward shift in the consumption rather than the investment function. He would probably agree that better policy, monetary and fiscal, would have made the Depression much less severe.

This is the general verdict on the second question: The Great Depression could have been avoided. Both monetary and fiscal policy were so inept that they contributed significantly to making the recession into the worst depression for which we have data. If there had been prompt, strong, expansive monetary and fiscal policy, the economy would have suffered a recession but not the trauma it did.

On the third question, could it happen again, there is agreement that it could not, except, of course, in the event of truly perverse policies. But these are less likely now than they were then. For one thing, we have history to help us avoid its repetition. Taxes would not again be raised in the middle of a depression nor would attempts be made to balance the budget. The Fed would seek actively to keep the money supply from falling. In addition, the government now has a much larger role in the economy. The higher level of government spending, which is relatively slow to change, and automatic stabilizers, including the income tax,[11] unemployment insurance, and Social Security, give the economy more stability than it had then.[12]

Turning to the fourth question, the role of the stock market crash remains in some dispute as a causal factor in the Depression. Clearly, the crash substantially reduced wealth, and thus contributed to a reduction in consumption demand, which helped worsen the recession. It is also true that it was easy for firms to raise funds to finance investment in the booming stock market of the later twenties, and impossible for them to do so in the early thirties. This too is a depressing factor. But whether the stock market crash was merely an accurate prediction of what was about to happen, or an autonomous factor, or even a self-fulfilling prophecy is not certain.[13] We are inclined to believe that it did play a substantial independent role in the Depression.

Finally, we want to return to the controversy between Friedman-Schwartz and Temin over the first question, what caused the Depression? We said that there was more agreement than there seemed to be. Why, then, is there controversy? The reason is that the thirties are seen as the period that set the stage for massive government intervention in the economy. Those opposed to an active role for government have to explain away the debacle of the economy in the thirties. If the Depression occurred because of, and not despite, the government (particularly the Fed), the case for an active government role in economic stabilization is weakened. Further, the thirties are a period in which the economy behaved in such an

[11] Recall from Chap. 3 that a proportional income tax reduces the multiplier.

[12] See Martin Baily, "Stabilization Policy and Private Economic Behavior," *Brookings Papers on Economic Activity*, 1978:1 (Washington, D.C. The Brookings Institution, 1978).

[13] John B. Kirkwood, "The Great Depression: A Structural Analysis," *Journal of Money, Credit and Banking*, November 1972, lays stress on the stock market crash in affecting consumption and investment, but does not attempt to explain the crash.

extreme way that competing theories have to be subjected to the test of whether they can explain that period. Those are the main reasons the dispute over the causes of the Great Depression continues to be so lively more than 50 years after it began.[14]

10-3 THE NEW ECONOMICS

The "New Economics" is a term that has come to be used to describe the analytical and philosophical approach to economic policy making used by the Kennedy and Johnson administrations in the 1960s. The analytical approach consists basically of the tools we have outlined in Chapters 3 through 7. The philosophy characterizing that approach to economics is a mix of activism and optimism. It is well characterized by a paragraph from the chapter, "Promise of Modern Economic Policy," in a book by Walter Heller, written in 1966 when the New Economics was at the pinnacle of esteem:[15]

> The significance of the great expansion in the 60's lies not only in its striking statistics of employment, income, and growth but in its glowing promise of things to come. If we can surmount the economic pressures of Vietnam without later being trapped into a continuing war on inflation when we should be fighting economic slack, the "new economics" can move us steadily toward the qualitative goals that lie beyond the facts and figures of affluence.

Walter Heller, now a professor at the University of Minnesota, was one of the chief architects of economic policy in the early sixties. He was chairperson of the Council of Economic Advisers (CEA) under both Presidents Kennedy and Johnson. The CEA is a body of professional economists that advises the President on economic policy. The Council became more influential in the Kennedy and Johnson adminstrations than it had been before, and it attracted as members and staff a succession of distinguished economists. Among these were James Tobin of Yale, Gardner Ackley of the University of Michigan, Robert Solow of MIT, Otto Eckstein of Harvard, Kenneth Arrow of Stanford, and the late Arthur Okun, then of Yale and afterward at the Brookings Institution, to name only a few.

[14] Among recent contributions are Michael Darby, "Three-and-a-Half Million U.S. Employees Have Been Mislaid: Or, an Explanation of Unemployment, 1934–1941," *Journal of Political Economy*, February 1976, who argues that unemployment is mismeasured after 1933 because those on government work relief programs are counted as unemployed. Adjusted for those individuals, the unemployment rate falls rapidly from 20.6 percent in 1933 to below 10 percent in 1936. See also Thomas Mayer, "Money and the Great Depression: A Critique of Professor Temin's Thesis," *Explorations in Economic History*, April 1978, and Karl Brunner (ed.), *Contemporary Views of the Great Depression* (Boston: Martinus Nijhoff, 1980).

[15] W. W. Heller, *New Dimensions of Political Economy* (New York: Norton, 1967), p. 58.

The New Economics emphasized the goal of reattaining full employment after the high unemployment levels of the late 1950s. The first goal of policy was to move to a full utilization of resources. The analysis of how that was to be done led to the application of a number of concepts, some of which, such as the full-employment budget surplus, we have already met. We shall briefly review the basic analytical concepts of the New Economics before concluding this section by discussing what was new in the New Economics.

The contrast between economic policy in the thirties and the sixties is marked. In the sixties, policy makers came into a not very difficult economic situation with well-thought-out theories and policies to apply. Those policies were based on the Keynesian analysis that developed in the thirties and out of the experience of the thirties. In the thirties, policy fumbled, and badly, for some way to get the economy moving again. The Roosevelt administration did run budget deficits, but most unwillingly, and it had no concept of the full-employment surplus; the Kennedy-Johnson adminstration planned a tax cut in 1963–1964 when the budget was in deficit, and sold the policy to a skeptical Congress.

Potential Output and the GNP Gap

To focus attention on the target of full employment and for use as an operating guide to policy, the Council (CEA), and particularly Arthur Okun, developed and stressed the concept of *potential output.* Potential output, or full-employment output, measures the level of real GNP the economy can produce with full employment. The full-employment rate of unemployment used in defining potential output in the sixties was 4 percent.[16] Chart 10-3 shows potential output for the 1953–1980 period.

Along with the concept and measurement of potential output went the notion of the *GNP gap*. The gap is simply the difference between actual and potential real output. For the years 1961–1965, actual GNP was below its potential level and the GNP gap was therefore positive. Chart 10-3 shows that at the beginning of 1961, the GNP gap was an extraordinary $60 billion, measured in 1972 dollars, or nearly 8 percent of GNP. A gap of that magnitude seemed clearly to call for expansionary policy. Either monetary or fiscal policy could be used to raise aggregate demand and increase actual output to a level closer to the economy's potential.

The notions of potential output and the GNP gap seem very simple, but they are important. They dramatize the costs of unemployment in easily understood terms—in terms of output lost due to unemployment—and make it easy to understand what alternative target levels of GNP at which policy makers might aim, would mean for the level of unemployment.

16 We introduced potential output in Chap. 1. Remember that we pointed out there that new measures of potential output take an unemployment rate of more than 5 percent to represent full employment.

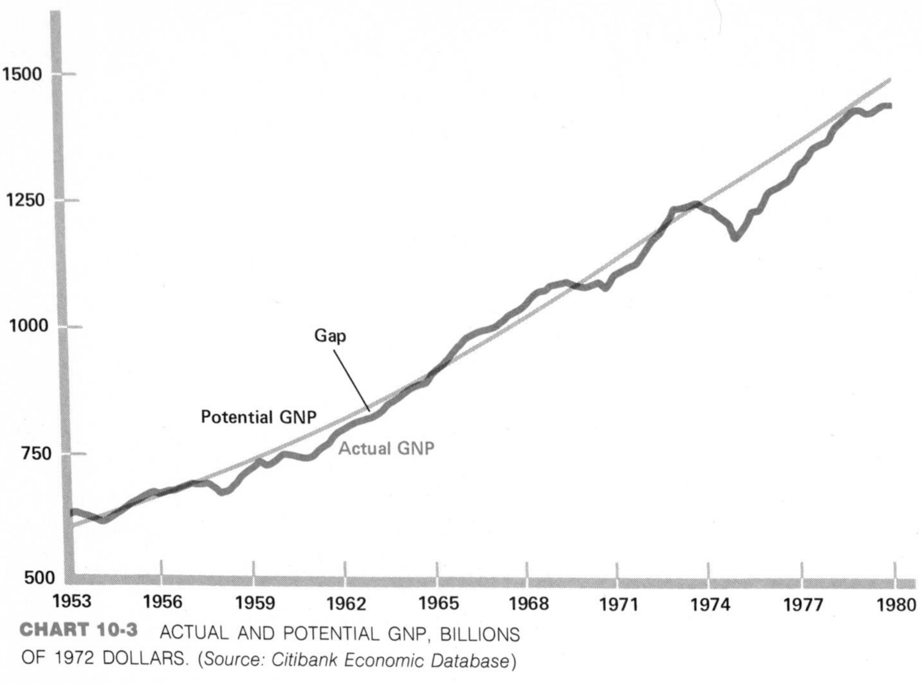

CHART 10-3 ACTUAL AND POTENTIAL GNP, BILLIONS OF 1972 DOLLARS. (*Source: Citibank Economic Database*)

The Full-Employment Budget Surplus

The full-employment budget surplus was discussed at some length in Chapter 3, and we will therefore be brief here. The concept had been introduced to the economics literature before the 1960s, most notably to study fiscal policy in the thirties. The concept is important and useful because it directs attention away from the actual budget, which is a misleading indicator of fiscal policy, toward the full-employment surplus—a more relevant, although still imperfect, indicator of policy.

The New Economists planned to use fiscal policy as the instrument with which to close the GNP gap. It was important to get across to Congress and the public the idea of the full-employment surplus because the unemployment rate was high in 1961 and the federal budget was in an actual deficit. Any proposals to increase spending or cut taxes would certainly imply a larger deficit. Members of Congress could be relied upon to look with great suspicion on any policy that might increase the budget deficit. By focusing attention on the full-employment budget, the New Economists appropriately succeeded in shifting attention away from the state of the actual budget to concern with how the budget would look at full employment—which had the side benefit of focusing attention on the full-employment issue itself.

Fiscal Drag and the Fiscal Dividend

Growth of potential output over time implies that aggregate demand must increase to maintain full employment. Suppose that income taxes increase with the level of income, but that government spending does not automatically increase along with income. In that case, the full-employment budget surplus increases over time as the economy grows. That increase in the full-employment surplus tends to exert a restraining effect on aggregate demand. The restraining influence on aggregate demand implied by a fixed level of government spending and a given tax structure[17] in a growing economy, and the resultant increase in the full-employment surplus, is called *fiscal drag*.

The policy implication of fiscal drag is that *fiscal dividends* should be paid. To offset the net deflationary effects of fiscal drag, government spending can be increased or tax rates can be reduced. These increases in spending or reductions in taxes are known as the fiscal dividend. How is the fiscal dividend possible? Suppose that potential output is rising and that taxes will rise along with it. To maintain a constant full-employment surplus, tax rates can be reduced. The same amount of taxes in total can be realized at lower tax rates if output rises. Alternatively, government spending can increase to match the increase in tax collections, so that the full-employment surplus remains constant despite the increase in output.[18]

Growth

The New Economics emphasized economic growth in two ways. First, there was the need for aggregate demand to grow in order to achieve full employment. In that respect, growth was a matter of achieving full employment and maintaining it. Second, there was an emphasis on achieving a high rate of growth of potential output itself. The emphasis was on investment spending to encourage growth in productive potential. We delay consideration of that aspect until Chapter 17.

The Behavior of Money Wages

We have to be brief in discussing the emphasis placed by the New Economists on the behavior of money wages relative to productivity, in affecting the rate of inflation, because we have not yet integrated the theory of inflation with our analysis of aggregate demand. At this stage we merely

[17] By "a given tax structure" we mean the set of rules, including tax rates, exemption levels, etc., used to calculate taxes. In Chaps. 14 and 16 we discuss the effects of inflation as also creating fiscal drag—an effect that has been very evident in the seventies.

[18] In the 1970s, there was concern that fiscal dividends are committed in advance. Certain government spending programs, such as Social Security, imply increasing government payments in the future, which will probably use up the fiscal dividend.

note that there was great concern over the behavior of money wages throughout the Kennedy and Johnson years, and that early in the period, in 1962, the Council of Economic Advisers set up *guideposts*[19] for the behavior of money wages. The basic guidepost was that money wages should not grow faster than the average rate of productivity increase in the economy. In 1965 and 1966, the guideposts were made more explicit and the rate of wage increase of 3.2 percent became the general criterion for noninflationary wage increases.

In setting up the criterion for noninflationary wage increases—that wages should not increase faster than labor productivity—the CEA also suggested that rapid investment could contribute to price stability. The notion was that rapid investment would increase the amount of capital employed in the production of output, and would thus increase the productivity of labor. For a given rate of wage increase, this greater productivity would mean less inflation. High investment spending was thus thought helpful in containing inflationary pressures.

As we have already noted, we shall not discuss wage behavior further in this chapter. By the end of Chapter 13, the apparatus for analyzing the proposals of the CEA for wage behavior and the role of investment and productivity increase in determining inflation will have been presented. At that stage you should return to this section to review the proposals of the CEA, which you will realize are what is now called supply-side economics.

What Was New?

What was new about the New Economics? Was the approach to stabilization policy along the lines of fiscal activism, potential output objectives, and the emphasis on the full-employment budget surplus in fact new? The answer here is not simple. It is true that the activism the CEA displayed was unprecedented. But it is true, too, that the tools and concepts the Council used were main-line professional macroeconomics. The idea of active fiscal policy as a countercyclical measure and the notion that there was nothing particularly desirable about a balanced budget were certainly not new.

Even so, the active use of fiscal policy met much resistance in the political process at the time. Herbert Stein, himself chairperson of the CEA under President Nixon, reviews the progress toward the major policy measure of the early sixties, the 1964 tax cut, in his book *The Fiscal Revolution*.[20] He shows how the Kennedy administration first had to get

[19] For an interesting, and sometimes amusing, discussion of the guideposts, see George P. Shultz and Robert Z. Aliber (eds.), *Guidelines* (Chicago: The University of Chicago Press, 1966). See, too, the evaluation in Otto Eckstein, "The Economics of the 1960s: A Backward Look," *Public Interest*, Spring 1970.

[20] Chicago: The University of Chicago Press, 1969.

accustomed to the idea that, during recession, a move toward an increased budget deficit was not a step toward fiscal irresponsibility. By the same token, Congress had to find its way toward expansionary fiscal policies, away from balanced budgets or tax cuts accompanied by offsetting reductions in public spending. Eventually, many recognized that a measure to expand aggregate demand was necessary in order to cope with high unemployment.

Thus, what was new about the New Economics was not the analysis, but the active and successful use of that analysis in the operation of fiscal policy.

10-4 THE 1964 TAX CUT

The first major economic policy action taken by the Kennedy-Johnson administration was the tax cut, embodied in the Revenue Act of 1964. That measure, enacted in February 1964, more than a year after the initial recommendation, provided for a permanent cut in income tax rates for individuals and corporations. The one-year lag provides an illustration of the decision lag of fiscal policy. Marginal tax rates for individuals that had ranged from 20 to 91 percent were reduced to a range of 14 to 70 percent. The tax rate for most corporations was reduced from 52 to 48 percent. It was estimated that the tax cut package amounted to a reduction in personal taxes of $10 billion and in corporate taxes of $3 billion. These tax cuts were very substantial. The personal tax cut of $10 billion was equivalent to a 20 percent reduction in personal tax payments and the corporate tax reduction amounted to 8 percent of corporate taxes.

The long-run effects of the tax cut are studied in this section in two ways. First, we provide some calculations of what the effects of the tax cut should have been, using the theory of Chapters 3 through 7 and estimates of the multipliers. Second, we look at the actual change in GNP and its components, and attempt to infer the contribution of the tax cut and to compare it with the predicted effects. We rely strongly on an important paper by Arthur Okun which develops an analysis of the tax cut and its expected macroeconomic impact.[21]

We do not go through Okun's entire analysis in this section; in particular, we do not review his calculations of the *dynamic effects* of the tax cut, corresponding to the dynamic multipliers shown in Chapters 5 and 9. These show how the tax cut was expected to affect GNP in each quarter after it took place, and are explained in the original article. The calculations are of interest especially in showing the differential speeds with which

[21] See Arthur Okun, "Measuring the Impact of the 1964 Tax Reduction," in W. W. Heller (ed.), *Perspectives on Economic Growth* (New York: Random House, 1968).

changes in the corporate tax rate and personal income tax affect the economy.

An important aspect of the analysis to follow is that it emphasizes fiscal policy and generally ignores monetary policy. It will be seen that we use the multiplier apparatus of Chapter 3, rather than the full IS-LM apparatus of Chapter 4. In Chapter 3, the interest rate was implicitly held constant. Accordingly, income expansion due to fiscal policy was not dampened in that chapter by increases in the interest rate. The assumption that the interest rate remained constant following the tax cut, which is required if we are to use the analysis of Chapter 3 rather than the full IS-LM analysis turns out to be justified. Monetary policy following the tax cut was *accommodating*. The Fed did allow the money supply to increase following the tax cut to keep the interest rate constant. If the money supply had not been increased, then the interest rate would have risen, and some investment spending would have been choked off. As Okun put it, "The monetary authorities supplied a good sound set of tires for the economy to roll on, but they did not contribute the engine."[22] The expansion was due to fiscal policy but it was supported, or accommodated, by an expansionary monetary policy. We will not discuss monetary policy further in this section.

*Long-Run Effects

We noted that the tax package consisted of a cut of about $10 billion in personal income taxes, and a cut in corporate profit taxes worth $3 billion. The cut in personal income taxes would increase disposable personal income and thereby increase consumption spending directly. The corporate tax cut, by raising corporate after-tax profits, would increase both investment spending and the payments of dividends out of the now higher profits. These increases in dividends would increase personal disposable income and thus consumption spending. Finally, both consumption and investment spending would increase in response to any changes in GNP—these are induced expenditures.

Tables 10-3 and 10-4 summarize these impacts on GNP. First, there are three components of the *direct* impact of the tax package on demand. Estimates of the direct effects of the tax cut on GNP depend on a number of *parameters*—that is, numerical values of coefficients like the long-run marginal propensity to consume and the propensity of corporations to pay dividends out of profits. In each case we use Okun's estimates of these parameters. In turn, they are based on a variety of studies to which Okun refers in the article cited above.

The first direct effect of the tax cut on aggregate demand arises from the $10-billion cut in personal income taxes. The long-run marginal

[22] Okun, cited in footnote 21, p. 44.

TABLE 10-3 DIRECT LONG-RUN EFFECTS OF 1964 TAX CUT

	Action	Effect	Explanation
1.	$10-billion cut in income taxes: $10 billion × 0.949 =	$9.49-billion increase in consumption	Long-run marginal propensity to consume (MPC) = 0.949
2.	$3-billion cut in corporate profit taxes $3 billion × 0.75 =	$2.25-billion increase in investment	Corporations invest 75% of after-tax profits
3.	$3-billion cut in corporate profit taxes: $3 billion × 0.625 = $1.875-billion increase in distributed profits $1.875 billion × 0.879 = $1.648-billion increase in personal disposable income $1.648 billion × 0.949 =	$1.56-billion increase in consumption	Firms distribute 62.5% of additional after-tax profits Only 87.9% of the dividends is available for spending after income taxes Long-run MPC is 0.949
4.	Total direct effect	$13.3-billion increase in aggregate demand	

propensity to consume is estimated at 0.949, which means that consumption spending increases by $9.49 billion as a result of the cut in personal income taxes. Second, the cut of $3 billion in corporate profit taxes is assumed to lead to an increase in corporate investment of $2.25 billion, on the assumption that firms invest 75 percent of their after-tax profits. Third, the increased dividends paid out by corporations increase consumption. The table shows three steps in the computation of that increase in consumption. Since corporations distribute 62.5 percent of their additional after-tax profits, there is an increase of $1.875 billion in dividends.[23] But those dividends are taxed, at the average rate of 12.1 percent, so that only 0.879 (= 1 − 0.121) of the increase in dividends remains as an increase in

[23] Note that the $3-billion cut in corporate taxes leads to an increase of $2.25 billion in corporate investment and a $1.875-billion increase in dividends. The total exceeds $3 billion, implying that corporations finance part of the increase in investment by borrowing.

TABLE 10-4 INDUCED LONG-RUN EFFECTS OF THE 1964 TAX CUT *(per dollar increase in income)*

		Effect	Explanation
1. Consumption	$1 × 0.505 = $0.505		Only about half the increase in GNP turns into increases in disposable income
	$0.505 × 0.949 =	$0.479 increase in consumption	Long-run MPC = 0.949
2. Investment	$1 × 0.206 = $0.206 increase in after-tax corporate profits		A dollar increase in income raises corporate after-tax profits by $0.206
	$0.206 × 0.75 =	$0.154 increase in investment	Corporations invest 75% of after-tax profits

disposable income. And then 0.949 of that increase in disposable income is consumed. The three direct effects of the tax cut add up to an increase in aggregate demand of $13.3 billion.

Table 10-4 shows the *induced* effects of the increase in income created by the tax cuts. There are two induced components of spending. First, it is estimated that only about half—0.505 is the estimate—of an increase in GNP represents an increase in disposable personal income. Then the long-run marginal propensity to consume is applied to the 0.505 to calculate the induced consumption resulting from a $1 increase in GNP. Second, there is induced investment as a result of an increase in GNP. A $1 increase in GNP leads to a 20.6-cent increase in after-tax corporate profits, of which 75 percent is invested. Thus there is a 15.4-cent increase in investment spending as a result of a $1 increase in GNP.

Applying the long-run propensity to consume, 0.949, to the change in disposable income, we have

$$\Delta C = 0.949\ \Delta Y_d = (0.949)\ (0.505\ \Delta Y) = 0.479\ \Delta Y \tag{1}$$

The induced change in investment is

$$\Delta I = (0.75)(0.206)\ \Delta Y = 0.154\ \Delta Y \tag{2}$$

These assumptions imply a long-run multiplier of 2.72, calculated using the equations of Chapter 3 together with Equations (1) and (2) as follows:

$$\Delta Y = \Delta A = \Delta \bar{A} + \Delta C + \Delta I$$
$$= \Delta \bar{A} + 0.479\ \Delta Y + 0.154\ \Delta Y \tag{3}$$

or

$$\Delta Y (1-0.479-0.154) = \Delta \bar{A} \tag{4}$$

$$\Delta Y = 2.72\ \Delta \bar{A} \tag{4a}$$

Now $\Delta \bar{A}$ is the change in spending of \$13.3 billion so that

$$\Delta Y = 2.72 \times \$13.3 \text{ billion} = \$36.2 \text{ billion} \tag{5}$$

which is the total effect on spending of the tax cut.

Table 10-5 suggests two ways of breaking down the total increase in GNP of about \$36 billion. We can attribute part of the increase in GNP to the cut in personal income taxes and part to the corporate income taxes, by reading across the table. The \$10-billion cut in personal taxes increases consumption by \$9.49 billion and, allowing for the multiplier, has a total effect of \$25.81 billion on demand (equal to \$9.49 billion × 2.72). The corporate tax cut of \$3 billion directly increases aggregate demand by \$3.81 billion, through its effects on investment and consumption. The total effects of the corporate tax cut on GNP are that \$3.81 billion times the long-run multiplier of 2.72, or \$10.3 billion. The corporate tax cut thus has a higher multiplier (10.36/3 = 3.45) than the multiplier associated with the personal tax cuts (25.8/10 = 2.58).

The second way of breaking down the effects of the tax cuts can be seen by reading down the columns of Table 10-5, which focus on the way in which the various components of aggregate demand are affected. Investment increases by \$7.8 billion. This is composed of the initial increase in investment of \$2.25 billion plus further induced investment of (0.154) × (\$36.2) = \$5.57 billion. Consumption demand increases by the initial increase of \$11.05 (= \$9.49 + \$1.56) plus induced consumption spending of \$17.34 billion (= 0.949 × 0.505 × \$36.2 billion).

This calculation of the long-run impacts of the tax cuts follows a

TABLE 10-5 TOTAL LONG-RUN EFFECTS OF THE 1964 TAX CUT *(in billions of dollars)*

	Consumption	Investment	GNP
Corporate tax cut	\$ 6.52	\$3.83	\$10.36
Personal tax cut	21.85	3.97	25.81
Total effect	\$28.39	\$7.80	\$36.17

Note: Numbers may not add up because of rounding.

multiplier approach similar to that outlined in Chapter 3 and illustrates the uses of that type of analysis. It is also appropriate to bear in mind the warnings of Chapter 9. Some of the numbers in Table 10-5 are estimated with a wide margin of uncertainty. In particular, the details of the way in which increases in corporate profits affect investment spending and dividends are quite uncertain. Thus, Table 10-5 represents Okun's best estimates, but, as he notes, "these estimates should be viewed as the center of a sizable range."[24] Indeed, many would consider multipliers in excess of 2 as unusually large.

*Lags and the Short-Run Effects of the Tax Cut

The long-run effects of the tax cut estimated in Table 10-5 were expected to take place over a period of years. From the viewpoint of policy, it is also important to calculate how rapidly the tax cuts would affect GNP. Chart 10-4 shows the predicted response of GNP to the tax cut in the first six quarters, that is, from the start of the tax cut at the end of the first quarter of 1964 to the second quarter of 1965. The lower shaded part of each bar shows the increase in GNP arising from an increase in consumption, and the upper part shows the contribution of increased investment spending to the increase in GNP. Chart 10-4 is nothing other than the dynamic multiplier of the tax cut. It is important to note how the GNP effects of the tax cut occur over time. They start with a minor impact on consumption but soon build up as both consumption and investment spending increase. By 1965/II, the increase in GNP has reached $25 billion, over 70 percent of the final $36 billion, with a third of it in increased investment and two-thirds in increased consumption. Further, as the chart suggests, the increase in GNP has not yet petered out. GNP is still growing in response to the fiscal expansion.

We will not now go any further into the details of the calculation of the dynamic effects shown in Chart 10-4, and refer the interested reader to the original Okun article.

A Look at the Data

In this section we look briefly at the actual data to see whether and how the tax cut worked. In doing so, we also illustrate the difficulties of evaluating the effects of past policy measures. These difficulties arise from the problem of deducing what would have happened if the policy measure had not been undertaken.

The analysis so far suggests plausible values for (1) the order of magnitude of the long-run effects and (2) the components of aggregate demand we expect to be affected. The problem in isolating the effects of the

[24] Okun, cited in footnote 21.

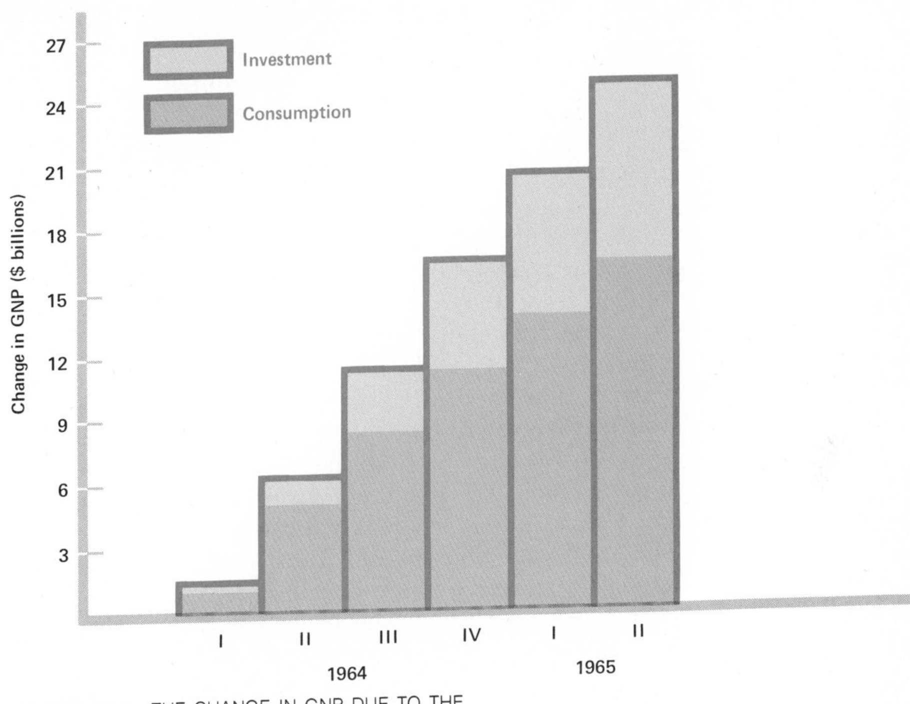

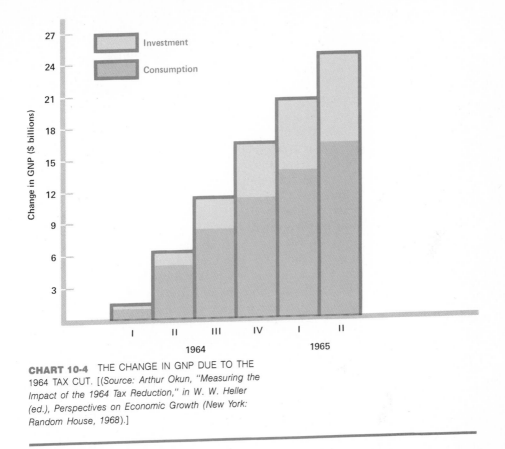

CHART 10-4 THE CHANGE IN GNP DUE TO THE 1964 TAX CUT. [(*Source: Arthur Okun, "Measuring the Impact of the 1964 Tax Reduction," in W. W. Heller (ed.), Perspectives on Economic Growth (New York: Random House, 1968)*).]

tax cut, however, is that there were a lot of other things influencing aggregate demand at the same time; particularly, adjustments to past changes in income were still affecting aggregate demand. There is no entirely certain and correct procedure that will identify the exact contribution of the tax cut to GNP. Ideally, we would like a procedure that allows us to find out what GNP would have been in the absence of the tax cut had everything else been the same. If we had that path of GNP, we would compare it with the path GNP actually took after the tax cut and attribute the difference, in a diagram like Chart 10-4, to the tax cut. The fact is that we cannot construct very exactly the *counterfactual* history of GNP and instead have to estimate what would have happened without the tax cut.

With this preface we can turn to the actual data. In particular, we will look at changes in real GNP and its components for the period 1963–1966, shown in Table 10-6. Consider first real GNP (in 1972 dollars). From 1962 to 1963, real GNP grew at 4 percent, a number that is approximately equal to estimates of potential GNP growth for that period.

If we assume, perhaps heroically, that GNP would have grown at 4 percent in the absence of the tax cut, we can attribute the difference between 4 percent and actual growth in 1964 and 1965 to the cut.

Choosing as the long run, a period of 3 years, we now compare the actual development of consumption and GNP in 1963–1966 with what would have happened along a 4 percent growth path. The difference, we assume, is due to the tax cut and we therefore compare it with our predictions in Table 10-5. The first row of Table 10-6 shows actual changes in real GNP and consumption from 1963 to 1966, and the second row shows the changes that would have occurred had consumption and GNP risen from their 1963 levels at a rate of 4 percent per year. In row 3, we take the difference. Here we find that GNP and consumption grew on average at rates higher than 4 percent, thus confirming the idea that the tax cut had an expansionary effect, raising the growth rate of demand above its trend rate.

In row 4, we report our predictions from Table 10-5, and we can now compare the last two rows. For GNP, our theoretical exercise predicted a cumulative increase of $36.2 billion, whereas we really have an increase (above trend) of $46.6 billion. Our model thus underestimates the expansion that took place. Conversely for consumption, the predicted expansion of $28.4 billion exceeds the actual expansion (above trend) of $22.1 billion. Considering the difficulty of specifying both the meaning of the long run in practice and of the way that history would have behaved without the tax cut, these comparisons fare quite well.

10-5 THE 1966 CREDIT CRUNCH

The credit crunch of the second half of 1966 was the first occasion in the post-World War II period that the Fed sharply cut back on monetary growth and caused rapid and, for the time, large increases in interest rates. For reasons to be explained in this section, banks and other financial institu-

TABLE 10-6 ACTUAL AND PREDICTED DEMAND DEVELOPMENT, 1963–1966 *(in billions of 1972 dollars)*

	GNP	Consumption
1. Actual change	150.3	84.7
2. 4 percent growth path	103.7	62.6
3. Difference (1 minus 2)	46.6	22.1
4. Predicted difference	36.2	28.4

Source: Economic Report of the President, 1979, and Table 10-5.

tions were not able to make their usual volume of loans. As Phillip Cagan describes the episode:[25]

> Increasingly, normally acceptable borrowers had to be disappointed, even though banks stretched their resources. During these months interest rates soared, and many corporations that borrow short-term funds on a regular basis began to doubt whether they would be able to meet upcoming financial commitments. The financial and business community developed a severe case of the jitters. Few had ever experienced a general financial stringency.

The crunch was the period of high interest rates, reduced availability of loans from financial institutions, and simple fear of financial disaster that prevailed from about August to October 1966.

In this section we analyze the causes and the consequences of the credit crunch.

The Onset of Inflation

The vigorous expansion in economic activity set off by the 1964 tax cut and supported by the accompanying monetary expansion led to a significant increase in inflation by 1965–1966. Chart 10-2 shows a clear break in the economy's inflation performance in 1965, with inflation increasing from the 1.0 to 1.5 percent range of 1961–1964 to the 2.9 to 5.4 percent range of 1966–1969. Unemployment fell to 4 percent by early 1966, and the economy not only reached the level of potential output, but was soon operating at a level of GNP above potential output. The increase in inflation led to the Federal Reserve policies that produced the credit crunch.

Monetary Policy and Disintermediation

In the last three quarters of 1966, the money supply was constant. The reduction in monetary growth, from an average of 4.5 percent in the preceding year to exactly zero, proved to be very deflationary. The demand for nominal balances was still growing because nominal income was increasing. By keeping the nominal money supply constant in the face of growing demand, the Fed forced up interest rates and thereby depressed spending. Chart 10-5 shows interest rates for 1965–1967, with the Treasury bill and commercial paper rates peaking in the fourth quarter of 1966.

The financial markets were affected not only by a relatively slow growth in the monetary base, but also by increased reserve requirements that were imposed on time deposits and, most important, by Regulation

[25] Phillip Cagan, "Monetary Policy," in Phillip Cagan et al., *Economic Policy and Inflation in the Sixties* (Washington, D.C.: American Enterprise Institute, 1972), pp. 99–101.

Q.[26] Regulation Q imposes ceilings on interest rates that banks are allowed to pay on their time deposits. As interest rates in the market rose, they soon hit the ceiling set by the Fed, and commercial banks found that they became uncompetitive in raising funds. The public preferred Treasury bills and commercial paper[27] rather than time deposits, whose regulated low yield now made them unattractive. As a consequence, commercial banks could not raise the funds with which to expand their lending.

Chart 10-5 compares the Fed discount rate, the yield on 4- to 6-month prime commercial paper, and the Regulation Q maximum rate. The period of the credit crunch coincides with the period in the chart in which the commercial paper rate was above the Regulation Q rate.

The process in which depositors withdraw funds from banks and other financial insititutions as a result of interest rate ceilings is known as *disintermediation.*[28] Because of the loss of funds, the banks can no longer make loans. Borrowers have to turn away from banks and raise funds by borrowing directly in the money market. Lenders and borrowers get together directly, avoiding the financial intermediaries and thus the regulation interest rate ceilings also. That is, firms no longer try to raise money for investment from bank loans but by selling debt (commercial paper) to investors in the money market.

You might think that this process of bypassing the financial intermedi-

[26] Regulation Q and disintermediation were discussed in Chap. 6.

[27] Commercial paper is a short-term bond (called a note) issued by firms for the purpose of borrowing for short periods (up to 6 months).

[28] A second and perhaps more important instance of disintermediation occurred in 1969. See Cagan, op cit., pp. 117–125.

CHART 10-5 INTEREST RATES AND REGULATION Q CEILING
(Sources: Survey of Current Business, 1969 Supplement, and Federal Reserve Bulletin)

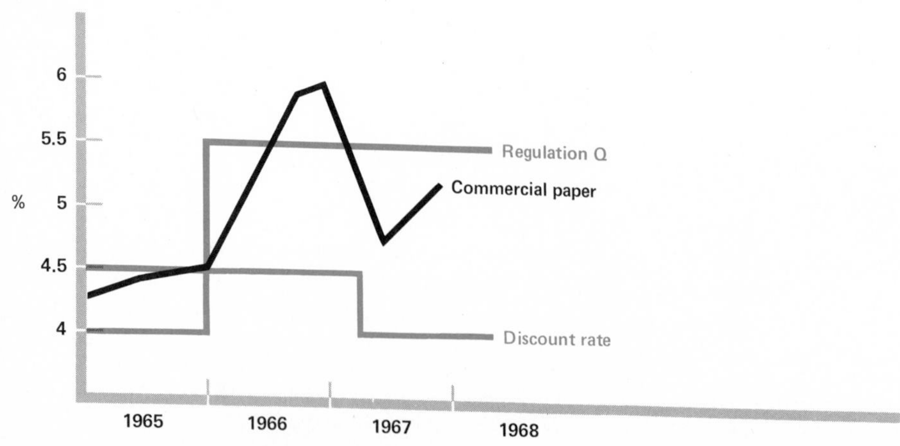

aries is quite unobjectionable since it gets the credit to those who need it most while giving lenders rates higher than those that Regulation Q will permit banks to pay. There are, however, two major problems. The first is that disintermediation inevitably hurts small business and consumers. They cannot place their credit demands directly in the market. They cannot issue commercial paper or other credit instruments in the way large corporations can. Indeed, it is precisely the role of banks and similar institutions to channel credit efficiently to these sectors and "intermediate" between borrowers and lenders. Regulation Q, when it becomes effective, therefore discriminates against consumer loans and small business credit. The other major problem arises for mortgages. Savings and loan associations specialize in mortgage credit which finances construction. Whenever ceiling interest rates on time deposits become effective, these institutions, exactly like banks, lose their competitiveness in attracting funds and consequently have a reduced volume of credit to loan out. This in turn means that less credit is available for construction, and as a consequence there is a strong impact on construction, as we see in Chart 10-6.[29]

The Fed's decision to allow interest rates to increase and stop monetary growth had been long delayed. In the two preceding years, the money stock had been allowed to grow to accommodate the fiscal expansion. Only in the face of sharply increased inflation did the Fed consider a move toward restraint and high interest rates, which have a strong impact on particular sectors of the economy, the most important being housing construction. Tight money meant, too, a more general slowdown in the growth of aggregate demand and therefore no further cuts in the unemployment rate. The choice between restraining aggregate demand to reduce inflationary pressure and monitoring high demand to reduce unemployment further was not then, nor is it usually, an easy one. It was already apparent to administration economists that rising defense expenditures were putting excessive demand pressure on the economy and that fiscal policy could offset that pressure. However, a tax increase did not come until 1968. In the meantime, at least in 1966, the full burden of restraining aggregate demand was taken up by the Fed in a "go-it-alone" tight monetary policy.

Effects of the Credit Crunch on Economic Activity

The tightness of monetary policy started to affect aggregate demand by late 1966. Private investment spending as shown in Chart 10-6 responded dramatically to the high interest rates and credit tightness. This was particularly true for residential construction, which declined sharply under the impact of tight credit. We note, too, the relative timing of reduced residential construction and the reduction in business fixed investment

[29] For further aspects of Regulation Q, see Albert Burger, "A Historical Analysis of the Credit Crunch of 1966," Federal Reserve Bank of St. Louis, *Review*, September 1969, pp. 13–30. Recall also that it is now planned to phase out Regulation Q by 1986.

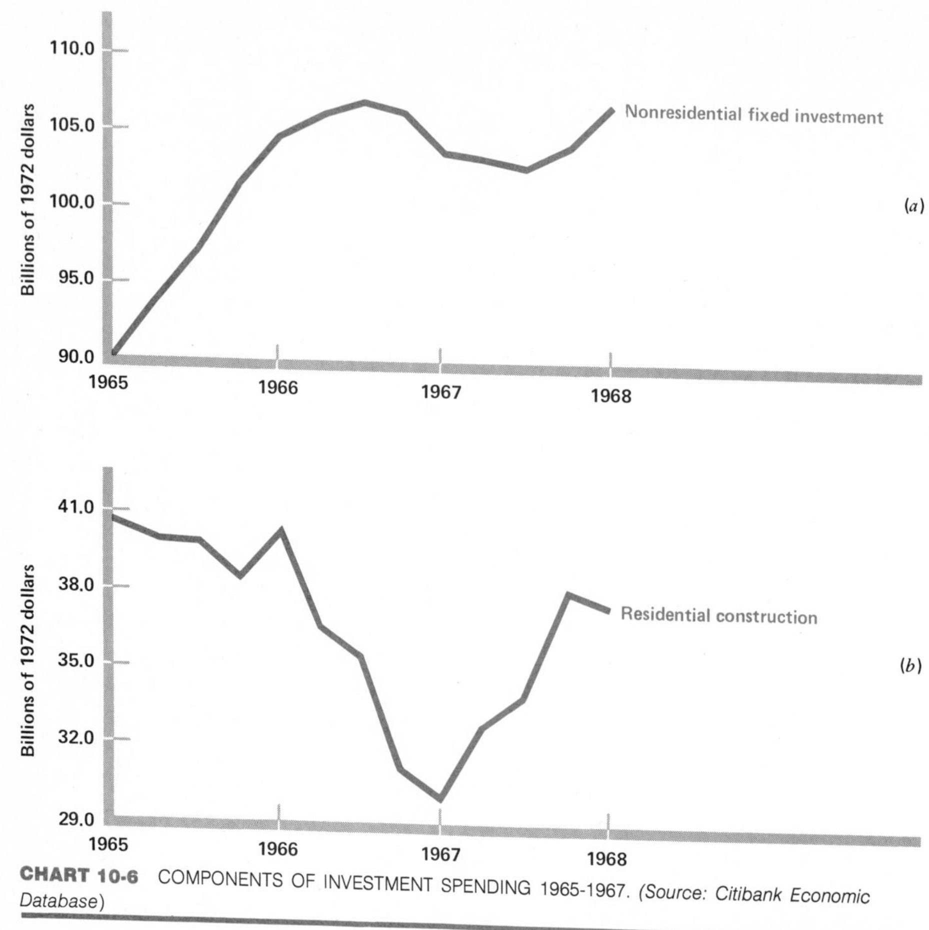

CHART 10-6 COMPONENTS OF INVESTMENT SPENDING 1965-1967. *(Source: Citibank Economic Database)*

spending. Residential construction reacted very quickly to tightness in money and credit markets. The adjustment in business investment was considerably slower.

The credit crunch was reflected in a sharp reduction in real income growth in 1966 and early 1967. From a high rate of growth of 8 percent in 1965, the rate of increase of real output fell as shown in Table 10-7. Much of

TABLE 10-7 REAL OUTPUT GROWTH: THE MINIRECESSION

1965	1966				1967				1968
	I	II	III	IV	I	II	III	IV	
8.1	7.6	3.6	3.1	4.8	−0.1	2.4	4.4	3.2	5.1

Source: Survey of Current Business, 1969 Supplement.

the slowdown of growth preceded the crunch itself but was probably a result of the fall in residential construction that began in the second quarter of 1966 as interest rates rose.

What accounts for the reduced real growth? The $5-billion reduction in housing construction and the flattening out of business fixed investment spending were each partially responsible. While residential construction accounts for less than 4 percent of GNP and the reduction in construction spending accounts for less than 1 percent of GNP, it is nevertheless sufficiently important a reduction to have started a dampening in real growth that is reflected in Table 10-7. Subsequently, as high interest rates slowed down business fixed investment, the economy entered a *minirecession* in early 1967. The minirecession was the short period of negative growth which, however, did not last long enough even to reduce output below its potential level. Real growth in the first quarter was close to zero. With a growing labor force, failure of real output and employment to grow means rising unemployment. We only record this fact here but will return to it in Chapter 13.

The effects of the 1966 credit crunch were soon overcome, and the economy returned once more to high growth rates of real spending and output. Charts of actual and potential output, such as Chart 10-3, show that the following period, 1968–1969, was one in which the GNP gap was negative and output was at, or even above, the full-employment level. The 1966 credit crunch made only a very transitory dent in growth performance for two reasons. One was the very sizable buildup of military spending, and the other was a monetary policy that resumed a highly expansionary path.

10-6 THE 1968 TAX SURCHARGE

Monetary policy in 1966 slowed down the growth rate of real output and produced the minirecession of early 1967. By late 1967, however, the economy had resumed a high growth rate of output and spending, despite declines in residential construction and business fixed investment. The explanation for the resumption of growth can be seen in Chart 10-7, which shows a rapid increase in federal government outlays between 1965 and 1967. The spending was in good measure for defense purposes, but there were, too, the Great Society programs of President Johnson. Along with the increased government spending went a more expansionary monetary policy, which we shall discuss.

The high level of employment combined with the increasing rate of inflation led administration economists to discuss the desirability of a tax increase to offset the expansionary impact of the high aggregate demand. Although the economy was still in a minirecession in the first quarter of 1967, it was clear that some restrictive policies were necessary in the face of high levels of government spending.

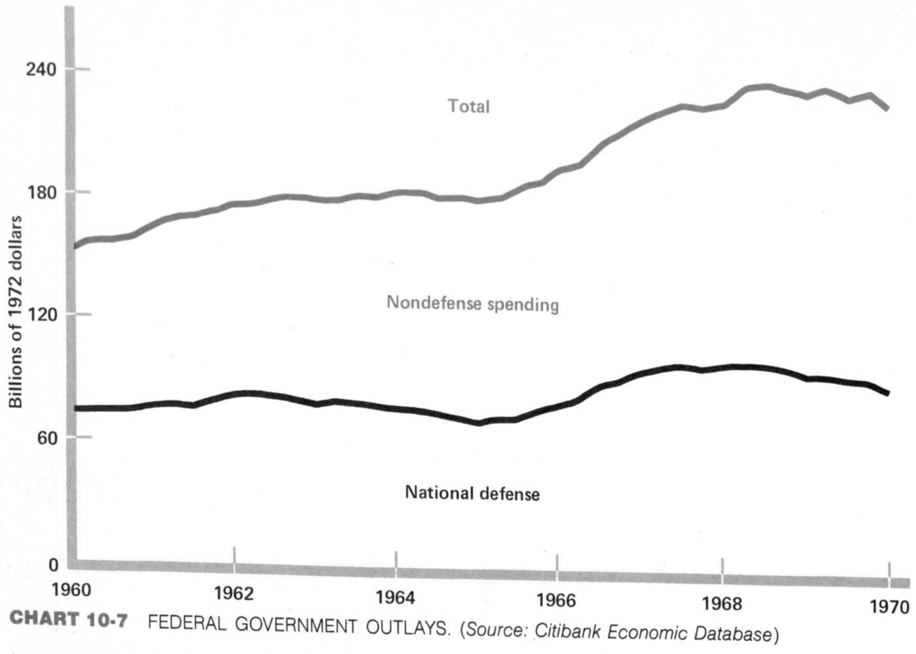

CHART 10-7 FEDERAL GOVERNMENT OUTLAYS. (*Source: Citibank Economic Database*)

There were three options for restrictive policy. The first was to run a tight monetary policy by reducing the growth rate of the money supply—the policy of 1966 and the credit crunch. Both the memory of the credit crunch and the impact of tight money on investment and particularly housing construction argued against the use of tight monetary policy.[30] Second, it might have been possible to cut government spending. Government spending on goods and services had grown in the last few years by more than $20 billion, and federal spending on goods and services had increased from 9 percent to 11 percent of GNP. However, military spending could not be cut because of the Vietnam war, and the administration was not eager to cut spending on its Great Society programs. This left the tax increase as the option that was chosen.

In January 1967 the administration asked Congress for a temporary tax surcharge, to start July 1. A tax surcharge is a proportional increase above existing taxes. Essentially, taxes are calculated using existing tax rates, exemptions, etc., and then, when the bill has been added up, a given percentage is added to it. Congress was reluctant to pass the legislation then, primarily because the minirecession was still on.

The tax surcharge was finally enacted only in June 1968, after a period of strong monetary expansion and an increase in the budget deficit. Chart 10-8 shows that the full-employment budget moved from a small surplus in

[30] Of course, the administration could not itself choose the course of monetary policy, but it could make its views known to the Fed.

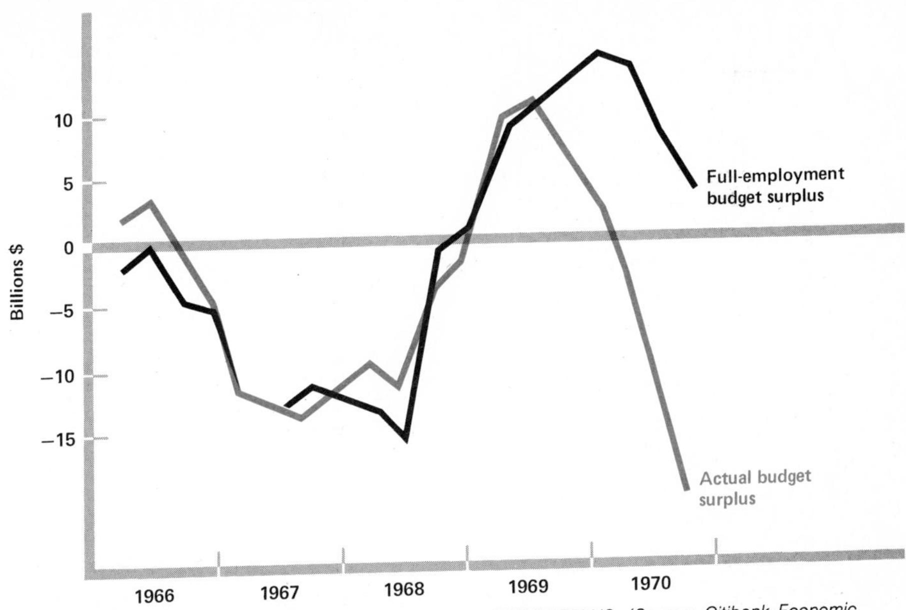

CHART 10-8 ACTUAL AND FULL-EMPLOYMENT BUDGET SURPLUS. (*Source: Citibank Economic Database*)

1966 to a large deficit by the middle of 1968. The shift to a full-employment deficit was largely the result of the increase in government spending.

The Tax Package

The Revenue and Expenditure Control Act of 1968 featured a 10 percent surcharge on income taxes paid by individuals, retroactive to April 1, 1968, and by corporations, retroactive to January 1, 1968. The act further provided for a reduction in some proposed federal expenditures and a ceiling on government spending for the fiscal year 1969. The surcharge was explicitly recognized as temporary and was due to expire in June 1969.

The tax surcharge was the main feature of the act. It was estimated that the surcharge would create an additional $10 billion in fiscal revenue per full year when estimated at the 1968 income level. The revenue effect shows up in Chart 10-8 as an increase in the full-employment budget surplus that moved from a deficit of $16 billion in the second quarter of 1968 to the much smaller deficit of $1 billion at the end of 1968.

Results of the Tax Surcharge

The question we have to address now is what amount of restraint in terms of reduced aggregate spending we would expect to arise from this restrictive fiscal action. The first guess is that we should simply reverse the analysis of the 1964 tax cut. Now we have a tax increase rather than a cut in taxes, but of roughly the same order of magnitude. There is, though, the potentially important difference that the 1968 surcharge was quite explicitly recognized as *temporary*. This means, in line with our analysis of the consumption function in Chapter 5, that individuals would plan to spread the current increase in tax liabilities over a much longer consumption and saving horizon. They would plan to finance the one-time extra tax liability by reducing saving a lot and reducing consumption rather little. By contrast, if the tax surcharge were viewed as permanent, more of it would come out of reduced consumption and quite a bit less out of reduced saving.

Was the 1968 tax surcharge effective in restraining aggregate demand? As usual, the question requires an estimate of what would have happened in the absence of the surcharge. Moreover, the point is still controversial among researchers.[31] The facts do suggest some answers, though. The most important fact that stands out is the sharp reduction in the saving rate in 1968–1969. Table 10-8 shows that the savings rate in 1968–1969 declined quite significantly and that the timing of the decline roughly accorded with the imposition of the surcharge.

What do we expect the savings rate to do in a permanent-income view of consumption behavior? We know that the tax surcharge will reduce personal disposable income and therefore should to some extent affect both consumption and saving. What happens, though, to the *fraction* of personal income saved? Figure 10-2 returns to the short-run and long-run consumption functions of Chapter 5. Starting from an initial equilibrium at point E with a disposable income of Y_d^0, we experience a transitory decline in disposable income to Y_d'. In the short run, the adjustment is to point E', with a relatively small adjustment in consumption and a relatively large decline in saving. If the decline in disposable income were maintained, we would ultimately move to point E'' on the long-run consumption function. In the short run, the ratio of consumption to income rises as we move from

TABLE 10-8 THE SAVINGS RATE IN RESPONSE TO THE 1968 TAX SURCHARGE

1967	1968				1969				1970
	I	II	III	IV	I	II	III	IV	
7.3	7.2	7.6	6.0	6.2	5.3	5.3	6.6	6.8	7.9

Source: W. L. Springer, "Did the 1968 Surcharge Really Work?" *American Economic Review*, September 1975.

[31] See A. Okun, "The Personal Tax Surcharge and Consumer Demand, 1968–1970," *Brookings Papers on Economic Activity*, 1971:1 (Washington, D.C.: The Brookings Institution, 1971), and W. L. Springer, "Did the 1968 Surcharge Really Work?" *American Economic Review*, September 1975, and the follow-up in the *American Economic Review*, March 1977.

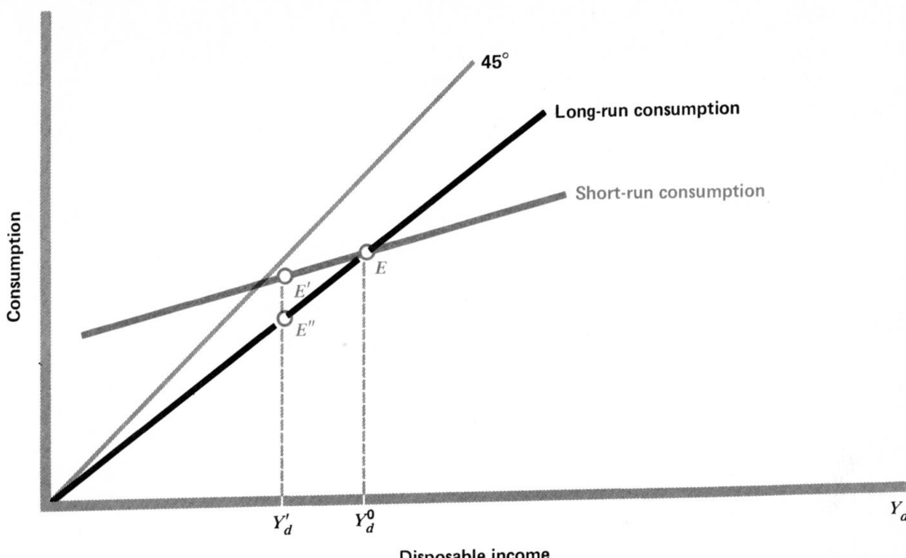

FIGURE 10-2 THE SHORT-RUN EFFECT OF A TRANSITORY TAX SURCHARGE

E to E'. It follows that the ratio of saving to income, the savings rate, declines. This is precisely the result observed in Table 10-8. Again, if the tax surcharge persisted, we would expect a downward shift of the short-run consumption function over time until point E'' was reached, with consumption and savings ratios back to the initial levels that they showed at point E. By contrast, if the tax increase were permanent, the adjustment would be directly from E to E'' with the savings rate remaining constant.

To illustrate the effect we are talking about, we look, in Table 10-9, at some numbers for the transition from the second to the third quarter of

TABLE 10-9 THE EFFECTS OF THE 1968 TAX SURCHARGE ON CONSUMPTION AND SAVING *(in billions of dollars at annual rates)*

	1968/II	1968/III	Change
Personal income	681	699	18
Less: Taxes, etc.	93	104	11
Equals: Personal disposable income	588	595	7
Less: Consumption	543	559	16
Equals: Personal saving	45	36	−9

Source: Survey of Current Business, 1973 Supplement.

1968 at the time the surcharge became effective. From the table it is quite apparent that a major part of the increased tax payments was financed by a reduction in saving. Taxes rose by $11 billion, of which $9 billion was financed by reducing saving. Consumption spending, in fact, increased along with personal income.

The evidence we are considering here would seem to argue quite strongly that the 1968 surcharge had only a minor effect on consumption spending. With most of the increase in taxes financed by a reduction in saving, the marginal propensity to consume out of disposable income appropriate for a transitory surcharge appears to be small. Indeed, marginal propensities to consume out of transitory income that have been suggested in the discussion of this tax increase range between 0.1 and 0.3.[32]

While there is no complete answer yet to the question of the effects of transitory changes in fiscal policy on aggregate demand, the basic outlines of the answer are clear. Both the theory of consumption of Chapter 5 and the experience of the tax surcharge of 1968 suggest that the impacts of temporary tax increases on consumption spending are relatively small. A transitory tax change of the 1968 type, scheduled to last a year, seems to have less than half the effect on consumption that a permanent change does.

Monetary Policy

Returning to the course of the economy in 1968, we note that real income continued to expand strongly despite the restrictive fiscal policy. The growth rate did decline a little. From a growth rate of real income of 4 percent at the beginning of the year, real growth fell to 3 percent at the end of the year. What sustained the increase in aggregate demand? We have seen that the reduction in the savings rate absorbed much of the restrictive fiscal policy. Beyond that, however, one has to look to monetary policy as a significant contributor to strength in aggregate demand. Table 10-10 shows the annual growth rates of money, first quarter to first quarter for M1.

[32] See R. Eisner, "What Went Wrong?" *Journal of Political Economy*, May/June 1971, and A. Blinder and R. Solow, "Analytical Foundations of Fiscal Policy," in A. Blinder et al., *The Economics of Public Finance*, (Washington, D.C.: The Brookings Institution, 1974), pp. 105–109.

TABLE 10-10 GROWTH RATE OF MONEY (M1)

1966/65	1967/66	1968/67	1969/68	1970/69
5.4	2.2	6.7	7.9	3.1

Source: Federal Reserve Bank of St. Louis.

It is striking that after the credit crunch of 1966, reflected in the very low growth rate of money for 1966 of 2.2 percent, money growth increased very sharply and was sustained at a high level around 7 percent for 2 years. From early 1967 until early 1969, money grew at a rate higher than it had for any 2-year period since the 1940s. This provides an explanation for the continued high level of aggregate demand and rapidly increasing inflation in this monetary expansion. Not only was monetary growth sufficiently vigorous to overcome the deflationary impact of restrictive fiscal policy, but it also contributed to expansion in aggregate demand and inflationary pressure. Indeed, in the period 1967–1968, inflation increased from the 3 percent that had prevailed in 1967 to 4.7 percent by late 1968.

Chart 10-9 helps interpret monetary policy. Here we show the interest rate on medium-term (3- to 5-year) Treasury bonds, the growth rate of money (M1), and the rate of inflation (CPI). The growth rate of the nominal quantity of money, after a decline in 1966–1967, increased sharply in 1968 and continued to be high in 1969. From this point of view, monetary policy was very expansionary in 1968, which thus helps explain why the fiscal

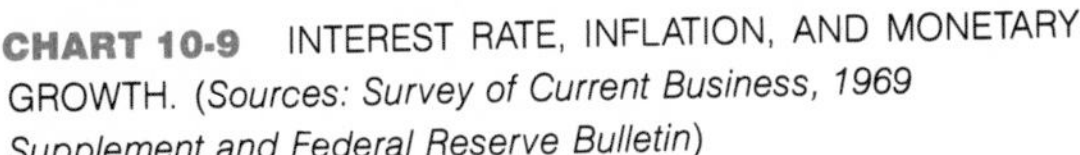

CHART 10-9 INTEREST RATE, INFLATION, AND MONETARY GROWTH. (*Sources: Survey of Current Business, 1969 Supplement and Federal Reserve Bulletin*)

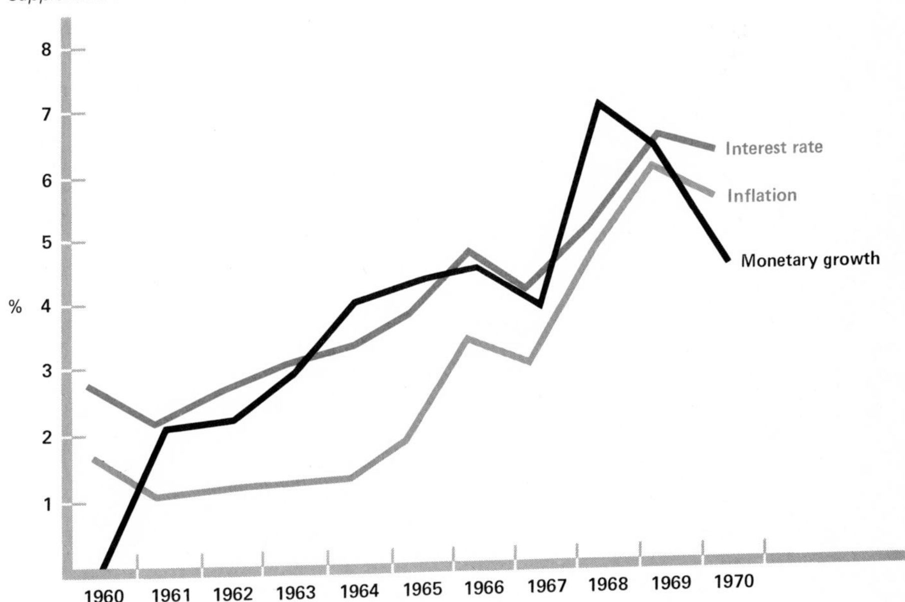

tightness, reflected in the sharp increase of the high-employment budget surplus in Chart 10-8, was not more deflationary in its impact on economic activity.

A look at interest rates might, on the contrary, suggest that monetary policy was tight. Interest rates increased from 1967 on and reached their highest level for the sixties in 1969. However, here it is important to return to the distinction between nominal and real interest rates. The expected real interest rate is the nominal interest rate minus the expected rate of inflation, and it is the expected real interest rate that is relevant for investment. In Chart 10-9 we show the actual rate of inflation. We do not have any exact measure of the expected rate of inflation, so that we cannot calculate the expected real rate of interest. But, since the actual rate of inflation increased throughout the sixties, with a particularly sharp acceleration in 1967, it is reasonable to suppose that the expected rate of inflation too rose through the sixties, and perhaps a little more rapidly in 1967 than earlier. In that case the expected real rate of interest would not have been rising as fast as the nominal interest rate, shown in Chart 10-9, and might even have been falling after 1967. If so, we could regard monetary policy as expansionary from the viewpoint of both the behavior of the growth rate of money and the behavior of expected real interest rates.

The interpretation of the economic events of 1968 is an important question in macroeconomics. One view is that the continued expansion was entirely due to the high growth of money *and* that fiscal policy does not matter. The other is that while both monetary and fiscal policy are potentially important, the effects of the fiscal policy in the form of the temporary surcharge were small compared with the effects of a strong monetary expansion. The view we have taken throughout this book is that both monetary and fiscal policy matter. The net effect will depend on the relative dosage and any special considerations that may be appropriate. For 1968 the net effect was undoubtedly caused by a monetary expansion that was more than sufficient to overcome the deflationary effects of the move toward a temporary budget surplus.

Why Did the Fed Do It?

In concluding this section, we must raise the question of why monetary policy was so very expansionary in the 1967–1968 period. There were two main factors. The first was a desire to avoid a repetition of the credit crunch, with its effects on housing and small business, and near financial panic. Second, the effects of the proposed tax surcharge in reducing aggregate demand were undoubtedly overestimated. The crucial distinction between the effects of permanent and transitory tax changes was not made. It was therefore anticipated that the tax increase would lead to a significant reduction in aggregate demand, and that monetary policy should cushion the anticipated shock. In a sense, the success of the tax cut of 1964 was partly responsible for the failure of the tax surcharge of 1968 because it led to an overestimate of the effectiveness of fiscal policy.

10-7 RESTRICTIVE MONETARY AND FISCAL POLICY IN 1969

The previous sections have shown how the New Economics was strikingly successful in moving the economy to full employment. When full employment was reached, however, the policies ran into trouble. As Walter Heller recognized:[33]

> The margin for error diminishes as the economy reaches the treasured but treacherous area of full employment. Big doses of expansionary medicine were easy—and safe—to recommend in the face of a $50 billion gap and a hesitant Congress. But at full employment, targets have to be defined more sharply, tolerances are smaller, the line between expansion and inflation becomes thinner. . . .

We do not yet have the analytical tools to discuss the economic policies and problems of the late sixties and early seventies. In this section we briefly set the scene for the discussion of recent policy, to be carried out in Chapter 16. The failure to coordinate monetary and fiscal policy, the failure to raise taxes to offset the increased defense spending in 1965–1967, and the failure to control monetary growth in 1967–1968 led inevitably to a buildup of inflation that left the incoming Nixon administration with inflation at the then "intolerably" high level of 5.4 percent. Unemployment in early 1969 was only 3.5 percent.

The low rate of unemployment allowed policy to shift to a fight against inflation. The incoming administration immediately reconsidered the budget for fiscal year 1970. Cuts in spending were proposed along with an extension of the surcharge at a 5 percent level and the repeal of the investment tax credit. Monetary policy, too, became more restrictive in 1969, with the growth rate of the money stock in the second half of the year being less than 2 percent, as compared with the nearly 8 percent growth rate in 1968. We will study the effects of these policies on the economy in Chapter 16.

REFERENCES

Bach, G. L., *Making Monetary and Fiscal Policy*, Brookings, 1971, chap. 6.

Brunner, K. (ed.), *Contemporary Views of the Great Depression*, Martinus Nijhoff, 1980.

[33] W. W. Heller, *New Dimensions of Political Economy* (New York: Norton, 1967), p. 69.

Diamond, J. J. (ed.), *Issues in Fiscal and Monetary Policy*, DePaul, 1971.

Cagan, Phillip, et al., *Economic Policy and Inflation in the Sixties*, American Enterprise Institute, 1972.

Friedman, M., *An Economist's Protest*, Horton, 1972.

———, *Dollars and Deficits*, Prentice-Hall, 1968.

——— and W. Heller, *Monetary vs. Fiscal Policy: A Dialogue*, Norton, 1969.

———, and A. Schwartz, *A Monetary History of the United States*, Princeton University Press, 1963.

Galbraith, J. K., *The Great Crash, 1929*, Hamish Hamilton, 1955.

Gordon, R. A., *Economic Instability and Growth: The American Record*, Harper & Row, 1974.

Heller, W., *New Dimensions of Political Economy*, Norton, 1967.

Kindleberger, C. P., *The World in Depression, 1929–1939*, University of California Press, 1973.

Okun, A., *The Political Economy of Prosperity*, Norton, 1970.

Poole, W., "Monetary Policy in the United States," *Proceedings of the American Academy of Political Science*, vol. 31, no. 4, 1975.

Stein, H., *The Fiscal Revolution in America*, The University of Chicago Press, 1969.

Temin, P., *Did Monetary Forces Cause the Great Depression?*, Norton, 1976.

Tobin, J., *The New Economics One Decade Older*, Princeton University Press, 1974.

APPENDIX: MAJOR CHANGES IN TAX LAWS IN THE 1960s*

Measure	Date recommended	Date enacted	Remarks
Investment tax credit	April 1961	October 1962	Provided a sizable incentive for new investment in depreciable equipment for domestic use. A 7 percent credit against income tax liabilities is allowed on most such investment.
Revenue Act of 1964	January 1963	February 1964	A permanent cut in income tax rates for all individual and corporate taxpayers. Personal taxes were cut by more than 20 percent and corporate taxes by about 8 percent. Before the cut, the marginal personal tax rates ranged from 20 to 91 percent; afterward, the range was 14 to 70 percent. For most corporations, the rate fell from 52 to 48 percent.

Measure	Date recommended	Date enacted	Remarks
Excise Tax Reduction Act of 1965	January 1965	June 1965	Repealed federal excise taxes on appliances, radios, television sets, jewelry, furs, and certain other items.
Tax Adjustment Act of 1966	January 1966	March 1966	Restored excise tax rates on transportation equipment and telephone services.
Temporary suspension of the investment tax credit	September 1966	November 1966	As of October 10, 1966, temporarily suspended the 7 percent investment tax credit.
Restoration of the investment tax credit	March 1967	June 1967	As of March 10, 1967, restored the 7 percent investment tax credit.
Revenue and Expenditure Control Act of 1968	January 1967	June 1968	Levied 10 percent surtax on personal income taxes effective April 1, 1968, and on corporate income effective January 1, 1968. The surtax was scheduled to expire on June 30, 1969. Postponed reduction in the respective 7 and 10 percent excise tax rates on automobiles and telephone services.
Extension of surtax	April 1969	August 1969	Extended the 10 percent surtax on personal incomes, previously scheduled to expire on June 30, 1969, to December 31, 1969.
Tax Reform Act of 1969	January 1969	December 1969	Increased personal exemptions and standard deductions. Introduced a maximum marginal rate of 50 percent on earned income. The maximum rate on unearned income remained at 70 percent. Extended the surtax from January 1, 1970, to June 30, 1970, at a 5 percent rate. Generally repealed the investment tax credit for corporations for property constructed, reconstructed, or acquired after April 18, 1969.

*During this period, Social Security tax rates were increased. This is not shown here.
Source: Adapted from ***Federal Reserve Bulletin***, various issues.

PROBLEMS

1 Using IS-LM curves, describe the competing "autonomous spending" and "monetary" explanations for the Great Depression.
2 Were interest rates high or low in the thirties?
3 Was the stock market crash responsible for the Depression?
4 The New Economics, while not theoretically novel in the early 1960s, was politically dangerous. President Kennedy ran, instead, on a balanced budget platform. How does such a fiscally conservative approach fit in with the New Economics? What would be the implications for stabilization policy of a commitment to a balanced budget every year? (Note that in the late seventies there were proposals to require the federal government to balance the budget.)
5 The New Economics is based on a Keynesian approach to macroeconomics, just as Chapters 3 and 4 are.
   (*a*) Indicate the problem of a GNP gap on the Keynesian cross diagram of Chapter 3. (*Note:* Indicate by a vertical line the level of potential output at one point in time.)
   (*b*) Draw on such a diagram the effect of a tax cut like the Revenue Act of 1964.
   (*c*) Show how a *negative* GNP gap can come about. What would be appropriate fiscal policy in such a case?
6 (*a*) Show in an IS-LM figure what the effect of the 1964 tax cut was. What would have happened if the Fed had kept the money supply constant?
   (*b*) Indicate the actual events of 1964–1965 on the IS-LM diagram, illustrating the meaning and effects of "accommodating" monetary policy.
7 Evaluate the general effectiveness and influence of monetary policy, using Chart 10-2 and the table below. What are the policy implications of long-delayed and unpredictable responses to changes in the money supply? What is the proper role of monetary policy in view of the experience of the 1960s?

GROWTH RATES OF M1 (*percent change, January to January*)

1960	1961	1962	1963	1964	1965	1966	1967	1968	1969
−0.3	3.0	1.7	3.7	4.0	4.8	1.5	7.1	7.9	3.8

Source: Federal Reserve Bulletin, various issues.

8 Explain why many people believe the the inflationary problems of the 1970s have their roots in the 1960s. How can this be so? What would be the cause? What could have been done to avoid such "heating up" of the economy, in this view?
9 The following quote is from a column by Milton Friedman in the December 9, 1968, issue of *Newsweek*. He goes on to point out that inflation rose dramatically during the Kennedy and Johnson years, as did government spending. Is this a fair appraisal of the New Economics? Would you agree or disagree with him? Explain.

The Nixon Administration will confront major economic problems in three areas: inflation, balance of payments, and the government budget. In each area, the New

Economics has managed in eight years to turn a comfortable, easy situation into a near crisis, to squander assets and multiply liabilities.

10 Discuss the notion of the monetary-fiscal policy mix. What determines the mix that is chosen. How did the effects of the mixes of 1966 and 1968 differ? Illustrate, using an IS-LM diagram. (Assume the level of income was the same.)

11 Explain the role of Regulation Q in the credit crunch of 1966.

3
PART

11
AGGREGATE SUPPLY

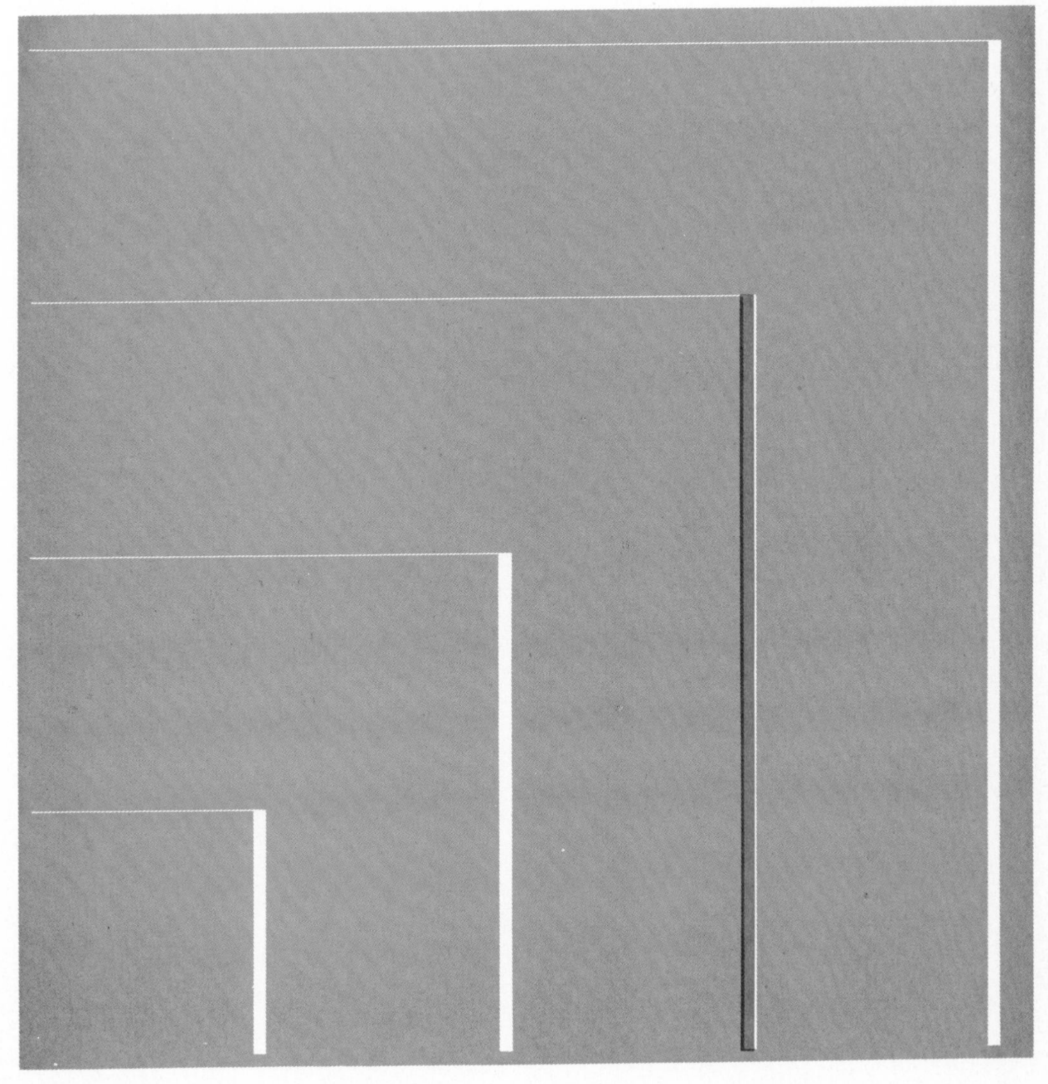

Up to this point we have discussed the determination of output on the assumption that prices are given and that firms supply all the output that is demanded at the current price level. But of course the aggregate price level changes over time, and changes in aggregate demand are likely to result in changes in both prices and output. We are now ready to begin our study of the determinants of the aggregate price level and its changes over time—that is, the rate of inflation. This chapter and the next develop the formal apparatus that enables us to study the simultaneous determination of the levels of output and prices.

Our analysis combines the theory of *aggregate demand* developed so far with a theory of *aggregate supply*. Aggregate demand and supply jointly determine the levels of output or income, and prices. The theory of aggregate supply will be developed in this chapter and combined with the theory of aggregate demand in Chapter 12.

Section 11-1 presents an intuitive preview and outline of the analysis of aggregate supply contained in the rest of the chapter. It is designed to be read by those interested in obtaining the essentials of the theory without necessarily going into details. Sections 11-2 through 11-6 develop the analysis of aggregate supply at a deeper level. Sections 11-7 and 11-8 contain further developments and refinements of interest to the more adventurous.

11-1 AGGREGATE DEMAND AND SUPPLY: A PREVIEW

In Chapter 4 we studied the aggregate demand side of the economy on the assumption that firms meet any level of demand at the prevailing level of prices, say P_0. The IS-LM framework allowed us to determine equilibrium output and spending as a function of fiscal and monetary policy variables. Monetary policy was represented by a given nominal money stock, M_0. In combination with the given price level, the nominal money stock implied a *real* money stock, M_0/P_0. The equilibrium level of spending was then a function of fiscal variables (and autonomous spending) and the level of real balances, or

$$Y^d = \beta\bar{A} + \gamma \frac{M}{P} \qquad \beta, \gamma > 0 \tag{1}$$

In Equation (1), Y^d denotes the equilibrium level of spending determined by the intersection of IS and LM curves. Equilibrium income or spending is written as a function of autonomous spending and fiscal variables, collected in the term $\bar{A}$, and as a function of the real money stock, M/P. The terms β and γ were developed as multipliers in Chapter 4 but need not concern us further until Chapter 12. From Equation (1) we note that an increase in the real money stock raises the equilibrium level of income. In terms of the analysis of Chapter 4, we have a rightward shift in the LM schedule and therefore a decline in equilibrium interest rates that leads to an increase in investment spending and hence to a rise in equilibrium income.

Suppose now that the nominal money stock is given and equal to M_0. What happens to aggregate demand if the price level declines? This raises the real money stock, lowers the interest rate, and raises real spending or aggregate demand. Conversely, if the price level increases, real balances will fall, interest rates will increase, and aggregate demand will fall. There is thus a relationship between the level of aggregate demand and the price level, *given the nominal money stock*. The higher the price level, the lower the level of aggregate demand, given the nominal money stock.

We show this relationship between the equilibrium level of real spending and the price level as the *aggregate demand schedule*, Y^d in Figure 11-1. The schedule slopes downward to reflect the fact that at a lower price level, the real money stock is higher, interest rates are lower, and aggregate demand is therefore higher. We will derive the schedule and study its properties at greater length in Chapter 12. For the present, we

FIGURE 11-1 AGGREGATE DEMAND AND SUPPLY

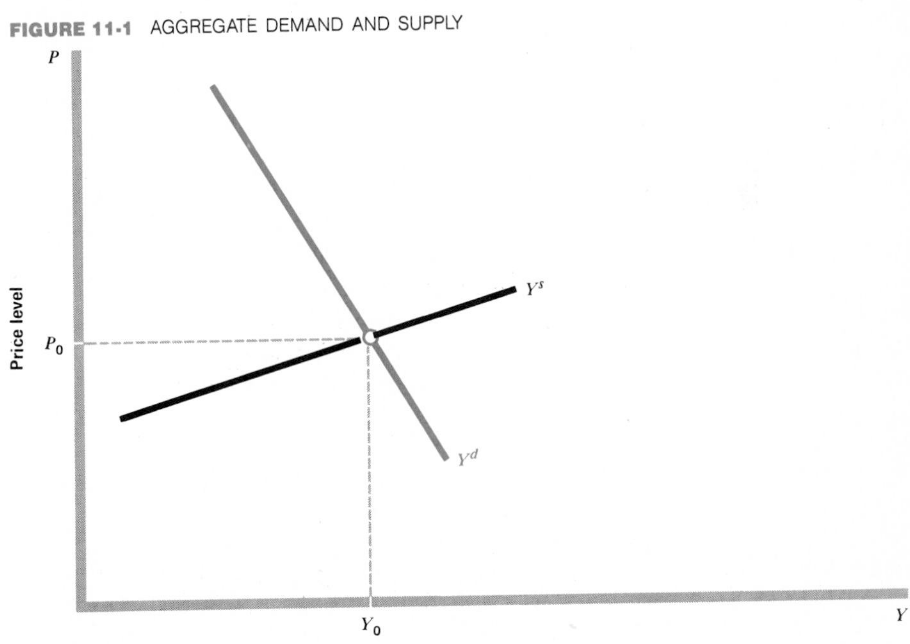

need retain only the fact that the schedule, representing Equation (1), is drawn for a given nominal money stock and given levels of autonomous spending and fiscal variables.[1]

Figure 11-1 also shows the aggregate supply schedule, Y^s. As we have drawn it, the schedule shows that increased output will be supplied only at a higher level of prices. Why does the schedule slope up? We will argue that firms base their prices on costs, primarily labor costs. When they expand their supply of output, firms also expand their input of labor. Using more labor will inevitably bid up wages somewhat—whether because overtime is necessary or because new workers have to be hired. Therefore the prices charged by firms will rise. We accordingly have an upward-sloping relationship between output and cost or prices. The slope of the aggregate supply curve reflects the increase in labor use and labor cost (and other costs) required to produce the increased output.

We will also develop in detail the important distinction between the short-run aggregate supply curve—a relatively flat schedule as drawn in Figure 11-1—and the long-run aggregate supply curve, which we will argue is vertical. Why are the short-run and long-run aggregate supply curves different?

The distinction between short-run and long-run supply mirrors the behavior of factor prices in responding to over- or underemployment of factors. (We can think of overemployment for the moment as substantial use of overtime.) Clearly, factor prices would rise and keep rising as firms bid for the overemployed factors, or they would keep falling if factors were underutilized. The important point, though, and an empirical one, is that factor prices and, in particular, wages, move slowly in response to unemployment or overemployment.

In the short-run, an increase in employment can be obtained at a relatively small increase in wages. Similarly, a reduction in employment and the resulting unemployment will lead to a relatively small decrease in wages.[2] Over time, though, overemployment will mean constantly rising wages and unemployment will imply falling wages. With firms passing on changes in costs into changes in prices, the implication is that the only position of stable prices is at the level of output corresponding to the full employment of labor.[3] At that level of employment, wages—and thus,

[1] We use the term "demand schedule" in obvious analogy with microeconomics, where the demand for an individual commodity is negatively related to its price. The word "aggregate" qualifies the analysis and reminds us that we are talking about the demand for *all* goods and services in the economy and the general level of prices, rather than about the relative price of an individual commodity.

[2] Indeed, we will argue in Chap. 15 that the response of wages to overemployment is likely to be greater than the response to unemployment, or that wages are less flexible downward than upward. This would imply that the aggregate supply curve would be flatter below the current level of output.

[3] In Chap. 13 we will introduce into the analysis the very important factor of expectations of inflation that will suggest that wages could be changing even at the full-employment level in order to maintain *real* wages—nominal wages divided by the price level—constant in the face of expected inflation. The verticality of the long-run aggregate supply curve can then be reinterpreted, as is shown in Chap. 13.

prices—will neither be falling because of unemployment nor rising because of overemployment. The long-run aggregate supply curve is thus vertical at the full employment output level.

The distinction between the short- and long-run supply curves arises because wages respond slowly to changes in labor demand. In the short run—of, say, a few months—we move along a given aggregate supply curve like Y^s in Figure 11-2. At an employment level such as that corresponding to the output level Y' in Figure 11-2, the wage rate is higher than it is at output level Y_0. But, because there is overemployment at Y', the wage is not only higher than at Y_0 but is also rising. Thus, in the next period some months later, wages at any given level of output, say Y_0, will be higher than they were in the previous period. Hence, the whole supply curve shifts up over time as long as the economy remains in a condition of overemployment.

Consider now an application of the model. We start with Figure 11-1, which shows that equilibrium output and prices are determined by the intersection of aggregate demand and supply. We assume until further notice that this demand-supply equilibrium is achieved instantaneously. Now turn to Figure 11-2, which again shows the aggregate demand

FIGURE 11-2 EFFECTS OF AN INCREASE IN AGGREGATE DEMAND

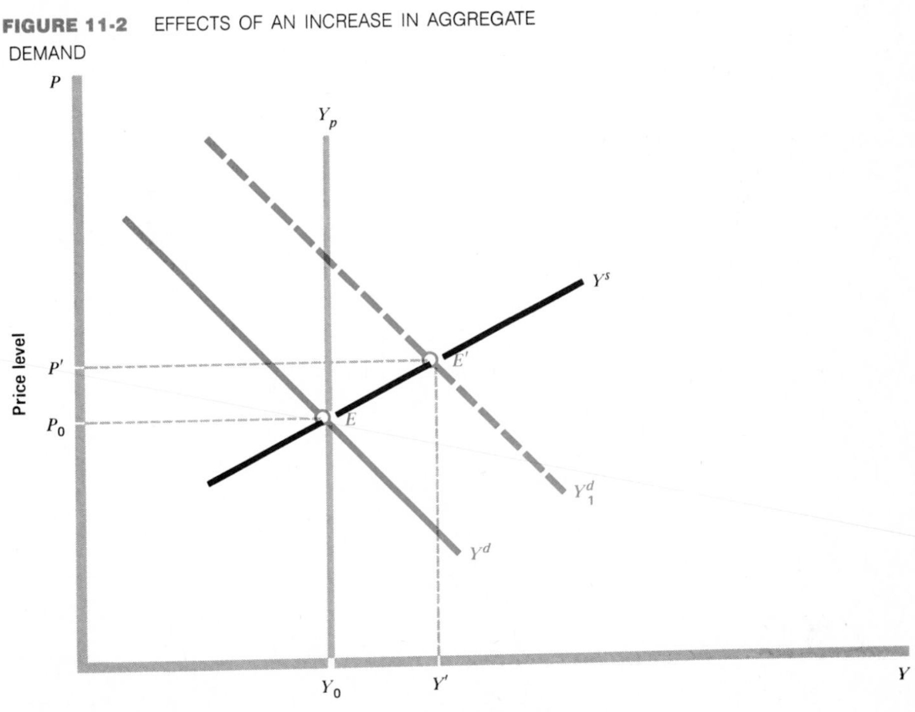

schedule, Y^d, and the short-run aggregate supply schedule, Y^s. It also shows the long-run aggregate supply curve, which is vertical at the level of potential output, Y_p. We start from a position of full equilibrium at point E.

Suppose that autonomous spending increases or, in terms of Chapter 4, that we have an upward shift of the IS schedule. For a given level of real balances, the shift implies an increase in equilibrium income or spending. In Figure 11-2 this is shown as a rightward shift of the aggregate demand schedule: at each level of prices and hence level of real balances, spending increases. At the initial level of prices, there is now excess demand leading firms to expand output. As firms hire more labor to produce the increased output, wages and labor costs rise and firms therefore charge higher prices. The new short-run equilibrium is at point E'. Both prices and output are higher at E' than at E. This is the first important point implied by the model:

- Changes in aggregate demand lead in the short-run to changes in both output and prices in the same direction. The extent to which the aggregate price level rises depends on the slope of the aggregate supply curve.

Inspection of Figure 11-2 will show that the change in short-run equilibrium output, from Y_0 to Y', falls short of the horizontal shift in demand. The increase in prices dampens the expansion of output since it reduces the level of real balances, raises interest rates, and thereby lowers spending. The extent of this damping effect obviously depends on the steepness of the aggregate supply curve, that is, on the extent to which an output expansion and the expansion of employment that lies behind it raise wages (and other costs) and prices. If, in the short run, wages and other costs do not respond at all to increased employment, the aggregate supply curve will be essentially flat and an increase in aggregate demand will in the short run be met by increased output. Point 2 is then the following:

- The extent to which changes in demand are met by changes in output as opposed to prices depends on the response of costs to an expansion in output and employment. If wage costs are very unresponsive in the short run, the supply curve is quite flat and shifts in demand are met at essentially constant prices.

Consider next the adjustment process. The short-run equilibrium at point E' in Figure 11-2 is one of overemployment. Wages are consequently increasing and firms' costs are rising. To supply the same level of output without reducing profits, firms will charge higher prices. This is shown in Figure 11-3 as an upward shift of the aggregate supply schedule to Y_1^s. The increase in costs resulting from overemployment leads to a new short-run equilibrium at point E''. The price level has increased and equilibrium

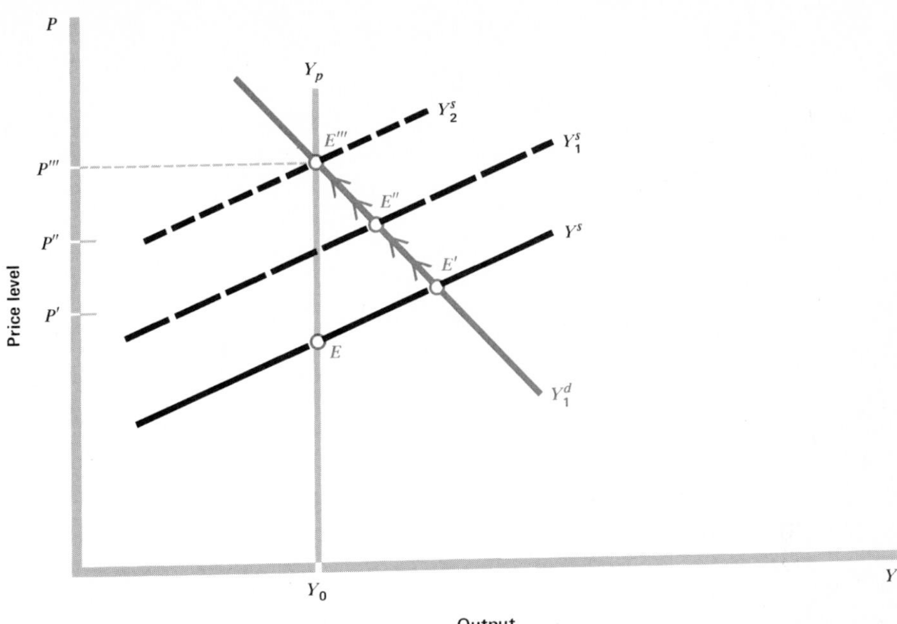

FIGURE 11-3 DYNAMIC ADJUSTMENT TO AN INCREASE IN AGGREGATE DEMAND

output has fallen, although it still exceeds the full-employment level. Thus, point E'' is only another short-run equilibrium and the process of wage and cost increases and the resulting upward shift in the supply curve will continue. Accordingly, we move, with a continually upward-shifting supply curve, along the aggregate demand schedule as indicated by the arrows. The process of cost and price increases continues until prices have risen sufficiently to reduce the level of real balances and hence of aggregate demand to the full-employment level, Y_p. Once Y_p is reached, there is no further tendency for wages to rise. At point E''', costs remain constant and the economy has reached a new long-run equilibrium. Accordingly, we have point 3:

- An expansion of output above normal will bring about overemployment and therefore rising wages and costs. Firms will pass on these cost increases into higher prices. The aggregate supply schedule shifts upward, thereby raising equilibrium prices and reducing equilibrium output along the aggregate demand schedule. The process continues until output declines back to the level of full employment. There is, of course, a parallel story for a decline in demand. The last point, already implicit in our analysis, is made by describing the adjustment mechanism that leads us from a position of short-run over-or underemployment back to full employment. The adjustment mechanism operates through changes in the levels of wages, costs, and prices on the real money stock. Changes in the *real* money stock in turn change interest rates and therefore real spending. The last point, then, can be put as follows:

- Adjustment from positions of over- or underemployment takes place through changes in the level of prices and real balances. Overemployment leads to higher prices and lower real balances, and hence to a contraction in demand, while underemployment leads to a fall in prices, increasing real balances, and therefore an expansion in demand.

We have now sketched the essential elements of the aggregate demand and supply framework. The remaining task is to make these elements more precise. On the aggregate demand side, we will look, in Chapter 12, at the exact way in which monetary and fiscal policy determine the position of the aggregate demand schedule. We will ask questions such as: By how much does a tax cut shift the aggregate demand schedule? Or, by how much does an increase in the *nominal* money stock shift the aggregate demand schedule?

In the rest of this chapter, we flesh out the theory of aggregate supply. The analysis starts in Section 11-2 with a frictionless *neoclassical* model of factor markets and output supply. In this idealized economy, factor and goods prices are fully flexible and adjust instantly to changes in demand. In such an economy, the aggregate supply curve is vertical in the short run as well as the long run, and output is always at the full-employment level. Aggregate demand changes affect the level of prices but not output. The neoclassical model provides a background against which it is easier to understand the development of the theory of aggregate supply in the rest of the chapter.

The basic theory rests on three elements: (1) the determination of the firm's level of employment, studied in Section 11-4; (2) wage behavior; and (3) pricing behavior. The last two elements are studied in Section 11-5. Short-run and long-run aggregate supply curves are examined in Section 11-6. The theory is then extended and made more realistic by a discussion of supply shocks and materials prices in Section 11-7. Section 11-8 discusses the cyclical behavior of productivity, prices, and the real wage.

11-2 THE FRICTIONLESS NEOCLASSICAL MODEL

The relationships between output and employment and between output and prices will be studied here in an idealized frictionless case. That is the case where wages and prices are flexible, where there are no costs either to workers in finding jobs or to firms in increasing or reducing their labor force, and where firms behave competitively and expect to sell all they produce at prevailing prices. That case will serve as a benchmark for the discussion of more realistic cases, but it also allows us to introduce such useful concepts as the production function and the demand for labor. Throughout, we will assume that labor is the only variable factor of production in the short run.

The Production Function

A production function provides a relation between the quantity of factor inputs, such as the amount of labor used, and the maximum quantity of output that can be produced using those inputs. The relation reflects only technical efficiency. In Equation (2) we write the production function

$$Y = F(N, \ldots) \tag{2}$$

where Y denotes real output, N is labor input, and the dots denote other cooperating factors (capital, for example) that are in short-run fixed supply. The production function is shown in Figure 11-4. It exhibits *diminishing returns*, which means that output increases proportionately less than labor input.

FIGURE 11-4 The Production Function and the Marginal Product of Labor

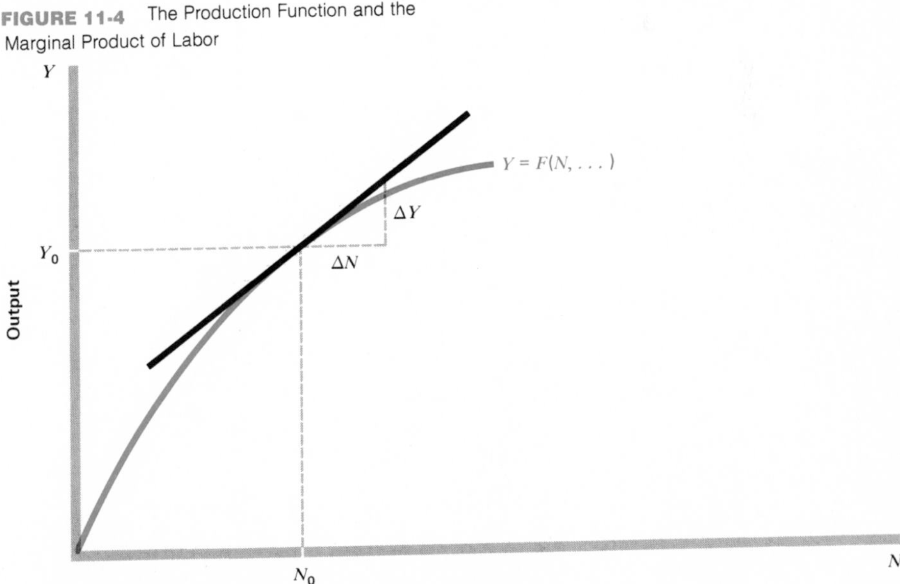

Diminishing returns are shown in the production function by the fact that it is not a straight line through the origin (constant returns) or an upward-curling line (increasing returns). Diminishing returns are explained by the fact that as employment increases and other inputs remain constant, each laborer on the job has fewer machines with which to work and therefore becomes less productive. Thus, increases in the amount of labor progressively reduce the addition to output that further employment can bring. An increase in the labor force will always raise output, but progressively less so as employment expands. The marginal contribution of increased employment is indicated by the slope of the production function, $\Delta Y/\Delta N$. It is readily seen that the slope flattens out as we increase employment, thus showing that increasing employment makes a positive but diminishing contribution to output.

Labor Demand

From the production function we can proceed to the demand for labor. We are asking how much labor a firm would want to hire. The rule of thumb is to continue hiring additional labor and expand production as long as the increase in the value of output exceeds the increase in the wage bill. A firm will hire additional workers as long as they will bring in more in revenue than they cost in wages. The contribution to output of additional labor is called the marginal product of labor and has already been identified in Figure 11-4 with the slope of the production function. That marginal product, as we have seen, is both positive—additional labor is productive—and diminishing, which means that additional employment becomes progressively less productive. We also noted that a firm will employ additional labor as long as the marginal product of labor, MPN for short, exceeds the cost of additional labor. The cost of additional labor is given by the real wage, that is, the nominal wage divided by the price level. The real wage measures the amount of real output the firm has to pay each worker. Since hiring one more worker results in an output increase of MPN and a cost to the firm of the real wage, firms will hire additional labor if the MPN exceeds the real wage. This point is formalized in Figure 11-5, which looks at the labor market.

The downward-sloping schedule in Figure 11-5 is the demand for labor schedule which is the MPN schedule; firms hire labor up to the point at which the MPN is equal to the real wage. The MPN schedule shows the contribution to output of additional employment. It follows from our reasoning that the MPN is positive but that additional employment reduces it, so that the MPN schedule is negatively sloped.

Now consider a firm that currently employs a labor force, N_1, and assume the real wage is $(w/P)_0$, where w is the money wage and P the price of output. At an employment level N_1 in Figure 11-5, the firm is clearly employing too much labor since the real wage exceeds the MPN at that

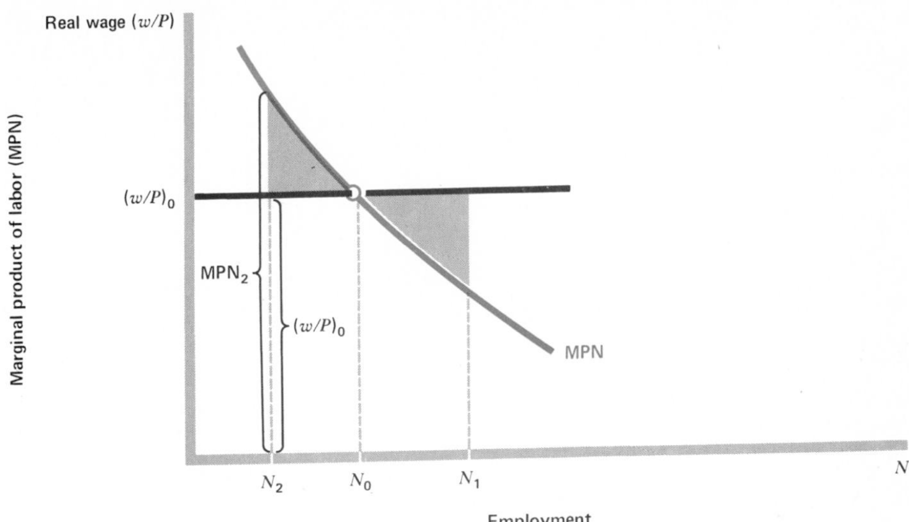

FIGURE 11-5 THE OPTIMAL EMPLOYMENT CHOICE FOR A GIVEN REAL WAGE

level of employment. What would happen if the firm should reduce employment? The reduction in employment would decrease output by the MPN times the change in employment, MPNΔN, and therefore reduce revenue to the firm. On the other side of the calculation, we have the reduction in the wage bill. Per unit reduction in employment, the wage bill would fall at the rate of the real wage, (w/P). The net benefit of a reduction in the employment level is thus equal to the vertical excess of the real wage over the MPN in Figure 11-5. It is apparent that at the level of employment N_1, excess is quite sizable, and it pays the firm to reduce the employment level. Indeed, it pays to reduce employment until the firm gets to point N_0. Only at that point does the cost of additional labor—the real wage—exactly balance the benefit in the form of increased output.

The same argument applies to the unemployment level N_2. Here employment is insufficient because the contribution to output of additional employment, MPN_2, exceeds the cost of additional employment, and it therefore pays to expand the level of employment. It is readily seen that the only level of employment that precisely balances the costs and benefits is the level N_0. Therefore, given *any* real wage, the firm's demand for labor is shown by the MPN curve.

Equilibrium in the Labor Market

We have now developed the relation between output and employment (the production function) and the optimal employment choice for a given real wage that is implied by the demand for labor. It remains to consider the determination of the real wage as part of labor market equilibrium. What we have not yet dealt with is the supply of labor.

We will make a quite simple assumption concerning labor supply. We will assume that the supply of labor is fixed at $\overline{N}$ and that it is independent of the real wage.[4] This is shown in Figure 11-6 as the vertical schedule, $\overline{N}\overline{N}$. The equilibrium real wage is clearly $(w/P)_0$.

How would the labor market get to that equilibrium? Suppose that the real wage fell whenever there was an excess supply of labor and that it rose whenever there was an excess demand. In terms of Figure 11-6, this would mean that the real wage would decline whenever it was above $(w/P)_0$. At $(w/P)_1$, for example, labor demand is only N_1 and thus falls short of labor supply. This would put downward pressure on the real wage, cause the real wage to fall, and make it profitable to expand employment. Exactly the reverse argument holds for real wages lower than $(w/P)_0$, where there is an excess demand for labor.

From Figure 11-6 we see that adjustment of the real wage would bring the labor market into full-employment equilibrium at a real wage $(w/P)_0$ and an employment level equal to the given labor supply $\overline{N}$. Figure 11-7 summarizes the complete equilibrium in the labor market and the

[4] The exposition of this chapter would be little affected if we assumed that labor supply increased as the real wage increased. The major change then would be that the full-employment level of employment would depend on the level of the real wage. You might want to experiment with an upward-sloping labor supply curve as you continue reading.

FIGURE 11-6 Equilibrium in the Labor Market

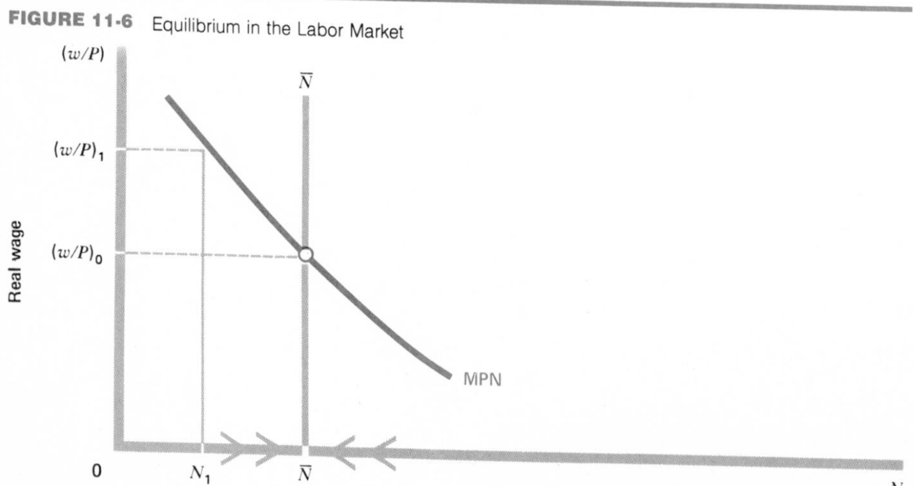

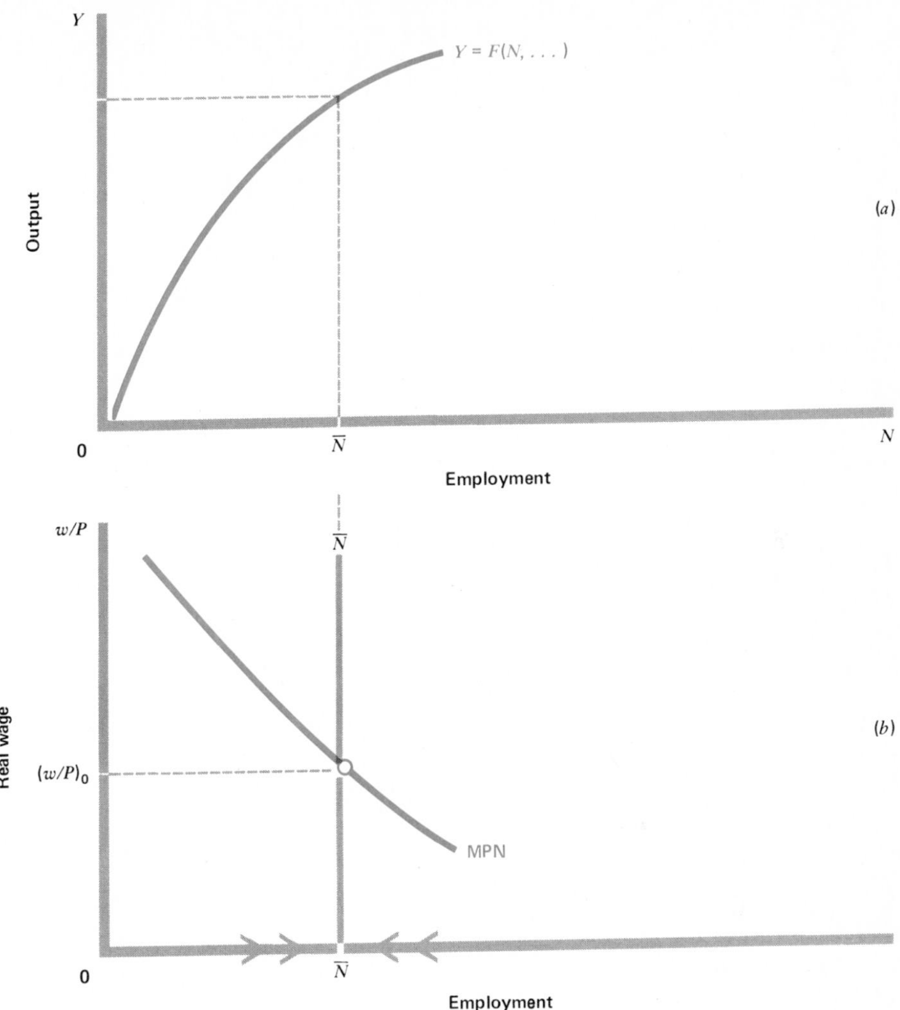

FIGURE 11-7 Equilibrium in the Labor Market and Full-Employment Output

corresponding level of *full-employment output* Y_p, which is the level of output associated with employment equal to the given labor supply.

Neoclassical Goods and Labor Market Equilibrium

We have now derived the full-employment supply of output and have to complete the neoclassical model by asking how *money* wages and prices are determined. How can we be sure that goods produced can be sold? Here we make two important assumptions: (1) goods prices will rise or fall instantaneously to clear the goods market, and (2) money wages will instantaneously rise or fall to clear the labor market. How will that adjustment work?

In the labor market, the flexibility of money wages ensures that at each price level the money wage rises or falls to achieve the necessary level of the real wage. We are therefore continuously in labor market equilibrium and, whatever the level of prices, firms will employ the full-employment labor force $\overline{N}$ and supply the corresponding level of output Y_p. This is shown in Figure 11-8 in the aggregate supply curve Y_pY_p. The aggregate supply schedule is vertical to show that the equilibrium level of output supplied—when the labor market is in equilibrium—is independent of the price level. If prices rose relative to wages, firms would be making profits. In an attempt to secure even larger profits, they would attempt individually to expand their employment level at the going money wage. In the aggregate, though, all they would do would be to compete for the given labor force and drive up the money wage until it had risen in proportion to the increase in prices, thus leaving real output unchanged.

Figure 11-8 includes an aggregate demand curve, Y^d, along with the vertical neoclassical aggregate supply function.[5] Aggregate demand and

[5] Recall from Sec. 1 that the aggregate demand curve slopes downward because increases in the price level reduce real balances, increase the interest rate, and reduce aggregate demand.

FIGURE 11-8 THE INTERACTION OF AGGREGATE SUPPLY AND DEMAND IN THE DETERMINATION OF THE EQUILIBRIUM PRICE LEVEL

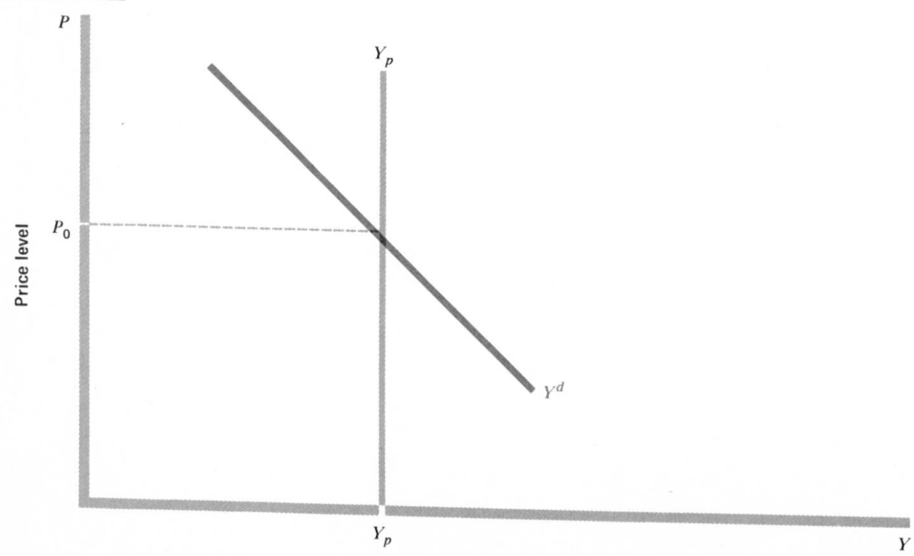

supply jointly determine the equilibrium price level, P_0. We need not be concerned yet with a full understanding of the details of the adjustment process of the price level in response to shifts in aggregate supply or demand. We need only recognize that it is plausible that the economy will converge to a full-employment equilibrium with all markets in equilibrium. Given the equilibrium price level P_0, the nominal wage will adjust so that the real wage is $(w/P)_0$. Furthermore, *if* wages and prices adjust rapidly, and *if* firms respond rapidly in their production decisions to changing conditions, and *if* labor moves rapidly between jobs as some firms expand and others contract, we would expect to be in equilibrium continuously. Any disturbance, such as an increase in the nominal money supply or an improvement in technology, would immediately be reflected in changes in wages and prices that would restore the full-employment equilibrium.

The neoclassical full equilibrium is a useful reference point for the study of more realistic descriptions of macroeconomics. We should expect to converge to the neoclassical equilibrium in the long run. But in the short run, problems of transactions costs and information problems associated with finding and taking jobs, together with simple stickiness of wages and prices due to contractual arrangements, will affect the adjustment process. If, for example, prices do not fall fast enough in response to a decline in the nominal quantity of money, we would expect to get transitory disequilibrium and unemployment. Such unemployment would not occur in the neoclassical model. It is exactly the range of issues such as short-run adjustment and unemployment with which the macroeconomics of the short run is concerned. We therefore retain the neoclassical analysis as a reference point and turn next to a discussion of the adjustment process under less ideal conditions.

The more realistic theory of aggregate supply we are about to develop differs from the neoclassical theory in three important respects. (1) Because it is costly to hire and fire workers, firms do not stay precisely on their neoclassical demand function for labor, as in Figure 11-6. Rather, they look ahead in making their hiring decisions, which are based on both the expected real wage and the level of output they expect to produce in the future. (2) The money wage adjusts only slowly. It takes unemployment to reduce the money wage or overemployment to increase it. (3) The prices charged by firms are based mainly on their costs of production. Since costs are largely wages, which respond slowly to demand, prices too respond slowly to demand. Thus the supply curve is relatively flat in the short run.

In the short run, changes in aggregate demand therefore have relatively little impact on prices. As William Nordhaus of Yale has put it: "After three decades, the major intellectual problem continues to be the fact that so little response to demand shifts comes through prices and wages."[6]

[6] William Nordhaus, "Inflation Theory and Policy," *American Economic Review*, May 1976, p. 62.

11-3 OUTPUT AND PRODUCTIVITY

The neoclassical analysis of the previous section suggests that the *average productivity of labor*—the level of output per unit of labor—should vary inversely with the level of output. Figure 11-4 implies that output per unit of labor falls as the level of output rises.[7] In fact, though, productivity varies procyclically, as can be seen in Chart 11-1. Output per work hour fell sharply during the recession of 1974–1975 and began to increase as the recovery from the recession got underway in 1975. Similarly, it began to fall again in 1979–1980 as the economy moved into a recession. The facts do not support the implication of Figure 11-4 for the behavior of productivity. It is thus clear that at least some element of the neoclassical analysis of Section 11-2 has to be amended.

The essential modification of the neoclassical analysis we shall make is to recognize that in the short run, firms will not necessarily be on their marginal product of labor schedule, MPN. As we argue in this section and the next, a firm need not react to changes in demand by changing its labor force or even its level of production. Even without changing its labor force,

[7] Be sure you can see from Fig. 11-4 that the ratio Y/N falls as Y rises.

CHART 11-1 THE PRODUCTIVITY OF LABOR, 1974–1979
(*Source: Citibank Economic Database*)

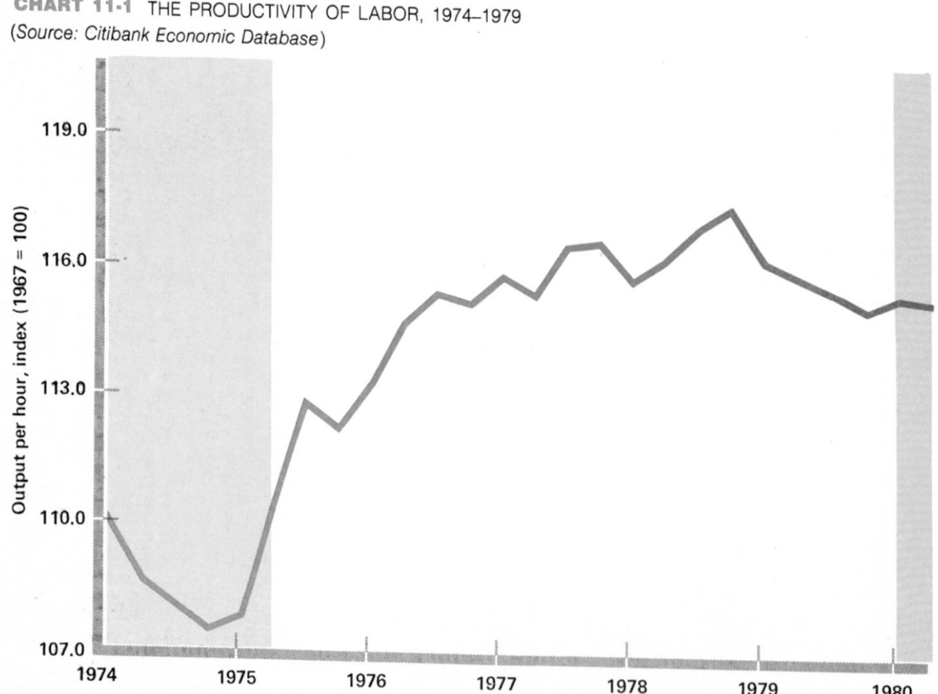

Note: Shaded region indicates recession.

a firm has two ways of meeting a change in demand. The first is to change its stock of inventories.[8] and the second is to adjust the rate at which the labor force works. In particular, if an increase in demand is viewed as *transitory* or temporary, the firm is likely to respond either by selling some goods held in inventory, by working its given labor force somewhat harder, perhaps including overtime, or by doing both. Similarly, in the face of a transitory decline in demand, the firm will retain its employees rather than lay them off, and it may therefore reduce hours of work or allow its inventories to build up.

The fact that variations in demand and sales may be seen as transitory suggests that we should analyze the firm's production decision separately from its employment decision, and that we should recognize that sales of goods can be made out of inventory without requiring production changes. To anticipate somewhat: If there are significant costs of hiring and firing labor, firms will want to have a relatively stable labor force but may still vary output as the demand for their goods varies.[9] Similarly, if there are significant costs to changing production rates, firms may want to stabilize production relative to sales, and thus allow inventories to fluctuate to meet very short-run movements in demand.[10]

We have now pointed to three possible adjustments a firm can make to a change in demand. It can adjust its inventory level, the rate at which its labor force works, or the size of its labor force. In the very shortest run, it is likely to respond to a change in demand by adjusting inventories. But inventories cannot be run down for very long, nor would firms want to keep accumulating them, and the adjustment of the rate at which the labor force works is likely to occur in the short run too. Then, over a slightly longer period, the firm will start adjusting its labor force as well. The rate of adjustment using each method will of course depend on how much information the firm has about the nature of the change in demand—the adjustment of the labor force will be made more quickly if the firm knows that the demand change is permanent.

The preceding argument suggests that as firms adjust both their hours of work and their labor force, we should expect to see an inverse relationship between the number of hours worked per week and the rate at which firms lay off workers. Chart 11-2 shows the average workweek of production workers in manufacturing, as well as the number of layoffs per 100 employees. It is evident that the layoff rate and the length of workweek move in opposite directions. This can be seen clearly in both the 1958 and 1974–1975 recessions, and also during the period of generally rising output from 1976 to 1979.

[8] Of course, inventories can be used in this way only in those industries where it is possible to store output.

[9] An early article drawing attention to the importance of costs of adjusting the labor force is that of Walter Oi, "Labor as a Quasi-Fixed Factor," *Journal of Political Economy*, October 1962.

[10] However, we do not examine inventory adjustment explicitly in the rest of this chapter.

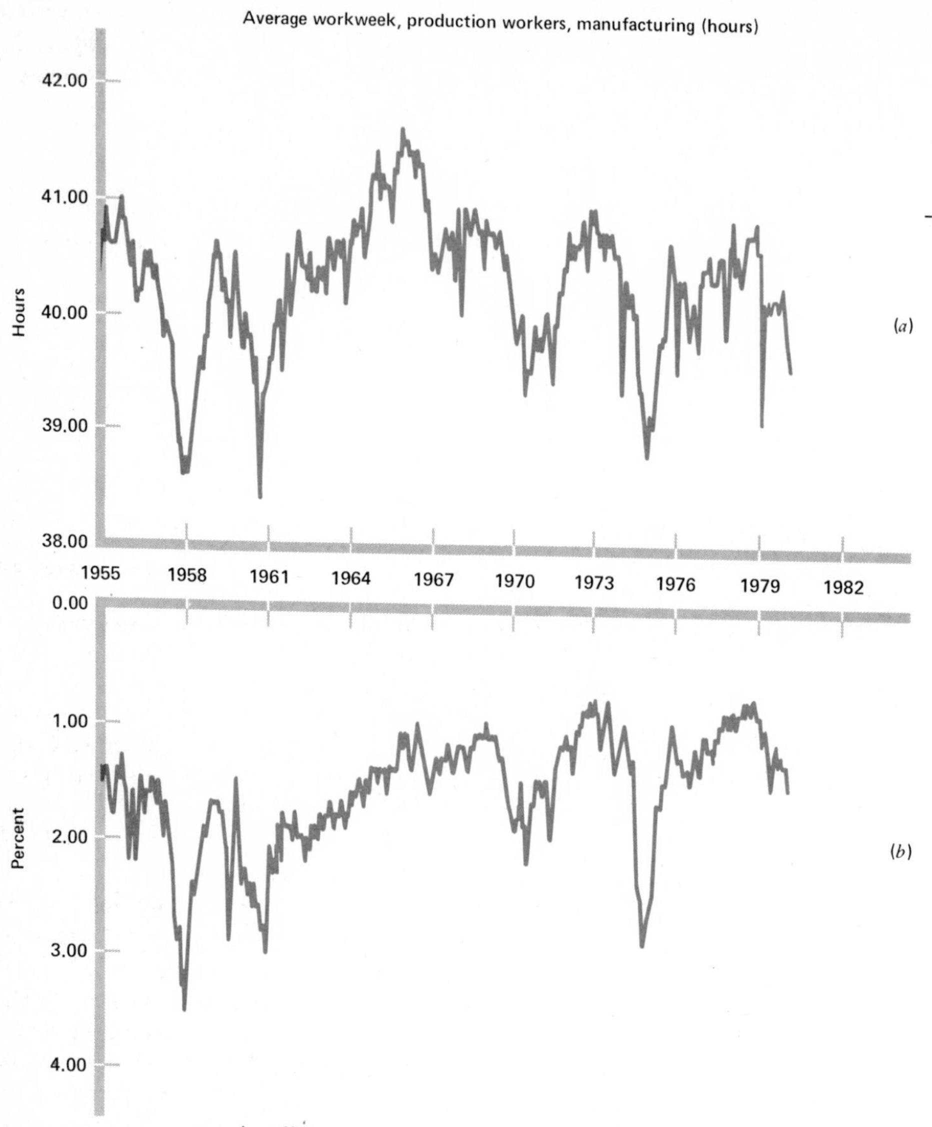

CHART 11-2 AVERAGE WORKWEEK AND LAYOFF RATE.
(*Source: Citibank Economic Database*)

We can return now to the productivity behavior shown in Chart 11-1. Why should labor productivity vary procyclically? The reason is simply that when output expands, firms have more work for their labor force to do, and labor works harder each hour that it is on the job.[11] Conversely, when output declines but firms are reluctant to lay off workers because the output decline may be temporary, the ratio of output to employment declines. Thus measured productivity—the ratio of output to employment—moves procyclically, or in the same direction as output. It is common to refer to firms' practice of not laying off workers in the face of a decline in demand as *labor hoarding.*

The major point of this section has been that the link between the firm's labor force and its output level is not automatic. In the presence of costs of adjusting the labor force—costs of hiring and firing labor and training new labor—the firm will not adjust its labor force completely in response to short-run changes in demand. Instead, the firm will adjust its labor force with a view to the level of output it will be producing over a longer period.

11-4 DETERMINATION OF THE LEVEL OF EMPLOYMENT

We now examine in more detail the firm's choice of employment level. How closely will employment move with output? We have already seen that firms can vary output as of a given employment level by using the labor force more or less intensively.[12] That is an efficient short-run adjustment, but it is clearly not a reasonable long-run strategy. A firm that expects a doubling in its output can achieve that output at much lower cost by increasing its labor force than by increasing the overtime work of its existing employees.

We have also argued that, unlike the neoclassical firms of Section 11-2, an actual firm will experience significant costs in changing employment in the short run. These costs arise from advertising, screening and interviewing new employees, and having to train those employees. Given these costs of changing employment, firms, in making their employment decisions, will look ahead to the levels of output they expect to be producing in the future.

What determines the average output the firm expects to produce over a longer period, such as a year or two, on which its present hiring decisions will in part be based? We refer to this output level as expected *normal*

[11] Another reason that labor productivity rises in the short run when output increases is that the firm has certain overhead labor—such as management—that is needed to keep the firm operating at all but that is not expanded with output.

[12] In this section, we will not be discussing inventory adjustment explicitly, although, as noted above, it is one way of meeting short-run changes in demand.

output. We can think of the typical firm as being a *monopolistic competitor* in the medium run of a year or two with which we are now concerned. The firm does not believe that it will be able to sell as much as it wants at the market price that will prevail for the industry, as the neoclassical firm of Section 11-2 believes. Rather, it believes that it will be faced by a downward-sloping demand curve for its output and will set its own price.[13]

Given the demand curve the firm believes it will face over the next year or two, it will choose the price and the corresponding level of output at which it expects to operate over the period. The choice will be made with the aim of maximizing profits. The firm will undoubtedly also take a longer view than just the next year or two, since it will take into account the effects of the prices it charges in the near future on demand in later periods, and also the possibility that high prices will attract competitors into the industry.[14]

The amount of labor the firm will want to have on hand to meet expected normal output will depend on both the firm's expected level of output and the real wage it expects to pay for labor. If the real wage is high, the firm will plan to use relatively little labor and more other factors to meet demand.

The implied labor demand curve is shown in Figure 11-9 as the downward-sloping schedule. At a real wage $(w/P)_0$, the firm (or firms in the aggregate) will want to have on hand an amount of labor N_0, given that they hold output expectations Y_0. A reduction in expected output shifts the demand curve for labor to the left. With expected output $Y_1 < Y_0$, the quantity of labor demanded at the real wage $(w/P)_0$ declines to N'.

A reduction in the real wage below $(w/P)_0$ would raise labor demand because firms would find it profitable to use more labor and undertake less investment to meet expected demand. However, in the period of a year or two for which the concept of expected normal output is relevant, we should not expect to see any substantial shifts in the level of the overall capital stock, and thus the demand curve for labor in Figure 11-9 would be quite steep.

In summary, we have argued that (1) the aggregate demand for labor and employment depends on output expectations and the expected real wage; (2) increased output expectations increase the employment level; and (3) a reduction in the expected real wage increases labor demand and employment.

[13] Actually, the monopolistic competition model is flexible enough to incorporate as an extreme case the assumption that the firm is a perfect competitor, and at the other extreme, that there is a fixed maximum amount it will be able to sell in the future—the case of a *sales constraint.*

[14] Considerations of potential competition have been emphasized by Paolo Sylos-Labini and Joe S. Bain. For an exposition, see Franco Modigliani, "New Developments on the Oligopoly Front," *Journal of Political Economy*, June 1958.

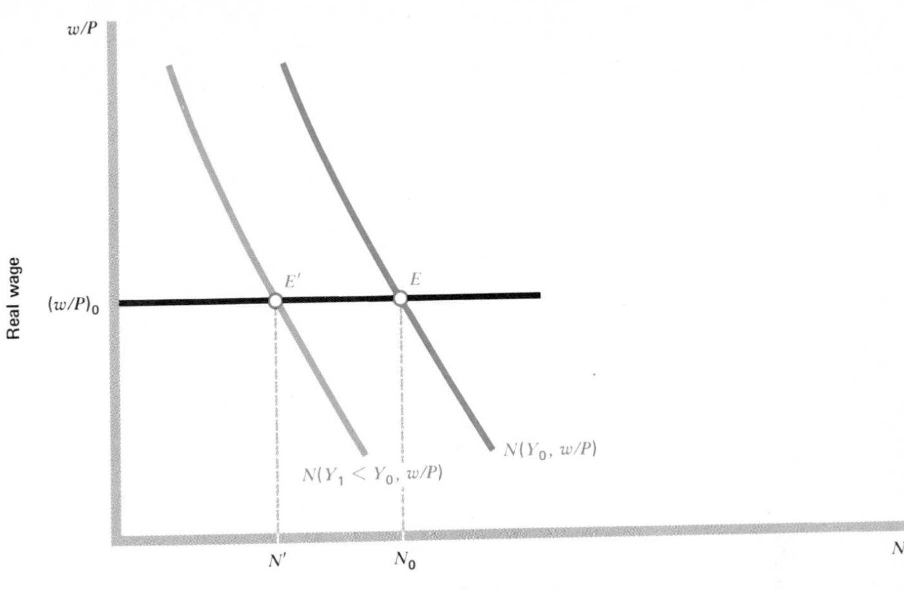

FIGURE 11-9 REDUCED OUTPUT EXPECTATIONS DECREASE THE DEMAND FOR LABOR AT EACH REAL WAGE

These considerations raise two questions: First, how do firms form their expectations about future output and real wages? Second, how do they respond to a change in demand they consider transitory?

We can start with the second question, which turns out to have a relatively obvious answer. If a firm faces a transitory increase in the demand for its output, but if at the same time it is costly to hire and fire additional labor, the firm will not expand employment substantially but, rather, will meet the increased demand out of inventories and through overtime. Obviously, though, the longer the increase in demand is expected to persist (or the less transitory it is) and the larger the increase in demand, the more likely it is that the firm will want to expand employment.

Next we turn to the always difficult question of expectations. We assume that firms expect the current level of real wages to persist. For output, we adopt a different convention. Here we recognize that if current demand is very low, firms do not believe that it will be low indefinitely. On the contrary, they expect demand to improve. Conversely, if demand is currently very high, firms anticipate some decline. Whether current demand is very high or low must obviously be judged relative to some bench mark. We take full-employment output Y_p to be the bench mark. The expectations formation we have just described can be formalized as

$$Y^e = \alpha Y + (1 - \alpha)\, Y_p \qquad 0 \leq \alpha \leq 1 \tag{3}$$

where Y^e is expected normal output.[15]

Equation (3) shows expected normal output Y^e as an average of full-employment output Y_p and current output Y. We treat the weight α in Equation (3) as given. If all disturbances causing the level of output to diverge from the full-employment level are believed to be entirely temporary, then α should be close to zero and changes in current output have almost no effect on expected output and therefore on employment. Conversely, if disturbances are expected to persist, and if it is believed that the economy takes a long time to move toward the full-employment level, then the weight α should be close to unity. Current output should receive a larger weight in the formation of expected output, and current employment would be more closely linked to current output.

In summary, the aggregate employment decision, taking all firms together, depends on expected output and the real wage. We can write a labor demand curve that is appropriate for the short run:

$$N = N\left(Y^e, \frac{w}{P}\right) = N\left(Y_p, Y, \frac{w}{P}\right) \tag{4}$$

The labor demand function shows that the total level of employment depends on expected output and the real wage. Expected output, in turn, depends on both potential output and the current level of output. At a given real wage, the higher the output, the higher the demand for labor. And, given the level of output, the lower the real wage, the higher the demand for labor.

11-5 WAGE AND PRICE SETTING

This section continues the derivation of the aggregate supply schedule by discussing wage and price setting. We will examine the relationship between the level of employment and wages, and then between wages and prices. Then, linking output to employment, employment to wages, and wages to prices, we will finally derive the aggregate supply schedule.

It is also worth recalling that we expect the aggregate supply schedule

[15] As we have noted frequently, modeling expectations with simple formulas is always difficult. You might want to consider the implications of an alternative formulation such as

$$Y^e = \alpha Y + (1 - \alpha)Y_p + \lambda(Y_{-1} - Y_p) \qquad 0 < \lambda < 1$$

as you continue reading. Is this formula a reasonable representation of how expectations might be formed?

to be flat in the short run—unlike the neoclassical schedule in Figure 11-7—but we expect the long-run aggregate supply schedule to resemble the vertical neoclassical supply function.

We will start in this section by examining the link between wage behavior and the level of employment. As for most of the elements of the theory of aggregate supply, empirical evidence on wage behavior is not yet conclusive. Most existing empirical evidence is related to the famous Phillips curve, introduced in Chapter 1 and reviewed in greater depth in Chapters 13 and 15. In the late fifties, the Phillips curve was treated as a relationship between the rate of unemployment and the rate of increase of *nominal* wages.[16] Wages would increase when (measured) unemployment was very low, and would stay constant and perhaps even fall if unemployment was very high. Later, the argument was modified to take account of the effects of expected changes in the price level on nominal wages,[17] but we defer that important modification to the later chapters on the Phillips curve.

For purposes of this chapter, it is sufficient to take the view that the state of the labor market determines the rate of change of money wages. Whenever employment is abnormally high, wages will be rising. Conversely, whenever employment is low, wages will be falling. This notion is consistent with the neoclassical view outlined in Section 11-2. But, in practice, the adjustment of the money wage to unemployment is not immediate, as assumed in the neoclassical analysis. Instead, wages move only slowly in response to labor market disequilibrium. In the short run, overemployment and underemployment are quite possible—even though the economy tends to move toward full employment in the absence of disturbances to aggregate demand and supply.

Once wage behavior has been studied, we move over to price behavior. The prices firms charge for their output are based mainly on the costs of producing output and in particular on the most important of those costs, the money wage, or the cost of labor. Accordingly, there will be a link between the unemployment rate and the behavior of the price level.

Wage Setting

The notion that the state of the labor market determines the behavior of money wages is formalized in Figure 11-10, where we show a demand for

[16] We should also note that the Phillips curve designation is now often used as we use it below: to describe a relationship between the rate of change of prices and the unemployment rate, rather than the wage-unemployment relation.

[17] Expected changes in the price level should affect nominal wages because labor and firms are both concerned with real wages. If the nominal wage for which labor contracts to sell its services remains fixed for, say, a year, then labor would be concerned with how the price level would change over the contract year, since the price level changes affect the real wage to be received. Hence, expected changes in the price level should affect the nominal wage.

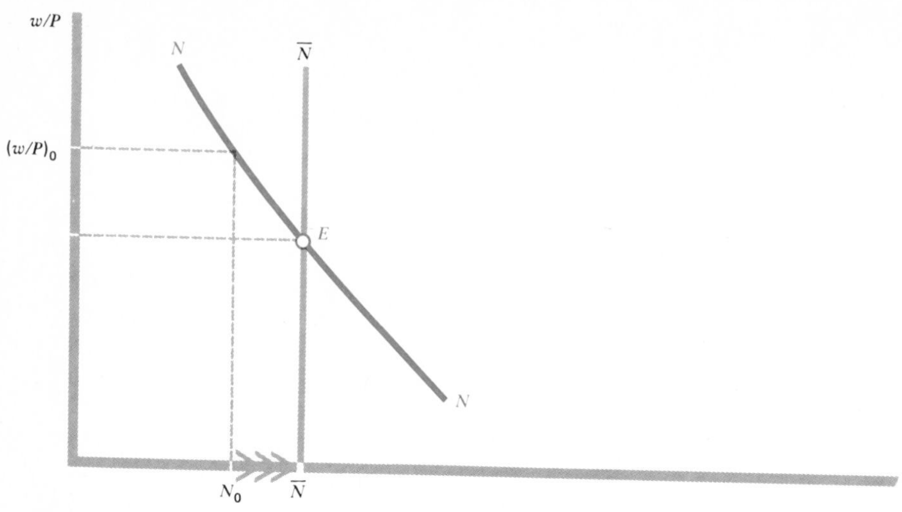

FIGURE 11-10 Adjustment in the Labor Market

labor curve (NN), drawn for the expected full-employment level of output, Y_p. We show, too, the supply of labor $\overline{N}$. If the real wage were initially at a level such as $(w/P)_0$, there would be unemployment of labor equal to the distance $N_0\overline{N}$. That unemployment would in turn cause wages to start declining—this is precisely the insight of the Phillips curve. Given the price level—the behavior of which we shall examine later—real wages would decline, adding to employment. However, the effect might be very slow because money wages might fall only slowly.

Now we will develop the simple notion illustrated in Figure 11-10 more formally. First, we have to explain that in this chapter we are abstracting from *frictional* unemployment—the unemployment that results from the rate at which people normally change jobs, and from the fact that it takes new workers some time to find their first job. This frictional unemployment is studied in detail in Chapter 15 under the name of the *natural rate of unemployment*, which can also be called the "full-employment rate of unemployment." Once we recognize that some unemployment is normal because of frictions in the labor market, we realize that overemployment is possible as well as underemployment. From now on we shall take $\overline{N}$ to be the level of employment that would exist at normal full employment. If the employment level is $\overline{N}$, we shall say that there is zero unemployment, even though the unemployment statistics, measuring also frictional unemployment, would report the actual unemployment rate at around 5 to 6 percent. Employment can exceed $\overline{N}$, in which case we say in this chapter that there is negative unemployment.

Wages respond to unemployment. If employment is below N, nominal wages will decline. Conversely, if employment is above $\overline{N}$—or unemployment is negative—wages will increase. This idea is formalized in Equation (5):

$$w = w_{-1}(1 - \epsilon u) \qquad 0 < \epsilon < 1 \tag{5}$$

where u is the unemployment rate and ϵ measures the responsiveness of wages to unemployment. Consider first the case where unemployment is zero, $u = 0$. In that case current wages w are equal to last period's wages, w_{-1}, so wages neither rise nor fall. Next we look at the case where there is some unemployment, $u > 0$. Now the term in parentheses is less than 1, and accordingly, current wages are less than last period's wages. Therefore, Equation (5) reflects the fact that unemployment causes wages to decline.

To emphasize the percentage rate of change of wages—or wage inflation—we can rewrite Equation (5):[18]

$$\frac{w - w_{-1}}{w_{-1}} = -\epsilon u \tag{5a}$$

The unemployment rate u in Equation (5) or (5a) is defined as the fraction of the full-employment labor force $\bar{N}$ that is not employed:

$$u \equiv \frac{\bar{N} - N}{\bar{N}} \tag{6}$$

Thus, if the full-employment labor force is equal to 100 people of whom 94 are employed, the unemployment rate is $u = (100 - 94)/100 = 6$ percent.[19] Using the definition of the unemployment rate in Equation (6), we can rewrite the *wage equation* as

$$w = w_{-1}\left[1 - \epsilon\left(1 - \frac{N}{\bar{N}}\right)\right] \tag{5b}$$

From Equation (5b) it is apparent that the current wage depends on two elements. One is last period's wage. Other things equal, the current wage is last period's wage. The other determinant of wages is employment, or more particularly, employment relative to the full-employment labor force $N/\bar{N}$. When employment exceeds the supply of labor, wages are rising, and when employment falls short, wages are falling.

[18] To get from Eq. (5) to Eq. (5a), we divide both sides by w_{-1} and subtract 1 from both sides of the equation to obtain $w/w_{-1} - 1 = -\epsilon u$, which can be rewritten as Eq. (5a).

[19] Recall that we are defining $\bar{N}$ as the full-employment labor force so that N can exceed $\bar{N}$. This also means that the unemployment rate as defined in Eq. (6) is not the same as the unemployment rate that is announced each month. The published unemployment rate measures unemployment as a fraction of the civilian labor force. Problem 9 at the end of this chapter asks you to relate the unemployment rate as measured in Eq. (6) to the published unemployment rate. Of course, our measure of u increases when the published unemployment rate increases, and vice versa.

In Figure 11-11 we show the current wage as a function of the level of employment, given the past wage w_{-1}. In studying the upper wage schedule, we first observe that when employment is equal to the full-employment labor supply $\overline{N}$, the current wage is equal to the past wage, or $w = w^0_{-1}$. Next we note that deviations from full employment affect the wage rate. An increase in employment, relative to $\overline{N}$, raises the wage and a reduction in employment lowers the wage.

In Figure 11-11 we also make the point that *if* employment were somehow kept below the full-employment level, then the money wage would keep on falling. To see that, we start at point E with full employment. Then we have a decline in employment because firms' output expectations decline. The decline in employment takes us to the employment level N_0, and the corresponding decline in money wages lowers the wage rate relative to last period. The money wage rate is now at w', having fallen from w^0_{-1}. The next step is to recognize that as we move ahead one period, unemployment is by assumption still the same, so there continues to be downward pressure on wages.

The new wage equation is based on the most recent money wage w'. It is shown as the lower schedule, crossing the $\overline{N}$ schedule at a wage rate $w_{-1} = w'$. The low employment level this period also exerts downward pressure on wages and we therefore move to point A'' with a further decline in wages. The process will continue in this manner until the falling money

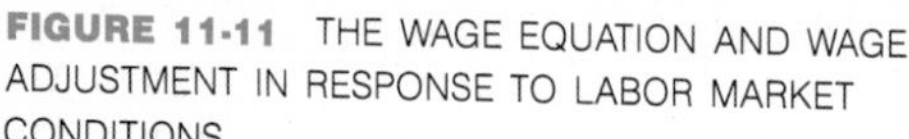
FIGURE 11-11 THE WAGE EQUATION AND WAGE ADJUSTMENT IN RESPONSE TO LABOR MARKET CONDITIONS

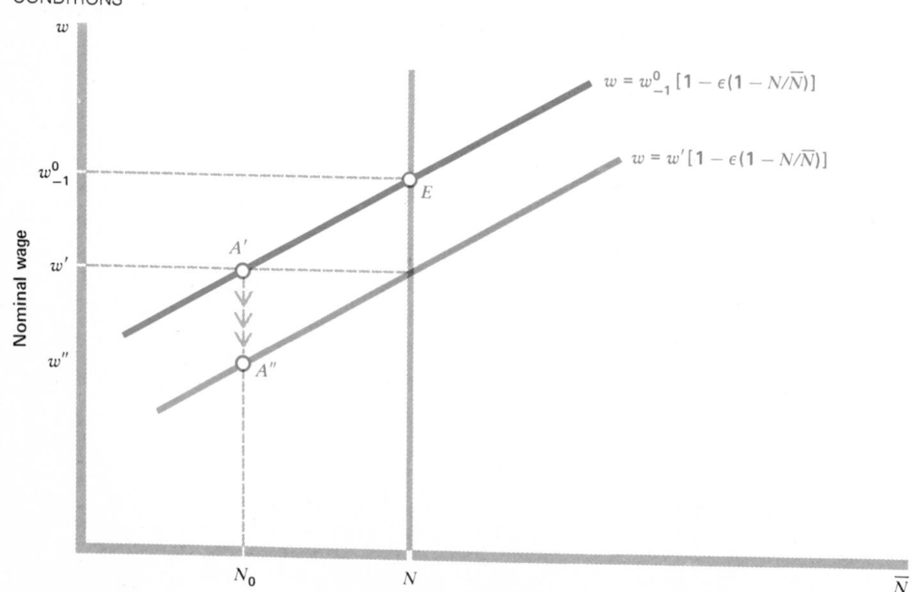

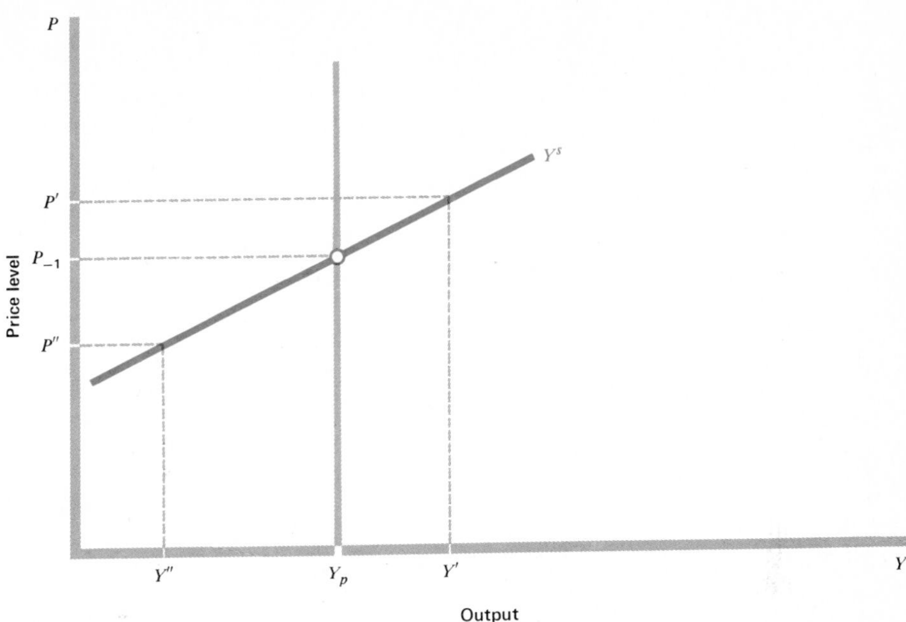

FIGURE 11-12 THE AGGREGATE SUPPLY CURVE

wages lower costs and prices sufficiently to expand aggregate demand and thereby raise output and employment.

In summary, we have said that wages are set on the basis of last period's money wage with an adjustment for the state of the labor market. When labor markets are tight, $N > \overline{N}$, wages are increasing. Conversely, when there is unemployment, $N < \overline{N}$, wages are falling. The slope of the wage equations in Figure 11-12 indicates the impact of a change in employment on the money wage rate. A steep schedule means that a change in current employment has a large impact on current money wages.

Price Setting

In the neoclassical framework of Section 11-2 it was assumed that prices are somehow adjusted by the "market." Now we shall instead assume that firms set prices, and that they set their prices on the basis of the costs of production. If a firm experiences an increase in costs, it will pass on that cost increase in the form of higher prices.[20]

[20] For some evidence on wage-price behavior, see Otto Eckstein (ed.), *Parameters and Policies in the U. S. Economy* (Amsterdam, North-Holland, 1976), chap. 3; and Otto Eckstein (ed.), *The Econometrics of Price Determination* (Washington: Board of Governors of the Federal Reserve, 1972). See also George L. Perry, "Slowing the Wage-Price Spiral: The Macroeconomic View," *Brookings Papers on Economic Activity*, 1978:2 (Washington, D.C.: The Brookings Institution, 1978).

We will proceed with two simplifying assumptions. First, labor costs are for the moment assumed to be the only variable cost. Second, prices are assumed to be based on wages, with a *markup* that allows for profits. Accordingly, increases in wages are assumed to be passed on into prices. With these simplifying assumptions, we can write the price level as

$$P = bw \qquad b > 1 \tag{7}$$

where b is a constant, the markup of prices over wages.[21]

We now have a relationship between prices and wages or labor cost. To go from here to an aggregate supply schedule, we have to use two further relations. One is wage equation (5) that links current wages to past wages and unemployment. Substituting for w in Equation (5) thus gives us

$$P = bw_{-1}(1 - \epsilon u) \tag{8}$$

In the present form, our price equation states that the level of prices set by firms will depend on last period's level of wages, w_{-1}, and on the unemployment rate. Prices are set higher, the higher wages were last period and the lower current unemployment is. The equation can be simplified by noting that last period's prices were proportional to the then prevailing wages, or

$$P_{-1} = bw_{-1} \tag{9}$$

We can thus substitute on the right-hand side of (8) to obtain a price equation in terms of past prices rather than wages:

$$P = bw_{-1}(1 - \epsilon u) = P_{-1}(1 - \epsilon u) \tag{10}$$

In this form we recognize the role of current unemployment in determining the movement of prices over time. If there is unemployment, wages and prices will have fallen relative to last period. Conversely, if there is overemployment ($u < 0$), firms will raise prices relative to the past level.

[21] We discuss four features of Eq. (7) later in the chapter. First, it simplifies by assuming labor is the only variable factor. We return to this point in Sec. 11-7. Second, it assumes that wages are passed on immediately into prices. In practice, an increase in wages is likely to be passed on slowly into prices, as firms initially respond to a cost increase by absorbing part of the change in costs so as not to lose customer goodwill. Problem 12 asks you to show that the slow pass-through of wages makes the aggregate supply curve flatter. Third, Eq. (7) implies that the real wage, w/P, is constant and equal to $1/b$. Fourth, Eq. (7) does *not* assume that price is based on the current average cost of production at each level of output. Since the productivity of labor increases with the level of output, average costs of production fall at a given wage rate as output rises. Rather, Eq. (7) implicitly assumes that price is based on the cost of production at some given level of output, particularly expected normal output. We return to points 3 and 4 in Sec. 11-8.

So far, we have a relation only between prices, past prices, and the level of unemployment. The aggregate supply schedule we are looking for, though, is a relation between prices and current output. To establish that link, we assume that the GNP gap—the excess of potential over actual output—is proportional to the unemployment rate.[22] That relation is summarized in (11):

$$u = h\,\frac{Y_p - Y}{Y_p} \qquad h > 0 \tag{11}$$

where h is a constant discussed in connection with Okun's law in Chapter 1. It remains for us to substitute the GNP gap in place of the unemployment rate in (10) to obtain

$$P = P_{-1}\left[1 - \epsilon h\left(1 - \frac{Y}{Y_p}\right)\right] \tag{12}$$

11-6 THE AGGREGATE SUPPLY CURVE

Equation (12) is precisely the relationship we have been aiming to derive—the short-run aggregate supply schedule. Since we have come some distance in doing so, we should review the route. First, we studied the factors determining firms' hiring decisions, arguing that firms base their hiring decisions on the level of expected normal output, which responds only slowly to changes in current output. Second, we discussed wage behavior, noting that wages respond only slowly to changes in the demand for labor. Thus, changes in aggregate demand affect hiring only slowly, and that in turn affects wages only slowly. Finally, we examined price-setting behavior, maintaining that prices are set mainly on the basis of costs. Making the simplifying assumptions that prices are proportional to wages and that wage changes are passed on directly into prices, we were able to derive Equation (12).

We can explore the properties of Equation (12) using Figure 11-12. First, suppose output is at the full-employment level, or $Y/Y_p = 1$. We note from (12) that in this case prices are at the level of the previous period, having neither risen nor fallen. Thus the aggregate supply schedule intersects the vertical schedule representing potential output at the price level P_{-1} that prevailed in the previous period. To supply a higher level of output, say Y', the firm has to increase employment above normal, raising

[22] Equation (11) is essentially Okun's law, mentioned in Chap. 1 and discussed in more detail in the appendix to Chap. 13. The basic notion underlying Eq. (11) is the obvious one that unemployment is lower when output is higher.

wages (perhaps through overtime) relative to their previous level. With increased labor costs, the firm will pass on these increased costs in the form of higher prices. Accordingly, for an output level Y', we have the supply price $P' > P_{-1}$. The converse is true for a decline in output below normal. If output declines, employment falls below normal, wages decline, and accordingly, firms charge a lower price, such as P'' at an output level Y''.

The Long-Run Aggregate Supply Curve

An important point about the aggregate supply curve, already made in the introduction to this chapter, is that the schedule does not stay put over time. Rather, wage and cost changes induced by over- or underemployment are passed on into higher or lower prices. In the long run, therefore, the aggregate supply curve will be vertical, as we now show.

Consider first Figure 11-13, where we again show a short-run aggregate supply schedule, Y^s, drawn for a given level of past wages, and therefore prices, P^0_{-1}. Suppose now that firms choose to supply a higher level of output Y', say because demand increases. At what price will that output be supplied? In the short run, the supply price is P', only a modest increase over the previous period's price. What happens next? The decline

FIGURE 11-13 THE RESPONSE TO THE AGGREGATE SUPPLY CURVE TO OVEREMPLOYMENT

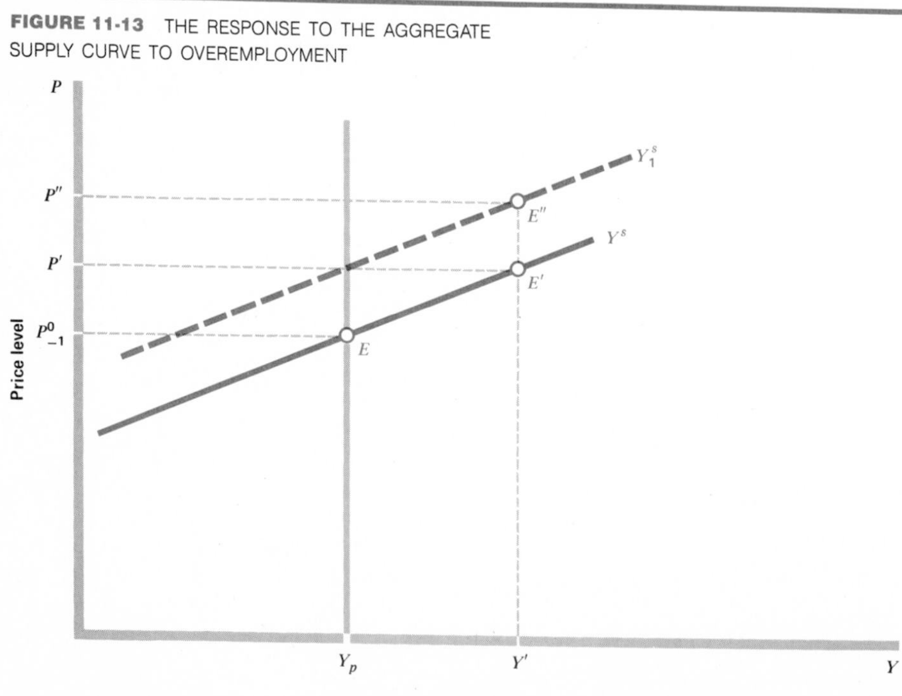

in unemployment implied by the output and employment expansion means that wages will increase [see Eq. (5)] and that therefore firms will charge higher prices. The aggregate supply schedule shifts upward to Y_1^s and the new price is P''. (Note the upward shift of the Y^s schedule is such that in the second period the supply schedule cuts the Y_p schedule at the price P'). As long as output is maintained above potential, wages will be rising and therefore prices will be rising or the supply schedule will keep shifting up.

The very important point, then, is that a level of output above full employment will be accompanied by ever-increasing prices. Conversely, if output were sustained below normal levels, wages and prices would keep falling. This is precisely the neoclassical adjustment process described earlier with the one exception that we think of it as spread out over time.

Over time the supply curve of Figure 11-13 will keep shifting unless output is at the full-employment level. We can thus conclude that the long-run aggregate supply curve is vertical—in the long run the price level can be constant only if output is at the full-employment level.

We shall now make this argument more formally, and in the process derive the Phillips curve implied by Equation (12). The rate of inflation can be determined from (12) by dividing both sides by P_{-1} and subtracting unity from both sides to obtain

$$\frac{P - P_{-1}}{P_{-1}} = h\epsilon\left(\frac{Y}{Y_p} - 1\right) \tag{13}$$

Equation (13) shows that if output is above normal, the rate of inflation is positive, and conversely, if output is below normal, prices will be falling or there is deflation. The price level keeps changing unless $Y = Y_p$.

We can write the inflation rate equation similarly using Equation (14), which is stated in terms of the unemployment rate rather than the GNP gap:

$$\frac{P - P_{-1}}{P_{-1}} = -\epsilon u \tag{14}$$

This is of course the Phillips curve written here as a relation between unemployment and the rate of inflation.[23] The relation is shown in Figure 11-14. When unemployment is positive, prices are falling because wages are falling. Conversely, when there is overemployment—u is negative—prices are rising, reflecting the rising wage costs that are brought about by excess demand in the factor markets. The inflation unemployment Phillips curve of Figure 11-14 will play a major role in the dynamic theory of aggregate supply we present in Chapter 13. However, recall that we have

[23] As noted earlier, the original Phillips curve was a relationship between the rate of change of *wages* and unemployment. The term is now used interchangeably to refer to equations like (5*a*) or (14).

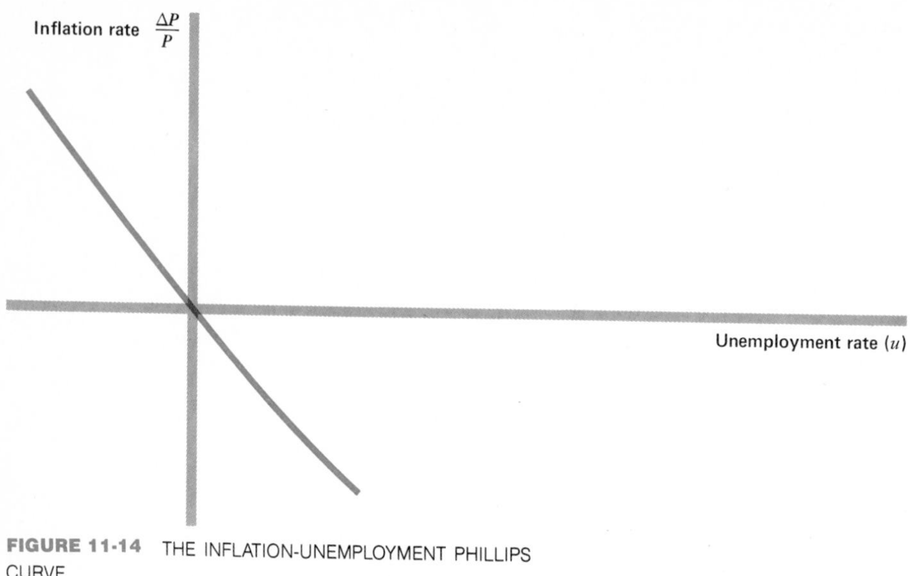

FIGURE 11-14 THE INFLATION-UNEMPLOYMENT PHILLIPS CURVE

here abstracted from the effects of the expected price level on the current wage rate. In Chapter 13 we will augment the Phillips curve of Figure 11-14 to take account of expected changes in the price level.

Figure 11-14 shows that the price level will keep changing unless $u = 0$. Therefore only at $u = 0$, or $Y = Y_p$, can the price level be constant. The long-run aggregate supply curve, showing the level of output consistent with a given price level in the long run, is therefore vertical at the level of potential output, Y_p.

We have now completed the derivation of the aggregate supply curve. Although we have had to simplify at every stage, and although the theory of aggregate supply is still in an unsettled state, the basic derivation we have presented is quite robust. Modifying it to take account of variable costs other than wages, of the slow pass-through of costs into prices, of possible variations in the markup, and so forth, will not change the basic outline of a supply curve that shows prices rising relatively little with output in the short run, and that is vertical in the long run. These are the essentials that are brought out by the analysis.

In the remaining sections of this chapter, we examine modifications and implications of the basic analysis.

*11-7 MATERIALS PRICES AND SUPPLY SHOCKS

In this section we extend the aggregate supply framework to discuss an important analytical and practical issue: the treatment of materials prices and *supply shocks*. A supply shock is a disturbance to the economy arising on the supply side of the economy—as, for instance, the increase in food prices in 1973–1974, and, of primary importance, the increases in oil prices in 1973–1974 and 1979–1980. The issue we have to discuss now is how to introduce materials prices—the prices of commodities like oil, zinc, or copper—into the analysis of aggregate supply. Our treatment of this issue makes a few critical simplifying assumptions, but even so, it will capture the essence of a supply shock.

The first step in introducing materials explicitly into the analysis is to recognize that materials are part of costs and that firms will take these costs into account in setting their prices. Next we note that as a matter of fact, materials prices are considerably more volatile than prices of finished goods and, in particular, that they rise relative to finished goods prices in expansions and fall during contractions. We represent this behavior of material prices in Equation (15):

$$P_m = vP + vP\left(\frac{Y}{Y_p} - 1\right) \tag{15}$$

The equation states that materials prices are proportional to the general price level, P, but that they contain a cyclical element. When output is above normal, material prices rise relative to the price level, and when there is a contraction in output, they fall relative to the price level. The full-employment level of material prices is $P_m = vP$.[24]

Our discussion of the pricing behavior of firms in the preceding sections already noted that firms base pricing decisions on normal costs, absorbing cyclical fluctuations in productivity. We will assume the same for materials prices, namely that firms base their pricing decisions on the average or cyclically adjusted price of materials, which we denote P_m' and which can be seen in Equation (15) to be given by $P_m' = vP$.

The extended pricing rule by firms is thus based on labor cost and *normal* material costs:

$$P = bw + cP_m' \tag{16}$$

Substituting for the normal or full-employment material price, we obtain

$$P = bw + cvP \qquad cv < 1 \tag{17}$$

[24] The *real* price of materials, P_m/P, is $P_m/P = v\,(Y/Y_p)$. Thus the real price of materials exceeds or falls short of v depending on whether output is above or below normal.

or

$$P = \frac{b}{1 - cv} w \tag{17a}$$

In the price equation the term c reflects the average use of materials per unit output and is taken as given in the short run. In the long run, though, it may well be a crucial parameter as an economy adjusts its technology to, for example, a change in the real price of oil.

From the revised pricing equation in (17), it is apparent that we are back to an equation like (7), provided the term $b/(1 - cv)$ remains constant. As long as that term is given, we can go ahead and substitute for wages and derive our aggregate supply schedule, the upward slope of which will reflect the cyclical movement of wages. Thus material prices will not make a fundamental difference to the aggregate supply schedule as long as two conditions are met. First, there is the assumption that firms absorb cyclical fluctuations in materials prices and price their goods on the basis of normal material costs. That assumption could easily be modified to allow for a cyclical effect of materials costs on prices. All the modification would do is make the aggregate supply schedule steeper (and nonlinear), as now both material prices and money wages rise during an expansion and fall in a contraction.[25] Second is the assumption that v remains constant, which we now modify.

An interesting application of our model concerns the case where there is an exogenous and permanent change in the real price of materials. The case in point is, of course, the oil price increase. How would we represent such a price increase in terms of our model? First we look at Equation (15) that shows material prices. An increase in the *real* price of materials implies that at each price level P, the price of materials is higher. Thus we can represent the increase in real materials prices as a rise in the factor of proportionality, v.[26]

The next step is to consider firms' adjustment to the increased real materials price. Since the materials price increase is considered permanent rather than transitory, firms will pass on the cost increase in the form of higher prices. In terms of Equation (17), we have an upward shift of the supply schedule at each level of wages.

In Figure 11-15 we show the effect of a materials price increase. We start at full employment with a price level P_0. Now a permanent increase in the real price of materials occurs. What happens to the aggregate supply schedule? At each level of output (and therefore of wages), costs rise and firms pass on the increased costs in the form of higher prices. Supply costs

[25] The interested student can verify this by substituting P_m as shown in Eq. (15) in place of P_m in the price equation. Solving for the price level P will yield an expression that is more strongly cyclical than Eq. (17*a*).

[26] Check Eq. (15) to make sure an increase in v indeed raises P_m/P at any given level of (Y/Y_p).

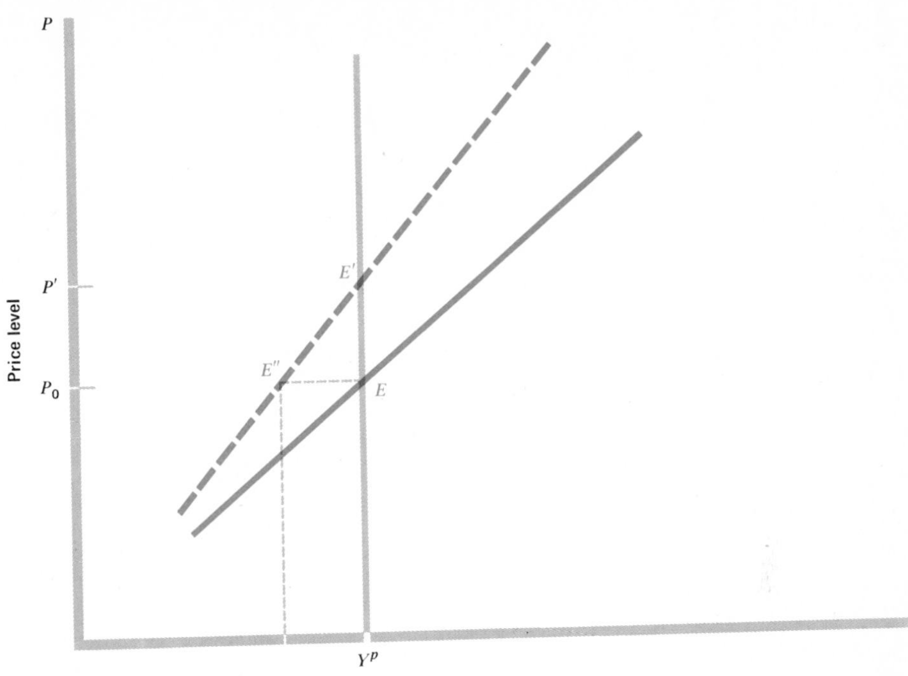

FIGURE 11-15 AN INCREASE IN THE PRICE OF MATERIALS

rise and therefore the whole aggregate supply schedule shifts upward. In addition, the supply curve becomes steeper.

A particularly interesting question, as we shall see in Chapter 16, is the policy choice for an economy faced with a supply shock such as the material price increase that shifts upward the aggregate supply schedule? One possibility is to attempt to maintain full employment at the cost of increased prices. This would correspond to an attempt to reach point E', and it would require an expansionary aggregate demand policy to accommodate the higher price level. Alternatively, there might be a strong preference for price stability and thus a point like E'' might be chosen. At E'', prices are held constant but output declines. Price stability is achieved by a recession sufficient to cut wage costs enough to offset the higher materials prices.

Our extended framework needs two more clarifying comments. The first concerns the full-employment level of output and the question of whether a change in real materials prices, such as the oil shock, reduces the economy's supply potential at full employment. The answer here is quite clearly yes. An increased real cost of materials makes the economy less productive, and even if all labor is employed, we produce less *net* output since we now pay more in real terms for one of the (imported) inputs. Therefore potential output declines. This is a very important fact to recognize because it means that in the face of a major supply shock, such as the oil price increase of 1973–1974, we have to revise our policy targets. It is necessary to make a downward revision in the level (not necessarily the growth rate) of the attainable output path that we can pursue.[27] As Figure 11-15 shows, this implies that the potential output line Y_p will shift to the left.

The second point concerns the behavior of nominal and real wages in the adjustment process. First we consider Equation (17*a*) to find the implication of the materials price increase for *real* wages, w/P. We immediately note that real wages are equal to

$$\frac{w}{P} = \frac{1 - cv}{b} \tag{17b}$$

and that, accordingly, the material price increase lowers real wages. The decline in real wages reflects the fact that the economy has become less productive or that the real price of another input, materials, has increased.[28] The important macroeconomic question is whether this *inevitable* fall in the real wage can be achieved with essentially stable prices or whether it takes inflation and recession—*stagflation*—to bring about the decline in real wages.

One conceivable adjustment to a materials price increase that is accepted as permanent is to have an offsetting reduction in domestic money wages so that the full-employment price level remains unchanged. (This also requires the use of aggregate demand policy, as we shall see in Chapter 12.) Alternatively, as already shown in Figure 11-15, we might have no change in money wages and therefore a rise in the level of prices. In the United States the latter outcome is more likely, as our experience in 1973–1974 suggests.

11-8 PRODUCTIVITY, WAGES, AND PRICES

In this section we take up the issues of the effects of changes in productivity on prices in the short and long runs, and the behavior of the profit rate.

We saw in Section 11-3 that productivity varies procyclically. The

[27] Estimates of the effect of the oil price increase on potential GNP are developed in Robert Rasche and John Tatom, "Energy Resources and Potential GNP," Federal Reserve Bank of St. Louis, *Reveiw*, June 1977.

[28] A subtle point to note is that the price level P is the price of finished goods and not a value-added price index like the GNP deflator. The former contains all costs including imported intermediate goods; the latter contains only labor and domestic materials costs.

question then arises of whether prices should not reflect productivity changes. When output is low, productivity is low, and the cost of production per unit of output is therefore high. Similarly, when there are transitory decreases in productivity because of weather or other disturbances, would prices not be increased? The empirical evidence here is that firms base their pricing decisions on *normal* or *standard unit labor cost*, not on actual or current unit labor cost. That means that firms look at average or cyclically adjusted costs in setting prices. The pricing rule in Equation (7), $P = bw$, thus does not reflect movements in costs arising from productivity changes in the short run. These transitory fluctuations in costs are largely absorbed by firms. Prices are more stable than unit labor costs.

The stability of prices relative to unit labor costs holds for the aggregate price level. However, when we look at the structure of different markets, we find that the prices of some goods, such as agricultural products and raw materials, are very flexible and move more than unit costs. The prices of manufactured products tend to be much more stable. The reason for their stability is presumably the concern of the manufacturers for retaining customer goodwill. The distinction between the behavior of prices in competitive and customer markets has been made by a number of economists, if not in exactly those words, and particularly by Arthur Okun.[29] The distinction is useful in thinking about the behavior of the prices of different goods during the trade cycle, and in understanding the stickiness of some prices.

The response of prices to long-run changes in productivity is different from the response to short-run changes. Productivity grows over time as a result of capital accumulation, learning, and new technology. The growth of productivity implies that as of given wages, costs per unit of output decline—with labor being more productive, it takes fewer hours to produce a unit of output. These permanent or trend increases in productivity do affect prices, since they change standard unit labor cost, as of a given nominal wage. But care is necessary here, since the wage itself is likely to adjust to the change in productivity. With labor being more productive, the neoclassical demand curve for labor in Figure 11-7 is likely to shift out to the right and the real wage will rise over time—as it has historically.[30]

We turn now to the third point in this section—the behavior of the profit rate during the trade cycle. In particular, it is well known that profits tend to rise as the economy expands and to fall as the economy contracts. The behavior of the profit rate is in fact fully consistent with the nonneoclassical theory of supply in this chapter. For we have noted that firms base their prices on normal unit costs. When there is an upswing, the productivity of labor increases and actual unit costs fall. But the prices firms

[29] Arthur Okun, "Inflation: Its Mechanics and Welfare Costs," *Brookings Papers on Economic Activity*, 1975:2 (Washington, D.C.: The Brookings Institution, 1975).

[30] Chapter 17 will discuss the historical behavior of productivity.

charge change relatively little. Therefore their profits rise. Conversely, on the downswing, unit labor costs rise relative to prices and firms have reduced profits.

We make one further point here. As we noted, the term b in Equation (7) is the markup of prices on wages, or more generally, on variable costs. It might seem plausible that firms would increase the markup as the demand for their output increases, and decrease markup as demand falls. That would imply that the real wage would fall as output expands (because P is increasing relative to w). However, evidence on the behavior of real wages during the trade cycle and of the markup is not yet definitive, and it is safest to say that there is no widely agreed-upon empirical evidence that the markup varies systematically with the cycle.[31]

11-9 SUMMARY

This chapter has covered a lot of very hard ground. The major point to be established was that output variations along the short-run aggregate supply schedule are accompanied by only moderate price increases. In the short run, the price level varies little with the level of output. Over time, however, wages, costs, and prices will keep rising if output is above normal and keep falling if output is below normal.

We summarize now the contents of the chapter.

1 The neoclassical theory of the demand for labor relates labor demand only to the real wage, given the quantity of other factors the firm is using. Competitive firms that are free to change the quantity of labor they use, costlessly and immediately, will hire labor up to the point where the real wage is equal to the marginal product of labor (MPN).
2 With wages and prices freely flexible, the equilibrium level of employment is determined in the labor market. The labor market is continuously in equilibrium at the full-employment level, and aggregate supply will therefore be the amount of output which that amount of labor produces. Given that the labor market is in equilibrium, the aggregate supply curve is vertical at the level of potential output—the aggregate supply curve is independent of the price level.
3 The aggregate supply theory we present starts from the recognition that it is costly for the firm to change the level of employment. In deciding how much labor to employ today, firms look ahead to the output level they expect to be producing in the future.
4 Firms accommodate temporary changes in demand largely by changing the amount of overtime their existing labor force works and by adjusting inventories.

[31] See Robert J. Gordon, "The Impact of Aggregate Demand on Prices," *Brookings Papers on Economic Activity*, 1975:3 (Washington, D.C.: The Brookings Institution, 1975).

5 The employment decision depends on both the real wage and the expected level of output. The expected level of output in turn depends on the full-employment level of output and the current level of output. Increases in expected output lead to increases in employment, and increases in the real wage reduce employment.
6 Current output affects current employment by affecting the expected level of output.
7 Nominal wages change in accordance with the state of excess demand in the labor market. When there is unemployment, wages fall, and when there is negative unemployment, wages rise. In this connection, it should be recalled that we abstract in this chapter from the existence of frictional unemployment.
8 Firms base the prices they charge on their costs of production. Thus, when wages rise because the level of employment is above the full-employment level, prices are increased too.
9 To assemble these elements: An increase in output is accompanied by an increase in prices. An increase in output resulting, say, from an increase in aggregate demand affects expected output, leading to an increase in employment. The increase in employment increases the nominal wage, which leads to some increase in the prices firms charge.
10 The full impact of changes in aggregate demand on prices occurs only over the course of time. A permanent increase in aggregate demand feeds slowly into an increased demand for labor, which in turn means wages rise slowly, which in turn means that prices are adjusted only over the course of time. If employment is somehow held above the full-employment level, wages and prices will continue to rise without end.
11 Material prices, along with wages, are a determinant of costs and prices. Firms base prices on normal or cyclically adjusted costs. Transitory changes in material prices are absorbed in profits. Permanent changes are passed on into changes in prices and therefore changes in real wages. Material price changes have been an important source of aggregate supply shocks.
12 Supply shocks, such as a material price increase, pose a difficult problem for macroeconomic policy. They can be accommodated through an expansionary aggregate demand policy with the effect of increased prices but stable output. Alternatively, they can be offset so that prices remain stable because of deflationary aggregate demand policy, but then output falls.

PROBLEMS

1 Using Figure 11-1, analyze the effects of an increase in the money stock on the price level and the level of output.

2 In Problem 1, what happens to the level of real balances as a result of the increase in the nominal money stock?

3 Suppose a new method of production is invented which increases the marginal product of labor at each level of employment.
  (*a*) What effect does this have on the (neoclassical) demand for labor?
  (*b*) What effect does it have on the equilibrium real wage if the supply of labor is fixed and independent of the real wage?
  (*c*) How would your answer to 3(*b*) be affected if the supply of labor increased with the real wage?

4 Suppose that the new method of production increases the average product of labor at each level of employment as well as the marginal product, and revert to the assumption that labor supply is independent of the real wage.
  (*a*) What effect does the invention have on the equilibrium level of real output?
  (*b*) What effect does the invention have on the equilibrium price level? (You will have to use the aggregate demand diagram here.)
  (*c*) What effect does the invention have on the *nominal* wage?
  (*d*) How are your answers to 4(*a*) to (*c*) affected if the supply of labor increases with the real wage?

5 What effect does a rightward shift in the supply curve of labor have on the aggregate supply curve, the equilibrium real wage, and the price level?

We move over now to the nonneoclassical aggregate supply curve developed in Sections 11-4 through 11-6.

6 (*a*) How do you account for the short-run behavior of labor productivity?
  (*b*) What does the neoclassical model imply about the short-run behavior of labor productivity, if one assumes that short-run fluctuations in output are accompanied by movements along a stable demand for labor curve of the sort presented in Figure 11-5?

7 (*a*) Given expected output, why does the real wage affect employment?
  (*b*) In the theory of aggregate supply presented in this chapter, how does the real wage behave (does it go up or down?) when there is an increase in output?

8 Suppose that all firms believed that the current level of output Y, whatever its level, was the long-run level of output Y^e, so that the weight α in Equation (3) was one.
  (*a*) How would that affect the slope of the aggregate supply curve? Be careful.
  (*b*) Explain for what particular aspect of the behavior of the economy in the short run the value of α in Equation (3) matters. Choose from (*i*) the slope of the aggregate supply curve, (*ii*) the behavior of the real wage, (*iii*) the behavior of labor productivity in the short run, and (*iv*) the behavior of the money wage in the short run. Explain your answer.

9 Suppose the natural rate of unemployment is 5 percent. How would the rate of unemployment u, defined in Equation (6), be related to the officially published unemployment rate, u_p, which includes frictional unemployment?

10 (*a*) How does the variable ϵ affect the slope of the aggregate supply curve?
  (*b*) How does the markup b affect the slope of the supply curve? Explain.

*11 How does an increase in materials prices P_m affect the aggregate supply curve?

*12 Assume, as in Section 11-5, that wages are the only variable cost. However, now assume that wages are passed on slowly into prices, so that Equation (7) is replaced by

$$P = b[cw + (1 - c)w_{-1}] \qquad 0 < c < 1 \tag{7a}$$

Use Equation (7a) together with the other equations to derive the aggregate supply curve. Note that the position of the supply curve will depend on the lagged wage rate. How does the slope of the aggregate supply curve compare now with the case in the text, for which $c = 1$?

12
INCOME, PRICES, AND UNEMPLOYMENT

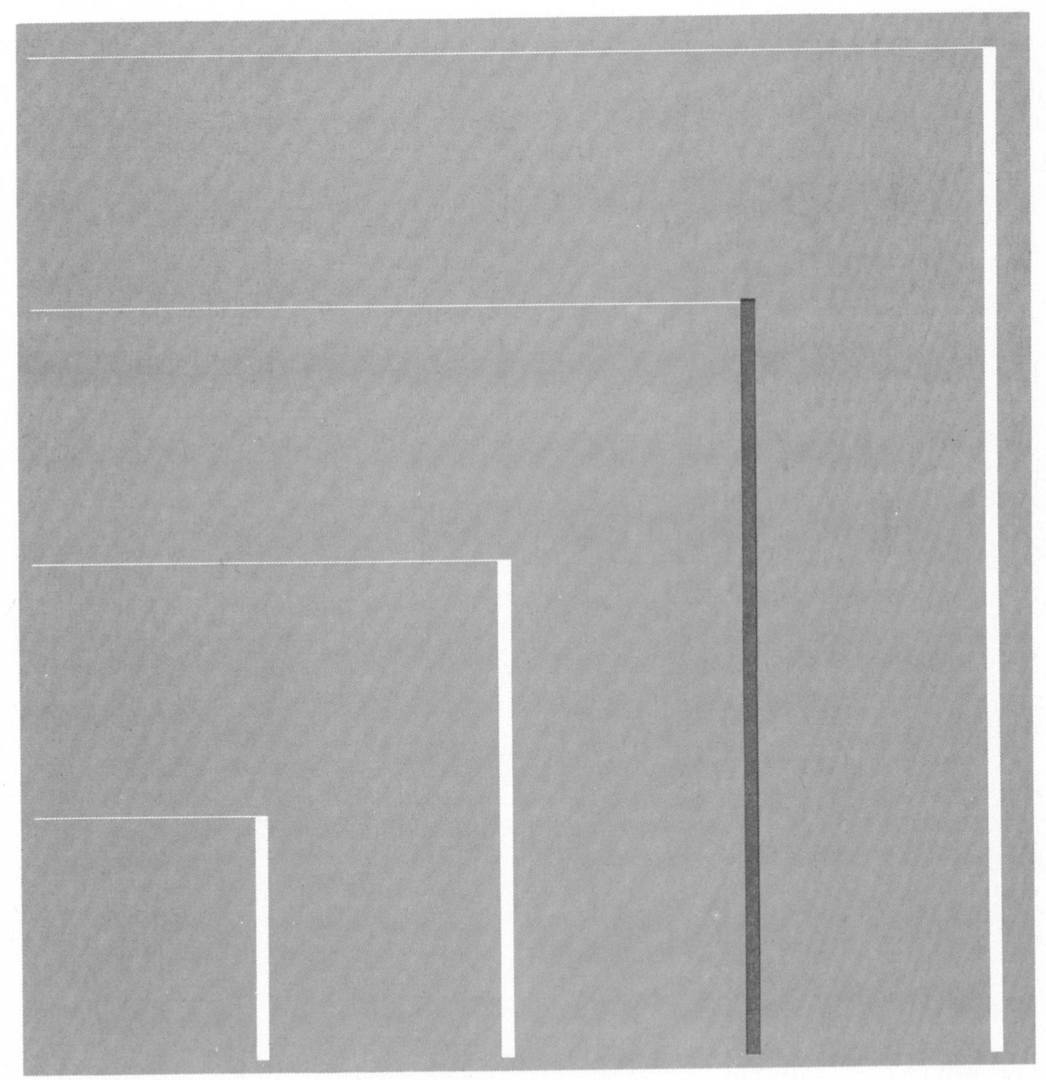

In this chapter we combine aggregate supply, studied in Chapter 11, with aggregate demand, as studied in Chapter 4 and outlined in Chapter 11. The resulting analysis leads to the simultaneous determination of most of the important macroeconomic variables—the level of output, the price level, interest rates, and (un)employment.[1] This chapter, therefore, extends the analysis of Chapter 4 by explicitly introducing the price level as one of the variables to be determined. Recall that throughout Chapter 4 we took the price level P to be fixed. The price level is, of course, far from constant. The extension of the IS-LM analysis to examine the determination of the price level is therefore an extremely important step.

The analysis in this chapter further differs from the IS-LM framework in that it is essentially dynamic. The discussion of the supply side in the previous chapter introduced the distinction between the short-run and the long-run aggregate supply curves. That distinction is important in this chapter because it is the basis on which we distinguish between the short-run, intermediate-run, and long-run effects of monetary and fiscal policies on output and prices.

12-1 AGGREGATE DEMAND

In this section we derive the *aggregate demand function* in more detail than in Chapter 11. The aggregate demand function is a relationship between the planned level of real spending or demand for goods and the level of prices, *given* the quantity of money and fiscal policy. Since it is a relationship between the quantity of goods demanded and the price level, and since it will be seen to be downward-sloping, it looks like the regular demand curve of microeconomics. In this case, however, we consider the *aggregate* demand for all goods and services as a function of the *aggregate* price level rather than the demand for a single good as a function of its (relative) price. Further, as we noted in Chapter 1, there is a lot behind the aggregate demand curve. It summarizes the equilibrium of both goods and assets markets.

In Chapter 4 we saw how the level of aggregate demand is determined by autonomous spending and the money stock. More formally, we can use the aggregate demand function, introduced in Equation (14) in Chapter 4:

$$Y = \beta\bar{A} + \gamma\frac{\bar{M}}{P} \tag{1}$$

$$\beta \equiv \frac{h\bar{\alpha}}{h + bk\bar{\alpha}} \qquad \gamma \equiv \frac{b\bar{\alpha}}{h + bk\bar{\alpha}}$$

[1] The only important macroeconomic variable that is not studied explicitly in this chapter is the inflation rate; its behavior is analyzed in detail in Chap. 13.

where the terms β and γ are, respectively, the "multipliers" associated with fiscal and monetary policy and incorporate the interaction between goods and money markets. The term $\overline{A}$ denotes autonomous spending, including fiscal variables, $\overline{M}/\overline{P}$ is the quantity of real balances, and Y is measured in *real* terms.

Equation (1) expresses the *joint* equilibrium of the goods and assets markets. It summarizes the basic results of Chapter 4: First, that the higher the level of autonomous spending (the farther out to the right the IS curve), the higher the equilibrium level of income; and, second, that the higher the real money supply (the farther to the right the LM curve), the higher the equilibrium level of income.

In deriving Equation (1), we explicitly assumed that any level of real output that was demanded could be produced, at the given price level. We thus ignored any constraints that might exist on aggregate supply. In this chapter, we shall explicitly consider the interaction of supply and demand. Accordingly, we do not treat Equation (1) as determining the level of output, but only as determining the level of demand *at a given price level.* If demand does not equal supply at that price level, then the price level is not an equilibrium price level and output is not at the equilibrium level either. The interaction of supply and demand determines the equilibrium levels of prices and real output, as shown in Chapter 11.

We shall now use Equation (1), together with the IS-LM analysis on which it is based, to study the relationship between the level of spending—the demand for goods—and the price level, given the nominal quantity of money and autonomous spending. It is obvious from inspection of Equation (1) that a higher price level implies lower real balances and therefore a lower equilibrium level of income and spending. This relationship is shown as the $Y^d(F,M/P)$ curve in Figure 12-1, where F represents the term $\beta\overline{A}$ in Equation (1).[2] To understand the relationship between aggregate demand and the price level that is shown in Figure 12-1, we turn to the IS and LM curves that underlie that relationship.

In Figure 12-2*a* we show the familiar IS and LM schedules. In Figure 12-2*b* we show the aggregate demand schedule. Consider first a price level P_0. Given fiscal policy, we have an IS curve. A given nominal quantity of money together with the price level P_0 will imply a quantity of real balances M/P_0 and an associated LM_0 curve. The equilibrium level of income is Y_0^d. Accordingly, we show point E_0 in the lower panel as one point on the aggregate demand schedule, or one combination of price and output levels such that both the goods market and money market are in equilibrium.

Consider next a lower price level P_1. Given the nominal quantity of money, the decline in the price level raises *real* balances to M/P_1, and

[2] We use the symbol F to emphasize that fiscal variables affect the position of the aggregate demand curve by affecting the term $\beta\overline{A}$.

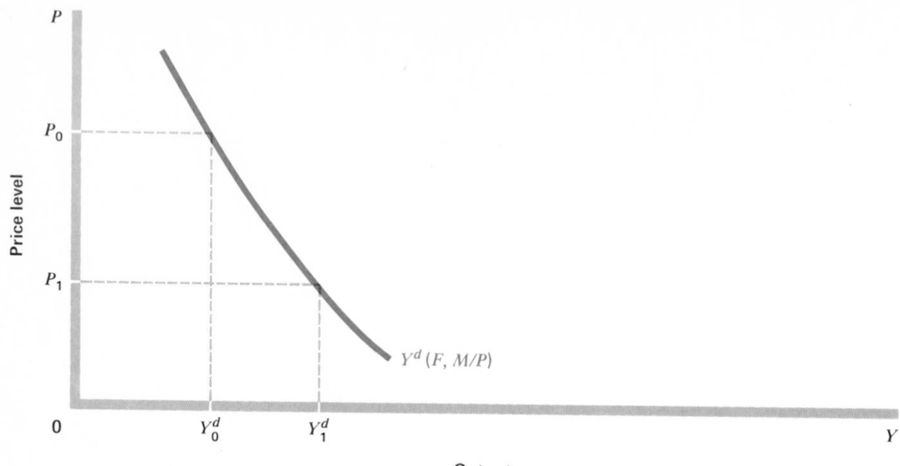

FIGURE 12-1 THE AGGREGATE DEMAND CURVE

therefore shifts the LM schedule to the right to LM′. The LM schedule shifts down and to the right because in order to induce the public to hold a larger quantity of real balances, income would have to be higher or interest rates would have to be lower. The new equilibrium level of income and spending is Y_1^d, and we record E_1 as another point on the aggregate demand schedule in Figure 12-2*b*. The schedule of points on the aggregate demand curve is obtained by considering all possible price levels. It is the schedule generated by the intersection of the IS and LM curves as the price level changes, namely, $Y^d(F,M/P)$ in Figure 12-1, that we refer to as the aggregate demand schedule. It is clear from the way we have derived the schedule that we can think of it as a *market equilibrium* schedule—the locus of points along which *both* the money market and the goods market are in equilibrium, given the value of autonomous spending and the nominal money supply.

Before we conclude this section, we want to give an economic interpretation of the aggregate demand relationship. Suppose that the goods and money markets are initially in equilibrium, so that we are at a point on the aggregate demand curve. Then let the price level increase. The higher price level reduces real balances and thereby creates an excess demand for real money balances at the given level of income. The excess demand for real balances raises interest rates. The increase in interest rates in turn reduces real spending by discouraging investment, and therefore leads to a decline in the equilibrium level of income. Thus the initial price increase leads to a decline in demand, so that the aggregate demand curve is negatively sloped.

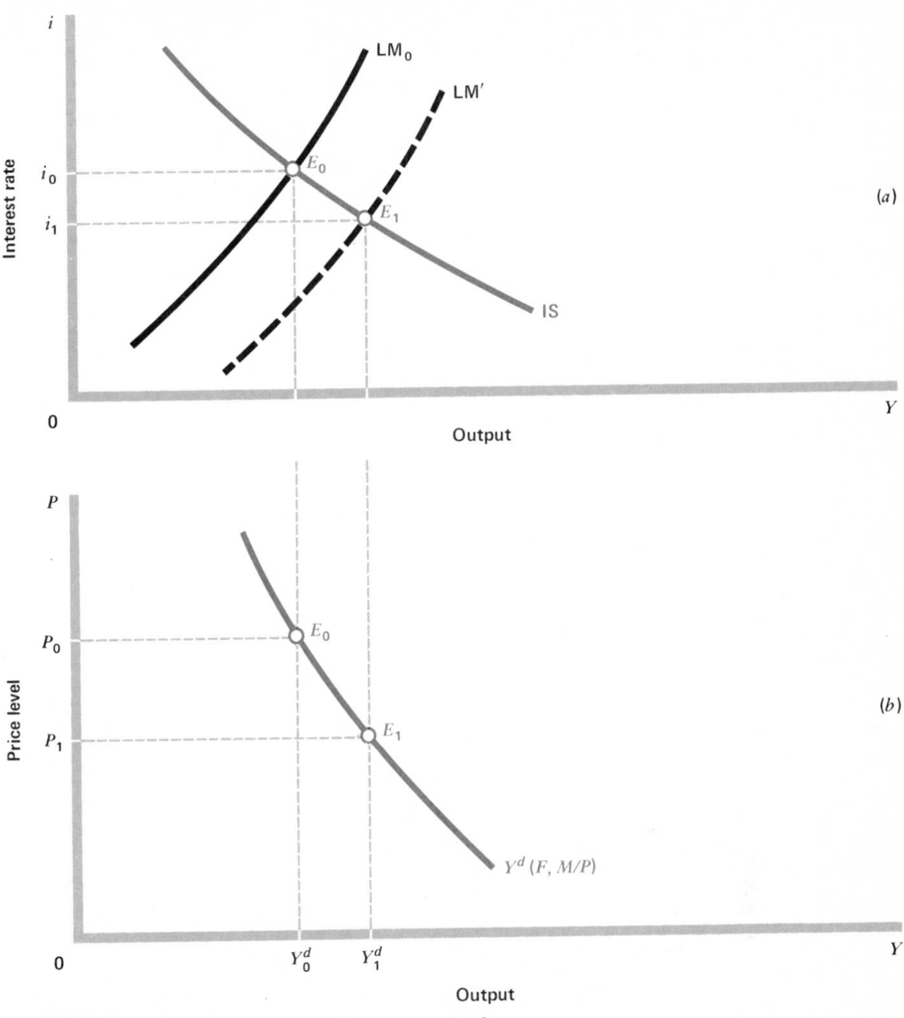

FIGURE 12-2 THE AGGREGATE DEMAND CURVE AS DERIVED FROM THE IS AND LM CURVES

There are two critical points to remember about the aggregate demand curve. The first is that autonomous spending and the nominal money supply are held constant as we move along the schedule. The second point can be seen by noting that the interest rate at E_1 in Figure 12-2 is lower than the interest rate at E_0—the point is that the interest rate declines as the level of income rises along the aggregate demand curve. The declining interest rate derives from the fact that with a given *nominal* quantity of money, a decline in the price level implies an increase in *real* balances. This increase in real balances lowers interest rates. The lower interest rate in turn raises investment spending and has an expansionary effect on aggregate demand and income. Thus, as we move down the aggregate demand curve, a falling rate of interest accompanies a rising level of real demand and a falling price level.

12-2 PROPERTIES OF THE AGGREGATE DEMAND SCHEDULE

There are two sets of questions we look at here: First, what determines the slope of the aggregate demand schedule? Second, how does the aggregate demand schedule shift in response to changes in fiscal policy and the nominal money supply?

The Slope of the Aggregate Demand Curve

The answer to the first question is fortunately very easy. We can draw on considerations developed in the discussion of monetary policy in Chapter 4. We asked there what determines the effectiveness of monetary policy—the increase in income associated with an increase in the money supply. We studied that question by increasing the money supply at a given price level, that is, by increasing the real money supply. The slope of the aggregate demand schedule in Figure 12-2 reflects the answer to exactly the same question. The reason that the question is the same is that Figure 12-2 relates a change in the real money supply to the resulting change in the equilibrium level of income and spending. However, this time the real money supply changes because the price level changes. The amount by which a given change in prices, and therefore in the real money supply, changes the equilibrium level of income and spending depends primarily on the response of money demand to the interest rate and the response of aggregate spending to the interest rate.

A low interest response of money demand and a high interest response of aggregate spending ensure a large effect of real money changes on output. The reason, as will be remembered from Chapter 4, is that a low interest response of money demand implies that a given change in real balances brings about a large change in interest rates. Given a change in interest rates, a large interest response of aggregate spending serves to translate the interest reduction into a large increase in spending. It follows, therefore, that the aggregate demand schedule is relatively flat—large changes in income and spending are associated with small changes in the price level—if monetary policy is very effective, that is, if the interest response of money demand is low and the interest response of spending is high.

The slope of the aggregate demand curve depends also on the multiplier $\overline{\alpha}$. Other things equal, a given reduction in the price level and an increase in real balances give rise to a larger increase in income and spending, the larger the multiplier or the larger the marginal propensity to spend. Accordingly, a large multiplier serves to flatten the aggregate demand function.[3]

The Effects of Monetary and Fiscal Policy Changes on the Aggregate Demand Curve

We turn now to the second question, which asks about the effects of changes in fiscal policy and the nominal money supply on the location of the aggregate demand curve. We are now examining the effects of variables that cause the entire aggregate demand curve to *shift*. In Section 12-1, by contrast, we were considering only movements along a *given* aggregate demand curve on which fiscal variables and the nominal money supply are kept constant. Before we proceed to a detailed graphical examination of the effects of an increase in the nominal money stock or expansionary fiscal policy on the aggregate demand curve, it is worth stepping back for a moment to ask what we expect to find.

We already know from Chapter 4 and Equation (1) that an increase in the nominal money supply increases aggregate demand as of a fixed price level. Thus we should expect an increase in the nominal money supply to shift the aggregate demand curve of Figure 12-1 outward, reflecting the increase in the demand for goods at a given price level that is caused by the change in the money stock. Similarly, we know that expansionary fiscal policy, such as an increase in government spending or a reduction in taxes, increases aggregate demand at a given price level. Accordingly, expansionary fiscal policy should also be expected to shift the aggregate demand curve outward.

We will now examine the effect of the policy changes in more detail. In Figure 12-3 we show the effects on the aggregate demand curve of an increase in the nominal quantity of money. Similarly, in Figure 12-4 we show the effects of an increase in government spending.

Consider first an increase in the nominal quantity of money. We are asking the following question: What is the effect of an increase in the nominal quantity of money on the equilibrium level of income and spending *at a given price level* P_0? The answer to that question will be the shift in the aggregate demand schedule. We know that for a given price level, an increase in the nominal quantity of money implies an increase in the real quantity of money. There is, therefore, a rightward shift in the LM curve to

[3] It will be useful for you to show the above propositions on the slope of the aggregate demand curve using Fig. 12-2. See prob. 2 at the end of the chapter.

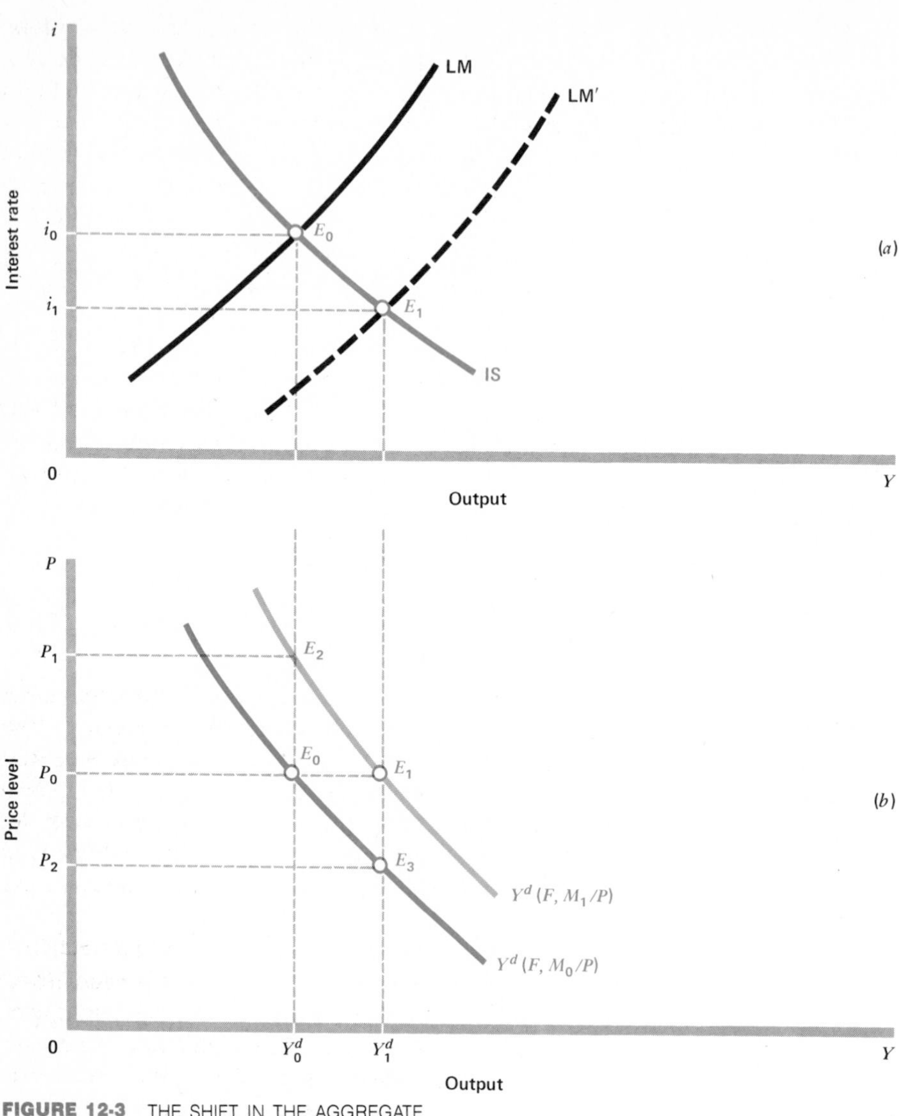

FIGURE 12-3 THE SHIFT IN THE AGGREGATE DEMAND CURVE DUE TO AN INCREASE IN THE NOMINAL MONEY SUPPLY ($M_1 > M_0$)

LM′, as in Figure 12-3*a*. As a consequence, the equilibrium level of income rises to Y_1^d. What happens is that at the given level of prices P_0, the higher nominal quantity of money implies a higher real quantity of money and therefore lower interest rates and higher equilibrium income and spending. We record this fact in Figure 12-3*b* by noting that point E_1 is a point on the new aggregate demand schedule.

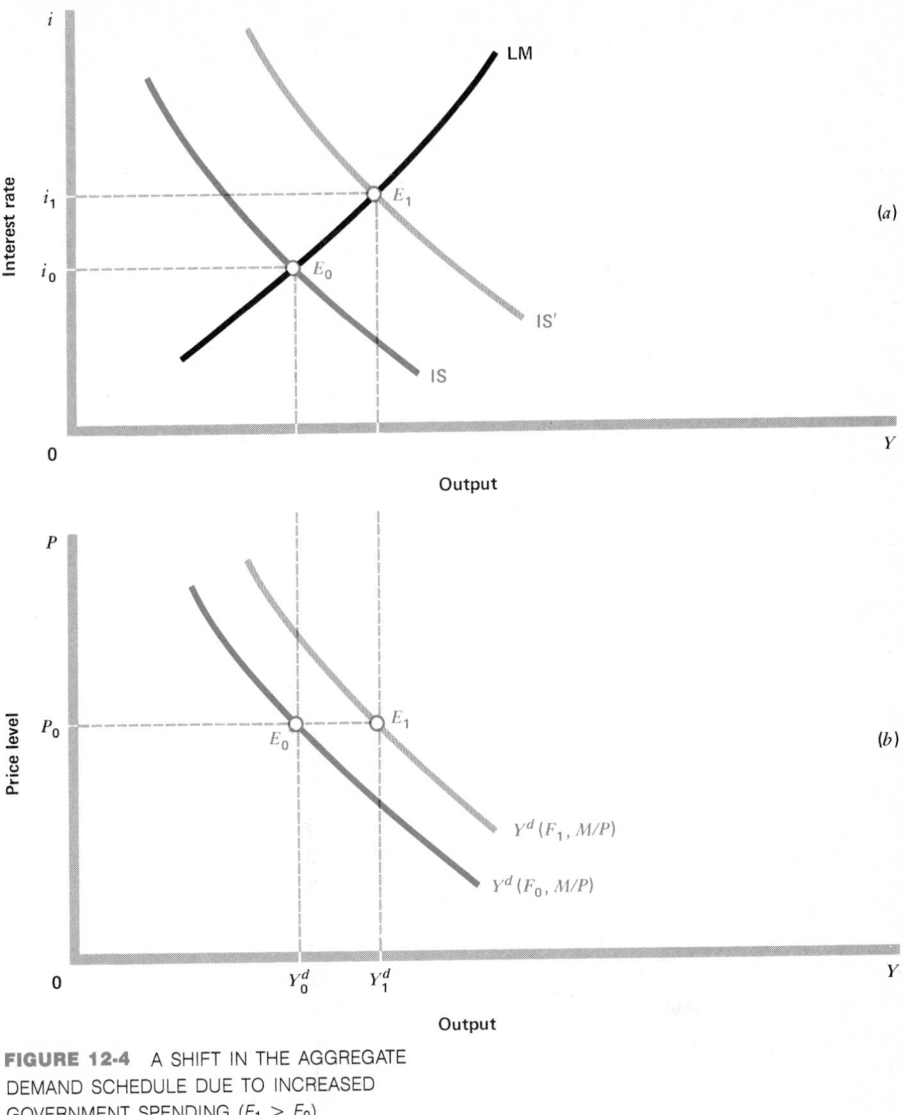

FIGURE 12-4 A SHIFT IN THE AGGREGATE DEMAND SCHEDULE DUE TO INCREASED GOVERNMENT SPENDING ($F_1 > F_0$)

The initial equilibrium price level was chosen arbitrarily. We could have started with any price level and thereby shown that the entire aggregate demand schedule shifts to the right.

There is an alternative and important way of recognizing the same point. When the nominal money supply increases, we could ask by how much the equilibrium price level would have to rise, at each level of income and spending, in order for aggregate demand to remain unchanged. It is clear from Equation (1) that aggregate demand would remain unchanged if the real money supply remained unchanged. Given an increase in the nominal money supply, we would therefore require prices to increase in such a way that M/P remains constant. In terms of Figure 12-3, this implies that an increase in the nominal money supply shifts the aggregate demand schedule up in exactly the same proportion as the increase in the nominal money stock. Thus the ratio P_1/P_0 in Figure 12-3 is the same as the ratio P_0/P_2, and each ratio is equal to M_1/M_0. This upward shift reflects an essential characteristic of aggregate demand, namely, that an equiproportionate increase in money and prices leaves the real money supply and therefore interest rates and real spending unchanged.[4]

Consider next the effect of an expansionary fiscal policy on the aggregate demand schedule. In Figure 12-4 we show that an expansionary fiscal policy in the form of increased government purchases or reduced taxes leads to an upward shift of the IS curve and a resulting increase in real income. At a given price level P_0, the fiscal expansion raises the equilibrium level of income and spending. In the lower graph this fact is recorded by point E_1 as a point on the new aggregate demand schedule. Since we could have started with any price level and corresponding LM curve in the upper panel, it is immediately apparent that, corresponding to the easier fiscal policy, we have a new aggregate demand schedule that lies everywhere to the right of the initial schedule. In fact, the rightward shift of the aggregate demand schedule at each price level, $\beta\Delta\bar{A}$, is related to the multiplier β in the equation for equilibrium aggregate demand, Equation (1). From the definition of β, it is apparent that the shift in the aggregate demand curve is larger, the larger the interest response of money demand, the lower the interest response of aggregate spending, and the smaller the income response of money demand.

Before proceeding, we summarize here the main points about aggregate demand: (1) The concept of aggregate demand provides a relation between the equilibrium level of income and spending and the level of prices. (2) The aggregate demand schedule is negatively sloped because a reduction in the price level raises real balances, reduces interest rates, and thereby raises the equilibrium level of income and spending. (3) An increase in the nominal quantity of money, or an expansionary fiscal policy, shifts the aggregate demand schedule up and to the right; equivalently, an expansionary monetary or fiscal policy raises the equilibrium level of income and spending at each level of prices.

[4] As a technical point, we refer to this property of the aggregate demand function as *homogeneity* of degree zero in money and prices. This means that an equiproportionate increase in money and prices leaves *real* demand unchanged.

12-3 THE INTERACTION OF AGGREGATE DEMAND AND AGGREGATE SUPPLY

As in Chapter 11, we now combine aggregate demand and supply to derive the full equilibrium of the system, including supply constraints. In Figure 12-5, we draw the aggregate demand schedule corresponding to a given fiscal policy and nominal quantity of money. The short-run aggregate supply curve was derived in Chapter 11. Its positive slope reflects the sluggish adjustment of wages to output changes.[5] The long-run supply curve is vertical and corresponds to the vertical Y_pY_p line at the level of potential output.

As we have drawn it, the initial equilibrium at E is one of underemployment. Output is below the level of potential output and, accordingly, the level of unemployment is above normal. How does the economy adjust over time from the equilibrium at point E? The high level of unemployment at E will imply declining wages. Declining wages in turn reduce costs and shift the supply schedule down and to the right over time. The downward shift in the supply schedule in turn causes equilibrium prices to decline, real balances to rise, interest rates to fall, and aggregate spending

[5] Recall that the aggregate supply curve developed in Chap. 11 explicitly does *not* take account of the role of expected inflation in affecting wages. We examine the very important role of expected inflation in Chap. 13.

FIGURE 12-5 THE INTERACTION OF AGGREGATE DEMAND AND SUPPLY

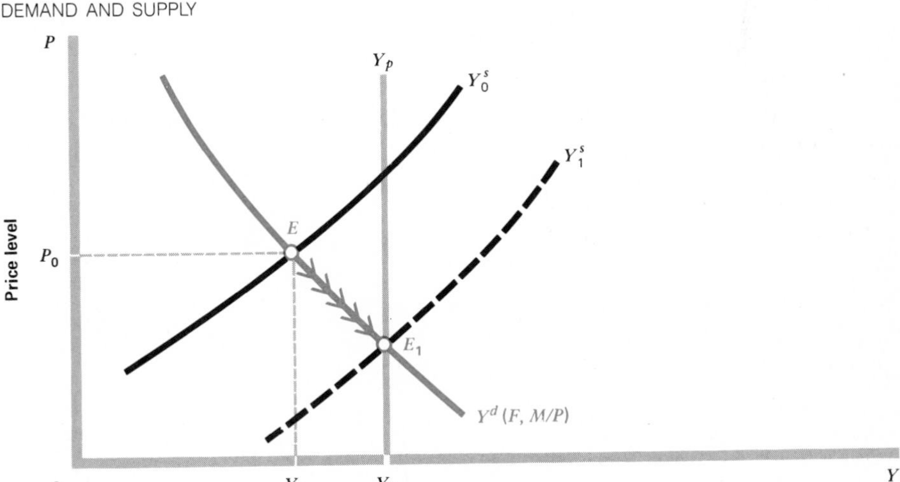

to increase. The adjustment process is therefore one of falling prices and increasing aggregate spending. The process of adjustment is represented by the arrows along the aggregate demand curve in Figure 12-5, which you will recognize as equivalent to Figure 11-3. This *automatic* process will continue until prices have declined sufficiently (and wages have also declined sufficiently) for aggregate demand to support the full-employment level of output Y_p at point E_1.

There is a critical lesson here. The point is that the levels of output and employment depend on aggregate demand which in turn depends on the real money supply, as we have seen in Equation (1). If wages are sluggish in the short run, then the real money supply (given the nominal supply of money) cannot rise fast enough to support full employment. Only over time and with protracted unemployment will wages decline to lower prices and raise real balances sufficiently to support full employment. In a world of perfect wage and price flexibility, we would always be at full employment. With sluggish wages and prices, by contrast, there is no assurance that we are always at full employment. Consequently, monetary and fiscal stabilization policy may be called upon to improve the macroeconomic performance implied by this *automatic* adjustment process.

Specifically, if aggregate demand, *at the current level of prices*, is insufficient to support the full-employment level of output, as at point E in Figure 12-5, an expansion in aggregate demand is called for. As we saw earlier, an expansion in the nominal quantity of money, or expansionary fiscal policy, would, by shifting the aggregate demand schedule, raise equilibrium income and spending at each level of prices. Expansionary aggregate demand policies can therefore be used to support full employment at the prevailing level of wages. In terms of Figure 12-5, expansionary policies shift the $Y^d(F,M/P)$ curve up and to the right. We have seen how the economy can undergo deflation to adjust the level of wages and prices to the prevailing quantity of money to reach the equilibrium at E_1. Alternatively, we may use monetary and fiscal policy to shift the aggregate demand curve to the right and thus move output to its full-employment level at the given wage rate.

There is a compelling logic to the argument that we should adapt the level of the nominal quantity of money to the prevailing level of wages and prices, rather than use unemployment or inflation to adapt wages and prices to whatever is the quantity of money. In the next two sections we shall study in considerably more detail how monetary policy and fiscal policy work in this more complete model. In particular, we are interested in the distinction between short-run and long-run effects of policies. The crucial point we shall make is that in the short run, both monetary and fiscal policy can be expansionary. In the long run, neither is expansionary, although fiscal policy retains some important real effects.

12-4 MONETARY POLICY

In this section, we examine the effects of an increase in the money stock. In Figure 12-6, we show the effect of an increase in the *nominal* quantity of money from M_0 to M_1 as a rightward shift in the aggregate demand schedule. As was shown in Figure 12-3, the aggregate demand schedule shifts upward in the same proportion as the increase in the nominal quantity of money. In Figure 12-6, we start with equilibrium at E, where output is at its potential level. In the short run, the increase in the money supply creates excess demand for goods at the initial price level. The excess demand in turn gives rise to an expansion in output and an increase in prices. The position of short-run equilibrium is at point E_1, where aggregate demand equals short-run supply. E_1 is also a point at which output exceeds potential output.

It is important to go behind the schedules for a moment to examine again the factors that account for the change in *real* output as a consequence of a change in the *nominal* quantity of money. On the supply side, the basic factor is the slow adjustment of nominal wages. The more sluggish the wages, the flatter the aggregate supply schedule and, accordingly, the larger the short-run expansion in output. Thus we retain the result from

FIGURE 12-6 THE EFFECTS OF MONETARY EXPANSION IN THE AGGREGATE DEMAND AND SUPPLY MODEL

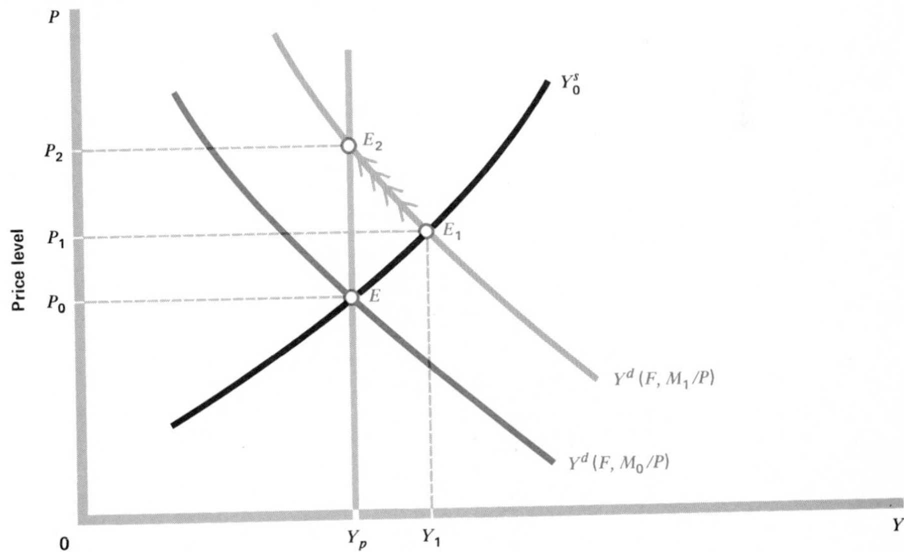

the supply side that sluggish wages imply that an increase in prices allows an expansion in real output.

On the aggregate demand side, we note that an increase in the nominal money stock also increases the real money stock *provided* prices do not rise to offset fully the increase in the nominal money supply. We recall from Section 12-2 that the increase in the nominal money supply shifts the aggregate demand schedule up in the same proportion as the increase in the money stock. Thus $(P_2 - P_0)/P_0$ in Figure 12-7 is the proportionate increase in the money stock. Since in the short run prices increase by only $(P_1 - P_0)/P_0$, we clearly have an increase in real balances. The increase in real balances causes a reduction in interest rates and, therefore, an increase in real aggregate demand. The fact that prices increase proportionately less than nominal money accounts for the expansion in real demand that sustains the higher level of output. At point E_1, therefore, we have a lower interest rate than at E, and that decline in the interest rate accounts for the higher level of real aggregate demand.

However, the short-run equilibrium at point E_1 is only transitory. The process of the shifting of the supply curve, caused by rising wages induced by overemployment, sets in, as in Figure 12-5. How long will the process continue? Wages will continue rising as long as output is above potential. So the supply schedule will keep shifting until point E_2 is reached. At that point, output has returned to normal: wages, prices, and the nominal

FIGURE 12-7 THE EFFECTS OF EXPANSIONARY FISCAL POLICY

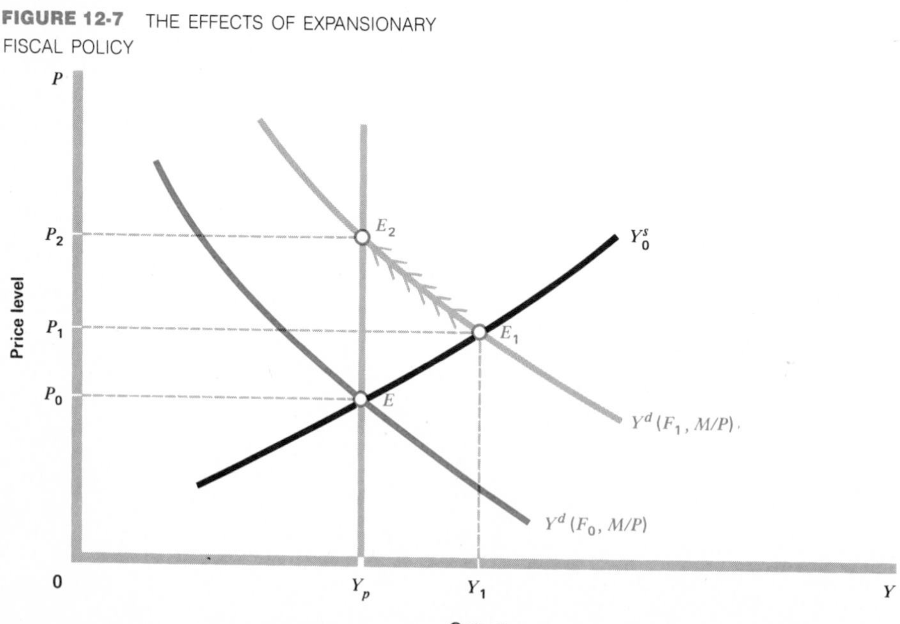

quantity of money *all* have increased in the same proportion. All real variables, including output and interest rates, have returned to their initial equilibrium.

The property of the economy whereby changes in the nominal quantity of money affect only nominal variables (the price level and wages), leaving all real variables unchanged, is referred to as the *neutrality of money*. We have just seen that money is neutral in the long run for an economy starting at full employment. We saw in Section 12-3 that when the economy is not initially at full employment, it adjusts over time until full employment is reached. Thus, even if the economy does not start at full employment, an increase in the money stock is neutral in the long run since it has no long-run effects on real variables. While it should be well understood that money is neutral in the long run, it should also be understood that monetary expansion causes an increase in output in the short run. Thus, money is not neutral in the short run. Accordingly, monetary policy can be used as a tool of stabilization policy to affect the behavior of real variables, such as the levels of output and unemployment.

12-5 FISCAL POLICY

Consider next the effects of an expansionary fiscal policy. Referring to Figure 12-7, we again start with a full-employment equilibrium at point E with output at its potential level Y_p. An expansion in government purchases or a cut in taxes will shift the aggregate demand schedule to the right and thus create an excess demand for goods at the initial level of prices. The resulting increase in output and prices serves to clear markets and establish a short-run equilibrium at point E_1. On the supply side, as in the discussion of monetary policy, we note that the sluggishness of wages allows an expansion in output and employment when prices rise. On the aggregate demand side at point E_1, a higher level of real spending is sustained by a higher level of government spending, or higher autonomous private spending due to tax cuts.

An important question concerns the interest rate at point E_1. Unlike the case of a monetary expansion, the interest rate at point E_1 is actually higher than at point E. It has increased to maintain balance between the demand for and supply of real balances. To establish that point, we observe that the increase in prices between E and E_1 implies that we have a lower quantity of real balances. Further, the expansion in output causes an increase in real money demand. To reduce the demand for real money to the new lower level of real supply, we clearly require a higher interest rate.

In the short run, a fiscal expansion raises output and employment. As in the case of monetary expansion, it will be more expansionary the flatter the aggregate supply curve—equivalently, the lower the responsiveness of costs to an expansion in output. Now consider again the adjustments that arise from the reduction in unemployment below normal. The resulting wage pressure will raise costs and thereby shift up the supply schedule. Again, the resulting price increase will reduce the real money supply, raise interest rates, and reduce real spending. In consequence, we will move up and along the aggregate demand schedule from E_1 to E_2 until output has returned to the potential level.

The next question to ask is, What will have happened once we return to the potential output level at E_2? It is apparent from Figure 12-7 that prices will have risen. The higher level of prices, given money, will have raised interest rates just sufficiently to reduce private real spending by exactly the increase in government spending. It is therefore true that, with long-run output given, increased purchases (absorption) of goods by the government leave fewer resources available for private purchases. The process by which the private sector is *crowded out*[6] in the long run is through higher prices and therefore higher interest rates.

The fact that in the long run private sector spending is displaced by increased government spending is entirely a consequence of the assumption that long-run output is fixed, so that if the government absorbs more, less is left to the private sector. This long-run crowding-out feature does not imply, however, that in the short run, government spending is ineffective in expanding output and aggregate demand. Again, it is critical to bear in mind that the long-run equilibrium is primarily an indication of a position to which the economy will adjust, given enough time. It should not be thought of as the point toward which the economy moves as the immediate short-run consequence of expansionary fiscal policy. It is true that the long-run interpretation of this model confirms the view that increased government spending always occurs at the expense of private real spending. While this view may be correct in the long run,[7] it does not establish the case against active fiscal policy as a tool of short-run stabilization.

The relationship between fiscal policy and interest rates can be inferred too from Figure 12-8, which includes the familiar IS curve. We have drawn in the initial IS schedule and the IS′ schedule corresponding to the increase in government spending. We also include a vertical line indicating potential output. Starting from the initial equilibrium at point E, the fiscal expansion first raises output and interest rates to some point like E_1. Subsequently, the rising prices cause the LM schedule (not drawn) to shift up and to the left so that the equilibrium moves along the IS′ schedule until potential output is reestablished. At that point, the interest rate will

[6] Crowding out was defined in Chap. 4. As an exercise, show the effect of a tax cut on the long-run level and composition of private spending.

[7] We say "may be" because we have here disregarded the effects of fiscal policy on the rate of investment and thus on the capital stock. See the problem set in Chap. 17 for further discussion.

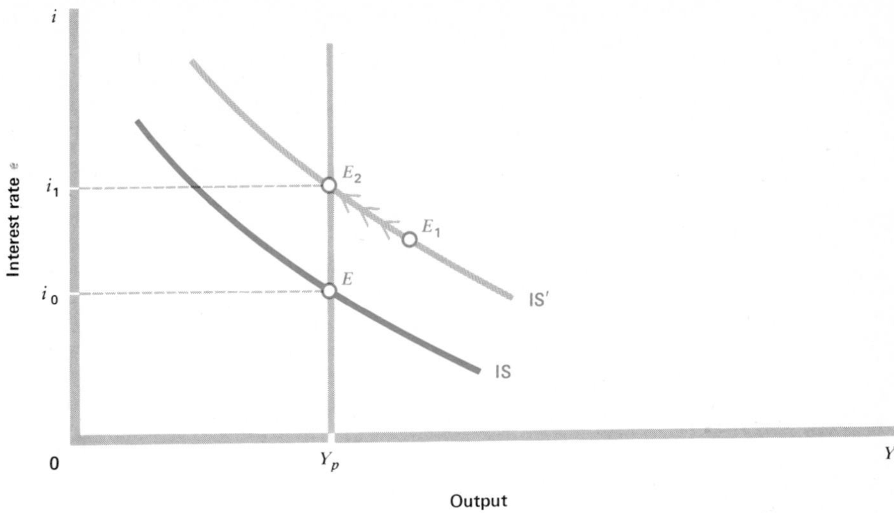

FIGURE 12-8 THE LONG-RUN EFFECT OF FISCAL EXPANSION ON INTEREST RATES

have risen just enough to restore goods market equilibrium at the initial level of output.

12-6 DISTURBANCES, POLICY RESPONSE, AND SUPPLY MANAGEMENT

The preceding discussion prepares us for an analysis of macroeconomic disturbances and policy responses. Now that we have extended the IS-LM framework to include aggregate supply as well as aggregate demand, we can consider disturbances that arise either on the supply or the demand side of the economy. On the demand side, we can consider disturbances such as autonomous changes in money demand or shifts in the consumption or investment functions. Each such change will shift the aggregate demand function and therefore disturb the macroeconomic equilibrium. On the supply side, we can look at disturbances, such as exogenous increases in materials costs or changes in taxes on goods or labor, that shift the supply schedule.

The extension of our basic IS-LM framework to include supply considerations allows us to discuss the new interest in fiscal policy as a tool of *supply management*. This view holds that fiscal policy in the form of variations in indirect taxes or payroll taxes can be used to offset supply disturbances, while both monetary and fiscal policy can be used to maintain aggregate demand at the full-employment level of output.

We will now go through the effects of an increase in payroll taxes on aggregate supply. The analysis will show that the supply side effects of such a policy are to *increase* prices and *reduce* output. Accordingly, a *cut* in payroll taxes can be used as a stimulative, and relative to other tax cuts, noninflationary stabilization policy.

To explore this view of fiscal policy effects on aggregate supply, we consider the case of an increase in payroll taxes, that is, taxes on wages. When there is a tax on wages, the wage paid to workers is less than the wage paid by employers. We assume that the wage paid to workers adjusts only with changes in the unemployment rate. More technically, we assume that in the short run the *incidence* of the payroll tax is on employers. Accordingly, an increase in labor costs due to payroll taxes will lead firms to pass on that cost increase in the form of higher prices. It follows that the supply schedule shifts up and to the left at each level of output. In Figure 12-9, we show that an increase in payroll taxes causes the economy to move from its initial equilbirium at point E to a new equilibrium at point E_1 with higher prices and lower output. An increase in payroll taxes raises prices because it raises costs, given the wage rate. Output declines because the cost and price increases reduce the real money supply, raise interest rates, and therefore reduce real spending.

FIGURE 12-9 THE SUPPLY EFFECT OF A PAYROLL TAX INCREASE

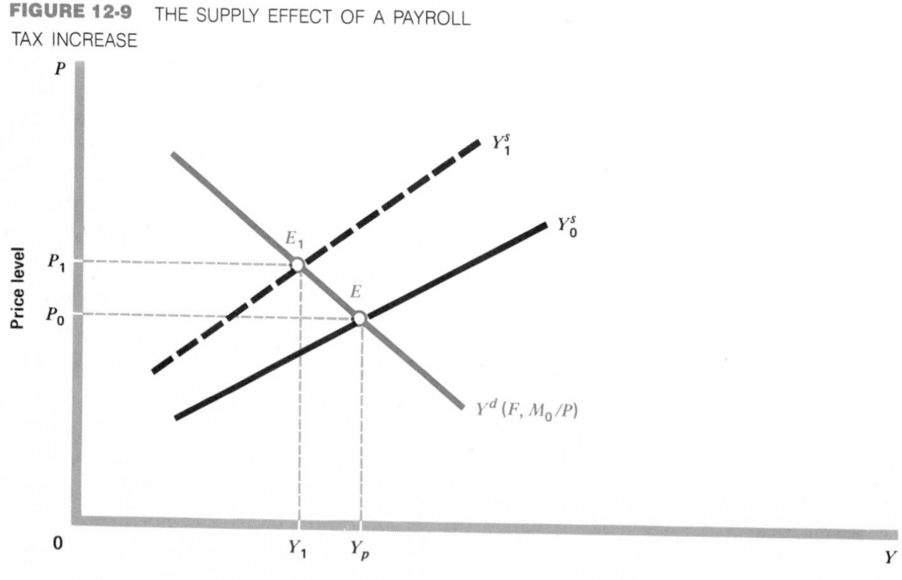

In Figure 12-9, we have *not* considered a second aspect of the payroll tax increase that operates on the aggregate demand side. A payroll tax increase obviously reduces disposable income at each level of output, since the government now collects more taxes. As a result, aggregate demand declines at each level of output unless this deflationary effect is offset by increased transfers or increased government spending. In the absence of such compensating policies, the aggregate demand schedule would therefore shift to the left in Figure 12-9 and further add to the output reduction, but at the same time make the effect on the price level ambiguous.

The preceding discussion suggests two questions about the choice of fiscal policies. First, there is the question of comparing payroll taxes, which have both supply and demand effects, with other fiscal policy instruments, such as changes in government spending or transfers. Second, there is the question of determining what type of disturbances would be best countered by policies that have supply effects and what type of disturbances should be countered mainly by aggregate demand policies.

The answers to these questions must rely on the general principle that policies should be geared as closely as possible to the disturbances they are supposed to offset. Thus, for aggregate demand disturbances, say an autonomous reduction in investment, the appropriate response is an aggregate demand policy. These policies, if timely and precisely set up, will maintain aggregate demand close to full employment and keep the price level constant. They therefore prevent the need to adjust output and prices to a transitory change in aggregate demand. We note also that in the case of aggregate demand variations, policies that mainly affect aggregate supply are inappropriate. They are inappropriate because they may stimulate output in the right direction but they do so at the cost of changing prices.

Consider next a disturbance that arises entirely on the supply side. Assume a temporary increase in raw material prices that raises costs and thus shifts the aggregate supply schedule upward. In the absence of policy changes, we would experience both an increase in prices and a reduction in equilibrium output, as shown in Figure 12-9. An appropriate policy response would be, for example, a cut in payroll taxes. The payroll tax cut would exert an offsetting effect by reducing costs, thus leaving the supply schedule unaffected. Again we remember, however, that the payroll tax cut reduces tax revenue and therefore exerts an expansionary effect on aggregate demand. To neutralize this side effect of the tax cut, we would require an offsetting cut in government spending or a cut in transfers.

It is clear from the preceding discussion that certain fiscal policy measures may be useful in coping with supply disturbances. This potential role in offsetting supply disturbances has led to the suggestion that supply management be used as a systematic part of macroeconomic stabilization policy. Fiscal policy changes in the form of payroll and indirect tax changes could, according to this new policy view, be used to offset inflationary supply shocks, while aggregate demand policies would continue to be used to maintain full employment.[8]

It is fair to say that there has been relatively little experience with fiscal policy as a tool of price and supply management. Nevertheless, the concept is intriguing.[9] Because there are at least three macroeconomic policy targets—full employment, price stability, and growth—successful stabilization policy may well require the use of fiscal policies that operate on aggregate supply as well as monetary and fiscal policies that affect both the level and composition of aggregate demand.

Yet another aspect of the new *supply side economics* emphasizes the impact of taxes on labor supply, capital formation, and productivity and hence on potential output. This aspect is taken up in Chapter 17.

12-7 SUMMARY

1 The aggregate demand function describes the equilibrium relationship between aggregate spending and the price level. The equilibrium in question is the simultaneous equilibrium of the goods and assets markets.
2 The aggregate demand curve slopes downward because an *increase* in the price level reduces real balances, increases the interest rate, and thereby *reduces* aggregate spending.
3 The aggregate demand curve is shifted up and to the right by an increase in the money stock or expansionary fiscal policy. At a given level of output, the aggregate demand curve shifts up in exactly the same proportion as the nominal money supply increases.
4 The short-run equilibrium of the economy is determined by the intersection of the short-run aggregate supply curve and the aggregate demand curve.
5 An increase in the money stock increases both output and the price level in the short run. In the long run, the aggregate supply curve shifts in response to positive or negative unemployment so that output moves back to its potential level.
6 In the long run, money is *neutral*, meaning that an increase in the money stock results only in an equiproportionate increase in prices.

[8] A special issue of *Brookings Papers on Economic Activity*, 1978:2 (Washington, D.C.: The Brookings Institution, 1978), is devoted to supply management. Janice Halpern and Alicia Munnell in "The Inflationary Impact of Increases in the Social Security Payroll Tax," *New England Economic Review*, March/April 1980, estimate, however, that changes in payroll taxes have only small effects on the price level.

[9] See, too, our further discussions in Chaps. 13 and 16.

7 Expansionary fiscal policy increases the levels of output and prices in the short run but only increases prices in the long run. Expansionary fiscal policy mainly *crowds out* other expenditures and has no effect on output in the long run.
8 *Supply management policies* are attempts to move the aggregate supply curve, for example, by changes in payroll taxes. There is, as yet, little experience with such policies. Conventional monetary and fiscal policies which move the aggregate demand curve are called *demand management policies*.
9 In deciding what policies to use in response to disturbances, the general rule is to use policies that most directly offset the effects of the disturbance. A shift in demand should be countered by a demand management policy and a supply shift should be offset by supply management policy.

PROBLEMS

1 (*a*) Explain why the aggregate demand curve slopes down.
(*b*) What happens to interest rates as we move down along this schedule, and why?
(*c*) What happens to the nominal stock of money as we move down along the aggregate demand curve? To the real money stock?

2 The text states that a higher multiplier $\bar{\alpha}$ would flatten out the aggregate demand curve.
(*a*) Give an economic interpretation of this fact.
(*b*) Use Equation (1) to prove this, noting that

$$\gamma \equiv \frac{b\bar{\alpha}}{h + bk\bar{\alpha}}$$

(If $\bar{\alpha}$ increases, what happens to γ? How is γ related to the slope of the aggregate demand curve?)

3 (*a*) What would be the effect on the aggregate demand curve of a cut in transfer payments?
(*b*) Would this effect be greater or smaller if the multiplier $\bar{\alpha}$ were higher?
(*c*) Verify this answer using Equation (1) and the fact that

$$\beta \equiv \frac{h\bar{\alpha}}{h + bk\bar{\alpha}},$$

*(*d*) Can you calculate $\Delta Y^d/\Delta R$ at a *fixed* level of price in terms of the variables we have already introduced? (Recall that R is transfer payments.)

4 Is it true that in the short run, expansionary fiscal or monetary policy can increase output only by also raising prices? Explain.

5 Suppose the aggregate supply curve were vertical. (Do you remember from Chapter 11 what would cause this?)

(*a*) What would be the effects of expansionary fiscal and monetary policy in the short run on output, prices, and interest rates?

(*b*) In the long run?

6 In the text it is noted that monetary policy is neutral in the long run even if the economy is not initially at full employment, as in Figure 12-5. Draw a diagram which demonstrates this fact and comment on the economic implications of this result. Does it seem to be a plausible one to you?

7 (*a*) Draw a diagram like Figure 12-7, indicating the effects of a tax increase in both the short and long runs.

(*b*) In what way is such a change in fiscal policy not neutral in the long run?

8 Suppose investors suddenly become more optimistic than in the past and decide to invest more at given levels of income and interest rates. Trace the effects of such a shift through the IS and LM curves to see its effect on equilibrium income as derived with the aggregate supply and demand curves. Explain the effects of the change in optimism on interest rates, prices, and income.

*9 A sales tax at the rate of 1 percent is imposed on all final goods. At the same time, income taxes are cut so as to maintain the budget in balance at the initial equilibrium. GNP initially is $1,500 billion.

(*a*) What is the size of the income tax cut?

(*b*) What is the short-run effect of the policy package on output and prices?

(*c*) What is the long-run effect on output and prices?

13

INFLATION, OUTPUT, AND UNEMPLOYMENT

13 INFLATION, OUTPUT, AND UNEMPLOYMENT

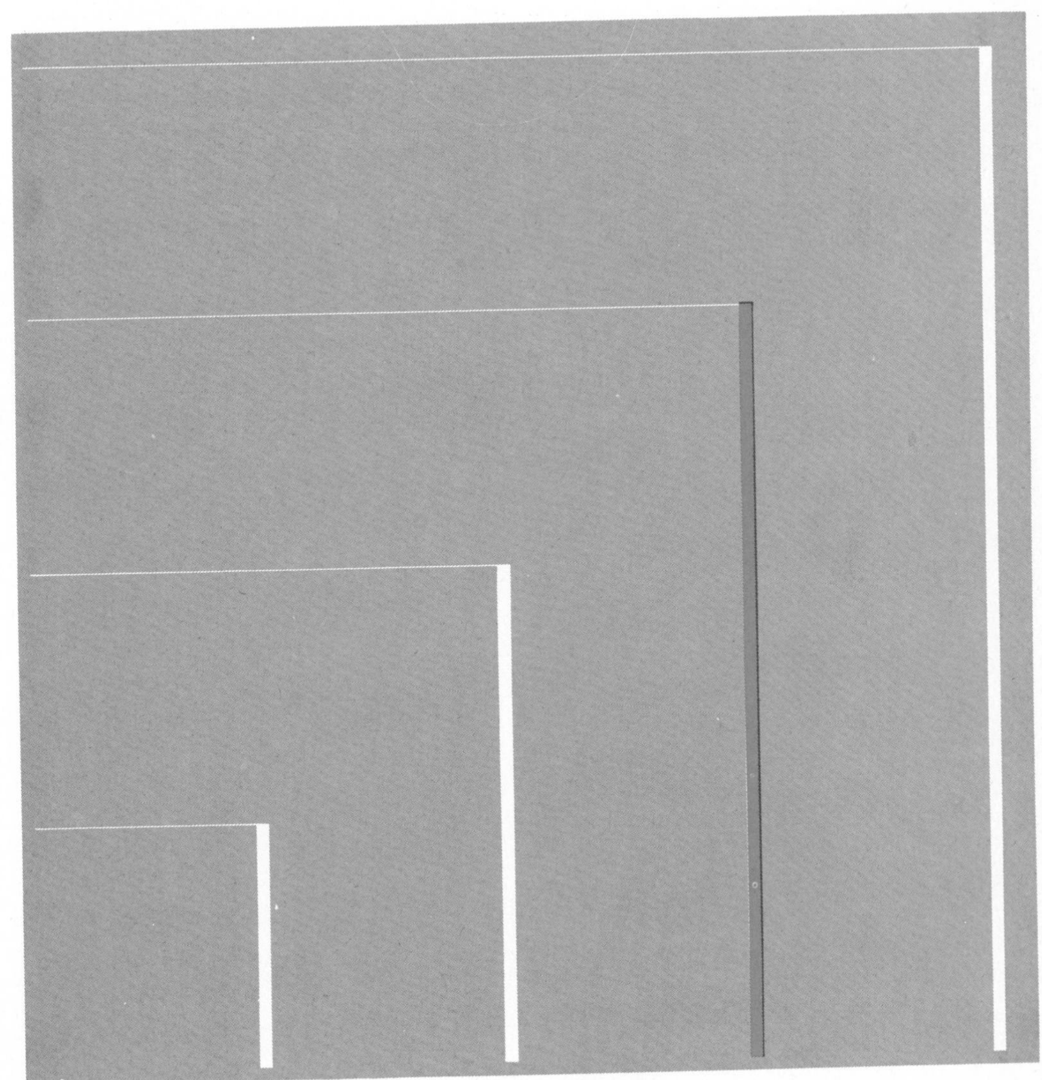

This chapter studies the behavior of inflation, unemployment, output, and interest rates. It is a direct extension of our work in Chapter 12, differing in only three respects. First, rather than focus on the level of prices, we look at its rate of change, the rate of inflation. Second, we give more explicit attention to dynamics, the question of how the economy moves from one period to the next in the adjustment process. Third, we introduce one element so far omitted from our theoretical model, inflationary expectations.

Our major aim is to develop a realistic framework to understand the behavior of the economy and to analyze such questions as: Why do inflation and unemployment sometimes increase together? Is inflation explained by lax monetary and fiscal policies? Can monetary and fiscal policies be used to raise the level of output permanently? Is it true that "inflation is always and everywhere a monetary phenomenon"?[1] Do high interest rates imply that monetary policy is tight?

Chart 13-1 points to the basic questions that we want to answer. The

[1] See Milton Friedman, *Dollars and Deficits* (Englewood Cliffs, N.J.: Prentice-Hall, 1968), p. 39.

CHART 13-1 INFLATION AND UNEMPLOYMENT
(Source: Citibank Economic Database)

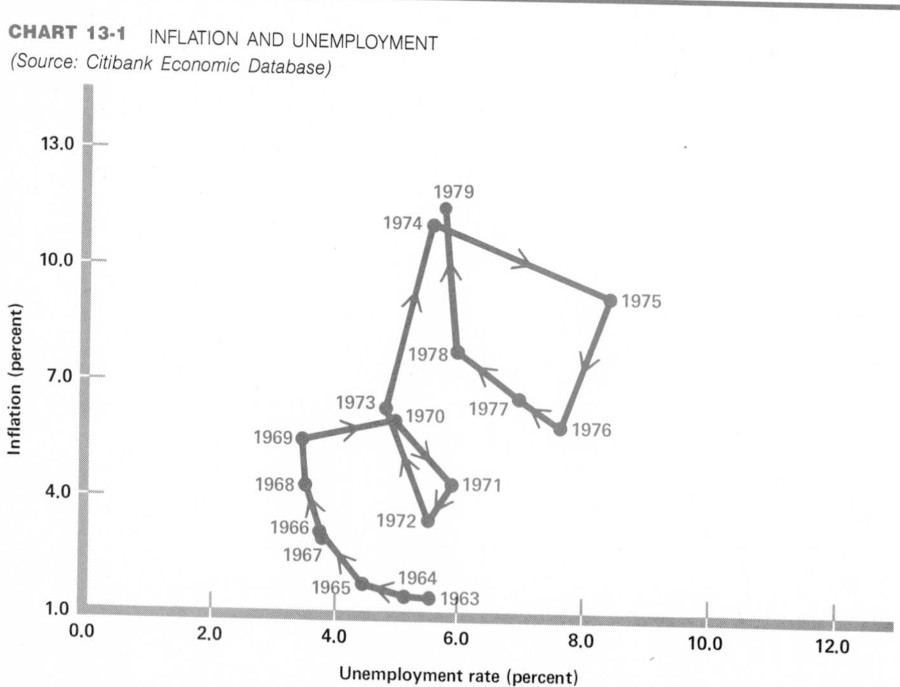

chart suggests that no extremely simple explanation—such as the view that unemployment declines when inflation increases—can account for the inflation-unemployment experience of the last two decades. In some periods, such as 1973–1974 and 1975–1976, inflation and unemployment move in the same direction. In other periods, for example, in 1974–1975 and 1976–1978, they move in opposite directions.

Chart 13-2 raises a second set of questions that will be dealt with in this chapter. Inflation and interest rates have both been rising since the 1950s. What relationship between inflation and interest rates accounts for this pattern?

The major element in explaining the unemployment-inflation and interest rate-inflation relations shown in the charts is inflationary expectations. We will show their place in the aggregate demand and supply framework and will demonstrate that the manner in which expectations are formed plays a crucial role in macroeconomic dynamics. The first place where inflationary expectations make their appearance is the Phillips curve—the relation between inflation and unemployment. In this chapter

CHART 13-2 INTEREST AND INFLATION *(Source: Citibank Economic Database)*

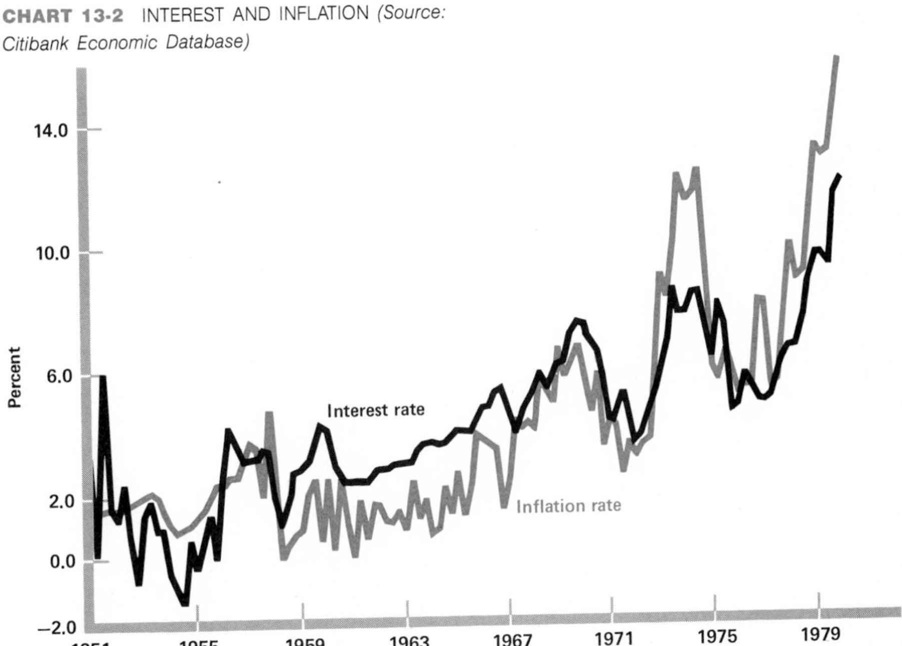

Note: Interest rate is market yield on 3-month Treasury bills. Inflation rate is the growth rate of the CPI over the following 3 months.

we will introduce an *expectations-augmented* Phillips curve. Inflationary expectations will also appear in the linkage between assets markets and goods markets. We introduce once again the relation between *nominal* and *real interest rates* and discuss the *Fisher relation*,[2] which argues that the real interest rate is unaffected by inflation in the long run but may change in the short run as the economy adjusts to changes in the inflation rate.

This chapter is written in two parts. The first sets out the basic results in an informal and intuitive manner. In Section 13-1, we introduce the long-run relation between monetary growth and inflation, the cornerstone of monetarism. We show that in the long run, inflation is indeed a monetary phenomenon. From that long-run perspective we turn next to the much more controversial question of the short-run determinants of inflation. In Section 13-2, we show that in the short run, inflation is determined not only by monetary policy but also by the stance of fiscal policy, by the behavior of autonomous spending, inflationary expectations, and supply shocks. This section thus previews the major results that are developed in the rest of the chapter.

13-1 MONEY AND INFLATION IN THE LONG RUN

In this section we look at the long-run relationship between money and the inflation rate. We consider a situation in which the money stock is growing at a constant rate, and in which inflation has settled down to a constant rate. Everybody is aware of the inflation, has adjusted to it, and expects it to continue. To begin with, we discuss an economy in which the growth rate of potential output is zero, and in which output has adjusted to its potential level. The long-run equilibrium we describe, with a constant rate of inflation and a constant output level, is also called a *steady state*. Later we shall modify our analysis to account for the possibility that potential output is growing over time.

In an economy with a constant growth rate of money and a constant level of output, and with everyone fully adjusted to the presence of inflation, there is a very simple relationship between the growth rate of money and the inflation rate. In such an economy, prices will rise at exactly the rate at which the nominal money stock is increasing.

We can formalize this relationship by denoting the *growth rate* of money by $m \equiv \Delta M/M$ and the rate of inflation by $\pi \equiv \Delta P/P$:

$$\pi = m \tag{1}$$

[2] Irving Fisher (1867–1947), no relation, was one of the great American economists, a health freak, an entrepreneur, and a poor stock market speculator.

Equation (1), which we will derive and discuss in detail below, is a central statement in macroeconomics. It points out that, in the long run, or on average, there is a link between monetary growth and inflation. More precisely, in a *stationary* economy—an economy where real income is constant—the rate of inflation is equal to the growth rate of the nominal quantity of money.

Before explaining Equation (1) in more detail, we look briefly at some evidence. Chart 13-3 shows the rate of inflation and the growth rate of money for the United States in the post-World War II period. The rates shown for each year are average rates over the past 4 years. Thus Chart 13-3 presents rough measures of long-run growth rates of money and the inflation rate. The chart suggests that the growth rate of money and the inflation rate do move together over long periods. However, the relationship is not exact. In part, this lack of an exact relationship reflects the role of other factors—such as fiscal policy changes, aggregate demand and supply disturbances, and shifts in money demand. A second factor making the relationship inexact is trend growth in output. We shall see later that the relationship, Equation (1), between the growth rate of the money stock and the inflation rate has to be modified to take account of the long-run growth in output.

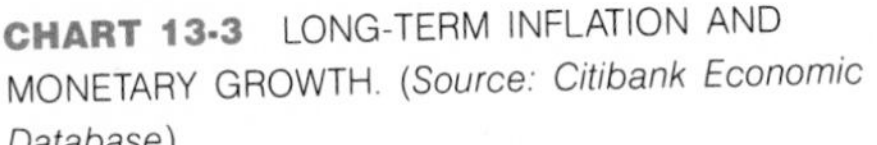

CHART 13-3 LONG-TERM INFLATION AND MONETARY GROWTH. (*Source: Citibank Economic Database*)

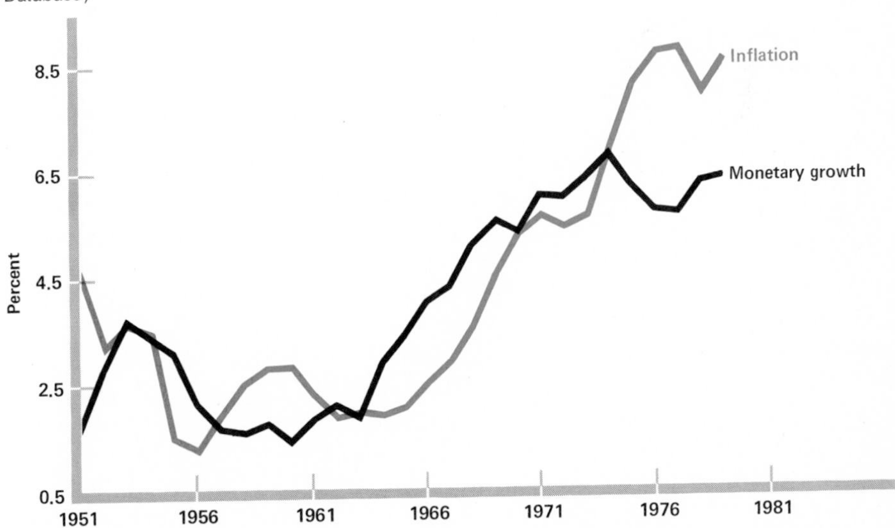

Note: Inflation and monetary growth are 4-year moving averages of annual growth rates of the GNP deflator and of M1. M1 is based on the old definition.

Now we return to Equation (1) to establish the long-run relation between inflation and monetary growth. For that purpose, we turn to the equilibrium condition in the money market, familiar from the LM curve:

$$\frac{M}{P} = L(i,Y) \tag{2}$$

or

$$M = PL(i,Y) \tag{2a}$$

Equations (2) and (2a) state that monetary equilibrium requires that money demand equals money supply. Equation (2) states this equilibrium condition in terms of real money demand and supply; Equation (2a) states the condition in terms of nominal money demand and supply.

Now consider long-run equilibrium where, by definition, all adjustments have taken place and, therefore, output and interest rates are constant. With output and interest rates constant, the demand for real money balances is constant. Therefore, to maintain the equality between the supply and demand for money, changes in the nominal money supply must be matched by corresponding changes in prices. For instance, if the stock of money were increasing by 5 percent per year, prices would have to be rising at the rate of 5 percent per year to maintain constant the real money supply M/P and thus maintain equilibrium in the money market. We have therefore established that in long-run equilibrium, money and prices must grow at the same rate.[3] That is precisely the message of Equation (1).

The argument that "inflation is always and everywhere a monetary phenomenon" is thus entirely correct as a description of long-run equilibrium. It is simply an implication of monetary equilibrium. The real money supply that yields monetary equilibrium is equal to the real money demand. To maintain a constant real money supply, an increasing nominal money stock has to be matched by rising prices. Thus, if the growth rate of the nominal money stock is 5 percent, the rate of inflation will be 5 percent. If the nominal money stock grows at the rate of 1000 percent, as it has in some hyperinflations, then the rate of inflation will be 1000 percent in long-run equilibrium.

Now we have to step back for a moment to ask how reasonable it is to look at the long run. After all, the economy is really never in long-run equilibrium. There is always some disturbance that upsets equilibrium and

[3] The same point can be made starting from Eq. (2a). With constant real output and constant interest rates there will be a given, constant *real* demand for money L. Looking at Eq. (2a), we see that if the left-hand side—the nominal quantity of money—is increasing at some rate, the right-hand side—the demand for nominal balances—must be increasing at the same rate. But in the steady state, the only factor changing on the right-hand side is the price level, since $L(\ )$ is constant. Therefore the price level must be increasing at the same rate as the nominal money stock.

causes inflation and output to be different from their long-run values. That point is well taken and indeed reduces the interest we would otherwise have in long-run equilibrium. But there is a different way of looking at long-run equilibrium which makes it a less precise but much more powerful concept. This alternative is to think of the long-run equilibrium as the *average* behavior of the economy over long time periods. To give an example, if on average over a 5-year period the money stock had grown at 10 percent per year, with some variation, say, between 8 and 12 percent, we would expect the inflation rate to be about 10 percent. It might be a bit lower or higher depending on economic disturbances during the period, but it would be roughly 10 percent. The reason this average interpretation of the long run is powerful is that we are not trying to be more precise than is reasonable. We wind up with only a rule of thumb, but it is a very sturdy one.

Output Growth and Long-Run Inflation

The relationship (1) between monetary growth and inflation requires a minor correction to account for output growth. It is clear that growth in real income raises real money demand, and that, therefore, the assumption of a constant demand for real balances is not appropriate when output is growing. How should we account for the effects of output growth on the relationship between monetary growth and inflation? For example, how does the average growth rate of real income of 3 percent in the United States in the post-World War II period affect Equation (1)?

In studying money demand in Chapter 7, we introduced the income elasticity of money demand. We noted there that the income elasticity of money demand is 0.7, which means that a 1 percent increase in real income raises real money demand by about 0.7 percent. Thus, if real income grows at the average rate of 3 percent, as it has in the United States, and if the income elasticity of money demand is 0.7, as it is in the United States, then real money demand grows at the average rate of 2.1 percent (=3 percent × 0.7) per year.

If real money demand is rising—say, at the rate of 2.1 percent per year—as a result of income growth, then monetary equilibrium requires that the real money supply increases at that same rate. The growth rate of the real money supply is just the difference between the growth rate of the nominal money stock and the rate of inflation. For instance, if the nominal money stock is increasing at 10 percent and the rate of inflation is 6 percent, the real money supply is growing at 4 percent. If the real money supply has to be growing at 2.1 percent to maintain monetary equilibrium, then the rate of inflation has to be 2.1 percent less than the rate of monetary growth, or, in symbols:

$$\pi = m - 2.1 \tag{1a}$$

Equation (1*a*) states that the rate of inflation is equal to the growth rate of money *less* an adjustment arising from real income growth.

Equation (1*a*) partially explains why, in Chart 13-3, there is some discrepancy between the average rate of monetary growth and the rate of inflation. We observe from the chart that monetary growth usually exceeds the inflation rate,[4] and Equation (1*a*) explains that fact by the growth in real money demand that results from real income growth.

Summary

Here we briefly summarize the long-run or average relation between inflation and monetary growth:

1 Inflation in the long run is a monetary phenomenon. By this we mean that increases in the growth rate of money are in the long run reflected one for one in the rate of inflation.
2 The higher the growth rate of the nominal money supply, the higher the rate of inflation.
3 The rate of inflation is lower, the higher the growth rate of real money demand. This means that inflation is lower, the faster the growth rate of output, and the more real money demand rises with increased real income or output.

The simple long-run relationship between monetary growth and inflation contains one extremely important lesson. If a country wants to reduce its average inflation rate, it has somehow to reduce the average growth rate of the money stock.

13-2 INFLATION AND OUTPUT IN THE SHORT RUN: AN OVERVIEW

Chart 13-4 shows the *short-run* rates of inflation and growth rate of money over the post-World War II period. The growth rates in this chart are annual rather than long-term averages. Comparing Charts 13-3 and 13-4, we can see clearly that the short-run link between money and inflation is weaker than the long-run relationship. The absence of a close link between the growth rate of money and the inflation rate in the short run suggests that there are other factors accounting for inflation in the short run. We now turn our attention to those factors. At the same time, we are interested in short-run fluctuations in output and unemployment in the economy and the relationship between these output fluctuations and inflation. Chapter 12

[4] However, that is not the case for 1975–1978. Do you know why? Think back to Chap. 7 and the recent behavior of the demand for money.

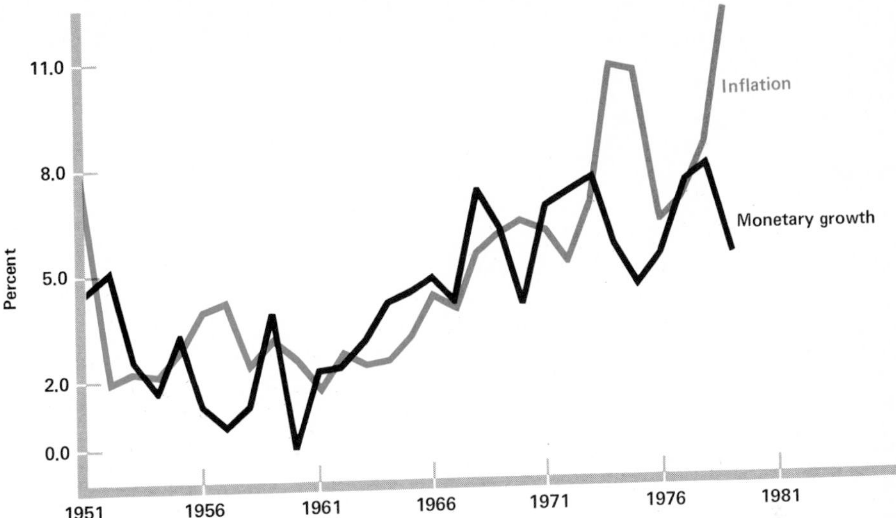

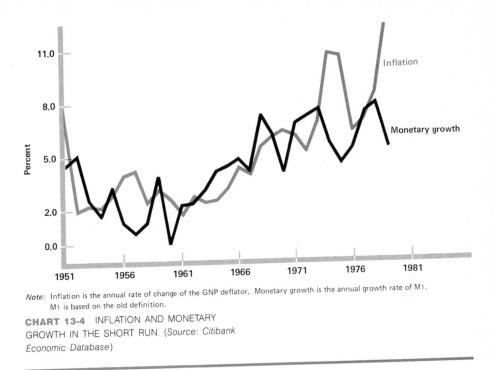

Note: Inflation is the annual rate of change of the GNP deflator. Monetary growth is the annual growth rate of M1. M1 is based on the old definition.

CHART 13-4 INFLATION AND MONETARY GROWTH IN THE SHORT RUN. (*Source: Citibank Economic Database*)

has already suggested that the behavior of the price level and the behavior of output are closely related in the short run, and we will again find that to be true.

In this chapter we reformulate the theory of Chapter 12 to include expectations of inflation. The expected rate of inflation affects both aggregate supply and aggregate demand. On the aggregate supply side, nominal wages adjust not only to unemployment, but also to expected inflation. Nominal wages adjust to expected inflation because both firms and workers are concerned with the *real* wages they will be paying or receiving over the course of their labor contracts. If prices are expected to increase at, say, 10 percent during the course of a labor contract, then nominal wages will tend, for that reason, to increase at a rate of 10 percent over the course of the contract. Wage rises are passed on into price rises, and the inflation rate thus reflects expected inflation.

On the aggregate demand side, expectations of inflation are important because different interest rates are relevant for spending decisions and for portfolio choices, for equilibrium in the goods and money markets. The expected *real* interest rate is relevant to the IS curve because, as we emphasized in Chapter 6, investment demand is affected by the expected real rate. However, as stressed in Chapter 7, the nominal interest rate is the cost of holding money, and it is therefore the nominal rate that is relevant to the LM curve. Since the difference between the expected real and nominal rates of interest is the expected inflation rate, and since aggregate demand is determined by the interaction of the goods and asset markets (IS and LM curves), the expected rate of inflation will affect aggregate demand. How? We will see that an increase in the expected rate of inflation *increases* aggregate demand. The essential reason is that an increase in the expected rate of inflation makes it more attractive to hold a real asset, such as capital, rather than a non-interest bearing asset like money. The desired capital stock and investment demand increases and therefore so does aggregate demand.

Preview

This preview gives an idea, although not a complete understanding, of what is to come. We start in Section 13-3 with the aggregate supply side, which establishes the link between actual inflation, expected inflation, and output. We develop the aggregate supply curve

$$\pi = \pi^* + h\epsilon\left(\frac{Y}{Y_p} - 1\right) \tag{3}$$

Equation (3) states that the actual inflation rate π is equal to the expected inflation rate π^* plus a term that depends on the difference between actual and potential output. The second term is already familiar from the development of aggregate supply in Chapter 11. When output is high relative to potential output, unemployment is low and wages are therefore rising and being passed on into price increases. The first element, the expected rate of inflation, means that there is a potential for inflation even at full employment. Wages, and therefore prices, will rise when output is at the full-employment level if inflation is expected and nominal wages adjust accordingly. Thus, on the supply side, the level of output (relative to potential) and the expected rate of inflation are the determinants of the inflation rate.

On the aggregate demand side, we develop Equation (4):

$$Y^d = Y^d_{-1} + \gamma f + \phi(m - \pi) + \eta(\pi^* - \pi^*_{-1}) \tag{4}$$

Equation (4) states that current real aggregate demand is equal to last period's aggregate demand, *plus* the increase that results from a change in fiscal policy, f, *plus* the increase that results from growth in real balances, $m - \pi$, plus the increase resulting from increases in the expected rate of inflation, $\pi^* - \pi^*_{-1}$.

Each of Equations (3) and (4) is a relationship between the inflation rate and the level of output, and we can, therefore, draw Equation (3) as the aggregate supply curve and Equation (4) as the aggregate demand curve.

Their intersection will determine the short-run inflation rate and level of output. Their movements over time determine how the inflation rate and output adjust to changes in monetary and fiscal policy variables.

Using the aggregate supply and demand curves, we will establish the following results:

1 In the long run, increases in the growth rate of money affect *only* the inflation rate, and not output, which returns to its potential level, Y_p.
2 The short-run equilibrium of the economy is determined by the current and last period's expected inflation rates, π^* and π^*_{-1}, last period's output, Y^d_{-1}, fiscal policy, f, and the growth rate of the money stock, m.
3 The short-run response to an increase in the growth rate of money is typically a rise in both output and inflation. The response to an expansionary change in the fiscal policy variable, f, is similar.
4 The behavior of expectations is crucial to the dynamic adjustment of the economy to changes in monetary and fiscal policy.

We are also interested in the behavior of real and nominal interest rates. The major results here are:

5 In the long run, an increase in the growth rate of money increases the nominal interest rate by the same amount as the money growth rate increases, leaving the real interest rate unchanged.
6 The short-run effects of an increase in the growth rate of money on interest rates depend on the behavior of expectations. If money growth increases and the expected inflation rate does not adjust, both the real and nominal interest rates fall initially. Then, as expected, inflation increases, and both the real and nominal interest rates rise, with the nominal rate rising faster.
7 Fiscal policy can affect the real interest rate in both the short and long runs.

*13-3 AGGREGATE SUPPLY: THE EXPECTATIONS-AUGMENTED PHILLIPS CURVE

This section develops the relation between inflation, aggregate supply, and inflationary expectations shown in Equation (3). Our starting point is the theory of aggregate supply developed in Chapter 11. We showed there [in Eq.(11), page 383] that wage and price adjustment in response to the level of over- or underutilization of labor and other resources implies a positive relation between inflation and the GNP gap. If output is above normal, wages and costs in general will be rising and firms will pass on these increasing costs into higher prices. Conversely, when output is below normal, declining costs lead to falling prices.

The equation

$$\pi = h\epsilon\left(\frac{Y}{Y_p} - 1\right) \tag{3a}$$

implied by Equation (13) on page 383, summarizes the effect on cost and price inflation of deviations of output from normal. The coefficient $h\epsilon$ in Equation (3*a*) captures on one hand the effect of unemployment on wages and on the other the relation between unemployment and the GNP gap that is known as Okun's law. Okun's law is reviewed in more detail in the appendix to this chapter. Here we need only the fact of a stable relation between unemployment and the gap—the higher the unemployment rate, the higher the gap. Thus we can look behind Equation (3*a*) and interpret wage behavior related to unemployment as the source of inflationary pressure or deflationary pressure as the economy deviates from full employment.

In Figure 13-1 we show Equation (3*a*)—still leaving aside inflationary expectations. The schedule labeled AS_0 shows the inflation rate associated with each level of output. At full employment, inflation is zero. With actual output above potential, wages and prices are rising, or there is inflation. With output below normal, there is deflation, or wages and prices are falling.

FIGURE 13-1 THE AGGREGATE SUPPLY SCHEDULE

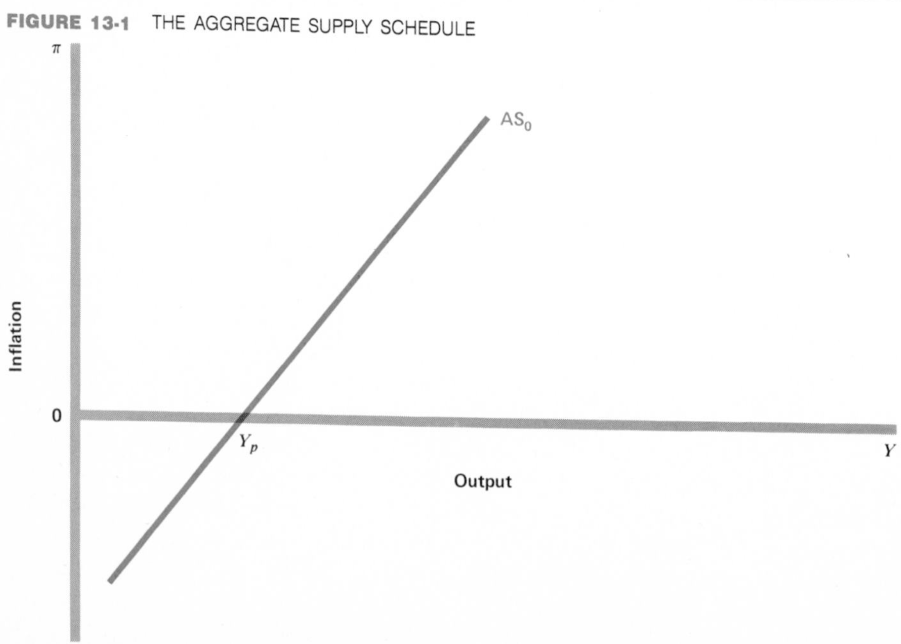

The extent to which the GNP gap affects inflation is summarized by the slope of the aggregate supply schedule or the term $h\epsilon$ in Equation (3*a*). This term reflects the relation between unemployment and the GNP gap h, and the sensitivity of money wages to unemployment ϵ. The higher either of these parameters, the higher the rate of inflation that is associated with a given level of the gap, or, in other words, the steeper the aggregate supply schedule. There is still another way of putting the same issue. The steeper the aggregate supply schedule, the more adverse the *inflation-output tradeoff*; that is, the more inflation we get from a given expansion in output and employment.

We will show presently that the position of the aggregate supply schedule shown in Figure 13-1 will be affected by the expected rate of inflation in a more complete model. Before we turn to that point, we discuss the concept and role of inflationary expectations.

Expectations

The role of inflationary expectations in influencing wage formation and therefore costs and prices is central to an understanding of the inflation process. Because labor contracts fix nominal wages for a given period ahead, labor will be concerned about its real wage over the period of the contract. A given money wage rate negotiated today will have less purchasing power 2 years from now if the inflation rate is 10 percent than if it is zero. Labor and firms, when they set current wages, will therefore look ahead to the inflation they expect over the period of the contract.

Typically, the environment is not one where the inflation rate has been constant for a long period and can be accurately predicted. More likely, the inflation rate in the recent past has varied somewhat and future inflation cannot be predicted with great accuracy. Given that uncertainty, we would assume expectations of inflation to be based in part on inflation rates actually experienced in the recent past. Labor would seek wage increases equal to the "habitual" rate of inflation that has recently been experienced, and thus find some insurance against the expected price increases.

Before proceeding to discuss how expectations are formed, we briefly reemphasize the critical role of inflationary expectations in the inflation process. Expectations are so critical because the simple fact that people expect inflation causes inflation. When wages increase because inflation is expected, costs increase and produce inflationary pressure as firms seek to pass on cost increases into higher prices.

When inflationary expectations are slow to adjust, monetary and fiscal policies will have quite large effects on the level of output and relatively small effects on the inflation rate. Two instances from recent economic history are relevant here. First, in the sixties, aggregate demand kept rising, partly as a result of the 1964 tax cut and then as a result of increases in government spending and monetary growth that were associated with the Vietnam war. However, inflation was very slow to develop, largely because the long period of moderate inflation of the late fifties and early sixties kept down expected inflation. Second, repeated attempts in the seventies to reduce existing inflation by restrictive monetary policy proved largely ineffective, resulting in unemployment rather than lower inflation. Expectations of inflation did not come down fast, and therefore actual inflation could not be reduced without substantially increasing unemployment.

Now we return once more to expectations formation. There is no generally accepted way in which to model inflationary expectations.[5] Traditionally, inflationary expectations have been regarded as some average of past inflation rates. One example is a weighted average of inflation rates in the past 4 years, with relatively heavy weight on the more recent past. We show such a weighted average for the postwar period in Chart 13-5, in which we observe the gradual upturn of this measure of inflationary expectations in the late sixties and the slow downturn after the 1973–1974 inflationary explosion. There is no particular advantage that attaches to a 4-year average, nor any evidence that makes us select that number. Nor need expectations be based only on the past behavior of the inflation rate.

[5] See Robert M. Solow, "Down the Phillips Curve with Gun and Camera," in David A. Belsley et al. (eds.), *Inflation, Trade and Taxes* (Columbus: Ohio State University Press, 1976).

CHART 13-5 ACTUAL AND EXPECTED INFLATION.
(*Source: Citibank Economic Database*)

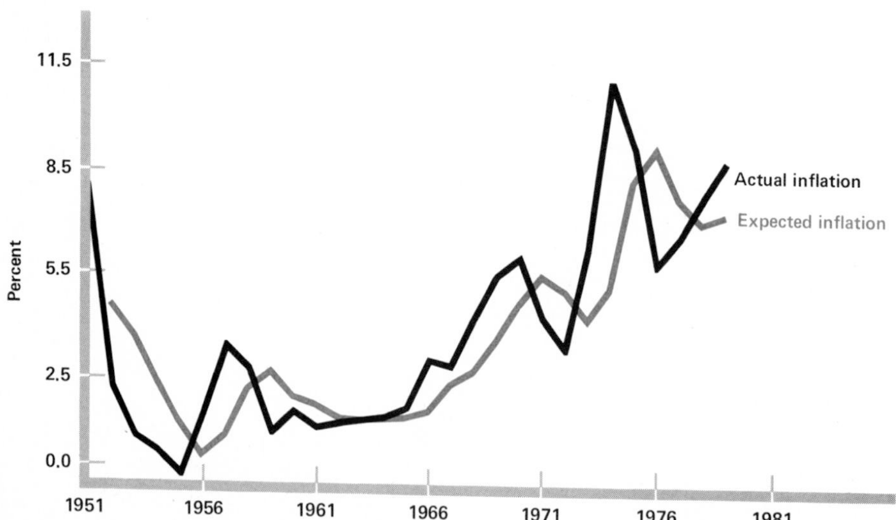

Note: The expected rate of inflation is a 4-year weighted average formed as follows: $\pi^* = 0.5\pi_{-1} + 0.3\pi_{-2} + 0.15\pi_{-3} + 0.05\pi_{-4}$ where the π_{-i} are the annual rates of inflation of the GNP deflator.

Any information that is available about the future course of monetary and fiscal policies would also be relevant to inflationary expectations.

For the purpose of the next few sections, we will make the simplifying assumption that the expected rate of inflation is equal to last period's rate of inflation:

$$\pi^* = \pi_{-1} \tag{5}$$

We adopt this oversimplified formulation only because it is easy to manipulate. Taking a long-run average over 3 to 5 years is more appropriate and important as a practical matter but really does not change the theory. All it does is to draw out the adjustment process over time and make for longer lags.

Later we will substitute for Equation (5) an alternative *perfect foresight* assumption which assumes individuals predict the inflation rate correctly:

$$\pi^* = \pi \tag{5a}$$

While Equation (5*a*) is difficult to believe as a literal description, it will help us see how important expectations are to the dynamic behavior of the economy. It will also bring out aspects of the *rational expectations approach* to macroeconomics, to be discussed in Section 13-6, and in Chapter 16.

Inflationary Expectations and Aggregate Supply

We now turn to the aggregate supply Equation (3), which includes inflationary expectations. Because both firms and workers are concerned with *real* wages, nominal wages adjust for expected inflation through the π^* term, as well as in response to the state of the labor market through the second term in (3), repeated here for convenience. The wage increases are then passed on into prices.

$$\pi = \pi^* + h\epsilon\left(\frac{Y}{Y_p} - 1\right) \tag{3}$$

Figure 13-2 shows the role of expectations in aggregate supply. We have reproduced the aggregate supply schedule AS_0, drawn for a zero expected inflation rate from Figure 13-1. An increase in the expected rate of inflation from zero to, say, $\pi^* = 5$ percent, will shift up the aggregate supply schedule so that now at full employment we would have a 5 percent rate of inflation. This is shown by the aggregate supply schedule AS_1. Conversely, a reduction in expected inflation below zero—the expectation of

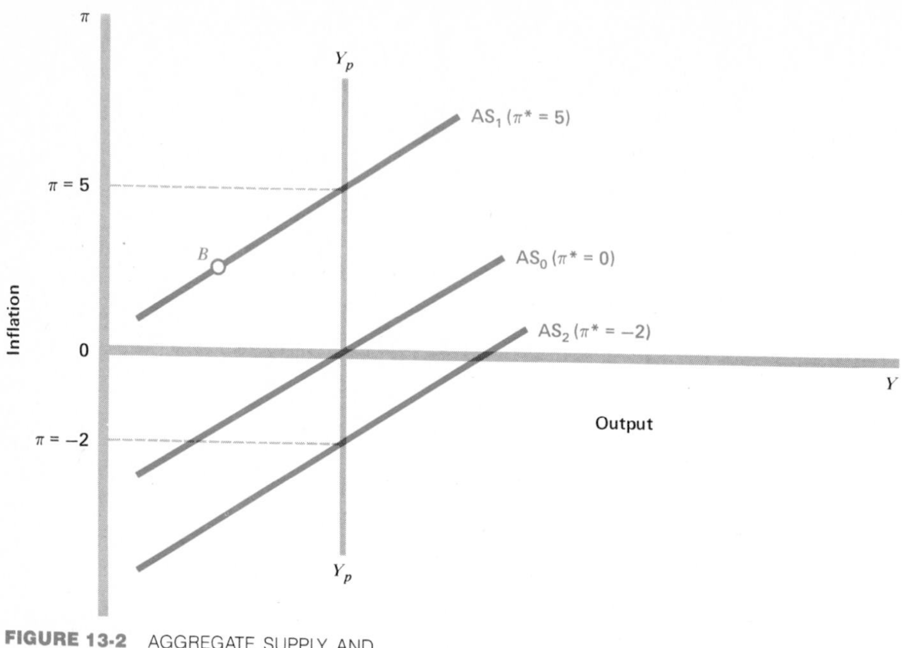

FIGURE 13-2 AGGREGATE SUPPLY AND EXPECTED INFLATION

deflation—will shift the aggregate supply schedule downward to AS_2. The schedule AS_2, drawn in Figure 13-2, reflects the expectation of prices falling at the rate of 2 percent. For higher rates of expected deflation, the aggregate supply schedule would shift down farther.

Embodying inflationary expectations in the aggregate supply schedule completes the picture of inflation and output on the supply side. Inflation depends on the state of the labor market, here measured by the GNP gap, and on inflationary expectations. Inflation is higher, the higher is actual output relative to potential output and the higher is expected inflation.

It is quite possible to have both inflation and unemployment (point *B*). That possibility arises when the expectation of inflation causes wages and prices to rise and unemployment does not exert sufficient dampening pressure on wage settlements to restore full employment. Clearly, this is the combination of facts observed in the seventies where persistent unemployment appeared together with inflation.

In concluding this section, we comment on a critical aspect of the aggregate supply schedule: In the long run, the aggregate supply schedule is vertical at the full-employment level. The long-run aggregate supply schedule is the schedule Y_pY_p. In the long run, the level of output is independent of the rate of inflation, as is the rate of unemployment. The reason for these strong results—sometimes referred to as the *long-run vertical Phillips curve*—is that expectations will ultimately adjust to the existing rate of inflation. Thus, by Equation (3), equality of actual and expected inflation implies that output is at the full-employment level whatever the rate of inflation. Deviations of output from the full-employment level require expectational errors or deviations of the inflation rate from its habitual level. In the long run equilibrium, by definition, there are no errors in expectations and therefore output is at the full-employment level.

*13-4 AGGREGATE DEMAND AND EXPECTED INFLATION

The preceding section showed that aggregate supply theory can be extended in a simple way to link output and the rate of inflation, taking account of inflationary expectations. In this section, we develop the link between aggregate demand and inflation, also taking inflationary expectations into account.

Aggregate Demand, Expected Inflation, and Interest Rates

In Chapters 11 and 12, we saw that aggregate demand depends on autonomous spending, including fiscal variables, and the real quantity of money. Taking explicit account of the fiscal variables, we can write aggregate demand as a function of fiscal and monetary variables:

$$Y^d = Y^d\left(F, \frac{M}{P}\right) \tag{6a}$$

Here F is a measure of fiscal policy, which we take to be represented by the full-employment budget deficit. In the aggregate demand function in Equation (6*a*), an increase in the full-employment deficit increases aggregate demand, as does an increase in the real money supply.

Equation (6*a*) omits the effects of expected inflation on aggregate demand. The importance of expected inflation arises from the distinction between real and nominal interest rates. The interest rate relevant to goods market equilibrium (the IS curve) is the expected real rate, and the interest rate relevant to money market equilibrium (the LM curve) is the nominal rate. Since the two rates differ by the expected rate of inflation, changes in the expected rate of inflation will affect aggregate demand.

We will now extend Equation (6*a*) to include inflationary expectations and the distinction between real and nominal interest rates. We will show that the extended aggregate demand function can be written

$$Y^d = Y^d\left(F, \frac{M}{P}, \pi^*\right) \tag{6}$$

and that increases in the expected rate of inflation increase aggregate demand.

For that purpose, we go back to the IS and LM curves of Chapter 4. In Figure 13-3, we show the LM schedule. On the vertical axis, we have the *nominal* rate of interest relevant for the choice between money and other financial assets.

In the goods market, however, the *real* interest rate is relevant since it determines the level of investment. In particular, we showed in Chapter 4, Equation (6*a*), that we can write the IS schedule as

$$Y = \overline{\alpha}(\overline{A} - bi_r) \tag{7}$$

where $\overline{A}$ denotes autonomous spending, $\overline{\alpha}$ is the multiplier, and i_r denotes the real rate of interest. If there are inflationary expectations, nominal and real interest rates will differ and we have to think about a way to introduce the IS schedule into Figure 13-3.

The critical step in reformulating the IS-LM model to include inflationary expectations is the relation

FIGURE 13-3 EFFECTS OF AN INCREASE IN THE EXPECTED INFLATION RATE ON THE REAL INTEREST RATE AND AGGREGATE DEMAND

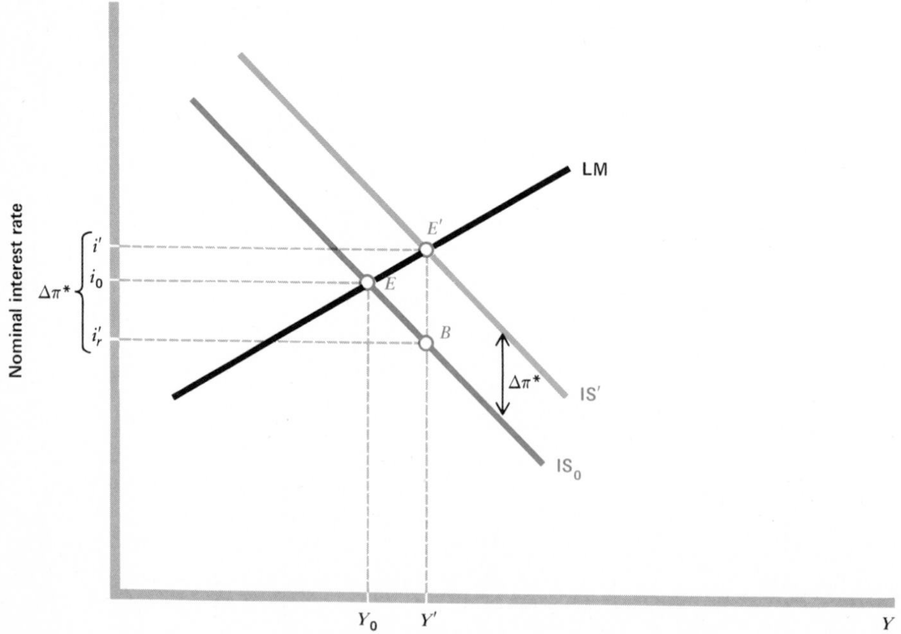

$$i_r = i - \pi^* \tag{8}$$

which states that the (expected) real rate of interest is the nominal rate less the expected rate of inflation. We can use Equation (8) to substitute for the real interest rate in (7) to obtain the following equation:

$$Y = \overline{\alpha}(\overline{A} - bi + b\pi^*) \tag{9}$$

In this form we recognize that equilibrium output in the goods market depends on both the nominal interest rate *and* the expected rate of inflation. In particular, for a given nominal interest rate, i, an increase in expected inflation will increase equilibrium output. What is the mechanism? Increased inflationary expectations, *given the nominal interest rate*, imply a lower real interest rate. This results in an increased incentive to invest, a rise in demand, and therefore a higher equilibrium output.

We also observe from Equation (9) that for a given rate of expected inflation, say π_0^*, we can draw the IS schedule as a function of the nominal interest rate. With given inflationary expectations, changes in the nominal rate correspond, one for one, to changes in the real rate. Accordingly, we draw in Figure 13-3 the schedule IS_0 corresponding to a given rate of expected inflation π_0^*. It is also clear that a change in expected inflation will shift the IS schedule. Increased inflationary expectations will shift the IS schedule up and to the right, since at each nominal interest rate they imply reduced real rates and hence an increased incentive to invest.

We can be more precise about the way in which changes in expected inflation shift the IS schedule. Note that since investment depends on the real rate, investment, and so equilibrium income, will remain unchanged if changes in inflationary expectations are precisely offset by changes in nominal interest rates. When inflationary expectations are up by two percentage points, demand and equilibrium income are unchanged only if nominal interest rates increase by the same amount. This implies, in terms of Figure 13-3, that a change in inflationary expectations, $\Delta\pi^*$, shifts the IS schedule upward by exactly the same amount, $\Delta i = \Delta\pi^*$.

We can now use our modified IS-LM model to show the effect of increased inflationary expectations on the equilibrium levels of income, nominal and real interest rates. Suppose then, as shown in Figure 13-3, that there is an increase in the expected rate of inflation. At the initial equilibrium nominal interest rate and income level, the money market remains in equilibrium. In the goods market, however, there is now an excess demand. The increased inflationary expectations have reduced the real interest rate at point E, investment spending increases, and accordingly, the IS curve shifts up by $\Delta\pi^*$ to IS′. At E the excess demand for goods causes an income expansion. As the economy moves to the new equilibrium at E', income rises. This rise in income raises money demand and hence equilibrium nominal interest rates. We thus have shown that an increase in inflationary expectations will raise equilibrium income and spending or aggregate demand, as shown in Equation (6).

What can we say about the impact of increased inflationary expectations on interest rates? Figure 13-3 allows us to describe the effect on both nominal and real interest rates. We already see that the nominal interest rate will rise to i'. But we also see that the nominal interest rate rises by less than the full increase in inflationary expectations, that is, $i' - i_0 < \Delta\pi^*$. This of course implies that the equilibrium real interest rate, i_r, corresponding to the equilibrium at point E', must have declined.

In fact, from the definition of the real rate—the nominal rate less the expected inflation—it is apparent that the new real rate is the interest rate corresponding to point B and shown as i_r' on the vertical axis. The increased inflationary expectations thus drive a wedge between nominal and real interest rates: Nominal rates rise and real rates fall.

How much does the real interest rate change? That clearly depends on the slopes of the IS and LM curves. At one extreme, we could have a flat IS curve, indicating extreme sensitivity of investment demand to the real interest rate. Then an increase in the expected rate of inflation would have little effect on the equilibrium real rate of interest and would affect the nominal rate almost one for one. The increase in aggregate demand is correspondingly large. Alternatively, the steeper the LM curve, the smaller the change in the real rate. In the extreme classical or quantity theory world in which the LM curve is vertical, the change in the expected rate of inflation again does not affect the real rate and only changes the nominal rate. In this case, though, income does not change either.

We defer further examination of interest rate behavior to Section 13-7. For the next few sections, we concentrate on the determination of output and inflation.

The Aggregate Demand Curve

We now use Equation (6) to derive an aggregate demand curve that relates the level of aggregate demand to the rate of inflation, as does Equation (4) in Section 13-2. From Equation (6), aggregate demand increases when the full-employment budget deficit expands, when real balances increase, and when the expected rate of inflation increases.

$$\Delta Y^d = \gamma f + \phi(m - \pi) + \eta\Delta\pi^* \tag{10}$$

In Equation (10), we see that the change in aggregate demand depends on the *change* in fiscal policy, f, on the *change* in the expected rate of inflation

$(\Delta\pi^* = \pi^* - \pi^*_{-1})$, and on the growth rate of real balances, $m - \pi$.[6] The growth rate of real money balances is equal to the growth rate of nominal balances less the rate of inflation. The terms γ and ϕ translate changes in the full-employment deficit and in real balances into changes in income, and therefore are related to the fiscal and monetary multipliers studied before. The term η summarizes the effects of expected inflation on aggregate demand, and thus depends on the slopes of the IS and LM curves.

Now, what is the interpretation of Equation (10)? If fiscal policy is expansionary, aggregate demand will rise. Thus an increase in the full-employment deficit, resulting from increased government spending or reduced taxes, raises aggregate demand. Similarly, aggregate demand rises if the real money supply grows (because nominal money grows faster than prices) or if the expected rate of inflation increases. These three factors will each raise aggregate demand relative to last period. We can underline that fact by writing aggregate demand this period, Y^d, as output (aggregate demand) last period, Y_{-1}, plus the change in demand arising from the three factors in Equation (10):[7]

$$Y^d = Y_{-1} + \gamma f + \phi(m - \pi) + \eta\Delta\pi^* \tag{10a}$$

where we have substituted $\Delta Y^d \equiv Y^d - Y_{-1}$.

We immediately recognize from Equation (10*a*) that we now have a relationship between aggregate demand and the rate of inflation. Given last period's income, expectations, the change in fiscal policy, and the growth rate of money (Y_{-1}, $\Delta\pi^*$, f, and m), we are left with a relationship between current demand and the current rate of inflation. Equation (10*a*) shows that the higher the rate of inflation, the lower is the level of aggregate demand

[6] Technical note: Equation (10) would follow from Equation (6) if (6) took the form

$$Y^d = \gamma F + \phi \ln (M/P) + \gamma\pi^*$$

where ln stands for the natural logarithm.

$$\begin{aligned} Y^d - Y^d_{-1} \equiv \Delta Y^d &= \gamma (F - F_{-1}) + \phi [\ln(M/P) - \ln(M_{-1}/P_{-1})] + \gamma (\pi^* - \pi^*_{-1}) \\ &= \gamma f + \phi [\ln(M/M_{-1}) - \ln(P/P_{-1})] + \gamma (\pi^* - \pi^*_{-1}) \\ &= \gamma f + \phi(m - \pi) + \gamma (\pi^* - \pi^*_{-1}) \end{aligned}$$

In the last step we use the fact that $\ln (M/M_{-1})$ is very close to $(M - M_{-1})/M_{-1} = m$ for moderate values of m. If Eq. (6) did not take this particular form, Eq. (10) could be looked on as a convenient approximation.

[7] In going from Eq. (10) to Eq. (10*a*), we substitute Y_{-1} in place of Y^d_{-1}. This is justified because, as we shall see below, last period's output was equal to last period's aggregate demand.

again, *given* Y_{-1}, $\Delta\pi^*$, f, m). There is a very simple explanation for this relationship. Given the growth rate of money m, the higher the rate of inflation, the lower the growth rate of real money balances, and therefore the smaller the increase in aggregate demand. Indeed, with inflation in excess of the growth rate of money, $m - \pi < 0$, real balances are declining and therefore real (and nominal) interest rates are increasing. In this case, current demand falls short of last period's demand because inflation has cut down the real money supply and thereby raised interest rates.

In Figure 13-4 we plot the aggregate demand schedule on the assumption that current changes in fiscal policy and expectations are zero ($f = 0$ and $\Delta\pi^* = 0$). The aggregate demand schedule is downward-sloping. Given the growth rate of money, a lower rate of inflation implies that real balances are higher and that therefore the interest rate is lower and spending is higher. The negative slope results from this connection between lower inflation and higher spending.

Given the negative slope of the curve, what determines its location? We observe from Equation (10*a*) (remember that we assume $f = 0$ and $\Delta\pi^* = 0$) that when $m = \pi$, current aggregate demand equals last period's output, $Y^d = Y_{-1}$. Thus the aggregate demand schedule passes through point B in Figure 13-4 where, at an inflation rate equal to the monetary growth rate, we have no change in real balances and therefore no change in spending. For a lower rate of inflation, current spending exceeds last period's. Conversely, for a higher rate of inflation, current spending falls short of last period's.

FIGURE 13-4 THE AGGREGATE DEMAND SCHEDULE

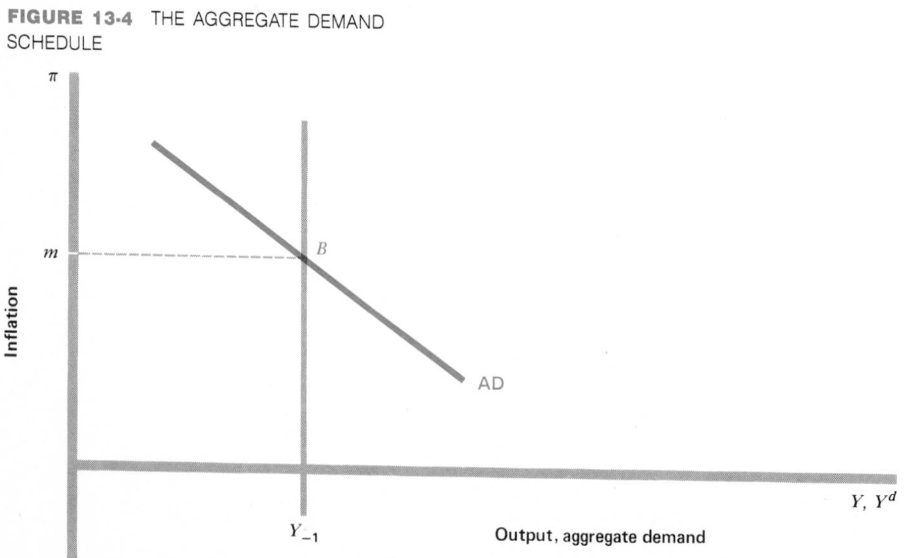

The aggregate demand schedule in Figure 13-4 is drawn on the assumption of a given growth rate of money m and zero change in fiscal policy and expectations. We now briefly ask how changes in these variables would affect aggregate demand. In Figure 13-5 we show that an increase in monetary growth to m' will shift upward the aggregate demand schedule to pass through point C. With higher monetary growth, we need higher inflation if real balances and therefore aggregate demand are to remain constant over time. From Equation (10a) it is apparent that an expansionary fiscal policy or an increase in the expected rate of inflation will likewise shift the aggregate demand schedule up and to the right. For each growth rate of nominal money and the rate of inflation, these changes provide extra expansionary force (over and above that from changing real balances) and therefore raise aggregate demand. Conversely, a move toward fiscal tightness or reduction in the expected rate of inflation shifts the aggregate demand schedule down and to the left.

In summary:

1 Current aggregate demand depends on past aggregate demand and the current stimulus that comes from fiscal expansion, growth in real balances, or increased expectations of inflation.
2 The aggregate demand curve is a downward-sloping relationship between the inflation rate and the level of output.

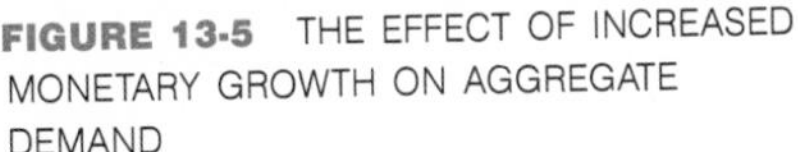

FIGURE 13-5 THE EFFECT OF INCREASED MONETARY GROWTH ON AGGREGATE DEMAND

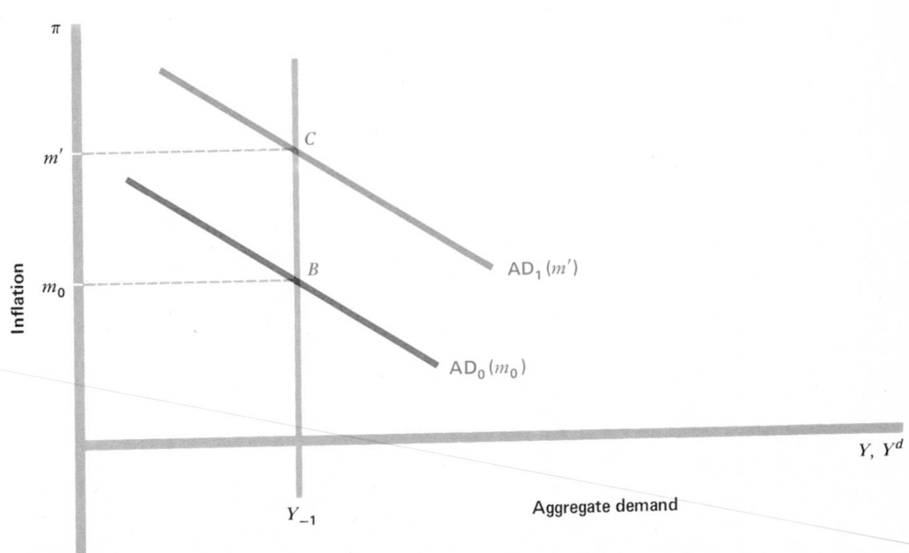

3 The position of the aggregate demand curve depends on last period's output (Y_{-1}), the growth rate of money (m), changes in the full-employment deficit (f), and changes in the expected rate of inflation ($\Delta\pi^*$). Increases in any of Y_{-1}, m, f, or $\Delta\pi^*$ increase aggregate demand and shift the aggregate demand curve upward.

*13-5 DETERMINING THE INFLATION RATE AND OUTPUT LEVEL IN THE SHORT RUN

To determine the inflation rate and the level of output in the short run, we put together our aggregate demand and supply curves. This is done in Figure 13-6. The intersection of the aggregate supply and demand curves at point E determines the inflation rate and the level of output this period, π_0 and Y_0, respectively.

Now, on what do the current rate of inflation and the level of output depend? They clearly depend on the positions of the aggregate supply and demand curves. Thus, changes in any of the variables that shift the aggregate supply and demand curves will affect the current inflation and output levels.

In Figure 13-6 we also show the consequences of an upward shift in the aggregate demand curve from AD_0 to AD_1. The equilibrium of the economy

FIGURE 13-6 THE DETERMINATION OF THE INFLATION RATE AND OUTPUT IN THE SHORT RUN, AND THE SHORT-RUN EFFECTS OF A SHIFT IN AGGREGATE DEMAND

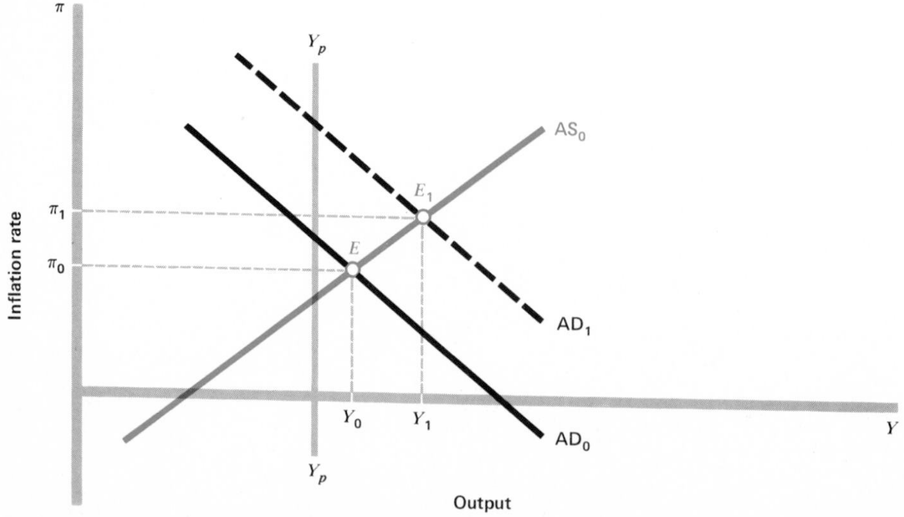

shifts from E to E_1, at which point both the inflation rate and the level of output are higher than they were at E. Upward shifts in the aggregate demand curve therefore result in increases in both the level of output and the inflation rate in the short run. We have already seen what determines the position of the AD curve and therefore what causes it to shift. The higher the lagged level of income Y_{-1}, the greater the change in the full-employment budget deficit f, the greater the increase in expected inflation, and the higher the growth rate of money, the higher the AD curve. Therefore, both the inflation rate and the level of output are higher in the short run, the higher last period's income, the greater the change in the full-employment budget deficit, the greater the increase in expected inflation, and the greater the growth rate of money.

Because the expected rate of inflation affects both aggregate supply and demand (even though in the latter case it is the *change* in expected inflation that is relevant), movements in the aggregate supply curve will in general be accompanied by shifts in the aggregate demand curve. Figure 13-7 shows the effects of an increase in the expected rate of inflation. The

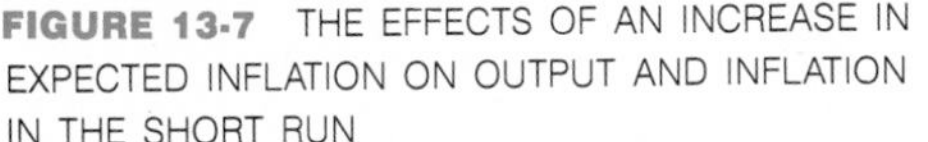

FIGURE 13-7 THE EFFECTS OF AN INCREASE IN EXPECTED INFLATION ON OUTPUT AND INFLATION IN THE SHORT RUN

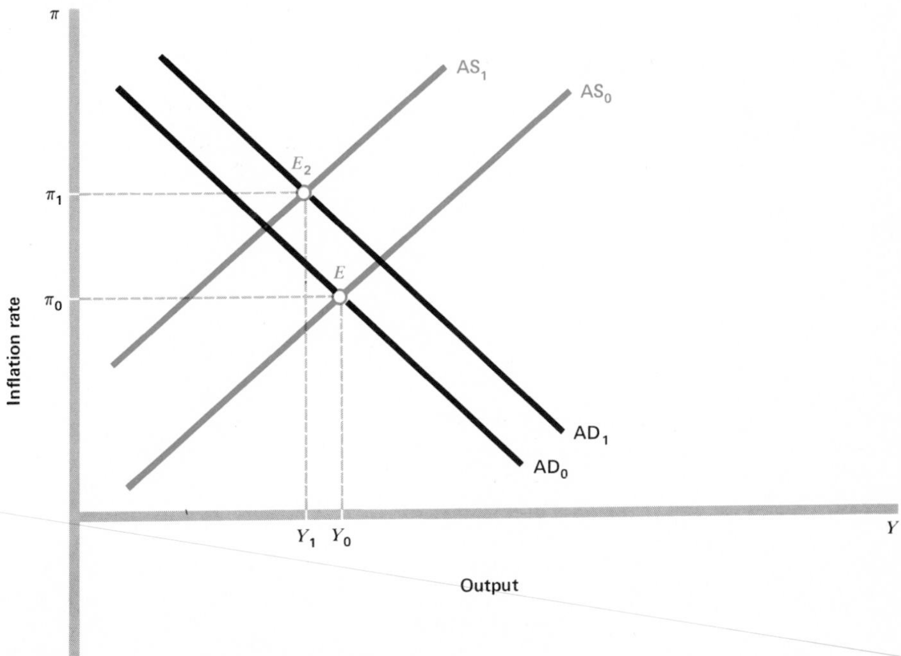

aggregate supply curve shifts up to AS_1, by the full amount of the increase in the expected rate of inflation, but the aggregate demand curve is shown shifting up less (to AD_1). The actual inflation rate rises and the level of output falls. The actual inflation rate rises by less than the expected inflation rate.

The result shown in Figure 13-7 clearly depends on the aggregate supply curve shifting more than the aggregate demand curve.[8] How reasonable is it that the aggregate demand curve should shift up by less than the increase in the expected rate of inflation? On careful examination, the condition depends essentially on the demand for real balances not being very interest-elastic. But we shall simply assume the condition is met because it is required if our aggregate supply-demand model is to be stable.[9]

Our preliminary analysis of aggregate supply and demand, in Figures 13-6 and 13-7, points to five factors affecting the inflation rate and the level of output in the short run: the expected rate of inflation, which determines the location of the aggregate supply curve, and the four other variables that determine the location of the aggregate demand curve. The four are the expected rate of inflation this period and last, the change in the full-employment budget surplus, the growth rate of nominal money, and the level of income last period. If policy makers want to change the behavior of the inflation rate, in the short run, they have to try to affect the expected inflation rate, the change in the full-employment budget surplus, or the growth rate of the money supply. The level of income and expected inflation last period are not variables that can be changed by policy makers today.

The analysis in this section, like that of Chapter 12, points to the potential role of *supply management*. If policy makers want to reduce the inflation rate in the short run, then they can use *demand management* policies which shift the AD curve downward. But such policies will tend to reduce output along with the inflation rate. If policies could be found to shift the AS curve downward, they would make it possible to reduce the inflation rate without reducing the level of income.

We now turn to the analysis of the effects of monetary and fiscal policy on the rate of inflation and the level of output in the short and long runs.

[8] Be sure you can see this. Experiment with your own version of Fig. 13-7.

[9] It is clear that if the aggregate demand curve shifts up by more than the increase in the expected rate of inflation, an increase in the expected rate of inflation will cause an even larger increase in the actual rate of inflation. If this higher inflation feeds back in turn into higher expected inflation, the potential for instability becomes clear. We thus assume henceforth that an increase in the expected rate of inflation shifts the aggregate demand curve up by less than the increase in the expected rate of inflation, as in Fig. 13-8. The condition is satisfied if η in Eq. (10) is less than ϕ. Use of the IS and LM curves shows that this condition is more likely to be satisfied, the smaller the coefficient h in the LM curve (which is different from the h in the aggregate supply curve).

*13-6 THE ADJUSTMENT OF OUTPUT AND INFLATION TO AN INCREASE IN MONETARY GROWTH

We have now looked at the short-run impact of shifts in the aggregate demand and supply schedules and can proceed to study the adjustment process that links short-run and long-run equilibria. In this section we examine the adjustment to an increase in the growth rate of money.

We start by using the expectations equation (5) in which the expected rate of inflation is the rate of inflation that occurred last period. Substituting that assumption about expectations into the aggregate supply curve, Equation (3), we have

$$\pi = \pi_{-1} + h\epsilon\left(\frac{Y}{Y_p} - 1\right) \tag{11}$$

as the aggregate supply curve. In this section we shall assume that the full-employment deficit is kept constant ($f = 0$), so that the aggregate demand curve is described by Equation (10*b*):

$$Y^d = Y_{-1} + \phi(m - \pi) + \eta\Delta\pi^* \tag{10b}$$

The point of departure of our analysis is the long-run equilibrium at point E in Figure 13-8. What does long-run equilibrium imply in the model shown by Equations (10*b*) and (11)? Long-run equilibrium implies that (1) the economy is at full employment, $Y = Y_p$; (2) actual and expected inflation are equal, $\pi = \pi^*$; (3) the rate of inflation is equal to the growth rate of

FIGURE 13-8 LONG-RUN EQUILIBRIUM

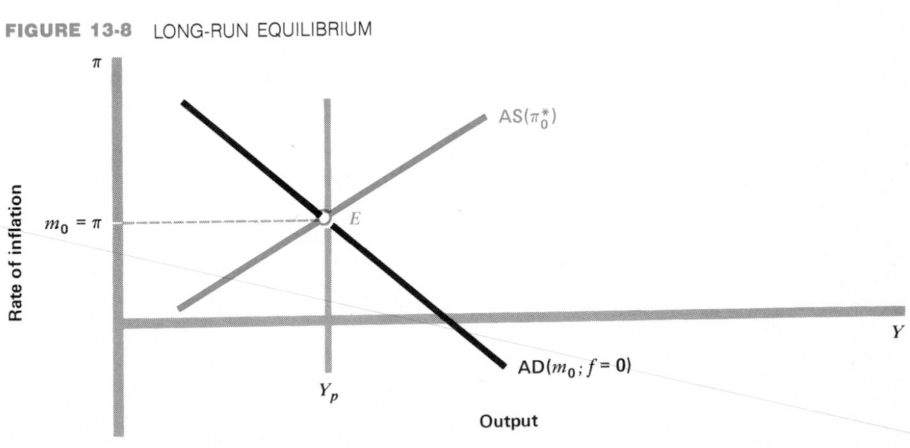

money, $\pi = m_0$; (4) aggregate demand equals aggregate supply, $Y^d = Y$; and (5) aggregate demand remains constant over time, $Y^d = Y_{-1}$.

These conditions are a full description of the equilibrium, but they are not all independent. Start with Equation (11) and note that equality of the actual and expected inflation rates implies that output is at the full-employment level.

Next consider Equation (10*b*) and note that equality of the growth rate of money and the rate of inflation, $\pi = m$, together with constancy of π^*, imply that current output equals past output. In other words, over time, aggregate demand remains constant. Finally, the condition that demand equals supply ensures that aggregate demand is equal to full-employment output.

Diagrammatically, in long-run equilibrium, the supply and demand curves intersect at point E in Figure 13-9. At E, the inflation rate is equal to the growth rate of money [by condition (3)], and output is at its potential level [by condition (1)].

Now, starting from a position of full equilibrium at point E in Figure 13-9, the growth rate of money rises from m_0 to m' and stays at that higher level indefinitely. In this figure the increased monetary growth is shown by an upward shift of the aggregate demand schedule to AD_1. The impact effect, with as yet unchanged expectations and therefore an unchanged supply schedule, is to raise both the rate of inflation and real output. Inflationary expectations, because they are sticky, keep down the actual rate of inflation and prevent it from responding fully to the increased monetary growth. Consequently, the real money supply expands and real output rises to meet the increased demand for goods. This takes us to point E_1. However, the economy will not remain at point E_1. The increased rate of inflation will be reflected in higher inflationary expectations and therefore in upward shifts of the aggregate supply and demand schedules. Similarly, the expansion in real output is reflected in a further upward shift of the aggregate demand schedule.

Accordingly, in period 2, the period after the rise in the growth rate of money, both the aggregate supply and demand curves shift. The aggregate supply curve shifts because the expected rate of inflation has increased— and π^* has increased because the inflation rate at E_1 is higher than the inflation rate at E. We can tell precisely how the supply curve shifts by looking at Equation (11). The new aggregate supply curve AS_2 crosses the Y_p line at precisely the inflation rate that occurred in period 1. The aggregate demand curve shifts up because both lagged output and the expected inflation rate have risen, as can be seen from Equation (10*b*).

In period 2 the inflation rate and level of output are determined at E_2. The inflation rate is undoubtedly higher than it was at E_1, and we have shown the output level at E_2 also to be higher than in the previous period. However, it is possible that output could be less in period 2 than in period 1, depending on the slopes of the aggregate supply and demand curves and

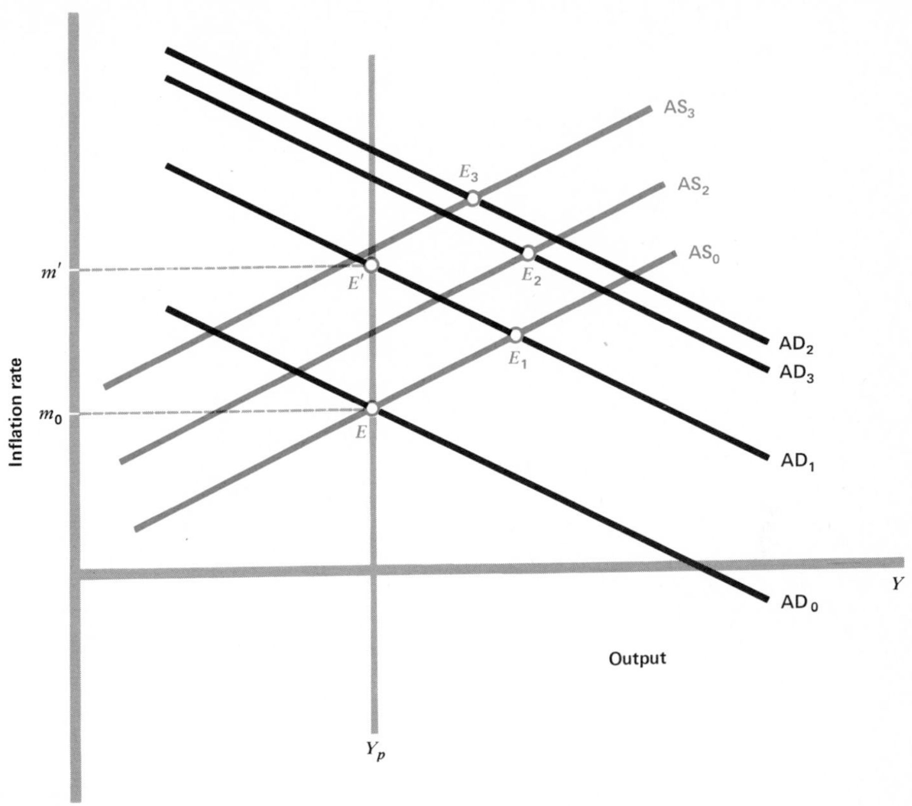

FIGURE 13-9 SHORT-RUN ADJUSTMENT TO A CHANGE IN THE GROWTH RATE OF MONEY

the extent to which the aggregate demand curve shifts from AD_1 to AD_2.

The two curves continue to shift in subsequent periods. As long as the inflation rate keeps rising, the aggregate supply curve will keep rising, since the actual inflation rate last period determines today's expected rate of inflation. The position of the aggregate demand curve is determined by the *level* of lagged output and the *change* of the expected inflation rate, $\Delta\pi^*$. Once $\Delta\pi^*$ is lower than $\Delta\pi^*$ last period (and that can happen even while the inflation rate is increasing)[10] and the level of output begins falling (that is, Y_{-1} is less than Y_{-2}), the aggregate demand curve will certainly

[10] Remember that we are referring to $\Delta\pi^* = \pi^* - \pi^*_{-1}$. Suppose that in three successive periods the expected inflation rate is 5, 8, and 9 percent, respectively. Then $\Delta\pi^*$, which in part determines the position of the AD curve, is 3 percent in the second period and only 1 percent in the third period, even though the expected inflation rate itself is still rising.

fall. Either falling output or a decrease in the change in the inflation rate will tend to cause the aggregate demand curve to fall. In Figure 13-9 we show the equilibrium in period 3 with a higher inflation rate and lower level of output than in period 2. In fact, in both periods 2 and 3, the rate of inflation is even higher than it will eventually be in the long-run equilibrium at E'.

It is not worth following the shifts of the aggregate supply and demand curves during the adjustment process in much further detail. Figure 13-10 shows the pattern of adjustment as the economy moves from E_1, its first-period equilibrium, to the eventual long-run equilibrium at E'. We do not include the shifting supply and demand curves that underlie the pattern of adjustment shown so as to keep the diagram clear. And we have, for convenience, smoothed the time path of adjustment. The first few points E_1, E_2, and E_3 that we traced in Figure 13-9 are also shown in Figure 13-10.

There are two special features of the adjustment process that deserve comment and that can be seen in Figure 13-10. First, given the expectations assumption (5), the economy does not proceed directly to the point of long-run equilibrium E'. Rather, the level of output will fall below Y_p at some stages in the adjustment process as a result of shifts in the aggregate supply and demand curves, and will, at other times, be above Y_p, as it is at E_1, E_2, and E_3. Similarly, the rate of inflation will sometimes be above its long-run equilibrium level m', as it is at E_2, and sometimes below it, as at E_1. Eventually, the economy settles down to its long-run rate of inflation m' and output level Y_p.

The *overshooting* of the inflation rate above its steady-state level during the adjustment process is not accidental or a result of our particular expectations assumptions. Rather, it is a common feature of the adjustment process of the economy to an increase in the growth rate of money. Why? At the new steady state, E', the level of output is the same as it was at E, but the inflation rate is higher. We would expect, and will show in Section 13-7, that the nominal interest rate is higher at E' than at E. That means the demand for, and level of, real balances is lower at E' than at E. The stock of real balances had to fall during the adjustment from E to E'. But real balances can fall only if the inflation rate exceeds the growth rate of money. Since money grew at the rate m' throughout the adjustment process, the inflation rate at some stage had to have exceeded m'. And this is precisely the overshooting feature.

The second important feature of the adjustment process is that in the course of the adjustment, there are times at which output decreases, while the inflation rate increases. For instance, between E_2 and E_3, in Figures 13-9 and 13-10, the inflation rate increases while output decreases. This inverse relationship between output and inflation is a result of the shifts of the supply curve caused by changes in the expected rate of inflation.

The inverse relationship between the rate of inflation and the level of output at some stages of the adjustment process predicted by our theory is

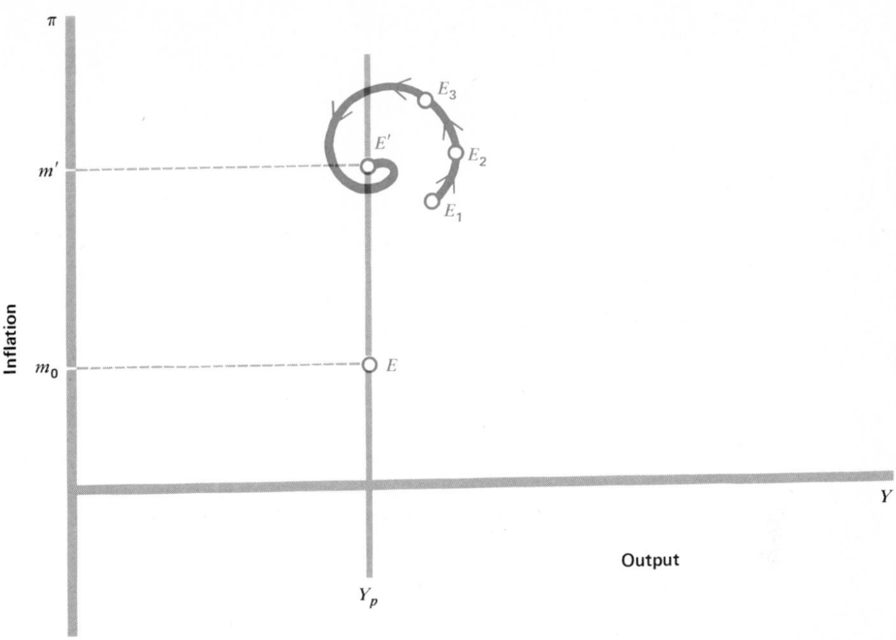

FIGURE 13-10 THE ADJUSTMENT PATH TO AN INCREASE IN MONETARY GROWTH

significant, for it often occurs in practice. However, it is widely believed that the Phillips curve implies that there cannot be such an inverse relationship. If one ignores the role of expected inflation in the Phillips curve, it is easy to conclude that periods in which the inflation rate and output move in opposite directions—and particularly periods in which output is falling while the inflation rate is rising—cannot be explained by economics. In fact, in 1973–1974 and early 1980 when both inflation and unemployment were increasing, there were complaints in the press that the laws of economics no longer seemed to be working. There is no law of economics that says the inflation rate and the level of output move in the same direction at all times. We should not be surprised if the level of output and the inflation rate move in opposite directions at some stages of the adjustment process. That is one of the major lessons of this section; it is the phenomenon of *stagflation*—stagnation with inflation.

The other major lesson, which we have mentioned several times, is that the details of the adjustment process depend on the formation of expectations. In a general way, it is easy to see that the details of the economy's adjustment must depend on the formation of expectations, since changing expectations are responsible for the way in which the aggregate supply curve shifts. We shall make the point more specifically now, however, by using the expectation assumption (5*a*), namely, that expectations show perfect foresight.

Perfect Foresight Expectations

The analysis so far has assumed that expected inflation is equal to last period's actual rate of inflation. This was taken up as a simple representation of expectations based on an average of past inflation rates. Now we change the expectations assumption quite radically. Specifically, we assume in Equation (5*a*) that people correctly foresee the inflation rate

$$\pi^* = \pi \tag{5a}$$

This expectations assumption, combined with the aggregate supply function Equation (3), has an extremely powerful implication. We repeat Equation (3) here:

$$\pi = \pi^* + h\epsilon\left(\frac{Y}{Y_p} - 1\right) \tag{3}$$

Now, if we substitute Equation (5*a*) into Equation (3), we see that we obtain

$$Y = Y_p \tag{12}$$

The implication of Equations (3) and (5*a*) together is that output is always at the potential level, which is what Equation (12) says.

Why? If we reexamine Equation (3), we will see that it says that output is at the potential level unless the expected and actual rates of inflation differ. By assuming perfect foresight expectations, we remove any differences between actual and expected inflation. What is the underlying economic story? The simple notion is that workers and firms in making their wage bargains plan to reach full employment, so that if their expectations turn out to be correct, there will be labor market equilibrium. Consequently, output will be at the potential level.

In particular, this means that the level of output is unaffected by expected changes in the growth rate of money, provided there is perfect foresight. Perfect foresight expectations are a special case of *rational expectations*, expectations which on average are right, and certainly not systematically wrong. The rational expectations notion, when used in a model like that of this section, indeed implies that monetary policy is ineffective, and members of the rational expectations school do take the view that monetary policy cannot be used systematically to affect output.[11]

We will not go into the details of the process of adjustment of the inflation rate to a change in the growth rate of money when there is perfect foresight. But it will be found that the inflation rate overshoots the steady-state inflation rate in the first period as a result of the effect of the increase in expected inflation on aggregate demand.

How reasonable is the result of the perfect foresight assumption that changes in the growth rate of money affect only the inflation rate and not the level of output? One possible objection should be disposed of, namely, that it is absurd to think that anyone can correctly predict the inflation rate. It is undoubtedly true that expectations will never be exactly correct, but the point is that if expectations are approximately correct, monetary policy will have little effect on output.

The more serious objection to the reasonableness of the result in Equation (12) criticizes the assumption underlying Equation (3). This is that the labor market works so smoothly that, in the short run, full employment will be attained if expectations of inflation are correct. In a context such as that of Chapter 11, in which prices do not adjust instantly to demand changes, monetary changes can have real effects through channels other than errors in expectations. If wage increases are passed on only slowly into price changes, then a change in the growth rate of money would only slowly be passed through into prices. This means the aggregate supply curve would move up only slowly in response to a change in monetary growth, and output should, as a consequence, increase. Realistically, stickiness of wage and price adjustment remains an essential feature of the adjustment process of the economy. We return to this point in Chapter 16, in connection with the further discussion there of the implications of rational expectations.

The major implication of the alternative expectations hypotheses is that the dynamic behavior of the economy is crucially affected by the way in which expectations are formed. With perfect foresight, changes in the rate of monetary growth leave output unaffected and cause the inflation rate to overshoot its steady-state level immediately. When expectations are formed on the basis of the lagged inflation rate, as in Equation (5), both output and inflation adjust slowly to the change in money growth. In this latter case, both output and inflation will at times be above, and at other times below, their steady-state levels during the adjustment process.

[11] The implications of perfect foresight and rational expectations for policy are being intensively studied by economists. We discuss the rational expectations school in more detail in Chap. 16. See Thomas J. Sargent and Neil Wallace, "Rational Expectations and the Theory of Economic Policy," *Journal of Monetary Economics*, April 1976, for an introduction to the approach.

Summary

The main points made in this section were:

1 If inflationary expectations are based in a simple way on the past behavior of the inflation rate, an increase in the rate of growth of the money stock increases both the inflation rate and the level of output in the short run. Both the rate of inflation and the level of output continue to fluctuate thereafter, tending eventually to move to the long-run equilibrium of the economy.
2 There are stages in the adjustment process of the economy to a change in the growth rate of money at which the level of output and the rate of inflation move in opposite directions. This occurs as a result of shifts in the aggregate supply curve caused by changes in expectations.
3 If expectations show perfect foresight, the response of the simple economy studied in this section to a change in the growth rate of money is very different. Output remains at its potential level throughout and the change in the growth rate of money affects only the inflation rate and not real income.
4 Even if expectations do show perfect foresight, changes in the growth rate of money can have effects on the level of real output if prices adjust only slowly to changes in demand. Such a mechanism was included in Chapter 11 and is omitted here only to keep the analysis relatively simple.

*13-7 FISCAL POLICY CHANGES

In the long run, the full-employment budget deficit is constant, and therefore f, the change in the full-employment deficit, is zero. Hence the inflation rate is in the long run independent of fiscal policy and is determined solely by the growth rate of money, as we saw in Section 13-1.

Fiscal policy may affect the level of potential output but not through channels we have been considering in this chapter. The route through which fiscal policy can affect the level of potential output is by affecting the mix of investment and consumption. If fiscal policy encourages investment, then the capital stock and level of potential output are likely to be higher in the long run. In this chapter, though, we have not included sufficient detail to study that allocative (between consumption and investment) role of fiscal policy. Instead, we treated fiscal policy as simply a method of affecting aggregate demand—and that is the way we shall continue to treat it in examining its short-run effects.

We will now consider what happens when there is an increase in the full-employment budget deficit, so that f, our measure of the *change* in the full-employment deficit, becomes positive in period 1. Thereafter, it reverts to zero. We assume the growth rate of money is constant at m_0. In the long run, we know, there are no effects of the fiscal policy change on either the inflation rate or the level of output.

Figure 13-11 is used for the analysis of the short-run effects of the increase in the full-employment deficit. The initial increase in the deficit moves the aggregate demand curve up from AD_0 to AD_1. We shall assume here that the expected rate of inflation is equal to last period's rate of inflation.[12] This ensures that the aggregate supply curve does not shift in the first period. The first-period equilibrium is, accordingly, at E_1, with both output and the inflation rate above their long-run levels.

Next period, both the supply and demand curves shift. The aggregate supply curve shifts up from AS_0 to AS_2 as a result of the change in the expected rate of inflation, which is now equal to last period's inflation rate. The aggregate demand curve is affected by the increases in lagged output and expected inflation, tending to cause the curve to shift upward, and by the fall in f, which is now back to zero, tending to cause the curve to shift

[12] In the problem set, we ask you to carry out this analysis under the alternative expectations assumption that the expected inflation rate is equal to the growth rate of money.

FIGURE 13-11 SHORT-RUN EFFECTS OF FISCAL POLICY

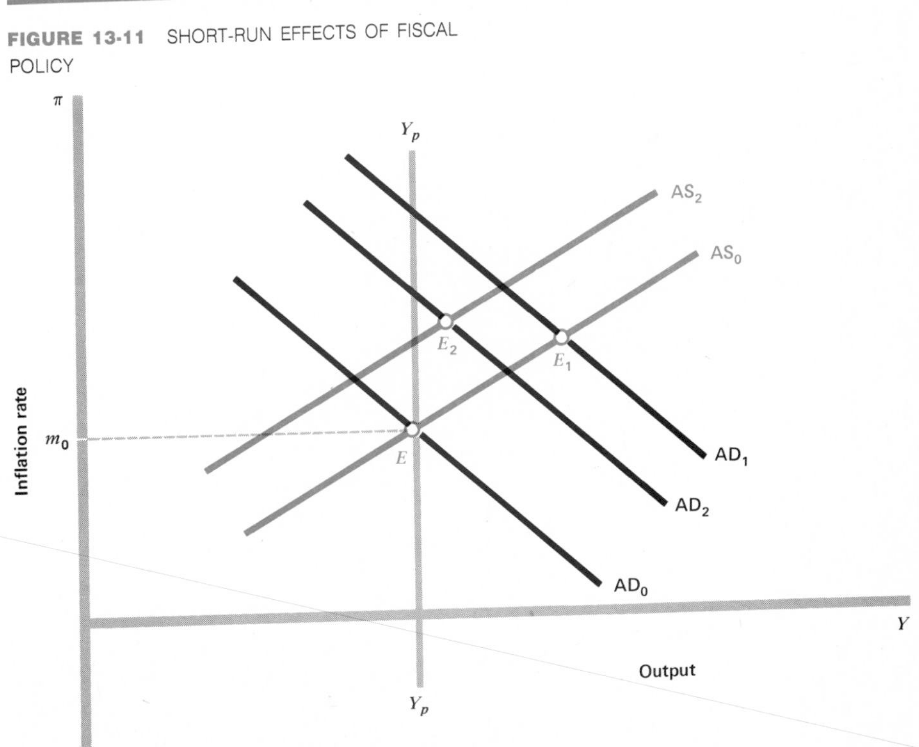

downward. The net effect of these three factors on the aggregate demand curve is ambiguous, but we assume that the curve shifts down in period 2 from AD_1 to AD_2. As a result of these two shifts, we show the level of output at E_2 as lower than that at E_1. However, if the aggregate demand curve shifts up, the level of output could be higher in the second period than in the first. Similarly, the inflation rate at E_2 may be either higher or lower than at E_1. Note that after period 2 the full-employment deficit is no longer changing.

In subsequent periods, the rate of inflation and the level of output both continue to change, moving eventually to their long-run equilibrium levels. During the process of adjustment, the inflation rate and the output rate move both above and below their long-run equilibrium levels.

The analysis of both this section and the last makes it very clear that quite complicated patterns of adjustment of the economy can result from very simple assumptions about the ways in which expectations adjust and in which aggregate demand is determined. We have simplified greatly here; for example, we have assumed that aggregate demand is determined solely by the current fiscal policy and current real balances, rather than also by lagged fiscal policy and real balances. We simplified the dynamics of the Phillips curve by omitting the influence of lagged unemployment rates. We used a very simple model of expectation formation. And even so, we do not get to tell a very simple story about how the economy adjusts to policy changes—or, for that matter, to other disturbances. This reinforces the message of Chapter 9 about the difficulties of stabilization policy, for it is precisely the dynamics of the response of the economy to changes in policy that policy makers have to be able to predict if they are to carry out successful policy.

*13-8 THE FISHER RELATION: REAL AND NOMINAL INTEREST RATES

We now return to the behavior of real and nominal interest rates, particularly during the adjustment process to an increase in the growth rate of money. We show that the real interest rate is, in the long run, unaffected by changes in the growth rate of money and consequent changes in the inflation rate, but that the real interest rate may change in the short run. This is fundamentally the argument made by Irving Fisher.[13] Correspondingly, the nominal interest rate adjusts one for one with the inflation rate in the long run, but not in the short run.

Our analysis combines the IS curve, Equation (7), with the diagrammatic apparatus of the previous sections. In particular, it will be convenient

[13] Irving Fisher, *The Theory of Interest* (New York: A. M. Kelly, Publishers, 1965). Reprint of 1930 edition.

to use Figure 13-10 to study real interest rate behavior in response to a change in the growth rate of money. We recall that underlying Figure 13-10 is the assumption that the expected rate of inflation is equal to last period's inflation rate.

Now Equation (7) is

$$Y = \overline{\alpha}(\overline{A} - bi_r) \tag{7}$$

In Figure 13-12 we reproduce Figure 13-10 in the top panel. In the bottom panel we draw the IS curve, Equation (7), with the real interest rate, i_r, on the vertical axis. We see immediately from both Equation (7) and the diagram that there is a unique real interest rate corresponding to each level of income. Thus, to study the real interest rate during the adjustment process, we concentrate on the behavior of real income.

Note first the long-run constancy of the real rate. Given fiscal policy, represented by $\overline{A}$ in Equation (7), there is a unique real interest rate corresponding to each level of income, and particularly to the level of potential output, Y_p. Since income in the long run is equal to Y_p, the real interest rate is in the long run equal to i_r^*.

Second, we consider the dynamic adjustment of the real interest rate following an increase in the growth rate of money. The real interest rate will decrease as long as income rises and increase as income falls. Thus, the real rate falls from i_r^* to i_r' as the economy moves from E to E_1 following the increase in the growth rate of money. The real rate continues to fall until income stops rising. The real rate then starts rising and continues to rise to above its steady-state level until income again turns around and begins to rise, at point B in Figure 13-12.

Figure 13-13 shows the time path of adjustment of the real rate to the change in monetary growth. Note particularly that the initial response of the real rate is to fall as the increase in the money stock reduces the nominal rate and expectations of inflation have not yet adjusted. Indeed, the fall in the real rate is the means by which monetary policy succeeds in increasing aggregate demand and output. Then later, as the inflation rate and price level rise, real balances fall, putting pressure on the nominal rate. At the same time, as expectations adjust, the real rate also rises.

Figure 13-13 also shows the behavior of the nominal interest rate. In the first period, the nominal rate falls from its initial i_0 level, since the expected rate of inflation has not yet changed. Then, in subsequent periods, the nominal rate rises relative to the real rate as the expected rate of inflation (equal in this analysis to last period's inflation rate) rises. The nominal rate starts falling before the real rate.[14] Then the nominal rate fluctuates around its new long-run equilibrium level, i'.

[14] Do you see why this is true? It is possible to read the nominal rate off Fig. 13-12. The expected rate of inflation each period is last period's inflation rate. Therefore, add to the current real rate the inflation rate last period to find the current nominal rate. You should experiment with this method, which we do not present formally since it clutters up the diagram.

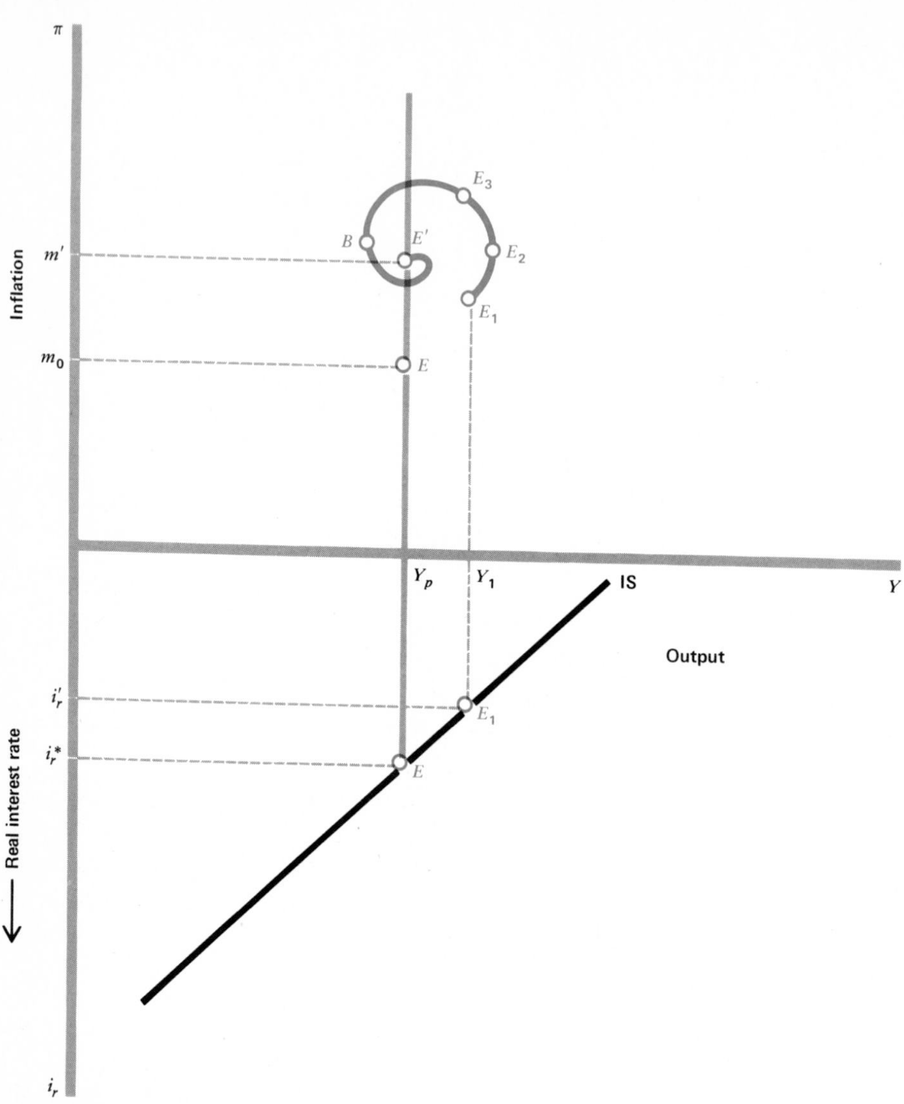

FIGURE 13-12 ADJUSTMENT OF OUTPUT, INFLATION, AND THE REAL INTEREST RATE TO AN INCREASE IN MONETARY GROWTH

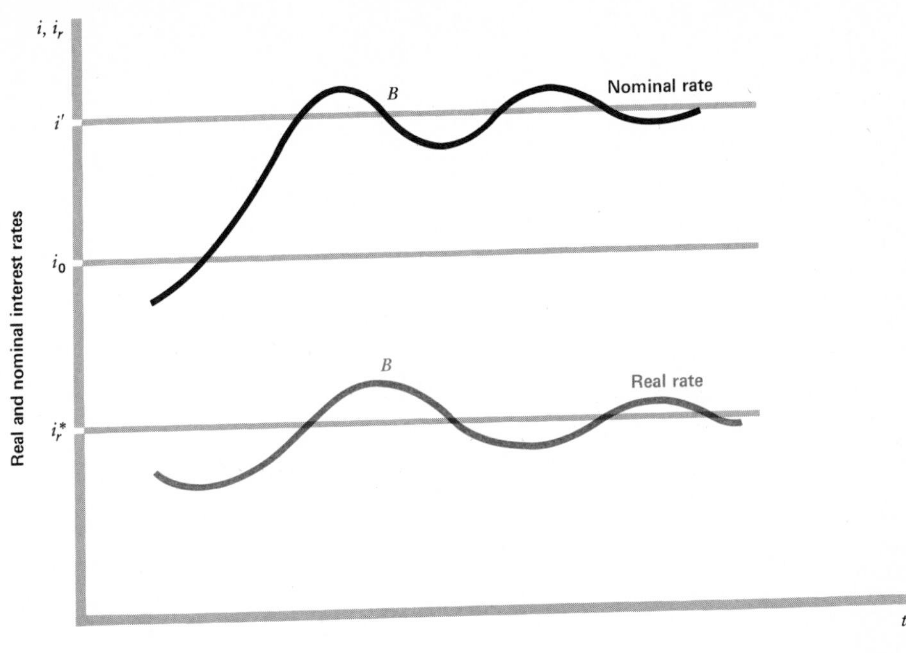

FIGURE 13-13 TIME PATHS OF THE REAL AND NOMINAL INTEREST RATES

What mechanisms are at work in affecting the behavior of the nominal rate? Initially, the nominal rate falls when the money supply increases, prices rise less, and real balances therefore increase. Later, as the level of income rises and the expected rate of inflation increases, the demand for money rises and the nominal rate increases.

What would be the adjustment pattern of real and nominal interest rates if there were perfect foresight? Then the real rate would not change at all, since the level of output does not change. The behavior of the nominal rate would be exactly parallel to that of the inflation rate, initially rising by more than the growth rate of money increases, and then reaching a new steady state where it has risen by exactly the same amount as the growth rate of money.

We now see that there is good reason for nominal interest rates to have risen during the postwar period, as shown in Chart 13-2. Those increases can be attributed to increases in the expected rate of inflation, which would cause an increase in investment demand if nominal rates remained at their initial level. However, the analysis has shown that, in the long run, the real rate is invariant to changes in the inflation rate.

Next, we want briefly to consider the effects of an increase in the full-employment deficit on real and nominal interest rates. We will not carry out the complete analysis, leaving that for you. But we should note that the IS curve in the lower panel of the diagram would shift out to the right and up. The impact effect of the increased full-employment deficit is to increase both the real and nominal interest rates. Then, during the adjustment process, both interest rates fluctuate around their new higher steady-state levels. In the long run, the real interest rate is increased, as is the long-run nominal rate.

We have three final brief comments. First, what is the connection between the analysis of Chapter 4, which showed that an increase in the money supply would reduce the interest rate, and the dynamic analysis of this section? Chapter 4, of course, did not include expectations of inflation and thus did not distinguish real from nominal interest rates. In addition, the price level was fixed in Chapter 4. We should regard the analysis of that chapter as indicating the *short-run* effects of an increase in the money stock on interest rates. With unchanged expectations, we do see from Figure 13-13 that both real and nominal rates fall in the short run when the growth rate of the money stock is increased. Then the implications of price flexibility and expectations of inflation begin to affect interest rates, and the results of Chapter 4 become inapplicable. Of course, the analysis of that chapter remains valuable, since we still use the basic IS-LM framework to study interest rate behavior in this chapter.

Second, we should note that the constancy of the real rate of interest discussed here should not be taken literally. We have omitted from the analysis any disturbances or shifts in the behavioral functions underlying the IS curve in the lower panel of Figure 13-12 and the aggregate supply and demand curves in the upper panel. Increases in investment demand or consumption demand would increase the real rate. Shifts in money demand would affect real and nominal rates in the short run, given the growth rate of money, as would other disturbances. There also are subtleties involving taxes that could upset the Fisher relation. But there is indeed a tendency for the real rate to be constant over long periods.

Third, the average real interest rate in the United States has been surprisingly low. In the period 1926–1978, the *ex post* real interest rate on Treasury bills averaged only 0.0 percent. Even the *ex post* real rate on long-term government bonds averaged only 0.6 percent.[15] The real return on common stocks over the same period averaged 6.1 percent.

Summary

1 An increase in the growth rate of money leaves the real interest rate

[15] These data are presented in Rober G. Ibbotson and Rex A. Sinquefield, *Stocks, Bonds, Bills, and Inflation: Historical Returns (1926–1978)* (New York: Financial Analysts Research Foundation, 1979).

unaffected in the long run and increases the nominal interest rate one for one.

2 An increase in the growth rate of money typically reduces both the real and nominal rates in the short run. Thereafter, the rates fluctuate around their steady-state values as the economy settles down to a new steady state.

3 Expansionary fiscal policy increases real and nominal interest rates in the short and long runs. Again, interest rates fluctuate around their steady-state values during the adjustment process.

4 The adjustment pattern for interest rates is heavily affected by the behavior of expectations of inflation.

13-9 SUMMARY

1 Using the aggregate supply-demand framework of Chapter 12, we can draw aggregate supply and demand curves relating the level of output to the inflation rate rather than the price level.

2 The short-run aggregate supply curve is upward-sloping—higher inflation rates are associated with higher levels of output, in the short run. The slope of the aggregate supply curve is greater, the more unemployment reacts to changes in output (the larger is h) and the more rapidly wages respond to changes in unemployment (the larger is ϵ). The position of the aggregate supply curve depends on the expected rate of inflation.

3 The long-run aggregate supply curve is vertical.

4 The short-run aggregate demand curve is downward-sloping. It is steeper, the less sensitive aggregate demand is to changes in real balances (the smaller is ϕ). The position of the aggregate demand curve depends on lagged output, the rate of change of the full-employment deficit, changes in expected inflation, and the growth rate of the money stock.

5 In the short run, the rate of inflation and the level of output are determined by the current and lagged expected rates of inflation, the lagged level of output, the change in the full-employment surplus, and the growth rate of the money stock. An increase in the expected rate of inflation increases the actual rate of inflation and reduces output. Increases in the last three variables increase both the rate of inflation and output.

6 In the long run, the level of output is equal to potential output. The rate of inflation is equal to the growth rate of the money stock.

7 In the short run, an increase in the growth rate of money produces increases in output and inflation if expectations are based on the past behavior of inflation. At stages during the adjustment process of the economy to the increased money growth, output and inflation will be moving in opposite directions.

8 If expectations show perfect foresight and if prices adjust immediately to wage changes, then output stays at its potential level when the growth rate of money rises.
9 In the short run, an increase in the full-employment deficit increases both output and the inflation rate. A one-time increase in the full-employment deficit has no permanent effects on the rate of inflation and the level of output.
10 The Fisher relation, that the real interest rate is independent of the inflation rate in the long run but varies during the adjustment process, is confirmed by the analysis of this chapter. Correspondingly, in the long run the nominal interest rate rises one for one with the inflation rate.
11 The behavior of output, unemployment, inflation,and interest rates is heavily affected by the way in which expectations are formed.

APPENDIX: OKUN'S LAW

One of the key rules of thumb in macroeconomics is the relationship between the unemployment rate and the GNP gap. This empirical relationship, developed by Arthur Okun and extensively used by the Kennedy-Johnson Council of Economic Advisers is stated in Equation (A1):

$$\text{GNP gap} = a(u - \bar{u}) \tag{A1}$$

where $\bar{u}$ is the natural rate of unemployment, taken in the 1960s to be 4 percent, and the parameter a was estimated in the sixties to be about 3. More recent estimates suggest a is now closer to 2½ and $\bar{u}$ to about 5½.[16] Okun's law as stated in Equation (A1) says that for every 1 percent unemployment above $\bar{u}$ percent, there is an a percent GNP gap. The GNP gap here is defined as the percentage shortfall of actual from full-employment output.

$$\text{GNP gap} \equiv \frac{Y_p - Y}{Y_p} \tag{A2}$$

Equations (A1) and (A2) allow us to calculate the loss in output due to unemployment. For example, if the unemployment rate is 7 percent, $\bar{u}$ is 5.5 percent, and a is 2.5, we have a 3.75 (2.5 × 1.5) percent GNP gap. With a level of potential output of $2,500 billion, this means a loss in output equal to $94 billion.

Okun's law describes the short-run relationship between the GNP gap and unemployment. The underpinnings of the law can be developed in terms of the determinants of short-run output. We write output as follows:

[16] For a description and discussion of some of these estimates, see Jeffrey Perloff and Michael Wachter, "A Production Function Non-Accelerating Inflation Approach to Potential Output," in *Carnegie-Rochester Conference Series*, vol. 10, Karl Brunner and Allan Meltzer (*eds.*), North-Holland.

$$Y = qh(1 - u)\overline{N} \tag{A3}$$

In Equation (A3), q is the productivity of labor, h is the average number of hours worked, u is the unemployment rate, and $\overline{N}$ is the labor force. Equation (A3) states that short-run output is equal to employment, $h(1 - u)\overline{N}$, times productivity, q. The total number of hours worked in the economy is equal to the fraction of the labor force employed, $1 - u$, times the labor force, $\overline{N}$, times the average number of hours worked, h. Employment times productivity or output per hour gives total output, Y.

Now from Equation (A3) it is apparent that there are four sources of increased output. Increased output can arise from an increased labor force, increased average hours worked, a reduction in the unemployment rate, or finally, an improvement in productivity. Okun's observation was that, in the short run, these sources of output growth move together in a relatively stable manner. This fact allows a simple relationship between output and employment, recognizing that unemployment itself is a proxy for all four of the sources of increased output. The detailed breakdown of the contribution to increased output of the various sources when the unemployment rate falls by 1 percent (e.g., from 5 percent to 4 percent), as measured by Okun, is shown in Table A13-1. More recent studies suggest the increased labor force and productivity contributions are smaller than shown in this table. However, there is not yet any consensus on the new estimates, and we shall use Okun's estimates in the rest of this appendix.

Consider a simple numerical example which illustrates the lesson of Table A13-1. Suppose the unemployment rate drops by two percentage points from 7 percent to 5 percent. Output then rises by 6 percent. Of that 6 percent increase, 2.1 percent arises from the output produced by those who were previously unemployed. Those previously employed now work longer each week on average, and that source of growth accounts for 0.8 percent of the increase in output. People who were not previously looking for work enter the labor force and obtain jobs (we discuss this point in more detail immediately below), and their production contributes 1.3 percent to output. Finally, output per hour worked rises, increasing output by the final 1.8 percent.

It is worth noting explicitly that the relationship between changes in output and changes in unemployment that we presented in Chapter 11 in the theory of aggregate supply is entirely consistent with Okun's law. Our theory relating output and unemploy-

TABLE A13-1 THE OUTPUT EFFECT OF A 1 PERCENT DROP IN UNEMPLOYMENT

Source of output change		Percent change in output
u	Jobs for the unemployed	1.05
h	Lengthened workweek	0.40
$\overline{N}$	Increased labor force	0.65
q	Improved productivity	0.90
Increase in output		3.00

Source: Arthur Okun, "Upward Mobility in a High-Pressure Economy," *Brookings Papers on Economic Activity*, 1973:2 (Washington, D.C.: The Brookings Institution, 1973).

ment included both changes in hours worked and in productivity, as does Okun's law. The only element of Table A13-1 we did not include is the change in labor force participation.

One important point about Table A13-1 is that increased labor input derives from two sources. The first source is the obvious one of the reduced unemployment rate—putting people who were looking for work back into productive activity. The second source is less obvious. The labor force itself typically increases when the unemployment rate drops. The point is that not all persons out of work are actually measured as "unemployed." To be counted as unemployed, an individual must engage in "specific job-seeking activity within the past four weeks." In a poor labor market, some people stop looking for work and are not counted in the official measures of the labor force. Once the labor market improves as the unemployment rate drops and employment prospects look brighter, such people reenter the labor market and the labor force $\bar{N}$ increases.

A second important point about the table is that a reduction in unemployment, or an increase in labor input, is usually accompanied by an improvement in productivity. Equivalently, productivity and output move in the same direction: output per worker increases when total output increases, and output per worker decreases when total output declines. The basic reason for this stems from the costs to firms of hiring and laying off workers, as discussed in Chapter 11.

Okun's law is only a rule of thumb, not a relationship that holds very precisely at each point in time. Even so, it has proved quite sturdy as a simple device to assess the required expansion in output to achieve a given unemployment target. Since the middle sixties, when the analysis was first developed, the unemployment rate taken to represent full employment has increased. Many argue that the full-employment unemployment rate now is approximately 5.5 percent rather than 4 percent. This obviously means that potential output is less than that corresponding to a 4 percent unemployment rate. It does not, however, impair the usefulness of either the concept of potential output and the GNP gap, or the relation between changes in output and changes in unemployment.

Finally, we shift to a somewhat longer-run perspective. It is often said that the economy has to grow at 3 percent just to keep the unemployment rate from rising. We want to use Equation (A3) to show why that should be. Suppose that the labor force were growing at some constant rate, say 1.5 percent, and the productivity of labor were growing at a constant rate, say, 1.5 percent.

Now, *given* those longer-run growth rates of productivity and the labor force, output will have to grow at 3 percent if unemployment is to remain constant. We return to Equation (A3) and turn it into a relationship among the growth rates of the variables in it:

$$g_Y = g_q + g_h + g_{1-u} + g_N \tag{A4}$$

In Equation (A4), g with a subscript denotes the growth rate of the particular variable. We shall assume that the number of hours worked per worker is constant, so that g_h is zero, and, accordingly:

$$g_Y = g_q + g_{1-u} + g_N \tag{A4a}$$

Now, what does Equation (A4a) tell us about the rate of output growth that is required to keep unemployment constant? Given $g_q = 1.5$ percent, and $g_N = 1.5$ percent, we have

$$g_Y = 1.5 + g_{1-u} + 1.5 = 3 + g_{1-u} \tag{A4b}$$

If the unemployment rate is to remain constant, we must have $g_{1-u} = 0$ and, accordingly,

$$g_Y = 3 \tag{A4c}$$

Equation (A4*c*) tells us that output has to grow at the sum of the growth rates of the labor force and productivity if unemployment is to remain constant. If output grows more slowly, then unemployment will be increasing.

How do Equation (A4*c*) and the statement that the economy has to grow at 3 percent to keep unemployment from rising relate to the Okun's law relationship between the unemployment rate and deviation of output from the potential output level? All that Equation (A4*c*) does is to tell us how fast potential output will be growing, given the assumed behavior of the labor force and productivity. Okun's law applies to short-run deviations of output around the path of potential output.

PROBLEMS

*1 (*a*) Explain how the size of h and the size of ϵ affect the slope of the aggregate supply curve. Be sure to provide an intuitive explanation along with any other explanation.
(*b*) Why is it the *product* $h\epsilon$ (rather than, for example, the sum $h + \epsilon$) that determines the slope of the AS curve?

2 Explain in words why the expected rate of inflation affects the position of the aggregate supply curve.

3 Suppose we have an economy where real output grows at the rate of 6 percent per year. The nominal quantity of money grows at the rate of 5 percent. The income elasticity of money demand is 0.5.
(*a*) What is the rate of inflation in long-run equilibrium?
(*b*) What is the growth rate of nominal income? (Remember that nominal income can grow because prices increase, real output rises, or both.)
(*c*) How would your answers to 3(*a*) and 3(*b*) change if the income elasticity of money demand was unity?

4 Suppose that the rate of inflation is 3 percent, that real wages are rising by 2 percent, and real balances are rising by 4 percent. What is:
(*a*) The rate of increase of nominal wages?
(*b*) The rate of growth of the nominal money stock?

*5 How far *upward* does the aggregate demand curve, Equation (10*a*), shift at a given level of income for:
(*a*) A 1 percent increase in the growth rate of the money stock?
(*b*) An increase of one unit in f?
(*c*) A one-unit increase in Y_{-1}?
(*d*) A 1 percent increase in the expected rate of inflation?

Explain why increases in each of those variables shift the AD curve up, and also try to explain the extent to which the curve is shifted in each case—5(*a*), 5(*b*), 5(*c*), and 5(*d*).

*6 (*a*) How does the ***slope*** of the aggregate demand curve determine the short-run effects on the rate of inflation and output of an increase in the growth rate of money—assuming that the expected rate of inflation is unaffected by the change in monetary growth?

(*b*) How does the slope of the AS curve affect the way in which a change in the growth rate of money changes the rate of inflation and output in the short run? Provide a verbal explanation along with any diagrams you draw in both cases.

7 (*a*) Suppose that there is a one-time increase in Y_p, which thereafter remains constant. How does that affect the ***long-run*** inflation rate?

(*b*) Suppose that Y_p began to grow steadily at a rate $\bar{x}$. How would that affect the long-run rate of inflation?

*8 Draw an aggregate supply-demand diagram like Figure 13-9, but with a very flat aggregate supply curve. Then, assuming that $\pi^* = \pi_{-1}$, allow the growth rate of money to increase and show how the supply and demand curves shift in the first two periods. Show what happens to the rate of inflation and the level of output in these periods, starting from the period in which the growth rate of money increases. Compare your results with those of Figure 13-9 and explain the reasons for any differences.

*9 Using the aggregate supply-demand diagrams of Chapter 12,

(*a*) Show how in steady state the aggregate supply and demand functions would be shifting up over time in such a way as to keep output constant.

(*b*) Analyze the ***first-period*** impact of an increase in monetary growth that does not affect expectations.

*10 Suppose the growth rate of money changes unexpectedly and that expectations are given by $\pi^* = m_{-1}$. Expectations are based on last-period's money growth. Analyze the short- and long-run effects of the changed money growth on output, inflation, and the real and nominal interest rates.

*11 In analyzing the effects of a change in f in one period, we assumed that the expected rate of inflation was given by Equation (5). Now use the alternative assumption that $\pi^* = m$, that people believe the inflation rate is determined exclusively by monetary growth.

(*a*) Analyze the dynamic consequences of a one-time increase in f.

(*b*) Does this expectations assumption show perfect foresight?

*12 Explain in words the mechanism whereby the nominal interest rate adjusts to inflation in the long run.

13 At the beginning of the chapter, in discussing Chart 13-1, we said that we wanted to be able to explain behavior such as that shown in the chart. How does the analysis of this chapter explain that behavior, particularly the periods when the unemployment rate and the inflation rate were increasing together?

*14 In Figure 13-3 we showed the effect of increased inflationary expectations on the equilibrium interest rate and level of output. In that figure we conducted the analysis with the nominal interest rate (i) on the vertical axis. Now show the same effects in a diagram that has the real interest rate on the vertical axis.

(*a*) Express the LM curve in terms of the real interest rate and expected inflation, using the relation, $i_r = i - \pi^*$.
(*b*) Draw the IS and LM schedules corresponding to the initial equilibrium.
(*c*) Consider the increase in inflationary expectations. Which schedules shift and by how much?
(*d*) Show in your diagram the change in the real interest rate.

14

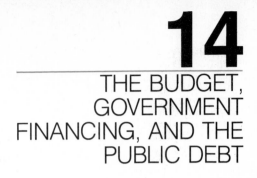

THE BUDGET, GOVERNMENT FINANCING, AND THE PUBLIC DEBT

The federal government's outlays for 1980 were over $500 billion, or more than 20 percent of GNP. The budget deficit for 1979 was nearly $30 billion, which means that the federal government spent about $30 billion more in that year than it received as taxes. The national debt at the end of 1979 was about $650 billion, or over $3,000 for every person in the United States. State and local governments spent about $330 billion in 1979, or almost 14 percent of GNP, compared with 5 percent in 1946.

Facts like these are frequently cited in discussions of the size and growth of the government's role in the economy, and as arguments in favor of a constitutional limitation on government spending or taxes. The facts naturally cause concern about the way the government affects the economy. But what does a large deficit mean for the behavior of the economy? Is it bound to lead to inflation? Is an ever-growing national debt certain to lead to economic disaster? This chapter will examine these and similar questions.

The chapter discusses a number of questions connected with the budget, government spending, and taxes. In Section 14-1 we describe the financing of the federal government budget deficit—that is, how the government pays for the excess of its spending over its income from taxes. In Section 14-2 we examine the facts about the federal budget, federal government spending, the financing of that spending, and the national debt. In Section 14-3 we study the effects on the economy of different methods of financing the budget and the economic significance of the national debt. Section 14-4 explores state and local government spending and financing. Section 14-5 briefly discusses the issue of the size of the government.

14-1 THE MECHANICS OF FEDERAL GOVERNMENT SPENDING AND FINANCING

In this section we examine how the federal government finances its spending. We are particularly interested in the relationship between the federal government's deficit and changes in the stocks of money and government debt.

How does the government pay for its spending? Directly, it pays for most of its spending with checks, drawn on a Federal Reserve bank. Aside from the fact that the check is drawn on a bank in which private individuals do not have accounts, a payment made by the government looks much like a check payment made by anyone else. Like an individual, the federal government must have funds in the accounts on which it writes checks. So the question of how the federal government finances its spending is the same as the question of how it makes sure that it has funds in the bank accounts (at the Federal Reserve System) on which it writes its checks.

The Treasury is the agency of the federal government that collects government receipts and makes payments for the government. The government's accounts at the Federal Reserve System are held and operated by the Treasury. The Treasury receives the bulk of its receipts from taxes.

In some years, taxes are less than federal government expenditures. Those are the years in which the federal government runs a budget deficit, as in 1979 and 1980. Total government expenditures consist of purchases of goods and services, G, and transfers, R. Denoting taxes by T and the deficit by BuD, with all variables measured in real terms, we know that

$$\text{BuD} \equiv (G + R) - T \equiv -\text{BuS} \tag{1}$$

Equation (1) reminds us that the budget deficit, BuD, is just the negative of the budget surplus, BuS. Thus in 1979, the deficit was $30 billion, or the surplus was minus $30 billion.

Now, how does the Treasury make payments when its tax receipts are insuffīcent to cover its expenditures? The answer is that it has to borrow. In describing how the Treasury borrows to finance its deficit, we shall step back a moment from the particular institutional arrangements of the United States economy and talk in general terms of a treasury financing its budget deficit by borrowing either from the public or from its central bank. We shall talk as if the Treasury can borrow directly from the central bank by selling it securities. Alternatively, it can sell securities (debt) to the public.[1]

When the Treasury borrows from the private sector, it sells Treasury securities or debt to the private sector. In return, it receives checks from individuals and firms (including banks) in exchange for the securities it sells them. These checks are deposited either in Treasury accounts at private banks or at the central bank, and can then be spent by the Treasury in the same way as tax receipts.

Alternatively, the Treasury can borrow from the central bank. This is done by the central bank's purchasing some of the debt of the Treasury. However, there is a major difference between the Treasury's borrowing from the public and from the central bank. When the central bank lends to the Treasury by buying Treasury debt, it pays for debt by giving the Treasury a check on the central bank—that is, by creating high-powered money. When the Treasury spends the deposit it has received at the central bank in exchange for its debt, it leaves the private sector with larger holdings of high-powered money. By contrast, when the Treasury borrows from the public, it receives and then spends high-powered money, thus leaving the amount of high-powered money in the hands of the public unchanged—except for a brief transition period between the sale of securities and

[1] Foreign central banks and financial institutions buy some U.S. Treasury securities and thus help finance the deficit. We shall treat sales of securities to foreign institutions as sales to the public.

expenditures by the Treasury. Since the stock of high-powered money is an important macroeconomic variable, the distinction between selling debt to the public and selling it to the central bank is in fact essential.

The distinction can be further clarified by noting that Treasury sales of securities to the central bank are referred to as *monetizing the debt*, meaning that the central bank creates (high-powered) money to finance the debt purchase. Yet another way of looking at the difference between sales to (borrowing from) the central bank and the public is to ask: What is the net change in the private sector's portfolio after the Treasury has made *and* financed its expenditures? Consider first the case of borrowing from the public or selling debt to the public. In this case, the public holds more debt, having bought the Treasury offering, and holds an unchanged quantity of high-powered money, since the Treasury spends the money it obtains from the debt sale to cover its deficit. Consider next the case where the deficit is financed by sale of debt to the central bank. In this event, the private sector's debt holding is unchanged while its holding of high-powered money is increased. The reason is that Treasury expenditures were financed by the creation of high-powered money by the central bank.

The government deficit can thus be financed in two ways: by sales of securities, or debt, to the private sector, and by borrowing from the central bank. Let ΔB_p be the change in the number of government bonds (securities) held by the private sector, ΔB_f be the change in the number of bonds held by the central bank, and P_b be the price in dollars paid for one bond. Let H be the stock of high-powered money. We have just seen that[2]

$$P \cdot \text{BuD} = P_b \Delta B_f + P_b \Delta B_p \simeq \Delta H + P_b \Delta B_p \tag{2}$$

Equation (2) is called the government's *budget constraint*. It states that the nominal budget deficit is financed by borrowing either from the central bank ($P_b \Delta B_f$) or from the private sector ($P_b \Delta B_p$). The change in the central bank's holdings of Treasury debt causes a corresponding change in high-powered money (ΔH), so that we can say that the budget deficit is financed either by selling debt to the public or by increasing the stock of high-powered money. It is in this sense that the central bank "monetizes" the debt.[3]

The view that the deficit is financed either by selling debt to the public or by increasing the stock of high-powered money looks at the government

[2] As we saw in Chap. 8, the stock of high-powered money may change for reasons other than open market operations. For that reason we use the symbol for "approximately equal to" ($\simeq$) in Eq. (2). The change in the central bank's holdings of government bonds is only approximately equal to the change in high-powered money.

[3] Note that the government budget constraint (2) also shows that for a given value of the deficit, changes in the stock of high-powered money are matched by offsetting changes in the public's holdings of government debt. A positive ΔH matched by a negative $P_b \Delta B_p$ is nothing other than an open market purchase.

sector as a whole, including or "consolidating" the central bank along with the Treasury in the government sector. When one thinks of the government sector as a whole, relative to the private sector, the transactions in which the central bank buys debt from the Treasury or lends to the Treasury are seen as mere bookkeeping entries within the government sector.

Now, in many countries it is useful to think of the government sector as a whole, without bothering to distinguish between the actions of the treasury and the central bank. However, in the United States it should always be remembered that the Fed retains considerable power and independence as to how it will act. Indeed, the Fed does not generally buy debt directly from the Treasury, and so does not directly finance the deficit in the way just described. The great bulk of Fed purchases of debt are made directly from the public. However, that should be thought of as only an institutional detail. For, although the Fed by and large does not buy directly from the Treasury, it does so indirectly by buying securities from the public. Suppose that the Fed is conducting open market purchases at the same time as the Treasury is selling debt to the public. The net effect of the combined Treasury sale of debt and Fed open market purchase is that the Fed ends up holding more Treasury debt, which is precisely what would happen if it bought directly from the Treasury.

In the United States the important institutional arrangement is that the Fed is largely responsible for the division of the total deficit BuD, in Equation (2), between the change in high-powered money and the change in government debt held by the private sector. There is no *necessary* association between the size of the government deficit in the United States and increases in the stock of high-powered money. If the Fed does not conduct open market purchases when the Treasury is borrowing, the stock of high-powered money is not affected by the Treasury's deficit.

Nonetheless, there have been occasions in the past when there was a more or less automatic association between Fed open market purchases and Treasury borrowing. This link was most direct when the Fed was essentially committed to maintaining constant the nominal interest rates on government bonds, in the period from 1941 to 1951. As we saw in Chapter 4, an increase in the government deficit tends to increase the nominal interest rate. If the Fed were committed to maintaining constant the nominal interest rate, an increase in the deficit would force it to conduct an open market purchase to keep the nominal interest rate from rising. Thus there would be a link between Treasury borrowing and Fed open market purchases.

The Fed's commitment to maintain constant nominal interest rates on government bonds ended formally in 1951 in the "Accord" between the Fed and the Treasury. Even though, after 1951, the Fed had no formal commitment to maintain constant nominal interest rates, its long-time policy of having target nominal interest rates—which could change from time to time—also led to an association between deficits and Fed open market purchases. For, given the Fed's target interest rates, Treasury borrowing which would have led to interest rate increases triggered Fed open market purchases to keep the interest rate from rising above its target level. Thus, for much of the fifties and sixties, there was a link between increased Treasury borrowing and Fed open market purchases.

Recently, the Fed has moved over to policies which concentrate on the behavior of the nominal money stock. A Fed commitment to producing a given money stock breaks the link between government deficits and the creation of high-powered money. Now the Fed creates high-powered money at a rate that should result in money's growing at the target rate, and the change in the stock of high-powered money is therefore not directly associated with the size of the government deficit.

We return now to Equation (2). We shall treat any indirect purchases of Treasury securities by the Fed—through open market purchases when the Treasury is running a deficit—as direct lending by the Fed to the Treasury. It follows from Equation (2) that when the budget is not balanced, the Treasury changes the net amount of *claims* on it held by the private sector and the Fed. Those claims are the securities the Treasury sells to the private sector and (indirectly) the Fed, and they represent claims for future interest payments. The total stock of such claims constitutes the *national debt*.[4] When the budget is in deficit, the national debt increases—the stock of claims against the Treasury increases. When the budget is in surplus, the national debt decreases. The Treasury takes in more taxes than it pays out, and can use the excess to retire (or buy back) previously issued debt.[5]

The national debt is a direct consequence of past deficits in the federal budget. The national debt increases when there is a budget deficit and decreases when the budget is in surplus. The way the national debt is divided between private sector claims on the Treasury and high-powered money depends on past monetary policy. If the Fed has financed a large proportion of each deficit in the past, then the ratio of high-powered money to the national debt is large. If the Fed has financed only a small part of each deficit in the past, then the ratio of high-powered money to national debt is small.

The Treasury sells securities more or less continuously. There is, for instance, a weekly Treasury bill auction, at which prospective buyers of

[4] Note that we are not counting in the national debt those claims on the Treasury that are held by government agencies other than the Fed. We regard those claims as canceling out within the government sector.

[5] Periodically, the Congress votes to raise the maximum amount of the debt the federal government can issue. The amount of debt subject to the ceiling imposed by Congress includes some of the debt owned by federal agencies along with what we are calling the national debt.

Treasury bills (lenders to the federal government) submit sealed bids specifying how much they are prepared to lend at different interest rates. The Treasury sells the amount of Treasury bills it has offered at the auction to the bidders who offer the highest prices, or the lowest interest rates.[6] Longer-term debt issues are less frequent. Issues of Treasury debt are not all made for the purpose of financing the budget deficit. Most debt issues are made to refinance parts of the national debt that are maturing. For example, the Treasury has to pay the amount it borrowed to a Treasury bill holder when the Treasury bill matures. Six months after a 180-day Treasury bill is issued, the Treasury has to pay the face amount of the Treasury bill to the holder. Typically, the Treasury obtains the funds to make those payments by further borrowing. The process by which the Treasury (with the help and advice of the Fed) finances and refinances the national debt is known as *debt management*. Only part of debt management is concerned with financing the current budget deficit. Most of it is concerned with the consequences of past budget deficits.

Summary

Five main points have been made in this section.

1. Federal government spending is financed through taxes and through borrowing, which is necessary when the budget is in deficit.
2. Borrowing may be from the private sector or indirectly from the Federal Reserve System.
3. Lending to the Treasury by the Fed changes the stock of high-powered money, whereas lending by the private sector to the Treasury to finance the deficit does not affect the stock of high-powered money.
4. The stock of claims held by the Fed and the private sector against the Treasury—the national debt—changes with the budget deficit. The national debt increases when there is a budget deficit and decreases when there is a budget surplus.
5. Because the deficit can be financed in two ways, there is no *necessary* connection between the budget deficit and changes in the stock of high-powered money. Equation (2), the government budget constraint, says only that the *sum* of changes in the stock of debt and changes in high-powered money is approximately equal to the budget deficit.

[6] Technically, there is no interest paid on Treasury bills. Instead, a Treasury bill is a promise by the Treasury to pay a given amount on a given date, say \$100 on June 30. Before June 30, the Treasury bill sells for a *discount* at less than \$100, with the discount implying a rate of interest. For instance, if the Treasury bill just described sold for \$97.50 on January 1, the holder of the bill for 6 months would earn a little more than 5 percent per annum, or 2.5 percent for 6 months.

14-2 BUDGETARY FACTS

In this section we briefly review some facts about the federal budget. Chart 14-1 shows actual and high-employment budget deficits[7] for the 1952–1979 period as a percentage of GNP. The actual budget has been in deficit every year since 1961, except for 1969. Before 1961 the actual budget was in surplus more often. The high-employment budget behaved differently. It was in almost continuous surplus from 1955 through 1969. Since 1970, the full-employment budget has been in deficit.

From the chart we see that both actual and high-employment budget deficits have on average been higher in the past 5 years than they were in earlier years. In particular, the actual budget deficit in 1975 reached the record level of $70 billion, or over 4 percent of GNP. We also see a sharp increase in the full-employment deficit in 1975 as a result of the $30-billion tax cut in that year.

Examine next Chart 14-2, which shows the size and Federal Reserve

[7] The high-employment or full-employment budget surplus was introduced in Chap. 3. The full-employment budget surplus is calculated at a level of GNP equal to potential output. Estimates of potential output are discussed in Chap. 17. As a result of recent downward revisions of estimates of potential output, new calculations of the full-employment budget for recent years show larger *deficits* than did previous estimates. (Be sure you can follow this statement.)

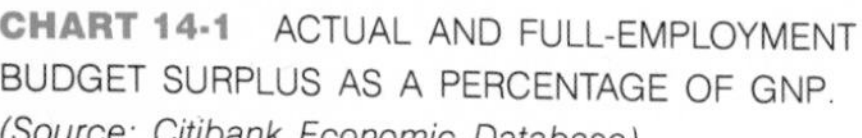

CHART 14-1 ACTUAL AND FULL-EMPLOYMENT BUDGET SURPLUS AS A PERCENTAGE OF GNP.
(Source: Citibank Economic Database)

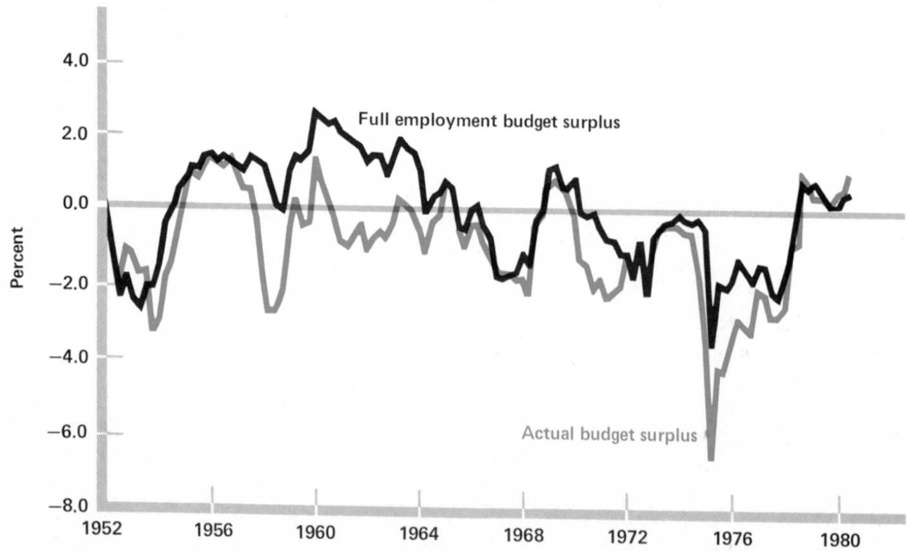

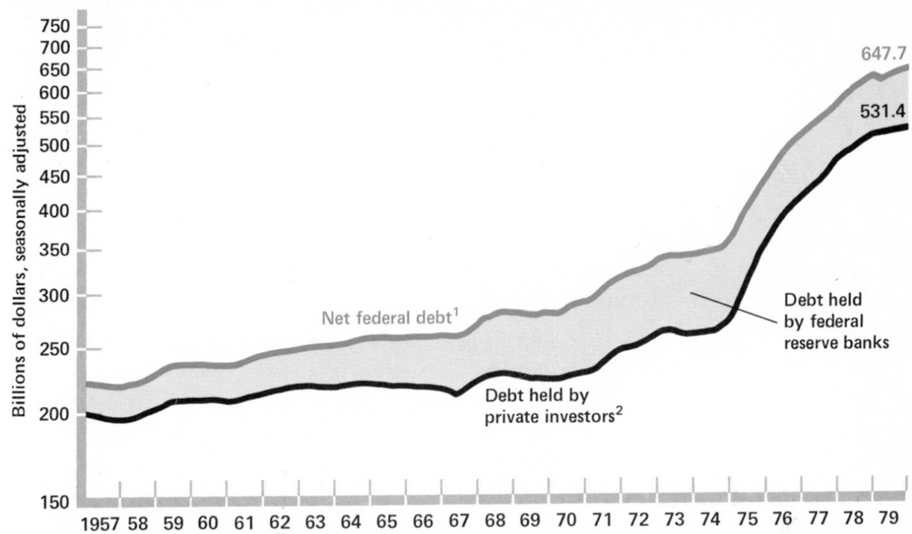

[1] Gross federal debt less debt held by United States government agencies and trust funds. This series includes debt held by the Federal Reserve System, private domestic investors (including state and local governments), and investments of foreign and international accounts in the United States.

[2] Defined to include both domestic and foreign holdings. Latest data plotted: fourth quarter. Latest data plotted: fourth quarter.

CHART 14-2 OWNERSHIP OF FEDERAL GOVERNMENT DEBT. *(Source: Federal Reserve Bank of St. Louis)*

holdings of federal government debt. Changes in the stock of debt correspond to the state of the actual budget surplus. The debt declined during 1956 and 1957, and again in 1961, years when the budget was in surplus. Similarly, the debt was increasing very rapidly with the budget deficits of 1967–1968 and again from 1970 to 1973. The largest post-World War II budget deficit, that of 1975, shows up in Chart 14-2 in the very sharp rise in the national debt during 1975. Subsequent large deficits have caused continued growth of the national debt.

As can be seen from the chart, part of the national debt is held by foreigners. Those foreigners may be either private individuals or official foreign institutions, such as foreign central banks. Foreign central banks hold reserves in the currencies of other countries, as we shall see in Chapter 18. Part of their reserves are held in dollars, in interest-bearing form, and that is what can be seen in Chart 14-2. Some of the national debt is held by international institutions, such as the World Bank (International Bank for Reconstruction and Development).

Chart 14-2 also shows the Federal Reserve System's holdings of federal debt. There is some similarity between the time patterns of the total debt and the Fed's holdings of the debt, but it is not strong. For instance, in late

1972, when the debt was rising rapidly, the Fed's holdings of debt fell. This reinforces the point, made at the end of Section 14-1, that there is no necessary connection between the size of the deficit and the Fed's holdings of government debt.

Although the national debt has been rising over the post-World War II period, it has not generally risen as fast as GNP. This can be seen in Chart 14-3, which plots the national debt as a percentage of GNP. In 1947, after the heavy borrowing by the federal government during the war, the debt was larger than GNP. By 1979 the debt was down to less than 30 percent of GNP. This is very much the historical pattern for the United States; the national debt usually rises substantially during wartime and then declines relative to GNP after wars. However, the debt did increase relative to GNP from 1975 to 1977 as a result of the large deficits. It is interesting to note that the debt has in fact fallen in real terms since the end of World War II. Over the 1945–1979 period, the nominal debt rose about threefold while the price level (CPI) rose by a factor of 3½. So, alarming as the growth of the national debt might appear, the debt has been declining rapidly in size (in the post-World War II period) relative to the economy as measured by GNP.

So far, we have presented some facts about the size of the budget deficit, its relation to the national debt, the financing of the deficit, and the size of the debt. We turn now to examine the budget itself in more detail. Table 14-1 presents the sources of the receipts by the federal government as a percentage of GNP. The major sources of receipts for the federal government are the individual income tax, the corporate income tax, and contributions to social insurance (Social Security.) The ratio of individual income taxes to GNP has remained fairly steady since 1955, though corporate profits taxes have declined as a percentage of GNP.[8] Social insurance taxes and contributions have increased rapidly as a share of GNP

[8] The share of profits in GNP has also declined over the period.

TABLE 14-1 FEDERAL RECEIPTS BY SOURCE *(as a percentage of GNP)*

Source	1955	1960	1965	1970	1975	1979
Individual income taxes	8	9	8	9	8	10
Corporate profits taxes	5	4	4	3	3	3
Social insurance taxes and contributions	2	3	4	5	6	7
Other taxes and receipts	3	3	2	2	2	1
Total receipts	18	19	18	20	19	21

Source: Citibank Economic Database. Totals may not add because of rounding.

TABLE 14-2 FEDERAL OUTLAYS BY MAJOR COMPONENT *(as a percentage of GNP)*

Major component	1955	1960	1965	1970	1975	1979
National defense	10	9	7	7	5	5
Benefit payments for individuals	4	5	5	6	10	9
Grants to state and local governments	1	1	2	2	4	3
Net interest	1	1	1	1	2	2
Other federal operations	1	2	3	5	2	2
Total budget outlays	17	18	18	21	23	21

Source: Citibank Economic Database.

over the past 25 years, and particularly in the past 10 years. Other taxes and receipts are largely indirect taxes, such as current excise taxes on tires, tobacco, and gasoline, as well as tariffs on imported goods. Reliance on indirect taxes has been declining over the past 25 years.

Table 14-2 shows how federal outlays are allocated among several broad categories of expenditure. In 1955 more than half the budget was devoted to national defense, and only one-sixth to transfer (benefit) payments to individuals. The share of national defense in the budget, and national defense spending as a share of GNP, have fallen in the past 20 years, with a temporary increase during the period of the Vietnam war. Transfer payments have increased rapidly since 1955, with the most rapid increase coming between 1970 and 1975. Now transfer payments exceed defense spending and account for nearly half of federal government outlays.

Table 14-3 shows the breakdown of transfer payments from 1965 to

TABLE 14-3 DOMESTIC TRANSFER PAYMENTS *(in billions of dollars)*

Fiscal year	Total	Retirement and disability*	Hospital and supplementary medical insurance	Food stamps	Veteran benefits and insurance	Unempolyment benefits	Other
1965	28.3	20.2	†	†	4.7	2.5	0.9
1970	52.0	32.9	6.7	0.6	6.9	3.0	1.9
1975	124.4	76.5	14.1	4.2	12.8	12.4	4.4
1979	186.7	122.7	28.1	5.7	14.0	9.6	6.6

*Includes black-lung benefits, supplemental security income benefits, and military retired pay.
†Less than $50 million.
Source: Special Analyses, Budget of the United States Government, Fiscal Years 1981 and 1976.

1979. In large part, the increase in transfer payments is due to rapid increases in payments for retirement (Social Security) and disability. Medicare payments too have increased rapidly. In part, the high level of transfer payments in 1975 was a result of the recession. This caused unemployment benefits to rise from $5 billion in 1974 to $12 billion in 1975. Nonetheless, even in 1975, unemployment benefits were only 10 percent of total transfer payments.

Grants to state and local governments have increased as a share of GNP in the past 25 years, as has net interest.[9] The reason net interest has increased as a share of GNP is not that the national debt has risen as a percentage of GNP (Chart 14-3 shows that the national debt fell as a percentage of GNP over the period) but that the interest rate paid by the federal government on the debt has risen rapidly.

So much for the facts about the federal budget. Next we consider what the facts mean.

[9] Because of rounding, Table 14-2 exaggerates the rise in net interest payments. The rise from 1 to 2 percent shown in the table is in fact a rise from 1.37 percent in 1955 to 1.69 percent in 1978.

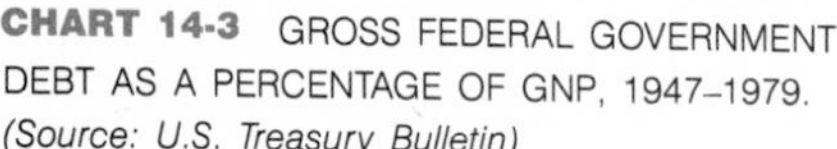

CHART 14-3 GROSS FEDERAL GOVERNMENT DEBT AS A PERCENTAGE OF GNP, 1947–1979. *(Source: U.S. Treasury Bulletin)*

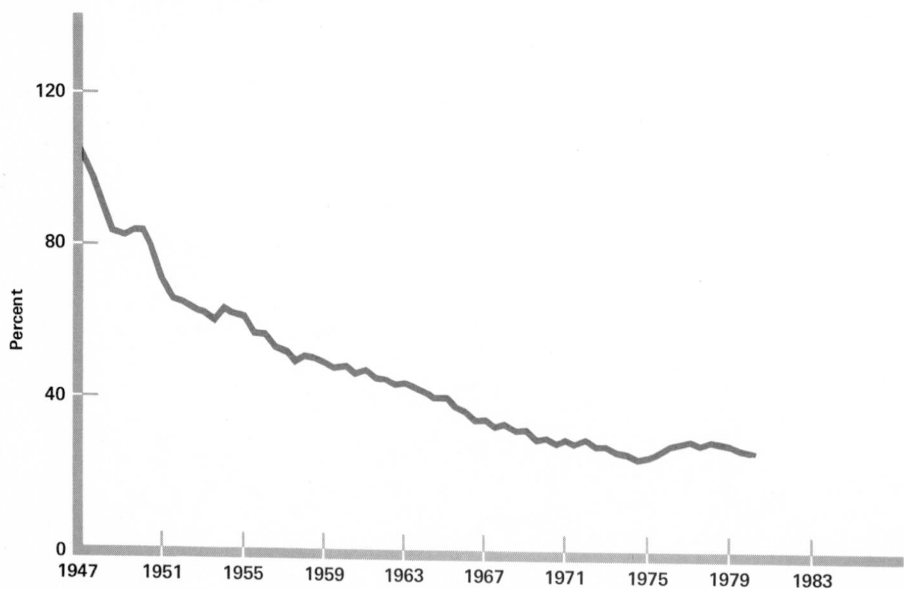

*14-3 THE BUDGET AND MACROECONOMIC EQUILIBRIUM

In earlier chapters we discussed the effects of monetary and fiscal policy on the equilibrium of the economy. In those chapters we measured fiscal policy by the full-employment deficit. We have now seen that the actual budget deficit affects the stock of government debt held by the private sector and/or the Fed. We did not take account of the interactions between the state of the budget and changes in the national debt in our earlier analysis. We now want to consider the effects of the creation or retirement of the debt associated with an actual budget deficit or surplus on the macroeconomic adjustment process. We first discuss the effects of a budget deficit that is financed by the Fed. Then we discuss the so-called *inflation tax*. Following that, we examine the effects of a deficit that is financed by borrowing from the private sector. Finally in this section, we briefly discuss the issue of the burden of the national debt.

Federal Reserve Financing of the Deficit

We distinguish between the effects of a temporary, say one-year, deficit that is financed by borrowing from the Fed and the effects of a continuing deficit. Suppose first that the budget is in deficit for a single year, and that the deficit is financed entirely by the Fed. Such a budget deficit might be caused by a one-year increase in government spending, which thereafter falls back to its original level.

Figure 14-1 reproduces the aggregate demand–aggregate supply framework of Chapter 12. We will use this framework to show that a transitory budget deficit financed by money creation permanently raises the price level, even though the increase in government spending does not persist. Government spending by assumption reverts to its initial level after one period. However, that transitory government spending is financed by creation of money and that increase in the money stock is permanent. As we saw in Chapter 12, an increase in the stock of money permanently raises the long-run price level.

Now consider the argument in more detail, using Figure 14-1 and starting from full equilibrium at point E. The initial increase in government spending will shift the aggregate demand schedule out and to the right to Y_1^d because the demand for goods and services is raised. The effect of increased spending in the short run is to raise output and prices.[10] If we ignored the financing of the deficit, we would conclude that the economy returns to point E once government spending declines to its initial level. In fact,

[10] The levels of output and prices in the short run would be given by the intersection of the Y_1^d curve and a short-run aggregate supply curve (not shown).

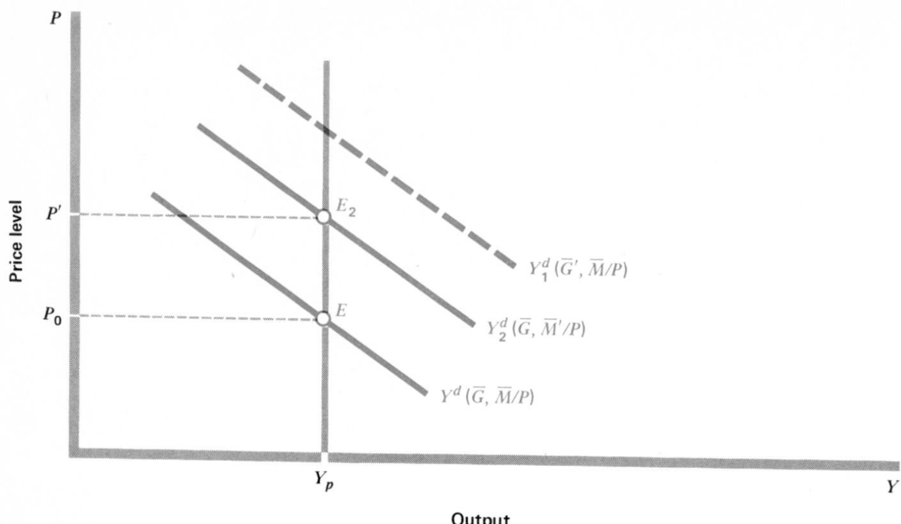

FIGURE 14-1 THE EFFECT OF A MONEY-FINANCED TRANSITORY INCREASE IN GOVERNMENT SPENDING

however, the government spending, when financed by the Fed, gives rise to an increase in the stock of money that will remain even after the government spending falls back to the initial level. The effect of that increase in the money stock, with government spending back at the initial level $\overline{G}$, is shown by the aggregate demand schedule Y_2^d. We are not concerned here with the adjustment process but rather with the long-run effects. These can be directly inferred from Figure 14-1 by recognizing that output in the long run will be unaffected by the money-financed transitory government spending. Accordingly, with output at the level Y_p, the long-run effect of the financing is to raise prices to the level P'. A transitory, money-financed deficit thus leads to a permanent increase in the level of prices. Note that the analysis implies that fiscal and monetary policy are interrelated through the financing of deficits.

Consider next the effects of a small *permanent* budget deficit financed by the Fed. Assume initially that the government keeps the deficit fixed in real terms. We assume a "small" real deficit because we shall argue presently that there is a maximum deficit that can be financed by money creation. Attempts to go beyond that maximum deficit lead to uncontrolled inflation. We have now to use the analysis of Chapter 13, since we shall be dealing with a process of continuing or ongoing inflation. Assume that the government increases its spending. That results in an increase in the full-employment deficit which shifts the aggregate demand curve AD in

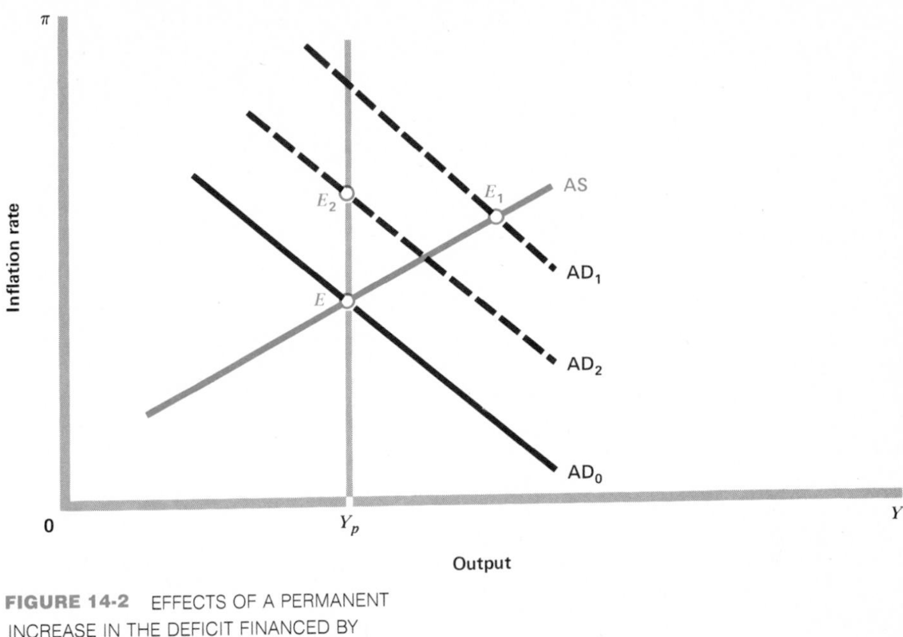

FIGURE 14-2 EFFECTS OF A PERMANENT INCREASE IN THE DEFICIT FINANCED BY BORROWING FROM THE FEDERAL RESERVE

Figure 14-2 out to the right. In addition, because the Fed is financing the deficit, the growth rate of the nominal money stock increases and shifts the aggregate demand curve farther out for that reason. These two factors shift the aggregate demand curve from AD_0 to AD_1 and move the economy from an equilibrium at E to E_1. Both the inflation rate and growth rate of output rise. Eventually, the aggregate demand curve shifts back to the left somewhat, as a result of the fact that the full-employment deficit is no longer increasing. However, because the money stock has to grow (at a higher rate) to finance the deficit, the aggregate demand curve remains permanently higher than it was initially, and the inflation rate at the new long-run equilibrium E_2 is permanently higher than it was initially at E.

Inflation and the Deficit

In the analysis of the permanent deficit above, we assumed that the deficit was fixed in real terms, that is, independently of the price level. In the United States economy, there are important elements of the tax system that depend on the price level. An increase in the price level tends to reduce the deficit unless definite action is taken to change tax rates. There are two main reasons for that. The first is that tax rates are fixed in relation to nominal income and are progressive. That is, taxes rise as a proportion of income as income increases. The second is that some government outlays are fixed in nominal terms, and hence decline in real value when the price level rises.

To make the first point, consider the example of a taxpayer shown in Table 14-4. We are comparing an initial situation with a price level of 100 and pretax nominal income of $20,000 with a later situation in which both the price level and pretax nominal income have doubled. Initially, taxes of $7,000 are paid on nominal income of $20,000. After the price level doubles, a higher proportion of nominal income, namely $20,000, is paid in taxes. That is because the income tax is progressive, which means that the real value of after-tax income falls with the price level and that the real value of taxes paid to the government rises with the price level—taxes increase from $7,000 to $20,000 in Table 14-4. In terms of the initial price level, taxes increase in real value by $3,000. Thus, with tax rates unchanged and a progressive tax system, inflation tends to raise real taxes and reduce the real deficit.

How important is the effect described in the above paragraph in the United States economy? Over the post-World War II period, there have been sufficient reductions of tax rates that the percentage of GNP paid in income taxes has remained fairly stable, as seen in Table 14-2. In the short run, with tax rates fixed, it has been estimated that the 12 percent inflation of 1974 increased the taxes received by the federal government by at least $20 billion in real terms.[11]

There have been a number of suggestions that the tax system be altered so that real taxes do not change with changes in the price level. These are proposals for *indexing* the tax system.[12] In an indexed tax system, tax brackets would increase in proportion to the price level. The result would be that changes in the price level would not affect *real* taxes. For

[11] See William Fellner, Kenneth W. Clarkson, and John H. Moore, *Correcting Taxes for Inflation*, American Enterprise Institute, 1975, and Milton Friedman. "Monetary Correction," in Herbert Giersch et al. (eds.), *Essays on Inflation and Indexation* (Washington, D.C.: American Enterprise Institute, 1974).

[12] See, for instance, Milton Friedman's article cited in footnote 11.

TABLE 14-4 EFFECTS OF INFLATION ON AFTER-TAX INCOME

Price level	Pretax income, nominal	Taxes, nominal	After-tax income, nominal	After-tax income, real
100	$20,000	$ 7,000	$13,000	$13,000
200	40,000	20,000	20,000	10,000

instance, in an indexed tax system, the nominal taxes in Table 14-4 would only double from $7,000 to $14,000 with doubling of the price level. Canada and some other countries have indexed parts of their income tax systems.

The major economic argument against indexation of the tax system is that a progressive tax system in nominal terms provides an automatic stabilizer for the economy in response to changes in the price level. We recall the role of automatic stabilizers from Chapter 3. The argument there was that a proportional income tax would reduce the marginal propensity to spend out of income and therefore would reduce the size of the multiplier. The argument here is that with progressive taxation of nominal income—that is, taxes that increase as a proportion of income as nominal income rises—we would have further stabilizing effects. With progressive taxation of nominal income, an increase in the price level such as would arise from an aggregate demand disturbance would be dampened because tax rates rise with the increase in nominal income and thus reduce multipliers. While a simple proportional tax system provides for a built-in stabilizer, the further benefits of progressive taxation for built-in stabilizer purposes are small. Thus the economic argument against indexation of the tax system is weak.

Aside from the progressive nature of the tax system in *nominal* terms, there is a second factor that leads increases in the price level to reduce the real deficit. Some of the payments the federal government makes are fixed in nominal terms. Of these, interest payments on the national debt are the major example. An increase in the price level reduces the real value of these payments and thus reduces the real deficit.

There are three major points in this part.

1 A temporary increase in government spending, financed by borrowing from the central bank, has a permanent effect on the price level because it increases the money stock.
2 A permanent increase in the real deficit, financed through borrowing from the Fed, permanently increases the inflation rate.
3 In the United States economy, a rising price level tends to reduce the real deficit, given real government spending on goods and services. That is mainly because tax rates are fixed in nominal terms and are progressive. Further, some budget outlays are fixed in nominal terms.

The Inflation Tax

In discussing the effects of a permanent real deficit, we said that it was possible that a deficit of given size could not be financed by borrowing from the central bank. To establish that fact, it is useful to think of inflation as a tax on the holdings of real money balances. To simplify the exposition, we shall talk only of equilibrium long-run inflation, in which the expected rate of inflation is equal to the actual rate of inflation.[13]

Inflation is a tax on the holdings of real balances because anyone who holds money when there is inflation loses part of the value of that money, owing to the inflation. A man starting the year with \$100 will have to add \$5 to his money holdings during the year merely to maintain their real value or purchasing power constant if there is 5 percent inflation. Alternatively, if he keeps his nominal money holdings constant at \$100 over the year, he loses 5 percent of the value of the money, owing to inflation. The effect of the inflation is thus the same as the effect of a tax on the holding of the money.

Let us spell out the argument more carefully. The value of the inflation tax is the amount that individuals have to add to their cash balances every year to maintain the real value of their cash balances constant. Let ΔM be the amount of nominal balances added to cash balances and P be the price level. Denote the real value of the inflation tax by T_I. Then

$$T_I = \frac{\Delta M}{P} \tag{3}$$

Now we can multiply and divide in Equation (3) by M to obtain

$$T_I = \frac{\Delta M}{M} \cdot \frac{M}{P} = \pi \cdot \frac{M}{P} \tag{3a}$$

In the absence of growth, and in the long run, $\Delta M/M$, the growth rate of the money stock, is equal to the rate of inflation π. Hence the inflation tax can be thought of as the inflation rate times holdings of real balances. In the long run, real balances are constant in the absence of growth, so that M/P is constant in the long run.

Now, how does the inflation tax behave as the inflation rate changes? At first glance, it might seem from Equation (3*a*) that the total inflation tax rises with the rate of inflation π. However, we know that holdings of real balances depend on the costs of holding real balances, and thus should be expected to fall as increases in the expected rate of inflation cause the

[13] Inflation is often rhetorically described as "the cruelest tax of all." This statement does not refer to the analysis we are about to carry out of inflation as a tax on real balances in the long run with the actual inflation equal to expected inflation. Instead, it applies to the effects of unexpected inflation on those who have saved in nominal assets—such as time deposits—for their retirement. Such individuals are obviously adversely affected by inflation. If the inflation is unexpected, they will find themselves with assets of lower real value than they had expected to have, and with a lower standard of living than they had planned.

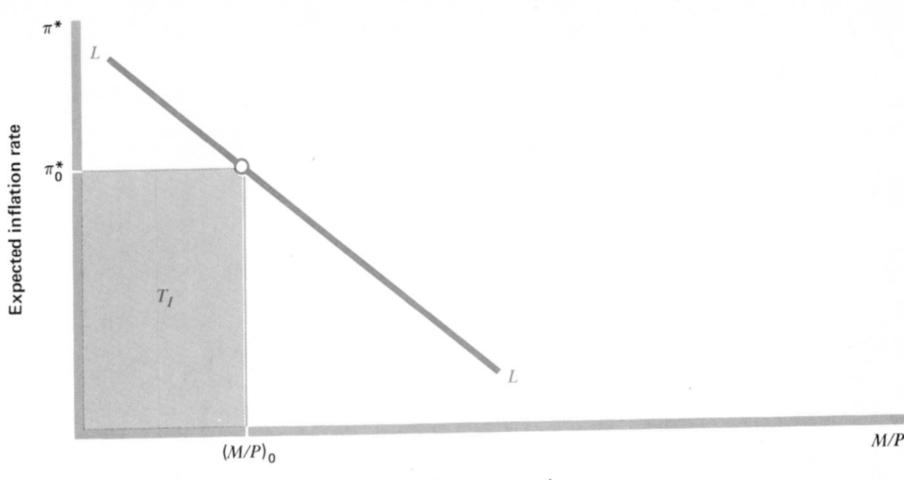

FIGURE 14-3 THE DEMAND FOR REAL BALANCES AS A FUNCTION OF THE EXPECTED RATE OF INFLATION

nominal interest rate, the cost of holding money, to rise. Figure 14-3 draws a demand curve for real balances (*LL*) as a function of the expected inflation rate, holding the real interest rate and real income constant. Since the real interest rate is constant, the *LL* curve in effect shows the demand for money as a function of the nominal interest rate. The *LL* curve is therefore downward-sloping.

In long-run equilibrium, in which the expected rate of inflation is equal to the actual rate, $\pi = \pi^*$, the inflation tax is given by the area of the rectangle shown in Figure 14-3. The tax from Equation (3*a*) is the product of the inflation rate and the level of real balances or the "tax base" and that is precisely given by the area of rectangles such as that shown, with sides of length π_0^* and $(M/P)_0$.

For the demand curve shown in Figure 14-3, the inflation tax as a function of the inflation rate is shown in Figure 14-4. As the inflation rate rises from zero, the total tax rises. Eventually though, increases in the inflation rate drive down the demand for money so much that the total tax revenue falls. T_I^* is the maximum inflation tax revenue. At a zero inflation rate, there is no tax and so no tax revenue. Thus, increases in the inflation rate from zero will increase total revenue from the inflation tax. Eventually, though, the tax rate becomes high enough to drive demand down to the

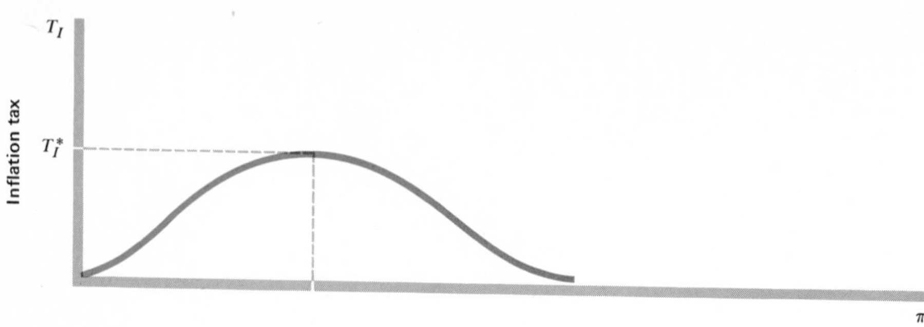

FIGURE 14-4 THE INFLATION TAX AS A FUNCTION OF THE RATE OF INFLATION

point where total revenue begins to decline.[14] There is nothing special about a tax on real balances as opposed to a tax on any other commodity in this regard.

Inflation is not referred to as a tax merely because individuals find that the real value of their money balances is reduced by inflation. The counterpart of the public's payment of the inflation tax—additions to nominal money balances so as to keep their purchasing power constant and thus offset the effect of inflation—is the government's receipt of the inflation tax. Thus the government collects the tax by buying goods and services from the private sector with the money the private sector adds to its nominal balances. This budgetary aspect of the inflation tax completes the reason why inflation can be thought of as a tax collected from money holders and accruing to the government. Furthermore, it is this tax aspect of money-financed deficits that has led some to argue that there are only two ways the deficit can be financed, taxation or borrowing from the public. The third way, borrowing from the Fed and corresponding money creation, it is argued, is in fact a form of taxation.[15]

Now, what does all this have to do with the budget and macroeconomic adjustment? The major point of this part is that, in long-run equilibrium,

[14] Can you show that the elasticity of demand for real balances with respect to the expected rate of inflation is one at the point of maximum revenue? Note that the "Laffer curve," which shows that income tax revenue first rises as the income tax rate rises and then falls as the tax rate reaches very high levels, is essentially the same as Fig. 14-4.

[15] It should be noted that in the United States and most other countries, only part of the money supply—high-powered money—is issued by the government. The inflation tax collected by the government is based on its "sales" of high-powered money, and not on the change in the total money supply. The commercial banks too may "collect" some of the inflation tax as the interest rates they charge on loans rise with inflation, while interest they pay on deposits is controlled by the Fed.

there is a maximum amount of revenue that can be raised through the inflation tax. Treasury borrowing from the Fed results in increases in the stock of high-powered money. That is, Treasury borrowing from the Fed is equivalent to the government's raising revenue through issues of high-powered money. But we have seen that there is a maximum amount of revenue that can be obtained in this way.

If the government attempts to raise more revenue than the maximum it can obtain through issues of high-powered money, and if it prints more high-powered money whenever it finds itself unable to cover its expenses, the rate of inflation will continue increasing. The public and the government will be competing for goods with the government printing money and the public trying to get rid of it. Eventually the economy will experience an extremely rapid inflation, or a *hyperinflation*. For instance, in the German hyperinflation of 1922–1923, the average rate of inflation was 322 percent *per month*.

Keynes, in a masterful description of the hyperinflation process in Austria after World War I, tells of how people would order two beers at a time because they grew stale at a rate slower than their price was rising.[16] Other stories include those of a woman who carried her (worthless) currency in a basket and found that, when she set down the basket for a moment, it was stolen, but the money was left.

To return now to the budget deficit, we see why the government could not finance a deficit in excess of the maximum revenue from the inflation tax by borrowing from the central bank. In other words, there are real deficits that simply can not, in the long run, be financed by borrowing from the central bank, that is, by the issuing of high-powered money. Attempts to finance in that way would lead to hyperinflation. The fear that hyperinflation will result from large budget deficits may be one of the arguments in the minds of those most concerned over the budget deficit. But it is foolish to assume that any budget deficit, however, small, will lead to a hyperinflation, even if it is financed by borrowing from the Fed.

The analysis of the inflation tax is not of great importance for the United States, with its well-functioning tax system and independent central bank. In other countries, with less well-developed tax systems, the printing of money may be one of the few ways the government has of obtaining resources. To put it differently, in some countries, large parts of government spending are financed by borrowing from the central bank and thus by inflation.

[16] See John Maynard Keynes, *A Tract on Monetary Reform* (New York: Macmillan, 1923), which remains one of the most readable accounts of inflation. See also Phillip Cagan, "The Monetary Dynamics of Hyperinflation," in Milton Friedman (ed.), *Studies in the Quantity Theory of Money* (Chicago: The University of Chicago Press, 1956).

Private Sector Financing of the Deficit

Once again we want to distinguish between the effects of a temporary budget deficit financed by borrowing from the private sector and the effects of a permanent budget deficit financed in that way. In this section, we consider the financing of a temporary deficit. We particularly want to compare the effects of financing by borrowing from the private sector with financing by the central bank, which was discussed above. We shall refer to financing of the deficit by borrowing from the private sector as *debt financing*, and to financing by borrowing from the Fed as *money financing*.

Figure 14-5 presents the familiar aggregate demand and supply diagram of Chapter 12. The initial effect of an increase in government spending is to move the aggregate demand curve out to Y_1^d from its initial position at Y^d. The extra government spending is financed by selling debt to the private sector. Thus the private sector accumulates government debt over the period during which government spending is at its higher level. Now, what effect does that higher stock of government debt held by the private sector have on aggregate demand?

Individuals holding government bonds regard those bonds as part of

FIGURE 14-5 EFFECT OF A TEMPORARY INCREASE IN GOVERNMENT SPENDING FINANCED BY BORROWING FROM THE PUBLIC

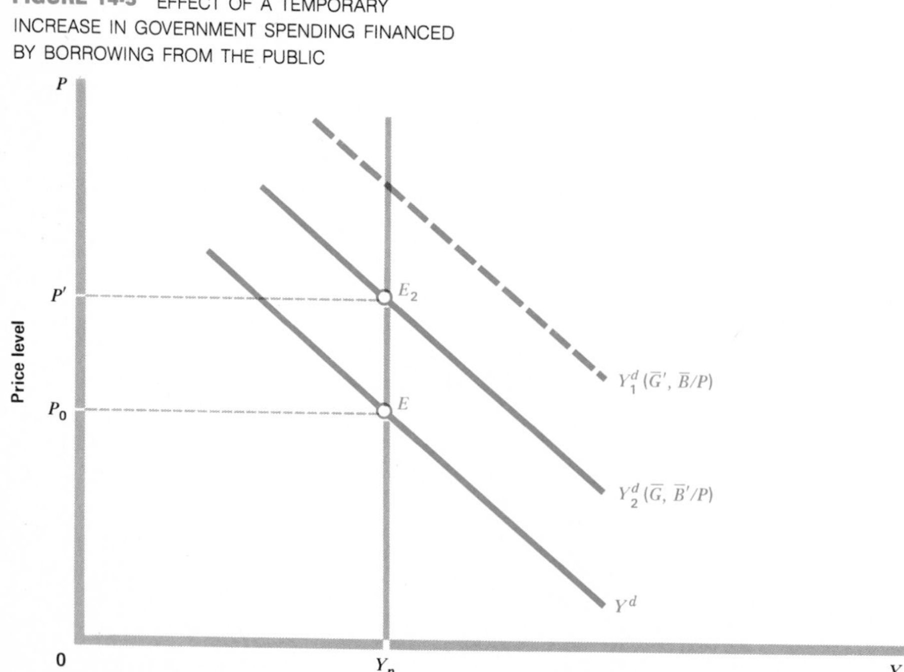

their wealth. Thus it would seem that given the level of income, aggregate demand should rise when the stock of government bonds rises, because individuals holding those bonds have higher wealth. The higher wealth increases consumption demand.[17] Accordingly, the aggregate demand curve would shift out to the right as a result of the increase in privately held wealth. Hence, we show the final aggregate demand curve—after government spending has returned to its original level—at Y_2^d, above the initial curve Y^d. The difference between the two aggregate demand schedules Y^d and Y_2^d arises from the higher stock of government bonds $\overline{B}\,'$, compared to $\overline{B}$ on the initial aggregate demand curve. Since the effects of the higher wealth on consumption demand are likely to be small, we show the final aggregate demand curve Y_2^d below the aggregate demand curve Y_1^d.

There are two complications to this analysis. The first is that the existence of the higher stock of debt raises the amount of interest payments in the federal budget. If the budget was originally balanced at point E, it may not be balanced at E_2. Of course, since the price level at E_2 is higher than at E, tax receipts may have risen at E_2 compared with E, and perhaps the budget would be balanced. But it need not be. If it were not, then further financing of the deficit would have to be undertaken, and that would have subsequent effects on the equilibrium. We discuss the effects of a permanent deficit below.

The second complication is related to the first. It is possible that individuals in the economy calculate their wealth taking into account the tax payments they will have to make in the future. Suppose that everyone believed that the national debt would eventually be paid off. Then everyone would know that at some point in the future, the federal government would have to run a surplus. Individuals might think the federal government would at some future date have to raise taxes in order to pay off the debt. To that extent an increase in the debt would increase their wealth and at the same time suggest to them that their taxes would be higher in the future. The net effect on aggregate demand might then be zero.[18] The issue raised by this argument is sometimes posed by the question, "Are government bonds wealth?"

There is another way of looking at this argument. Now, instead of concentrating on wealth, we concentrate on disposable income. An increase in the debt raises disposable income for the private sector because it raises the interest payments the private sector receives. The federal government has to finance those interest payments in some way. Suppose that it financed them by raising taxes or reducing other transfer payments. Then disposable income would be unaffected, despite the higher debt. Consump-

[17] Recall the discussion of wealth as a factor in consumption spending in Chap. 5.

[18] For an eclectic, but difficult, view of this argument, see Robert J. Barro, "Are Government Bonds Net Wealth?" *Journal of Political Economy*, December 1974.

tion demand in this case would be little affected by the increase in the national debt. With such a combined change in the debt and taxes that leaves the budget balanced in the long run, the aggregate demand curve would return to its initial position at Y^d. There would be no (or little) long-run effect from the higher debt if the higher debt did not result in an unbalanced budget.

The theoretical and empirical issue of whether an increase in the national debt increases aggregate demand is not yet settled. It is difficult to isolate the effects of changes in the debt on consumption demand in empirical studies of consumption. The theoretical arguments we have are not conclusive. We are not certain whether individuals do take account of their future tax liabilities when they calculate their wealth. Thus we have to leave this question in an unresolved state.

There is one important difference between debt financing and money financing of a given short-run budget deficit. Money financing of the deficit, as we saw in Chapter 12, tends to reduce the interest rate in the short run compared with debt financing. That is because money financing increases the nominal money stock, whereas debt financing does not. In the short run, then, debt financing reduces the level of investment compared with money financing. That is one of the issues connected with the crowding-out question that we studied in Chapter 4.

We want also to compare the effects on the price level of money and debt financing of a temporary increase in government spending. There is no question that the price level is higher with money financing than with debt financing. There are two reasons. First, money financing increases the money stock and debt financing does not. The higher the money stock, the greater the aggregate demand at any given price level. Second, we attributed a price level rise in the case of debt financing to the wealth effect of a greater stock of debt on consumption. While there is some argument about whether bonds are wealth, there is no question that money is wealth. So the wealth effect on consumption is larger in the case of money financing than debt financing. That, too, means that aggregate demand at any given price level will be higher with money than with debt financing.

We now summarize the effects of a temporary budget deficit financed by debt creation. Such financing probably increases aggregate demand, but because of the possible effects of anticipated future tax liabilities on consumption, that is not certain. Debt financing, starting from a balanced budget and if not compensated for by higher taxes or reductions in other transfer payments, leads to a permanent deficit in the budget. Debt financing raises the interest rate and reduces investment in the short run as compared with the effects of money financing.

We turn now to a permanent real deficit. An attempt to run a permanent real deficit financed by debt must imply reductions in other transfer payments or increases in taxes. For, as the debt accumulates over time, interest payments on the debt increase. Without changes in other variables affecting the deficit, the deficit would continue to increase through the increasing interest payments. Such a policy cannot be maintained forever because eventually government spending and other transfers would be reduced to zero and taxes would have to continue to increase forever. That cannot be done forever without having adverse effects on the level of output. Therefore we conclude that attempts to finance a given real deficit purely through debt financing cannot be viable in the long run in an economy that is not growing.[19]

We have now discussed the two extreme cases of financing of the deficit purely through the creation of high-powered money and purely through borrowing. In practice, neither of these extremes is followed.

Chart 14-2 shows the Fed's holdings of public debt, as well as the total national debt. The Fed's holdings of debt increase most of the time along with increases in the total debt outstanding, indicating that the Fed has been monetizing part of the deficit. But the Fed has certainly not habitually financed the entire deficit, or even some fixed share of it. The link between federal government budget deficits and Fed holdings of government debt is not automatic.

We should also note that the discussion of the financing of permanent deficits fixed in real terms represents the analysis of an abstract case in the sense that few governments make decisions to run permanent deficits fixed in real terms. The results of the analysis are nonetheless useful. We saw that an increase in the real deficit financed through money creation increases the steady-state rate of inflation, provided that the inflation tax could generate that amount of revenue. That result is indicative of the inflationary effects of the financing of deficits through the printing of high-powered money. We also saw that a permanent increase in the real deficit could not in the long run be financed purely through borrowing from the private sector, since the interest on the debt would also have to be financed.

The Burden of the Debt

We stated at the beginning of the chapter that the national debt now exceeds $3,000 per person in the United States. That seems to be a heavy debt for each individual to bear. It is the notion that every person in the country has a large debt that makes the existence of the debt seem so serious.

However, we should realize that corresponding to the debt that individuals each have as their share of the national debt, there are Treasury bonds and bills that every person on average has. By and large, we owe the

[19] The long-run effects of debt-financed changes in government spending are analyzed in a widely discussed paper by Alan Blinder and Robert Solow, "Analytical Foundations of Fiscal Policy," in A. S. Blinder et al., *The Economics of Public Finance* (Washington, D.C.: The Brookings Institution, 1974).

national debt to ourselves. Each individual shares in the public debt, but many individuals own claims on the government that are the other side of the national debt. If there is a debt for individuals taken together, it arises from prospective taxes to pay off the debt. The taxes that different individuals would pay to retire the debt would also vary among the population. To a first approximation, one could think of the liability that the debt represents as canceling out the asset that the debt represents to the individuals who hold claims on the government.

You will recognize that we are now discussing the question of whether the debt is counted as part of wealth for the population as a whole. Earlier, we started from the view that the government bonds and Treasury bills that individuals hold are part of their wealth. We then asked whether the possibility that all individuals consider the future tax liabilities connected with the hypothetical paying off of the debt at some future date meant that on balance the debt was not part of the wealth. In this section we started from the other side: we first talked of the national debt as a debt, and then pointed out that there were assets held by individuals corresponding to that debt. We pointed out earlier that it was not yet certain whether individuals taken together in fact count the national debt as a part of wealth. There certainly does not seem to be any argument that the liability represented by some possible paying off of the debt at some unknown future time outweighs the value of the assets that individuals hold at present. At this level, then, there is no persuasive argument that the debt is a burden in the sense that the economy as a whole regards the national debt as a reduction in its wealth.

The only factor ignored in the previous paragraph is that part of the debt is owned by foreigners. In that case, for the United States economy as a whole, part of the asset represented by the debt is held by foreigners, while the future tax liability accrues entirely to residents. Then that part of the debt held by foreigners might represent a net reduction in the wealth of United States residents.

Although the debt is not a burden in the fairly crude sense in which one asks whether individuals regard themselves as being poorer because of the existence of the debt (leaving aside the part of the debt owned by foreigners), there are more sophisticated senses in which it might be a burden. The most important sense in which there is a possible burden arises from the potential long-run effects of the debt on the capital stock. We saw earlier that debt financing increases the interest rate and reduces investment. That would mean that the capital stock would be lower with debt financing than otherwise. If individuals regard the debt as part of their wealth, then they tend to increase their consumption at a given level of income, which results in a smaller proportion of GNP being invested.[20]

[20] For articles dealing with the burden of the debt, see J. M. Ferguson (ed.), *Public Debt and Future Generations* (Chapel Hill: University of North Carolina Press, 1964).

In the long run, that would result in a lower capital stock and thus a lower level of real output. In that sense, then, the debt could be a burden. Moreover, the debt might be a burden because debt servicing in the long run could require higher tax rates. If those tax rates have adverse effects on the amount of work that individuals do, then real output would be reduced. But it is far from certain that higher tax rates in fact reduce the amount of work that individuals do.

Thus, if the debt is a burden, it is a burden for reasons very different from those suggested by the statement that every person in the United States has a debt of $3,000 as a share of the national debt. The major possible source of burden arises from the possible effects of the national debt on the capital stock.

14-4 STATE AND LOCAL GOVERNMENT SPENDING AND FINANCING

Chart 14-4 shows state and local government expenditure (on purchases of goods and services and transfers) as a percentage of GNP annually since 1946. State and local government expenditure has increased markedly as a percentage of GNP. In 1979 the share was about 13 percent.

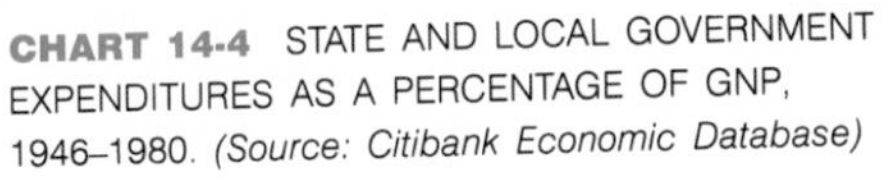

CHART 14-4 STATE AND LOCAL GOVERNMENT EXPENDITURES AS A PERCENTAGE OF GNP, 1946–1980. *(Source: Citibank Economic Database)*

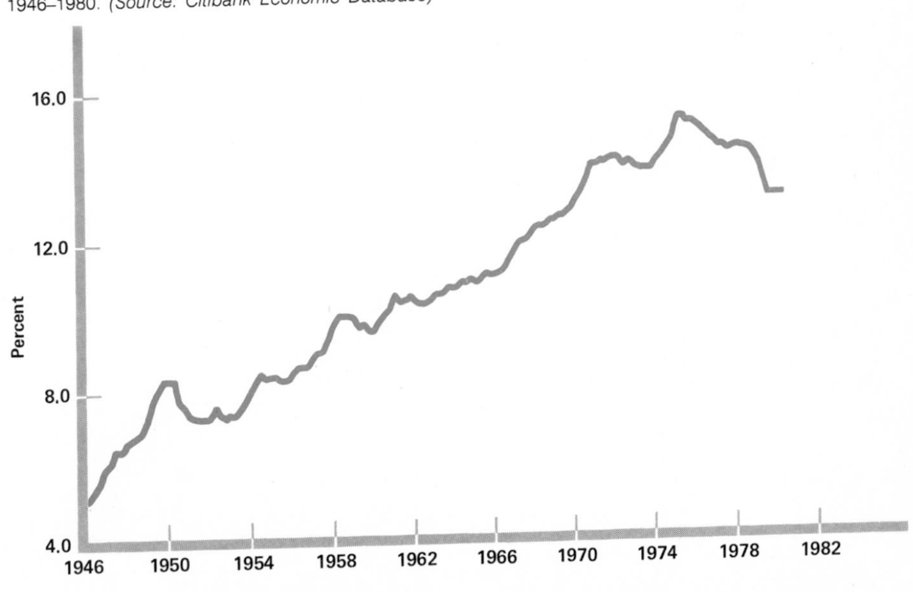

Most of state and local government spending is on purchases of goods and services. In 1979, state and local purchases were 13 percent of GNP, and thus constituted an important component of aggregate demand. In fact, state and local governments purchase more goods and services than the federal government does. The relative purchases of goods and services can be seen in Chart 14-5. In 1979, state and local governments spent $310 billion on goods and services, compared with $166 billion for the federal government. The rapid increase in state and local government purchases relative to federal purchases of goods and services began in the late sixties. The goods and services that state and local governments buy are typically education, highways, hospitals, fire protection, garbage removal, and police protection. State and local governments spend relatively small amounts on transfer payments. With regard to interest payments, state and local governments actually on balance receive more interest than they pay out. This is a result of the budget surpluses they have been running which have enabled them, taken together, to purchase federal securities. Although many state and local governments run deficits (e.g., New York City) and have to borrow, thus accounting for the existence of state and local government securities, others run surpluses and purchase securities issued by the federal government.

The major sources of state and local government revenues are indirect

CHART 14-5 PURCHASES OF GOODS AND SERVICES: FEDERAL, STATE, AND LOCAL GOVERNMENTS. *(Source: Citibank Economic Database)*

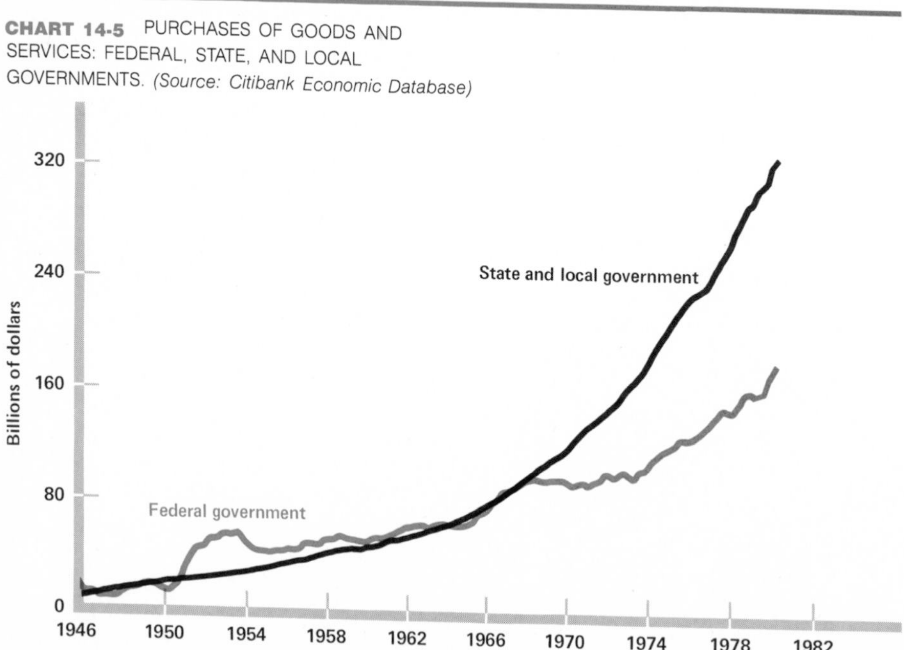

taxes, largely the sales tax. Other large sources of funds are state income taxes, property taxes, and grants-in-aid from the federal government.

State and local government financing differs from federal financing mainly in that the state and local governments cannot borrow from the Fed. Thus, when a state or local government runs a deficit, it has to borrow by selling securities to the private sector.

Two major questions arise in connection with state and local governments' role in the economy. The first concerns the determinants of state and local government spending. In large part, this is determined through the political process. Although state and local spending as a proportion of GNP has been rising, it would not be wise to assume that this trend will continue. The political reaction to increasing taxes, especially at the local level, may well reverse, or at least halt, the trend shown in Chart 14-5.

The second question concerns the effects of state and local government spending on the economy. Here the analysis of federal government spending and taxing of earlier chapters is relevant. There are multiplier effects for changes in state and local spending just as there are for changes in federal spending.

14-5 THE SIZE OF THE GOVERNMENT

A recurring theme in political discussion concerns the size of the government and taxation. A vocal part of the electorate argues that the size of the government has been increasing almost continuously in the past 25 years, that much of government spending is wasteful, that the tax burden is excessive, and that the role of government should therefore be curtailed. Constitutional provisions have been passed in some states limiting government spending or taxes, and there are several proposals for amending the United States Constitution either to require a balanced budget or else to limit spending to a certain fraction of GNP.[21]

There is no simple test that will tell us whether we get our money's worth from government spending in general. There have been a number of studies of particular government programs showing that they work less effectively than was originally expected, perhaps very badly, and arguing that it would be better if the programs were abandoned and the problem left to the free market to handle. Even the Social Security system and the food stamp program have received substantial criticism. The approach that looks at individual programs to examine their success and suggest changes is clearly the most careful way to evaluate government spending.

[21] See Bruce K. MacLaury, "Proposals to Limit Federal Spending and Balance the Budget," in Joseph A. Pechman (ed.), *Setting National Priorities: The 1980 Budget* (Washington, D.C.: The Brookings Institution, 1979) for a discussion of some of the proposals.

But many critics of government prefer to take a broader approach, on the ground that the government has a permanent tendency to expand independently of the merits of the particular programs it runs at any one time. Two arguments make for this view. The first is that the political incentives operate that way. All members of Congress are against government spending in general and in favor of spending in their own districts. To get spending in their respective districts, they have to support spending in other districts. The second argument is that the bureaucratic incentives operate that way. Once a bureaucracy has been set up, it needs to expand, to find things to keep itself busy and important. Thus, it is argued, overall limits on government spending have to be imposed to keep politicians and bureaucrats under control.

What are the facts? Table 14-5 summarizes some post-World War II trends. If we look at the size of federal government expenditures, we see them at a relatively low level just before the Korean war, rising sharply during that war, and then falling back somewhat. There was a slow increase in federal spending from the mid-fifties to the mid-seventies. Note, however, the change in the composition of federal spending. Federal government purchases of goods and services are now a smaller percentage of GNP than they were in 1949–1951. It is the other components of federal outlays, particularly transfer payments, that account for the increase. We see also a substantial increase in the size of state and local governments. We should note that some of the state and local expenditures are financed by grants from the federal government, so that it would not be appropriate to

TABLE 14-5 GOVERNMENT SPENDING AS A PERCENTAGE OF GNP *(calendar years)*

	Federal expenditures			
Year	Total	Purchases of goods and services	Other	State and local expenditures
1949–51	15.9	8.7	7.2	7.6
1952–54	20.4	14.6	5.8	7.7
1955–59	18.1	11.3	6.8	9.0
1960–64	19.1	10.8	8.3	10.4
1965–69	19.7	10.7	9.0	11.8
1970–73	20.7	8.8	11.9	13.8
1974–75	22.2	8.0	14.2	14.8
1976	22.7	7.6	15.1	14.5
1977	22.3	7.7	14.6	14.1
1978	21.9	7.3	14.6	14.3
1979	20.8	6.9	13.9	13.9

Source: Economic Report of the President.

add the first and last columns of the table to find total government expenditure. Even so, there has been a substantial increase in the size of total government expenditure in the post-war period, with state and local government having expanded more than the federal government.

Despite the historical record, there is nothing inevitable about growth in the federal budget as a share of GNP, and there are signs that we can expect the federal budget (and state and local government budgets) to show smaller growth in the next few years than in the recent past. Indeed, Table 14-5 suggests that total government spending as a percentage of GNP may have stopped rising and even begun to fall.

14-6 SUMMARY

1 Federal government expenditures are financed through taxes and borrowing. The borrowing takes place directly from the public, and may be indirectly from the Fed.
2 Under present institutional arrangements, there is no necessary link between Treasury borrowing and changes in the stock of high-powered money. Federal Reserve financing of the deficit increases the stock of high-powered money.
3 When the Fed tries to control the level of interest rates, it creates an automatic link between Treasury borrowing and the creation of high-powered money.
4 Federal government receipts come chiefly from the individual income tax, the corporate income tax, and social insurance taxes and contributions. The share of the last category has increased rapidly in the postwar period, especially since 1965.
5 Federal government expenditures are chiefly on defense and transfer payments to individuals. The share of defense in federal expenditure has fallen over the past 25 years, while the share of transfers has risen.
6 A temporary increase in government spending financed by an increase in the stock of high-powered money increases the price level permanently.
7 A permanent increase in government spending financed by money creation results in a permanent increase in the inflation rate.
8 Inflation can be regarded as a tax on real balances. The federal government collects the tax through the quantity of high-powered money that it provides during inflation to meet the increased demand for high-powered money. There is a maximum revenue that can be raised through the inflation tax.
9 A temporary increase in government spending financed by debt creation increases the price level permanently.
10 Debt financing of a permanent increase in government spending is not

viable if potential output remains fixed. The interest payments on the debt would continually increase, making for a rising deficit that has to be funded by borrowing.

11 The major sense in which the national debt may be a burden is that it may lead to a decline in the capital stock in the long run.

12 In the late sixties and early seventies, the share of state and local government expenditure in GNP has increased steadily and now amounts to about 13 percent of GNP.

PROBLEMS

1 What effect does a federal government surplus have on the stock of money and the stock of debt? Explain in detail the mechanics of how the stocks of money and bonds are affected.

2 Suppose the Treasury issues $1 billion in Treasury bills which are bought by the public. Then the Fed conducts open market purchases of $300 million. Effectively, how has the debt been financed?

3 Under what circumstances are fiscal and monetary policy related rather than existing as two completely independent instruments in the hands of the government?

4 In some countries there is virtually no capital market in which the government can borrow, and only a rudimentary tax system, so that taxes produce only very small revenues.

(*a*) What is the relationship between monetary and fiscal policy in such countries?

(*b*) What does the inflation tax analysis imply about the ability of the government in such a country to spend a large share of GNP permanently?

5 Analyze the difference in the impact on the interest rate, investment, and the price level of a temporary change in government spending, financed by money creation and borrowing, respectively.

6 What would be the effect of inflation on real income taxes if income taxation was:

(*a*) Regressive?

(*b*) Proportional?

(*c*) Indexed?

*7 Recall that the elasticity of demand for real balances with respect to the expected inflation rate (see Figures 14-3 and 14-4) is defined as

$$\frac{\Delta(M/P)}{\Delta\pi^*}\,\frac{\pi^*}{(M/P)}$$

Prove that if $[\pi_0^*,(M/P)_0]$ is the point in Figure 14-3 where T_I is maximized, then at π_0^* this elasticity is 1.

*8 Analyze the effects on the economy of a permanent increase in the level of government spending financed by money creation.

*9 Trace the path the economy follows when there is a permanent increase in government spending that is financed by borrowing from the public. Take account of the size of the deficit in each period. (Do not follow this sequence of events for more than three periods. Use the diagrams of Chapter 13.)

10 Examine Chart 14-5 and then calculate how the share of total government purchases (by federal and state and local governments) of goods and services in GNP changed from 1965 to 1979. (You will have to use one of the charts in Chapter 1 that shows the level of GNP.) How have total government purchases changed relative to the size of the federal budget? Why is there so much more concern about the size of the federal budget than about total government purchases of goods and services?

11 Some people say that a huge government debt is a burden in that individuals on average owe over $3,000 as their share of the debt. Others point out that a large debt means individuals own large amounts of government securities and thus are wealthier. Who is right?

15

STABILIZATION POLICY: THE PHILLIPS CURVE AND THE TRADEOFFS BETWEEN INFLATION AND UNEMPLOYMENT

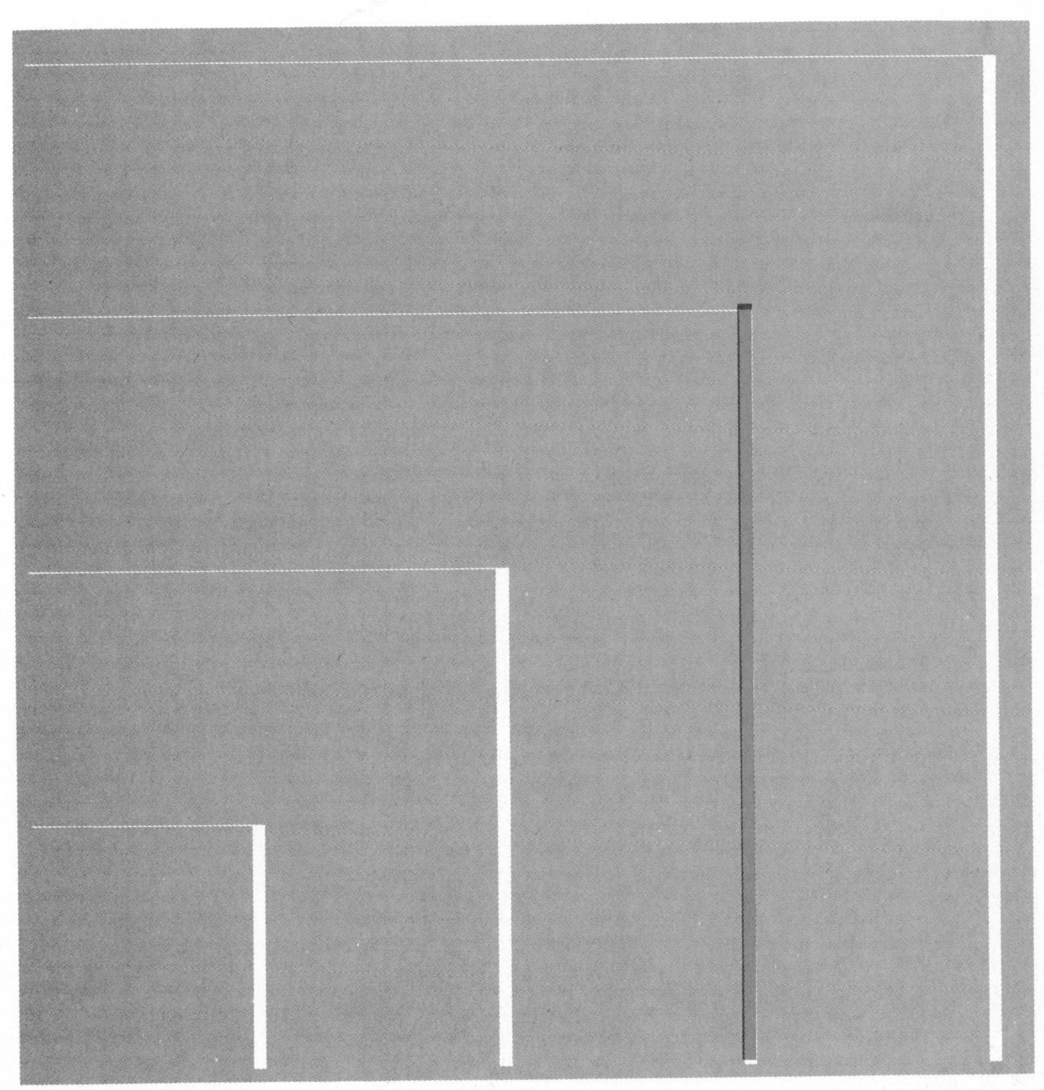

In mid-1979, economic forecasters were all predicting the 1980 recession. The inflation rate then had been running at an annual rate of over 12 percent for 6 months. Some members of Congress and economists argued strongly for a tax cut to try to head off the coming recession. But the Carter administration, supported by the Fed's belief that it was more important to try to reduce the inflation rate, refused to support a tax cut. Similarly, in the early part of the recovery from the recession in 1975, monetary and fiscal policy were only moderately stimulative. The policy decision was to move the economy along a path of relatively slow but safe recovery, to make inroads on inflation in preference to a rapid reduction in unemployment.

These policy choices reflect an assessment of the relative costs of inflation and unemployment. They certainly reflect the judgment that there is a cost to inflation, and that this cost is sufficiently important to warrant a period of unemployment in order to reduce inflation. The policies imply, too, the belief that inflation can be reduced in the long run without the cost of a permanently higher rate of unemployment. This chapter investigates the premises of such policy choices. We address the questions of the costs of inflation and of unemployment, the meaning of unemployment, and the *tradeoff* between inflation and unemployment.

You will find that the problems in this chapter do not have definite answers. These problems are among the most lively and controversial in current economic research. Furthermore, the inflation-unemployment problem is the key issue in political economy. It is a campaign platform issue, and it is frequently an issue of legislation. The Humphrey-Hawkins Act, passed by Congress in 1978, sets policy goals of 4 percent unemployment and 3 percent inflation by 1983. The act raises the question of whether either or both of these goals is feasible. Although the policy answers in this area are few, recent research has substantially increased understanding of the nature of unemployment and the costs of inflation, and it is well worth laying out the relevant considerations and analyzing the areas of agreement and controversy.

This chapter starts by revisiting the Phillips curve of Chapter 13 and investigating the tradeoff between inflation and unemployment. In Chapter 13 we argued that in the short run while the expected inflation rate is constant, the Phillips curve is relatively flat. This implies a short-run tradeoff between inflation and unemployment: in the short run, the unemployment rate can be reduced at the cost of higher inflation. By contrast, we argued that in the long run, the unemployment rate is equal to the natural rate. This indicates that there is no long-run tradeoff between inflation and unemployment, or alternatively, that the long-run Phillips curve is vertical. That view is not universally held. It has been argued that lower unemployment can be bought *in the long run* at the cost of higher inflation. We examine the arguments and evidence about the slope of the long-run Phillips curve in Section 15-1.

In Section 15-2 we study the structure of United States unemployment, emphasizing the flows in and out of the unemployment pool. The natural rate of unemployment is the focus of Section 15-3. We discuss the concept, some estimates of the natural rate, and methods of lowering the rate. Sections 15-4 and 15-5 explore the costs of unemployment and inflation, respectively. Section 15-6 examines alternative strategies—steady but slow versus cold turkey—for ending inflation.

15-1 IS THE LONG-RUN PHILLIPS CURVE VERTICAL?

In Figure 15-1 we show two long-run Phillips curves. The vertical long-run curve P_VP_V was introduced in Chapter 13. Its essential property is the implication that in the long run, the unemployment rate is independent of the rate of inflation, and equal to the *natural rate*, u. The downward-sloping long-run curve, P_NP_N, by contrast, implies that in the long run, there is a *tradeoff* between inflation and unemployment. According to the negatively sloped curve, the economy can in the long run operate either with a high rate of inflation and low rate of unemployment, say at point A, or with a low rate of inflation and high rate of unemployment, at a point like B.

If there is a long-run tradeoff, as along the P_NP_N curve, then policy makers must make the important choice between running a high-pressure economy in which inflation is high but there is little unemployment and jobs are easy to find and a low-pressure economy in which prices are stable but jobs are difficult to find. If the long-run curve is vertical, such as P_VP_V, there is no such choice. Indeed, if the long-run curve is vertical but policy makers mistakenly think there is a choice, they may be tempted to increase the inflation rate to try to reduce the unemployment rate, as P_NP_N suggests they can. But all they will get in the long run is more inflation and no less unemployment, as indicated by the P_VP_V curve. The issue is clearly important.

The view that there is a long-run tradeoff was widely accepted in the sixties, but does not now command much support. In the remainder of this section, we consider (1) why the view that there is a long-run tradeoff was held and (2) what the implications of a long-run vertical Phillips curve are.

The main reason the long-run tradeoff view was accepted in the sixties was that it seemed to fit the facts. The original Phillips curve, estimated by Phillips on the basis of almost a century's data, was negatively sloping. Since a century is quite long enough to be the long run, it looked as though there was a negative long-run relationship. Similarly, you will see if you go back to Chart 13-1 that in the sixties the inflation and unemployment rates in the United States were negatively related, as on $P_N P_N$. And even a decade is long enough to be the long run.

Of course, experience in the United States and other countries since then does not suggest that there is a negative long-run Phillips curve, as a further look at Chart 13-1 will confirm. Indeed, if anything, the long-run relationship looks positively sloped.[1]

At a theoretical level, the downward-sloping curve was initially accepted because the role of expectations of inflation was ignored. In terms of the Phillips curve used in Chapter 13,

$$\pi = \pi^* - \varepsilon(u - \overline{u}) \tag{1}$$

the expected rate of inflation, π^*, was omitted from early formulations of the curve.

Since the early sixties was a period of low and relatively constant inflation, ignoring expectations of inflation did little harm to predictions made using the Phillips curve. The important change in ideas came in the late sixties and early seventies when the Phillips curve seemed to be shifting. It was apparent in 1971 that the 5 percent inflation then being experienced along with a 6 percent unemployment rate was inconsistent with the Phillips curve fitted on data from the fifties and sixties. It became clear that a Phillips curve without expectations was unstable.

At that time, and even a little earlier, concentration shifted to the role of expectations of inflation in the process of wage bargaining. The suggestion was that when inflation was expected, labor would want its wage agreements to reflect the expected inflation, and firms would be willing to go along with the proposals since the prices they would expect to charge would also rise with expected inflation. The argument was advanced originally by Milton Friedman and Edmund Phelps,[2] and it leads to the *expectations-augmented Phillips curve*, Equation (1).

What are the implications of a Phillips curve, such as Equation (1), that is vertical in the long run? There is, first, the implication that there is no long-run tradeoff between inflation and unemployment. However, Equation (1) does suggest that there could be a short-run tradeoff, as long as the expected rate of inflation does not adjust to actual inflation. The idea here is that the public takes time to catch on to the rate of inflation, and that by the time it has recognized an inflation rate, say of 5 percent, the government could already have moved the rate of inflation up to 6 percent. Then, by the time the public has begun to expect 6 percent inflation, the actual rate of

[1] Milton Friedman, in his Nobel Prize lecture, argued that the long-run curve is positively sloped. See "Inflation and Unemployment," *Journal of Political Economy*, June 1977.

[2] See Milton Friedman, "The Role of Monetary Policy," *American Economic Review*, March 1968, and Edmund Phelps, *Inflation Policy and Unemployment Theory* (New York: Norton, 1973).

inflation could be moved to 7 percent—and so on. However, it is hard to believe that the public would not eventually come to understand that the inflation rate was accelerating. One can then argue that the acceleration of the inflation rate could be ever-increasing; but again, the public should ultimately catch on. Thus, even if it is possible to affect the unemployment rate through aggregate demand policy in the short run, it is not possible to do so in the long run.

Second, there is the implication of Equation (1), seen in Chapter 13, that if expectations are *rational*, that is, if people are on average right about expected inflation even in the short run, aggregate demand policy cannot be used systematically to affect unemployment in the short run either. This is *not* necessarily an implication of the long-run Phillips curve's being vertical, even though it is an implication of Equation (1). For example, suppose wages adjust slowly to changed expectations and prices in turn adjust slowly to wages. Under these conditions, aggregate demand policy can be used to affect unemployment in the short run even if expectations are rational, since then we are essentially in the fixed price or slowly adjusting price economy studied in Chapter 4. However, in the long run, as prices fully adjust, the Phillips curve will be vertical.

The vertical long-run Phillips curve generated controversy in the sixties since it seems to suggest that *nothing* can be done about long-run unemployment, which will settle down to the natural rate $\overline{u}$, whatever aggregate demand policies are followed. However, whether the long-run Phillips curve is vertical or downward-sloping, it may be possible to reduce the natural rate $\overline{u}$ through labor market policies. These are policies designed to make the labor market more efficient. In terms of Figure 15-1, labor market policies would imply a leftward shift of the vertical long-run Phillips curve by reducing $\overline{u}$. Indeed, the idea of shifting the Phillips curve was discussed long before the issue of long-run vertical versus downward-sloping curves arose.

While there is now considerable agreement on a long-run vertical Phillips curve, that agreement is not unanimous.[3] Nor, for that matter, do we feel completely confident that the Phillips curve is vertical at *all* rates of inflation. Therefore we would not be surprised to see that the long-run Phillips curve has a shape such as that shown in Figure 15-2. At positive rates of inflation (to which our actual experience since 1945 is essentially limited), the curve is for all practical purposes vertical. At negative rates of inflation, it may well be practically horizontal. Even high unemployment will not cause prices to fall rapidly. The basis for the Phillips curve of Figure 15-2 is the suggestion that money wage behavior is asymmetrical.

[3] See, for example, Robert Solow, "Down the Phillips Curve with Gun and Camera," in David A. Belsley et al. (eds.), *Inflation, Trade and Taxes* (Columbus: Ohio State University Press, 1976), and James Tobin, "Inflation and Unemployment," *American Economic Review*, March 1972.

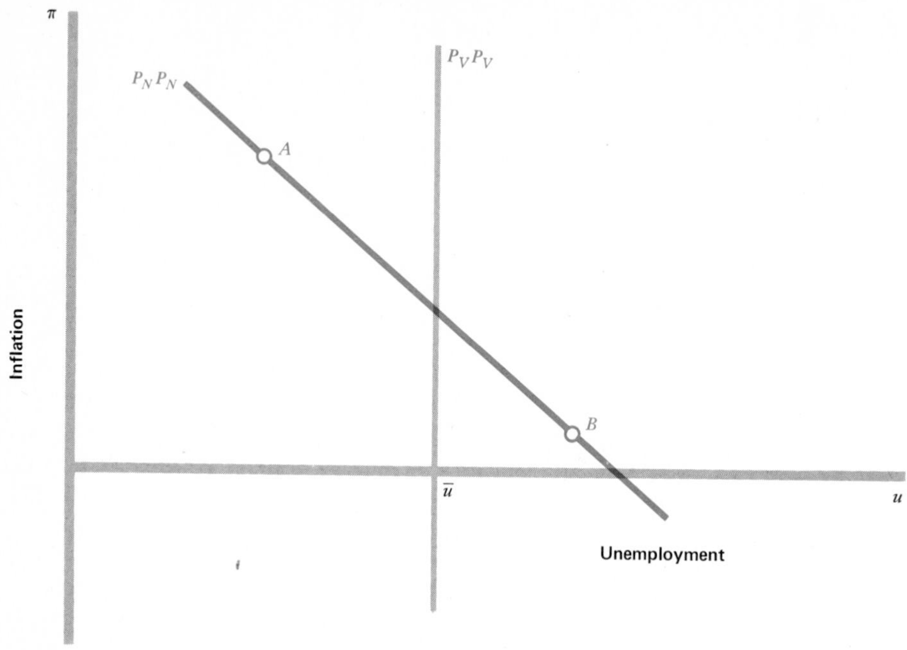

FIGURE 15-1 VERTICAL AND NEGATIVELY SLOPED LONG-RUN PHILLIPS CURVES

Wages rise in the face of excess demand for labor or expected inflation, but do not fall at the same rate in the event of even heavy unemployment or expected deflation.[4] There is some evidence for that view, and, if it is correct, the long-run Phillips curve might well be kinked, as in Figure 15-2.

What practical conclusions can we draw from our discussion of the Phillips curve here and in Chapters 11 and 13? The first important point is that the short-run Phillips curve with given expectations and/or sticky wages and prices may well be quite flat—large reductions in unemployment can be achieved with little increase in inflation. The next proposition is that expectations adjust and shift the Phillips curve up after an expansion of aggregate demand and reduction of unemployment. The expectations adjustment certainly raises the inflation cost of sustaining a lower unemployment level. The last proposition is that there is no *usable* long-run

[4] In fact, money wages might not fall at all but simply remain constant. In that event, the rate of decline in prices would at most be equal to the rate of productivity growth. This is so because the rate of change of prices is approximately equal to the rate of change of wages less the growth rate of productivity. Accordingly, with money wages constant, productivity growth puts a floor under the rate of deflation.

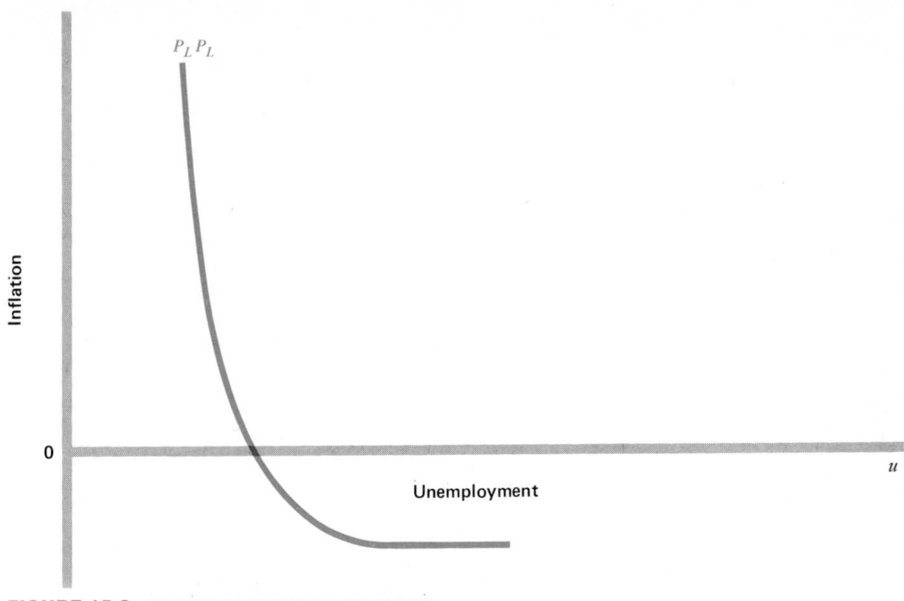

FIGURE 15-2 THE LONG-RUN PHILLIPS CURVE WITH MONEY WAGES THAT ARE STICKY DOWNWARD

inflation-unemployment tradeoff in the United States economy. This means that for all practical purposes, the long-run Phillips curve is vertical and that expansionary aggregate demand policies cannot be used to reduce long-run unemployment. In the short run, though, increases in aggregate demand can be used as a means of reducing unemployment.

15-2 THE ANATOMY OF UNEMPLOYMENT

It is time to take a closer look at unemployment, now that we have reviewed the inflation-unemployment tradeoff. We will emphasize three central facts about United States unemployment:

1 There are substantial flows of individuals in and out of unemployment each month, and most people who become unemployed in any given month remain unemployed for only a short time.
2 Much of United States unemployment is constituted of people who will be unemployed for quite a long time.
3 There is considerable variation of unemployment rates across different groups in the labor force.

The first and second facts may seem contradictory. A numerical example should make it clear that there is no necessary contradiction. Suppose that the labor force consists of 100 (million) people, and that 5 people become unemployed each month. Suppose that four of those people are unemployed for precisely 1 month, and one person will be unemployed for 6 months. Suppose also that the economy is in a steady state, so that this situation has repeated itself every month for years.

We ask first how many people are unemployed at any one time, say September 30. There will be five people who became unemployed September 1, one person who became unemployed August 1 (and who has been unemployed for 2 months), and so on, back to the person who became unemployed April 1, and whose 6 months of unemployment will end the next day, on October 1. In total, there will be ten people unemployed. So the unemployment rate is 10 percent. Of the ten, six will suffer a 6-month spell of unemployment before they again become employed. This is consistent with the second fact. But, remember that we started with five people becoming unemployed each month, four of whom remain unemployed for only a month. And that is consistent with the first fact, that most people who become unemployed within a given month remain so for only a short time. We shall return to this example later in this section.

The third fact, variation of unemployment rates across different groups in the labor force, can be examined using the relationship between the overall unemployment rate, u, and the unemployment rates, u_i, of groups within the labor force. The overall rate is a weighted average of the unemployment rates of the groups:

$$u = w_1 u_1 + w_2 u_2 + \cdots + w_n u_n \tag{2}$$

The weights, w_i, are the fraction of the civilian labor force that falls within the specific group, say, black teenagers.

Equation (2) makes it clear that the overall unemployment rate either could be made up of unemployment rates that are much the same for different groups in the labor force, or else could conceal dramatic differences in unemployment rates among groups categorized, say, by age, race, and sex. Fact 3 is that the aggregate rate does conceal substantial differences in unemployment rates. For instance, in 1979, the aggregate unemployment rate averaged 5.8 percent: white unemployment was 5.1 percent, and nonwhite unemployment was 11.3 percent. In terms of Equation (2), we have

$$5.8\% = (0.89)\ 5.1\% + (0.11)\ 11.3\% \tag{2a}$$

where the shares of the two groups in the labor force are 89 percent and 11 percent, respectively.

We now turn to a more detailed examination of the three central facts about the anatomy of unemployment.

Flows In and Out of Unemployment

An unemployed person is defined as one who is out of work *and* who (1) has either actively looked for work during the previous 4 weeks, or (2) is waiting to be recalled to a job after having been laid off, or (3) is waiting to report to a new job within 4 weeks.

Figure 15-3 shows how people enter and leave the *unemployment pool.* A person may become unemployed for one of four reasons: (1) The person may be a new entrant into the labor force, looking for work for the first time or else be a reentrant—someone returning to the labor force after not having looked for work for more than 4 weeks. (2) A person may quit a job in order to look for other employment and register as unemployed while searching. (3) The person may be laid off. The definition of *layoff* is a suspension without pay lasting or expected to last more than 7 consecutive days, initiated by the employer "without prejudice to the worker." The latter qualification means that the worker was not fired but rather will return to the old job if demand for the firm's product recovers. A firm will typically adjust to a decline in product demand by laying off some labor. A firm may also rotate layoffs among its labor force so that the individual

FIGURE 15-3 FLOWS IN AND OUT OF THE UNEMPLOYMENT POOL

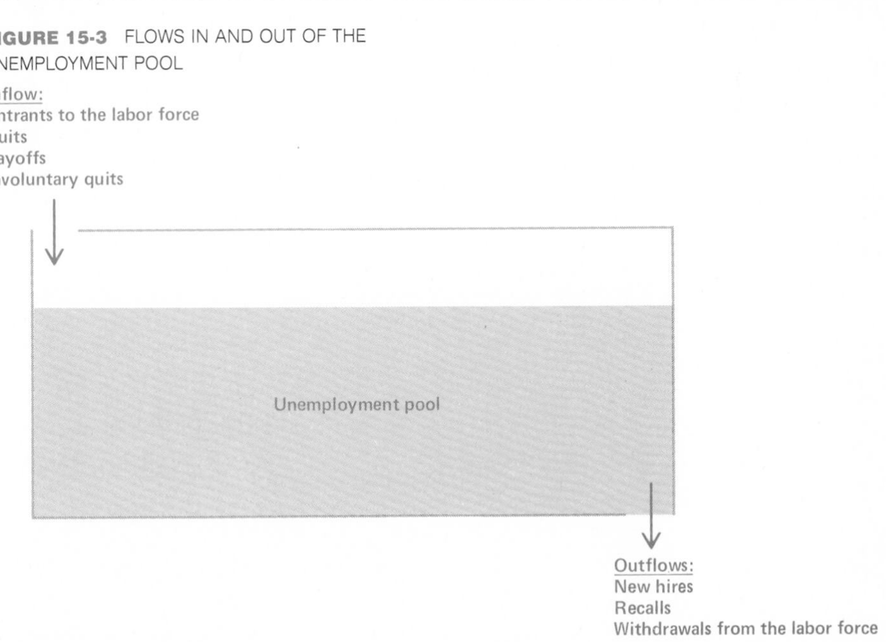

laid-off worker may expect a recall even before product demand has fully recovered. In manufacturing, it appears that over 75 percent of laid-off workers return to jobs with their original employers.[5] (4) A worker may lose a job to which there is no hope of returning, either because he is fired or because the firm closes down. This last way of becoming unemployed is referred to as "involuntary quits."

These sources of inflow into the pool of unemployment have a counterpart in the outflow from the unemployment pool. There are essentially three ways of moving out of the pool of unemployment. (1) A person may be hired into a new job. (2) Someone laid off may be recalled. (3) An unemployed person may stop looking for a job and thus, by definition, leave the labor force. Such a person may plan to look for a job again soon.

Recent research has concentrated on the flows into and out of unemployment.[6] The research starts from the recognition that the flows are large relative to the average level of unemployment. A first way of looking at the flows in and out of unemployment is by obtaining direct estimates of the rate at which the labor force turns over in manufacturing establishments. Those data, for the months of May 1975 and May 1979, respectively, are presented in Table 15-1. They support our conclusions about large flows in and out of the pool of unemployment. "Accessions" are names added to the payroll of a company in a given month. Thus, in May 1979, manufacturing companies on average added 4.1 names to their payrolls per

[5] See Martin Feldstein, "Temporary Layoffs in the Theory of Unemployment," *Journal of Political Economy*, October 1976.

[6] Robert E. Hall, "Why Is the Unemployment Rate So High at Full Employment?" *Brookings Papers on Economic Activity*, 1970:3 (Washington, D.C.: The Brookings Institution); Stephen T. Marston, "Employment Instability and High Unemployment Rates," *Brookings Papers on Economic Activity*, 1976:1 (ibid.); and Kim B. Clark and Lawrence H. Summers, "Labor Market Dynamics and Unemployment: A Reconsideration," *Brookings Papers on Economic Activity*, 1979:1 (ibid.).

TABLE 15-1 LABOR TURNOVER RATES IN MANUFACTURING *(per 100 employees)*

	May 1975		May 1979	
Total accessions	3.9		4.1	
New hires		2.0		3.1
Recalls		1.9		1.0
Total separations	3.9		4.0	
Quits		1.3		2.0
Layoffs		1.8		1.0
Other, including involuntary quits		0.8		1.0

Source: Citibank Economic Database.

100 employees. "Separations" are names removed from the payrolls during the month. In May 1979, manufacturing companies on average removed 4 names from their payrolls per 100 employees. Note first that the levels of accessions and separations (per 100 employees) are consistently high, each in the vicinity of 4 percent per month. Second, note that even when the unemployment rate was at the high level of 8.9 percent in May 1975, accessions were equal to 3.9 percent of the manufacturing work force. Even in the depths of the recession, firms were hiring new people and calling back workers who had earlier been laid off. Perhaps even more surprising, in May 1975, 1.3 percent of the workers in manufacturing quit their jobs voluntarily. Table 15-1 presents a remarkable picture of movement in the labor force. People are taking and leaving jobs even during times of very high unemployment.

A second way of looking at flows in and out of unemployment is to consider the *duration* of spells of unemployment. A spell of unemployment is defined as a period in which an individual remains continuously unemployed. Given the unemployment rate, the shorter the average spell of unemployment—the time the individual is unemployed—the larger the flows. For instance, in the example at the beginning of this section we had a 10 percent unemployment rate with five people becoming unemployed each month. We could also have a 10 percent unemployment rate if ten people became unemployed each month and each one remained unemployed for exactly one month. In the earlier example, the average spell is longer than a month since four out of five spells end in a month, but one out of five lasts 6 months. (The average spell is thus 2 months.) The shorter the average duration, the larger the flows of labor through the unemployment pool, given the overall unemployment rate.

As Table 15-2 shows, in 1974, a year in which unemployment was 5.6 percent, or about the natural rate, 60 percent of all spells ended within a month, and the average completed spell of unemployment lasted less than 2 months. Again, the suggestion is one of considerable movement of labor in and out of unemployment. We should note, though, one perhaps surprising feature of Table 15-2, which is that almost half the spells of unemployment ended in withdrawal from the labor force, rather than in employment in a new job, Indeed, recent research[7] suggests that the distinction between being unemployed and being out of the labor force is not a very sharp one, and that individuals move quite easily in both directions—between being unemployed (meaning essentially that they looked for a job in the past 4 weeks) and not employed (out of the labor force).

Now that we have a picture of the labor market as being in a constant state of movement, we can ask about the factors changing the rate of unemployment and those determining the overall level of unemployment.

[7] See, for example, the Clark and Summers article cited in footnote 6.

TABLE 15-2 CHARACTERISTICS OF COMPLETED SPELLS OF UNEMPLOYMENT, BY DEMOGRAPHIC GROUP, 1974, AND FOR ALL GROUPS, 1969 AND 1975

	1974					1969	1975
	Males		Females				
Characteristic	16–19	20 and over	16–19	20 and over	All groups	All groups	All groups
Proportion of spells ending within one month	0.71	0.47	0.70	0.60	0.60	0.79	0.55
Mean duration of a completed spell (months)	1.57	2.42	1.57	1.91	1.94	1.42	2.22
Proportion of spells ending in withdrawal from the labor force	0.46	0.26	0.58	0.55	0.45	0.44	0.46

Source: Kim B. Clark and Lawrence H. Summers, "Labor Market Dynamics and Unemployment: A Reconsideration," ***Brookings Papers on Economic Activity***, 1979:1 (Washington, D.C.: The Brookings Institution, 1979). Copyright © 1979 by the Brookings Institution, Washington, D.C.

Figure 15-3 makes it clear that unemployment increases when the flow into unemployment exceeds that out of the pool. Thus, increases in quits and layoffs increase unemployment, as does an increase in the flow of new entrants into the labor market, since new entrants typically take time to find a job once they decide to become employed. Unemployment is reduced by increases in hiring rates and by unemployed workers leaving the labor force.

Table 15-3 and Chart 15-1 provide some information about the breakdown of the reasons for unemployment. The categories in this table do not precisely match those in Figure 15-3. Nevertheless, they, together with Chart 15-1, show the importance of variations in the rate of job loss, as well as the reentry rate, in affecting the overall rate of unemployment. When unemployment was very high, as in May 1975, job loss was by far the most important reason for unemployment. The data also show the importance of the reentrant category, which is consistent with the earlier comment that flows both from unemployment to "out of the labor force" and in the reverse direction are large.

The Unemployment Rate and the Time Unemployed

We turn now to the second fact to be established in this section. We noted earlier that the average duration of a spell of unemployment is quite short—under 2 months—and that most spells of unemployment end within

TABLE 15-3 UNEMPLOYED PERSONS BY REASON FOR UNEMPLOYMENT

	May 1975 (percent)		May 1979 (percent)	
Job losers	57.6		39.9	
Layoffs		N.A.		12.0
Other job losers		N.A.		27.9
Job leavers	9.2		16.1	
Reentrants	23.5		29.8	
New entrants	9.6		14.2	
Total	100.0		100.0	

Note: N.A.-not available.
Source: Employment and Earnings, June 1975 and 1979.

CHART 15-1 REASONS FOR UNEMPLOYMENT. *(Source: Economic Indicators, December 1976 and July 1979)*

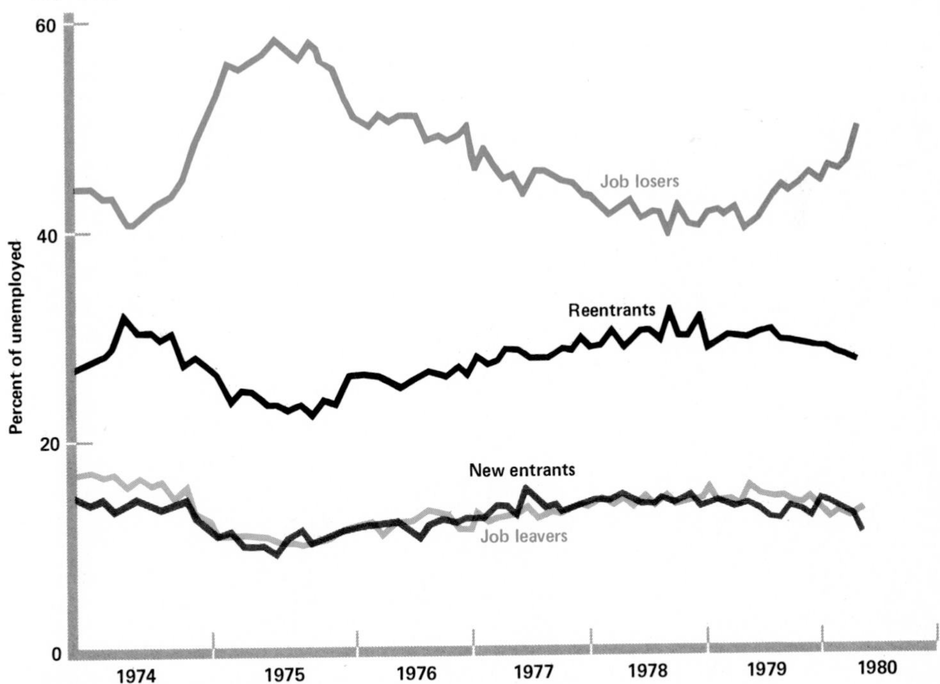

Source: Economic Indicators; December 1976, July 1979, and May 1980.

a month. But, as the example with which we started this section showed, it is still possible that much of unemployment can be traced to people who are unemployed for long spells. Indeed, given the fact that a spell of unemployment ends when someone either withdraws from the labor force or finds a job, it is possible for a person to have several spells of unemployment within the year and not actually work at all that year.

Table 15-4 provides information about the proportion of unemployment that consists of people who are unemployed for different lengths of time within the year.[8] In 1974, only 4.2 percent of total unemployment within the year was accounted for by people who were unemployed for 1 to 4 weeks, even though most spells of unemployment end within a month. Nearly 42 percent of unemployment (the sum of the last two rows in Table 15-4) was accounted for by people who were unemployed for 27 or more weeks, or more than 6 months.

If instead of looking at unemployment we looked at nonemployment data—adding together the time individuals are unemployed and the time they are not in the labor force—we would find long-term *nonemployment* to be even more important than long-term unemployment. For instance, in 1974, over 50 percent of total time not employed could be attributed to those not employed for 40 or more weeks.

These data establish that despite the substantial flows in and out of unemployment, much of aggregate unemployment (and also nonemployment) is accounted for by people who remain unemployed for a substantial time. Thus, if one believes that unemployment is a more serious problem when it affects only a few people intensely, rather than many people a little,

[8] The *total* amount of time unemployed (over all spells of unemployment) is counted for an individual who experiences more than one spell of unemployment.

TABLE 15-4 PERCENTAGE OF UNEMPLOYMENT ACCOUNTED FOR BY TIME UNEMPLOYED *(per unemployed person)*

All groups	1969	1974	1975
Weeks of unemployment (percent of weeks)			
1–4 weeks	5.7	4.2	2.6
5–14 weeks	27.8	22.4	15.6
15–26 weeks	31.6	31.7	27.0
27–39 weeks	19.1	21.1	22.3
40 weeks or more	15.8	20.7	32.5
	100.0	100.0	100.0

Source: Adapted from Kim B. Clark and Lawrence H. Summers, "Labor Market Dynamics and Unemployment: A Reconsideration," *Brookings Papers on Economic Activity*, 1979:1 (Washington, D.C.: The Brookings Institution, 1979). Copyright © 1979 by The Brookings Institution, Washington, D.C.

these data suggest that unemployment is a more severe problem than the aggregate unemployment rate indicates. The next set of data we review, those on the distribution of unemployment by age, race, and sex groups, support that view.

The Distribution of Unemployment

The third important fact about the anatomy of unemployment is that unemployment is distributed very unevenly across the population. Table 15-5 and Chart 15-2 show unemployment rates by age, sex, and race categories. The message from the data is clear. First, there are some differences in unemployment rates between males and females, given age and race. However, these differences are relatively small. Second, nonwhite unemployment is substantially higher than white unemployment, with the unemployment rate for black teenagers (not shown in the table) being twice the corresponding rate for white teenagers. In fact, in all age and sex groups, black unemployment rates are at least 1½ times as large as white unemployment rates. And third, unemployment rates fall as age rises, up to the age of 65.

TABLE 15-5 RATES OF UNEMPLOYMENT, BY AGE, SEX, AND RACE

	Unemployment rate (percentage of labor force)	
	1975	1979
Males		
16–19	20.1	15.8
20–24	14.3	8.6
25–64	5.6	3.3
Females		
16–19	19.7	16.4
20–24	12.7	9.6
25–64	7.0	4.8
White		
Males	7.2	4.4
Females	8.6	5.9
Nonwhite		
Males	13.7	10.3
Females	14.0	12.3
All workers	8.5	5.8

Note: Unemployment rates are for persons 16 or more years of age unless otherwise indicated. *Sources:* U.S. Department of Labor, *Monthly Labor Review*, and *Economic Report of the President*.

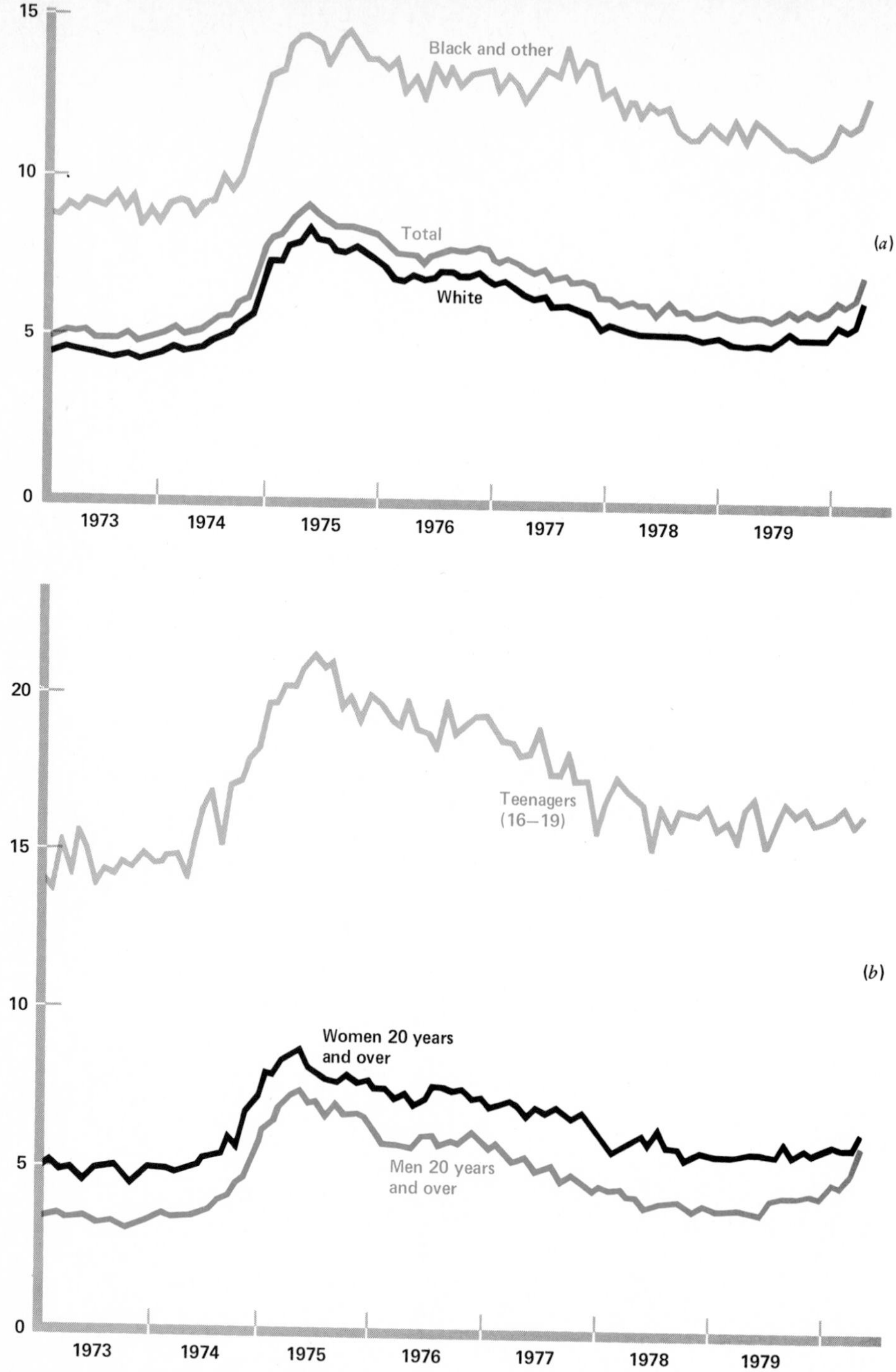

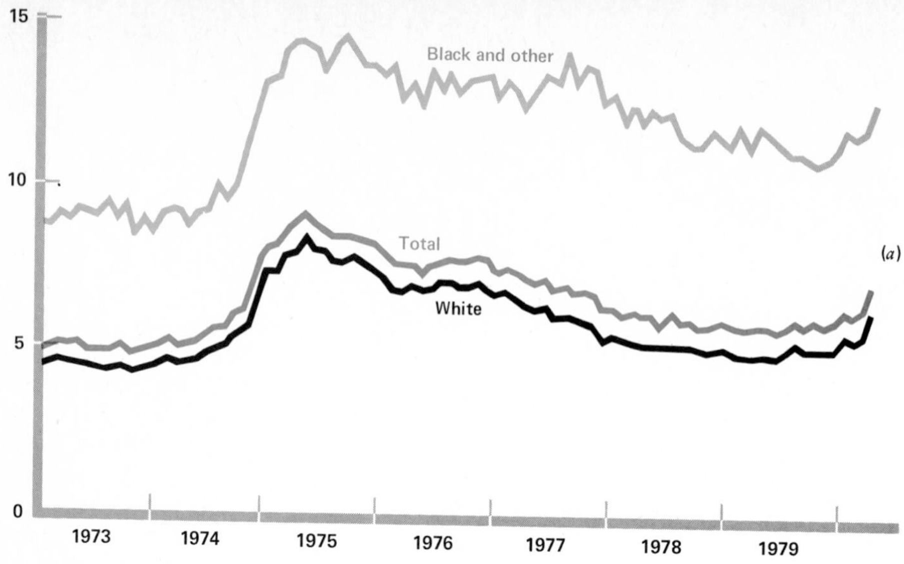

15
10
5
0
Black and other
Total
White
(a)
1973
1974
1975
1976
1977
1978
1979
20
15
10
5
0
Teenagers
(16–19)
(b)
Women 20 years
and over
Men 20 years
and over
1973
1974
1975
1976
1977
1978
1979

Source: Economic Indicators; December 1976, July 1979, and May 1980

CHART 15-2 SELECTED UNEMPLOYMENT RATES.
(Source: Economic Indicators, December 1976, July 1979, and May 1980.)

Table 15-2 presents data on the duration of unemployment spells by age and sex characteristics. The duration of unemployment differs across groups in the labor force, lengthening particularly with age.[9] Table 15-2 also shows data on the proportion of spells of unemployment ending in withdrawal from the labor force. Spells of unemployment are more likely to end in withdrawal from the labor force among young males than among older males; this difference does not exist between younger and older females.

The evidence tells an unambiguous story. Unemployment is much higher among the young than among the older. But the nature of the unemployment is different. The young tend to be unemployed more often and for short spells, whereas older workers are unemployed less often but for longer periods. It should also be noted that about half the teenage unemployed are, in fact, at school and looking for part-time work. To the extent that long periods of unemployment are a more serious concern than short periods, a given rate of unemployment (say 5 percent) among older workers is a more serious concern than the same rate of unemployment (5 percent) among youths. But the level of unemployment among the young is so high that youth unemployment is indeed a severe problem.

We have now reviewed the three central facts about United States unemployment experience:

1 There are substantial flows through the pool of unemployment each month.
2 Nonetheless, most unemployment is accounted for by people who will be unemployed for several months during the year.
3 There are substantial variations in unemployment rates across different labor force groups.

We turn next to the natural rate of unemployment.

15-3 THE NATURAL RATE OF UNEMPLOYMENT

The *natural rate of unemployment* is also called the full-employment level of unemployment, or the long-run equilibrium level of unemployment. In

[9] *Technical note:* If you consult one of the sources of labor market data, such as *Monthly Labor Review* or *Employment and Earnings*, you will find figures on the duration of unemployment by characteristic, along with overall rates of unemployment. These duration data refer to the length of time the individual has been unemployed to date, *not* to the length of a *completed spell* of unemployment. Going back to our example at the beginning of this section, the duration data in the official sources would show five people who have been unemployed 1 month, one person unemployed 2 months, and one each unemployed for 3, 4, 5, and 6 months. The average duration would be computed as $[(5 \times 1) + (1 \times 2) + (1 \times 3) + \cdots + (1 \times 6)]/10 = 2.5$ months. Of course, the duration as reported in the official sources would increase together with the duration of completed spells. Thus the comparative duration rates shown in the official sources agree fully with the statements here, and are well worth examining.

this section, we first discuss the determinants of the natural rate of unemployment, then examine estimates of changes in the natural rate since the fifties, and finally consider proposals for reducing it.

Figure 15-3 points to the factors causing the unemployment rate to change. Increases in the rate of entry to the labor force, or quits, or layoffs, or involuntary quits cause the unemployment rate to rise. Increases in hiring, or recalls, or withdrawals from the labor force, cause the unemployment rate to fall. Each of these factors is in part determined by economic variables, such as the level of aggregate demand and the actual and expected real wage rate. When aggregate demand rises (at a given real wage), firms increase their hiring. When aggregate demand falls, firms lay off workers. Thus there is an immediate link between the factors emphasized in Figure 15-3 and aggregate demand. However, it should be noted that the relationship between aggregate demand and the variables affecting the rate of unemployment is not unambiguous. For instance, an increase in the demand for labor increases quits at the same time as it reduces layoffs. A man thinking of leaving his job to search for another would be more likely to quit when the job market is good and demand is high than when there is heavy unemployment and the prospects of finding a good job quickly are low. In fact, it can be seen from Table 15-1 that quits and layoffs moved in the opposite direction between May 1975 and May 1979: quits rose from 1.3 percent to 2 percent per month, while layoffs fell from 1.8 percent to 1 percent per month. When the unemployment rate is constant, flows in and out of unemployment just balance each other. These flows can match at any level of unemployment, as they did in 1975. The *natural rate of unemployment*, however, is that rate of unemployment at which flows in and out of unemployment just balance,[10] *and* at which expectations of firms and workers as to the behavior of prices and wages are correct.

The determinants of the natural rate of unemployment can be thought of in terms of the duration and frequency of unemployment. The *duration* of unemployment is the average length of time a person remains unemployed, which depends on (1) the organization of the labor market, in regard to the presence or absence of employment agencies, youth employment services, etc.; (2) the demographic makeup of the labor force, as discussed above; (3) the ability and desire of the unemployed to keep looking for a better job; and (4) the availability and types of jobs. If all jobs are the same, an unemployed person will take the first one offered. If some jobs are better than others, it is worthwhile searching and waiting for a good one. If it is very expensive to remain unemployed, say, because there are no unemployment benefits, an unemployed person is more likely to accept a job

[10] We should recognize that when the labor force is growing and the unemployment rate is constant, the pool of unemployed grows over time. For example, with a labor force of 90 million and 5 percent unemployment, total unemployment is 4.5 million people. With a labor force of 100 million and 5 percent unemployment, there are 5 million unemployed, and the unemployment pool has grown by a half-million people.

offer than to continue looking for a better one. If unemployment benefits are high, then it may be worthwhile for the unemployed person to continue looking for a better job rather than to accept a poor job when one is offered.

The behavior of workers who have been laid off is also important when considering the duration of unemployment. Typically, a worker who has been laid off returns to the original job and does not search for another job. The reason is quite simple: once a worker has been with a firm for a long time, she has special expertise in the way that firm works which makes her valuable to that firm but is not of great benefit to another employer. In addition, she may have built up seniority rights, including a pension. That means that such an individual could not expect to find as good a job if she searched for a new one. Her best course of action may be to wait to be recalled.

There are two basic determinants of the *frequency* of unemployment. The first is the variability of the demand for labor across different firms in the economy. The second is the rate at which new workers enter the labor force. Even when aggregate demand is constant, some firms are growing and some are contracting. The contracting firms lose labor and the growing firms hire more labor. The greater this variability of the demand for labor across different firms, the higher the unemployment rate. Further, the variability of aggregate demand itself will affect the variability of the demand for labor. Second, the more rapidly new workers enter the labor force—the faster the growth rate of the labor force—the higher the natural rate of unemployment.

The four factors affecting duration and the two factors affecting frequency of unemployment are the basic determinants of the natural rate of unemployment.

You should note that the factors determining the level of the natural rate of unemployment are not immutable. The structure of the labor market and the labor force can change. The willingness of workers to remain unemployed while looking for, or waiting for, a new job can change. The variability of the demand for labor by different firms can shift. As Edmund Phelps has noted, the natural rate is not "an intertemporal constant, something like the speed of light, independent of everything under the sun."[11] Indeed, the natural rate is difficult to measure, and estimates of it have changed over the past few years from about 4 percent in the 1960s to near 5.5, or even 6, percent in the early eighties.

Estimates of the Natural Rate of Unemployment

Estimates of the natural rate of unemployment typically try to adjust for changes in the composition of the labor force, and perhaps for changes in

[11] See E. Phelps, "Economic Policy and Unemployment in the Sixties," *Public Interest*, Winter 1974.

the natural rate of unemployment of the various groups in the labor force. We can write an equation very similar to Equation (2) for the natural rate, $\bar{u}$:

$$\bar{u} = w_1\bar{u}_1 + w_2\bar{u}_2 + \cdots + w_n\bar{u}_n \tag{2b}$$

Equation (2*b*) says that the natural rate is the weighted average of the natural rates of unemployment of the subgroups in the labor force.

Estimates of the natural rate generally start from some period when the labor market was thought to be in equilibrium and when the aggregate unemployment rate, as well as the unemployment rates of the groups in Equation (2*b*), were at their natural levels. This period is usually taken to be the mid-1950s, and the aggregate natural rate for that period is assumed to be 4 percent. The natural rate estimated for each group will differ from 4 percent: for teenagers it will be much higher, for prime-age males it will be lower, and so on.

The first adjustment made to the 4 percent rate follows from the fact that the composition of the labor force has been changing since the mid-1940s. The weight of teenagers and women in the labor force has been rising. Holding the $\bar{u}_i$ constant, the changing composition of the labor force is taken into account by changing the weights, w_i, in Equation (2*b*) to reflect the current composition of the labor force rather than that of the mid-fifties. The result is a rise in the natural rate.

The second adjustment that is typically undertaken is to assume that the natural rate for each group may depend on the relative size of that group in the labor force, that is, on the weight w_i. The idea here is that one type of labor is not a perfect substitute for another, and that the more of some type of labor there is, the higher the unemployment rate for that group.[12]

Table 15-6 presents for selected years estimates of the full-employment rate of unemployment made by the Council of Economic Advisers. There are other estimates of the natural rate; they differ in their method of calculation, but they all include adjustments for the composition of the labor force, and they all show the natural rate rising substantially since the fifties.[13] Estimates of the natural rate at the end of the seventies and the beginning of the eighties cluster around 5.6 percent.

[12] See also W. Fellner (ed.), *Contemporary Economic Problems*. (Washington, D.C.: American Enterprise Institute, 1980). For details of the method of adjustment, see Peter K. Clark, "Potential GNP in the United States, 1948–1980," in *U.S. Productive Capacity: Estimating the Utilization Gap*, Working paper 23 (St. Louis, Mo.: Washington University, Center for the Study of American Business, 1977). Clark was then on the Council of Economic Advisers and his paper describes the method used by the Council to arrive at measures of the full-employment unemployment rate.

[13] See, for instance, George L. Perry, "Potential Output and Productivity," *Brookings Papers on Economic Activity*, 1977:1 (Washington, D.C.: The Brookings Institution, 1977), and Jeffrey Perloff and Michael Wachter, "A Production Function—Nonaccelerating Inflation Approach to Potential Output," in Karl Brunner and Allan Meltzer (eds.), *Carnegie-Rochester Conference Series*, vol. 10, (North-Holland Amsterdam)

TABLE 15-6 ESTIMATES OF THE NATURAL RATE OF UNEMPLOYMENT, 1955–1979

Year	Full-employment unemployment rate
1955	4.0
1960	4.2
1965	4.5
1970	4.7
1975	5.1
1979	5.2

Source: Peter K. Clark, "Potential GNP in the United States, 1948–1980," in *U. S. Productive Capacity: Estimating the Utilization Gap*, Working paper 23 (St. Louis, Mo.: Washington University, Center for the Study of American Business, 1977).

Reducing the Natural Rate of Unemployment

Discussion of methods for reducing the natural rate of unemployment tends to focus on the distribution of unemployment across different groups in the labor force.[14] Unemployment rates are lowest among mature white males. If unemployment rates for other groups of workers could be reduced toward those levels. the overall unemployment rate would obviously drop.

The place to start is with teenage unemployment. We have pointed out earlier that teenagers are unemployed more frequently than others. Reasons for their unemployment may be examined with the help of Table 15-7. It can be seen that many of the unemployed teenagers are new entrants to the labor force, and also that more teenagers than adult males

[14] See Martin S. Feldstein, "The Economics of the New Unemployment," *Public Interest*, 33, Fall 1973, and Robert E. Hall, "Prospects for Shifting the Phillips Curve through Manpower Policy," *Brookings Papers on Economic Activity*, 1971:3 (Washington, D.C.: The Brookings Institution, 1971).

TABLE 15-7 UNEMPLOYED PERSONS BY REASON FOR UNEMPLOYMENT BY SEX, AGE, AND RACE *(in percent)*

	Males, 20+		Females, 20+		Both sexes, 16 to 19		White		Nonwhite	
	1975	1979	1975	1979	1975	1979	1975	1979	1975	1979
Total unemployed (percentage distribution)	100.0	100.0	100.0	100.0	100.0	100.0	100.0	100.0	100.0	100.0
Job losers	74.9	63.6	50.0	37.3	25.5	20.5	56.0	43.6	52.8	40.5
Job leavers	8.5	14.1	13.9	16.3	8.7	11.8	10.9	15.6	7.9	10.0
Reentrants	14.5	19.3	31.9	40.0	29.9	29.0	23.5	28.7	32.0	32.0
New entrants	2.1	3.0	4.2	6.3	35.8	38.6	9.6	12.1	13.2	17.4

Source: Employment and Earnings.

are reentrants to the labor force. The unemployment rate among teenagers could be reduced if the length of time teenagers take to find a first job were reduced, and also if their entry and exit from the labor force were made less frequent. In order to reduce delays in the finding of jobs, it has been suggested that a Youth Employment Service should be set up to help school leavers locate jobs.

One of the main reasons teenagers enter and leave the labor force often is that the jobs they hold when they are working are not particularly attractive. It is a matter of some controversy as to how to improve existing jobs. Martin Feldstein has suggested that part of the reason jobs are unappealing is that the minimum wage is too high to make it worthwhile for employers to spend more money training the labor they hire in order to make their employees more skilled in their line of work.[15] He points to the apprentice system in other countries, in which young workers either receive very low pay or else pay to get jobs while they are learning skills. He argues that a reduction in the minimum wage would help make such on-the-job training more attractive to employers in the United States. He also suggests that there should be a system of scholarships for this type of training, since he doubts that a lower minimum wage by itself would be sufficient to encourage the right amount of on-the-job training. Similarly, there might be a case for the payment of wage subsidies to encourage firms to hire teenagers who might otherwise be unemployed.

By contrast, Peter Doeringer and Michael Piore[16] doubt that measures such as reducing the minimum wage will do much to improve the nature of jobs in what they call the *secondary labor market.* They suggest that there are a host of noneconomic factors affecting the kinds of jobs that are typically available in the economy. The major economic variables they cite as determining the nature of jobs are the stability and level of aggregate demand. They argue that the instability of aggregate demand is the major reason firms rely on temporary labor and subcontracting to meet high levels of demand. If demand were maintained at a high *and* stable level, firms would have more incentive to create good stable jobs for their entire work force.

When we move away from teenage unemployment to other categories of unemployment, it is clear from Table 15-7 that reentry rates into the labor force are much higher for all categories other than mature males. This suggests that these other groups, too, move in and out of the labor force. Thus the same policies that might increase the stability of teenage employment should be expected to work for these groups. These would include policies to provide such workers with more training, perhaps in government manpower training schemes. There have been a number of

[15] Martin Feldstein, "The Economics of the New Unemployment," cited in footnote 14.

[16] Peter B. Doeringer and Michael J. Piore, "Unemployment and the 'Dual Labor Market'," *Public Interest*, 38, Winter 1975.

such programs, the success of which is difficult to evaluate.[17] They would also include attempts to create "job banks" which would make it possible to match the characteristics of available jobs with those of workers looking for jobs. Better day-care facilities would also contribute to more stable labor market participation.

Finally, we return to the system of unemployment benefits. Unemployment benefits are not taxed, but wages are. It appears that unemployment benefits typically are about 50 percent as high as after-tax wage incomes.[18]

A high level of unemployment benefits makes it less urgent for an unemployed person to obtain a job. Further, the fact that a laid-off worker will not suffer a large loss from being unemployed makes it more attractive for an employer to lay off workers temporarily than to attempt to keep them on the job.

There seems to be little doubt that unemployment compensation does add to the natural rate of unemployment. This does not imply, though, that unemployment compensation should be abolished. What is appropriate is a scheme that will create less incentive for firms to lay off labor while at the same time ensuring that the unemployed are not exposed to economic distress.[19] This is obviously a difficult trick to carry off.

It has become fashionable to argue that unemployment does not present a serious social problem because the unemployed essentially choose to be unemployed and live off unemployment compensation. This argument is wrong in assuming that all unemployment is covered by unemployment benefits. In fact, insured unemployment is less than two-thirds of total unemployment.

15-4 THE COSTS OF UNEMPLOYMENT

The costs of unemployment are so obvious that this section might seem superfluous. Society on the whole loses from unemployment because total output is below its potential level. The unemployed as individuals suffer both from their income loss while unemployed and from the low level of self-esteem that long periods of unemployment cause.[20]

This section provides some estimates of the costs of forgone output

[17] Robert E. Hall, "Why Is the Unemployment Rate So High," *Brookings Papers*, 1970:3, and "Prospects for Shifting the Phillips Curve," ibid., 1971:3 (Washington, D.C.: The Brookings Institution, 1971): and Martin Feldstein, cited in footnote 5.

[18] Data on unemployment benefits and after-tax incomes are published in the *Monthly Labor Review*.

[19] See Feldstein, "The Economics of the New Unemployment," cited in footnote 14, for discussion of the ways in which the current system could be improved.

[20] See Robert J. Gordon, "The Welfare Cost of Higher Unemployment," *Brookings Papers on Economic Activity*, 1973:1 (Washington, D.C.: The Brookings Institution, 1973); and Edmund S. Phelps, *Inflation Policy and Unemployment Theory* (New York: Norton, 1972).

resulting from unemployment, and clarifies some of the issues connected with the costs of unemployment and the potential benefits from reducing unemployment. We distinguish between cyclical unemployment, associated with short-run deviations of the unemployment rate from the natural rate and "permanent" unemployment that exists at the natural rate.

Cyclical Unemployment

We have already studied Okun's law, which estimates the short-run loss of output associated with an increase of one percentage point in the unemployment rate. The cost of this increase in the unemployment rate in the short run is a fall of two and a half percentage points in the level of real output. This is the fundamental cost of cyclical unemployment.

Are there any other costs of unemployment or, for that matter, offsetting benefits? It is possible to imagine offsetting benefits. We do not discuss here the benefit arising from a temporary reduction in the inflation rate accompanying a temporary increase in unemployment, but rather focus on the costs of unemployment taken by itself. A possible offsetting benefit occurs because the unemployed are not working and have more leisure. However, the value that can be placed on that leisure is small. In the first place, much of it is unwanted leisure.

Second, there is a fairly subtle issue that we shall have to explore. If a person were free to set her hours of work, she would work up to the point at which the marginal value of leisure to her was equal to the marginal return from working an extra hour. We would then be able to conclude that if her workday were slightly reduced, the overall loss to her would be extremely small. The reason is that she acquires extra leisure from working less, at the cost of having less income. But she was previously at the point where the marginal value of leisure was equal to the after-tax marginal wage, so that the benefit of the increased leisure almost exactly offsets the private loss of income. However, the net marginal wage is less than the value of the marginal product of an employed person to the economy. The major reason is that society taxes the income of the employed person, so that society as a whole takes a share of the marginal product of the employed person. When the employed woman in our example stops working, she loses for herself only the *net* of tax wage she has been receiving. But society also loses the taxes she has been paying. The unemployed person values her leisure at the net of tax wage, and that value is smaller than the value of her marginal product for society as a whole. Therefore, the value of increased leisure provides only a partial offset to the Okun's law estimate of the cost of cyclical unemployment.

Note that we do not count both the individual's personal loss of income and the Okun's law estimate of forgone output as part of the cost of unemployment. The reason is that the Okun's law estimate implicitly includes the individual's own loss of income—it estimates the total loss of output to the economy as a whole as a result of the reduction of employment. That loss could in principle be distributed across different people in the economy in many different ways. For instance, one could imagine that the unemployed person continues to receive benefit payments totaling close to her or his previous income while employed, with the benefit payments financed through taxes on working individuals. In that case, the unemployed person would not suffer an income loss from being unemployed, but society would still lose from the reduction in total output available.

However, the effects of an increase in unemployment are, in fact, borne heavily by the unemployed themselves. There is thus an extra cost to society of unemployment that is very difficult to quantify. The cost arises from the uneven distribution of the burden of unemployment across the population. Unemployment tends to be concentrated among the poor, and that makes the distributional aspect of unemployment a serious matter. It is not one we can easily quantify, but it should not be overlooked. Further, there are many reports of the adverse psychic effects of unemployment that, again, are not easy to quantify but should not be ignored.[21]

"Permanent" Unemployment

The benefits of reducing the natural rate of unemployment are more difficult to estimate than the costs of cyclical unemployment. It is clear that the Okun's law estimate of a 2½ percent change in output resulting from a change of one percentage point in the unemployment rate is not appropriate here. The reason is that the increase in output associated with cyclical changes in unemployment results in part from the fact that the labor put back to work in the short run is able to use capital that had not been fully utilized when unemployment was high. However, in the long run, which is relevant when considering a reduction in the natural rate of unemployment, it would be necessary to invest to provide for the capital with which the newly employed would work. The Okun 2½:1 ratio is therefore too high for the long-run benefits of reducing the natural rate of unemployment. One estimate of benefit is that a reduction of one percentage point in the natural unemployment rate from 5 percent would increase long-run output by only 0.76 percent.[22]

The available estimates of the social benefits of a reduction in long-run

[21] See Harry Maurer, *Not Working* (New York: Hold, Rinehart and Winston, 1979), and Kay L. Schlozman and Sidney Verba, *Injury to Insult* (Cambridge: Harvard University Press, 1979).

[22] See Robert J. Gordon, cited in footnote 20. Can you see how a number like this would emerge if the economy's production function is Cobb-Douglas with a labor share of about ¾?

unemployment cannot be narrowed down to very solid numbers. Even more difficult is the estimate of an "optimal" long-run unemployment rate. Here. we ask the question whether any—and, if so, how much—unemployment is desirable in the long run. A first guess at the answer to that question is that all unemployment is wasteful, since the unemployed labor could usefully be employed. However, that answer is not totally persuasive. Those people who are unemployed in order to look for a better job are performing a valuable service not only for themselves. They are also performing a service for society by attempting to put themselves into a position in which they earn the most and are the most valuable. Because the composition of demand shifts over time, we can expect always to have some firms expanding and some contracting. This is true even with a stable level of aggregate demand. Those who lose their jobs will be unemployed and they benefit both society and themselves by not taking the very first job that comes along, but rather searching for the optimal employment. Accordingly, we can conclude that some unemployment is a good thing in an economy in which the composition of demand changes over time. It is one thing to recognize this and quite another to pin down the optimal rate of unemployment numerically. Gordon's estimate in the article cited in footnote 20 is 2 percent. Feldstein[23] has argued that the unemployment rate could be lowered to less than 3 percent and perhaps even close to 2 percent, though he has cautiously avoided specifying the precise number.

15-5 THE COSTS OF INFLATION

The costs of inflation are much less obvious than those of unemployment. There is no direct loss of output from inflation, as there is from unemployment. In studying the costs of inflation, we again want to distinguish the short run from the long run. In the case of inflation, though, the relevant distinction is between inflation that is *perfectly anticipated* and taken into account in economic transactions, and *imperfectly anticipated*, or unexpected inflation. We start with perfectly anticipated inflation because that case provides a useful bench mark against which to judge unanticipated inflation.

Perfectly Anticipated Inflation

Suppose that an economy has been experiencing a given rate of inflation, say 5 percent, for a long time, and that it is correctly anticipated that the

[23] In "The Economics of the New Unemployment," cited in footnote 14.

rate of inflation will continue to be 5 percent. In such an economy, all contracts would build in the expected 5 percent inflation. Borrowers and lenders will both know and agree that the dollars in which a loan will be repaid will be worth less than the dollars which are given up by the lender when making the loan. Nominal interest rates would be 5 percent higher than they would be in the absence of inflation. Long-term wage contracts will increase wages at 5 percent per year to take account of the inflation, and then build in whatever changes in real wages are agreed to. Long-term leases will take account of the inflation. In brief, any contracts in which the passage of time is involved will take the inflation into account. In that category we include the tax laws, which we are assuming would be indexed. That is, as discussed in Chapter 14, the tax brackets themselves would be increased at the rate of 5 percent per year.[24] Inflation has no real costs in such an economy, except for a minor qualification to be noted below.

That qualification arises because the interest rate that is paid on money might not adjust to the inflation rate. No interest is paid on currency—notes and coin—throughout the world, and no interest is paid on demand deposits in many countries. It is very difficult to pay interest on currency, so that it is likely that the interest rate on currency will continue to be zero, independent of the perfectly anticipated inflation rate. Interest can be, and in some states is already, paid on demand deposits. Thus it is reasonable to expect that in a fully anticipated inflation, interest would be paid on demand deposits, and the interest rate paid on demand deposits would adjust to the inflation rate. If so, the only cost of perfectly anticipated inflation is that the inflation makes it more costly to hold currency.

The cost to the individual of holding currency is the interest forgone by not holding an interest-bearing asset. When the inflation rate rises, the nominal interest rate rises, the interest lost by holding currency increases, and the cost of holding currency therefore increases. Accordingly, the demand for currency falls. In practice, this means that individuals economize on the use of currency by carrying less in their wallets and making more trips to the bank to cash smaller checks than they did before. The costs of these trips to the bank are often described as the "shoe-leather" costs of inflation. They are related to the amount by which the demand for currency is reduced by an increase in the anticipated inflation rate, and they are trivial.

We should add that throughout this discussion, we are assuming inflation rates that are not too high effectively to disrupt the payments system. This disruption was a real problem in some instances of hyperinflation, but it need not concern us here. We are abstracting, too, from the cost

[24] The taxation of interest would have to be on the *real* (after-inflation) return on assets for the tax system to be properly indexed.

of "menu change." This cost arises simply from the fact that with inflation—as opposed to price stability—people have to devote real resources to marking up prices and changing pay telephones and vending machines as well as cash registers. These costs are there, but one cannot get too excited about them. On balance, the costs of fully anticipated inflation are trivial.

The notion that the costs of fully anticipated inflation are trivial does not square well with the strong aversion to inflation reflected in policy making and politics. The most important reason for that aversion is probably that inflations in the United States have not been steady, and that the inflationary experience of the United States is one of imperfectly anticipated inflation, the costs of which are substantially different from those discussed in this section.

There is a further line of argument that explains the public aversion to inflation, even of the fully anticipated, steady kind we are discussing here. The argument is that such a state is not likely to exist, that it is a mirage to believe that policy makers could and would maintain a steady inflation rate at any level other than zero. The argument is that policy makers are reluctant to use restrictive policy to compensate for transitory increases in the inflation rate. Rather than maintain a constant rate of inflation in the face of inflation shocks, the authorities would accommodate these shocks and therefore validate them. Any inflationary shock would add to the inflation rate rather than being compensated by restrictive policy. In this manner, inflation, far from being constant, would, in fact, be rising as policy makers validate any and every disturbance rather than use policy to rigidly enforce the inflation target. Zero inflation, it is argued, is the only target that can be defended without this risk.[25]

Although there are many examples of countries with long inflationary histories, there does not appear to be any tendency for the inflation rate of those countries to increase over time. The argument thus seems weak. However, it is true that the inflation rate has been more stable in countries with low rates of inflation than in countries with inflation rates that are on average higher,[26] perhaps providing a germ of validity to the notion.

Imperfectly Anticipated Inflation

The idyllic scene of full adjustment to inflation painted here does not describe economies that we actually know. Modern economies include a

[25] See William J. Fellner, introductory essay in William J. Fellner (ed.), *Contemporary Economic Problems* (Washington, D.C.: American Enterprise Institute, 1973).

[26] Arthur M. Okun, "The Mirage of Steady Inflation," *Brookings Papers on Economic Activity*, 2:1971 (Washington, D.C.: The Brookings Institution, 1971).

variety of institutional features representing different degrees of adjustment to inflation. Economies with long inflationary histories, such as those of Brazil and Israel, have made substantial adjustments to inflation through the use of indexing. Others in which inflation has been episodic, such as the United States economy, have made only small adjustments for inflation.

One of the important effects of inflation is to change the real value of assets fixed in nominal terms. A doubling of the price level, such as the United States experienced in the period from 1960 to 1977, cuts the purchasing power of all claims or assets fixed in money terms in half. Thus, someone who bought a 20-year government bond in 1960 and expected to receive a principal of, say, $100 in constant purchasing power at the 1980 maturity date, actually winds up with a $100 principal that has purchasing power of less than $50 in 1960 dollars. The more than doubling of the price level has effectively reduced the real value of the asset by over one-half. It has transferred wealth from creditors—holders of bonds—to debtors. This effect operates with respect to all assets fixed in nominal terms, in particular, money, bonds, savings accounts, insurance contracts, and some pensions. Obviously, it is an extremely important effect since it can certainly wipe out the purchasing power of a lifetime's saving that is supposed to finance retirement consumption. In 1979 the total value of assets fixed in nominal terms was about $7 trillion, or about $30,000 per head. An increase of one percentage point in the price level would reduce the real value of these assets by $70 billion, or an amount equal to 3 percent of GNP.

Those figures by themselves seem to explain the public concern over inflation. There appears to be a lot riding on each percentage-point change in the price level. That impression is slightly misleading. Many individuals are both debtors and creditors in nominal assets. Almost everyone has some money, and is thus a creditor in nominal terms. Many of the middle class own housing, financed through mortgages whose value is fixed in nominal terms. Such individuals benefit from inflation because it reduces the real value of their mortgage. Other individuals have borrowed in nominal terms to buy consumer durables, such as cars, and to that extent have their real indebtedness reduced by inflation.

Table 15-8 shows the net position of different sectors in the economy in terms of the amounts of nominal assets they own or owe. In other words, the table shows the net debtor or creditor status in terms of nominal or "monetary" assets and liabilities.[27] The household sector shows up as a net monetary creditor, with the government the offsetting major monetary debtor. Nonfinancial corporations are to a large extent monetary debtors

[27] Table 15-8 is an updated version of a similar table in G. L. Bach and James B. Stephenson, "Inflation and the Distribution of Wealth," *Review of Economics and Statistics*, February 1974.

TABLE 15-8 NET DEBTOR OR CREDITOR STATUS IN NOMINAL ASSETS OF MAJOR ECONOMIC SECTORS *(in billions of dollars)*

	1960	1970	1979
Households	+350	+695	+1,544
Unincorporated businesses	−23	−86	−265
Nonfinancial corporations	−88	−264	−664
Financial corporations	+24	−14	−42
Governments	−251	−341	−664

Note: A plus sign indicates a net monetary creditor.
Source: Federal Reserve Flow-of-Funds. Accounts Assets and Liabilities Outstanding.

reflecting their debt-financed capital structure. Similarly, financial corporations are net monetary debtors. For example, the banks' net debtor position is reflected by their liabilities in the form of debt and deposits, while their assets include some real assets like land and structures.

The important point about Table 15-8 is the recognition that a change in the price level brings about a major redistribution of wealth between sectors. Thus an inflation rate of 10 percent in 1979 would have resulted in a transfer of $66.4 billion from the household sector to the government. Obviously, we must be careful in assessing the implications of that statement. A redistribution of wealth from corporations to the household sector, for example, means that as a household the average person has gained, but as owner of a corporate stock, the average household has lost. This singles out transfers between the government and the private sector as particularly important because here the offset is much less immediate.

We are talking here about inflation because that is the current issue. It should be apparent, though, that much the same problems arise with deflation or falling prices. Thus, from 1929 to 1933, the consumer price index fell by almost 25 percent, and that decline meant an extremely large increase in the real value of liabilities, in particular, the real debt of farmers. Inflation redistributes wealth within society from creditors to debtors, and deflation redistributes income from debtors to creditors.

However, we must go beyond Table 15-8 in two respects. First, that table really indicates the vulnerability of different sectors to inflation. It does not tell us to what extent inflation was anticipated when the contracts behind the figures in Table 15-8 were drawn. The 10 percent inflation referred to above might have been correctly anticipated, so that the wealth transfers occurring as a result of the inflation would not cause any surprises.

However, that does not mean that the creditors would not benefit from higher rates of inflation, and the debtors from lower rates. Second, the gains and losses from these wealth transfers basically cancel out over the economy as a whole. When the government gains from inflation, the private sector may have to pay lower taxes later. When the corporate sector gains from inflation, owners of corporations benefit at the expense of others. If we really did not care about the distribution of wealth among individuals, the costs of unanticipated inflation would be negligible. Included in the individuals of the previous sentence are those belonging to different generations, since the current owners of the national debt might be harmed by inflation—to the benefit of future taxpayers.

The costs of unanticipated inflation are thus largely distributional costs. There is some evidence[28] that the old are more vulnerable to inflation than the young in that they own more nominal assets. Offsetting this, however, is the fact that Social Security benefits are indexed, so that a substantial part of the wealth of those about to retire is protected from unanticipated inflation. There appears to be little evidence supporting the view that the poor suffer unduly from unanticipated inflation.

Inflation redistributes wealth between debtors and creditors, as shown in Table 15-8, because changes in the price level change the purchasing power of assets fixed in money terms. There is room, too, for inflation to affect income positions by changing the distribution of income. A popular line of argument has always been that inflation benefits capitalists or recipients of profit income at the expense of wage earners. Unanticipated inflation, it is argued, means that prices rise faster than wages and therefore allow profits to expand.[29] For the United States in the postwar period, there is no persuasive evidence to this effect. There is evidence that the real return on common stocks—that is, the real value of dividends and capital gains on equity—is reduced by unanticipated inflation. Thus, equity holders appear to be adversely affected by unanticipated inflation.[30]

The last important distributional effect of inflation concerns the real value of tax liabilities. We recall from Chapter 14 that a failure to index the tax structure implies that inflation moves the public into higher tax brackets and thus raises the real value of its tax payments or reduces real disposable income. Inflation acts as though Congress had voted an increase in tax

[28] See Bach and Stephenson, cited in footnote 27.

[29] Louis De Alessi, "Do Business Firms Gain from Inflation? Reprise," *Journal of Business*, April 1975. See also Nancy Jianakoplos, "Are You Protected from Inflation?" Federal Reserve Bank of St. Louis, *Review*, January 1977.

[30] See Charles R. Nelson, "Inflation and Rates of Return on Common Stocks," *Journal of Finance*, May 1976. See also Franco Modigliani and Richard Cohn, "Inflation, Rational Valuation and the Market," *Financial Analysts Journal*, March–April 1979, for a controversial view of the reasons why inflation affects the stock market.

schedules. An estimate of this overtaxation due to the approximately 10 percent inflation from 1973 to 1974 is $7 billion (in 1974 dollars) on account of increased personal income taxes alone.[31]

The fact that unanticipated inflation acts mainly to redistribute wealth, the net effects of which redistribution should be close to zero, has led to some questioning of the reasons for public concern over inflation. The gainers, it seems, do not shout as loudly as the losers. Since some of the gainers (future taxpayers) have yet to be born, this is hardly surprising. There is also a notion that the average wage earner is subject to an illusion when both the nominal wage and the price level increase. Wage earners are thought to attribute increases in nominal wages to their own merit rather than to inflation, while the general inflation of prices is seen as causing an unwarranted reduction in the real wage they would otherwise have received. It is hard to know how to test the validity of this argument.

It does appear that the redistributive effects of unanticipated inflation are large, and that, accordingly, some parts of the population could be seriously affected by unanticipated inflation. It is difficult to be more precise in discussing this complicated question, which, like others in this chapter, remains the subject of ongoing research.

*15-6 SHORT-RUN AND LONG-RUN TRADEOFFS ONCE AGAIN

Chapter 13 studied the determination of the rates of inflation and unemployment and the response of the economy to various shocks. In this section, we ask what the scope for stabilization policy might be in response to shocks. We have already (in Chapter 9) considered issues of uncertainty about the dynamic response of the economy and the size of multipliers. We have now reviewed some evidence on the costs of inflation and unemployment. The remaining question is this: How fast should policy makers try to reach their target? Given the long-run unemployment rate, there is a unique long-run growth rate of money that will satisfy the inflation target. The problem is to know whether, from some initial situation, one should try to proceed to that inflation target at maximum speed—and suffer a large unemployment cost in the transition—or whether, on the contrary, a more gradual approach is called for.

Assume the economy to be in full equilibrium with an inflation rate of 10 percent and that a move to a lower long-run rate of inflation is planned. Further, assume that only monetary policy will be used to achieve that reduction in inflation. Now a first possibility arises if the government

[31] See William Fellner et al., *Correcting Taxes for Inflation* (Washington, D.C.: American Enterprise Institute, June 1975), p. 8.

commands total credibility with the public and all prices and wages adjust freely. In that case, it is sufficient to announce and implement a reduction in monetary growth to the new long-run target level. The inflation rate will immediately respond because the credibility that the government commands will instantaneously be reflected in a revision of expectations to the new lower rate of inflation. The free adjustability of prices and wages will ensure that the expectations are immediately reflected in actual price behavior.

It is more likely that the government does not command such credibility, so that expectations continue to be formed—entirely or predominantly—on the basis of past observations of inflation. That case is analyzed in Figure 15-4. The initial equilibrium is at point E, and the long-run target is at point E'. Now we shall examine two strategies which we refer to as *gradualist* and *cold turkey*. A gradualist policy involves a gradual reduction in monetary growth toward the new long-run level, while a cold-turkey policy goes for an immediate reduction in the inflation rate to the long-run level.

The gradualist approach is a compromise. It recognizes that in the transition to the new long-run equilibrium, unemployment will occur, and

FIGURE 15-4 ALTERNATIVE ADJUSTMENT POLICIES

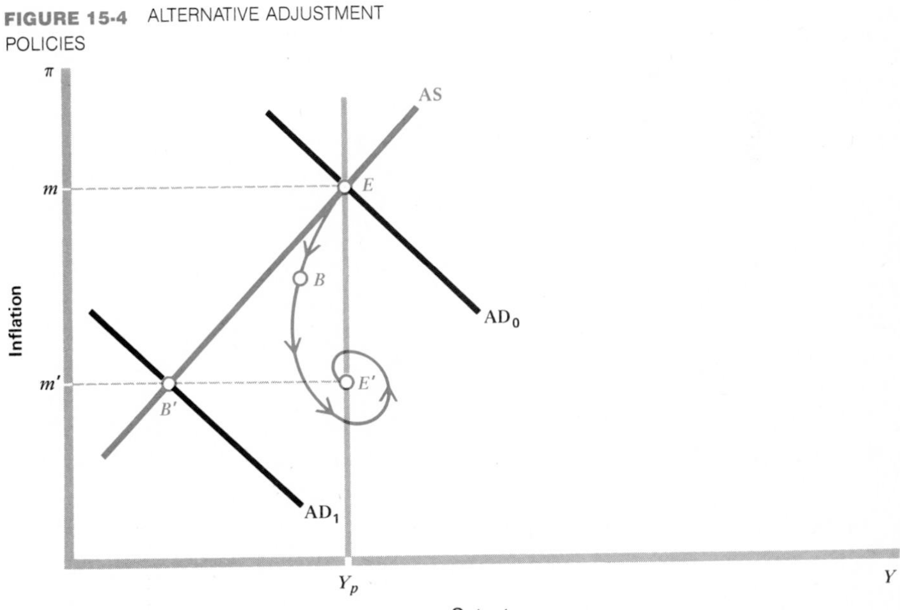

that inflation can be reduced faster with a more restrictive policy. The gradualist approach recognizes, too, that more rapid adjustment of inflation will imply higher unemployment. The compromise is to achieve the target of reduced inflation over time.

Figure 15-4 illustrates the two policy options. The gradualist approach is shown by the cyclical adjustment path. Starting at point *E*, monetary growth with this strategy is reduced somewhat, so that there is an immediate reduction in inflation but also some increase in unemployment because output declines (say, at point *B*). Over time, the reduction in inflationary expectations shifts the aggregate supply schedule downward and the decline in output and reduction in inflationary expectations shift the aggregate demand schedule down. With this improvement in the inflation-unemployment tradeoff, further reductions in monetary growth become possible until the new long-run equilibrium at point *E′* is reached. The approach to that equilibrium may well be cyclical,[32] but the outstanding aspect of the policy is not to seek an immediate full achievement of the inflation target.

The cold-turkey strategy immediately implements the new inflation target by sharply reducing monetary growth *below* the new long-run level *m′*. The strategy is to reduce inflation immediately to the new long-run level. This requires a reduction in the growth rate of money over and above what is appropriate in the long run. This is shown by the shift of the aggregate demand schedule to AD_1 in Figure 15-4. The cold-turkey policy immediately moves to point *B′*. The reduction in output and the sharp increase in unemployment exert a sufficiently deflationary effect to cut down the rate of inflation. From then on the policy faces the problem of building up aggregate demand without raising inflation as the economy moves from *B′* to the long-run equilibrium at point *E′*.

How should we evaluate the two policies? Figure 15-5 shows the implications for inflation and unemployment of the two paths. It is apparent that the cold-turkey strategy involves much higher unemployment in the short run. It has the compensating advantage that it achieves the target inflation immediately and that, perhaps, it is a more credible demonstration of policy intent. If the latter were true, it might be argued that expectations adjust faster and that, accordingly, the adjustment process might be faster. By comparison, the gradualist approach chooses adjustment to reduced inflation along a path that involves a lower unemployment rate with the offsetting cost of an inflation rate that declines less rapidly. Also, because the policy reduces inflation only gradually, it may act more

[32] In principle, a careful economic policy could move the economy from *E* to *E′* without a cyclical approach. In practice, a direct approach requires more knowledge of the economy than the policy maker is likely to have.

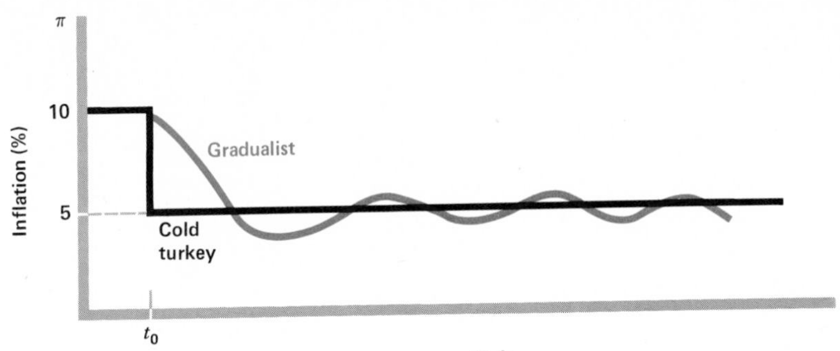

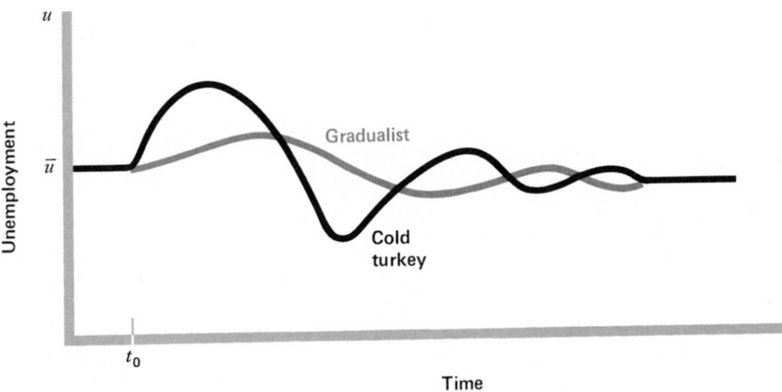

FIGURE 15-5 ALTERNATIVE PATHS OF INFLATION AND UNEMPLOYMENT

slowly in causing people to revise downward their expectations and therefore may lengthen the adjustment process.

In choosing between the policies, the policy maker has to trade off more unemployment now for less inflation. In addition, though, the policy maker has to recognize the lagged effects of monetary policy and must be aware of the possible inaccuracies of predictions or information about the economy.

How is the policy maker to choose among paths of the type shown? This depends to a large extent on her evaluation of the costs of inflation and unemployment. Someone who is persuaded that the costs of inflation are low would not be willing to incur much unemployment to reduce the inflation rate. Even if such a policy maker agreed that ultimately a lower rate of inflation was desirable, she would not do anything as extreme as is implied by the cold-turkey policy. Rather, she might chip away over time at the inflation rate, slowly trying to move the economy toward a lower rate, but always remaining acutely conscious of the effects of her policies on unemployment. Someone believing that inflation undermines the political fabric of democracy, and that some unemployment does not, would be willing to incur the costs of high unemployment in the short run to rid the country of the curse of inflation. But how is she to choose?

The discussion of the costs of inflation and unemployment in Section 15-5 suggested that the aggregate costs of cyclical unemployment are relatively easy to measure. Okun's law is useful in this regard. However, there are distributional costs of unemployment that are more difficult to quantify. The costs of unanticipated inflation also are largely distributional and equally difficult to quantify. Thus, although economic analysis can help in identifying the costs of inflation and unemployment, it cannot pin them down accurately. Further, the weights given to the losses suffered by different groups of people are likely to vary between policy makers. If it were demonstrated that unanticipated inflation hurt group X and benefited group Y, that would not guarantee that all policy makers would agree on the costs of unanticipated inflation. Some policy makers would regard damage done to group X as not very costly if not beneficial, and benefits for group Y as a good thing. Other policy makers would doubtless have an opposite view.

This section has raised the question of how fast policy makers should attempt to reach their targets. There is the final question, though, of choosing long-run targets and recognizing that the cost of adjustment may be excessive compared with the benefits. Those who hold this view argue that inflation should be stabilized at the current level, rather than reduced. They contend that a stable rate of inflation removes some, and perhaps most, of the cost of inflation, so that the residual benefits of reducing inflation may look small compared with the adjustment costs. Thus Herbert Stein, a chairperson of the Council of Economic Advisers in the Nixon administration and now a professor at the University of Virginia, has argued:[33]

> It will probably not be possible for us to establish the expectation of something like zero inflation without our going through a period in which that actually is the rate. Nothing the government says will be believed without such a demonstration, and the demonstration is likely to be extremely painful. . . . The rate has been around 6 percent for over seven years, and interest rates, wage contracts, annuities, and many other arrangements have been adjusted to it. On balance what seems crucial is to try to assure that the rate does not rise above 6 percent, or gets back promptly if it does.

[33] Herbert Stein, "Fiscal Policy: Reflections on the Past Decade," in William Fellner (ed.), *Contemporary Economic Problems* (Washington, D.C.: American Enterprise Institute, 1976), p. 83.

Beyond that, if opportunities arise to get the rate lower, they should be taken, but no great sacrifice should be made in order to achieve that.

15-7 SUMMARY

1 The long-run Phillips curve is essentially vertical. In the long run, there is no inflation-unemployment tradeoff.
2 The short-run Phillips curve is flatter than the long-run schedule because expectations are sticky and wages and prices are slow to adjust. But the Phillips curve shifts over time as expectations adjust to the actually realized rate of inflation.
3 In the long-run labor market policies, rather than inflation, must be used to reduce the natural rate of unemployment.
4 The anatomy of unemployment for the United States reveals frequent and short spells of unemployment. With near full employment in 1974, more than half the spells of unemployment lasted less than 4 weeks.
5 Nonetheless, a substantial fraction of United States unemployment is accounted for by those who are unemployed for a large portion of the time.
6 There are significant differences in unemployment rates across age groups, sex, and race. Unemployment among black teenagers is highest and that of white adults is lowest. The young, women, and minorities have significantly higher unemployment rates than middle-aged male whites.
7 The concept of the natural rate of unemployment singles out that part of unemployment which would exist even at full employment. The unemployment arises in part because of a high frequency of job changes, in particular for teenagers. The high frequency is explained partly by the poor quality of jobs available to people without training. The natural rate of unemployment is hard to conceptualize and even harder to measure. The consensus is to estimate it around 5.6 percent, up from the 4 percent of the mid-fifties.
8 Policies to reduce the natural rate of unemployment involve labor market and aggregate demand policies. The economy needs a stable, high level of aggregate demand. Disincentives to employment and training, such as minimum wages, and incentives to extended job search, such as untaxed unemployment benefits, also tend to raise the natural rate.
9 The cost of unemployment is the psychic and financial distress of the unemployed as well as the loss of output. The loss of output is only little compensated by the unemployed's enjoying leisure. For one

thing, a large part of unemployment is involuntary. For another, the social product of labor exceeds the wage rate because of income taxes.

10 The economy can adjust to perfectly anticipated inflation by moving to a system of indexed taxes and to nominal interest rates that reflect the expected rate of inflation. In the absence of regulations that prevent these adjustments (such as usury laws or interest rate ceilings), there are no important costs to perfectly anticipated inflation. The only costs are those of changing price tags periodically and the cost of suboptimal holdings of currency.

11 Imperfectly anticipated inflation has important redistributive effects among sectors. Unanticipated inflation benefits monetary debtors and hurts monetary creditors. The government gains real tax revenue, and the real value of government debt declines.

12 Optimal adjustment in reducing the rate of inflation involves the policy choice between a strategy that lowers inflation fast with high initial unemployment and an alternative slow and gradual policy. The assessment of these policy options involves the costs and benefits of inflation and unemployment. The lower the cost of unemployment and the higher the cost of inflation, the more likely that a rapid adjustment is appropriate. The faster expectations adjust and the more credible the policy, the faster it can be implemented without generating high unemployment.

PROBLEMS

1 During the 1960s and again in 1978–1979, an effort was made to improve the Phillips curve relationship through the use of wage-price guideposts and presidential jawboning. The idea was to give firms guidelines publicly for determining nominal wage increases. How would such a policy reduce inflation? Would you expect it to work in the short run? In the long run? What factors determine its effectiveness?

2 One frequently hears of the wage-price spiral. The underlying idea is that wage increases cause price increases, and these in turn cause more wage increases. These feed on one another in a never-ending spiral. Can the economy get caught in such a spiral? How would it get in? Out? Explain this notion in terms of the Phillips curve.

3 Discuss strategies whereby the government (federal, state, or local) could reduce unemployment in or among:

(*a*) Depresssed industries
(*b*) Unskilled workers
(*c*) Depressed geographical regions
(*d*) Teenagers

Include comments on the *type* of unemployment you would expect in these various groups (i.e., relative durations of unemployment spells).

4 Discuss how the following changes would affect the natural rate of unemployment. Comment also on the side effects of these changes.
   (*a*) Elimination of unions
   (*b*) Increased participation of women in the labor market
   (*c*) Larger fluctuations in the *level* of aggregate demand
   (*d*) An increase in unemployment benefits
   (*e*) Elimination of minimum wages
   (*f*) Larger fluctuations in the *composition* of aggregate demand

5 Discuss the differences in unemployment between men and women in view of Tables 15-2, 15-5, and 15-7. What does this imply about the types of jobs (on average) the different sexes are getting?

6 Some people say that inflation can be reduced in the long run without an increase in unemployment, and so we should reduce inflation to zero. Others say a steady rate of inflation at, say, 6 percent is not so bad, and that should be our goal. Evaluate these two arguments and describe what, in your opinion, are good long-run goals for inflation and unemployment. How would these be achieved?

7 In the past 10 years, Americans' awareness of inflation has increased markedly.
   (*a*) Suppose people now adjust their expectations more rapidly than earlier because of this experience. What are the implications in terms of the effects of policy?
   (*b*) Suppose, instead, that people now take the view that inflation is going to be 6 percent no matter what the government does. What would this do to government efforts to reduce inflation below that figure? Explain.

*8 How would the model in Chapter 13 be affected if a long-run Phillips curve like P_NP_N in Chart 15-1 were used, rather than a vertical long-run Phillips curve? Trace the short- and long-run effects of a decrease in the full-employment surplus in such a model.

9 The following information is to be used for calculations of the unemployment rate. There are two major groups, adults and teenagers. Teenagers account for 10 percent of the labor force and adults for 90 percent. Adults are divided into men and women. Women account for 25 percent of the adult labor force. The following table shows the unemployment rates for the groups.

Group	Unemployment rate (u)
Teenagers	14.0%
Adults:	
Men	4.5%
Women	6.0%

   (*a*) How do the numbers in this table compare (roughly) with the numbers for the United States economy?
   (*b*) Calculate the aggregate unemployment rate.
   (*c*) Assume the unemployment rate for teenagers rises from 14 to 20 percent. What is the effect on female unemployment? (Assume 60 percent of the teenagers are men.) What is the effect on the aggregate unemployment rate?
   (*d*) Assume the share of women in the adult labor force increases to 40 percent.

What is the effect on the adult unemployment rate? What is the effect on the aggregate unemployment rate?

(*e*) Relate your answers to methods of estimating the natural rate of unemployment.

10 Use the ***Economic Report of the President*** to find the unemployment data for the years 1969, 1975, and 1979. Use, as labor force groups, males and females, 16 to 19 years of age and 20 and over (that is, four groups). Then calculate what 1975 and 1979 unemployment would have been if each group in 1975 and 1979 had the unemployment rate of the group in 1969. What does the answer tell you?

*11 In the ***Economic Report of the President***, you will find data on the duration of unemployment. (You should now read footnote 9 in this chapter again.) Compare the distribution of unemployment by duration in 1969, 1975, and 1979. What relationship do you find between duration and the overall unemployment rate?

12 How feasible are the goals of the Humphrey-Hawkins Act for 1983? (They are given in the introduction to this chapter.)

16

ECONOMIC POLICY 1969–1980: THE PROBLEMS OF INFLATION AND UNEMPLOYMENT

16

ECONOMIC POLICY 1969–1980: THE PROBLEMS OF INFLATION AND UNEMPLOYMENT

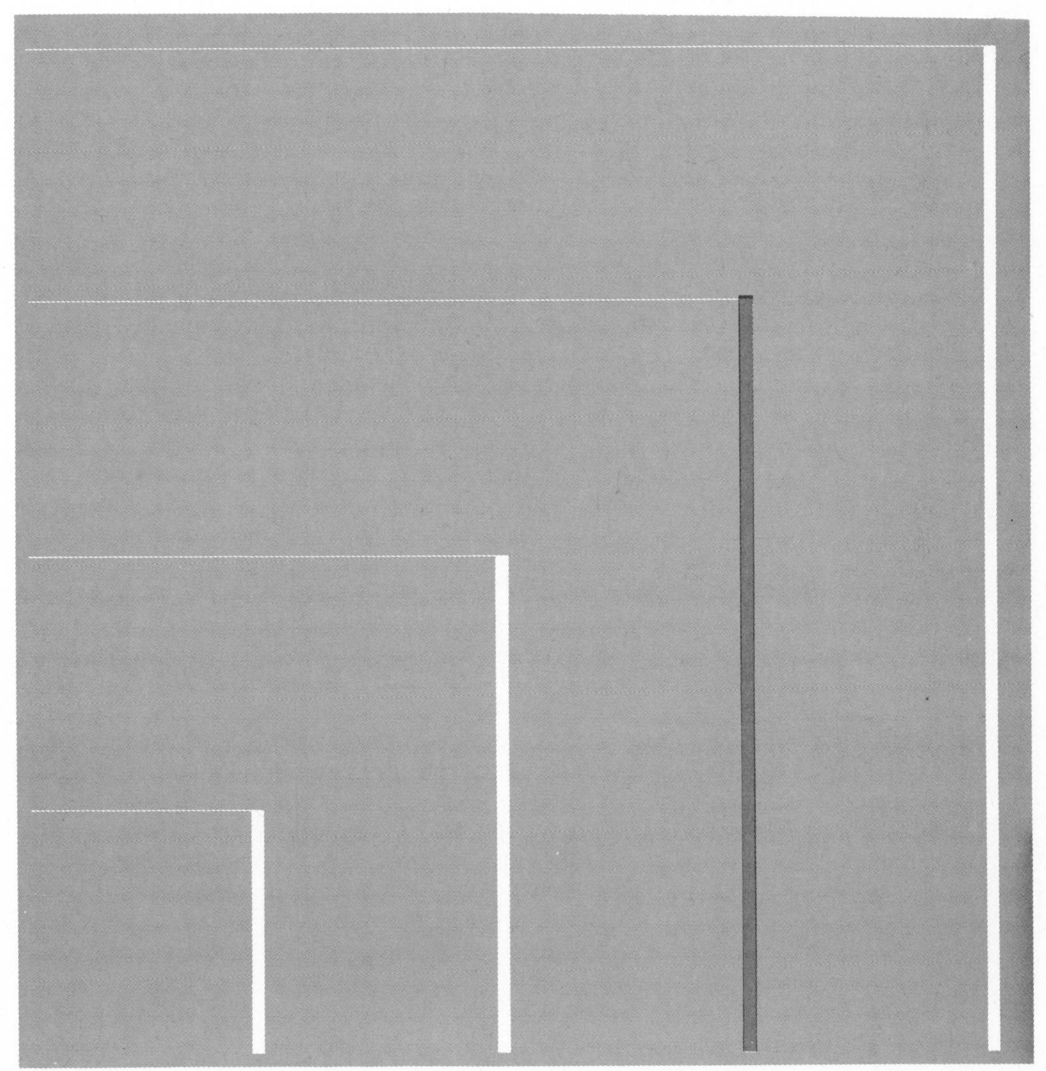

This chapter follows up on our Chapter 10 discussion of economic policy in the 1960s. The Kennedy administration came into office in 1961 with an inheritance of low inflation and high unemployment, as we saw in Chapter 10. The sixties was a period of expansionary economic policy, with the consequence that the Nixon administration took over in 1969 with an altogether different scene. Unemployment was down to 3.5 percent, but inflation was above 5 percent.

The policy problems of the 1969–1980 period initially revolved around attempts to reduce inflation. These attempts led to a recession in 1970–1971, during which the inflation rate fell very little. The economy boomed during 1972–1973, but was then faced with unprecedentedly large supply shocks in the form of increases in agricultural and oil prices in 1973–1974. Attempts to deal with the supply shocks through restrictive demand policies were unsuccessful, and the economy in 1975 was in its deepest recession of the postwar period. Recovery began at the end of 1975 and continued into 1979. By mid-1980 the economy was once more in a recession.

The period 1969–1980 saw two recessions and two recoveries and, in 1979, the onset of yet another recession. Average growth performance in the period was much lower than in the sixties, and by 1979, inflation had become quite solidly entrenched at around 9 percent. The stubborn persistence and indeed acceleration of inflation made it increasingly the number one macroeconomic policy problem.

The understanding of macroeconomics increased significantly during this period. The period started with demand management policies based largely on control of the money supply. It brought renewed use of monetary and fiscal policies as stabilization tools. The importance of supply shocks produced increased attention to the potential role of supply management tools. Economic targets were reexamined and there were major revisions of the estimates of potential output and normal unemployment. Policy makers emerged from the experience of the seventies with the recognition that "there is a lesson to be drawn from past policy mistakes. The history of monetary and fiscal policies demonstrates that we have a great deal to learn about implementing discretionary policies."[1]

The use of active discretionary policy was increasingly questioned during the period. The view that active use of stabilization policy might be destabilizing was discussed in Chapter 9, and had long been argued by adherents of *monetarism*. Monetarist views were influential in the formulation of policy in the early part of the period. In the latter part of the 1970s, a more sophisticated critique of discretionary policy, developed by the *rational expectations school*, gained influence.

Changing views about policy were accompanied in the early part of the

[1] *Annual Report of the Council of Economic Advisers*, 1976, p. 20.

decade by a change in the cast of policy makers and in the economic theories of their advisers. Keynes—and fiscal policy—had made the cover of *Time* magazine in 1965. In 1969 Milton Friedman—and monetarism—made the *Time* cover. Friedman's monetarist theories laid heavy stress on money stock behavior affecting GNP. Monetarism was strong in the early 1970s. But as much as the failure of the 1968 tax surcharge marked the end of the magic of the New Economics, so the failure of gradualist policies in 1969–1971 was to mark the end of the magic of monetarism. Economics would emerge from the 1960s and 1970s more balanced, less activist, less monetarist, and less self-confident.

In this chapter we focus on both the policy issues of the 1970s and the theories of economic policy that help explain the policy choices that were made and their failure or success. We start with a discussion of monetarism, and then move on to examine economic policy during the decade. After providing a broad overview of macroeconomic developments in the seventies, we discuss the 1969–1973 and 1973–1980 periods in more detail. We conclude with a discussion of supply management and of the rational expectations approach to macroeconomics, which provides a possible explanation for the emergence of persistent high inflation.

16-1 MONETARISM

Milton Friedman and monetarism are almost synonymous. Monetarism appears, however, in many shades and covers quite a spectrum from a harder monetarism than the Friedman variety to eclectic Keynesianism. In that spectrum one would include distinguished economists such as Karl Brunner of the University of Rochester and Allan Meltzer of Carnegie-Mellon, Thomas Mayer of the University of California at Davis, Phillip Cagan of Columbia University, and David Laidler and Michael Parkin of the University of Western Ontario, to name only some of the most prominent. Monetarism is not confined to academic economists. Indeed, the Federal Reserve Bank of St. Louis has long been a haven of a monetarist perspective on macroeconomics. If monetarism admits of some diversity, it nevertheless comes down to the proposition that money is extremely important for macroeconomics, that money is more important than other things such as fiscal policy, and, in some variants, that money is virtually *all* that matters.

Friedman's views on macroeconomics have been laid out in a series of scholarly articles, books, and popular writing.[2] Outstanding among his

[2] Some of Friedman's major articles are reprinted in *The Optimum Quantity of Money* (Chicago: Aldine, 1969). See also his book *A Program for Monetary Stability* (New York: Fordham University Press, 1959), and Milton Friedman and Anna J. Schwartz, *A Monetary History of the United States, 1867–1960* (Princeton, N.J.: Princeton University Press, 1963).

publications is *A Monetary History of the United States, 1867–1960*, a book written jointly with Anna J. Schwartz of the National Bureau of Economic Research. Despite its length, the *Monetary History* is an absorbing book that skillfully relates the behavior of the economy to the behavior of the stock of money. The book generally attributes changes in the level of prices and in economic activity—including the Great Depression—to movements in the stock of money.

What are the main features of monetarism?

Emphasis on the Stock of Money

Monetarism emphasizes the importance of the behavior of the money stock in determining (1) the rate of inflation in the long run and (2) the behavior of real GNP in the short run. Friedman has said:[3]

> I regard the description of our position as "money is all that matters for changes in *nominal* income and for *short-run* changes in real income" as an exaggeration but one that gives the right flavor of our conclusions.

The view that the behavior of the money stock is crucial for determining the rate of inflation in the long run is consistent with the analysis of Chapter 13, as we noted there. The view that the behavior of the money stock—by which Friedman usually means the *growth rate* of the money stock—is of primary importance in determining the behavior of nominal and real GNP in the short run is not one we have accepted. Our treatment so far has given emphasis to *both* monetary and fiscal variables in determining the short-run behavior of nominal and real GNP. But there is no doubt that monetary variables play an important role in determining nominal and real GNP in the short run.

An important part of monetarism is the insistence that changes in the growth rate of money—accelerations and decelerations—account for changes in real activity. Instability in monetary growth is mirrored in variability in economic activity. Thus Friedman argues:[4]

> Why should we be concerned about these gyrations in monetary growth? Because they exert an important influence on the future course of the economy. Erratic monetary growth almost always produces erratic economic growth.

[3] "A Theoretical Framework for Monetary Analysis," *Journal of Political Economy*, March/April 1970, p. 217.

[4] "Irresponsible Monetary Policy," *Newsweek*, Jan. 10, 1972. Reprinted in Friedman's collection of public policy essays, *There's No Such Thing as a Free Lunch* (La Salle, Ill.: Open Court Publishing, 1975), p. 73.

Monetarists point to a number of economic expansions and recessions as being caused by monetary accelerations and decelerations. These would certainly include the 1966 slowdown of economic activity in response to the credit crunch, the failure of the 1968 tax surcharge because it was swamped by expansionary monetary policy, and the 1970 and 1980 recessions.

Friedman's view of the primary importance of money is based in part on his careful historical studies, in which he was able to relate the booms and recessions of United States economic history to the behavior of the money stock. In general, it appeared that increases of the growth rate of money produced booms and inflations, and decreases in the money stock produced recessions and sometimes deflations. In part, his view of the primary importance of money is based on a theoretical analysis of the effects of fiscal policy, as discussed in Chapter 14's analysis of the different methods of financing the government budget deficit. We showed there that a money-financed deficit has a larger permanent effect on the price level than a debt-financed deficit.

These permanent effects are long-run effects. It is less clear why Friedman places primary emphasis on monetary policy—as opposed to fiscal policy—in affecting the behavior of real and nominal GNP in the short run.

Long and Variable Lags

Monetarism has emphasized that although the growth rate of money is of prime importance in determining the behavior of GNP, the effects of changes in the growth rate of money on the subsequent behavior of GNP occur with long and variable lags. On average, it takes a long time for a change in the growth rate of money to affect GNP, so the lag is long. In addition, the time it takes for this change to affect GNP varies from one historical episode to another—the lags are variable. These arguments are based on empirical and not theoretical evidence. Friedman estimates the lags may be as short as 6 months and as long as 2 years.

The Monetary Rule

Combining the preceding arguments, Friedman argues against the use of active monetary policy. He suggests that because the behavior of the money stock is of critical importance for the behavior of real and nominal GNP, and because money operates with a long and variable lag, monetary policy should not attempt to "fine-tune" the economy. The active use of monetary policy might actually destabilize the economy, because an action taken in 1980, say, might affect the economy at any of various future dates, such as in 1981 or 1982. By 1982, the action taken in 1980 might be inappropriate for the stabilization of GNP. Besides, there is no certainty that the policy will take effect in 1982 rather than 1981. For example, suppose that the economy is currently in a recession, and that the money supply is increased rapidly today to increase the growth rate of real GNP. Today's increase in the growth rate of money might affect GNP within 6 months, and achieve its purpose. However, it might work only in 2 years, by which time GNP might well already have increased without the aid of the monetary policy action. And if the expansionary monetary policy affects an economy by then close to full employment, inflation will result.

Thus Friedman reaches the conclusion that although monetary policy has powerful effects on GNP, it should not be actively used lest it destabilize the economy. Accordingly, he argues that the money supply be kept growing at a constant rate, to minimize the potential damage that inappropriate policy can cause.[5]

The Unimportance of Interest Rates

In the IS-LM model of Chapter 4, changes in the money stock affect the economy primarily by affecting interest rates, which in turn affect aggregate demand and thus GNP. Accordingly, the level of interest rates seems to provide a guide to the effects of monetary policy on the economy. When interest rates are low, monetary policy seems to be expansionary, encouraging investment and thus producing a high level of aggregate demand. Similarly, high interest rates seem to indicate contractionary policy. Further, the Fed is able to control interest rates through open market operations. For instance, when it wants to reduce interest rates, it carries out open market purchases, buying bonds and raising their price. Since the Fed can control the level of interest rates, and since interest rates provide a guide to the effects of monetary policy on the economy, it seems perfectly sensible for the Fed to carry out monetary policy by controlling interest rates. When the Fed judges aggregate demand should be expanded, it lowers interest rates, and when it judges aggregate demand should be reduced, it raises interest rates. Through the 1950s and most of the 1960s, the Fed did carry out its monetary policy by attempting to set the level of interest rates.

Friedman and monetarism brought two serious criticisms of the Fed procedure of attempting to set interest rates as the basis for the conduct of monetary policy. The first is that the behavior of nominal interest rates is not a good guide to the direction—whether expansionary or contractionary—of monetary policy. The real interest rate, the nominal interest rate minus the expected rate of inflation, is the rate relevant to determining the

[5] For a concise statement, see Milton Friedman, "The Case for a Monetary Rule," *Newsweek*, Feb. 7, 1972. Reprinted in *There's No Such Thing as a Free Lunch*, op. cit., pp. 77–79. Arguments about active policy making were discussed in Chap. 9.

level of investment, as we saw in Chapter 6. But a high nominal interest rate, together with a high expected rate of inflation, means a low real rate of interest. Thus monetary policy might be quite expansionary in its effects on investment spending even when nominal interest rates are high. Consequently, Friedman and other monetarists argue that the Fed should not concentrate on the behavior of nominal interest rates in the conduct of monetary policy.

The second criticism is that the Fed's attempts to control nominal interest rates might be destabilizing. Suppose the Fed decides that monetary policy should be expansionary and that the interest rate should be lowered. To achieve these goals the Fed buys bonds in the open market, increasing the money supply. The expansionary monetary policy itself tends to raise the inflation rate. It thus tends to raise the nominal interest rate as investors adjust their expectation of inflation in response to the behavior of the actual inflation rate. But then the Fed would have to engage in a further open market purchase in an attempt to keep the nominal interest rate low. And that would lead to further inflation, further increases in nominal interest rates, and further open market purchases. The end result is that an attempt to keep nominal interest rates low may lead to increasing inflation. Therefore, Friedman argues, the Fed should not pay attention to the behavior of nominal interest rates in the conduct of monetary policy,[6] and should, rather, keep the money supply growing at a constant rate.

Each of these arguments on the dangers of conducting monetary policy by reference to nominal interest rates is important. It is indeed correct that real, and not nominal, interest rates provide the appropriate measure of the effects of monetary policy on aggregate demand. It is also true that the Fed could, by attempting to keep nominal interest rates low forever, destabilize the economy. However, once the latter danger has been pointed out, the probability that the Fed will destabilize the economy by operating with reference to interest rates is reduced. The use of interest rates as a guide to the direction of monetary policy does not mean that the Fed has to attempt to keep the interest rate fixed forever at some level. Instead, it may aim each month or quarter for an interest rate target that it regards as appropriate for the current and predicted economic situation.

The monetarist case for concentrating on the behavior of the money stock in the conduct of monetary policy is a strong, but not conclusive, one. The major weakness in the argument is that the demand for real balances may change over time and indeed has done so, as in 1975. A simple numerical example should help make the point. Suppose that real income is constant, and that the nominal interest rate is constant. Suppose also that

[6] The details of the argument are spelled out in Friedman's "The Role of Monetary Policy," *American Economic Review*, March 1968.

the demand for real balances is constant. Then if the money supply grows at, say, the rate of 5 percent, the price level, too, will grow at 5 percent, so that the stock of real balances remains constant. Now suppose, instead, that the demand for real balances is falling by 2 percent per year. Then if the nominal money supply increases at 5 percent per year, the price level has to increase at 7 percent per year to keep the supply of real balances equal to the demand. Thus, shifts in the demand for money affect the rate of inflation, given the growth rate of money. In this example, if the demand for real balances grew at 5 percent per year, 5 percent money growth would not be inflationary at all. These shifts in demand raise the possibility that concentration on the behavior of the nominal money stock may be seriously misleading and inappropriate for the conduct of monetary policy.

The possibility is not purely hypothetical. For instance, in late 1975, the money stock was growing very slowly, at about 2 percent, although nominal interest rates were low and real income was rising. Given rising real income and constant interest rates, the demand for real balances should, according to the demand for money function of Chapter 7, have been increasing. However, real balances were actually falling at the time, despite the rising real income. This suggests that the demand for money was shifting—that people were reducing their demand for real balances at given levels of interest rates and income. The question then was whether the Fed should attempt to increase the growth rate of the money stock, despite the low level of interest rates. Given the low nominal interest rates, real interest rates were assuredly low, since inflationary expectations at the end of 1975 cannot have been for less than 5 percent inflation over the coming 2 years. The low level of interest rates suggested that monetary policy was expansionary, and the low rate of growth of the money stock suggested, on the contrary, that monetary policy was contractionary. In this event, the Fed argued that monetary policy was expansionary despite the low growth rate of the nominal money stock, and that faster growth of the money stock was not needed for the recovery to continue. And the Fed was right. In that case, concentration on the behavior of the money stock as a guide to monetary policy would have been inappropriate and inflationary.

Given the possibility, and the actual experience, of shifts in the demand for money, we see that the behavior of the money stock is not a perfect guide to the conduct of monetary policy. Neither is the behavior of nominal interest rates. However, the behavior of the nominal money stock and the behavior of nominal interest rates both provide some information about the direction in which monetary policy is pushing the economy, imperfect as each measure is. Accordingly, the Fed should pay attention to the behavior of both interest rates and the supply of money in the conduct of its monetary policy.[7]

[7] The argument is worked out in Benjamin M. Friedman, "Targets, Instruments, and Indicators of Monetary Policy," *Journal of Monetary Economics*, October 1975.

The Importance of Fiscal Policy

Friedman has frequently, if tongue in cheek, said that fiscal policy is very important. Although we noted earlier that he argues fiscal policy itself is not important for the behavior of GNP, he does contend that it is of vital importance in setting the size of government and the role of government in the economy. Friedman is an opponent of big government. He has made the interesting argument that government spending increases to match the revenues available. The government will spend the full tax collection—and some more. Accordingly, he is in favor of tax cuts as a way of reducing government spending.

In the shorter run, Friedman has pointed to the size of the government deficit as one of the variables that does affect the growth rate of the money stock. That is in part due to the Fed's concern over the behavior of interest rates. When the deficit is large, interest rates tend to rise unless the Fed monetizes the debt, as we saw in Chapter 14. Large deficits, therefore, tend to be associated with rapid monetary expansion, and for that reason have an expansionary effect on the economy. But since there is no inherent reason why a deficit has to be financed by money creation, the link between deficits and expansion is not an immutable one, but rather a result of the way the Fed behaves. Friedman stands out in arguing that fiscal policy does not have strong effects on the economy except to the extent that it affects the behavior of money. Thus he has remarked:[8]

> To have a significant impact on the economy, a tax increase must somehow affect monetary policy—the quantity of money and its rate of growth. . . .
>
> The level of taxes is important—because it affects how much of our resources we use through the government and how much we use as individuals. It is not important as a sensitive and powerful device to control the short-run course of income and prices.

The Inherent Stability of the Private Sector

The final aspect of monetarism we consider here is the monetarist view that the economy, left to itself, is more stable than when the government manages it with discretionary policy, and that the major cause of economic fluctuations lies in inappropriate government actions. This view is quite fundamental in that it underlies many other monetarist positions, and it may be the litmus test for distinguishing monetarists from other macroeconomists. It is because this point is so fundamental that a major stage in the acceptance of monetarism occurred when Friedman and Schwartz published their *Monetary History of the United States*. In it they provided

[8] Milton Friedman, "Higher Taxes? No," *Newsweek*, Jan. 23, 1967. Reprinted in *There's No Such Thing as A Free Lunch*, op. cit., p. 89.

evidence for the view that the Great Depression was the result of bad monetary policy rather than private sector instability, arising, say, from autonomous shifts in consumption or investment demand.

Summary: We Are All Monetarists

From the viewpoint of the conduct of economic policy, the major monetarist themes are (1) an emphasis on the growth rate of the money stock, (2) arguments against fine tuning and in favor of a monetary rule, and (3) a greater weight that monetarists, as compared, for example, with Keynesians, place on the costs of inflation relative to those of unemployment.

Although we describe these as the major monetarist propositions relating to policy,[9] it is not true that macroeconomists can be neatly divided into two groups, some subscribing to the monetarist religion and the others to a less fundamentalist faith called neo-Keynesianism. Most of the arguments advanced by Friedman and his associates are technical and susceptible to economic analysis and the application of empirical evidence. Many of those propositions are now widely accepted and are no longer particularly associated with monetarism. As Franco Modigliani has remarked, "We are all monetarists now." He adds that we are monetarists in the sense that all (or most) macroeconomists believe in the importance of money.

Much of the analysis of this book would, a few years ago, have been considered monetarist. For example, we have assumed the Phillips curve is vertical, a proposition that was originally associated with monetarism. We have laid considerable stress on the behavior of the money stock and less stress on the behavior of interest rates. We have emphasized that fiscal policy has little long-run effect on inflation. Older readers will doubtless detect other places at which we appear monetarist to their eyes. That is all to the good. If economists did not modify their analyses in the light of new theories and evidence, the field would be barren.

Friedman and his associates have indeed changed macroeconomics. The forceful and persuasive way in which he has emphasized the role of money has changed the views of most economists on the importance of monetary policy. It is always possible that those views would have changed anyway, in the light of the increasing inflation of the last decade. The fact remains, however, that it was Friedman, and not someone else, who hammered away at the importance of money. Fortunately, we are beyond

[9] For a range of views on monetarism, see Karl Brunner, "The Monetarist Revolution in Monetary Theory," *Weltwirtschaftliches Archiv*, 1970; Jerry Stein (ed.), *Monetarism* (Amsterdam, North-Holland, 1976); Franco Modigliani, "The Monetarist Controversy," *American Economic Review*, March 1977; and Thomas Mayer, *The Structure of Monetarism* (New York: Norton, 1978).

the stage at which it is useful to think in terms of monetarists versus Keynesians.

16-2 OVERVIEW

In this section, we sketch the main economic events of the period 1969–1980. The period can be split into subperiods corresponding to the cycles of recession and recovery of economic activity. In Table 16-1 we show these subperiods and note the official dating of peaks and troughs of the cycles. Remember in this context that the practical definition of a recession is negative growth in real output for two successive quarters. Table 16-2 gives annual rates of inflation, growth, and unemployment for the decade.

In Chart 16-1 we show the unemployment rate and the rate of inflation in the consumer price index (CPI).[10] The shaded areas show the peak-to-trough part of each of the business cycles as recorded in Table 16-1. Chart 16-2 shows data on actual and potential output; we have again shaded the recession part of each cycle.

The 1969–1973 Period

The first cycle starts from the low unemployment rate of 3.5 percent but also from an inflation rate of about 5 percent which seemed high at the time. Given the low unemployment rate, inflation was the major economic problem, so restrictive monetary and fiscal policies were adopted, and they produced the 1969–1970 recession. An important aspect of the policy episode was the notion of *gradualism*, the idea of a slow deceleration in economic activity so as to achieve a reduction in inflation without a substantial decline in economic activity. Gradualism notwithstanding, the policies did lead to a recession.

In an attempt to end the recession, a set of expansionary policies

[10] Inflation rates and growth rates, unless otherwise stated, always refer to the rate of change over the same quarter of the previous year.

TABLE 16-1 CYCLES IN ECONOMIC ACTIVITY, 1969–1980

	Peak	Trough	Peak
1969–1973	December 1969	November 1970	November 1973
1973–1980	November 1973	March 1975	January 1980

Source: Digest of Business Conditions.

TABLE 16-2 INFLATION AND GROWTH, 1969–1979 *(annual percentage rates)*

	1969	1970	1971	1972	1973	1974	1975	1976	1977	1978	1979
Inflation (CPI)	5.4	5.9	4.2	3.3	6.2	11.0	9.1	5.8	6.5	7.7	11.3
Growth of output	2.6	−.3	3.0	5.7	5.5	−1.4	−1.3	5.9	5.3	4.4	2.3
Unemployment	3.5	5.0	6.0	5.6	4.8	5.6	8.5	7.7	7.0	6.0	5.8

Source: Citibank Economic Database.

known as the New Economic Policy, or NEP, was adopted. The policy package included price controls to cope with the ongoing high inflation and also a vigorous expansion in demand. As Chart 16-1 shows, inflation did indeed decelerate substantially, partially as a consequence of the preceding recession and partially because of controls. The GNP gap shown in Chart 16-2 reveals that the economic slack that had developed in the recession was altogether eliminated by early 1973. Indeed, the economy had achieved overemployment.

The period raises three major questions. The first is why gradualism failed. The second concerns the effectiveness of price controls. The third

CHART 16-1 UNEMPLOYMENT AND INFLATION, 1969–1979. *(Source: Citibank Economic Database)*

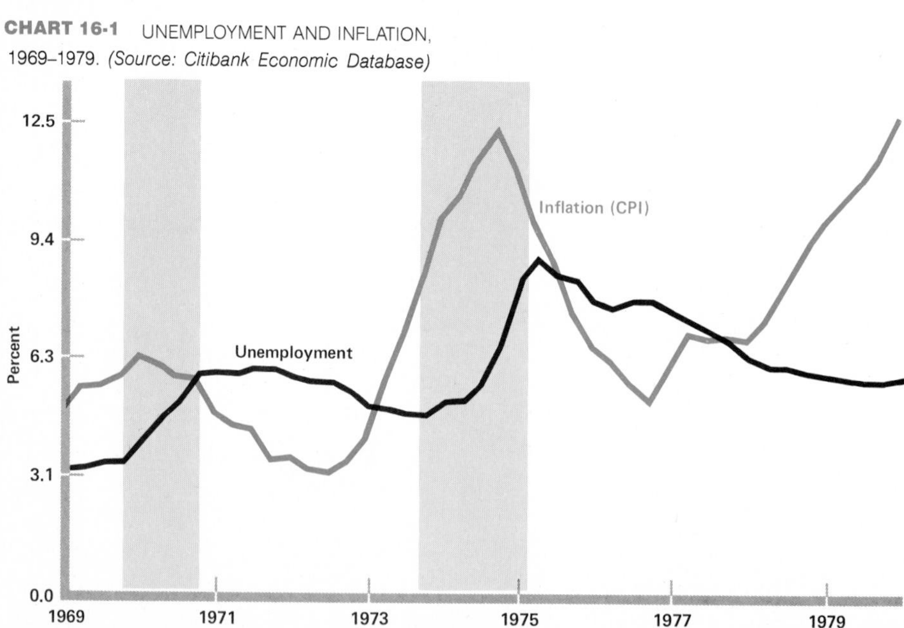

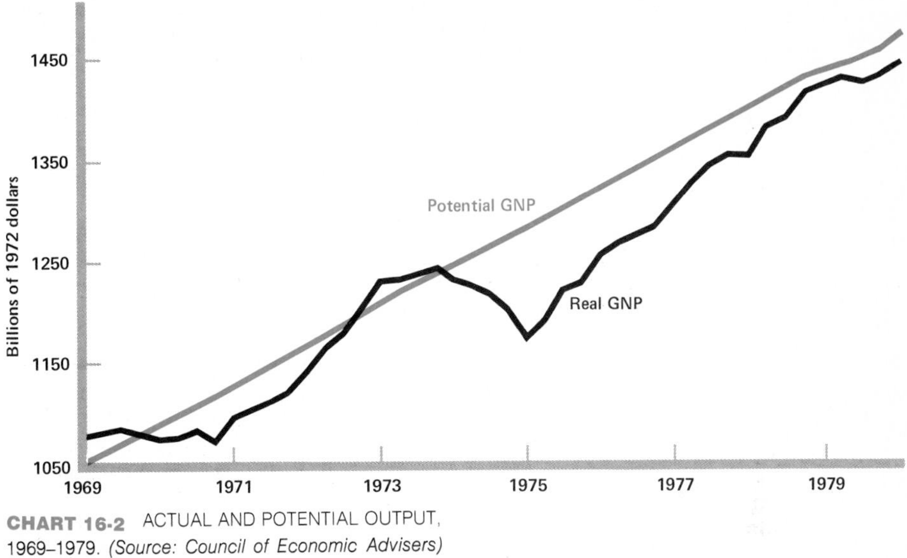

CHART 16-2 ACTUAL AND POTENTIAL OUTPUT, 1969–1979. *(Source: Council of Economic Advisers)*

question is why monetary and fiscal policies in the 1971–1973 recovery period were overexpansionary. The last point is particularly important since it accounts, in part, for the inflation explosion in 1973–1974. The poor policy performance has led as measured a critic as Phillip Cagan to comment that "the failure of policy in 1972 and early 1973 to restrain monetary growth was a monumental blunder."[11]

The 1973–1980 Period

The second cycle corresponds to the period from late 1973 to January 1980. By late 1973 the progressive softening of price and wage controls, together with expansionary policies, had brought inflation up to 6 percent. Once again, inflation became a chief concern of policy. At the same time, the oil price shock and reductions in food supplies exerted strong inflationary pressure along with a reduction in real aggregate demand. Throughout 1974, the economy moved into a decline, as shown by GNP growth in Table 16-2, although unemployment increased only slowly. There was a quite determined effort to choke off inflationary pressures by tight monetary and fiscal policies. By late 1974 and early 1975, the economy had moved into a

[11] Phillip Cagan, "Controls and Monetary Policy," in Cagan et al., *A New Look At Inflation*, (Washington, D.C.: American Enterprise Institute, 1973), p. 27.

recession that proved to be the deepest in the postwar period. Unemployment reached almost 9 percent, and at the depth of the recession in the first quarter of 1975, the GNP gap was 9 percent.

The recession called for expansionary policies. The administration was concerned, however, that too rapid a recovery would be reflected in continuing high inflation. The choice, therefore, was for a moderate recovery path. A tax cut was passed in early 1975. Monetary policy remained relatively tight, but an unpredicted increase in velocity or decline in money demand offset the monetary tightness and furthered the expansion.

The upswing of economic activity starting in the second quarter of 1975 lasted over 4 years. Growth remained high, though uneven, throughout, and unemployment fell progressively to below 6 percent. By the end of 1978, the GNP gap amounted to only 2 percent and in the view of many, full employment had been attained. The big policy problem that had developed by then was persistent high inflation.

This period raises a large number of interesting issues. The first is the idea of a supply shock in the form of material and oil price increases in 1973–1974 that raised inflation and led to a contraction of demand. The second issue concerns an assessment of stabilization policies in the recovery. The third problem is that of inflation and the question of why recessions seem to have become so much less effective in reducing inflationary pressure.

16-3 GRADUALISM, 1969–1971

The major economic problem confronting the new Nixon administration in 1969 was inflation. The low unemployment rate of 3.5 percent allowed policy to shift entirely to a fight against inflation. It was decided that the fight should be a slow one. In his review of the period, Cagan notes:[12]

> The concept of a "tradeoff" between inflation and unemployment had been widely discussed and was very much in the minds of policymakers. There was general agreement that any success in slowing inflation would produce a higher rate of unemployment. The unemployment would reflect a gap between potential and actual output, and this pressure of excess capacity in commodity and labor markets would bring down the rate of inflation. The policymakers thus had a choice: Larger excess capacity would bring inflation under control faster, but would also require a higher peak level of unemployment. The challenge to policy was to follow a thin line, bringing about reasonable if not spectacular reductions in inflation at the cost of moderate unemployment in the short run.

[12] Phillip Cagan, "Monetary Policy," in Cagan et al., *Economic Policy and Inflation in the Sixties* (Washington, D.C.: American Enterprise Institute, 1972), p. 104.

The plan was thus to reduce the inflation rate gradually in order to avoid excessive increases in the unemployment rate. This is precisely the type of choice that was discussed at the end of Chapter 15.

Policy Actions

Both monetary and fiscal policies became sharply contractionary in 1969 and 1970. In Chart 16-3 we show the growth rate of nominal money (M1). Nominal M1 had grown at about 7 percent in 1968. Throughout 1969, M1 growth declined, reaching 4 percent in the last quarter and falling to near 3 percent in the first quarter of 1970. This amounted to a very sharp reduction in nominal money growth. Indeed, nominal money growth in 1969–1970 fell short of inflation, so that the real money stock was actually falling.

The deceleration in monetary growth was clearly excessive, given the administration's goal of avoiding large-scale unemployment. In August 1969, Friedman noted:[13]

> The Federal Reserve System has done it again. Once more it is overreacting as it has so often done in the past. . . . Some retardation in growth and some increase in unemployment is an inevitable, if unwelcome by-product of stopping inflation. But there is no need—and every reason to avoid—a retardation of the severity that will be produced by a continuation of the Fed's present monetary overkill.

As Chart 16-3 shows, the deceleration of monetary growth stopped early in 1970 as the unemployment rate began rising. From 1970, money growth rose gradually but continually, increasing from only 3 percent in the first quarter of 1970 to 7 percent by the middle of 1971. By that time, money growth had accordingly returned to its level in the late 1960s.

The tightening of fiscal policies is shown in Chart 16-4. Here we report the full-employment budget surplus, and it is quite apparent that there was a sharp turnaround in the second half of 1968 and in 1969. The full-employment budget moved from a deficit of about \$16 billion in the first half of 1968 to a surplus of around \$17 billion in 1969. The major fiscal measures are shown in the appendix to this chapter. Note that the fiscal tightening came substantially from the 1968 Revenue and Expenditure Control Act, the belated fiscal response to the overexpansion of the 1960s. The act provided for surtaxes on personal and corporate incomes. These surtaxes were extended in 1969–1970. The fiscal tightening reflects also, of course, *fiscal drag*. As real income (full employment) rises over time and

[13] Milton Friedman, *An Economist's Protest* (New York: Horton, 1972), p. 54. In his analysis, reprinted from one of his *Newsweek* columns, Friedman blames the Fed's behavior on its attention to interest rates.

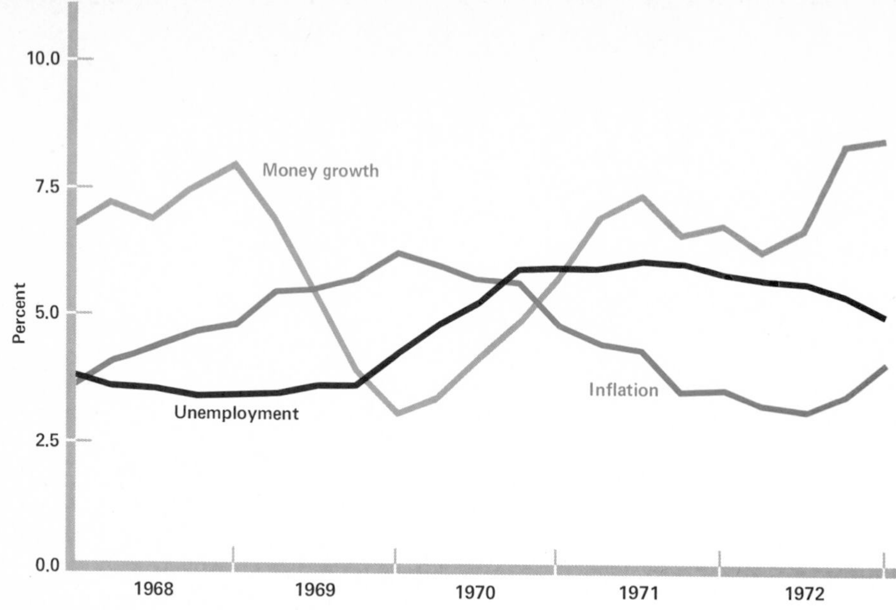

CHART 16-3 THE GROWTH RATE OF MONEY (M1) AND THE RATES OF INFLATION AND UNEMPLOYMENT, 1968–1972. *(Source: Citibank Economic Database)*

CHART 16-4 FULL-EMPLOYMENT BUDGET SURPLUS, HALF-YEARLY AVERAGES AT ANNUAL RATES. *(Source: Citibank Economic Database)*

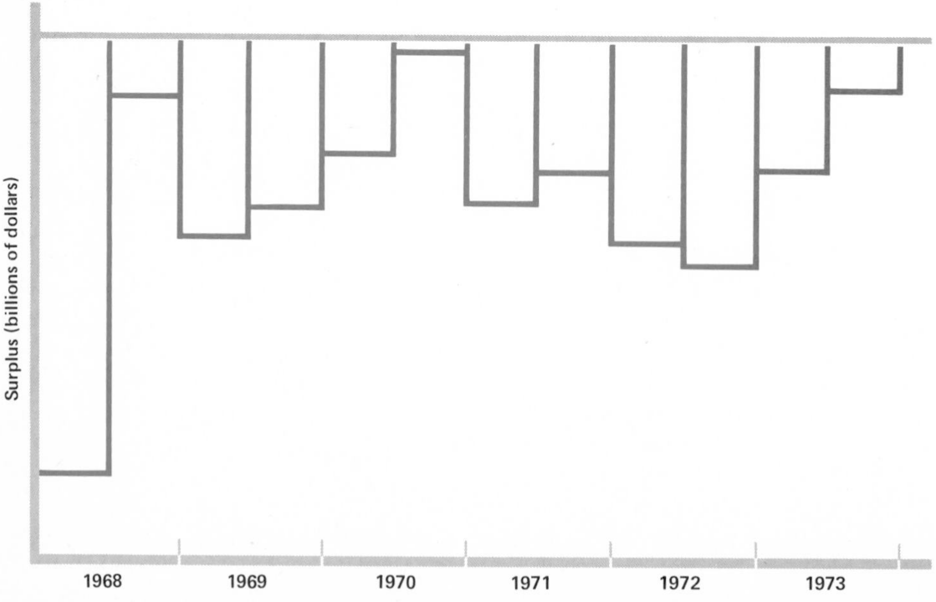

prices increase, taxpayers move into higher tax brackets and thus pay an increasing share of their incomes in taxes.

The fiscal tightening, much like the deceleration in monetary growth, started to be reversed in early 1970. From a surplus of $7 billion for 1969 the full employment budget moved to a deficit of $8 billion by 1971. The monetary and fiscal expansions in 1970–1971 reflect the standard expansionary response of stabilization policies to a recession.

The Results of Policy

The restrictive policy measures of 1969 brought about the recession of 1970. Fiscal tightening reduced aggregate demand. Monetary deceleration raised interest rates, as shown in Chart 16-5, and this rise in interest rates also contributed to the contraction of spending. Output declined and unemployment increased. The GNP gap was near zero in 1969 and rose to nearly 4.5 percent by late 1970. The unemployment rate reached nearly 6 percent.

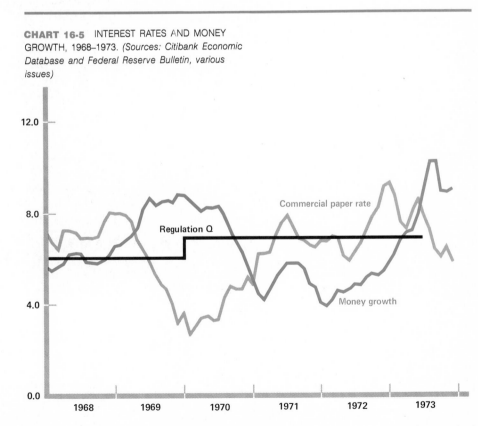

CHART 16-5 INTEREST RATES AND MONEY GROWTH, 1968–1973. *(Sources: Citibank Economic Database and Federal Reserve Bulletin, various issues)*

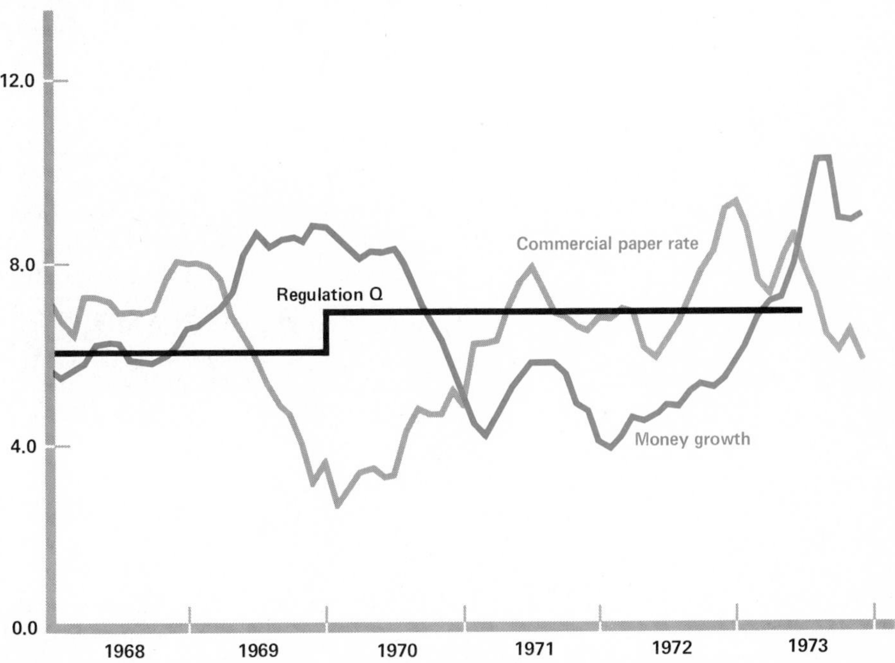

The reversal of monetary and fiscal policies in 1970, as shown in Charts 16-3 and 16-4, ensured that the recession was neither very long nor particularly deep. By early 1971, real GNP was growing again, although only at a moderate pace.

The problem with gradualism was that the policy seemed to have almost no effect on inflation. As Chart 16-3 shows, the recession made practically no dent in the inflation rate; the rate of change of the consumer price index was even higher in 1970 than in 1969. There were some signs that the inflation rate was falling in early 1971, but the rate was still around 4 percent. The costs of unemployment had indeed been borne by the economy—the unemployment rate rose from 3.5 percent to 6 percent—but the benefits in the form of a reduction in the inflation rate had been small. The inflation rate had fallen only from 5 percent in early 1969 to 4 percent in early 1971.

What Went Wrong?

The 1970 recession eliminated the reduction in unemployment achieved during the long period of expansion in the 1960s. It failed, however, to eliminate the inflation that had built up during those years. On the contrary, even during the recession year of 1970, inflation actually increased. While the response of aggregate demand, output, and unemployment entirely conforms to our theories, the failure of inflation to decelerate is clearly puzzling.

We argued in Chapter 11 that prices are based largely on the behavior of costs, and particularly on wages. Table 16-3 presents data on rates of increase of wages (compensation of labor, including benefits), the CPI, and the GNP deflator. The table shows that the rate of increase of compensation barely slowed down during 1969 and 1970. Accordingly, we turn to the behavior of wages to explain the failure of inflation to slow down.

Why did wage inflation fail to fall? There are two main reasons, both connected with expectations of inflation, which we emphasized in Chapter 13. Recall that we argued there that wages would adjust for expected inflation.

TABLE 16-3 INFLATION AND PRODUCTIVITY, 1965–1970 *(average annual percentage rates of increase)*

	1965–1968	1966–1969	1967–1970	1969	1970
Compensation	6.7	6.6	7.2	6.8	7.1
GNP Deflator	3.6	4.2	5.0	5.0	5.4
CPI	3.3	4.1	5.2	5.4	5.9
Productivity	2.8	1.8	1.4	0.2	0.7

Source: Federal Reserve Bank of St. Louis.

Now, first, the rate of inflation had been rising through the 1960s. Expectations of inflation probably adjusted slowly to this rising trend. As expectations adjusted, they were built into the rate of increase of wages. The recession itself would, given expectations, tend to reduce the rate of wage inflation. But the adjustment of expectations was working in the opposite direction, offsetting the dampening effect of the recession on wages.

The rising trend of inflation is not the only reason we can see for rising rates of increase of compensation and for the belief that the inflation rate would not fall. The other reason is that the administration itself, perhaps unintentionally, encouraged the belief that the anti-inflationary policies were less than wholehearted. Frequently, administration economists referred to the economic recovery that was ahead—once the economy had passed through the valley of the small recession that was needed to get rid of inflation. Such statements suggested that the administration would not allow any period of unemployment to be protracted, and that expansionary policies should be expected to follow soon after unemployment began to increase.

A contributory factor in keeping the inflation rate high is the behavior of productivity growth which, Table 16-3 shows, fell during this period. As we saw in Chapter 11, productivity usually falls during recessions. But, as we shall argue in Chapter 17, there was probably also a reduction in the trend rate of productivity increase at this time, which contributed to the inflation. Given the rate of wage increase, costs and therefore prices were rising faster than they would have, had productivity growth been higher.

While there are explanations of the persistence of inflation through the recession, it is nonetheless true that the slowness of the inflation rate to respond to changes in aggregate demand and increases in unemployment during the 1969–1971 period was a surprise to many economists. For instance, Milton Friedman, despite his usual emphasis on the long lags of monetary policy, wrote in May 1969:[14]

> If the Fed continues its present policy of moderate growth in the money supply, we should start seeing results in the near future. By summer or early fall, the rise in income should start slackening. The effect will first be on output. However, by fall at the latest, the pace of price rise should start coming down.

This recession episode illustrates the difficulty of reducing inflation through restrictive aggregate demand policies. Looking back on the inflation experience in the past 10 years, the Council of Economic Advisers has noted:[15]

[14] In *An Economist's Protest* (New York: Horton, 1972), pp. 51–52.

[15] *Economic Report of the President*, 1978, p. 140.

> The inflation would not have persisted during the 1970 recession, if wages and prices were more sensitive to economic slack. On the basis of the experience of that period, and the similar one more recently, estimates of the size and duration of the demand restraint and output loss that it takes to slow inflation have been revised sharply upward.

There are three major lessons from the 1969–1971 experience. The first is the pervasiveness of lags. It took several quarters for each change in policy to have its effects on nominal GNP. Thus the restrictive policies starting in 1969 had their major impact on nominal GNP only in 1970. Similarly, the increase in the growth rate of money in 1970 began to affect the behavior of GNP only in 1971. Indeed, there is also a lag between changes in real GNP and unemployment, as can be seen in Table 16-2.

Second, it can be very difficult to influence inflationary expectations. Despite the repeated statements of the policy makers that inflation was going to be reduced, and that anti-inflationary policies would be followed, there is little evidence that expectations of inflation were much reduced during 1969. And then, when it became apparent in 1970 that the administration was *not* going to allow substantial unemployment to develop to kill inflation, those expectations turned out to be justified.

The third lesson is one that you have no doubt already learned. There is substantial uncertainty about the effects of policy on the economy, and particularly about the timing of those effects. Those uncertainties stem largely from the factors analyzed earlier—lags and expectations formation.

The 1970 Credit Crunch and Crisis Averted

One very interesting episode in the middle of the 1969–1971 period warrants special attention. As a result of the slow monetary growth of late 1969, interest rates rose sharply toward the end of 1969, and stayed high through the first half of 1970. The behavior of the commercial paper rate is shown in Chart 16-5. From 1968 on, the rate on commercial paper repeatedly exceeded the interest rate that commercial banks and other financial intermediaries were allowed to pay on their deposits. The Fed sets maximum rates on time deposits under Regulation Q. Thus, Chart 16-5 shows the Regulation Q ceiling for interest rates on time deposits of $100,000 or more,[16] as well as the rate on 4- to 6-month commercial paper.

Chart 16-5 reminds us of the adverse effect on financial intermediaries of market rates that exceed maximum deposit rates. When market interest rates rise above deposit rates, as happened in 1968–1970, there will be disintermediation. Financial institutions become uncompetitive in raising

[16] Interest rate ceilings are published in the *Federal Reserve Bulletin*. Regulation of interest rates on large deposits (CDs) was suspended in May 1973.

funds through deposits, and consequently they have to contract and cannot expand their loan business. As was noted in Chapter 10 in connection with the 1966 credit crunch, financial disintermediation is particularly harmful for mortgage lending. Accordingly, the construction industry was badly affected by these high market rates, given the interest rate ceilings that channeled funds away from institutions specializing in financing construction loans.

A specific episode we want to discuss is the bankruptcy of the Penn Central Railroad. Penn Central had been borrowing heavily in the commercial paper market. Then, in June 1970, the company declared its bankruptcy. Holders of commercial paper issued by Penn Central thus suffered capital losses. More importantly, though, there was concern that other companies might be drawn into bankruptcy next, since Penn Central was one of the largest corporations in the country. Lenders were therefore reluctant to buy commercial paper, which made it difficult for corporations that had been relying on borrowing in that market to obtain financing.

The situation had all the earmarks of a financial panic, in which a lack of confidence reduces the amount of lending that lenders are willing to undertake, and thereby makes it difficult for borrowers to obtain funds and can perhaps force them into bankruptcy. One of the original functions of a central bank is to act as *lender of last resort.* When a financial panic threatens, the panic can be prevented if the central bank steps in to ensure that funds are available to make loans to firms that are perfectly sound but, because of panic, are having trouble raising funds. In June 1970, the Fed did act as a lender of last resort. It encouraged banks to raise funds by removing the deposit ceiling rate for large-denomination and short-maturity deposits, and to lend the borrowed funds in the commercial paper market. It also made it clear to the banks that they would be able to borrow freely from the Fed in order to lend to firms needing to borrow.

The decisive action prevented a financial panic, and the money markets successfully weathered the Penn Central storm without major distress. Here was an instance of a successful Fed policy action that is little known outside the financial markets.

New Economic Policy and the 1971–1972 Boom

Pressures for a change in economic policy, and particularly *wage and price controls*, had been rising through 1970 and 1971 as the inflation rate remained high while the unemployment rate climbed to 6 percent. Wage and price controls are governmental measures to affect the prices firms charge and the wages labor earns *directly*, rather than through the slow roundabout route of affecting aggregate demand and expectations. The controls can vary from a wage-price freeze, in which no changes in prices or wages are allowed, to weak jawboning, in which the administration uses its powers of persuasion to suggest to firms that they not raise prices or wages.

Wage-price controls had been used in the United States during World War II and the Korean war, and there had been periodic attempts at jawboning through the Kennedy administration. A related type of policy, incomes policy, has been widely used in Western European countries, usually to no great success over periods of more than a few years.[17]

The Nixon administration had emphatically rejected even the notion of jawboning, believing that it both interfered with the operation of free markets and had no effect on inflation. The Democrat-controlled Congress had fewer inhibitions, and in 1970 passed legislation authorizing the President to impose wage and price controls—a power the President did not then think he would ever want to use.

Progress at disinflation through the recession had been very slow. Chart 16-3 reveals some decline in inflation, but the rate remained high, near 5 percent. The forthcoming 1972 election contributed to the pressure to do something, since it would have been less than desirable to have to run on a record of an economic policy which had reduced the inflation rate by 1 percent at the cost of 2.5 percent unemployment. Something had to be done.

On August 15, 1971, the *New Economic Policy* was unveiled. The policy proposed fiscal measures to reduce both government spending and taxes. It also imposed a 90-day wage and price freeze, which subsequently became known as phase I of the wage-price control program. The freeze meant just that: prices and wages were not allowed to be changed for 90 days. The 1972 *Economic Report of the President* makes the case for the freeze.[18]

> The chief virtues of the freeze were its decisiveness, comprehensiveness and administrative simplicity. The President's announcement that practically all wage and price increases were prohibited left no doubt of a drastic change in the upward trend of prices and wages. Equally important, a freeze could be—and was—imposed immediately, precluding anticipatory price and wage increases and providing time to prepare and set in motion more lasting and flexible measures.

Why would a freeze work in reducing inflation? Two points are to be recognized. First, we have noted that inflationary expectations accounted for much of the difficulty in reducing actual inflation. The imposition of wage-price controls in the form of a freeze solves that problem by the stroke of a pen. Second, the idea of a freeze, announced and imposed without prior warning, has the dramatic advantage of forestalling anticipatory price increases. If a long debate preceded the imposition of controls, many firms

[17] See Lloyd Ulman and Robert Flanagan, *Wage Restraint: A Study of Incomes Policy in Western Europe* (Berkeley: University of California Press, 1971).

[18] *Economic Report of the President*, 1972, p. 16.

would find the time to hike their (list) prices prior to the controls and thus frustrate the entire program by accelerating inflation rather than containing it.

The Controls Program

After the wage-price freeze came phase II, a more flexible program for control of wages and prices. Wages could now be increased at 5.5 percent per year, with special allowances for gross inequities and low-paid workers. Prices could be raised to pass along increases in costs. Some small firms and agricultural and imported commodities were exempt from wage-price controls.

Phase II ran from November 1971 to January 1973, when it was, logically enough, replaced by phase III, a yet more flexible set of controls. Phase III ran through June 1973, by which time the inflation rate had reached the vicinity of 10 percent. Another price freeze was imposed then, to be replaced by phase IV in August 1973. The controls ran out in April 1974. Details of the various phases are not vital beyond the facts that agricultural and imported commodities were exempt from price controls, and that phase III was more flexible than phase II.[19]

Fiscal and Monetary Policy

The pattern of fiscal policy in the expansion of 1971–1973 is shown in Chart 16-4. Fiscal policy was expansionary through 1972. The major elements of the fiscal policy package were an investment tax credit, a reduction in personal income taxes, and repeal of excise taxes on automobiles. The reduction in revenues was only partially offset by an increase in Social Security taxes, so that the net effect of the measure was expansionary. The full-employment budget moved from a $2-billion surplus in 1970 to a deficit of $8 billion and $17 billion in 1971 and 1972, respectively. Only in 1973 did fiscal policy turn more restrictive as a consequence of Social Security tax increases and the fiscal drag implied by inflation.

Chart 16-3 reveals also the very expansionary stance of monetary policy. Following the sharp deceleration in money growth in 1969, there was a rapid acceleration. Money growth returned by 1971 to the 7 to 8 percent range and thus ran substantially ahead of the rate of inflation. Accordingly, the real money stock was rising, thereby reinforcing the fiscal stimulus. Through the end of 1972, there was no attempt to use monetary policy to moderate the pace of the boom that was developing. That the boom was taking place was perfectly clear. We shall have to ask why Fed policy was so expansionary through 1972.

[19] See *Economic Report of the President*, 1974, p. 91, for a table listing details of the various phases.

The Behavior of the Economy

The imposition of the wage-price freeze in August 1971 had an immediate effect on the inflation rate. The rate was less than 2 percent for the 3 months of the freeze. The inflation rate was not cut to zero by the freeze because some commodities were excluded. At the end of the freeze, there was a temporary bulge in the inflation rate as some catching up on price increases took place—with the permission of the Price Commission that was administering the price controls. Nonetheless, it is clear from Chart 16-3 that there was a definite reduction in the inflation rate after the imposition of wage and price controls. That reduction lasted through 1972.

As for the behavior of real GNP, we have already commented on the rapid rate of growth of output through the six quarters from 1971/I. Housing investment expanded especially rapidly as interest rates fell, and consumption spending rose fast. The unemployment rate was slow in responding to the growth rate of output, but it did eventually fall sharply toward the end of 1972, moving rapidly from 5.6 percent in October to 5.1 percent in December. It is clear once again that unemployment responds only with a lag to changes in real output. By the second half of 1972, economic slack as measured by the GNP gap had been eliminated. The gap was zero in the fourth quarter of that year.

On the surface then, 1972 was, as President Nixon claimed, "a very good year for the American economy."[20] But the expansionary policy of the period, and the failure of monetary and fiscal policy to restrain the boom as it developed, stored up trouble for the next few years.

Did the Controls Work?

The rate of inflation did fall after the imposition of wage and price controls in 1971. The question we discuss in this section is whether the fall in the inflation rate was due to the imposition of controls, or whether it might have occurred anyway. The reason to believe the inflation rate might have fallen anyway is that in the first half of 1971, it was lower than in 1970. If that improvement had been maintained, the inflation rate might have dropped even without controls to the same level that it attained with them.[21]

Evidence on the effects of controls is difficult to interpret. Given

[20] *Economic Report of the President*, 1973, p. 3.

[21] A study by Edgar L. Feige and Douglas K. Pearce of the Universities of Wisconsin and Houston, respectively, suggests that the controls had no major effect on inflation other than during the freeze. See their article "Inflation and Incomes Policy: An Application of Time Series Models," in Karl Brunner and Allan Meltzer (eds.), *The Economics of Price and Wage Controls* (Amsterdam: North Holland, Carnegie-Rochester Conference Series, 2, 1976).

monetary and fiscal policies, controls could have worked either indirectly, through expectations, or directly, by preventing wage and price increases that would have taken place even after allowing for the effects on expectations. We cannot, however, be sure of the proportions in which the reduction in inflation was due to (1) the effect of controls on expectations; (2) the direct effects of controls in prohibiting wage and price increases that would, after allowing for the lower expectations of inflation, have occurred; and (3) the lagged effects of the high unemployment rate of 1971.

There is evidence, from surveys that directly asked people about their expectations, that inflation expectations were reduced by the imposition of controls.[22] Cagan estimates that about one-third of the reduction in inflation from 1971–1972 was due to expectations. There is also evidence that controls reduced the inflation rate by holding back price rises by more than would normally have occurred given the rate of wage increase.[23] This evidence bears on point 2 above. If controls held back price increases relative to wage increases, then they would have reduced profit margins and this profit reduction appears to have happened. Somewhat less than one-third of the 3 percent reduction in the inflation rate from 1971 to 1972 can be attributed to the reduction of prices relative to wages.

The remaining reduction in the inflation rate—somewhat over 1 percent—can then be attributed to two factors. First, controls might directly have reduced the rate of wage increase, even after taking account of expectations. This factor also relates to point 2 above. Finally, there is point 3—the lagged effects of unemployment on wage inflation. Some estimates indicate that the credit is about evenly divided between these last two sources.[24]

We should note that wage-price controls were introduced in 1971 at a time when there was unemployment and excess capacity in the economy. The controls therefore did not generate excess demands in individual markets by preventing prices from rising to clear the market. This accounts for there being very few shortages during 1972. In contrast, one can think of trying to introduce wage and price controls in an economy at a high level of employment and inflation. In such an economy, the controls would soon lead to shortages and other microeconomic distortions. Any effects that controls would have on expectations in those circumstances would impose a heavier cost in terms of shortages than did controls in 1972.

[22] Phillip Cagan "Controls and Monetary Policy," in Cagan et al., *A New Look at Inflation* (Washington, D.C.: American Enterprise Institute, 1973).

[23] Robert J. Gordon, "Wage-Price Controls and the Shifting Phillips Curve," *Brookings Papers on Economic Activity*, 1972:2 (Washington, D.C.: The Brookings Institution, 1972).

[24] See Robert Gordon's article, cited in footnote 23.

Why Did the Fed Do It?

The failure of the Fed to slow down the growth rate of money and run a tighter monetary policy toward the end of 1972 is difficult to explain fully. Two factors provide part of the explanation. First, as can be seen from Chart 16-5, interest rates were rising over the course of the year. Although the Fed had formally decided in early 1972 to pay more attention to the growth rate of money and less to interest rates than it had previously, it was still concerned about rising interest rates. It may have interpreted increases in interest rates as contractionary rather than as the reflection of the effects of increasing real output on money demand.[25] Second, the unemployment rate was slow in responding to the expansion of real output that began in 1971. It was only toward the end of 1972 that the unemployment rate began its fall from the 6 percent level down to 5 percent. The Fed may have waited to see more definite results of its policies on unemployment before it regarded the recovery from the earlier recession as truly underway.

Nonetheless, the monetary growth data of Chart 16-3 reflect inappropriate Fed policy. In particular, the rapid growth in the second part of 1972 was inappropriate for the stabilization of the economy.[26]

16-4 SLOWDOWN, RECESSION, AND INFLATION, 1973–1975

The 1973–1975 period is one of the most interesting from the viewpoint of economics of the post-World War II period—though to be sure, "May you live in interesting times" is a curse and not a benediction. The course of increasing inflation and a deepening recession is shown in Chart 16-6. Here we show the inflation rate of the consumer price index and the GNP gap for each quarter in the 1973–1976 period.

The vigorous expansion that followed the 1970 recession came to an end at the beginning of 1973. Real growth had been high enough not only to eliminate the GNP gap caused by the recession but, in fact, to move the economy beyond potential output. The economy spent the last three quarters of 1973 in a *growth recession* with output still growing, but growing at a rate below potential. The rapid deceleration of economic activity in the growth recession was not recognized at the time because GNP estimates were in error and would show up only later in revised GNP data.

[25] A lively analysis of policy in 1973 is presented in Franco Modigliani, "A Critique of Past and Prospective Economic Policies," *American Economic Review*, September 1973. See also Otto Eckstein, *The Great Recession* (Amsterdam: North-Holland, 1978) for an econometric model evaluation of the events and policies.

[26] One reason for the Fed's attention to the behavior of interest rates in 1972 was its fear that Congress was about to impose controls on interest rates. To avoid such controls, the Fed may have wanted to act so as to prevent interest rates rising to levels that would incur congressional wrath and action.

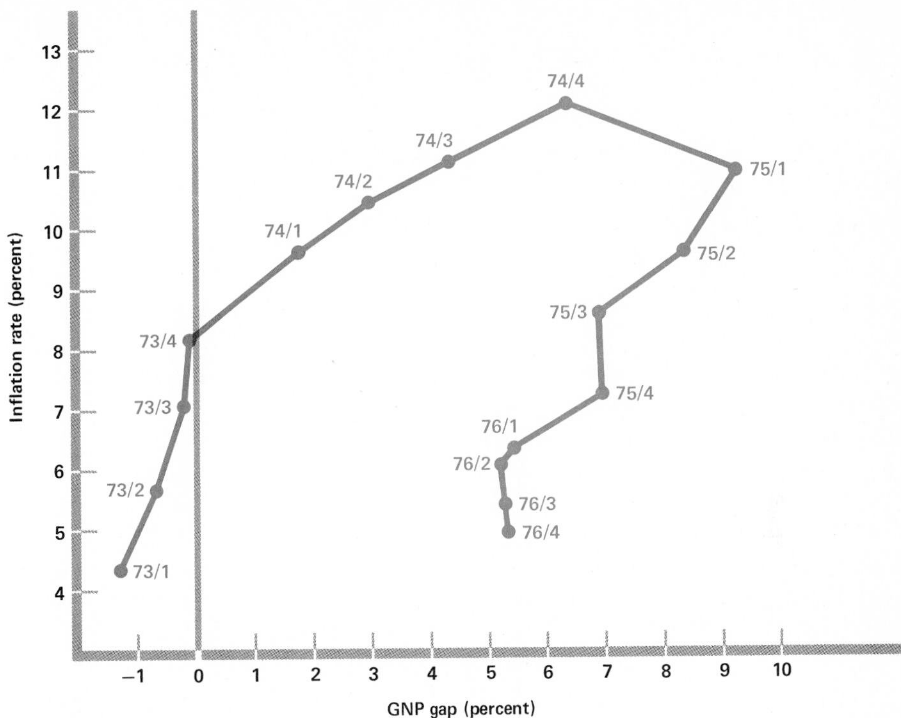

CHART 16-6 INFLATION AND THE GNP GAP, 1973–1976. *(Source: Economic Report of the President)*

At the end of 1973, the economy, already buffeted by food price increases and heading toward a recession, was struck by the Arab oil embargo and oil price increase. Real GNP growth became sharply negative in the first two quarters of 1974 and moderated a little in the third quarter. Growth collapsed in the last quarter of 1974 and the first quarter of 1975, with spectacular negative growth rates for those quarters of minus 7.5 percent and minus 9.2 percent, respectively. The recovery began in the second quarter of 1975. The protracted period of slow and negative growth and the sharpness of the recession at the end of 1974 were unprecedented in the post-World War II period.

Low and negative growth rates of real GNP in 1974 and the first quarter of 1975 meant a growing GNP gap. In Chart 16-6 we show how economic slack increased sharply from full employment at the end of 1973 to a GNP gap of nearly 9 percent early in 1975. The increasing GNP gap was, of course, also reflected in rising unemployment—an increase from 4.8 percent at the end of 1973 to near 9 percent in mid-1975, as can be seen in Chart 16-1.

The purpose of this section is to describe the events of the 1973–1975 period in somewhat more detail, paying particular attention to the effects of policy, and exogenous shocks such as the food, oil, and materials price increases on the economy. We shall also be asking whether the recession had to be as bad as it was.

The Supply Shock and the Inflation Explosion

The 1973–1975 recession was accompanied by a veritable explosion of inflation. Inflation more than doubled from the level of about 5 percent in the first years of the seventies to near 12 percent toward the end of 1974. We now analyze the sources of that inflation explosion and its role in bringing about and deepening the recession.

There were three main sources of the sharp increase in inflation. All three arose on the supply side. The first was the impact of high employment on labor compensation and thereby on costs and prices. The second factor was the substantial increase in food prices due to poor harvests in Russia and other countries. The third source of sharply rising prices was the oil and materials price increase. We shall first look at some facts and then formalize our discussion, using the aggregate demand and supply framework.

Table 16-4 shows inflation rates for various price indexes and for labor compensation. For labor compensation, we note a substantial increase in 1973 that must be explained by the fact that full employment had been reached. Subsequent increases in 1974 and 1975 reflect both labor's attempts, through higher wage increases, to keep up with sharply rising consumer prices, and the dampening effect of economic slack. Note that compensation was increasing at a lower rate than inflation, and that, accordingly, real wages were declining in 1974.

The most important source of increased inflation was the sharp rise in materials prices. Materials prices inflation, as shown in Table 16-4, was as high as 36 percent in 1973, and that increase in costs must of course show

TABLE 16-4 INFLATION RATES FOR PRICE AND COST INDICES: 1972–1975

	1972	1973	1974	1975
Compensation	6.3	8.2	9.1	10.0
Crude materials prices	10.9	36.4	12.7	0
Food stuffs and feed	11.6	41.1	5.2	1.3
Fuel	6.9	10.6	33.3	23.7
Other	10.1	32.5	27.2	−8.3
Producer prices	1.8	9.1	15.3	10.2
Consumer prices	3.3	6.2	11.0	9.1

Source: Citibank Economic Database.

up in producer and consumer prices, as was indeed the case in 1974 and 1975.

Consider now in more detail the inflationary burst in materials prices shown in Table 16-4. Food and feed stuffs showed a record inflation in 1973 of more than 40 percent. This reflected largely poor harvests in the United States and abroad, and was an isolated shock that unfortunately came altogether at the wrong time. The second event was inflation of fuel prices brought about through the OPEC embargo and price increase. This showed up particularly in 1974 and 1975 with inflation rates for fuels of 33 and 24 percent. The last item is the inflation rate of "other" materials prices that was around 30 percent in both 1973 and 1974, but was actually negative in 1975. This inflation reflected the worldwide economic expansion of the early 1970s and the resulting shortages. It reflected also the dollar depreciation to which we return, and a substantial speculative bubble caused by producers' fears that material shortages, as in the case of oil, might bring about production disruption.

The bubble in materials prices was both extreme and short-lived. From the 36 percent inflation for crude materials in 1973, we were down to zero in 1975 as the recession, taking hold, reduced industrial demand for materials, and as good harvests eliminated inflation of agricultural prices.

Inflation of materials prices raises costs to producers of finished goods and therefore must show up in their prices. Consequently, the 1973–1974 materials price explosion is reflected in the 1973–1975 producer prices. From only 2 percent inflation in 1972, producer price inflation increased to 15 percent in 1974. The producer price inflation was matched, though on a reduced scale, in a sharply increased rate of inflation for consumer prices.

In summary, a combination of materials price shocks, from oil and food, sharply increased costs and brought about a general acceleration of price inflation relative to that of wages. We turn next to a macroeconomic analysis of the effect of materials price increases on the price level and employment, using the analytical framework developed in Chapter 11.

*The Material Price Supply Shock: An Analytical Treatment

We show now how the aggregate demand and supply framework can be used to analyze the macroeconomic impact of a materials price increase, such as that of 1973–1974. In Figure 16-1 we draw the aggregate demand schedule, Y^d. The schedule is drawn for a given nominal money stock and a given fiscal policy. We also draw the initial aggregate supply schedule Y^s and our initial equilibrium—say mid-1973—at point E. The price level is P_0, and we should think of P as the consumer or producer price index for finished goods.

Given the wage rate, a materials price increase means that firms experience an increase in costs. To produce the same level of output firms

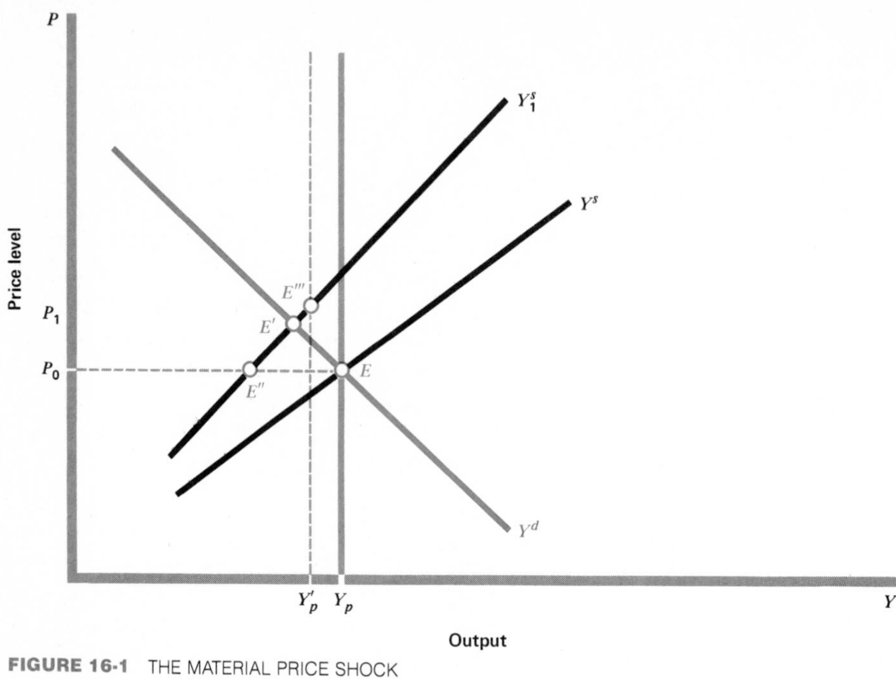

FIGURE 16-1 THE MATERIAL PRICE SHOCK

would have to be compensated by higher prices. Thus the aggregate supply schedule shifts upward to Y_1^s. As shown in Chapter 11, it also becomes steeper. For a given aggregate demand schedule, the materials price increase thus leads to a rise in equilibrium prices and a decline in output. The economy will move to point E', corresponding to the situation in 1974–1975.

We show also in Figure 16-1 a reduction in the level of potential output to Y_p'. The increase in oil prices reduced the level of potential output in the United States, since firms would not find it profitable to supply the same level of output as before at full employment of labor, given the increase in costs. However, although the level of *potential output* falls, the full-employment level of *employment* does not change, since the oil price increase does not reduce the labor force.

In the move from E to E', there is a rise in prices and a decline in output. We show output at E' below its new potential level, so that there is unemployment at that point. We discuss policy responses to the shock later, but note possibilities here. One policy is to attempt to keep the price level constant at the original level, P_0. This would require a contractionary aggregate demand policy, a policy that *offsets* the inflationary impact of the supply shock, by shifting the aggregate demand curve to intersect Y_1^s at E''. Such a policy obviously produces a large increase in unemployment and a fall in output. Over time, aggregate demand could then be expanded as the aggregate supply curve shifts down under the impact of unemployment, so as to maintain the price level at P_0.

The second possibility is to *accommodate* the increase in prices by expanding aggregate demand in an attempt to maintain full employment. The policy here would be to shift the aggregate demand curve so as to intersect the new aggregate supply curve Y_1^s at E'''. Of course, this results in a price level even higher than that at E'.

It is important to recognize that there is no easy alternative in the face of a supply shock. The reduction in potential output will lead to a higher price level in any event, given existing monetary and fiscal policies. Policies to offset this inflation will produce further unemployment. Policies to fight the unemployment at E' will produce more inflation.

There is an important qualification that we have to introduce at this point. We cannot treat *all* increases in materials, food, and energy prices as if they were exogenous and independent of the inflation process we are analyzing. After all, these prices too are affected by aggregate demand. But the cartel-induced increase in fuel prices, and the rise in agricultural prices caused by poor harvests, were exogenous, providing a substantial supply shock to the economy.

Economic Policy Responses: 1973–1975

We have shown above how the food, fuel, and materials price increases raise costs. We turn now to the policy responses to that shock and, in particular, consider the extent to which policies accommodated or suppressed the price shock.

Wage-price controls were in effect, with softening, until early 1974. The controls became progressively less effective as the economy approached full employment and exceptions had to be allowed to avoid shortages. At the same time, exemption of food and imports from controls meant that some of the major price shocks could be directly passed through into consumer prices. In this context, we have to mention, too, the depreciation of the dollar in the early 1970s. The depreciation meant that dollar prices of imports increased sharply.[27]

Table 16-5 shows the monetary and fiscal response to growing inflation and rising economic slack. The table shows, on a half-yearly basis, nominal money growth and the full-employment budget surplus (as a percent of GNP). The growing slack notwithstanding, the fight against inflation

[27] For a detailed discussion of the effects of depreciation of the exchange rate on domestic prices, see Chaps. 18 and 19.

TABLE 16-5 MACROECONOMIC VARIABLES: 1973–1976

	1973		1974		1975		1976
	I	II	I	II	I	II	I
M1 growth	8.3	6.7	5.8	5.2	3.9	4.8	5.3
Inflation (CPI)	4.8	7.5	10.2	11.8	10.4	8.0	6.2
Growth of output	6.8	4.1	−.3	−2.5	−3.8	1.3	7.0
Unemployment	4.9	4.8	5.1	6.1	8.5	8.4	7.6
Full-employment surplus/GNP	−.8	−.3	−.2	−.2	−2.1	−2.0	−1.5

Note: Numbers are for half-years to reduce inessential detail.
Source: Citibank Economic Data base.

remained the priority until the end of 1974. Monetary growth sharply declined in 1973–1974 from 8 percent to near 5 percent. Monetary policy thus quite certainly did not accommodate the supply shock. On the contrary, it was deliberately contractionary.

Fiscal policy showed a tightening in the first half of 1973 as the full-employment budget deficit fell by half a percentage point, measured as a fraction of GNP. The tightening largely reflected the effect of price increases on full-employment income taxes. Until late 1974, fiscal policy remained inactive. Indeed, discussion of fiscal policy in the fall of 1974 considered further tightening to fight inflation rather than recession.

The price shock in combination with the restrictive aggregate demand policy sent the economy into a deep recession. In the fourth quarter of 1974 and the first quarter of 1975, real GNP declined sharply. In these two quarters, unemployment rates for the total labor force grew from 5.6 percent to 8.2 percent. The sharp rise in unemployment brought about a dramatic, though of course belated, reversal of priorities. Fiscal policy became sharply expansionary through the tax cut of early 1975, and monetary policy allowed interest rates to decline substantially.

Fiscal policy measures were enacted very expeditiously. In February 1975, the administration proposed an income tax rebate for households, an increased investment tax credit, and public service employment programs. By March, Congress had already enacted the measure, having substantially increased the size of the fiscal package. The policies show up in Table 16-5 as an increase in the full-employment budget deficit of almost two percentage points, measured as a fraction of GNP. Fiscal policy thus was very strongly supportive of an expansion, and remained so for the rest of 1975.

Fiscal policy operated, of course, not only through the discretionary measures such as rebates or increased investment tax credits, but also through built-in stabilizers. The extent to which built-in stabilizers came into action can be assessed from a comparison of the changes in actual and full-employment federal budgets.

Table 16-6 shows that the actual budget deficit increased from $10 billion to $70 billion. The full-employment deficit, by contrast, increased by only about $30 billion. The difference of $30 billion is a reflection of the operation of built-in stabilizers. These are reduced taxes as income declines, unemployment benefits, and other transfer payments. In the recovery to 1976, we see the same point in the opposite direction. Here the full-employment deficit narrowed by $4 billion, but the recovery reduced the actual deficit by as much as $17 billion.

What evaluation can we place on economic policy in the 1973–1975 period? It is quite apparent that once the depth of the recession was recognized, economic policy—both monetary and fiscal—moved very strongly to support an expansion and to avoid the threat of depression on the scale of the 1930s. What is more debatable is whether economic policy—inadvertently or deliberately—made the recession worse than it need have been. We now take up this issue.

The growth recession at the end of 1973 was exacerbated by the oil price increase, which led quickly to a deepening and worsening of the recession. Given the large cost in terms of output forgone and the high levels of unemployment that resulted, the cost in inflation of accommodating the oil price increase would, in our judgment, have been worth bearing. In particular, there is little justification for the reduction of monetary growth in mid–1974. However, as our earlier discussion showed, there is no policy that could have been used that would not have implied a reduction in real GNP to reflect the lower real standard of living that Americans could achieve with the new higher price of oil.

It is much easier to decide what policy should have been than to decide what it will be. Unfortunate as the economic experience of the 1973–1975 period was, policy makers did not make colossal blunders. They were making policy in a difficult environment, with less than perfect knowledge.

TABLE 16-6 THE FULL-EMPLOYMENT AND ACTUAL FEDERAL BUDGETS: 1974–1976 *(in $ billions)*

	1974	1975	1976
Full-employment surplus	9.3	18.2	13.4
Actual surplus	−10.7	−70.6	−53.6

Source: Economic Report of the President, 1980.

In the first place, no one knew how long the oil cartel would last. Second, there was not then a good body of economic theory to help them analyze the way to deal with supply shocks. Economists had concentrated largely on demand shocks for the past 30 years.

Third, as we have noted several times, the data the policy makers were receiving were quite poor. The money stock data are revised frequently, and the growth rates of money change with each revision. We have also mentioned that the real GNP data available in 1973 considerably overestimated the growth of real GNP in the middle two quarters of the year. Thus the Fed was not alerted as early as it might have been to the slowdown in GNP growth that was then taking place.

Indeed, data problems were so bad that, in December 1974, Geoffrey H. Moore, a respected business-cycle expert and former Commissioner of Labor Statistics, said,[28] "I can't help thinking how ironic it would be if by overdeflating the current dollar figures in a well-intentioned effort to get rid of the effects of inflation, we should have talked ourselves into a recession." Moore was saying that the real GNP data, even then, were subject to so much uncertainty that it was doubtful whether the economy was in a recession at all.

Making policy under such circumstances is difficult. Since there is no point in not using hindsight when it is available, we can now argue that policy was excessively expansionary in 1972, and that it should have accommodated the oil price increase in 1974. The first argument is probably widely accepted, while the second is controversial and reflects our judgment of the costs of inflation and unemployment. It is in any event clear that the economy would have shown some fluctuations in output and prices under the best of policies, given the disturbances that occurred in the 1973–1975 period.

16-5 THE RECOVERY, 1975–1979

Chart 16-7 shows the essentials of the recovery from the 1973–1975 recession. The GNP gap declined from a 1975 average of 8.3 percent to a level of only 2 percent in 1979.[29] Inflation initially decelerated in 1976, but then accelerated again in 1977 and 1978 and reached new post-World War II peaks in 1980. We turn now to a closer analysis of the real expansion and the path of inflation.

[28] *New York Times*, Dec. 8, 1974, Business & Finance Section.

[29] Indeed, as will be discussed in Chap. 17, some estimates of potential GNP imply that the gap had been eliminated by early 1979.

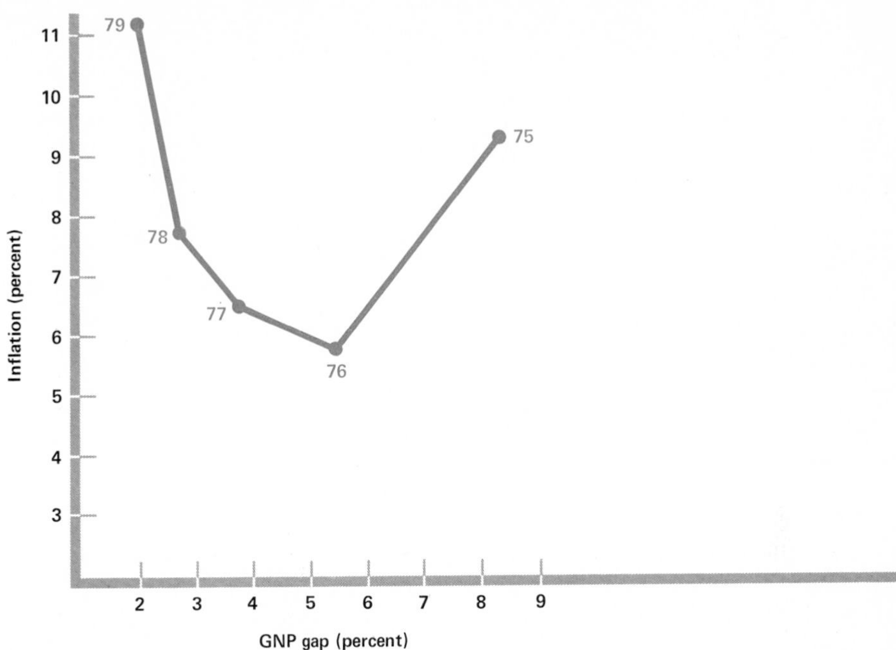

CHART 16-7 THE 1975–1979 RECOVERY. *(Source: Economic Report of the President)*

The Expansion

We have already considered the monetary and fiscal policies pursued in 1975 and 1976. These policies proved effective in raising aggregate demand and expanding output. As can be seen in Table 16-2, real growth in 1976 was nearly 6 percent, near 5 percent in 1977, and still 4 percent in 1978. There was, accordingly, a long and strong expansion sufficient to return the economy to near full employment as well as to generate over 10 million jobs from 1975 to 1979 (for a labor force of 103 million people by 1979).

Table 16-7 summarizes the behavior of policy variables from 1975 to 1979. We see that fiscal policy was essentially passive, with the full-employment surplus changing very little after an increase from 1974 to 1975. Interest rates remained low in 1975 and 1976, and then began a steady and accelerating climb through 1978 and into 1979. The growth rate of M1 was low in 1975 and 1976 and then increased. The low growth rates of M1 in the early part of the period caused some concern that monetary growth would not be sufficient to support the recovery that was desired. But, in the event, velocity increased without any rise in interest rates,

TABLE 16-7 MACROECONOMIC VARIABLES, 1975–1979

	1975	1976	1977	1978	1979
Full employment surplus (% of GNP)	−2.0	−1.6	−1.8	−1.1	−.3
Growth rate of M1	4.8	6.5	8.1	8.2	7.7
Growth rate of M2	12.8	14.1	10.9	8.2	8.8
Treasury bill rate (%)	5.8	5.0	5.3	7.2	10.0
Inflation (%)	9.2	5.7	6.5	7.7	11.3
Unemployment	8.5	7.7	7.0	6.0	5.8

Source: Economic Report of the President and Citibank Economic Database.

indicating a shift in the demand function for money that we have discussed in Chapter 7. The growth rates of the money aggregates in the first part of the period were at or below their target ranges, but from the end of 1976 through the end of 1978, the growth rate of M_1 was consistently above the target range set by the Fed.

It is clear from Table 16-7 that fiscal policy did not provide any further impetus for continued recovery after 1975, and that monetary policy was really expansionary only in 1977, if at all. The reason for ambiguity about the direction of monetary policy is that interest rates and the growth rate of money tell a different story—indeed, the data suggest that the growth rate of money responded in part to the pressure of rising interest rates in 1977 and 1978, in an attempt to keep the momentum of the recovery alive. We should, after all, recall that although the recovery proceeded fast, it started from the highest unemployment rate of the postwar period, and that unemployment came in sight of the 5.5 percent estimated natural rate level only in 1978. A slower growth rate of money in 1977 and 1978 would have resulted in less inflation, but it would also have slowed real growth. As often happens, the Fed had to weigh the tradeoff between inflation and unemployment in setting policy.

One dramatic episode in monetary policy took place in late 1978. The United States balance of payments had been in deficit throughout the year, and the dollar had been depreciating or falling in value relative to foreign currencies. As we shall see in Chapters 18 and 19, the belief that a currency is about to depreciate leads to actual depreciation, as happened in October 1978, when the dollar began to fall rapidly against other currencies. Foreigners believed that monetary policy in the United States was too expansionary and would lead to continued dollar depreciation. Eventually, the Fed put together a policy package announcing that it would restrict monetary growth and would, if necessary, borrow abroad in order to buy up the dollars that foreign speculators were selling. The November package was successful in stopping the continuing depreciation of the dollar, which then began to appreciate against major foreign currencies, particularly the Japanese yen.[30]

If policy did not provide much expansionary impulse to the economy during 1976–1978, what did? An important factor in the fast recovery was the behavior of inventories. Chart 16-8 shows output and final sales for the business sector. In 1973 and 1974, output mostly exceeded final sales and, in consequence, inventories were building up. We note that production was declining during the period but sales were falling even more rapidly. By the end of 1974, the process was dramatically reversed with a substantial cut in production and an output level that remained below sales for three quarters. The lagged adjustment of production reveals why unemployment rose sharply only at the end of 1974, and the gradual, but protracted, buildup of inventories in 1973 and 1974 explains why the cut in production and employment was so substantial when it came. Once inventories had

[30] If this entire episode appears mysterious at this stage, you should be able to understand it better after reading Chaps. 18 and 19.

CHART 16-8 INVENTORIES AND SALES, 1973–1976.
(Source: Citibank Economic Database)

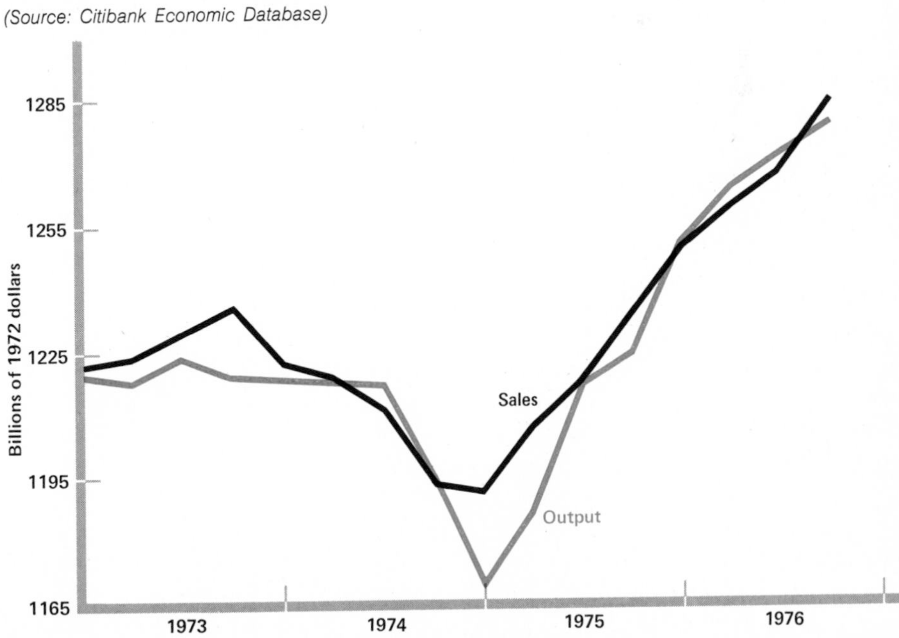

been run down to normal levels, production and employment recovered quite rapidly. The inventory behavior helps explain the timing of the recession and the recovery.

In addition, the recovery was supported by a significant increase in the rate of investment, particularly, in 1975 and 1976, of residential investment. Business investment grew at 7 percent per year in real terms from 1975 to 1979. The recovery was thus largely generated by the private sector, given monetary and fiscal policies that did not restrain that impetus.

Inflation in the Recovery

Chart 16-7 showed that the recovery was accompanied initially by a decline in the inflation rate. But by early 1979, the economy was back to double-digit inflation, even though output was not above the potential level. As with the 1971 recovery, we are left with the question of why the recession failed to reduce the inflation rate more, and we have also to ask why inflation accelerated sharply in 1979.

Before we launch into the discussion, though, we should emphasize that the high unemployment of 1975 did lead to a substantial reduction in the inflation rate. The less than 6 percent inflation of 1976 contrasts favorably with the 11 percent of 1974 and the more than 9 percent of 1975. But from 1976 the inflation rate increased each year.

Table 16-8 presents data on labor compensation and inflation for the years 1975 to 1979. We see that the rate of increase of labor compensation did rise over the period, leading through the markup pricing discussed in Chapter 11 to increasing inflation. The rate of growth of productivity slowed over the period, also contributing to an increase in the inflation rate. The decline in the rate of increase of productivity will be discussed in Chapter 17. Before we turn to the key question of the reasons for the behavior of the rate of increase of compensation, we look at two extra inflationary factors.

The first factor is the large depreciation of the dollar from mid-1977 to

TABLE 16-8 INFLATION IN THE RECOVERY *(average annual percentage rates)*

	1975	1976	1977	1978	1979
Compensation	10.0	8.4	7.9	8.6	8.9
Productivity	2.0	3.5	1.6	0.5	−1.1
Unit labor cost	7.8	4.7	6.2	8.0	10.2
Producer prices	9.2	4.6	6.2	7.8	12.5

Note: Data for compensation, productivity, and unit labor costs are for the nonfarm business sector.
Source: Citibank Economic Database.

1979. The falling value of the dollar contributed to increases in import prices and, in particular, to a resurgence of high commodity-price inflation. Much as in 1974–1975, rising prices of commodity imports contributed to increasing inflation. The second factor, the increases in oil prices that began early in 1979, did not contribute to the acceleration of inflation in 1977 and 1978, but dominated the very high inflation of 1979 and early 1980. The events of 1978–1980 were in many ways a replay of the 1973–1975 recession.

We are still left with the task of explaining the behavior of compensation, or wages. As in the recovery from the recession of 1969–1971, wage inflation continued because labor correctly believed that inflation would continue. We thus have a very difficult situation in which actual inflation depends on the rate of increase of wages, which in turn depends on expected inflation. The result is that inflation occurs because it is expected—with some role for the state of demand. High unemployment reduces the rate of increase of wages below the expected rate of inflation.

However, the evidence is that the effectiveness of unemployment in reducing the rate of wage increase below the expected rate of inflation is weak. Why this should be so is one of the central puzzles of macroeconomics. The rational expectations approach to which we turn shortly suggests some answers. Before we discuss the rational expectations approach to macroeconomics, though, we briefly discuss another development resulting from the recent inflationary experience—that of *supply management*.

16-6 NEW APPROACHES

In this section we consider two developments in macroeconomics in the 1970s, supply management and rational expectations.

Supply Management and TIP

The approach to aggregate supply developed in Chapters 11 and 13 emphasized the role of costs of production in affecting prices. This emphasis suggests that government policies that affect firms' costs can be used to influence inflation directly. For instance, firms pay Social Security taxes for their employees and pass these costs on into prices. Reductions in Social Security taxes might therefore be expected to reduce the prices charged by firms. At a time when inflation is increasing, it might make sense to reduce the rate of Social Security taxation to offset the increasing inflation.

Such a notion is attractive, but it does leave the question of what other taxes might be used to replace the Social Security tax and what their effects on the price level might be. We should also note that empirical work has not been able to tie down the effects of changes in Social Security taxes on the inflation rate very precisely. Nonetheless, it is plausible that at least in the short run, reductions in such taxes could reduce the rate of inflation. This is why it has been suggested that increases in Social Security taxes, offset by reductions in income taxes, are inflationary.[31]

The notion of supply management applies also to a variety of new policies that have been suggested to affect prices through tax incentives. TIP—tax-based incomes policy—would offer firms or workers incentives to keep price or wage rises low. For example, in 1978 the Carter administration proposed *real wage insurance* as a means of reducing the rate of wage increase. The proposal was that unions contracting for a wage increase of 7 percent or less would be compensated by the government for any fall in real wages resulting from inflation in excess of 7 percent; thus, union members would maintain their real wages. For example, if the inflation rate was 10 percent, the Treasury would pay workers who had satisfied the terms set for eligibility for the "insurance" an amount equal to 3 percent of their wages, so as to keep the real wage at the level it would have been had the inflation rate been 7 percent. The payment might be direct or a reduction in taxes. The Congress did not accept the proposal.

The idea behind real wage insurance depends on the relationship between the rate of wage increase and subsequent price behavior. If the rate of wage increase can be reduced, then the rate of price increase will fall. Thus, the Carter administration hoped that by setting up incentives to keep the rate of wage increase at 7 percent or less, it would get the inflation rate down, so that the promised insurance payments would be unnecessary. As events turned out, of course, the oil price increase in 1979 provided an extra inflationary force that would have made the scheme very expensive for the Treasury.

Ingenious as most forms of TIP are, they share a serious failing. The problem is that there does not appear to be any simple form of TIP that could be implemented without creating a bureaucratic mess. We thus doubt that TIP will be activated in the United States.[32] We do expect, though, that the supply aspects of taxes discussed here will be increasingly taken into account in future years in choosing tax packages.

Tax policies that encourage savings and investment, in order to promote capital accumulation, and policies to encourage increased labor supply also come under the heading of *supply-side economics*.

It is obvious that the reemergence of aggregate supply as an important element in analyses of the economy will lead to an increasing emphasis on these policies in the next few years.

[31] Substantial increases in Social Security taxes are planned for early 1981. It has been suggested that these taxes should be replaced by general income taxes. For a discussion of the impact of such a policy change on the price level, see Janice Halpern and Alicia Munnell, "The Inflationary Impact of Increases in the Social Security Payroll Tax," *New England Economic Review*, March/April 1980.

[32] A special issue of the *Brookings Papers on Economic Activity*, that of 1978:2 (Washington, D.C.: The Brookings Institution, 1978) is devoted to TIP and similar policies.

We turn next to a second development that can be traced to the inflationary experience of the last decade—the rise of the rational expectations school of macroeconomics.

*The Rational Expectations School

The failure to reduce inflation in the 1970s and the apparent inability of macro policy to achieve its goals have led to a reconsideration of the premises of modern macroeconomics. The reconsideration places great emphasis on expectations, on the credibility of policies, and on the limited scope for discretionary stabilization policies. The general emphasis on expectations and the credibility of policies is widely shared. Indeed, we have explained much of the behavior of the inflation rate and wage increases by appealing to expectations of inflation and the belief that anti-inflationary policies would not be long-lived. But the emphasis and its implications have been taken further by a group of economists who have developed the *rational expectations* approach to macroeconomics. Among the leading members of the school are Robert Lucas of the University of Chicago, Thomas Sargent and Neil Wallace of the University of Minnesota, and Robert Barro of the University of Rochester.[33] Some would add the more eclectic Robert Hall of the Hoover Institution and Stanford University to this list.

The notion of rational expectations itself assumes that individuals use information efficiently and do not make systematic mistakes in their expectations.[34] This assumption is made on occasion by almost all macroeconomists, and its use does not qualify the user automatically as a member of the rational expectations school. One other assumption is made by those we identify as belonging to the school. It is that markets always clear, and that economic agents set wages and prices (given their information) so as to achieve full employment, maximize profits, and maximize economic welfare.

The strongest form of rational expectations has three major implications. The first is that there is no involuntary unemployment. Why? Because anyone who expects to be unemployed, or who is currently unemployed and would prefer to work, can find work by asking for it at a wage below the existing wage. If, at the existing wage, the individual prefers not to work but rather to continue searching for a job, then the

[33] For an introduction, see Thomas Sargent and Neil Wallace. "Rational Expectations and the Theory of Economic Policy," *Journal of Monetary Economics*, April 1976. See also Robert E. Lucas, Jr., "Understanding Business Cycles," in Karl Brunner and Allan Meltzer (eds.), *Stabilization of the Domestic and International Economy*, Carnegie-Rochester Conference Series, vol. 5.

[34] In Chap. 13, we discussed the implications of *perfect foresight* for the adjustment of the economy to a change in the money stock, and we showed that in that case, the price level jumped immediately to its new level and output stayed at its full-employment level. Perfect foresight is a special case of rational expectations that holds when there is no uncertainty.

unemployment is voluntary. Of course, the theory recognizes that there is some normal level of unemployment corresponding to individuals who are between jobs or looking for their first job.

If there is no involuntary unemployment, why, then, does the level of output vary? Here the theory points to two factors. The first consists of changes in the level of potential output. The second, more important, involves mistakes in perceiving the current economic situation. Suppose that individuals do not know the aggregate price level in the current period. Of course, they do know the wage at which they can work. They have to form an estimate of the *real* wage on the basis of the price level they expect to hold during the period. Now, if the price level should turn out to be unexpectedly high, then individuals overestimate the real wage and work harder than they would if they knew the true situation. Thus, *unexpectedly* high prices lead to a higher level of output than at full employment. Individuals are working harder than they would at full employment.

This mechanism is very subtle,[35] and it is regarded by some as implausible. It clearly requires that individuals do not have complete information about the current state of the economy. Otherwise, with all markets clearing, the economy would be at the full-employment level of output. Indeed, one of the consequences of the development of the rational expectations school has been a growing emphasis on the information that individuals use and process in making their economic decisions.

The second implication follows closely from the first. It is that the level of output cannot be affected by changes in monetary policy unless those changes are not perceived by individuals in the economy. For, suppose that it is believed and known that the money supply has changed. Then individuals know the price level should be higher and adjust their prices and wages accordingly so as to produce full employment immediately.[36] If there is a lag in the publication of data on the money stock, individuals will adjust prices to the level of the money stock they expect. If the money stock turns out to be higher than expected, aggregate demand will be higher, and output will rise because of the mechanism, described earlier, in which individuals mistakenly work harder, believing the real wage is above the level at which it currently is. We thus arrive at the most famous proposition advanced by the rational expectations school, that *with regard to monetary policy only unexpected changes in the stock of money affect the level of output*.

[35] The mechanism is discussed in more detail in Robert E. Lucas, Jr., "Understanding Business Cycles," cited in footnote 33.

[36] Recall the application of perfect foresight expectations in Chap. 13 that produced precisely this adjustment.

If only unanticipated changes in the stock of money affect the level of output, then monetary policy cannot affect the level of output except by producing *surprises*. This leads to the third implication: Under these circumstances, there appears to be no role for monetary policy systematically to affect output or unemployment. Any systematic policy, such as increased monetary expansion in a recession (remember that recessions are possible as a result of surprises), would be predicted by market participants, and wages and prices would be set accordingly. Unless the Fed had better information or shorter reaction lags than the market, it could not, according to this theory, have a systematic *real* effect.

This theory might seem successful in explaining why monetary policy apparently has little effect on the level of output. But it requires us to interpret changes in output as largely the result of imperfect information. And it also has the apparently implausible implication that the Fed should find it easy to reduce the inflation rate. So long as the Fed announces that it will be reducing the growth rate of money, say to zero, market participants should adjust wages and prices accordingly, and the system will remain at full employment but at a lower rate of inflation.

Members of the rational expectations school argue that a mere announcement by the Fed of a change of policy would not actually lead to changed expectations, since the Fed has been pursuing a particular policy pattern for a long time. It would take actions rather than words for market participants to be convinced that the policy had in fact changed. We return to this point below.

Relative Wages, Wage Contracts, and Rational Expectations

The strongest form of the rational expectations theory just outlined, which assumes market clearing in every period and attributes fluctuations to imperfect information, is not widely accepted. There are, however, models that share the basic premise of rational expectations but also recognize economic institutions such as long-term contracts and the importance of the relative wages of various groups in the labor market.[37] Relatively simple amendments here go far in removing some of the least plausible implications of the strong market-clearing form of rational expectations theory.

Suppose we have 2-year labor contracts and that half the contracts in the economy come up for renewal every year. Suppose further that we start from price stability and that an unanticipated decline in the money stock occurs. If all wages and prices were instantaneously flexible, they would immediately decline in proportion to the fall in money and no real effects

[37] The discussion here follows a paper by John Taylor, "Staggered Wage Setting in a Macro-Model," *American Economic Review*, May 1979.

would arise. This does not occur, however, if we have long-term contracts that fix nominal wages. With a lowering in the money stock, there is potentially a decline in employment. Unemployed workers whose wages come up for renewal now have the choice of reducing their wages enough to become employed. If they did so, their wages would of course have to fall substantially compared with wages of those whose contract has another year to run. This change in *relative* wages may be as objectionable to unions as the fact of unemployment. Current wages will thus be set somewhere in between the full-employment level and the level of wages on contracts still running. That means wages do *not* adjust immediately to money changes, that is, wages are less than fully flexible. It takes some time until the whole wage structure adjusts. The fact that we have long-term, nonsynchronized wage setting, and that relative wages matter, directly implies the possibility of extended periods of wage stickiness and unemployment.

The model is thus able to explain wage stickiness and unemployment occurring at the same time. It also explains simultaneous wage inflation and unemployment. Suppose there is a contraction in demand, as we have just discussed, and that labor knows that policy will be expansionary in the future. Then those whose wages are currently up for renegotiation recognize that if they set too low a wage, they will be out of line with the wages that will be set next year by a group that will then be facing strong demand. Accordingly, even with the possibility of current unemployment, the prospect of expansionary aggregate demand policies in the future will make current economic slack less effective in dampening wage and price inflation. Rational expectations enter here in that the groups currently setting their wages look ahead and ask themselves what will be the macroeconomic environment in which other groups set their wages next period. If the policy setting next period is expected to be expansionary, this fact will already be anticipated in this year's wages.[38]

The relative wage model, combined with rational expectations, thus has two important features: first, wages are sticky downward in the face of unemployment; and second, wage inflation may persist in the face of unemployment. The extent of persistence is determined by, among other things, the degree to which the policy setting is accommodative or not.

Expectations and Disinflation

What does the rational expectations approach have to suggest about the possibilities of reducing inflation in the United States economy? In its most extreme form, the approach would argue that only the announcement of a

[38] Similar implications follow if workers are concerned about the real wages they will be receiving in future years, rather than relative wages.

permanently lower growth rate of nominal money is necessary. There are few who take such a suggestion seriously, and even the Federal Reserve Bank of Minneapolis, which has vigorously supported the rational expectations view, argues that a program of disinflation should be both announced and gradual.[39]

> Once the program of gradually slowing aggregate demand has begun, and the government has unambiguously demonstrated its determination to carry it out, the costs of the program will decline. When the new approach is well-known and understood, then even large steps will not lead to higher unemployment. As surprises gradually disappear, so will the high costs of fighting inflation with macroeconomic policies.

It is widely recognized that a policy of disinflation would bring about a period of unemployment. In terms of the theory of rational expectations, the slack is needed to show that the Fed is indeed serious about the new anti-inflationary policy. The question is whether economic slack can or should be maintained long enough to reduce the underlying rate of inflation.

Chart 16-9 throws some light on the question. Here we show real growth and inflation experience for the postwar business cycles in the United States. In each case we measure the cycle from peak to peak and look at average inflation and real growth through recession and recovery. The startling fact is that from one recession to the next, in the postwar period, inflation has *always* increased. There have been variations in real growth, with the 1960s standing out as a high growth period, but business-cycle history has been unambiguously one of rising inflation in this period. Policy has failed to stabilize inflation and, instead, has tended to accommodate rising inflation. Given this historical record, what are the chances for inflation stabilization in the United States? We cannot do better than quote Cagan on this point:[40]

> Market decisions about wages and prices are guided at least in part by rational expectations of the direction of policy. To the extent that prices behave according to the theory of rational expectations, the trend rate of inflation can persist in the face of slack demand, and the proclaimed desire of policy makers to subdue inflation only if they are generally not believed to be capable of translating the desire into effective action. Since the evidence suggests that the economic capability exists, the lack of credibility concerns the political capability. In such circumstances and in view of our past experience, the desire to subdue inflation is obviously not enough and must be confirmed by performance. The conclusion appears inescapable, therefore, that the

[39] Federal Reserve Bank of Minneapolis, "Eliminating Policy Surprises: An Inexpensive Way to Beat Inflation," *1978 Annual Report*, p. 7.

[40] Phillip Cagan, *Persistent Inflation* (New York: Columbia University Press, 1979), p. 249.

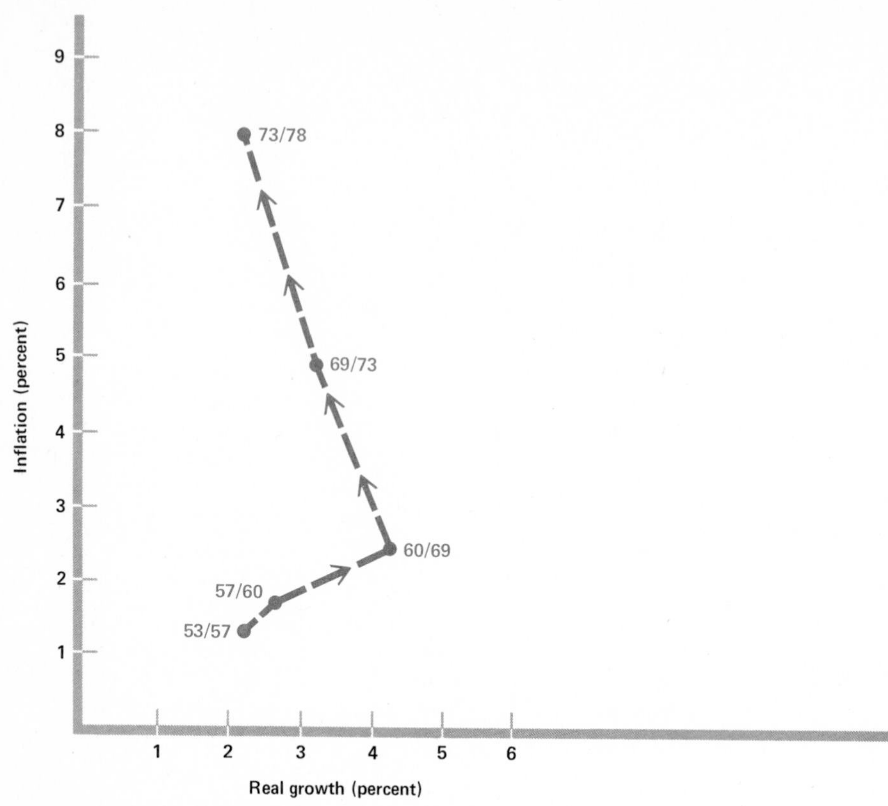

CHART 16-9 INFLATION AND REAL GROWTH IN POSTWAR BUSINESS CYCLES. *(Source: Economic Report of the President)*

reduction of inflation requires the maintenance of slack demand, and the less that policy hides an intention to maintain slack, the faster the reduction will be.

Whether or not the costs of the protracted slack justify the gains in reduced inflation is, of course, the key issue of political economy.

APPENDIX: MAJOR TAX CHANGES, 1970–1978

Measure	Date recommended	Date enacted	Remarks
Revenue Act of 1971	August 1971	December 1971	Accelerated by 1 year scheduled increases in personal exemptions and the standard deduction retroactive to August 15, 1971. Reinstated the 7 percent investment tax credit.
Tax Reduction Act of 1975	February 1975	March 1975	For individuals: authorized a 10 percent rebate on 1974 taxes up to a maximum of $200, temporarily increased the percentage standard deduction for 1975, and allowed a 5 percent tax credit up to $2,000 for the purchase of a newly built principal residence between March 1975 and December 1976. For business: increased the investment tax credit to 10 percent and lowered corporate tax rate on earnings of less than $50,000.
Revenue Adjustment Act of 1975	October 1975	December 1975	Increased the standard deduction. Provided a tax credit for each taxpayer equal to the greater of $35 for each personal exemption or 2 percent of the first $9,000 of taxable income.
Tax Reform Act of 1976	November 1975	October 1976	Attempted to close selected tax shelters. Replaced the former standard percentage deduction with a flat amount.
Tax Reduction and Simplification Act of 1977	February 1975	May 1977	Extended through 1978 the general tax credit enacted in December 1975. Provided a tax credit to employers in 1977 and 1978 of $2,100 for each new worker hired.
Revenue Act of 1978	January 1978	October 1978	Adjusted personal income tax structure to reflect past inflation, and reduced corporate taxes and capital gains taxes.

17
LONG-TERM GROWTH AND PRODUCTIVITY

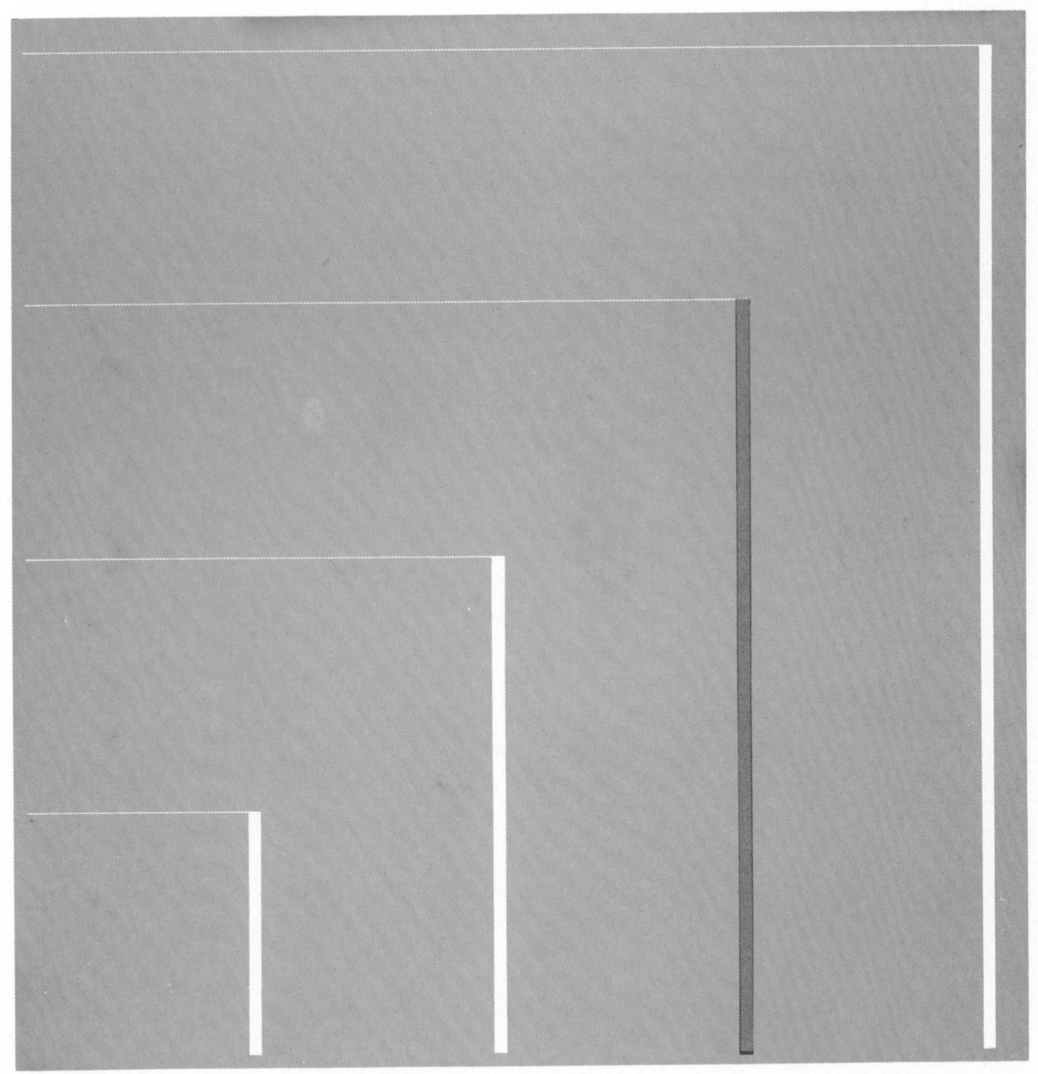

This chapter discusses long-term growth and potential output. In earlier chapters we were concerned with the maintenance of full employment and the behavior of output relative to the full-employment or potential level of output. In this chapter we shall ask what determines the growth rate of potential output over time. Over long periods, actual output on average stays close to potential output despite short-run fluctuations, so that we will also be discussing the long-run behavior of actual output.

The question we are asking is brought out by Chart 17-1, which shows the evolution of real output (in 1972 dollars) in the United States economy from 1889 to 1979. Over that period, real output grew more than eighteenfold, or at an annual rate of about 3.3 percent. Growth theory asks what factors account for the increase in output over time, and what behavior an economic system will show along the *growth path* of full-employment output.

In discussing these questions, we go to fundamentals. We step back from the aggregate demand and supply framework and ask how the

CHART 17-1 REAL GNP IN THE UNITED STATES, 1889–1979. (*Sources: U.S. Department of Commerce, Long-Term Economic Growth, 1973,* and *The National Income and Product Accounts of the United States, 1929–1974, 1977; and Citibank Economic Database)*

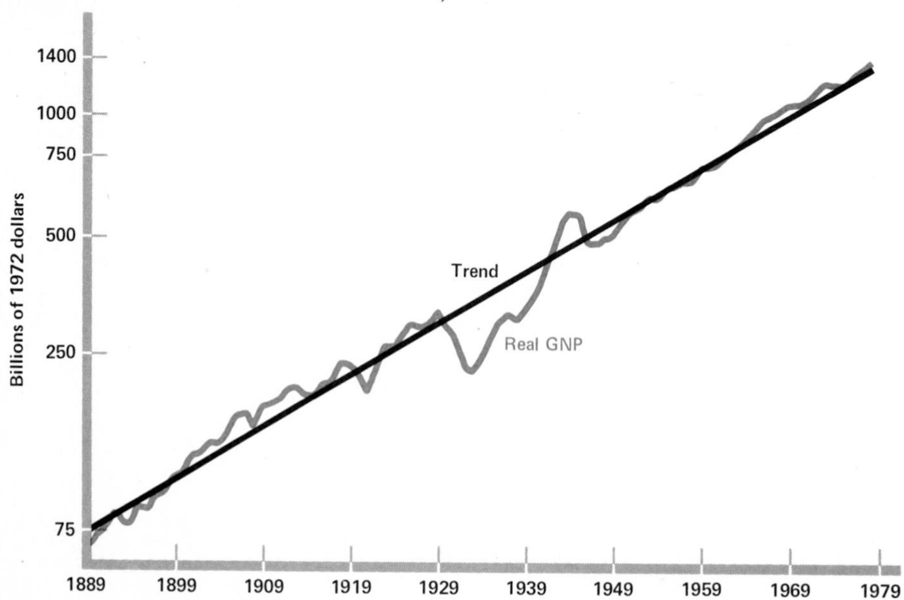

economy would behave over time if there were always full employment. With full employment, output would be determined by *factor supplies*—by the availability of capital and labor to produce goods. Over time, output would be determined by the growth in factor supplies and by changes in the productivity of factors of production.

This in turn raises the questions of what determines the growth of factor supplies, and how the growth in factor supplies translates into income and output growth. The simple theory we present emphasizes two elements: (1) the production function that relates factor inputs—capital and labor—and the state of technology to output or GNP and (2) the savings rate.

The production function relates growth in factor supplies to growth in output. And the savings rate determines what part of current output is saved and invested (added to the capital stock), and thus results in an increase in the input of capital. Because we assume that output is continuously at the full-employment level, we also assume that any output that is saved is automatically added to the capital stock, and we do not separately discuss the determinants of the rate of investment.

Chart 17-1 has already introduced the major questions raised in this chapter: What determines the growth rate of output in the long run? In particular, what made real output in the United States grow at the average annual rate of 3.3 percent over the past 90 years? For many purposes, though, we are interested not in the level of total real output but rather in the level of output in relation to population, or in real per capita output.

The average growth rate of per capita income has been about 1.9 percent per year over the 1889–1979 period. The growth rate of output per head is equal to the growth rate of total output minus the growth rate of population, as shown in Table 17-1. Output per head has increased fivefold over the past 90 years. The average person in 1979 had 5 times the amount of output or income at his or her command than did the average person in 1889. Most of our ensuing analysis concentrates on the determinants of output growth per capita. We want to know why per capita output grew to produce the extraordinary fivefold increase over the past 90 years.

There are two central messages from the simple growth theory we study here. (1) The savings rate determines the rate of growth of per-capita

TABLE 17-1 AVERAGE ANNUAL GROWTH RATES, 1889–1979

Average growth of output	3.3%
Less: Average growth of population	1.4%
Equals: Average growth of output per head	1.9%

Source: U.S. Department of Commerce, *Long-Term Economic Growth, 1860–1970* (1973), and *Economic Report of the President*.

output in the short and medium terms. The larger the fraction of output saved and invested, the larger the growth rate of full-employment output. (2) In the long run, the growth rate of output per head depends on the rate of technological change (improvements in methods of production). Total output growth depends on the rate of technological change and the growth rate of the population. In the long run, the savings rate determines only the *level* and not the *growth rate* of the capital stock and output per capita. The higher the savings rate, the higher the amount of capital.

This preview has laid out both the questions to be asked in this chapter and some of the answers. We now turn to a more detailed analysis. In Section 17-1, we introduce the production function, which provides the framework for our analysis. In Section 17-2, we look at the empirical evidence on sources of growth in the United States. Here we explain the growth in output, shown in Table 17-1, in terms of the growth in capital, growth in labor input, and improvements in technology. In Section 17-3, we examine measures of United States potential output in the postwar period. Section 17-4 turns to growth theory and formalizes the relationships among saving, population growth, and growth in capital. Section 17-5 briefly discusses the question of *limits of growth* that has become an important issue of public concern.

17-1 SOURCES OF GROWTH IN REAL INCOME: THEORY

In this section we ask the question: What are the sources of growth in real output over time? The simple answer is: first, growth in the availability of factors of production and, second, improvements in technology. If output is at the full-employment level, then there are only two ways of obtaining an increase in output: (1) to have more factors of production and/or (2) to be able to use existing factor supplies more effectively. The latter possibility means that we are producing more effectively because of either a more efficient allocation of resources or more effective technology.

The Production Function

The preceding remarks can be formalized by writing down a *production function*. A production function tells us how much output or real GNP is produced by given amounts of factor inputs. Denoting real output by Y, capital or machines by K, and the labor force by N, we have

$$Y = AF(K,N) \tag{1}$$

where we treat A as a constant.[1] Equation (1) states that output Y is a

[1] The term A used here has no connection with aggregate demand, which was denoted by that letter in other chapters.

function of the inputs of capital and labor. An increase in either input will raise output. We impose a particular property on the production function, namely, *constant returns to scale*. Constant returns to scale means that if all inputs increase in some proportion, then output will increase in that proportion. For example, if both capital and labor were to increase by 10 percent, output would increase by 10 percent. With constant returns to scale, the productivity of factors is independent of the scale of production. Constant returns to scale imply that output per head, Y/N, is independent of the scale of operation. Output per head or labor productivity depends on the amount of capital per worker, $k \equiv K/N$. The higher the amount of capital cooperating with each laborer, the more productive the laborer, or the higher the output per person.

Constant returns imply a simple relationship between labor productivity or output per worker, Y/N, and capital per worker, $k \equiv K/N$. The more capital per head we have, or the more capital-intensive the economy, the larger is output per head. We can write this relationship as

$$x = Af(k) \tag{1a}$$

where $x \equiv Y/N$ denotes output per head. We have already noted that in Equation (1*a*) an increase in the amount of capital per head k will make labor more productive and therefore raise output per worker. We add now the further assumption of diminishing returns *not* to scale but to capital intensity. As we keep raising the amount of capital per head k, labor becomes more productive and therefore output rises. However, the increase in output becomes progressively less. Additional capital cooperating with a given labor force is invariably productive but at a diminishing rate.

In Figure 17-1 we illustrate the properties of the production function that we have discussed so far.[2] In particular, we note that (1) output per head x is an increasing function of capital per head k, which is called the capital-labor ratio; and (2) the contribution to output of progressive increases in the capital-labor ratio diminishes. The latter aspect is captured in Figure 17-1 in the flattening out of the production function.

The contribution of an increase in capital per head to the amount of output per head is called the marginal productivity of capital. We note from Figure 17-1 that an increase in the capital-labor ratio from k_0 to k' raises output by $\Delta x = \text{MPK}\ \Delta k$. The term MPK denotes the marginal product of capital, which is given in Figure 17-1 by the slope of the production function.

The idea of the marginal product of capital is best understood in the

[2] The production function was also discussed in Chaps. 6 and 11.

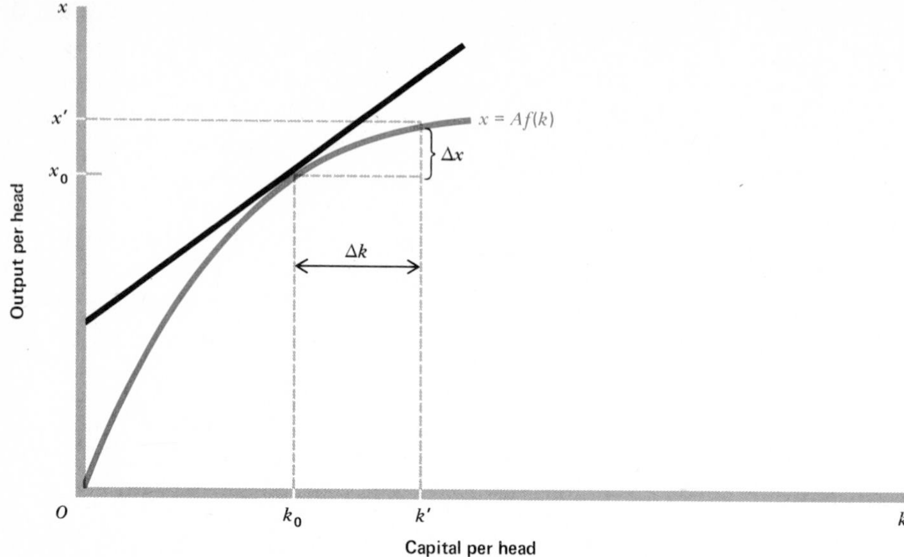

FIGURE 17-1 THE PRODUCTION FUNCTION

following manner. We start off from a capital-labor ratio k_0, where we produce an amount of output per head x_0. Next we have an increase in the capital-labor ratio to k'. Obviously, output per head will increase, and we can read off from the production function that it rises to x'. Thus we have an increase in output of $\Delta x = x' - x_0$ that is brought about by an increase in capital per person of $\Delta k = k' - k_0$. Forming the ratio $\Delta x/\Delta k \equiv \text{MPK}$, we are looking at the increase in output due to the increase in capital or at the marginal product of capital. For sufficiently small changes in the capital-labor ratio we can use the slope of the production function to translate a change in capital into the corresponding change in output. Thus the marginal product of capital is given by the slope of the production function.

Sources of Growth

This exercise has prepared us for a discussion of a first source of growth. We have seen that growth in the amount of capital per head increases output per head. Therefore, one of the sources of long-term growth in output per head is that capital has grown faster than labor and therefore has caused the capital-labor ratio to rise.

A second source of growth is reflected in the constant term A in Equation (1*a*). Let this term represent the state of technology. An improvement in technology would mean that we could produce a larger quantity of output per head with the same amount of capital per head. Given capital and labor, improved technology raises factor productivity and therefore output. In terms of Figure 17-2, an improvement in technology is shown by an upward shift of the production function and thus a higher amount of output associated with each capital-labor ratio. Our second source of growth in output per head is therefore improvement in technology, or *technical progress.*[3]

We have now seen that there are two sources of growth in output per head: (1) increases in the amount of capital per head, which contribute to output by an amount Δx = MPK Δk; and (2) technical progress, which contributes to output an amount $\Delta x = f(k)\,\Delta A$. We can therefore write the total change in output per head as

$$\Delta x = \text{MPK}\ \Delta k + f(k)\ \Delta A \tag{2}$$

If we divide both sides by the level of output per head x, we obtain a much more convenient expression:

[3] *Warning:* Technical progress in general implies that more output can be produced with the same inputs. The particular form of technical progress represented by increases in the constant term A in Eq. (1*a*) implies that the marginal products of both capital and labor increase by the same ratio. Other forms of technical progress imply changes in the *relative* productivities of capital and labor. We choose the form in which A increases for expositional convenience. For more details on technical progress, see R. M. Solow, *Growth Theory* (New York: Oxford University Press, 1970), pp. 33–38, and the very readable treatments in Daniel Hamberg, *Models of Economic Growth* (New York: Harper & Row, 1971) and Philip A. Neher, *Economic Growth and Development* (New York: Wiley, 1971).

FIGURE 17-2 TECHNOLOGICAL PROGRESS

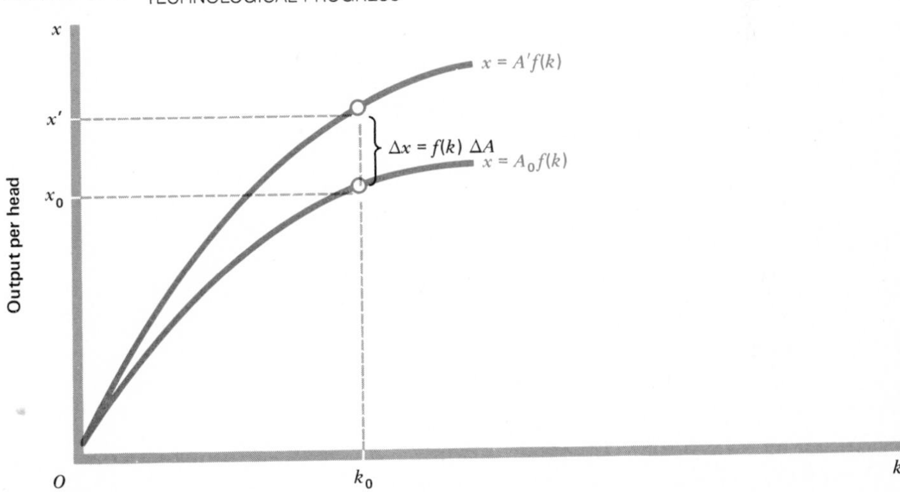

$$\frac{\Delta x}{x} = \theta \frac{\Delta k}{k} + \frac{\Delta A}{A} \tag{3}$$

where the term $\theta \equiv (\text{MPK})k/x$ is capital's share in income.[4] It is capital's share in income because in a competitive economy, the owners of capital are paid for the services of capital an amount equal to capital's marginal product. Accordingly, the marginal product—the return per unit of capital—times the stock of capital divided by total income, $(\text{MPK})k/x$, is the fraction of income that accrues to capital.

Equation (3) tells us that growth in output per head is equal to growth in capital per head times the share of capital in income plus the rate of technical progress, $\Delta A/A$. To take an example, assume that capital per head grows at the rate of 2 percent. Assume, capital's share in income, quite realistically for the United States, is $\theta = 0.35$. Then, if the rate of technical progress is 1.1 percent, the growth rate of output is 0.35×2 percent + 1.1 percent = 1.8 percent. In fact, this is approximately the long-term growth rate in output per capita in the United States, as we noted earlier in commenting on Table 17-1.

Growth in capital per head and technology are the only sources of growth in output per head. However, if we are interested in growth of total output—as opposed to output per head—we have to take account of increases in the size of the labor force. If we hold technology constant and hold constant the amount of capital per person but increase the size of the labor force, we expect output to increase. We can use Equation (3) to make this point by recognizing that the growth rate of output per worker is equal to the growth rate of output less the growth rate of the labor force, $\Delta x/x \equiv \Delta Y/Y - \Delta N/N$. Similarly, the growth rate in the capital-labor ratio is the growth rate of capital less the growth rate of labor, $\Delta k/k \equiv \Delta K/K - \Delta N/N$. Using these substitutions in Equation (3) yields

$$\frac{\Delta Y}{Y} = \frac{(1 - \theta)\Delta N}{N} + \frac{\theta \Delta K}{K} + \frac{\Delta A}{A} \tag{4}$$

Equation (4) conveniently summarizes the three sources of growth. The growth contributions of capital and labor are weighted by their respective shares in income. Equation (4) implies, as we assumed at the outset, constant return to scale. This is apparent from the fact that, say, a 10 percent increase in both capital and labor will increase output in the same proportion.

[4] In more detail, dividing the term $\text{MPK}\Delta k$ in Eq. (2) by x, we have $[(\text{MPK}\Delta k)/x]$. Now multiply and divide by k to obtain $[(\text{MPK} \cdot k)/x](\Delta k/k)$. Now $\text{MPK}k$ is the marginal product of capital times the amount of capital per head, or the amount of income received by capital divided by the number of workers. The derivation of the $\Delta A/A$ term in Eq. (3) is left for the problem set at the end of the chapter.

17-2 EMPIRICAL ESTIMATES OF THE SOURCES OF GROWTH

The previous section prepares us for an analysis of empirical studies that deal with sources of growth. Equation (4) suggests that the growth in output can be explained by growth in factor inputs, weighted by their shares in income, and by technical progress. An early and famous study by Robert Solow of MIT dealt with the period 1909–1949 in the United States.[5] Solow's surprising conclusion was that over 80 percent of the growth in output per labor hour over that period was due to technical progress, that is, to factors other than growth in the input of capital per labor hour. Specifically, Solow estimated for the United States an equation similar to Equation (4) that identifies capital and labor growth along with technical progress as the sources of output growth. Of the average annual growth of total GNP of 2.9 percent per year over that period, he concluded that 0.32 percent was attributable to capital accumulation, 1.09 percent per annum was due to the increases in the input of labor, and the remaining 1.49 percent was due to technical progress. Per capita output grew at 1.81 percent, with 1.49 percent of that increase resulting from technical progress.

The very large part of the growth contribution that is taken up by "technical progress" makes that term really a catchall for omitted factors and poor measurement of the capital and labor inputs. Further work therefore turned quite naturally to explore this residual, that is, growth not explained by capital accumulation or increased labor input.

Perhaps the most comprehensive of the subsequent studies is that by Edward Denison.[6] Using data for the period 1929–1969, Denison attributed 1.8 percent of the 3.4 percent annual rate of increase in real output to increased factor inputs. Output per labor hour grew at the rate of 2.09 percent, of which 1.59 percent was due to technical progress. Denison's findings thus support Solow's estimate that most of the growth in output per labor hour is due to technical progress. Table 17-2 shows a breakdown of the increased factor input into its various components.

Technical progress explains almost half the growth in output, with growth in total factor inputs accounting for the other half of growth. Consider now the breakdown between the various components of increased factor use. Here increases in the labor force get a very large credit for their contribution to growth. Why? Because labor grows very fast? The answer is provided by Equation (4), which suggests that labor's growth rate has a

[5] "Technical Change and the Aggregate Production Function." *Review of Economics and Statistics*, August 1957.

[6] *Accounting for United States Economic Growth 1929–1969* (Washington, D.C.: The Brookings Institution, 1974). See also Denison's *Accounting for Slower Economic Growth: The United States in the 1970s* (ibid., 1980).

TABLE 17-2 SOURCES OF GROWTH OF TOTAL NATIONAL INCOME, 1929–1969

Source of growth	Growth rate (percent per annum)
Total factor input	1.82
Labor: 1.32	
Capital: 0.50	
Output per unit of input	1.59
Knowledge: 0.92	
Resource allocation: 0.30	
Economies of scale: 0.36	
Other: 0.01	
National income:	3.41

Source: E. Denison, *Accounting for United States Economic Growth 1929–1969* (Washington, D.C.: The Brookings Institution, 1974), p. 127.

relatively large weight because labor's share of income is relatively large. The counterpart is obviously the relatively low share of capital. Thus, even if capital and labor grew at the same rate, the fact that they have different shares in income—labor having a share of about 65 percent and capital having a share of about 35 percent—implies that labor would be credited with a larger contribution toward growth.

Next we look at the various sources of increased factor productivity or increased output per unit factor input. Here the striking fact is the importance of advances in knowledge that account for almost two-thirds of the contribution of technical progress toward growth. Two other sources of increased factor productivity are worth recording. One is the increase in productivity that stems from improved resource allocation. Here we can think of people leaving low-paying jobs or low-income areas and moving to better jobs or locations, thus contributing to increased output or income growth. An important element is relocation from farms to cities.

The remaining significant part of technical progress is *economies of scale*. This is a bit troublesome because we assumed away economies of scale in deriving Equation (4). In deriving that equation, we explicitly assumed constant returns to scale, but we find now that more than 10 percent of the average annual growth in income is due to an expanding scale of operation. As the scale of operation of the economy expands, fewer inputs are required per unit output presumably because we can avail ourselves of techniques that are economically inefficient at a small-scale level but yield factor savings at a larger scale of production.

The major significance of Denison's work, and the work in this area of others, including Simon Kuznets and J. W. Kendrick, is to point out that there is no single critical source of real income growth. The early suggestion by Solow that growth in the capital stock makes a minor, though not negligible, contribution to growth stands up well to the test of new research. Capital investment is certainly necessary—particularly because some technological improvements require the use of new types of machines—but it is clear that there are other sources of growth that can make an important contribution. Furthermore, since for most purposes we are interested in output per head, we have to recognize that we are left with only technical progress and growth in capital to achieve increased output per head. Here we have to ask, What are the components of technical progress? Advances in knowledge stand out as a major source and point to the roles of research, education, and training as important sources of growth.[7]

17-3 POTENTIAL OUTPUT AND PRODUCTIVITY

The idea of potential output became a central concept in macroeconomic policy making in the 1960s. Potential output and the associated concept of the GNP gap provided policy makers with a target for policy setting.

Potential output is a measure of the output the economy can produce when factors of production are fully employed. Using the production function

$$Y = AF(K,N) \tag{1}$$

we obtain a measure of potential output by calculating the level of Y that corresponds to full-employment levels of input K (capital) and N (labor).

Typically, we are interested in both past and future levels of potential output. Past levels of potential output are of interest for judging past macroeconomic performance. Future levels of potential output are useful for guiding policy and for providing a baseline for expectations of future output.

Early estimates of potential output were made by Arthur Okun. He assumed that potential output corresponded to a level of labor input [N in Equation (1)] that prevailed when unemployment was 4 percent.[8] Although he did not then use the phrase, we would now say that 4 percent was his estimate of the natural rate of unemployment.[9] Okun also assumed that

[7] A collection of useful papers on the sources of growth are contained in Edmund Phelps (ed.), *The Goal of Economic Growth* (New York: Norton, 1969).

[8] Arthur M. Okun, "Potential GNP: Its Measurement and Significance," reprinted in his book, *The Political Economy of Prosperity* (New York: Norton, 1970).

[9] We have not explicitly discussed the meaning of the full-employment level of capital [(K in Eq. (1)]. The amount of capital used in production does vary over the cycle as the number of shifts worked, using particular machinery and hours of work, vary. *Capacity utilization*, a number estimated by the Fed among others, attempts to measure the extent to which capital is being employed. Some standard rate of capacity utilization, such as 87.5 percent, is typically used to calculate full employment K in (1). Of course, the levels of employment of capital and labor move very much together over the cycle.

potential output grew at 3.5 percent per year. This estimate corresponded to postwar experience of growth rates of output between periods when there was full employment of labor.

There are two steps in estimating potential output. The first is to estimate the production function, Equation (1), and the second is to estimate the full-employment levels of capital and labor and any other inputs that might be taken into account. For example, recent studies have tried to incorporate energy as a factor of production, in order to estimate the impact of the energy crisis on potential output.[10]

Projections of future potential output are typically made by calculating the growth rate of potential GNP. For this purpose it is useful to turn to Equation (4), derived from Equation (1):

$$\frac{\Delta Y}{Y} = (1 - \theta)\frac{\Delta N}{N} + \theta\frac{\Delta K}{K} + \frac{\Delta A}{A} \tag{4}$$

Output grows as a result of increases in factor inputs and technical progress. Therefore, to predict potential output growth, it is necessary to predict the full-employment levels of factor inputs and the growth rate of technical progress. As mentioned earlier, inputs would include not only capital and labor as in Equation (4) but also other factors, such as energy, that might be important.

The growth rate of the labor input depends on the growth rates of the different demographic groups in the labor force and their participation rates—that is, the percentage of each group in the labor force. It also depends on the natural rate of unemployment for each group. The rate of growth of capital depends on future rates of investment. If energy is treated explicitly as a factor, then predictions of the rate of change of energy use have to be made.

Predicting these variables is obviously difficult. For instance, our energy use depends in part on OPEC's future policy decisions, which we cannot confidently know now. Similarly, investment fluctuates a great deal. And we have also to predict technical progress, which almost by its nature is not firmly predictable.

Because of the complexity of the complete calculation of future output growth using Equation (4), a shortcut is typically taken. Specifically, the productivity of labor, which we denote Z (not to be confused with Z used elsewhere in the book) is measured by

$$Z = \frac{Y}{N} \tag{5}$$

[10] Robert Rasche and John Tatom, "Energy Resources and Potential GNP," Federal Reserve of St. Louis, *Review*, June 1977; and Jeffrey Perloff and Michael Wachter, "A Production Function-Nonaccelerating Inflation Approach to Potential Output," in Carnegie-Rochester Conference Series, vol. 10, Karl Brunner and Allan Meltzer (eds), (Amsterdam: North Holland).

where Y is the level of output and N is the level of labor input. That is, productivity is the *average* product of labor. Now if we turn (5) around, we can write $Y = NZ$ and then see that

$$\frac{\Delta Y}{Y} = \frac{\Delta N}{N} + \frac{\Delta Z}{Z} \tag{6}$$

The growth rate of output is equal to the growth rate of labor input plus the rate of growth of productivity.

We turn now to estimates of potential output that are based on this approach.

Estimates of Potential Output

Chart 17-2 presents actual GNP and the estimates of potential GNP used by the Council of Economic Advisers through 1976. The latter series is labeled "1976 potential." By the 1976 measure, output was below potential even at the height of the 1972–1973 boom. This estimate was entirely consistent with the official view that the natural rate of unemployment was

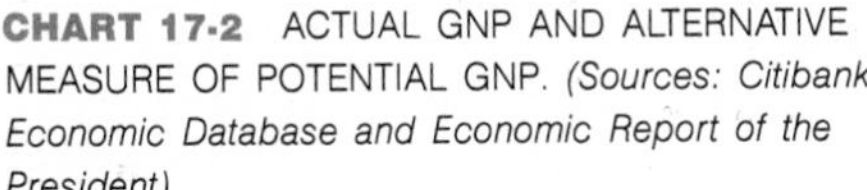
CHART 17-2 ACTUAL GNP AND ALTERNATIVE MEASURE OF POTENTIAL GNP. *(Sources: Citibank Economic Database and Economic Report of the President)*

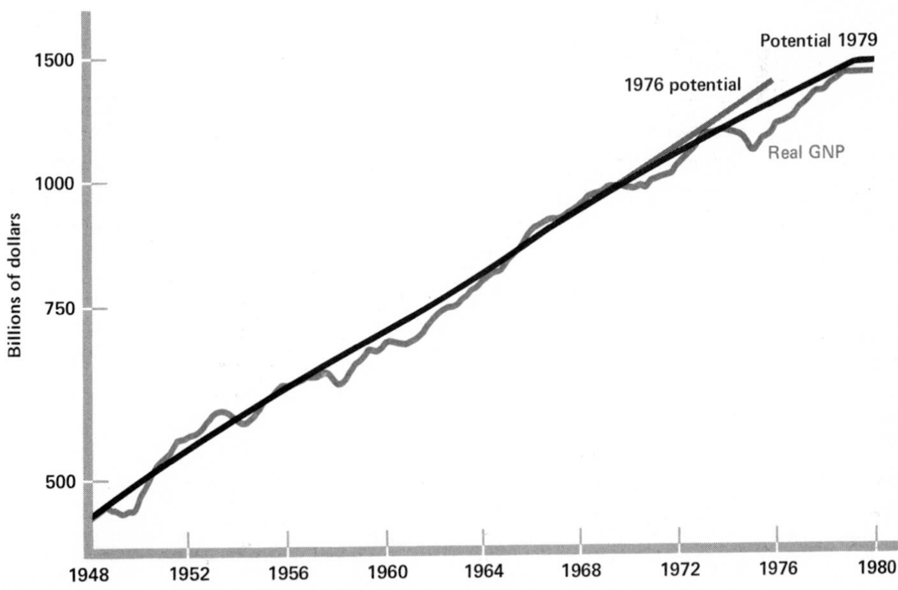

Note: Prior to 1968, potential GNP is estimated to have grown at 4 percent.

4 percent, well below the 1973 level of 4.8 percent. By the 1976 measure, output in 1975 was a full 13 percent below potential.

The Council decided in 1977 to revise its estimate of potential output and its growth rate. The estimate of the *level* of potential output was reduced because it was by then clear that the full-employment level of unemployment was higher than 4 percent. The estimate of the natural rate of unemployment was raised by the Council to 4.9 percent to reflect the increased proportion of young people and women in the labor force and their higher unemployment rates. The *growth rate* of potential output was revised down to 3.5 percent from about 4 percent (to which it had been raised in the mid-sixties) to reflect the slowdown in productivity growth compared with the sixties. We shall discuss reasons for the productivity slowdown later in this section. The revised estimate of potential GNP reduced the estimated 1975 GNP gap to 9.5 percent.

In 1979 the Council again revised its estimates of the level and rate of growth of potential output. The natural rate of unemployment for 1979 was estimated to be 5.1 percent, and the growth rate of potential output since 1973 was estimated to be only 3 percent. This revision reduced the estimated 1975 GNP gap to a little over 7.5 percent. The new series is shown in Chart 17-2 as "Potential 1979." This is the series we have used in other chapters of the book to calculate the GNP gap.

There is as yet no consensus on measures of potential GNP and its growth rate. Indeed, the studies cited in footnote 10 suggest that even the most recent "Potential 1979" series of the Council of Economic Advisers is an overestimate. This view results partially from differences in estimates of the natural rate of unemployment: Perloff and Wachter[11] calculate the natural rate of unemployment to be about 5.5 percent rather than the Council's 5.1 percent.

What about estimates of future potential GNP? Using an approach based on Equation (6), the Council of Economic Advisers predicts that potential output will grow at about 3 percent over the next few years. They estimate that the growth rate of the labor input from 1979 to 1983 will be 1½ percent per year. How did they arrive at this estimate? The labor force is expected to grow at 1¼ percent per year, hours of work for each worker are predicted to fall by ½ percent per year, and the participation rate of labor is expected to rise by ¾ percent per year, leading to 1½ percent growth in the labor input (1½ = 1¼ − ½ + ¾). The Council predicts that productivity will grow at 1½ percent per annum, leading from Equation (6) to a predicted growth rate of potential output of 3 percent. This is a full 1 percent below the estimated growth rate of potential output in the late sixties. It is clear that this gloomy forecast for the growth rate of potential output would have been more optimistic if productivity had been expected

[11] As cited in footnote 10.

to grow at the nearly 3 percent rate of 1948 to 1973 rather than 1.5 percent. What accounts for the change in the productivity outlook?

Productivity

Table 17-3 shows the record of productivity growth in the postwar United States economy. The record is one of falling productivity growth, with the experience of the 1973–1979 period being particularly poor. A slowdown of nearly 2 percent in the growth rate of productivity is very large,[12] and the data in the table have been the subject of both research and concern.

We look to six factors in accounting for the productivity slowdown. The first is the rate of investment. The capital-labor ratio in the United States increased less rapidly after 1973 than before: from 1948 to 1973, the capital-labor ratio grew 3 percent per year, but after 1973 it grew only at 1¾ percent. This 1¼ percent fall leads to a reduction in the rate of productivity increase of about 0.35 percent.[13]

Second, changes in the structure of the labor force affect productivity. In general, worker productivity increases with experience for at least several years after workers enter the labor force. Thus, increases in the number of inexperienced workers can reduce the rate of productivity increase temporarily; for the post-1973 period, the decline from this source is put in the vicinity of 0.3 percent per year.

The third factor leading to a decline in the rate of productivity growth is increasing regulation of industry. Two points have to be made here. One is that the benefits of regulation—such as pollution control—are typically not included as part of output. If the value of the increased volume of clean air that we have been "buying" through the costs of pollution controls in this decade were included in GNP, productivity growth would not have declined as much as it has. Second, it is obviously very difficult to

[12] How much lower would output be after 20 years if output grew at 2 percent rather than 4 percent?

[13] Problem 5 at the end of this chapter asks you to make the calculation underlying this sentence.

TABLE 17-3 LABOR PRODUCTIVITY GROWTH, PRIVATE BUSINESS ECONOMY, 1948–1978 *(percentage rate of increase of output per hour)*

	1948–1955	1955–1965	1965–1973	1973–1977	1977–1979
Rate of productivity increase	3.4	3.1	2.3	1.0	−0.2

Source: Economic Report of the President.

measure the effects of regulation on output. In some industries, such as mining, where there have been both a sharp fall in productivity and increased safety regulation, it is clear that the regulations have been a major cause of the productivity decrease. Estimates of the total decline in productivity increase due to increased regulation are in the vicinity of 0.3 percent yearly.

The fourth factor is the decline in United States spending on research and development. The decline here is almost entirely in government research spending. Although much of the government research of the fifties and sixties was on space and defense, some part of that research spending did end up increasing productivity in the private sector, particularly in the area of miniaturization, such as hand computers. It is also claimed that as a result of increased regulation of the private sector, more research and development are directed at meeting government regulations and less at fundamental innovation than was the case in the sixties. These effects have not been measured.

The fifth factor is the shift in the composition of output in the United States and other developed countries, particularly toward the service sector. Productivity growth in the service sector has been slower than average in the entire postwar period. Further, the *level* of productivity in this sector has been lower than average productivity. As an increasing proportion of the labor force moves into the lower productivity sectors, the growth rate of productivity falls. As a complement of this shift, we should note the end of the shift of factors out of agriculture. Worldwide, economic development is associated with a shift of labor from agriculture, where productivity is relatively low, to industry, where it is relatively high. While this shift takes place, the rate of increase of productivity is above its trend level. Once the shift stops, the rate of increase of productivity returns to trend. In the United States, the shift of labor out of agriculture was complete by the mid-sixties, and no gains in productivity from that source can be anticipated.

The final factor we consider is the rapid rise in the price of energy in 1973. This was a one-time shock that reduced productivity, since it made the use of energy and thus machinery more expensive, and thus led firms to attempt to economize on energy use. To the extent that the *real* price of energy will continue to rise, we can expect the energy shortage to have a permanent impact on the *growth* rate of productivity in the United States.

Where do these six factors leave us? Poor productivity performance has led to public concern that the rate of investment is too low; this concern will likely lead to policies to encourage investment. Such policies have received much attention recently, as part of supply-side economics. Thus the first factor—the decline in the rate of increase in the capital-labor ratio—may well be reversed. The second factor, the increasing percentage of less experienced workers, will continue for some time as the participation rates of women increase. But with the passing of the baby boom of the postwar period, we can look forward to (if those are the right words) an aging labor force, and this second factor will reverse itself. We hesitate to predict the future of regulation, but suspect that the rate of increase of regulation will fall, also in part in response to the new emphasis on aggregate supply. Research and development—the fourth factor—will probably be encouraged by more favorable tax treatment in the near future. But spending on basic research does not automatically produce new knowledge that translates into higher productivity, and the outlook on this score is uncertain. The shift in the composition of output toward services will probably continue. And prospects on the energy front do not look good for the next decade at least. Thus, the overall prospect for productivity is that the growth rate should make some comeback from the dismal performance of 1973 to 1979, but that we cannot soon expect to repeat the outstanding performance—unique in the nation's history—of 1948 to 1973.

In summary, then, it is clear that potential output did not grow in the seventies at a rate even close to the 4 percent rate of the sixties. This can be attributed in part to an increase in the natural rate of unemployment, and in part to the many factors that reduced the growth rate of productivity. It is the future behavior of productivity, and especially that part of productivity increase due to technical progress, that is crucial for the long-run growth of the United States economy.

*17-4 GROWTH THEORY

In this section we will be concerned with growth of output from a theoretical point of view rather than in terms of the historical record. We ask what determines output growth in the short and long runs. You will see that we have already answered that question when we recognized in Equation (4), that factor growth and technical progress are the sources of output growth. The next step, therefore, is to ask, What determines the growth of factor inputs? We take a rather simple formulation here by (1) assuming a given and constant rate of labor force growth, $\Delta N/N \equiv n$, and (2) assuming that there is no technical progress, $\Delta A/A = 0$. With these assumptions we are left with the growth rate of capital. Capital growth is determined by saving, which in turn depends on income. Income or output in turn depends on capital. We are thus set with an interdependent system in which capital growth depends, via saving and income, on the capital stock. We now study the short-run behavior, the adjustment process, and the long-run equilibrium of that interdependent system.

Steady State

We start by discussing the steady state of the economy. Here we ask whether in an economy with population growth and saving, and therefore growth in the capital stock, we reach a point where output per head and capital per head become constant. In such a steady state, current saving and additions to the capital stock would be just enough to equip new entrants into the labor force with the same amount of capital as the average worker uses.

These ideas can be made more concrete by returning to Equation (3), recognizing that we assume zero productivity growth. We therefore have

$$\frac{\Delta x}{x} = \frac{\theta \Delta k}{k} \tag{3a}$$

Equation (3*a*) states that growth in output per head is proportional to growth in the stock of capital per head, $\Delta k/k$. Clearly, to reach a steady state where output per head is constant, we would have to reach zero growth in the stock of capital per head. Our focus is therefore on the determinants of the growth rate of capital per head.

Capital per head, $k \equiv K/N$, grows as current saving provides resources to be invested and added to the capital stock per worker. Capital per head declines to the extent that population growth reduces the amount of capital average workers each have at their disposal.

More precisely, the rate of growth of capital per head is equal to the difference between the growth rate of capital, $\Delta K/K$, and the growth rate of population, $n \equiv \Delta N/N$:

$$\frac{\Delta k}{k} = \frac{\Delta K}{K} - n \tag{7}$$

where we use the shorthand notation n for the given rate of growth of the labor force. Equation (7) shows that capital per head grows if the capital stock grows faster than the labor force. Combining this with Equation (3*a*), we realize that output per head grows if capital grows faster than the labor force:

$$\frac{\Delta x}{x} = \theta\left(\frac{\Delta K}{K} - n\right) \tag{8}$$

where we have substituted Equation (7) in Equation (3*a*).

Equation (8) implies that output per head will be constant when capital and labor grow at the same rate. In other words, we will be in the steady state when output per head is constant because $n = \Delta K/K$. The next step in the analysis is to link growth in the capital stock to income and saving.

The growth rate of the capital stock $\Delta K/K$ is determined by additions to the capital stock, that is, by investment and thus by saving. Additions to the capital stock are equal to investment, which in turn is equal to saving, less depreciation:

$$\Delta K = \text{saving} - \text{depreciation} \tag{9}$$

We assume that a constant fraction s of income or output is saved. Accordingly, saving is equal to sY. We assume that the depreciation rate of capital is d percent per year, so that total depreciation is at the rate of dK per year. Substituting for saving and depreciation in Equation (9) yields

$$\Delta K = sY - dK \tag{9a}$$

We have to do some more work on Equation (9a) before we arrive at a final equation that describes the growth process. The further modifications of Equation (9a) are (1) to turn it into percentage change form by dividing both sides by the capital stock and (2) to get it into per capita form by subtracting the growth rate of labor from both sides. Undertaking these two operations, we have

$$\frac{\Delta K}{K} - n = \frac{sY}{K} - n - d \tag{9b}$$

We note that the left-hand side is the growth rate of the capital-labor ratio. The right-hand side is made up of three terms. First, we have saving per unit of capital, which is equal to total investment per unit of capital. However, to get to the growth of capital per person, we have to subtract both depreciation and growth of the labor force, which are the remaining two terms in Equation (9b). A final simplification of Equation (9b) is obtained by multiplying and dividing the saving term (sY/K) by the labor force N to obtain $s(Y/N)\ (N/K)$. This allows us to replace that term by sx/k, using the production function in per capita terms:

$$\frac{\Delta k}{k} = \frac{sx}{k} - (n + d) \tag{10}$$

or

$$\Delta k = sx - (n + d)k \tag{10a}$$

Equation (10) is the final form of our growth model. It describes the growth rate of the capital stock in terms of saving behavior, population growth, and depreciation.

The growth process can be studied in terms of Figure 17-3. Here we reproduce the production function in per capita terms from Figure 17-1. We have added the savings function, which, for each capital-labor ratio, is simply the fraction s of output. Thus, for any capital-labor ratio, say k_0, the corresponding point on the saving schedule tells us the amount of saving per head $sx(k_0)$ that will be forthcoming at that capital-labor ratio.

We know that all saving is invested so that gross investment or gross additions to the capital stock, in per capita terms, are equal to sx_0, given a capital-labor ratio of k_0. We know, too [from Equation (10*a*)], that the increase in the capital-labor ratio falls short of that gross addition for two reasons:

1 Depreciation reduces the capital-labor ratio, and part of gross investment must be devoted to offsetting depreciation. In particular, if the depreciation rate is d, then an amount dk is required as a depreciation allowance. For example, if the depreciation rate was 10 percent and the capital-labor ratio was ten machines per person, then each year the equivalent of one machine would depreciate and would have to be replaced, that is, 10 percent times ten machines equals one machine.
2 Growth in the labor force implies that with a given stock of capital, the capital-labor ratio would be declining. To maintain the amount of capital per head constant, we have to add enough machines to the stock of capital to make up for the growth in population.

It follows that we can write the investment required to maintain constant the capital-labor ratio in the face of depreciation and labor force growth as $(n + d)k$. That amount of investment is required to maintain constant the capital-labor ratio. When saving and hence gross investment are larger than $(n + d)k$, the stock of capital per head is increasing. If saving and gross investment are less, then we are not making up for depreciation and population growth, and, accordingly, capital per head is falling. We can therefore think of the term $(n + d)k$ as the *investment requirement* that will maintain constant capital per head and therefore, from Equation (1*a*), output per head.

In Figure 17-3 we show this investment requirement as a positively sloped schedule. It tells us how much investment we would require at each capital-labor ratio just in order to keep that ratio constant. It is positively sloped because the higher the capital-labor ratio, the larger the amount of investment that is required to maintain that capital-labor ratio. Thus, with the depreciation rate of 10 percent and a growth rate of population of 1 percent, we would require an investment of 1.1 machines per head per year at a capital-labor ratio of 10 machines per head to maintain the capital-labor ratio constant. If the capital-labor ratio were 100 machines per head, the required investment would be 11 machines (= 100 machines per head times 11 percent).

We have seen that the saving schedule tells us the amount of saving and gross investment associated with each capital-labor ratio. Thus, at a capital-labor ratio of k_0 in Figure 17-3, saving is sx_0 at point A. The investment requirement to maintain constant the capital-labor ratio at k_0 is equal to $(n + d)k_0$ at point B. Clearly, saving exceeds the investment requirement. More is added to the capital stock than is required to maintain constant the capital-labor ratio. Accordingly, the capital-labor ratio grows. Not surprisingly, the increase in the capital-labor ratio is equal

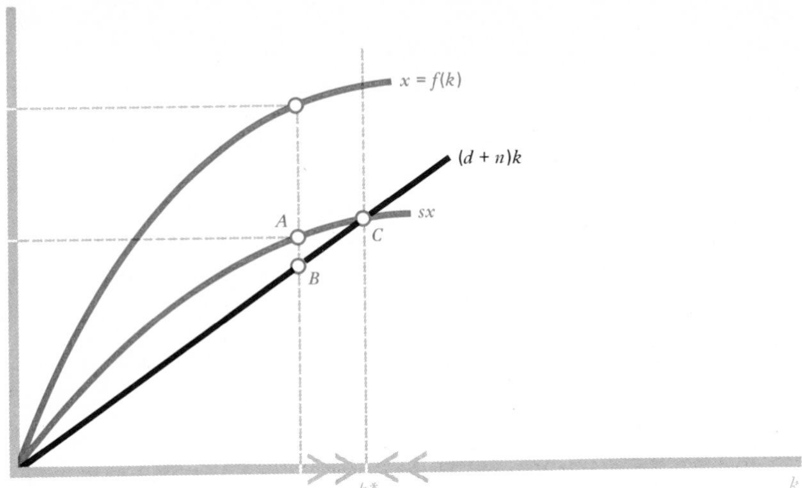

FIGURE 17-3 SAVING, INVESTMENT, AND CAPITAL ACCUMULATION

to actual saving or investment less the investment requirement and is thus given by the vertical distance AB.

In the next period, capital per head will be higher. You immediately recognize the line of argument we are taking. From Figure 17-3 it is clear that with a somewhat higher capital-labor ratio, the discrepancy between saving and the investment requirement becomes smaller. Therefore the increase in the capital-labor ratio becomes smaller. However, the capital-labor ratio still increases, as indicated by the arrows.

The adjustment process comes to a halt at point C. Here we have reached a capital-labor ratio k^* such that saving and investment associated with that capital-labor ratio exactly match the investment requirement. Given the exact matching of actual and required investment, the capital-labor ratio neither rises nor falls. We have reached the *steady state*. We can make the same argument by starting with an initial capital-labor ratio in excess of k^*. From Figure 17-3 we note that for high capital-labor ratios, the investment requirement is in excess of saving and investment. Accordingly, not enough is added to the capital stock to maintain the capital-labor ratio constant in the face of population growth and depreciation. Thus, the capital-labor ratio falls until we get to k^*, the steady-state capital-labor ratio.

To review our progress so far:

1 Capital and labor are used to produce output according to a production function assumed to have constant returns to scale.
2 To maintain the capital-labor ratio constant, saving and investment have

to be sufficient to make up for the reduction in capital per head that arises from population growth and depreciation.

3 With saving a constant fraction s of output, we established that the capital-labor ratio moves to a steady-state level k^* at which output and therefore saving (investment) are just sufficient to maintain constant the capital-labor ratio.

4 The convergence to a steady-state capital-labor ratio k^* is ensured by the fact that at low levels of the capital-labor ratio, saving (investment) exceeds the investment required to maintain capital per head and therefore causes the capital-labor ratio to rise. Conversely, at high capital-labor ratios, saving (investment) falls short of the investment requirement, and thus the ratio declines.

Now we can turn to a more detailed study of the characteristics of steady-state equilibrium and the adjustment process. First, we recognize what a steady-state equilibrium really means. We note that the steady-state level of capital per head is constant, and thus, from the production function, that the steady-state level of output per head is also constant. The steady state is reached when all variables, in per capita terms, are constant. This means that in the steady state, output, capital, and labor all grow at the same rate. They all grow at a rate equal to the rate of population growth, and therefore output and capital remain constant in per capita terms. Note particularly that the steady-state growth rate is equal to the rate of population growth and therefore is not influenced by the saving rate. (Recall that we are assuming no technical progress.) To explore this property of the steady state in more detail, we turn now to an investigation of the effects of a change in the saving rate.

A Change in the Saving Rate

In this subsection we address the puzzling question of why the long-run growth rate should be independent of the saving rate. If people save 10 percent of their income as opposed to 5 percent, should we not expect this to make a difference to the growth rate of output? Is is not true that an economy in which 10 percent of income is set aside for additions to the capital stock is one in which capital and therefore output grow faster than in an economy saving only 5 percent of income?

We show here that an increase in the saving rate does the following: (1) In the short run, it raises the growth rate of output; (2) it does not affect the long-run growth rate of output; and (3) it raises the long-run *level* of capital and output per head.

Consider now Figure 17-4 with an initial steady-state equilibrium at point C, where saving precisely matches the investment requirement. At point C, exactly enough output is saved to maintain the stock of capital per

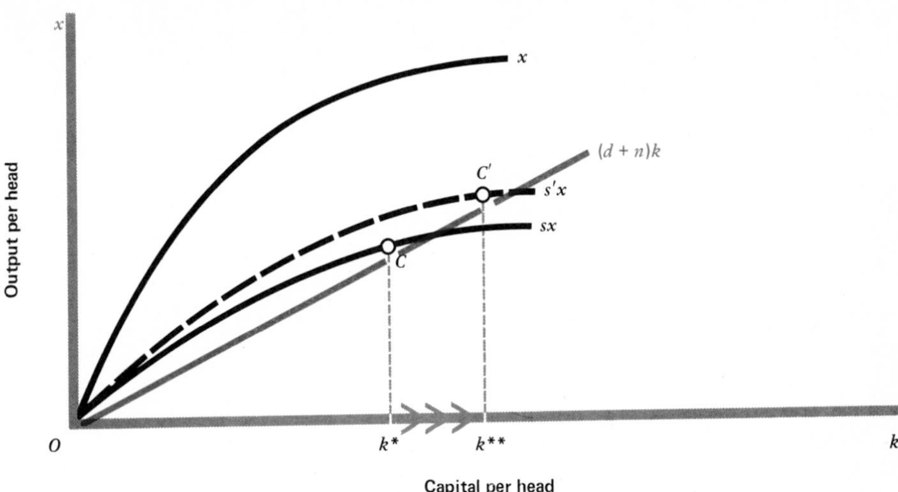

FIGURE 17-4 AN INCREASE IN THE SAVING RATE

head constant in the face of depreciation and labor force growth. Next consider an increase in the saving rate. For some reason, people want to save a larger fraction of income. The increased saving rate is reflected in an upward shift of the saving schedule. At each level of the capital-labor ratio, and hence at each level of output, saving is larger.

At point C, where we initially had a steady-state equilibrium, saving has now risen relative to the investment requirement and, as a consequence, more is saved than is required to maintain capital per head constant. Enough is saved to allow the capital stock per head to increase.

It is apparent from Figure 17-4 that the capital stock per head will keep rising until we reach point C'. At C', the higher amount of saving is just enough to maintain the higher stock of capital. at point C', both capital per head and output per head have risen. Saving has increased as has the investment requirement. We have seen, therefore, that an increase in the saving rate will in the long run raise only the *level* of output and capital per head, as shown in Figure 17-4, but not the *growth rate* of output per head.

The transition process, however, involves an effect of the saving rate on the growth rate of output and the growth rate of output per head. In the transition from k^* to k^{**}, the increase in the saving rate raises the growth rate of output. This follows simply from the fact that the capital-labor ratio rises from k^* at the initial steady state to k^{**} in the new steady state. The only way to achieve an increase in the capital-labor ratio is for the capital stock to grow faster than the labor force (and depreciation). This is precisely what happens in the transition process where increased saving per head, due to the higher saving rate, raises investment and capital growth over and above the investment requirement and thus allows the capital-labor ratio to rise.

In summary, the long-run effect of an increase in the saving rate is to raise the level of output and capital per head but to leave the growth rate of output and capital unaffected. In the transition period, the rates of growth of output and capital increase relative to the steady state. In the short run, therefore, an increase in the saving rate means faster growth, as we would expect.

Figure 17-5 summarizes these two results. Figure 17-5*a* shows the level of per capita output. Starting from an initial long-run equilibrium at

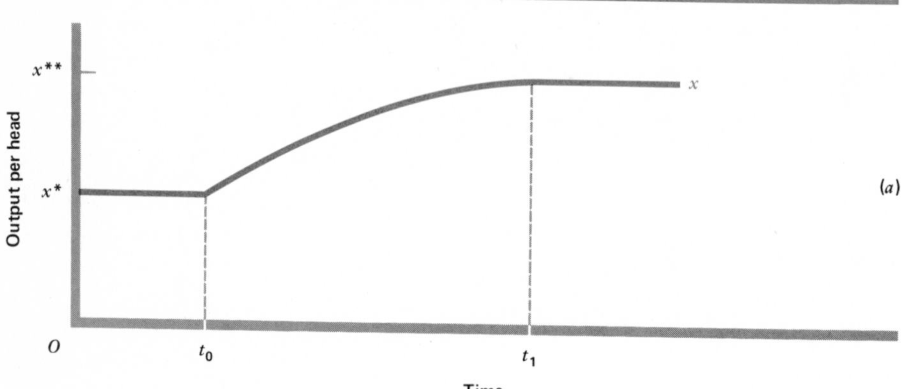

FIGURE 17-5a THE TIME PATH OF PER CAPITA INCOME

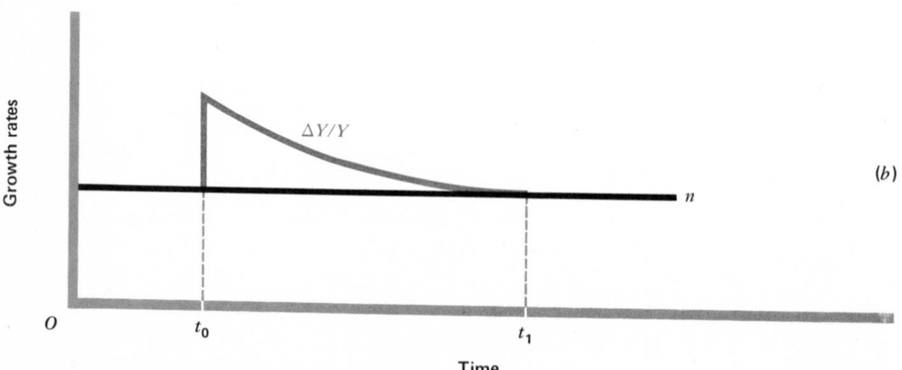

FIGURE 17-5b THE TIME PATH OF THE GROWTH RATE OF OUTPUT

point t_0, the increase in the saving rate causes saving and investment to increase, the stock of capital per head grows, and so does output per head. The process will continue at a diminishing rate. In Figure 17-5*b* we focus on the growth rate of output and capital. The growth rate of output is equal to the growth rate of population in the initial steady state. The increase in the saving rate immediately raises the growth rate of output because it implies a faster growth in capital and therefore in output. As capital accumulates, the growth rate decreases, falling back toward the level of population growth.

Population Growth

The preceding discussion of saving and the influence of the saving rate on steady-state capital and output makes it easy to discuss the effects of increased population growth. The question we ask is, What happens when the population growth rate increases from n to n' and remains at that higher level indefinitely? We will show that such an increase in the rate of population growth will raise the growth rate of output and lower the level of output per head.

The argument can be conveniently followed in Figure 17-6. Here we show the initial steady-state equilibrium at point C. The increase in the growth rate of population means that at each level of the capital-labor ratio, it takes a larger investment just in order to maintain the capital-labor ratio

FIGURE 17-6 AN INCREASE IN THE RATE OF POPULATION GROWTH REDUCES PER CAPITA INCOME

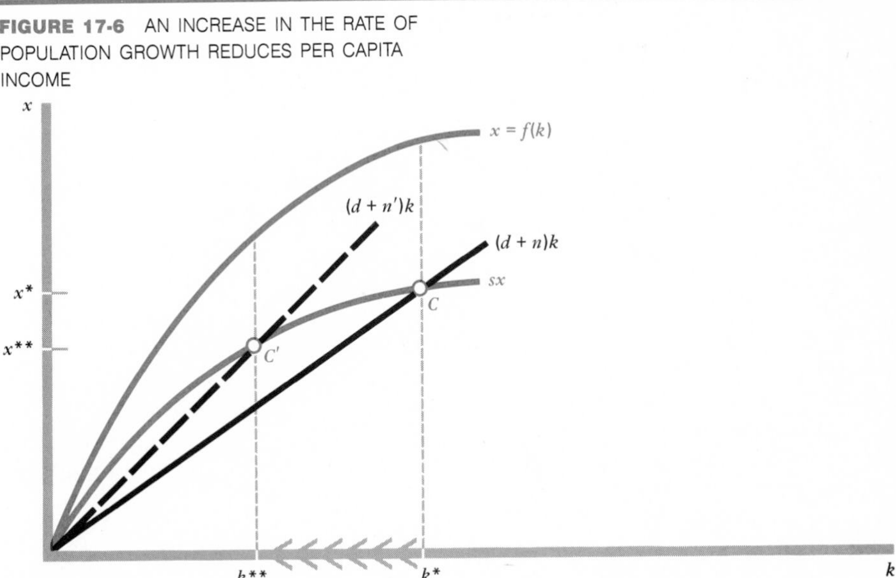

constant. Suppose we had ten machines per head. Initially, the growth rate of population is 1 percent and depreciation is 10 percent, so that we require per year 11 percent times 10 machines, or 1.1 machine, just to offset population growth and depreciation and thus maintain capital per head constant. To maintain the capital-labor ratio constant in the face of a higher growth rate of population, say 2 percent, requires a higher level of investment, namely, 12 percent as opposed to 11 percent. This is reflected in Figure 17-6 by an upward rotation of the investment requirement schedule.

It is clear from the preceding argument that we are no longer in steady-state equilibrium at point C. The investment that was initially just sufficient to keep the capital-labor ratio constant will no longer be sufficient in the face of higher population growth. At the initial equilibrium, the higher population growth with unchanged saving and investment means that capital does not grow fast enough to keep up with labor force growth and depreciation. Capital per head declines. In fact, capital per head will keep declining until we reach the new steady-state equilibrium at point C'. Here the capital-labor ratio has declined sufficiently for saving to match the investment requirement. It is true, too, that, corresponding to the lower capital-labor ratio, we have a decline in output per head. Output per head declines from x^* to x^{**}.

The decline in output per head as a consequence of increased population growth points to the problem faced by many developing countries. Fast growth in population, given the saving rate, means low levels of income per head. Indeed, in poor countries one can trace poverty, or low income per head, to the very high rate of population growth. With population growth, saving will typically be too small to allow capital to rise relative to labor and thus to build up the capital-labor ratio to achieve a satisfactory level of income per head. In those circumstances, and barring other considerations, a reduction in the rate of population growth appears to be a way of achieving higher levels of steady state per capita income and thus an escape from poverty.

Technical Progress[14]

The review of the empirical sources of growth showed that technical progress contributed almost one-half the average annual growth in real income between 1929 and 1969. So far, we have omitted technical progress from our growth model and simply studied the economy on the assumption of a given rate of population growth and given saving behavior. In such an

[14] The treatment is deliberately brief since technical progress in growth theory is a somewhat technical and taxonomic matter. The reader is referred to Robert Solow, *Growth Theory* (New York: Oxford University Press, 1970) for an exposition of these issues.

economy we saw that the growth rate of output converges to a steady-state growth rate exactly equal to the growth rate of population. As a consequence, in the steady state output per head is constant. In the steady state, saving, investment, and capital accumulation are just sufficient to maintain the capital-labor ratio constant and thereby ensure that output grows at the rate of population growth.

What happens, though, once we allow for technical progress which, after all, has historically been so important? Ths historical record shows that for the period 1929–1969, real income per head grew at the rate of 2.13 percent (= 3.41 − 1.28).[15] Three-quarters of that increase in real income per head was due to technical progress.

How do we incorporate technical progress in the analysis? First we note that with technical progress we have an additional source of growth. We would therefore expect that, even with a constant capital-labor ratio, output per head can be growing. In this sense we would expect technical progress—that is, a continuously shifting production function—to add to real growth per head. The next question is whether the economy would actually settle down to steady-state growth. Here the answer depends on the precise form that technical progress takes. If technical progress takes the form of a uniform increase in the productivity of factors so that at a given capital-labor ratio, output increases in the proportion of technical progress, then a steady state will in general not exist. The economy keeps growing at a rate faster than the rate of population growth and at a rate that is *not* constant.

By contrast, if technical progress were *labor-augmenting*, a steady state would exist. Here the idea is that technical progress renders a given labor force more effective. Technical progress of this variety operates as though it increased the growth rate of the labor force. With this special type of technical progress, the economy will indeed settle down to a steady state where output per head grows at a constant rate equal to the rate of technical progress. Thus, technical progress is in fact compatible with steady-state analysis; more important, it contributes to long-run growth in real income per head.

17-5 THE LIMITS OF GROWTH

This section briefly introduces the important and necessarily speculative question of where the economy is heading. The discussion becomes more general and raises the question of whether limited resources and the

[15] The average growth rate of total population from 1929 to 1969 was 1.28 percent. This is slightly less than the growth rate of labor hours of 1.32 percent shown in Table 17–2.

pressure of population on scarce land and food will ultimately bring the growth process to a dramatic halt. Are growing economies heading toward stagnation or even disaster?

We have first to raise the question of population and space. The world, being of finite size, cannot accommodate an ever-growing population. It is therefore quite apparent that unless other planets can be colonized, population growth has to decline. In fact, one of the serious problems of our time is that this is recognized and indeed happening in rich countries that can still cope relatively well with growing populations, while population growth has not been significantly reduced in poor countries. Although space is not yet clearly a problem in these countries, food shortages and poverty are certainly major problems.

The second preliminary point we have to raise concerns food. Even though we recognize that there is still a lot of space in the world to accommodate the physically growing world population, the question of food is a very serious one. Will there be enough food for the 5 billion people who are expected to be in the world by 1990? Experts agree to a significant extent that the food problem is largely a matter of distribution and income inequality, not a problem of the inability of the globe to produce enough food. With the right incentives, food can be produced, but there is the obvious problem that the poor may not be able to afford the costly food that could be produced. These issues are sufficiently important to warrant detailed study, and we refer the reader to an article by Lance Taylor and the references contained in it.[16]

There is a related question that we want to raise here. It is whether, abstracting from food considerations, we expect real income per head to keep growing. The question is whether the world will progressively encounter factors of production in limited supply that prevent continued growth. Factors that are essential to the production process, such as oil and minerals, are *exhaustible resources*, the available stocks of which appear to limit the growth process. This was clearly as true a hundred years ago as today and a question that could have been, and was, raised at that time.[17] With the benefit of hindsight, we would argue that new deposits of these resources have been discovered in the past at a rate much in excess of that at which we have used up resources. If anything, in the last hundred years the supplies of *known* resources have grown. This is the standard retort of the growth-oriented economist. The argument is perfectly valid as a matter of historical record, though it obviously is true, too, that the more we discover, the less there is to be discovered in the future.

A more important challenge to the limits set by exhaustible resources

[16] Lance Taylor. "The Misconstrued Crisis: Lester Brown and World Food," *World Development*, 1975. See also the World Banks *World Development Report* (Washington, D.C.: 1980) International Bank for Reconstruction and Development.

[17] See W. S. Jevons, *The Coal Question*, 1865, reprinted (New York: Augustus M. Kelley, 1965).

is technical progress. There is no doubt that much technical progress takes the form of inventions and processes that dispense with, or save on, scarce resources used up in production. The expectation or hope, then, is that the same technical progress that in the last century has proved an important source of real growth will continue to keep up real growth in per capita income in the face of limitational factors and exhaustible resources. More particularly, it is hoped and expected that economic incentives will divert resources to inventions and innovations precisely in the field of exhaustible and limited resources and ensure that they will not prove a bottleneck to the growth process.

There is no assurance that the right technical progress will come along and bail us out when coal, oil, and copper run short in supply. Perhaps one should not bank on technological progress, innovation, and ingenuity to help us out. At the same time, it would be irresponsible to dismiss entirely the extraordinary record of technical progress that has contributed around one-half the average growth in real income. There will surely continue to be technical progress. The major problem of social policy then becomes the channeling of resources in the right direction to ensure that research and effort are devoted to solving society's bottleneck problems. The market mechanism itself is a powerful instrument to achieve precisely that purpose, but may in some instances need a helping hand.

There is one further potential contributor to real growth in the face of limited resources. That is *economies of scale*. We have assumed in the previous section that production is subject to constant returns to scale and that productivity of factors is independent of the scale of operation of the economy. This implies that as capital and labor expand, output expands at the same rate without any gains in growth from the fact that the economy has become, as it were, a larger plant. Now the historical record reviewed here shows that returns to scale accounted for 10 percent of the annual average growth rate in real income in the United States economy from 1929 to 1969. As the economy expanded its use of capital and labor, output expanded more than proportionately, even holding the state of technology constant. Like technical progress, economies of scale are a potential counterweight against exhaustible resources. While exhaustible resources tend to put limits to growth, technical progress and economies of scale are sources of growth that help overcome or offset these limitational factors. Again, the only thing one can do is to point to their important role in history and argue that while nobody can or will guarantee their ocntinued benefit, there will surely be some contribution to growth that we should expect from economies of scale.

The subject of this section is one that cannot have a definite conclusion. This is a controversial question and an important one.[18] The

[18] William Nordhaus, "World Dynamics: Measurement without Data," *Economic Journal*, December 1973.

only message we can convey is that, historically, there have been important counterweights to the role of exhaustible resources, and that these will continue to make an important contribution toward growth in real per capita income. That balance is important to bear in mind and, indeed, to stimulate by the right social policies toward research and invention.

17-6 SUMMARY

1 A production function links factor inputs and technology to the level of output. Growth of output, changes in technology aside, is a weighted average of input growth with the weights equal to income shares. The production function directs attention to factor inputs and technological change as sources of output growth.
2 Growth theory studies the determinants of intermediate-run and long-run growth in output. Growth in factor supplies—labor and capital—and productivity growth or technological progress are the sources of growth. Saving behavior determines capital accumulation.
3 In United States history over the 1929–1969 period, growth in factor inputs and technical progress each accounted for roughly one-half the average growth rate of 3.4 percent of output. Growth in the stock of knowledge, along with growth in labor input, was the most important source of growth.
4 Per capita output grows faster, the more rapidly the capital stock increases and the faster is technical progress. In United States history since 1889, output per head has grown at an average rate of 1.8 percent.
5 Potential output grew at nearly 4 percent in the sixties, but its growth rate has fallen to around 3 percent since then. The fall is in large part due to the decline in productivity growth. The prospects for a return to the high productivity growth rates of the 1948–1973 period are slim, but some improvement from the poor performance of the late seventies is likely so long as rising energy prices do not disrupt the economy repeatedly.
6 The concept of steady-state equilibrium points (in the absence of technical change) to the conditions required for output per head to be constant. With a growing population, saving must be just sufficient to provide new members of the population with the economywide amount of capital per head.
7 The steady-state level of income is determined by the saving rate. In the absence of technical change, the steady-state growth rate of output is equal to the rate of population growth.
8 An increase in the growth rate of population raises the steady-state growth rate of total output and lowers the level of steady-state output per head.

9 An increase in the saving rate transitorily raises the growth rate of output. In the new steady state, the growth rate remains unchanged, but the level of output per head is increased.
10 With technical change, per capita output in the steady state grows at the rate of technical progress. Total output grows at the sum of the rates of technical progress and population growth.
11 Limits of growth pose a serious question for continued increases in real per capita income or even the maintenance of current consumption standards. The historical record is one of technological progress that offsets limitational factors and scarce resources. There is no certainty that this offset will continue, but public policy can make a contribution in that direction.

PROBLEMS

1 Which of the following government activities have effects on the long-term growth rate? Explain how they can do so.
   (*a*) Monetary policy
   (*b*) Labor market policies
   (*c*) Educational and research programs
   (*d*) Fiscal policy
   (*e*) Population control programs

*2 The assumption of constant returns to scale in the production function Equation (1) can be summarized as

$$F(bK, bN) = bF(K,N) \qquad \text{for any } b > 0$$

Using this fact, derive Equation (1*a*) from Equation (1) and explain why k is the only determinant of x.

*3 (*a*) Use the fact from microeconomics that capital is paid its marginal product to show that θ is the fraction of total income which is paid to capital.
   (*b*) Derive the $\Delta A/A$ term in Equation (3) from Equations (2) and (1*a*). Explain why, if $\Delta A/A = 0$, real output does not grow as rapidly as the capital-labor ratio.

*4 Present and explain the step-by-step derivation of Equation (4), using Equation (3) and the formulas leading up to Equation (4).

5 In Section 17-3, we related the growth rate of the capital-labor ratio to the growth rate of productivity. Use Equations (4) and (6) to show that

$$\frac{\Delta Z}{Z} = \theta\left(\frac{\Delta K}{K} - \frac{\Delta N}{N}\right) + \frac{\Delta A}{A}$$

Explain why a 1¼ percent fall in the growth rate of the capital-labor ratio would reduce the growth rate of productivity by about 0.3 percent.

6 Draw a figure like Figure 17-3 which indicates the adjustment process when $k_0 > k^*$. How does the adjustment process work? Explain Figure 17-3 in terms of the saving = investment identity.

7 (*a*) In the absence of technical progress, what happens to output per head and total output over time? Why?
(*b*) What is the long-run effect of the saving rate on the *level* of output per capita? On *growth* of output per capita?

8 Evaluate this statement: "The saving rate cannot affect the growth of output in the economy. That is determined by the growth of labor input and by technical progress."

*9 Suppose we assume a production function of the form

$$Y = AF(K,N,Z)$$

where Z is a measure of the natural resources going into production. Assume this production function obeys constant returns to scale and diminishing returns to each factor [like Equation (1)].
(*a*) What will happen to output per head if capital and labor grow together but resources are fixed?
(*b*) What if Z is fixed but there is technical progress?
(*c*) Interpret these results in terms of the limits to growth.

*10 Use the model of long-run growth to incorporate the government. Assume that an income tax at the rate t is levied and that, accordingly, saving per head is equal to $s(1 - t)x$. The government spends the tax revenue on public consumption.
(*a*) Use Figure 17-3 to explore the impact of an increase in the tax rate on the steady-state output level and capital per head.
(*b*) Draw a chart of the time path of capital per head, output per head, and the growth rate of output.
*(*c*) Discuss the statement: "To raise the growth rate of output, the public sector has to run a budget surplus to free resources for investment."

11 Use Figure 17-3 to explore the impact of a *once-and-for-all* improvement in technology.
(*a*) How does technical progress affect the level of output per head as of a given capital-labor ratio?
(*b*) Show the new steady-state equilibrium. Has saving changed? Is income per head higher? Has the capital stock per head increased?
(*c*) Show the time path of the adjustment to the new steady state. Does technical progress transitorily raise the ratio of investment to capital?

12 Consider an economy where a baby boom *transitorily* raises the growth rate of population from n to n'. After a few years, the growth rate of population falls back to the rate n.
(*a*) What is the impact of the baby boom on steady-state output per head?
(*b*) Show the adjustment process of the economy as the growth rate of population increases and then falls back to the initial level. Draw the time path of the variables shown in Figure 17-5.

13 Discuss the statement: "The lower the level of income, the higher the growth rate of output."

4
PART

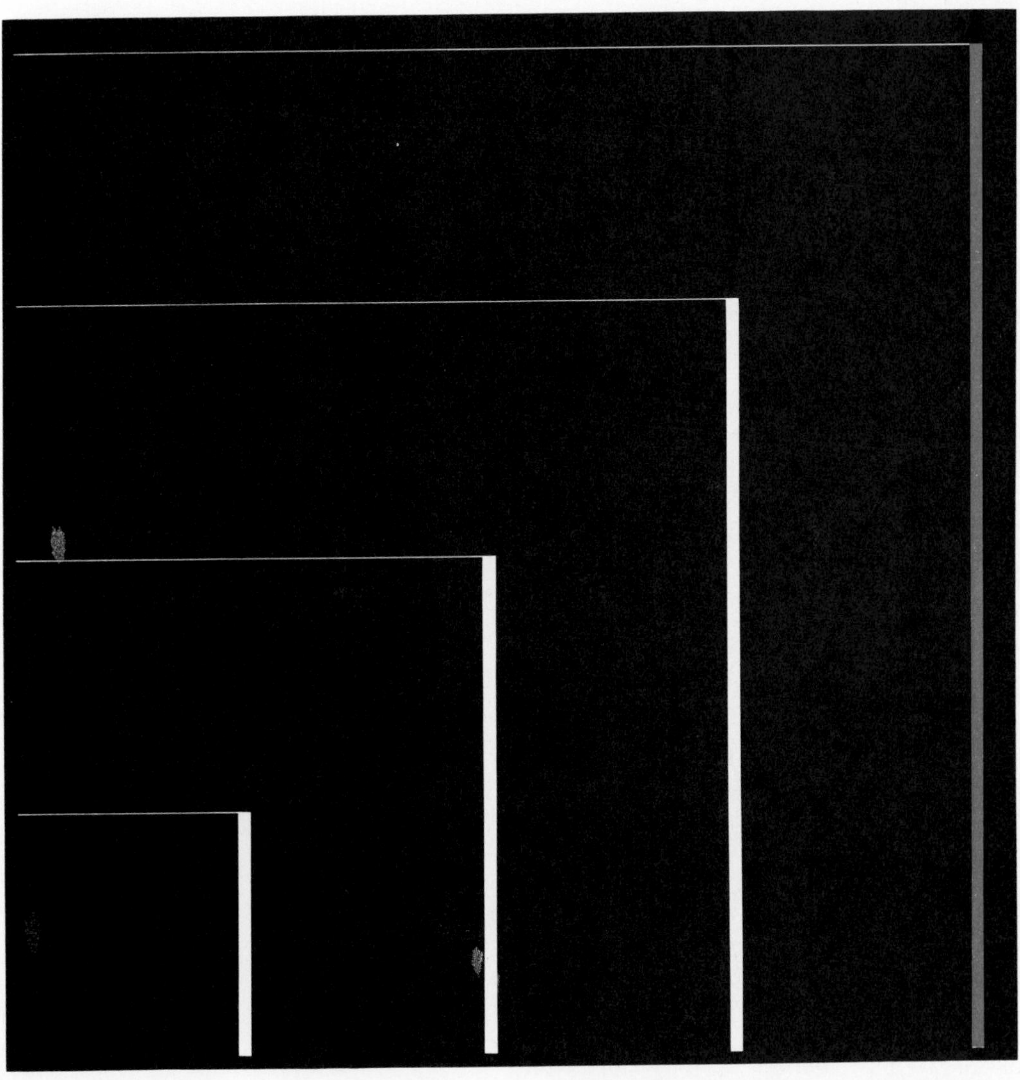

18

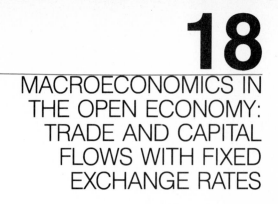

MACROECONOMICS IN THE OPEN ECONOMY: TRADE AND CAPITAL FLOWS WITH FIXED EXCHANGE RATES

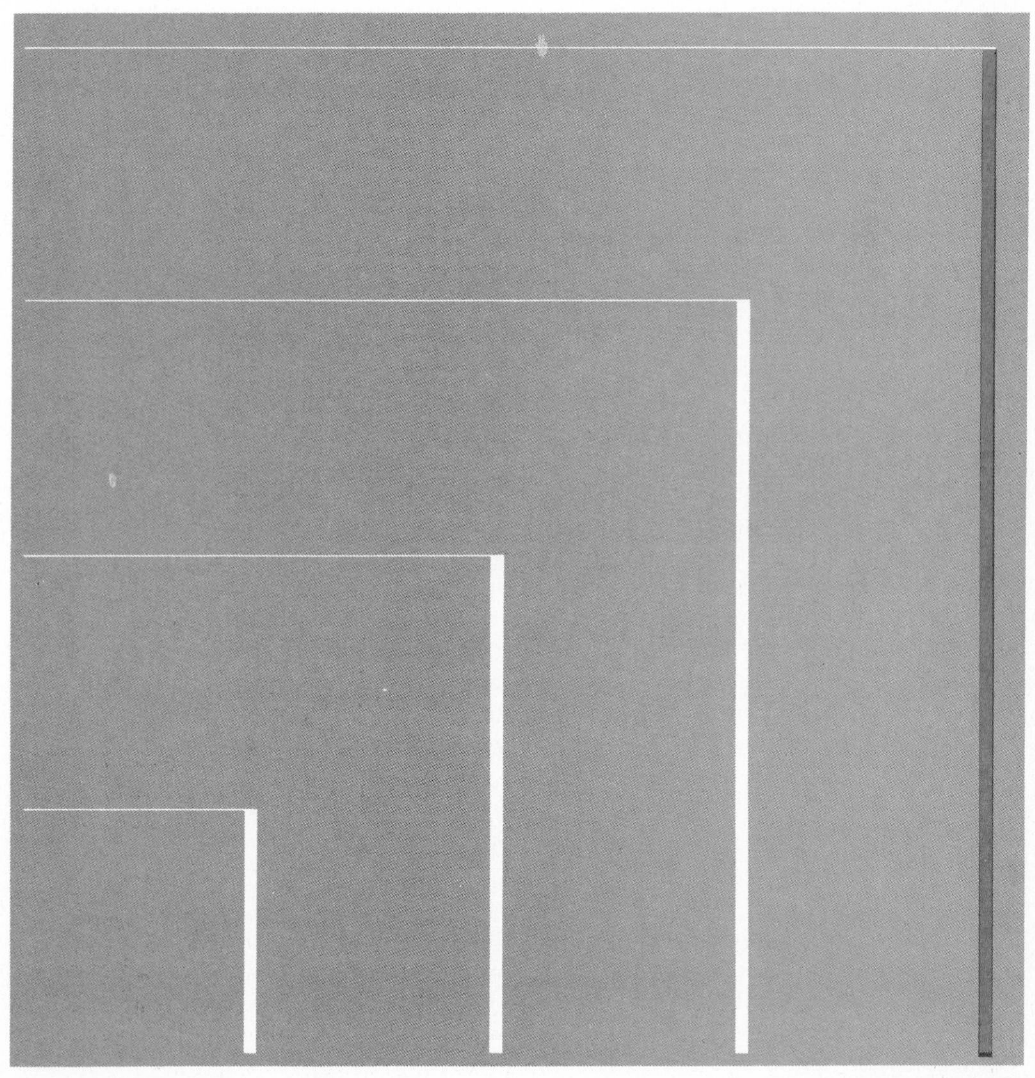

This is the first of two chapters analyzing foreign trade and its effects on the economy. It extends the macroeconomics we have learned to open economies—economies that trade with others. Trade among economies takes place in both goods and services—Americans buy German cars and Europeans buy American brokers' services, and in assets—Americans buy Japanese stocks and Arabs buy American real estate. Since all economies engage in international trade, all economies are open.

The degree of openness, as measured by the ratio of imports to GNP, varies widely. For the United States, the import-GNP ratio rose from about 3.5 percent in 1946 to more than 10 percent after the oil price increase in 1973. Britain imports an amount equal to about 40 percent of GNP, and the Netherlands about 50 percent. Trade is more important for most other economies than for the United States. Nonetheless, even for the United States, events connected with trade, such as the increase in oil prices in 1973–1974 and 1979-1980, can have serious effects on the economy.

This chapter begins with a brief description of the balance of payments accounts—the record of the country's transactions with other economies. Section 18-1 also describes the two basic exchange rate systems—*fixed* and *flexible rate* systems. In the fixed exchange rate system, central banks fix the dollar price of foreign currencies and stand ready to buy and sell foreign currencies at that price. The world was essentially on a fixed rate system from 1946 to 1973, though there were occasional adjustments of exchange rates during that period. In the flexible exchange rate system, the exchange rate is determined in the foreign exchange market and can change from moment to moment. After 1973, exchange rates between the dollar and other currencies were allowed to float, to be determined by the supply and demand for foreign exchange.

The rest of this chapter analyzes trade in goods and assets in a fixed exchange rate system. Section 18-2 abstracts from trade in assets and examines the way in which foreign trade affects goods market equilibrium, and the determinants of the balance of trade in goods and services. Section 18-3 examines the effects of devaluation and looks at the financing of deficits. Trade in assets is studied in Section 18-4, as are the implications of such trade for the conduct of monetary and fiscal policy. Chapter 19 presents an analysis of international trade under flexible exchange rates.

18-1 THE BALANCE OF PAYMENTS AND EXCHANGE RATE REGIMES

The *balance of payments* is the record of the transactions of the economy with the rest of the world. There are two main accounts in the balance of payments: the *current account* and the *capital account*. The current account records trade in goods and services, as well as transfer payments.

Services include freight, royalty payments, and interest payments. Transfer payments consist of remittances, gifts, and grants. We talk of a current account surplus if exports exceed imports plus net transfers to foreigners, that is, if receipts from trade in goods and services and transfers exceed payments on this account.

The capital account records purchases and sales of assets, such as stocks, bonds, and land. There is a capital account surplus, or a net capital *in*flow, when our receipts from the sale of stocks, bonds, land, bank deposits, and other assets exceed our payments for our own purchases of foreign assets.

Closely related to the current account are certain subaccounts that we mention here for completeness. The *trade balance* simply records trade in goods. Adding trade in services to the trade balance, we arrive at the *balance on goods and services.* Finally, adding net transfers, we arrive at the current account balance.

The simple rule for balance of payments accounting is that any transaction that gives rise to a payment by United States residents is a deficit item. Thus, imports of cars, use of foreign shipping, gifts to foreigners, purchase of land in Spain, or making deposits in a bank in Geneva are all deficit items. Surplus items by contrast would be United States sales of airplanes abroad, payments for United States licensing of foreign firms to use American technology, pensions received by United States residents from abroad, or foreign purchases of GM stocks.

The overall *balance of payments* is the sum of the current and capital accounts. If both the current account and the capital account are in deficit, then the overall balance of payments is in deficit. When one account is in surplus and the other is in deficit to precisely the same extent, the overall balance of payments is zero—neither in surplus nor in deficit.

Table 18-1 shows the United States balance of payments accounts for selected years. The current account—net payments for goods, services, and transfers—was in surplus throughout the 1960s. The pattern changed

TABLE 18-1 THE UNITED STATES BALANCE OF PAYMENTS ACCOUNTS *(in billions of dollars)*

	1960	1965	1970	1975	1978	1979
Current account	2.8	5.4	2.3	18.3	−13.5	− 0.3
Capital account	−5.4	−6.3	−12.4	−30.2	−31.7	−13.2
Errors and omissions	−1.0	− .5	− .2	5.9	10.7	28.7
Official reserve transactions	3.6	1.4	9.4	5.9	34.5	−16.3

Note: Numbers may not add because of rounding. Minus sign denotes a deficit.
Source: Economic Report of the President and *Economic Indicators.*

dramatically in the seventies, with the current account being in deficit in several years, and substantially so in 1978, as the table shows. The capital account reflects the rate of *net* purchases of assets from the rest of the world. The United States capital account has been consistently in deficit, and increasingly so in recent years. One reads in the press of foreigners investing in the United States by buying American firms, which tends to create a capital account surplus. (Be sure you know why.) However, the table shows that such capital inflows have been too small in total to create an overall capital account surplus.

Since any transaction which gives rise to a payment by United States residents to foreigners is a deficit item, an overall deficit in the balance of payments—the sum of the current and capital accounts—means that United States residents make more payments to foreigners than they receive from foreigners. Since foreigners want to be paid in their own currencies,[1] the question arises of how these payments are to be made.

In Table 18-1, the "Official reserve transactions" entry measures the overall balance of payments deficit.[2] When the overall balance of payments is in deficit[3]—when the sum of the current and capital accounts is negative—Americans have to pay more foreign currency to foreigners than is received. The Fed and foreign central banks provide the foreign currency to make payments to foreigners, and the net amount supplied is "official reserve transactions." When the United States balance of payments is in surplus, foreigners have to get the dollars with which to pay for their excess of payments to the United States over their receipts from sales to the United States. The dollars are provided by the central banks.

Before proceeding, we should dispose of the "Errors and omissions" entry. That entry arises because not all transactions between United States residents and foreigners are recorded. The federal government collects data on current and capital account payments, and also has data on official reserve transactions. If all transactions were recorded, the official reserve transactions would exactly balance the recorded current and capital account transactions. However, in practice the numbers do not add up, and the "Errors and omissions" entry is included to reconcile the recorded sum of

[1] An exception occurs if foreigners want to be paid in dollars to add to their assets. In that case, we conceptually separate out, first, our demand for imports, which gives rise to payments in foreign currency that appears in the current account, from, second, foreigners' demand for dollars, which appears in the capital account as an inflow.

[2] The presentation of balance of payments statistics as in Table 18-1 was stopped in mid-1976 after a review committee suggested that official reserve transactions are not a full measure of foreign exchange intervention. See "Report of the Advisory Committee on the Presentation of Balance of Payments Statistics," *Survey of Current Business*, June 1976.

[3] For the moment we ignore the "Errors and omissions" entry in Table 18-1 and talk as if it were zero. If it were zero, official reserve transactions would be precisely equal to the sum of current and capital account deficits.

current and capital accounts with the entry "Official reserve transactions." It is believed that most of the sometimes vast "Errors and omissions" are in the capital account.

Fixed Exchange Rates

We now return to the way in which central banks, through their official transactions, *finance* balance of payments surpluses and deficits. At this point we want to distinguish between fixed and floating exchange rate systems.

In a fixed rate system, foreign central banks stand ready to buy and sell their currencies at a fixed price in terms of dollars. In Germany, for example, the central bank, the Bundesbank, would buy or sell any amount of dollars in the 1960s at 4 Deutsche marks (DM) per United States dollar. The French central bank, the Banque de France, stood ready to buy or sell any amount of dollars at 4.90 French francs (FF) per United States dollar. The fact that the central banks were prepared to buy or sell *any* amount of dollars at these fixed prices or exchange rates meant that market prices would indeed be equal to the fixed rates. Why? Because nobody who wanted to buy United States dollars with French francs would pay more than 4.90 francs per dollar if dollars could be gotten at that price from the Banque de France. Conversely, nobody would part with dollars in exchange for francs for less than 4.90 francs per dollar if the Banque de France, through the commercial banking system, was prepared to buy dollars at that price.

In a fixed rate system, the central banks have to finance any balance of payments surplus or deficit that arises at the official exchange rate. They do that simply by buying or selling all the foreign currency that is not supplied in private transactions. If the United States were running a deficit in the balance of payments vis-à-vis Germany so that the demand for marks in exchange for dollars exceeded the supply of dollars in exchange for marks from Germans, the Bundesbank would buy the excess dollars, paying for them with marks.

Fixed exchange rates thus operate like any other price support scheme, such as in agricultural markets. Given market demand and supply, the price fixer has to make up the excess demand or take up the excess supply. In order to be able to ensure that the price (exchange rate) stays fixed, it is obviously necessary to hold an inventory of foreign exchange that can be sold in exchange for domestic currency. Thus, foreign central banks held *reserve* inventories—of dollars, and gold that could be sold for dollars—that they would sell in the market when there was an excess demand for dollars. Conversely, when there was an excess supply of dollars, they would buy up the dollars, as in our example of a United States balance of payments deficit vis-à-vis Germany.

What determines the amount of foreign exchange intervention—buying or selling of dollars in the foreign exchange market—that a central bank would have to do in the fixed exchange rate system? We already have the answer to that question. The balance of payments measures the amount of foreign exchange intervention needed from the central banks. So long as the foreign central bank has the necessary reserves, it can continue to intervene in the foreign exchange markets to keep the exchange rate constant. However, if a country persistently runs deficits in the balance of payments, the central bank eventually will run out of foreign exchange, and will be unable to continue its intervention.

Before that point is reached, the central bank is likely to decide that it can no longer maintain the exchange rate, and will *devalue* the currency. In 1967, for instance, the British devalued the pound from $2.80 per pound to $2.40 per pound. That meant it became cheaper for Americans and other foreigners to buy British pounds, and thus affected the balance of payments. We shall study the way in which devaluation affects the balance of payments in Section 18-3.

We have so far avoided being specific on exactly which central banks did the intervening in the foreign exchange market in the fixed rate system. It is clear that if there were an excess supply of dollars and an excess demand for marks, either the Bundesbank could buy the dollars in exchange for marks, or the Fed could sell marks in exchange for dollars. In practice, during the fixed rate period, each foreign central bank undertook to *peg* (fix) its exchange rate vis-à-vis the dollar, and most foreign exchange intervention was undertaken by the foreign central banks. The Fed was nonetheless involved in the management of the exchange rate system, since it frequently made dollar loans to foreign central banks that were in danger of running out of dollars.

Flexible Exchange Rates

We have seen that the central banks have to provide whatever amounts of foreign currency are needed to finance payments imbalances under fixed exchange rates. In flexible rate systems, by contrast, the central banks allow the exchange rate to adjust to equate the supply and demand for foreign currency. If today's exchange rate against the mark were 60 cents per mark, and German exports to the United States increased, thus increasing the demand for marks by Americans, the Bundesbank could simply stand aside and let the exchange rate adjust. In this particular case, the exchange rate could move from 60 cents per mark to a level such as 62 cents per mark, making German goods more expensive in terms of dollars and thus reducing the demand for them by Americans. We shall in Chapter 19 examine the way in which exchange rate changes under floating rates affect the balance of payments. The terms *flexible rates* and *floating rates* are used interchangeably.

Indeed, in a system of *clean floating*, central banks stand aside completely and allow exchange rates to be freely determined in the foreign exchange markets. The central banks do not intervene in the foreign exchange markets in a system of clean floating, and official reserve transactions would, accordingly, be zero in such a situation. That means the balance of payments would be zero in a system of clean floating: the exchange rate would adjust to make the current and capital accounts sum to zero.

In practice, the flexible rate system, since 1973, has not been one of clean floating. Instead, the system has been one of *managed* or *dirty floating*. Central banks have intervened to buy and sell foreign currencies, in attempts to influence exchange rates, and official reserve transactions have, accordingly, not been zero. Table 18-1 shows that there were official reserve transactions in 1975, for example. The reasons for this central bank intervention under floating rates are discussed in Chapter 19.

Terminology

The use of language with respect to exchange rates can be very confusing. In particular, the terms *depreciation* and *appreciation*, and *devaluation* and *revaluation*, will recur throughout this chapter and the next.

A *depreciation* of the exchange rate is an increase in the domestic currency price of foreign exchange. Thus, if the dollar price of marks moves from 40 cents per mark to 60 cents per mark, we talk of a depreciation of the dollar, or an appreciation of the mark. When our currency depreciates, we pay more units of domestic money per unit of foreign money. Conversely, an appreciation means that the domestic currency price of foreign money falls—we pay fewer dollars per unit of foreign money.

A further clarification concerns the difference between devaluation (revaluation) and depreciation (appreciation). The term *devaluation* is used to refer to the adjustment of a fixed exchange rate, such as the sterling devaluation of 1967 from $2.80 per pound to $2.40 per pound. A *depreciation*, by contrast, refers to an increase in the dollar price of foreign exchange under a flexible exchange rate system. There is no substantial economic difference between depreciation and devaluation.

Summary

1 The balance of payments accounts are a record of the transactions of the economy with other economies. The capital account describes transactions in assets, while the current account covers transactions in goods and services and transfers.
2 Any payment to foreigners is a deficit item in the balance of payments. Any payment from foreigners is a surplus item. The balance of payments

deficit (or surplus) is the sum of the deficits (or surpluses) on current and capital accounts.

3 Under fixed exchange rates, central banks stand ready to meet all demands for foreign currencies arising from balance of payments deficits or surpluses at a fixed price in terms of the domestic currency. They have to *finance* the excess demands for, or supplies of, foreign currency (that is, the balance of payments deficits or surpluses, respectively), at the pegged (fixed) exchange rate by running down, or adding to, their reserves of foreign currency.

4 Under flexible exchange rates, the demands for, and supplies of, foreign currency can be made equal through movements in exchange rates. Under clean floating, there is no central bank intervention and the balance of payments is zero. But central banks sometimes intervene in a floating rate system, engaging in so-called dirty floating.

The remainder of this chapter is concerned with the operation of a system of fixed exchange rates. We begin in Section 18-2 by abstracting from the capital account and dealing only with trade in goods. Section 18-3 examines the reasons for, and effects of, devaluation. Section 18-4 introduces the capital account and discusses the impact of trade in assets on the conduct of monetary and fiscal policy.

18-2 TRADE IN GOODS, MARKET EQUILIBRIUM, AND THE BALANCE OF TRADE

This section is concerned with the effects of trade in goods on the level of income, and the effects of various disturbances on both income and the trade balance—which, from now on, we use as shorthand for the current account. We also examine policy problems which arise when the balance of trade and the level of income require different corrective actions. The section concludes by introducing the important notion of the *policy mix*.

In this section, we shall be fitting foreign trade into the IS-LM framework, which is the basic income determination model of Chapter 4, and which continues to underlie the aggregate demand function used in later chapters. As in Chapters 3 and 4, we assume that the price level is given, and that output that is demanded will be supplied. As you no doubt appreciate by now, this assumption enables us to develop the details of the analysis most simply. It is both conceptually and technically easy to relax the assumption, and we shall briefly do so later. But it is important to be clear on how the introduction of trade modifies the analysis of aggregate demand, and for that reason we start from a familiar and basic level.

A word of warning is in order before you start working through the following sections. The exposition here assumes you are thoroughly at home with the IS-LM analysis, and therefore proceeds quite rapidly.

However, the material is not inherently more difficult than that of earlier chapters and should, with careful and active reading, be totally accessible.

Domestic Spending and Spending on Domestic Goods

In this subsection we want to establish how foreign trade fits into the IS-LM income determination model of Chapter 4. With foreign trade, part of domestic output is sold to foreigners (exports) and part of spending by domestic residents falls on foreign goods (imports). If we go back to income determination as studied in Chapters 3 and 4, it is apparent that the foreign trade complication will require some modification of our analysis.

The most important change is that it is no longer true that domestic spending determines domestic output. What is true now is that spending on domestic goods determines domestic output. Spending by domestic residents falls in part on domestic goods but in part on imports. Part of the typical American's spending is for imported beer, for instance. Demand for domestic goods that determines output, by contrast, includes exports or foreign demand along with part of spending by domestic residents.

The way in which external transactions affect the demand for domestic output was examined in Chapter 2. We provide a reminder by looking at the definitions:

$$\text{Spending by domestic residents} \equiv A \equiv C + I + G \tag{1}$$

$$\text{Spending on domestic goods} \equiv A + NX \equiv (C + I + G) + NX \tag{2}$$

where NX is the trade balance (goods and services) surplus. The definition of spending by domestic residents $(C + I + G)$ remains that of the earlier chapters. Spending on domestic goods is total spending by domestic residents, *less* their spending on imports *plus* foreign demand or exports. Since exports minus imports is the trade surplus, or net exports, NX, spending on domestic goods is spending by domestic residents plus the trade surplus.

With this clarification we can return to our models of income determination. We will continue to assume, as in Chapter 4, that domestic spending depends on the interest rate and income, so that we can write

$$A = A(Y,i) \tag{3}$$

Further, we assume for the present that foreign demand for our goods or exports X is given and equal to $\overline{X}$. Domestic demand for foreign goods, or imports Q, is assumed to depend only on the level of income, so that $Q = Q(Y)$. As income rises, part of the increase in income is spent on imports, while the rest is spent on domestic goods, or saved.

Now the trade balance is

$$NX \equiv X - Q = \overline{X} - Q(Y) \tag{4}$$

With our assumptions, the trade balance NX is a function only of the level of income. The trade balance is shown as a function of income in Figure 18-1. Imports are small at low levels of income, so that given the fixed level of exports, there is a trade surplus, $NX > 0$. As income rises, import spending increases until we reach income level Y_B, where imports match exports, so that trade is balanced. A further increase in income gives rise to a trade deficit. We can thus write

$$NX = NX(Y, \overline{X}, \ldots) \tag{4a}$$

where $\overline{X}$ denotes the given level of exports and the dots denote the other variables, such as exchange rates and prices, which we hold constant for now. We repeat that, as in Chapters 3 and 4, we assume that domestic prices are given. Here we shall also assume that foreign prices are fixed. These assumptions are relaxed below.

Goods Market Equilibrium

There is equilibrium in the domestic goods market when the amount of output produced is equal to the demand for that output. The value of output

[4] We are thus implicitly assuming that all factors of production are owned by domestic residents, who in turn own no factors of production abroad. If foreigners owned some of the factors of production located in our country, part of the value of output produced would be paid to foreigners and the value of output produced would exceed the income of domestic residents unless our residents earned more from their ownership of foreign factors than we paid to foreign owners of domestic factors.

FIGURE 18-1 THE TRADE BALANCE AS A FUNCTION OF INCOME

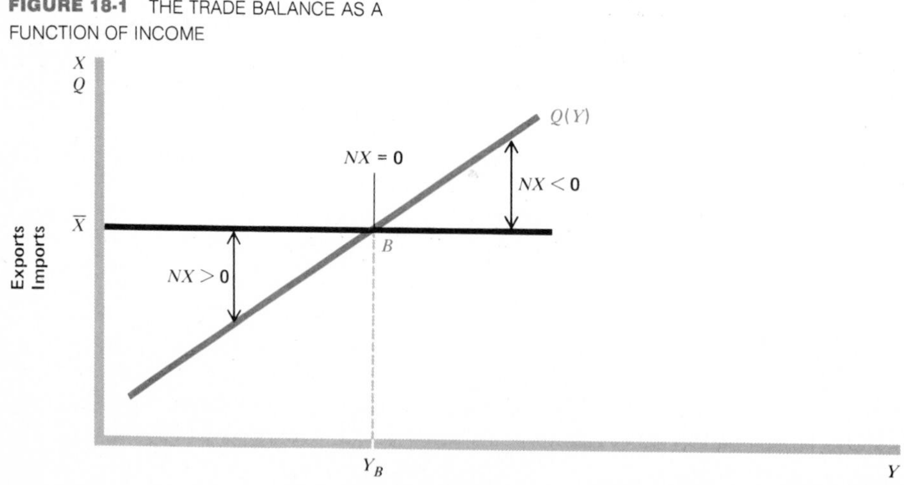

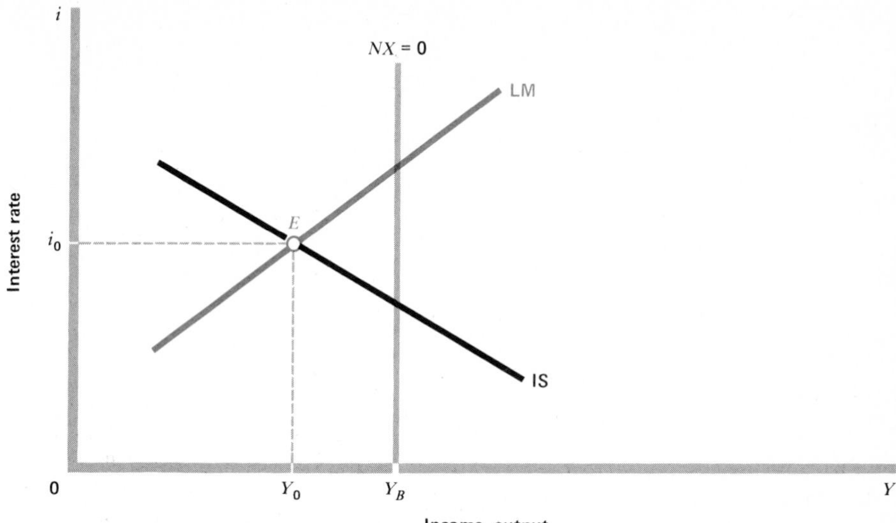

FIGURE 18-2 GOODS AND MONEY MARKET EQUILIBRIUM

produced continues to be equal to income.[4] The equilibrium here is different from that in Chapter 3 in that the demand for domestically produced goods includes net exports:

$$Y = A(Y,i) + NX(Y,\overline{X}, \ldots) \tag{5}$$

Figure 18-2 illustrates the goods market equilibrium condition (5). We still refer to it as a goods market equilibrium schedule, or IS curve, though it is important to recognize that now the trade surplus, or net exports, *NX*, appears as a component of demand for output. The schedule is downward-sloping because an increase in output gives rise to an excess supply of goods: the increase in income is only partly spent on domestic goods, the rest being saved or spent on imports. To compensate for the excess supply, interest rates would have to decline to induce an increase in aggregate demand. The IS schedule is drawn for the given level of foreign demand $\overline{X}$.

We have also shown, in Figure 18-2, the trade balance equilibrium schedule $NX = 0$. Given exports, we see from Figure 18-1 and Equation (4) that there is some level of income, Y_B, at which import spending exactly matches export revenue, so that trade is balanced. Points to the left of the $NX = 0$ schedule are points of trade surplus. Here income and hence import spending are low relative to exports. Exports accordingly exceed imports. Points to the right of the $NX = 0$ schedule, by contrast, are deficit points. Here income and hence import spending are too high relative to exports for trade to be balanced. Finally, we have drawn, too, the LM schedule, which is precisely the same as in our study of the closed economy.

Equilibrium Income and the Balance of Trade

The next question to address, using Figure 18-2, is where the short-run equilibrium of the economy will be. It will be at point E, the intersection of the IS and LM curves. The reason is: Trade need not be balanced. In the short run, a trade balance deficit can be financed by running down foreign exchange reserves and a surplus can be financed by building up reserves. The assumption then is that the central bank finances the trade deficit by selling foreign exchange and thus maintains the exchange rate at its pegged level in the face of a trade and balance of payments deficit, or that the bank purchases foreign exchange if there is a surplus.[5] We assume the goods and money markets clear sufficiently quickly so that equilibrium is determined at point E in Figure 18-2. As we have drawn the equilibrium, the trade balance is in surplus.

Disturbances

How do internal and external disturbances—shifts in the level or composition of spending, or changes in exports—affect equilibrium income and the balance of trade? To answer that question, it is important to remember that both the IS and the trade balance schedules are drawn for a given level of exports, $\overline{X}$.

We can think of three types of disturbances, the effects of which we will briefly analyze in turn: (1) an increase in autonomous domestic spending that falls on our own goods, (2) an increase in exports, and (3) a shift in demand from domestic goods to imports. Before going through the exercises, we want to indicate the results we expect to find. There are two results that we should expect. First, any increase (decrease) in spending on our goods should result in an increase (decrease) in equilibrium income. Second, we would expect the trade balance to worsen if domestic income expands, but we would expect it to improve if exports rise or if there is an autonomous decline in imports. It is not so clear how an increase in exports affects the trade balance. Say exports increase and, as a consequence,

[5] We are abstracting here from a complication that is suggested by our study of the money supply process in Chap. 8. We saw there that foreign exchange transactions have an effect on high-powered money and thus on the money supply. Thus, a trade deficit would cause the central bank to lose foreign exchange and, as a counterpart, would cause the monetary base and the money supply to fall. We assume that the central bank automatically engages in offsetting open market operations that keep the money supply constant. In the case of a deficit, such a "sterilization operation" would require a purchase of debt in the open market to offset the reduction in the monetary base due to the trade deficit, as we saw in Chap. 8.

domestic income rises. This income increase, in turn, raises import spending, and we are not certain whether the net effect on the trade balance is an improvement or a worsening. What we can show is that the net effect is actually an improvement—induced import spending dampens but does not offset the trade balance improvement resulting from an increase in exports.

The Effects of an Increase in Autonomous Spending

With these preliminary remarks, we can proceed to our analysis. First, consider an autonomous increase in our spending on domestic goods, perhaps because of expansionary fiscal policy. In Figure 18-3 we show the effect to be a shift in the IS curve. At the initial equilibrium E, there is an excess demand for goods and, accordingly, the equilibrium income level will increase. The new equilibrium is at point E', where output and interest rates have risen and where we have a reduction in the trade surplus. The expansion in output will have increased import spending, and thus at E' the trade surplus is less than at E. The first lesson is, therefore, that expansionary domestic policies or autonomous increases in spending will raise income but will, too, cause a worsening of the trade balance.

There is a second point worth making, and that concerns the size of the income expansion induced by an expansionary policy. By comparison with a closed economy, we have less of an expansion in an open economy.

FIGURE 18-3 THE EFFECTS OF AN INCREASE IN DOMESTIC SPENDING

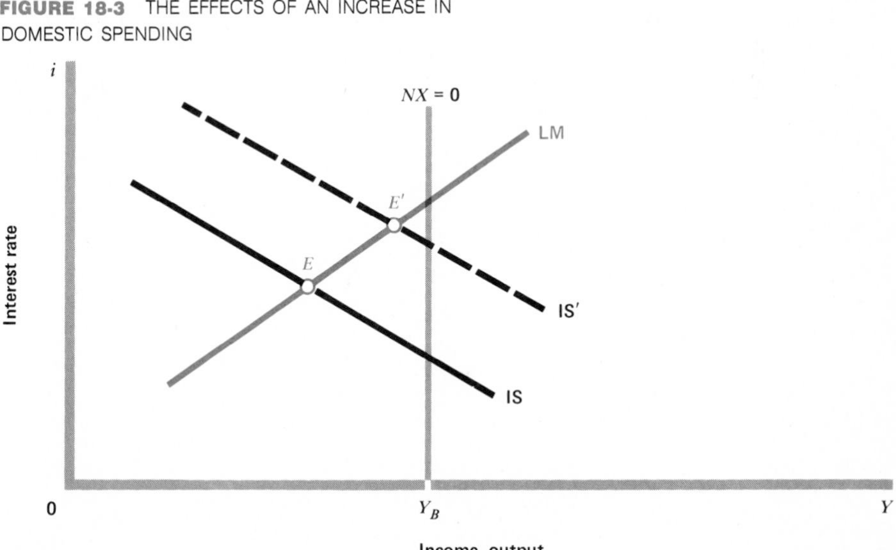

Multipliers are smaller because induced spending on domestic goods is less. Induced spending is less than in a closed economy because part of an increase in income is now spent on imports rather than domestic goods. Imports are a *leakage* from the domestic multiplier process. Because the spending on imports induced by income increases does not increase demand for domestic output, they reduce the size of the multipliers. Indeed, the larger the fraction of an increase in income that is spent on imports, the smaller the multiplier, because there is relatively little induced spending on domestic goods.

The Effects of an Increase in Exports

The next disturbance we consider is an increase in exports. An increase in exports raises the demand for domestic goods and thus shifts the IS curve to the right (to IS′), as shown in Figure 18-4. At the same time, the increase in exports implies that at each level of income the trade balance is improved and that, therefore, the trade balance equilibrium schedule shifts out and to the right. It takes a higher level of income to generate the import spending to match the higher level of exports. Thus, the trade balance schedule shifts to $NX' = 0$. Starting from a position of balanced trade at point E, we find that the increase in exports raises equilibrium income and improves the balance of trade at point E'. The first part is quite intuitive. Higher demand for our goods leads to an increase in equilibrium output. The trade balance

FIGURE 18-4 THE EFFECT OF AN INCREASE IN EXPORTS

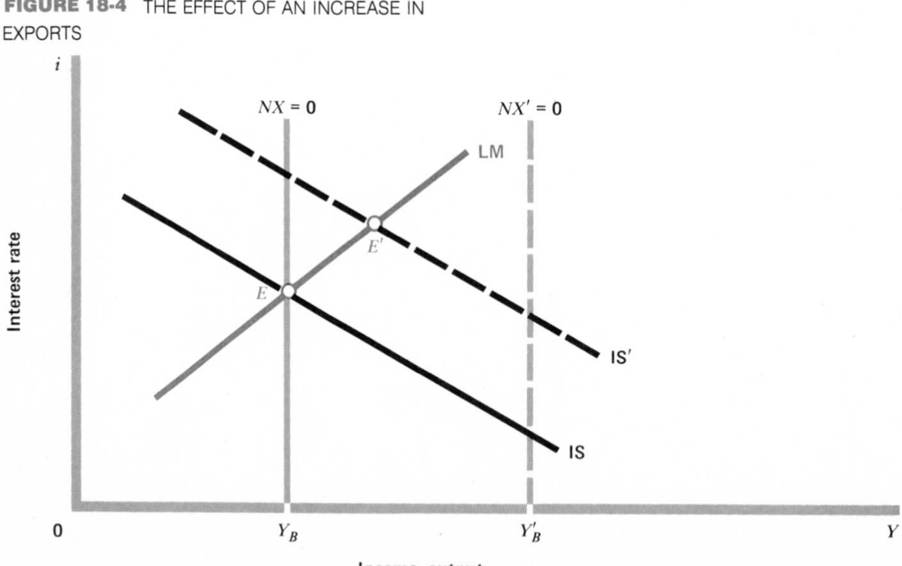

improvement, though, is less intuitive. Clearly, the increase in exports by itself improves the trade balance, but the increase in income leads to increased import spending which, it seems, could perhaps offset the direct improvement from the export increase. This is in fact not the case, and we leave the demonstration of that result as a problem.[6]

A Shift in the Composition of Demand

The last disturbance we consider is a shift in demand from imports to domestic goods. You will recognize that this has the same effects as an increase in exports. It means increased demand for domestic goods and also an improvement in the trade balance.

Internal and External Balance

We have now constructed and used, in Figures 18-2 through 18-4, our basic diagrammatic apparatus for embodying trade in the IS-LM model. We can draw on the analysis of income and trade balance determination to ask about economic policy making. From a policy perspective we would want to be able to achieve both *internal* and *external* balance. Internal balance means that output is at the full-employment level Y_p. External balance is interpreted here as trade balance equilibrium.

It is clear enough why internal balance should be an aim of policy. But why is external balance desirable? In a fixed exchange rate world, balance of payments deficits cannot be maintained indefinitely, as the financing of the deficits requires the country to use its reserves of foreign currency. Such reserves will run out in the face of continual deficits. Hence, a country on a fixed exchange rate cannot aim to run a balance of payments deficit[7] indefinitely. On the other side, a country on fixed rates wants to avoid running a permanent surplus because that causes it to acquire foreign currencies to add to its reserves indefinitely. Since the foreign exchange could be used to buy and consume foreign goods, the country is permanently forgoing some consumption it could otherwise have had, when it chooses to run permanent balance of payments surpluses.

The policy problem is illustrated in Figure 18-5. The problem is that for a given level of exports we may not be able to achieve *both* internal and external balance. In Figure 18-5, we have drawn the trade balance schedule, $NX = 0$, for the given level of exports. We have drawn, too, the full-employment level of output Y_p, and the two lines do not coincide.

We can break up Figure 18-5 into three regions, as shown in Table

[6] See problem 3 at the end of this chapter.

[7] In the absence of capital movements, and grants, remittances, etc., the balance of payments is equal to the balance of trade.

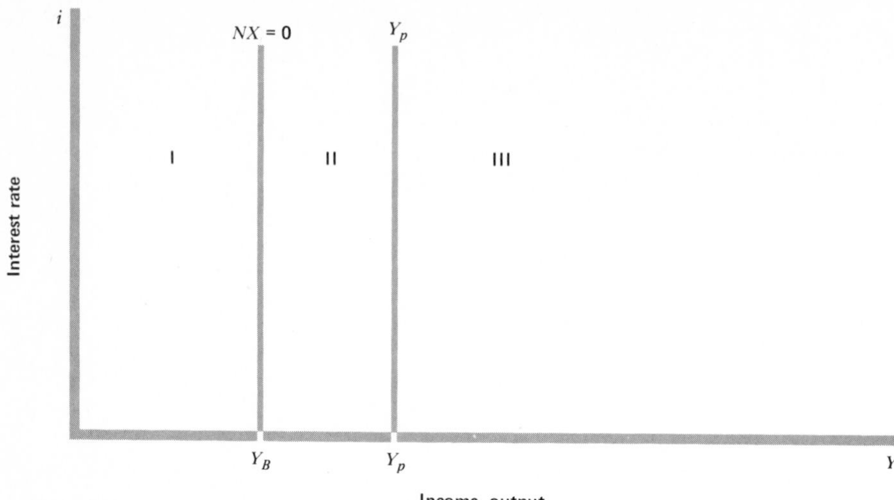

FIGURE 18-5 INTERNAL AND EXTERNAL BALANCE AND THE POLICY DILEMMA

18-2. To the left of the trade balance schedule, as we saw before, we have a trade surplus and to the right we have a deficit. To the left of the Y_p schedule, we have underemployment and to the right we have overemployment.

From a policy viewpoint, regions I and III present no problem. In region I we want to pursue an expansionary policy so as to raise employment *and* reduce the trade surplus. Until we get to trade balance equilibrium, there is no issue, since both the internal and external targets call for expansionary policies. Similarly, in region III we want to pursue restrictive policies to reduce overemployment and the trade deficit. Until we get to full employment, there is no issue. The dilemma area is region II. Here we have to choose whether we want to use tight policies to achieve trade balance equilibrium, or expansionary policies to achieve full employment. Not only are we unable to reach both targets simultaneously by manipulating aggregate demand, but any attempt to reach one target gets us further away from the other. Such a situation is called a *policy dilemma*,

TABLE 18-2 EXTERNAL AND INTERNAL BALANCE CONFLICT

	I	II	III
Employment	Under	Under	Over
Trade balance	Surplus	Deficit	Deficit

and it can always arise when there are more targets of policy than instruments with which to move the economy toward its targets. In our case we have only one policy instrument—aggregate demand policies—but we have two independent targets—external and internal balance.

The policy dilemma that is pointed out by Figure 18-5 can be solved by finding another policy instrument to cope with the multiple targets. It is quite apparent that what is needed is some policy that shifts the trade balance schedule to the right until it overlaps with the full-employment level of output line, Y_p. An obvious policy would be to cut down on imports at each level of income. Such a policy would reduce import spending at each level of income and thus shift the trade balance schedule to the right.

How can we cut import spending? We can use any of a number of tools, among them tariffs and exchange rate changes. Tariffs are excise taxes on imported goods. A tariff would raise the cost of imports to domestic residents and thereby divert demand away from imports to domestic goods. A 10 percent tariff on imported shoes, for instance, makes imported shoes more expensive relative to domestically made shoes, and shifts demand to locally made shoes. A devaluation, as we shall see, would achieve the same effect by raising import prices relative to the prices of domestically made goods. In summary, the point is that if we have a trade deficit at full employment—as is the case in Figure 18-5—we require a policy that directly affects the trade balance so as to give us trade balance equilibrium at full employment.

The Use of Expenditure Switching and Expenditure Reducing Policies

The argument of the previous subsection needs to be spelled out in more detail to focus attention on a subtle and important point: policies to shift spending from imports to domestic goods generally also affect aggregate demand in the goods market. Accordingly, policies to shift the $NX = 0$ line generally have to be accompanied by policies that adjust aggregate demand.

Figure 18-6 shows a situation in which the level of output in the economy is at Y_p, but the balance of payments is in deficit, since the $NX = 0$ line is to the left of Y_p. As we saw earlier in this chapter, aggregate demand policies cannot, in this case, both keep us at full employment and reduce the trade deficit. Consider using a tariff which shifts demand from imports to domestic goods. By using the tariff, we reduce import spending and shift the trade balance line to the right until it coincides with the full-employment line.

But the tariff will also affect the demand for domestic goods. The spending which at a given level of income no longer goes to imports goes to domestic goods instead. We are simply *switching* expenditures from imports to domestic goods. Accordingly, the tariff shifts the IS curve out to the right to IS′. We therefore have to use a further policy to offset the

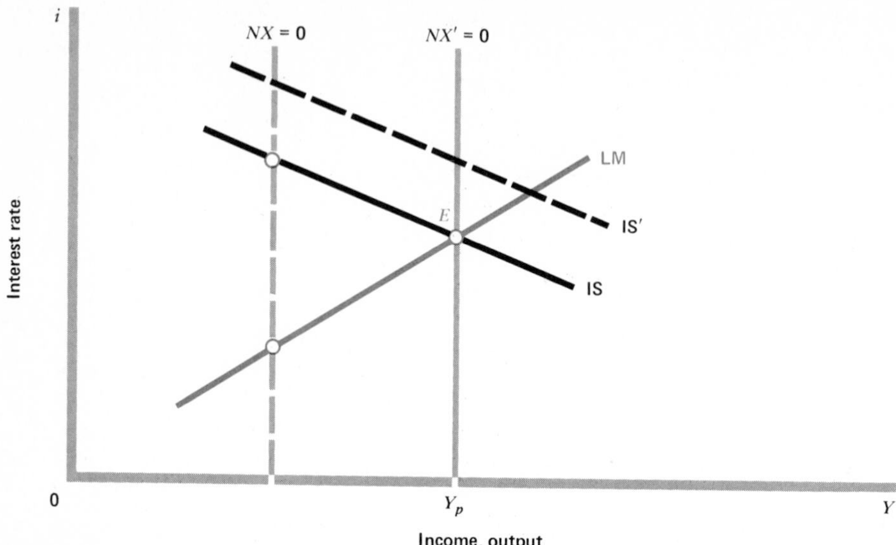

FIGURE 18-6 THE POLICY DILEMMA WITH A BALANCE OF TRADE DEFICIT

expansionary effect of the tariff in the domestic goods market. We could use either monetary or fiscal policy to shift the economy's equilibrium back to the full-employment level Y_p.

The important point, then, is that, in general, it is necessary to combine both *expenditure switching* policies, which shift demand between domestic and imported goods, and *expenditure reducing* (or *expenditure increasing*) policies, to cope with the targets of internal and external balance. This point is of general importance and continues to apply when we take account of capital flows and other phenomena omitted in this section.

Interdependence and Repercussion Effects

The next topic to be taken up in this section is the interdependence of income determintion in the world economy. An increase in income in one country (country A), by spilling over into imports, will affect demand for output abroad and thus will lead, in turn, to a foreign expansion in imports from country A. These *spillover effects* in the income determination process have two implications: (1) Countries, in general, cannot decide on appropriate stabilization policies without knowing what policies or income levels will prevail abroad and hence what the world demand for their exports will be. This suggests that coordination of stabilization policy between countries is desirable. (2) One country's income and import expansion spills over to increases in income abroad. But, in addition, the foreign income increase which the spillover induces leads to increased foreign import demand. There is thus a *repercussion effect* that we have so far ignored by assuming that export demand is autonomous. The repercussion effect is the additional effect on country A's income caused by the reaction of foreign countries' income to an initial increase in aggregate demand in country A.

We consider first the problem posed by spillover effects. It is actually a very important one. For example, during the 1975 world recession, some countries, like Germany, were relying on the United States recovery to pull them out of their own recession. How? It was expected that United States monetary and fiscal policies would stimulate the United States level of income and therefore United States imports. With part of United States imports coming from Germany, this would have led to increased German exports. Increased exports, in turn, mean increased income and employment. Thus, a recovery in Germany could clearly have been started off by an increase in exports. For obvious reasons, such a recovery is called an *export-led recovery*.

A critical question in the policy decision to wait for an increase in foreign demand rather than to undertake domestic action must be the size of the impacts of one country's income growth on another country's exports and thus on the latter's income. In the specific context of Germany, the question would be by how much would a 1 percent increase in United States income, say, increase German income. If the number were of the order of 0.5 percent, then United States growth could make an important contribution to German recovery, and disregard of United States policy could lead to serious policy errors.

Table 18-3 provides estimates of the size of repercussion effects and the importance of international linkages. The table, derived from an econometric model of the OECD, shows income multipliers associated with an expansion in one country on that country itself and on other countries.[8] Consider first the case of the United States. An increase of one percentage point in United States autonomous spending would raise United States income by 1.47 percent. What is the impact on selected other countries? Looking at the top row, we find that German income growth rises by about ¼ percent and the same is true for Japan. Thus, the United States expansion does affect these countries, although the size of the effect is not overwhelming. The comparison with Canada is of interest here. A United States

[8] The OECD (Organization for Economic Cooperation and Development) is a grouping of industrialized countries, based in Paris and serving as a framework for international policy discussion. Among the members are the few listed in Table 18-3, plus Italy, the United Kingdom, France, and seventeen others.

TABLE 18-3 THE INTERNATIONAL TRANSMISSION OF AGGREGATE DEMAND DISTURBANCES

Initiating country/group (1 percent increase in autonomous spending)	Affected country or group *(percentage change in income)*				
	United States	Germany	Japan	Canada	OECD
United States	1.47	.23	.25	.68	.74
Germany	.05	1.25	0.6	0.6	.23
Japan	.04	.05	1.26	.06	.21
Canada	.06	.03	.03	1.27	.10
OECD	1.81	2.38	1.84	2.32	2.04

Source: OECD Occasional Paper, "The OECD International Linkage Model," January 1979.

expansion by 1.47 percent raises Canadian income growth by nearly 0.7 percent. Thus Canada appears considerably affected by United States expenditure disturbances. The last entry in the top row of Table 18-3 shows the impact of a United States expansion on industrialized countries as a group. The impact here is to increase the group's combined income by three-quarters of a percentage point.[9]

Consider for comparison a Canadian expansion. The multiplier for Canadian income growth of a 1 percent increase in Canadian autonomous spending is 1.27, about the same as for the United States. The impact on the rest of the world is quite minor, though. The most substantial impact is on the United States (0.06 percent induced income growth) and only 0.03 percent increased growth for Germany or Japan.

What determines the size of multipliers and spillover effects? There are three chief factors to be taken into account in interpreting the multiplier patterns revealed in Table 18-3. First, the size of the country is important. A Canadian expansion, for example, induces only a small percentage increase in United States income because a given dollar change in Canadian income and imports will be only a small fraction of United States income. By contrast, a given increase in United States income and imports will be a relatively large fraction of Canadian income.

The second important determinant of multiplier patterns is openness to trade. The spillover effects of an expansion in any one country on the rest

[9] Do you see why the relative effect on total OECD income (0.74 percent) of a 1 percent increase in United States autonomous spending is smaller than the relative effect on United States income (1.47 percent)?

of the world will be more substantial, the more open the expanding economy.[10]

The third point to note is the extent to which trade patterns are reflected in the multipliers. The United States, for example, benefits relatively more from a Canadian expansion than does Germany. This reflects the fact that Canada has a high marginal propensity to import from the United States in comparison with its propensity to import from Germany.

Table 18-3 allows us to study not only the effects of an individual country's expansion and the induced spillovers but also the effect of a simultaneous joint expansion in all industrialized countries. The last row of the table provides the multipliers for this experiment. Clearly, if all countries expand together—each raising autonomous expenditure by 1 percent—the multiplier effects are much more substantial. Each country benefits not only from its own expansion and its repercussion effects through induced expansion abroad but also from the autonomous foreign expansion. Accordingly, the multipliers are around 2 in this case, while being in the range of 1.2 to 1.5 for the case of an isolated expansion.

We can now return to the question of export-led recoveries and ask what contribution United States real growth could have made to Germany. That answer from Table 18-3 is that the impact would not have been large. In the short run, United States autonomous spending would have to increase by more than 4 percent (1/0.23) to raise German income by only one percentage point. The transmission effect in this instance would have been quite small, although for a case like Canada, United States growth is a critically important determinant of Canada's short-run growth performance.

Interdependence, Relative Growth, and the Current Account

The effects of changes in the level of income in one country on income in another, studied in the preceding section, are transmitted through changes in the levels of imports and exports. The spillover and repercussion effects therefore also produce effects on the current account.[11] A country that is growing rapidly will tend to increase its imports relatively fast. The current

[10] There is, however, an offset to this, since a more open economy (as measured by the marginal propensity to import) will have a smaller multiplier, so that a given demand expansion will induce a smaller increase in imports. The net effect of more openness, though, is to increase the spillover effects. In problem 6 at the end of this chapter, we ask you to check this statement using the standard multiplier model of Chap. 3, extended to allow for trade.

[11] Estimates of current account effects of expansion in different countries are provided in OECD Occasional Paper, "The OECD International Linkage Model," January 1979.

account of the rapidly growing country will therefore tend to go into deficit.

Such effects have been important for the United States in the past few years. Table 18-4 presents relevant facts on income growth and the current account. The "Big Six" are Japan, Germany, France, the United Kingdom, Canada, and Italy, the United States' major trading partners within the OECD. Consider first 1975, the trough of the worldwide recession. United States income fell absolutely by 1.3 percent, more of a decline than the 0.3 percent fall abroad. With the substantial fall in income at home relative to that abroad, our *net* imports fell very substantially, and, consequently, the current account shows a record surplus for that year. The magnitude of the worldwide recession in 1975 reflects the fact that the decline in activity in each area spread, through multiplier effects, throughout the world, thus deepening the recession. In 1976, growth patterns were roughly the same, and the United States experienced a reduction in the current account, surplus. An interesting year is 1977. Here United States growth ran substantially ahead of growth abroad. The consequence was a massive turnaround in the United States current account, a deficit of $14 billion. With nearly matching growth rates, there remained a deficit in 1978.

A word of warning is needed here. The behavior of the current account reflects more than relative income growth. Other factors, such as changes in the exchange rate, exogenous shocks such as the oil price increase, shifting trade patterns due to the emergence of new competitors and the spread of technology abroad, all affect the current account as well. Even so, Table 18-4 is highly suggestive in pointing to the United States' *relative* cyclical performance as an essential determinant of the current account.

External Balance, Money, and Prices

The analysis has been developed so far on the assumption that domestic prices do not respond at all to changes in demand. This is a convenient assumption for expository purposes, but we know it is not realistic. We

TABLE 18-4 REAL INCOME AND THE UNITED STATES CURRENT ACCOUNT

	1975	1976	1977	1978	1979
		Real income growth *(percent per year)*			
United States	−1.3	5.9	5.3	4.4	2.3
Big Six	− .3	5.4	3.3	4.3	4.3
		Current account *(billions of dollars)*			
United States	18.3	4.6	−14.1	−13.5	−0.3

Source: Economic Report of the President and *OECD Economic Outlook.*

therefore show now how a more complete model—parallel to the aggregate demand and supply analysis of Chapter 12—would look in an open economy.

We start by reviewing the main points of Chapter 12. Aggregate demand depends on the level of prices. A higher level of prices implies lower real balances, higher interest rates, and lower spending. In an open economy, the relation is slightly more complicated because now an increase in our prices reduces demand for our goods for two reasons. The first is the familiar higher interest rate channel summarized above. The second reason arises because an increase in our prices makes our goods less competitive with foreign-produced goods. When the prices of goods produced at home rise, and given the exchange rate, our goods become more expensive for foreigners to buy, and their goods become *relatively* cheaper for us to buy. An increase in our prices is thus an increase in the *relative price* of the goods we produce, and shifts demand away from our goods toward imports, as well as reducing exports.

In summary, then, an increase in our price level reduces the demand for our goods both by increasing the interest rate (and reducing investment demand) and by reducing net exports—by making the goods we produce relatively more expensive than foreign-produced goods. In Figure 18-7 we show the downward-sloping demand schedule for our goods, D. Demand is

FIGURE 18-7 OPEN ECONOMY MACROECONOMIC EQUILIBRIUM WITH PRICE ADJUSTMENT

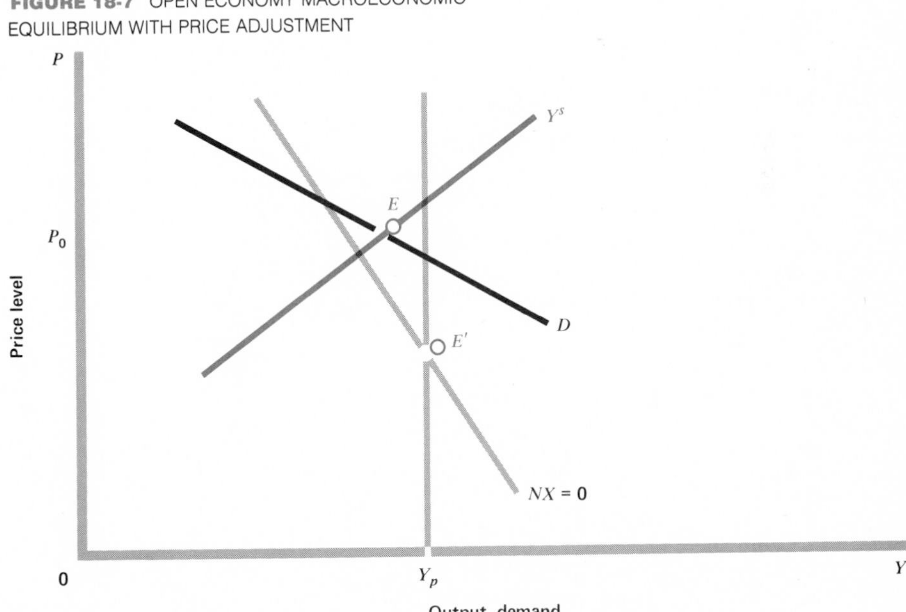

equal, as before, to aggregate spending by domestic residents, A, plus net exports, NX:

$$D \equiv A + NX \tag{6}$$

The demand for domestic goods, D, is drawn for a given level of foreign prices, a given nominal money supply, and given fiscal policy. Remember, too, that the exchange rate is fixed. An increase in the nominal money stock shifts the schedule upward, as does expansionary fiscal policy. We have shown, too, the short-run aggregate supply schedule, Y^s, and the full-employment level of output, Y_p. Initial equilibrium is at point E, where we have unemployment.

Next we look at the trade balance equilibrium schedule, $NX = 0$. An increase in our income raises imports and worsens the trade balance. To restore trade balance equilibrium, domestic prices would have to be lower. This would make the home country more competitive, raise exports, and reduce imports. Thus, we show the trade balance equilibrium schedule as downward-sloping.[12] We assume that it is steeper than the demand schedule for domestic goods. The schedule is drawn for a given level of prices abroad. The short-run equilibrium at point E is one where the home country has a trade deficit. Our prices are too high or our income is too high to have exports balance imports. To achieve trade balance equilibrium, we would have to become more competitive, thus exporting more and importing less. Alternatively, we could reduce our level of income in order to reduce import spending.

The Adjustment Process

Consider next the policy options from an external and internal balance point of view. At point E there is unemployment and a deficit. To restore full employment, we could expand aggregate demand, or else wait for wages and prices to fall sufficiently to raise the demand for our goods through the interest rate and increased net exports channels. From an external point of view, we have to achieve a decline in income or in prices to restore balance.

Point E' is a point at which we have both internal and external balance. At E', we have full employment and balanced trade. But we cannot get to that point except through a protracted recession that cuts domestic prices sufficiently to shift the aggregate supply schedule down. This adjustment

[12] We assume that a decline in prices improves the trade balance. This requires that exports and imports are sufficiently responsive to prices. There is a possibility that a reduction in our price level (which reduces the prices of our exports) lowers our revenue from exports—because the increased sales are not sufficient to compensate for the lower prices. We shall assume that this possibility does not occur. We assume, too, that import spending does not depend on the interest rate.

process would indeed occur if the government did not pursue any stabilization policy and simply pegged the exchange rate. The process is sufficiently important to deserve more attention.

First we look at the aggregate demand side. We remember that there is a link between the central bank's holdings of foreign exchange and the domestic money supply, assuming now no sterilization, as defined in footnote 5. When the central bank pegs the exchange rate, selling foreign exchange, it reduces domestic high-powered money and therefore the money stock. This is exactly what happens in the case of a deficit. Thus the trade deficit at point E implies that the central bank is pegging the exchange rate, selling foreign exchange to keep the exchange rate from depreciating, and reducing the domestic money stock. It follows immediately that over time the aggregate demand schedule (which is drawn for a given money supply) will be shifting down and to the left. On the aggregate supply side, we remember that unemployment leads to a decline in wages and costs, which is reflected in a downward-shifting aggregate supply schedule. Over time, therefore, the short-run equilibrium point E moves down as both demand and supply schedules shift. The points of short-run equilibrium move in the direction of point E', and the process will continue until that point is reached. (The approach may be cyclical, but that is not of major interest here.)

Once point E' is reached, we have achieved long-run equilibrium. Because the trade balance is in equilibrium, there is no pressure on the exchange rate and therefore no need for exchange market intervention. Accordingly, there is no influence from the trade balance on the money supply and thereby on aggregate demand. On the supply side, we have reached full employment. Therefore wages and costs are constant, so that the supply schedule is not shifting. At point E' we have a combination of relative prices, demand, and employment that gives both internal and external balance. The adjustment of the level of prices ensures that we can have—in the long run—both full employment and trade balance equilibrium.

The adjustment process we have just described is called the *classical adjustment process*. It relies critically on price adjustments and an adjustment in the money supply based on the trade balance. The adjustment process "works" in the sense that it moves the economy to a long-run equilibrium of internal and external balance. However, the mechanism is far from attractive. There is no good case for a protracted recession simply to achieve a cut in prices. A preferable policy is to resort to expenditure switching policies, or to exchange rate changes, as a means of achieving internal and external balance.[13]

[13] An exchange rate depreciation or shifts in demand from imports to domestic goods would shift both the net export schedule and the aggregate demand schedule up and to the right.

The Monetary Approach to the Balance of Payments

How important are monetary considerations in explaining balance of payment problems? Is it true that balance of payments deficits are a reflection of an excessive money supply? These questions must be raised because it is frequently suggested that external balance problems are monetary in nature.

There is a simple first answer. It is obviously true that for any given balance of payments deficit, a sufficient contraction of the money stock will restore external balance. The reason is that a monetary contraction, by raising interest rates and reducing spending, generates a contraction in economic activity, a decline in income, and therefore a decline in imports. It is equally true that this result could be achieved by tight fiscal policy, so there is nothing especially monetary about this interpretation of remedies for external imbalance.

A more sophisticated interpretation of the problem recognizes the link, examined in the previous section, between the balance of payments deficit, foreign exchange market intervention, and the money supply. The automatic mechanism is for a sale of foreign exchange—as arises in the case of deficits—to be reflected in an equal reduction in the stock of high-powered money. The central bank merely sells one asset (foreign exchange) and buys another (high-powered money). This process will automatically lead to a decline in the stock of money in deficit countries and an increase in the money stock in surplus countries. Given that the money supply is thus linked to the external balance, it is obvious that this adjustment process must ultimately lead to the right money stock so that external payments are in balance. This process was shown in Figure 18-7.

The only way the adjustment process can be suspended is through *sterilization operations*. We discussed this in Chapter 8 on the money supply. There we noted that central banks frequently offset the impact of foreign exchange market intervention on the money supply through open market operations. Thus, a deficit country that is selling foreign exchange and correspondingly reducing its money supply may offset this reduction by open market purchases of bonds that restore the money supply. Clearly, with such a practice, the automatic adjustment mechanism is suspended. Persistent external deficits are possible because the link between the external imbalance and the equilibrating changes in the money stock is broken. It is in this sense that persistent external deficits are a monetary phenomenon: the central bank actively maintains the stock of money too high for external balance.

The emphasis on monetary considerations in the interpretation of external balance problems is called the *monetary approach* to the balance of payments.[14] The monetary approach has been used extensively by the

[14] For a collection of essays on this topic, see Jacob Frenkel and Harry G. Johnson (eds.), *The Monetary Approach to the Balance of Payments* (London: Allen & Unwin, 1976). See also International Monetary Fund, *The Monetary Approach to the Balance of Payments* (Washington, D.C., 1977).

International Monetary Fund (IMF) in its analysis and design of economic policies for countries in balance of payments trouble. We can give the flavor of the approach by describing typical IMF procedure in analyzing a balance of payments problem.

We start with the balance sheet of the monetary authority, typically the central bank, as in Table 18-5. The monetary authority's liabilities are high-powered money, as explained in Chapter 8. But we recognize on the asset side that it can hold both foreign assets—including foreign exchange reserves, gold, and claims on other central banks or governments—and domestic assets, or *domestic credit.* Domestic credit consists of the monetary authority's holdings of claims on the public sector—government debt—and claims on the private sector—usually loans to banks.

From the balance sheet identity, we have

$$\Delta NFA = \Delta H - \Delta DC \tag{7}$$

where ΔNFA denotes the change in net foreign assets, ΔH the change in high-powered money, and ΔDC the change in domestic credit. In words, the change in the central bank's holdings of foreign assets is equal to the change in the stock of high-powered money minus the change in domestic credit.

Now the important point about Equation (7) is that ΔNFA is the balance of payments: recall from Section 18-1 that official reserve transactions, which is all that ΔNFA is, are equal to the balance of payments.

The first step in developing a stabilization policy package is to decide on a balance of payments target, ΔNFA^*. We want to ask how much of a deficit we can afford and then adjust policies to make the projected deficit no larger. The target will be based largely on the availability of loans and credit from abroad and the possibility of drawing down existing reserves. The next step is to ask how much the demand for money in the country will increase. The planned changes in the stock of high-powered money ΔH^* will have to be just sufficient to produce, via the money multiplier process, the right increases in the stock of money to meet the expected increase in demand. Then, given ΔNFA^* and ΔH^*, Equation (7) tells the monetary authority how much domestic credit it can extend consistent with its balance of payments target and expected growth in money demand. Typically, a stabilization plan drawn up by the IMF will include a suggested limit on the expansion of domestic credit.

TABLE 18-5 BALANCE SHEET OF THE MONETARY AUTHORITIES

Assets	Liabilities
Net foreign assets (NFA)	High-powered money (H)
Domestic credit (DC)	

The limit provides a *ceiling on domestic credit expansion*. The adoption of such a numerical ceiling could be useful in helping the central bank avoid the temptation of expanding its loans to the government or private sector in the face of rising interest rates or government budget deficits.

The simplicity of Equation (7) raises an obvious question. Since all it takes to improve the balance of payments is a reduction in the rate of domestic credit expansion, why not balance payments immediately and always? To answer this question, we need to understand the channels through which the curtailment of domestic credit improves the balance of payments.

Essentially, controlling domestic credit means operating a tight money policy. Consider an economy that is growing and has some inflation, so that the demand for nominal balances is rising. If domestic credit expansion is slowed, then domestically supplied increases in the money stock are lower than the increase in demand, and an excess demand for money develops. This, in turn, causes interest rates to rise and spending to decline. The increase in interest rates tends to improve the capital account and the reduction in spending tends to improve the current account, thus leading to a balance of payments improvement. That is, the monetary approach as used by the IMF relies on restrictive monetary policy to control the balance of payments. But there is a subtle difference between domestic credit ceilings and ordinary tight money. In an open economy with fixed exchange rates, the money stock is endogenous. The central bank cannot control the money stock, since it has to meet whatever demand arises for foreign currency. But it can make "money" tight by reducing the growth of domestic credit. That will imply that the only source of money growth becomes an increase in foreign exchange reserves or foreign borrowing. That means the economy has to go through enough of a recession or rise in interest rates to generate a balance of payments surplus.

The use of domestic credit ceilings is a crude policy to improve the balance of payments. But the simplicity of the conceptual framework, and the apparent definiteness of the policy recommendations to which it leads, frequently make it the best policy tool available, particularly if dramatic action is needed.

Proponents of the monetary approach have also argued that depreciation of the exchange rate cannot improve the balance of payments except in the short run. The argument is that in the short run, the depreciation does improve a country's competitive position and that this very fact gives rise to a trade surplus and therefore to an increase in the money stock. Over the course of time, the rising money supply raises aggregate demand and therefore prices until the economy returns to full employment and external balance. Devaluation thus exerts only a transitory effect on the economy which lasts as long as prices and the money supply have not yet increased to match fully the higher import prices.

The analysis of the monetary approach is entirely correct in its insistence on a longer-run perspective in which prices and the money stock adjust and the economy achieves internal and external balance. It is also correct in arguing that monetary or domestic credit restraint will improve the balance of payments, though the mechanism through which this policy works is more difficult than proponents of the approach typically indicate. The approach is misdirected when it suggests that exchange rate policy cannot, even in the short run, affect a country's competitive position. More important, exchange rate changes frequently occur from a position of deficit and unemployment. In that case, a depreciation moves the economy toward equilibrium. It eases the adjustment mechanism by achieving an increase in competitiveness through an increase in import prices rather than through a recession-induced decline in domestic prices.

Summary

We have covered a lot of ground at a hard pace, and it is worthwhile seeing where we have been and where we are going. In this section we amended our previous analysis to allow for trade in goods. As yet, we have not taken into account trade in assets. We were assuming that the exchange rate was fixed, and that the central bank had enough reserves to meet any demands for foreign currency that might occur as a result of balance of payments deficits. Through most of the section, we assumed that domestic and foreign price levels were fixed. This assumption was relaxed at the end.

The major points were:

1 The introduction of trade in goods means that spending by domestic residents is no longer equal to the demand for domestically produced goods. Some of the demand for goods of our residents goes for imports, and some of the demand for our goods comes from foreigners, to whom we export.
2 There is equilibrium in the goods market when the demand for our goods, consisting of spending by domestic residents, plus net exports, is equal to the output of domestic goods, which is equal to the income of domestic residents under specified conditions.
3 In short-run equilibrium, there is no guarantee that trade balances. In our simplest model, there is a unque level of income at which trade balances, and which is not necessarily the income level at which the economy comes into short-run equilibrium.
4 An increase in autonomous demand for domestic goods increases domestic output and worsens the trade balance. An increase in imports reduces domestic output and worsens the trade balance. An increase in exports increases domestic income and reduces the trade deficit. A shift in demand toward domestically produced goods increases the level of income and reduces the trade deficit, or increases the trade surplus.
5 Because trade does not necessarily balance in short-run equilibrium,

there may be a *policy dilemma* in attempting both to move income to the potential output level and to balance trade. An increase in the level of income, to move it closer to potential, may well worsen the trade balance.

6 The use of *expenditure switching* policies, which change the relative prices of domestic and imported goods, combined with *expenditure reducing* policies, can move the economy to full employment with balanced trade.

7 Because foreigners' demands for our goods—our exports—are their imports, and because their imports depend on their level of income, the demand for our goods depends on the foreign level of income. Further, because an increase in their income increases our exports and increases our level of income, and therefore our imports, there are *repercussion effects* by which a change in foreign income eventually induces an increase in the demand for their goods through exports. The size of these interdependence and repercussion effects depends on the relative size and openness of the economy. A small economy may be very dependent on a larger one, but a large economy's level of income does not depend much on the income level in small foreign economies.

8 Once we allow for price flexibility with fixed exchange rates, we use the analytical apparatus of Chapter 12. We see that price flexibility ultimately leads an economy to full employment with balanced trade. The mechanism involves changes in the domestic money supply which occur as the central bank keeps selling foreign exchange to domestic residents in exchange for domestic currency (essentially an open market sale of foreign currency). The falling money stock reduces our prices and therefore improves the balance of trade. Policy can be used actively to bring about adjustments without relying on this automatic and slow-moving mechanism.

9 The monetary approach to the balance of payments emphasizes the central bank's balance sheet identity, Equation (7), which shows that sufficient contraction of domestic credit will improve the balance of payments. The process through which this improvement comes about will require higher interest rates and lower domestic income. We should also note that the link between the balance of payments and the domestic stock of money, which is central to the monetary approach, can easily be broken through sterilization operations by the central bank.

So much for where we have been. In the next section, we compare the alternatives of *financing* a trade deficit by the central bank's drawing down its reserves (or by borrowing) with adjustment through *devaluation*. Then in Section 18-4 we introduce trade in assets, so-called *capital mobility*, and analyze its implications for stabilization policy.

18-3 FINANCING OF DEFICITS AND DEVALUATION

In a fixed exchange rate system, it is possible for the central bank to use its reserves to finance temporary imbalances of payments—that is, to meet the excess demand for foreign currency at the existing exchange rate arising from balance of payments deficits. Other ways of *financing* temporary payments imbalances are also available. A country experiencing balance of payments difficulties can borrow foreign currencies abroad. The borrowing may be undertaken either by the government (usually the central bank) or by private individuals. Although borrowing may be undertaken to finance both current and capital account deficits, we concentrate in this section on the current account.

A current account deficit cannot be financed by borrowing from abroad without raising the question of how the borrowing will be repaid. Clearly, if the counterpart of the current account deficit is productive domestic investment, there need be little concern about paying back the interest and capital borrowed. The investment will pay off in terms of increased output, some of which may be exported, or which may replace goods that previously were imported. The investment would thus yield the foreign exchange earnings with which to *service* (make payments on) the debt. However, problems may well arise in repaying the foreign debt if borrowing is used to finance consumption spending.

Maintaining and financing a current account deficit indefinitely or for very long periods of time is impossible. The alternative to financing deficits is *adjustment* of the current account through policy measures to reduce the deficit. We examined in Section 18-2 one method of adjusting a current account deficit, through the imposition of tariffs. However, tariffs cannot be freely used to adjust the balance of trade, partly because there are international organizations and agreements such as GATT (General Agreement on Tariffs and Trade) and the IMF (International Monetary Fund) that outlaw, or at least frown on, the use of tariffs. Tariffs have generally fallen in the post-World War II period as the industrialized world has moved to desirably freer trade between countries.

Another way of adjusting a current account deficit is to use restrictive domestic policy. In this regard, it is worth repeating that a trade deficit reflects an excess of expenditure by domestic residents and the government over income. In Chapter 2 we showed that

$$NX \equiv Y - (C + I^a + G) \tag{8}$$

where NX is the trade surplus and I^a is actual investment. Thus, a balance of trade deficit can be reduced by reducing spending $(C + I + G)$ relative to income (Y). The trade deficit can, accordingly, be eliminated by reducing aggregate demand, by reducing C, or G, or I. In terms of Figure 18-6, the trade deficit can be eliminated by using restrictive monetary and/or fiscal policy to shift the intersection of the IS and LM curves to the level of income at which trade balances. The costs of such a policy, in terms of unemployment, are obvious.

The unemployment that typically accompanies adjustment through recession and the desirability of free trade, which argues against the use of tariffs, both suggest that an alternative policy for reconciling internal and external balance be considered. The major policy instrument for dealing with payments deficits in the dilemma situation is *devaluation*—which usually has to be combined with restrictive monetary and/or fiscal policy. A devaluation, as we noted in Section 18-1, is an increase in the domestic currency price of foreign exchange. Given the nominal prices in the two countries, devaluation increases the relative price of imported goods in the devaluing country and reduces the relative price of exports from the devaluing country.

Table 18-6 shows the effects of an exchange rate shift on relative prices. Recall that we are assuming that nominal prices in the home currency in each country are fixed. We assume that we (Americans) produce and export Chevrolets and they (Germans) produce and export VWs. The Chevrolet is priced at $5,000 and a VW at DM10,000. These prices, in terms of the respective producer's currencies, are assumed to remain constant. Now, at an exchange rate of $0.40 per mark, the relative price of a VW in terms of Chevrolets is $4,000/$5,000 = 0.8, meaning that a VW costs 80 percent as much as a Chevrolet. Next, consider a devaluation of the dollar by 50 percent. The table shows that the dollar price of a VW rises and that the mark price of a Chevrolet declines. Both in the United States and in Germany, Chevrolets become *relatively* cheaper, or VWs become relatively more expensive. The dollar devaluation lowers the mark price of United States goods and raises the dollar price of German goods. The exchange ratio for German and United States cars now becomes $6,000/$5,000 = 1.20, so that a VW now costs 20 percent more than a Chevrolet. Clearly, the increase in the relative price of German goods will affect the pattern of

TABLE 18-6 THE EFFECT OF EXCHANGE RATE CHANGES ON RELATIVE PRICES

	Volkswagen	Chevrolet
Dollar price		
(a) $0.40/DM	$4,000	$5,000
(b) $0.60/DM	$6,000	$5,000
DM price:		
(a) $0.40/DM	DM10,000	DM12,500
(b) $0.60/DM	DM10,000	DM 8,333

demand, increasing both United States and German demands for Chevrolets at the expense of the demand for VWs.

How does a devaluation assist in achieving internal and external balance? Let us take first a special case of a country that has been in full employment with balance of trade equilibrium, as shown by point E in Figure 18-8. Now let there be an exogenous decline in export earnings, so that the $NX = 0$ schedule shifts to the left to $NX' = 0$. At the given exchange rate and relative prices—that is, prices of domestic goods relative to world prices—the foreign demand for domestic goods is assumed to decline. In the absence of domestic policy intervention, and with fixed rates, the short run and intermediate-run adjustment would be one of a decline in output and income. The IS schedule moves to the left as a result of the fall in exports and the resultant income decline at the point E' lowers imports, but not enough to make up for the loss of export revenue. The net effect is therefore unemployment and a trade deficit.

Next, we ask how the home country can adjust to the loss of export markets. One possibility is for the home country to go through an adjustment process of declining domestic wages and prices as the high unemployment slowly reduces wages or slows down their rate of increase. Such an adjustment would, over time, lower domestic costs and prices as compared with the prices of foreign goods. The home country would gain in competitiveness in world markets and thus restore export earnings and employment. There is no doubt that this is a feasible adjustment process, and, indeed, is the process that would occur by itself, given enough time.

An alternative solution is to recognize that in order to restore full employment and export earnings, the home country must become more competitive in the prices charged for exports and imports. To restore competitiveness, domestic costs and prices have to decline *relative* to foreign prices. That adjustment can occur in two ways: (1) through a decline in domestic costs and prices at a given exchange rate and (2) through a depreciation of the exchange rate with unchanged domestic costs and prices.

The latter strategy has the obvious advantage that it does not require a protracted recession to reduce domestic costs. The adjustment is done by a stroke of the pen—a devaluation of the currency. Why would a devaluation achieve the adjustment? *Given* prices of foreign goods in terms of foreign currency (e.g., the mark prices of German goods), a devaluation, as shown in Table 18-4, raises the relative price of foreign goods. The effect is to induce an increased demand for American goods and a reduction in demand for imports in the United States.

The case we have just considered is special, however, in one important respect. The economy was initially in balance of trade equilibrium at full employment. The disturbance to the economy took place in the trade account. Accordingly, if we could move the $NX = 0$ locus back to the full-employment level of income—as we could with a devaluation—both internal and external balance would be attained. Put differently, the reason there was an internal balance problem of unemployment in Figure 18-8 was the reduction in exports and consequent external balance problem. Both problems could thus be cured through devaluation.

In general, we cannot cure *both* internal and external problems by a simple devaluation. The general case will require expenditure shifting through, say, a devaluation and a policy affecting the level of spending. To make that point, we look at the case of an increase in domestic spending that falls entirely on imports. This is studied in Figure 18-9, where we start from a full equilibrium at point E. The increase in import spending comes entirely at the expense of saving, and consequently there is no change in demand for domestic goods and thus no shift in the IS curve. The trade balance schedule, however, shifts to the left. Since people now spend more on imports at each level of income, a lower income level is required to achieve trade balance. Thus, the trade balance schedule shifts to $NX' = 0$. Now it is apparent that the only effect of the disturbance is to create a trade deficit. There is no counterpart to that disturbance in the domestic goods market.

Suppose, next, we correct the trade deficit by devaluation, thus shifting the trade balance schedule back to the full-employment level of output. This does not solve the entire problem because the devaluation now diverts demand from foreign to domestic goods, and thus the IS curve shifts

FIGURE 18-8 THE EFFECTS OF A DECLINE IN EXPORTS ON INCOME AND THE TRADE BALANCE

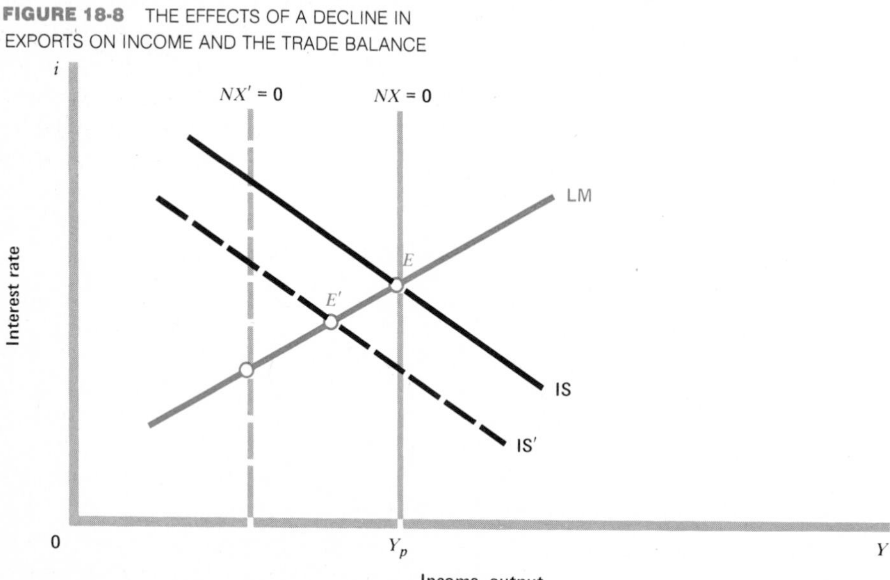

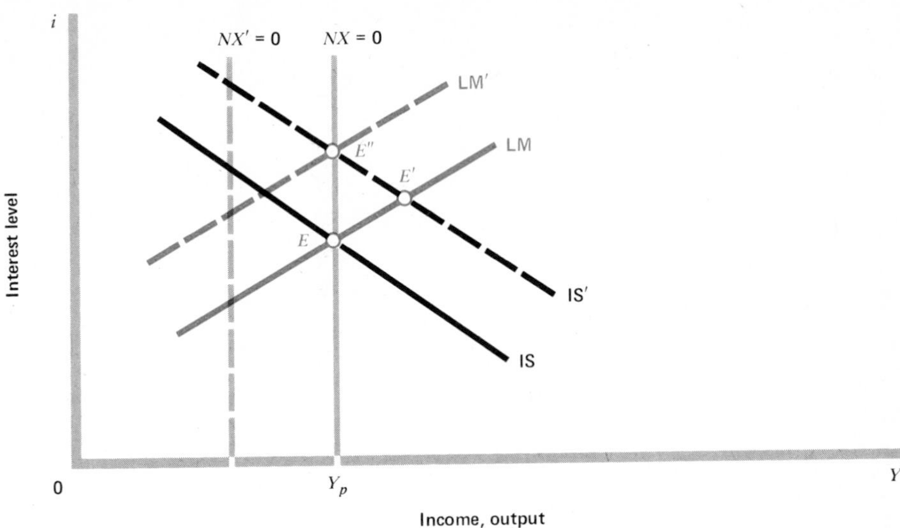

FIGURE 18-9 A DEVALUATION AND TIGHT MONEY TO RESTORE INTERNAL AND EXTERNAL BALANCE

out and to the right to IS′. The devaluation thus gives rise to overemployment and a deficit at E'. Clearly, we need a further instrument. We need tight monetary or fiscal policy to accompany the devaluation.

We show, in Figure 18-9, the use of a tight monetary policy. The monetary tightening shifts the LM curve to LM′ and restores full equilibrium at point E''. The point that we have made is that, in general, we need two instruments—affecting expenditure *level* and *composition*—to achieve internal and external balance. A devaluation shifts spending away from foreign goods and toward domestic goods and thus is an important ingredient of the policy mix. A further instrument is required to achieve the proper level of aggregate spending. In Figure 18-9, the level of spending at E' is excessive, and accordingly, either tight money or tight fiscal policy is required to complete the policy mix.

We should not fool ourselves into believing that just because full employment can be maintained, current account adjustment with a devaluation is costless. Current account adjustment involves not only a cut in spending to the level of income, but also, in many instances, a worsening of the *terms of trade*—the price of exports relative to imports. Foreign goods become more expensive, thus reducing the purchasing power of the goods we produce. Therefore our standard of living falls.

Finally, a comment on the role of the exchange rate in a fixed rate system. In the fixed rate system, the exchange rate is an *instrument of policy*. The central bank can change the exchange rate for policy purposes, devaluing when the current account looks as though it will be in for a prolonged deficit. In a system of clean floating, by contrast, the exchange rate moves freely to equilibrate the balance of payments. In a system of dirty floating, the central bank attempts to manipulate the exchange rate while not committing itself to any given rate. The dirty floating system is thus intermediate between a fixed rate system and a clean floating system.

18-4 CAPITAL MOBILITY AND THE POLICY MIX

So far, we have been assuming that trade is confined to goods and services and does not include assets. Now we allow for trade in assets and see the effects of such trade on the equilibrium of the economy and its desired policy mix.

One of the striking facts about the international economy is the high degree of integration or linkage among financial or capital markets—the markets in which bonds and stocks are traded. In particular, the capital markets are very fully integrated among the main industrial countries. Yields on assets in New York and yields on comparable assets in Canada, for example, move closely together. If rates in New York rose relative to those in Canada, investors would turn to lending in New York, while borrowers would turn to Toronto. With lending up in New York and borrowing up in Toronto, yields would quickly fall into line. Chart 18-1 shows the yields on United States short-term securities and their Canadian counterpart.[15] It is quite apparent that the yield differential is consistently small. There is impressive evidence in Chart 18-1 of the linkage of international capital markets that ensures consistency among interest rates in different countries. That consistency arises because capital flows—lending to and by foreigners—to countries with higher interest rates soon equalizes such rates.

The high degree of capital market integration that is reflected in Chart 18-1 suggests that any one country's interest rates cannot get too far out of line from those in the rest of the world without bringing about capital flows that tend to restore yields to the world level. As we have noted, if Canadian yields fell relative to United States yeilds, there would be a capital outflow from Canada because lenders would take their funds out of Canada and borrowers would try to raise funds in Canada. From a point of view of the balance of payments, this implies that a decline in relative interest rates—a decline in our rates relative to those abroad—will worsen the balance of payments because of the capital outflow—lending abroad by United States residents.

[15] The yield on Canadian securities in Chart 18-1 is "covered," which means that it is without exchange risk. Any yield differential in Chart 18-1 is *not* a reflection of exchange risk.

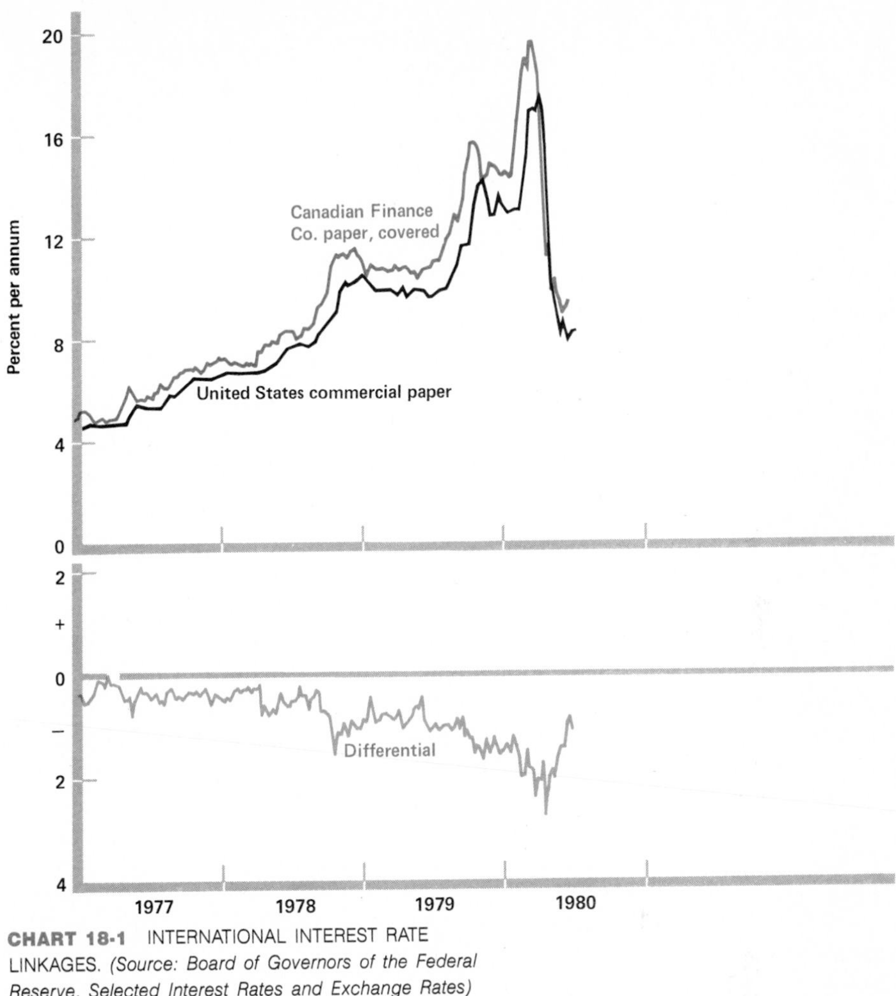

CHART 18-1 INTERNATIONAL INTEREST RATE LINKAGES. *(Source: Board of Governors of the Federal Reserve, Selected Interest Rates and Exchange Rates)*

The recognition that changes in our interest rates affect capital flows and the balance of payments has important implications for stabilization policy. First, because monetary and fiscal policies affect interest rates, they have an effect on the capital account and therefore on the balance of payments. The effects of monetary and fiscal policy on the balance of payments are limited *not* to the trade balance effects discussed in Section 18-2 but extend to the capital account. The second implication is that the way in which monetary and fiscal policies work in affecting the domestic economy and the balance of payments changes when there are international capital flows. We will examine the monetary-fiscal policy mix that can be used to achieve internal and external balance, and see that capital flows can be used to *finance* the trade balance and thus help in achieving overall balance of payments equilibrium.

The Balance of Payments and Capital Flows

We can introduce the role of capital flows in a framework in which we assume that the home country faces a given price of imports and a given export demand. In addition, we assume that the world rate of interest is given and that capital flows into the home country at a rate that is higher, the higher the home country's rate of interest. That is, foreign investors purchase more of our assets, the higher the interest rate our assets pay relative to the world interest rate. In Figure 18-10 we show the rate of capital inflow CF, or the capital account surplus, as an increasing function of the rate of interest. At the world interest rate, i^*, there are no capital flows. If the domestic interest rate is higher, there will be an inflow, and conversely, if the domestic interest rate is lower, there will be a capital outflow.

Next we look at the balance of payments. The balance of payments surplus BP is equal to the trade surplus NX, plus the capital account surplus CF:

$$B = NX(Y,\overline{X}, \ldots) + CF(i) \tag{9}$$

In Equation (9) we have shown the trade balance as a function of income and the capital account as a function of the domestic interest rate. We remember from Section 18-2 that an increase in income worsens the trade balance. We have just learned that an increase in the interest rate raises capital inflows and thus improves the capital account. It follows that

FIGURE 18-10 INTEREST-RESPONSIVE CAPITAL FLOWS

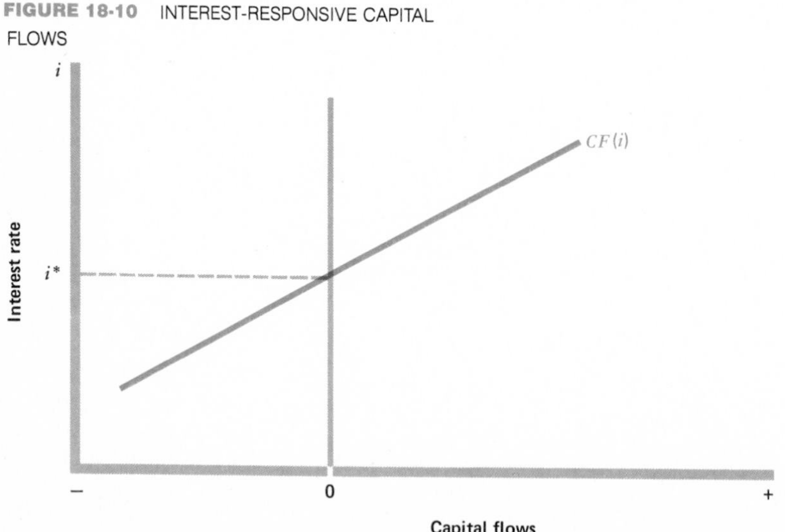

when income increases, an increase in interest rates could maintain overall balance of payments equilibrium. The trade deficit would be offset by a capital inflow. That idea is extremely important because it suggests that in the short run we can get out of the internal-external balance dilemma of Section 18-2.

The problem, we remember, was to achieve simultaneously internal and external balance from a position of deficit and unemployment or surplus and boom. The presence of interest-sensitive capital flows suggests that we can run an expansionary domestic policy without necessarily running into balance of payments problems. We can afford an increase in domestic income and import spending, provided we accompany it by an increase in interest rates so as to attract a capital inflow. But how can we achieve an expansion in domestic income at the same time that interest rates are increased? The answer is that we use fiscal policy to increase aggregate demand to the full-employment level and monetary policy to get the right amount of capital flows.[16]

Internal and External Balance

In Figure 18-11 we show the positively sloped schedule $BP = 0$, derived from Equation (9), along which we have balance of payments equilibrium. To derive the slope of the $BP = 0$ line, start with an income expansion, which raises imports and worsens the balance of payments. To restore balance of payments equilibrium, interest rates have to be higher to attract the capital flows that finance the trade deficit. Thus to maintain payments balance, an income increase has to be matched by a higher interest rate, and the $BP = 0$ line is therefore upward-sloping.

The schedule is drawn for given exports and a given foreign interest rate. The higher the degree of capital mobility, the flatter the schedule. If capital is very highly responsive to interest rates, then a small increase in the interest rate will bring about very large capital flows and thus allow the financing of large trade deficits. The larger the marginal propensity to import, the steeper the schedule. An increase in income worsens the trade balance by the increase in income times the marginal propensity to import. Thus, a high propensity to import means that a given increase in income produces a large deficit and thus requires a large increase in interest rates to bring about the right amount of capital flows to offset the trade deficit. Points above and to the left of the $BP = 0$ schedule correspond to a surplus,

[16] The idea of the policy mix for internal and external balance was suggested by Robert Mundell in his important paper, "The Appropriate Use of Monetary and Fiscal Policy under Fixed Exchange Rates," *I.M.F. Staff Papers*, March 1962. Mundell's work on international macroeconomics has been extraordinarily important, and the adventurous student should certainly consult his two books: *International Economics*, (New York: Macmillan, 1967) and *Monetary Theory* (Pacific Palisades, Calif.: Goodyear, 1971).

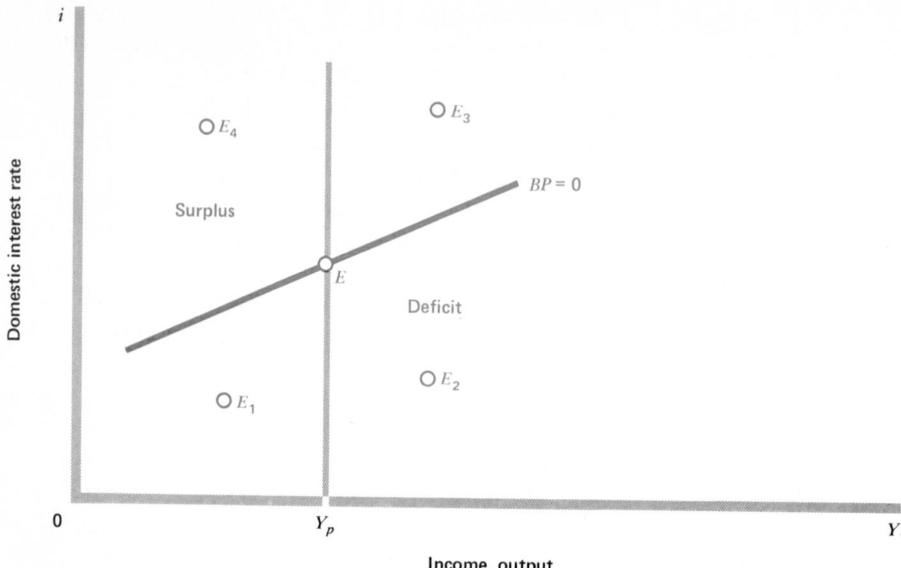

FIGURE 18-11 INTERNAL AND EXTERNAL BALANCE

and points below and to the right to a deficit. We have also drawn, in Figure 18-11, full-employment output Y_p. The full equilibrium with both internal and external balance is at point E.

We can talk about policy problems in terms of points in the four quadrants of Figure 18-11. Each such point would be an intersection of an IS and an LM curve and the question is how to use monetary and fiscal policy—shifting the IS and LM curves—to get to full equilibrium. Thus, point E_1, for example, corresponds to a case of unemployment and deficit. Point E_2, by contrast, is a case of deficit and overemployment. What are points E_3 and E_4?

The Policy Mix

Suppose that the economy is at point E_1. The appropriate policy to produce internal and external balance requires a higher level of employment for internal balance and higher interest rates and/or a lower level of income for external balance.

In terms of the analysis of Section 18-2, there is a policy dilemma at E_1 because employment considerations suggest income should be raised and balance of payments considerations suggest it should be reduced. However, now there is a way out of the dilemma. Suppose we reduce the money supply and thus raise interest rates. To offset the effects of the higher interest rates on income, we could use expansionary fiscal policy. Clearly, we would keep income constant and reach balance of payments equilibrium by getting interest rates high enough. However, we can do better. We can use fiscal policy to get us all the way to full employment and use tight money, in the form of higher interest rates, to achieve balance of payments equilibrium. Thus we can get to point E with both internal and external balance.

The lesson we have just derived is that under fixed exchange rates, we should expand income through fiscal policy whenever there is unemployment and use tight money whenever there is a balance of payments deficit. The combination of policies moves us to both internal and external balance. With a situation like point E_4, we want to use the same principle, but the economic conditions are different. Here we have a surplus and unemployment. Accordingly, we need expansionary fiscal policy to achieve full employment and expansionary monetary policy to reduce interest rates. Point E_4 is actually *not* a dilemma situation, since any form of expansionary policy moves us in the right direction with respect to both targets.

We leave it to you to work through the remaining cases and note here merely the principle: Under fixed exchange rates and with capital mobility, we use monetary policy to achieve external balance and fiscal policy to achieve full employment. What is the experience with such a rule? There is little doubt that tight money, for balance of payments reasons, is the oldest remedy in the policy maker's medicine chest. Since monetary policy is a flexible tool, attainment of external balance in the short run through tight money is relatively easy.

Limitations of the Policy Mix

The argument for a policy mix is persuasive, but it overlooks three important limitations. The first problem is that fiscal policy may not be sufficiently flexible to implement the needed policy mix. The discussion of lags in Chapter 9 made the point that the inside lag for fiscal policy is quite long. If fiscal policy cannot be modified readily, then all the policy maker can do is control the balance of payments, *or* employment, through monetary policy. We are back in a dilemma situation, because there are two targets—internal and external balance— but only one instrument—namely, monetary policy. The second point is that a country will typically not be indifferent to the level of domestic interest rates. Even if fiscal policy were sufficiently flexible to implement the policy mix, it would still be true that the composition of domestic output would depend on the mix. Thus, a country that attempts an expansion in aggregate demand, together with tight money, effectively restricts the construction sector and investment spending in general. The notion of a policy mix with monetary policy devoted to the balance of payments therefore overlooks the fact that the interest rate determines the composition as well as the level of aggregate spending.

The final consideration concerns the composition of the balance of payments. Countries are not indifferent about the makeup of their balance of payments between the current account deficit and the capital account surplus. Even if the overall balance is in equilibrium so that one target is satisfied, there is still the problem that a capital account surplus or capital inflow means net external borrowing: our country's debts to foreigners are increasing. Those debts will eventually have to be repaid.

Under a system of fixed exchange rates, there are circumstances under which a country—much like an individual—will find it useful to borrow in order to finance, say, a current shortfall of export earnings. However, continued large-scale borrowing from abroad is not consistent with a fixed exchange rate over long periods. Large-scale borrowing eventually places the country in a position where the interest payments it has to make to foreigners become a major burden for the economy. Faced with the prospect of continued foreign borrowing on a large scale in order to maintain its exchange rate fixed, a country would be well advised to implement adjustment policies that improve the current account balance. Such policies would typically be a devaluation accompanied by restrictive monetary and/or fiscal policy to reduce domestic demand pressures.

18-5 SUMMARY

1 The balance of payments accounts are a record of the international transactions of the economy. The current account records trade in goods and services, as well as transfer payments. The capital account records purchases and sales of assets. Any transaction that gives rise to a payment by United States residents is a deficit item for the United States.
2 The overall balance of payments is the sum of the current and capital accounts. If the overall balance is in deficit, we have to make more payments to foreigners than they make to us. The foreign currency for making these payments is supplied by central banks.
3 Under fixed exchange rates, the central bank maintains constant the price of foreign currencies in terms of the domestic currency. It does this by buying and selling foreign exchange at that fixed exchange rate. For that purpose, it has to keep reserves of foreign currency.
4 Under floating or flexible exchange rates, the exchange rate may change from moment to moment. In a system of clean floating, the exchange rate is determined by supply and demand without central bank intervention to affect the rate. Under dirty floating, the central

bank intervenes by buying and selling foreign exchange in an attempt to influence the exchange rate.

The remainder of the chapter studies the role of international trade in goods and assets under fixed exchange rates:

5 The introduction of trade in goods means that some of the demand for our output comes from abroad and that some spending by our residents is on foreign goods. There is equilibrium in the goods market when the demand for domestically produced goods is equal to the output of those goods.
6 In short-run equilibrium, the balance of trade may be in deficit. If there is no trade in assets, there may be a policy dilemma in that balanced trade and full employment cannot be attained merely through the manipulation of aggregate demand by fiscal and monetary policy. Expenditure switching policies that change the allocation of spending between imports and domestic goods are needed to solve the problem.
7 Over longer periods, there is an automatic adjustment mechanism in the economy which eventually leads to full employment at balanced trade under fixed exchange rates. A balance of trade deficit leads to a reduction in the domestic money stock which eventually leads to falling domestic prices that, given the foreign price level, switch spending away from imports and increase foreign demand for our goods. In the long run, domestic wages will also adjust to ensure full employment.
8 However, there are alternative mechanisms for achieving balanced trade without going through an adjustment process involving falling domestic prices. A devaluation, combined with restrictive aggregate demand policies, can lead to balance of payments equilibrium from a situation of trade deficit at more than full employment.
9 The introduction of capital flows points to the effects of monetary and fiscal policy on the balance of payments through interest rate effects on capital flows. An increase in the domestic interest rate, relative to the world interest rate, leads to a capital inflow that can finance a balance of trade deficit.
10 Policy dilemmas can then be handled by combining restrictive monetary policies to improve the balance of payments through higher interest rates and capital inflows, with expansionary fiscal policy to increase domestic employment.
11 However, such policies cannot be used in the long run to maintain balanced payments at the fixed exchange rate. The interest burden of the policies would, in the long run, be excessive, and the exchange rate could not be maintained. If balance of payments deficits are not

temporary, then adjustment policies, such as devaluation, with accompanying monetary and fiscal changes, have to be undertaken to correct the imbalance.

PROBLEMS

1 This problem formalizes some of the questions about income and trade balance determination in the open economy. We assume, as a simplification, that the interest rate is given and equal to $i = i_0$. In terms of Figures 18-1 and 18-2, the monetary authorities hold constant the interest rate so that the LM curve is flat at the level $i = i_0$.

We assume aggregate spending by domestic residents is

$$A = \overline{A} + cY - hi \qquad 1$$

Import spending is given by

$$Q = \overline{Q} + mY \qquad 2$$

where $\overline{Q}$ is autonomous import spending. Exports are given and equal to

$$X = \overline{X} \qquad 3$$

You are asked to work out the following problems:

(*a*) What is the total demand for domestic goods? The balance of trade?
(*b*) What is the equilibrium level of income?
(*c*) What is the balance of trade at that equilibrium level of income?
(*d*) What is the effect of an increase in exports on the equilibrium level of income? What is the multiplier?
(*e*) What is the effect of increased exports on the trade balance?

2 Suppose the marginal propensity to save is 0.1 and the marginal propensity to import is 0.2.
(*a*) What is the open economy multiplier?
(*b*) Assume there is a reduction in export demand of $\Delta\overline{X}$ = \$1 billion. By how much does income change? By how much does the trade balance worsen?
(*c*) What policies can the country pursue to offset the impact of reduced exports on domestic income and employment as well as the trade balance?

3 It has been suggested that, the smaller the marginal propensity to import, the larger the cost of adjustment to external imbalance. What is the rationale for this argument? Do you agree?

4 It has been argued that a central bank is a necessary condition for a balance of payments deficit. What is the explanation for this argument?

5 Consider a country that is in a position of full employment and balanced trade.

You are asked to discuss which type of disturbances can be remedied with standard aggregate demand tools of stabilization:

(*a*) A loss of export markets
(*b*) A reduction in saving and a corresponding increase in demand for domestic goods
(*c*) An increase in government spending
(*d*) A shift in demand from imports to domestic goods
(*e*) A reduction in imports with a corresponding increase in saving

Indicate in each case the impact on external and internal balance as well as the appropriate policy response.

*6 Derive the formula $1\ (m + s)$ for the foreign trade multiplier, assuming the demand for imports is $Q = \bar{Q} + mY$. Use the formula to discuss the impact on the trade balance of an increase in autonomous domestic spending. In your discussion, comment on the proposition that the more open the economy, the smaller the domestic income expansion. Comment, also, on the counterpart proposition that the more the economy opens, the more the trade balance worsens. What measures openness? What does this imply about the extent of spillover effects as a function of m?

*7 Consider a world with some capital mobility: The home country's capital account improves as domestic interest rates rise relative to the world rate of interest. Initially, the home country is in internal and external balance. (Draw the IS, LM, and $BP = 0$ schedules.)

Assume now an increase in the world rate of interest.

(*a*) Show the effect of the foreign interest rate increase on the BP schedule.
(*b*) What policy response would immediately restore internal and external balance?
(*c*) If the authorities took no action, what would be the adjustment process along the lines described by the "monetary approach to the balance of payments"?

*8 Consider again the case of a country that faces some capital mobility. Here we ask what monetary fiscal policy mix should be pursued to offset the following disturbances:

(*a*) A transitory gain in exports
(*b*) A permanent gain in exports
(*c*) A decline in autonomous spending
(*d*) An increased rate of capital outflow (at each level of domestic interest rates)

*9 This question is concerned with the repercussion effects of a domestic expansion once we recognize that as a consequence output abroad will expand. Suppose that at home there is an increase in autonomous spending, $\Delta\bar{A}$, that falls entirely on domestic goods. (Assume constant interest rates throughout this problem.)

(*a*) What is the resulting effect on income, disregarding repercussion effects? What is the impact on our imports, ΔQ?
(*b*) Using the result for the increase in imports, we can now ask what happens abroad. Our increase in imports appears to foreign countries as an increase in their exports and therefore as an increase in demand for their goods. In response, their output expands. Assuming the foreign marginal propensity to save is s^* and the foreign propensity to import is m^*, by how much will a

foreign country's income expand as a result of an increase in its exports?

(c) Now combine the pieces by writing the familiar equation for equilibrium in the domestic goods market: Change in supply, ΔY, equals the total change in demand: $\Delta\overline{A} + \Delta X - m\,\Delta Y + (1 - s)\,\Delta Y$, or

$$\Delta Y = \frac{1}{s + m}(\Delta\overline{A} + \Delta X)$$

Noting that foreign demand ΔX depends on our increased imports, we can replace ΔX with the answer to 9 (*b*) to obtain a general expression for the multiplier with repercussions.

(d) Substitute your answer for 9(*b*) in the formula for the change in foreign demand, $\Delta X = m^* \,\Delta Y^*$.

(e) Calculate the complete change in our income, including repercussion effects. Now compare your result with the small-country case. What difference do repercussion effects make? Is our income expansion larger or smaller with repercussion effects?

(f) Consider the trade balance effect of a domestic expansion with and without repercussion effects. Is the trade deficit larger or smaller once repercussion effects are taken into account?

10 Use the central bank balance sheet to show how a balance of payments deficit affects the stock of high-powered money under fixed exchange rates. Show, too, how sterilization operations work.

11 Discuss the manner in which income, price adjustments, and money supply adjustments interact in leading the economy ultimately to full employment and external balance. Choose as an example the case where a country experiences a permanent increase in exports.

12 In relation to external imbalance, a distinction is frequently made between imbalances that should be "financed" and those that should be "adjusted." Can you think of a classification of disturbances that give rise, respectively, to imbalances that require adjustment and those that should more appropriately be financed?

19

TRADE AND CAPITAL FLOWS UNDER FLEXIBLE EXCHANGE RATES

19

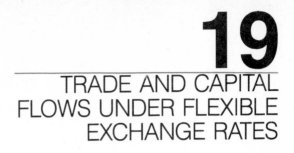

TRADE AND CAPITAL FLOWS UNDER FLEXIBLE EXCHANGE RATES

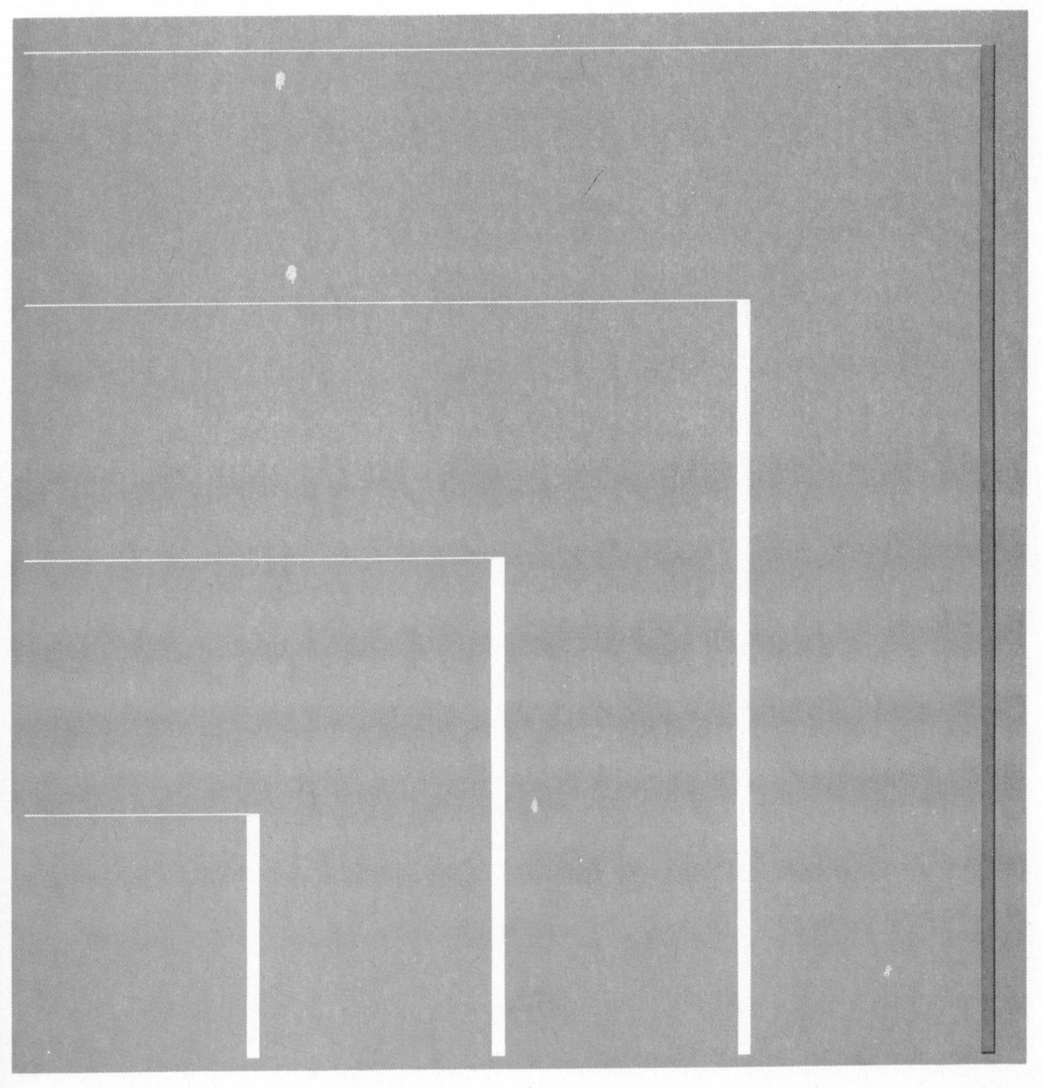

This chapter is concerned with flexible exchange rates and events in the world economy since 1973. The world moved to a flexible exchange rate system in 1973 as the fixed exchange rate system that had existed since 1945 collapsed. The fundamental cause of the collapse of the fixed rate system—also called the *Bretton Woods system*, after the town in New Hampshire in which the conference setting up the system was held—was the incompatibility of macroeconomic targets among countries.

During the sixties, and again in 1971–1973, some countries, including Britain and the United States, pursued expansionary policies. Other countries—the hard-currency countries, particularly Germany—wanted lower inflation rates than the world economy was experiencing and followed less expansionary policies. With fixed exchange rates, the lower rate of inflation in Germany than in the United States meant that German goods were becoming progressively cheaper relative to United States goods. As a result, Germany ran increasingly large balance of payments surpluses, while the United States (and Britain) had large deficits. Under such circumstances, the countries with large surpluses have to revalue their currencies, or the deficit countries have to devalue, to correct the payments imbalances.

A fixed exchange rate system with free capital flows between countries is badly equipped to deal with revaluations or devaluations that are widely anticipated. To understand this point, we turn to the case of Germany in 1973. There were recurrent rumors in 1973 that the Deutsche mark would be revalued once more.[1] The rumors arose because the exchange rate adjustment of 1971 had not appreciably reduced the United States balance of payments deficit. The belief in an imminent Deutsche mark revaluation led to large capital outflows from the United States and inflows into Germany.

Why would the belief that the mark was about to be revalued lead to a capital inflow into Germany? Suppose people expect the mark will be revalued from 30 cents per mark to 40 cents per mark. A holder of $1 million today could buy DM3.33 million for his dollars at the price of 30 cents each. Then, after the devaluation, he could exchange his DM3.33 million for $1.33 million, receiving 40 cents for each mark. The operation nets a profit of 33 percent. Since there is no risk that the mark will be devalued, there is very little risk in buying it, and hence the belief in impending revaluation leads to large purchases of marks by holders of other currencies. If there is no revaluation, there is hardly any loss, and if there is a revaluation, there is a large profit.

As a result of the expected revaluation, the German Bundesbank had to buy about $10 billion in foreign exchange to meet foreign demands for marks at the existing exchange rate, in the 5 weeks from the end of January

[1] The Deutsche mark had been revalued in 1961, 1969, and 1971. In 1971 a number of other currencies also had their exchange rates adjusted.

to the first of March 1973. Recall from Chapters 8 and 18 that central bank purchases of foreign exchange increase the domestic money supply. Now the $10 billion that the Bundesbank purchased by selling marks amounted to almost 20 percent of the German money supply at that time. Thus, in order to defend the exchange rate, the Bundesbank was being forced to expand the German money supply at an extraordinary rate. The large increase in the money supply in turn created the fear—indeed, the certainty—that the capital inflow would have substantial inflationary effects. The way out was to stop intervening in the foreign exchange market and thus to gain control of monetary policy for purposes of domestic stabilization. But once the Bundesbank decided to stop intervening in the foreign exchange market, it left the exchange rate to be determined by supply and demand in that market. That is, it chose to allow a flexible exchange rate regime.

A country which is expected to devalue also faces an intractable problem under fixed exchange rates. In that case, the expected devaluation produces an outflow of capital from the currency. Suppose that the pound was expected to be devalued. Then holders of pounds would buy other currencies in exchange for their pounds.[2] With the Bank of England committed to supporting the exchange rate, it would have to buy the pounds that others were selling. In so doing, it would rapidly reduce its reserves of other currencies and would eventually run out of reserves to exchange for the pounds. Thus it would be forced to devalue.

The general point is that a fixed exchange rate system is not viable if countries pursue policies which lead to different rates of inflation and there is free mobility of capital. The countries with lower inflation rates will eventually have to revalue or those with higher inflation rates will have to devalue. It is thus always clear in which direction there will be a revaluation or devaluation. Capital can flow with little risk and with the promise of large gains in anticipation of exchange rate changes. And, as the capital starts flowing, countries with surpluses are forced to accept increases in their money supplies they do not want, and deficit countries face the risk of running out of reserves.

There were, in the early seventies, increasingly large-scale flows of capital in anticipation of exchange rate changes. The German decision to float the exchange rate in 1973 was merely the particular event which marked the end of the fixed rate system, rather than the fundamental cause of the change of system. The fundamental cause was the incompatibility of the economic policies being followed by different countries.

What is the system that has emerged since 1973? There are three chief characteristics. The first is the formation of *currency areas.* For instance, in

[2] To see why expected devaluation produces a flight of capital, reverse the example of the expected mark appreciation above.

1973, some countries in the European Economic Community (EEC) joined Germany in a currency area with fixed exchange rates that is called the *snake*. The snake is an arrangement, shown in Chart 19-1, whereby exchange rates between partner countries can fluctuate only within narrow limits. However, the exchange rates of all the currencies in the currency area fluctuate relative to the United States dollar. If the small margin of fluctuation within the snake were eliminated, the shaded band in Chart 19-1 would collapse to a fixed rate within the snake—a fixed rate between Dutch guilders and marks, for example—and a floating rate of the mark-guilder relative to the United States dollar.

In 1979 Europe went further in an attempt to create a common currency area—an area with fixed exchange rates among the members—by setting up the *European Monetary System* (EMS). The EMS is an extension

CHART 19-1 THE EUROPEAN ECONOMIC COMMUNITY SNAKE AND THE FRENCH FRANC IN RELATION TO THE DOLLAR. *(Source: Organization for Economic Cooperation and Development. Economic Outlook, July 1976)*

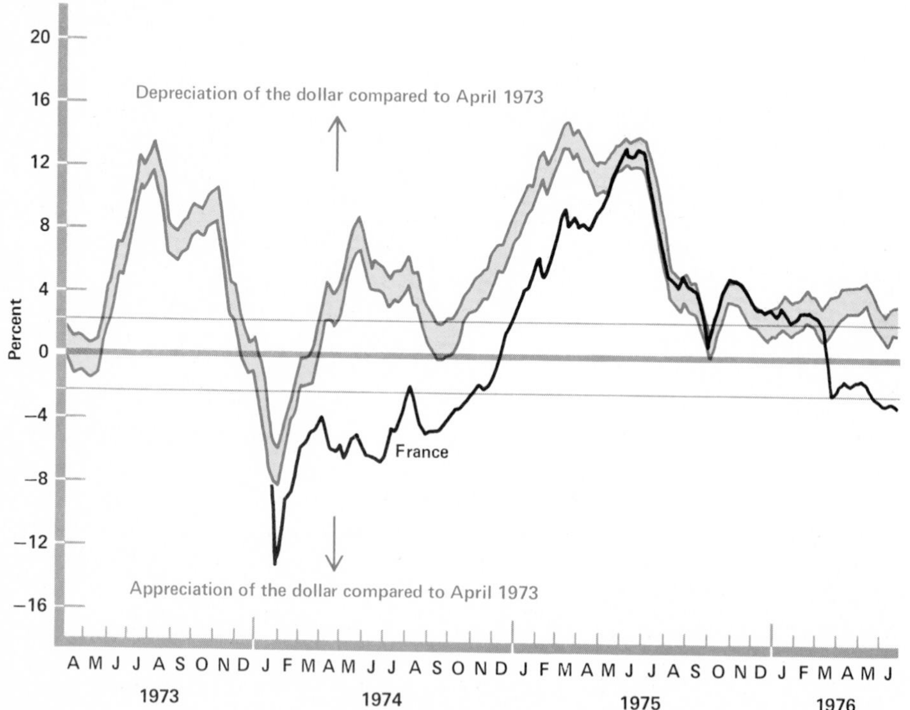

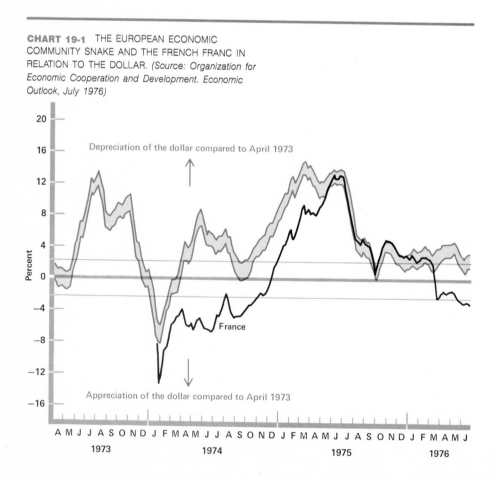

of the snake that includes France and, with special arrangements, Italy and the United Kingdom. Beyond providing for fixed exchange rates between members of the group (within narrow margins), the EMS has worked out a detailed system of intervention and corrective policies should an individual country get out of line with the group. It also provides ample financing for countries that may find it difficult to keep in step with the other members of what is clearly intended to be a low inflation, hard currency club.

The second fact about exchange rate experience since 1973 is also apparent from Chart 19-1. There have been large *fluctuations* in rates in the floating rate period. Movements in the exchange rates between the snake currencies and the dollar have been described as "wild gyrations," and whatever they are called, they have been large. The question arises of where these movements come from and whether central banks should intervene in the market to smooth exchange rate movements.

This leads us to the third fact—*dirty floating*. Rates have in practice not been determined by the free interplay of private demand and supply but have, on the contrary, been significantly affected by official intervention. Central banks have intervened almost daily in the foreign exchange markets to smooth out short-run fluctuations. They well may have also attempted—with some success—to fight longer-run exchange rate movements.

The extent of intervention has increased in the past few years. It is worth noting that in 1978, for example, foreign central banks purchased in excess of $35 billion in attempts to prevent their currencies from appreciating. The intervention was conducted chiefly by the large, industrialized countries. The highest quarterly figure was reported by Japan, which showed a gain in reserves of $10 billion in the last quarter of 1978. This was a time when the yen was appreciating sharply against the dollar and when the Carter administration (on November 1) undertook a substantial stabilization program to shore up the dollar.

The dirty floating of the period since 1973 obviously again raises the question of why central banks intervene to affect the exchange rate, rather than leave it to the market to set the rate. A final question that is raised by the floating rate regime concerns world trade and capital flows. Prior to 1973, a flexible rate system was viewed with suspicion. The argument was that flexible rates create uncertainty and thus reduce trade and lending in the world economy. The question is important because such an effect, should it occur, would obviously have repercussions at the macro level by forcing countries to be in trade balance. It turns out, though, that world trade did not decline after the move to flexible exchange rates and large payments imbalances continue to be financed through capital flows.

The plan of this chapter is as follows. In Section 19-1 we extend the analysis of Section 18-4 of a Keynesian model with capital mobility and sticky prices to a world of flexible exchange rates. In Section 19-2, we round out the model by looking at a world of flexible prices. The analysis of Section 19-2 leads to a review of the chief determinants of exchange rates. Sections 19-1 and 19-2 are the core of the chapter. Section 19-3 introduces exchange rate measures that are widely used and that deal with the difficulty that the exchange rate of a currency, say the dollar, often appreciates against one currency (for example, the French franc) while it depreciates against another (say, the yen). The question that arises is whether the dollar is on the average appreciating or depreciating, and by how much? Sections 19-4 and 19-5 offer some signifigant extensions of, and qualifications to, the theoretical sections. Section 19-4 discusses exchange rate expectations and international interest rate differentials, while Section 19-5 deals with real wage stickiness and with the important possibility that the trade balance responds perversely to exchange rate changes in the short run—the so-called J curve.

19-1 EXCHANGE RATES AND EQUILIBRIUM OUTPUT

We start with a model of output and exchange rate determination. Our discussion will extend the analysis of Chapter 18, where we looked at income determination in an open economy. In that chapter, we assumed capital mobility, sticky prices, demand-determined output, and fixed exchange rates. Here, we maintain all these assumptions except the last and now allow the exchange rate to be flexible. Our analysis will proceed as follows: First, we shall review the role of exchange rates in determining the relative prices of imports and domestically produced goods and thereby the demand for domestic output. Next, we develop the equilibrium conditions in the goods and money markets and in the external balance. Finally, we use our model to show the implications of monetary and real disturbances for the level of output and the exchange rate. These results can then be directly compared with those for the fixed exchange rate world analyzed in Chapter 18. After making the comparison, we proceed in the following sections to alternative assumptions about capital mobility and to a discussion of longer-term adjustments of prices and output.

Exchange Rates and Relative Prices

A central price in an open economy is the relative price of goods produced in the rest of the world in terms of goods produced at home. If the price of goods we produce falls relative to the price of the goods foreigners produce, then the demand for our goods tends to rise. If American goods become cheaper, then both Americans and foreigners will tend to buy more

American goods and fewer foreign goods. Given income or spending levels, a decline in the relative price of our goods makes us more competitive and, as a consequence, raises *net* exports and creates demand for domestic output.[3]

The price of our goods relative to foreigners' goods is clearly central to the operation of a flexible exchange rate system, and we have to ask how to measure it. We define the relative price as the ratio of import prices to domestic prices, *both measured in the same currency*. Define P^* as the price of goods produced abroad measured in foreign currency (yen per unit), e as the exchange rate measured in \$/yen, and P as the dollar price of our goods. The relative price of foreign goods in terms of domestic goods, *the terms of trade*, is then defined as

$$\frac{eP^*}{P} \equiv \text{terms of trade or relative price of imports} \tag{1}$$

The term eP^* measures the price of foreign goods in terms of dollars, and P of course measures the price of domestic goods in terms of dollars. If import prices (eP^*) rise relative to domestic prices (P), we say there has been a worsening or deterioration of the terms of trade. For example, the repeated increases in oil prices worsened the importing countries' terms of trade and meant that more units of exports (Cadillacs or cornflakes) had to be given up to buy a barrel of oil.

We have now defined the relative price of imports or foreign goods in terms of domestic goods and have argued that it is important in determining the demand for domestic output. We consider next the relation between exchange rates and relative prices. Here we make, for the moment, the strategic assumption that both foreign prices, P^*, and domestic prices, P, are given. This implies that the terms of trade move *one for one* with the exchange rate. If the exchange rate depreciates (e rises), then import prices increase in home currency and thus, with our prices given, the *relative* price of imports rises. Exchange depreciation thus raises the relative price of imports or makes domestic goods relatively cheaper. Therefore, exchange depreciation leads to increases in net exports and in demand for domestic goods.

The question of the effect of changes of the exchange rate on the terms of trade is a crucial one, to which we return in Section 19-2. We shall argue there that changes in the exchange rate set off forces that in the longer term tend to offset the effects of the initial exchange rate change on the terms of

[3] We should note, pending further discussion, that we assume that elasticities are large enough for a decline in relative price to raise net exports. We return to this important issue in more detail in Sec. 19-5, under the subheading, "Relative Prices and the Trade Balance: The J Curve."

trade. But in the short run with sticky prices, exchange rate changes do change relative prices.

Relative Prices, Net Exports, and Demand for Domestic Output

The demand for domestic output comes from both domestic residents and the rest of the world. We showed in Chapter 18 that we can write demand for domestic goods as the sum of total spending by domestic residents (including spending on imports), A, plus *net* exports or the trade surplus, NX. Domestic aggregate spending depends on interest rates, i, and income, Y. Net exports depend on foreign income, which we take as given, domestic income, and relative prices, eP^*/P.

$$NX = NX(Y, eP^*/P) \tag{2}$$

We recall from Chapter 18 that a rise in income reduces net exports because it leads to increased import spending. In Equation (2) we also include the relative price as an explicit determinant of net exports. A rise in the relative price of imports leads to an increase in net exports because it lowers our imports and raises our exports.

We consider next the equilibrium condition in the domestic goods market. Output is assumed to be determined by demand, and prices are given. Equilibrium requires that output equal the demand for domestic goods or, equivalently, aggregate spending plus the trade surplus:

$$Y = A(i,Y) + NX\,(Y, eP^*/P) \tag{3}$$

We show in Figure 19-1 the IS schedule that represents goods market equilibrium *given* an exchange rate, say e_0. What happens to the IS schedule if the exchange rate depreciates?

Exchange depreciation will, under our assumptions, raise the relative price of imports or lower the relative price of our own goods. With our own goods more competitive, there is increased net demand arising from increased net exports. Thus, for a given interest rate and income level, exchange depreciation must lead to an excess demand for our goods. To restore equilibrium, output would have to rise or interest rates would have to increase. In Figure 19-1, we accordingly show that exchange depreciation shifts the IS schedule up and to the right. The schedule IS′ is drawn for a higher relative price of imports. Conversely, an appreciation and fall in import prices would of course lead to an excess supply of our goods and a downward shift of the IS schedule.

We now develop the remaining parts of our model of exchange rate and output determination, namely, the money market equilibrium condition and the balance of payments.

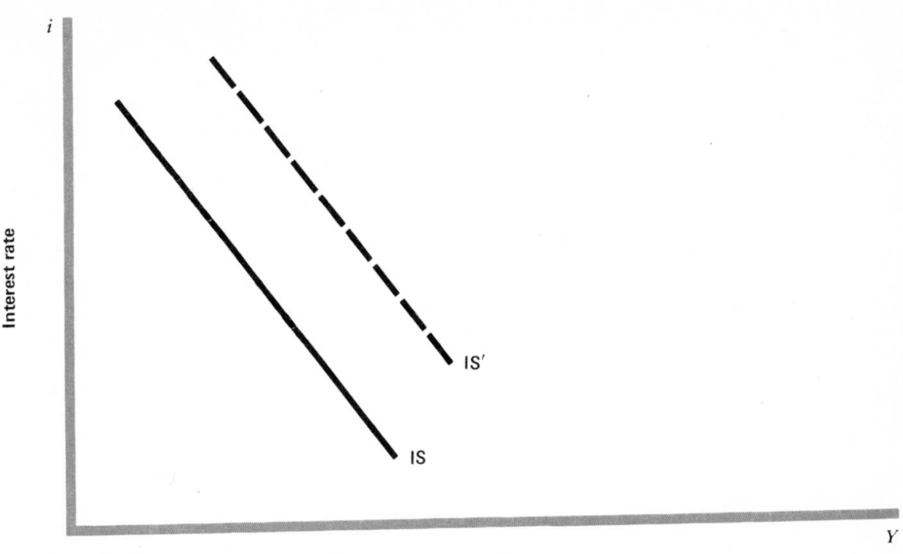

FIGURE 19-1 EFFECTS OF EXCHANGE RATE DEPRECIATION ON THE IS CURVE

Monetary Equilibrium and Payments Balance

The condition of monetary equilibrium is the familiar LM schedule of earlier chapters. Given prices, P, and nominal money, M, we have a given real money stock, M/P. Equilibrium in the money market requires that the demand for real money balances equal the existing real money stock:

$$\frac{M}{P} \equiv L(i, Y) \tag{4}$$

Real money demand in (4) is a decreasing function of the interest rate and an increasing function of the level of income. The LM schedule is shown in Figure 19-2 for a given real money stock.

We draw on the discussion of capital mobility in Chapter 18 to develop our balance of payments equation. The balance of payments surplus, BP, is equal to net exports, NX, plus the net rate of capital inflow, CF.

$$BP = NX(Y, eP^*/P) + CF(i, i^*) \tag{5}$$

We have already introduced the fact that the trade balance depends on income and relative prices. We now have added the rate of capital flow as a function of our interest rate, i, and the given interest rate abroad, i^*. If our interest rate increases relative to that in the rest of the world, then there will be a net capital inflow.

For the present, we make the simplifying assumption that capital mobility is very high, so that we can have payments balance only at the world interest rate. If our interest rate were lower, there would be large-scale capital outflows swamping any current account surplus. Conversely, with a higher interest rate than the rest of the world, the capital inflows would swamp any deficit in the current account. We represent this assumption of high capital mobility in Figure 19-2 by a flat BB schedule. Points above it correspond to a balance of payments surplus and points below it to a deficit.

Adjustment to a Real Disturbance

We have now completed our model, represented by Equations (2) through (5) and Figure 19-2, and can ask how the economy will adjust to disturbances. In particular, we want to know how various changes affect our level of output, the interest rate, and the exchange rate. The first change we

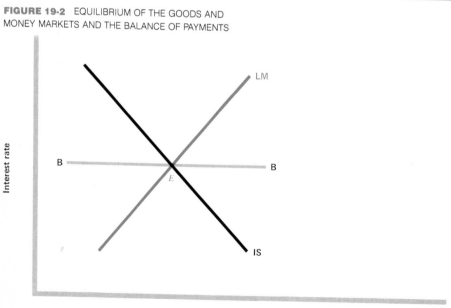

FIGURE 19-2 EQUILIBRIUM OF THE GOODS AND MONEY MARKETS AND THE BALANCE OF PAYMENTS

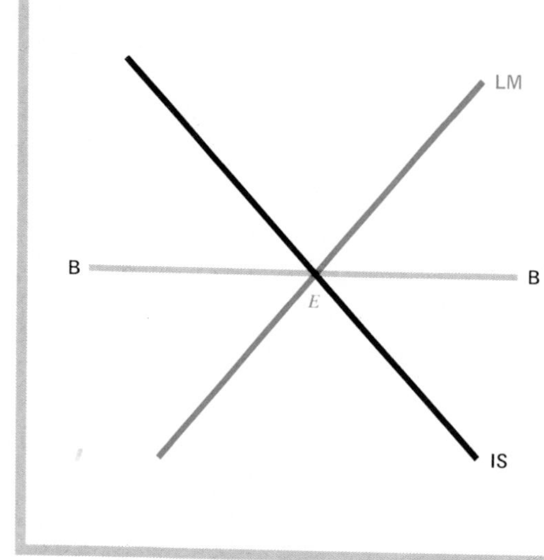

look at is an exogenous rise in the world demand for our goods, or an increase in exports. The change in export demand is a *real* disturbance to the economy.[4]

Starting from an initial equilibrium at point E in Figure 19-3, we see that the increase in foreign demand implies an excess demand for our goods. At the initial interest rate, exchange rate, and output level, demand for our goods now exceeds the available supply. For goods market equilibrium, at the initial interest rate and exchange rate, we require a higher level of output. Accordingly, the IS schedule shifts out and to the right.

Now consider for a moment point E', where the goods and money markets clear. Here, output has increased to meet the increased demand. The rise in income has increased money demand and thus raised equilibrium interest rates. But is point E' an equilibrium? It is not, because the balance of payments is not in equilibrium. In fact, we wold not reach point E' at all. The tendency for the economy to move in that direction, as we show now, will bring about an exchange rate appreciation that will take us all the way back to the initial equilibrium at E.

[4] Disturbances that, by contrast, originate in the money market, are called *nominal*.

FIGURE 19-3 EFFECTS OF AN INCREASE IN THE DEMAND FOR EXPORTS

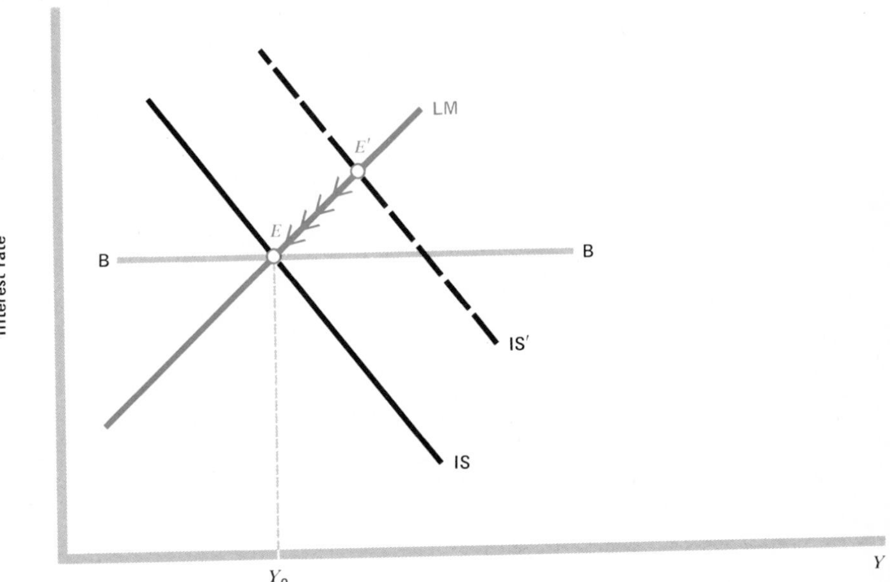

Suppose, then, that the increase in foreign demand takes place and that, in response, there is a tendency for output and income to increase. The induced increase in money demand will raise interest rates and thus will bring us out of line with interest rates internationally. The resulting capital inflows immediately put pressure on the exchange rate. The capital inflow causes our currency to appreciate.

The exchange appreciation means, of course, that import prices fall and that domestic goods become relatively more expensive. Demand shifts away from domestic goods and net exports decline. In terms of Figure 19-2, the appreciation implies that the IS schedule shifts back from IS′ to the left. Next, we have to ask how far the exchange appreciation will go and to what extent it will therefore dampen the expansionary effect of increased net exports.

The exchange rate will keep appreciating as long as our interest rate exceeds the world level. This implies that the exchange appreciation must continue until the IS schedule has shifted back all the way to its initial position. This adjustment is shown by the arrows along the LM schedule. Only when we return to point *E* will output and income have reached a level consistent with monetary equilibrium at the world rate of interest.

We have now shown that under conditions of perfect capital mobility, an expansion in exports has no lasting effect on equilibrium output. With perfect capital mobility, as a result of the increase in export demand, the tendency for interest rates to rise leads to currency appreciation and thus to a complete offset of the increase in exports. Once we return to point *E*, net exports are back to their initial level. The exchange rate has of course appreciated. Imports will increase as a consequence of the appreciation, and the initial expansion in exports is in part offset by the appreciation of our exchange rate.

We can extend the usefulness of this analysis by recognizing that it is valid not only for an increase in exports. The same analysis applies to a fiscal expansion. A tax cut or an increase in government spending would lead to an expansion in demand in just the same way as increased exports do. Again, the tendency for interest rates to rise leads to appreciation and therefore to a fall in exports and increased imports. There is, accordingly, complete *crowding out* here. The crowding out takes place not as in Chapter 4 because higher interest rates reduce investment but because the exchange appreciation reduces net exports.

The important lesson here is that real disturbances to demand do not affect equilibrium output under flexible rates with perfect capital mobility. We can drive the lesson home by comparing a fiscal expansion under flexible rates with the results we derived for the fixed rate case. In Chapter 18, we showed that with fixed rates, fiscal expansion under conditions of capital mobility is highly effective in raising equilibrium output. For flexible rates, by contrast, a fiscal expansion does not change equilibrium output. Instead, it produces an offsetting exchange rate appreciation and a shift in the composition of domestic demand toward domestic goods and away from net exports.

We turn next to the analysis of a monetary disturbance.

Adjustment to a Monetary Disturbance

We now show that under flexible exchange rates, an increase in the money stock leads to an increase in income and a depreciation of the exchange rate. The analysis uses Figure 19-4. We start from an initial position at point E and consider an increase in the nominal quantity of money, M. Since prices are given, we have an increase in the real money stock, M/P. At E there will be an excess supply of real balances. To restore equilibrium, interest rates would have to be lower or income would have to be larger. Accordingly, the LM schedule shifts down and to the right to LM′.

We ask once again whether point E' is the new equilibrium. At E', goods and money markets are in equilibrium (at the initial exchange rate), but it is clear that interest rates have fallen below the world level. Capital outflows will therefore put pressure on the exchange rate. The exchange

FIGURE 19-4 EFFECTS OF AN INCREASE IN THE MONEY STOCK

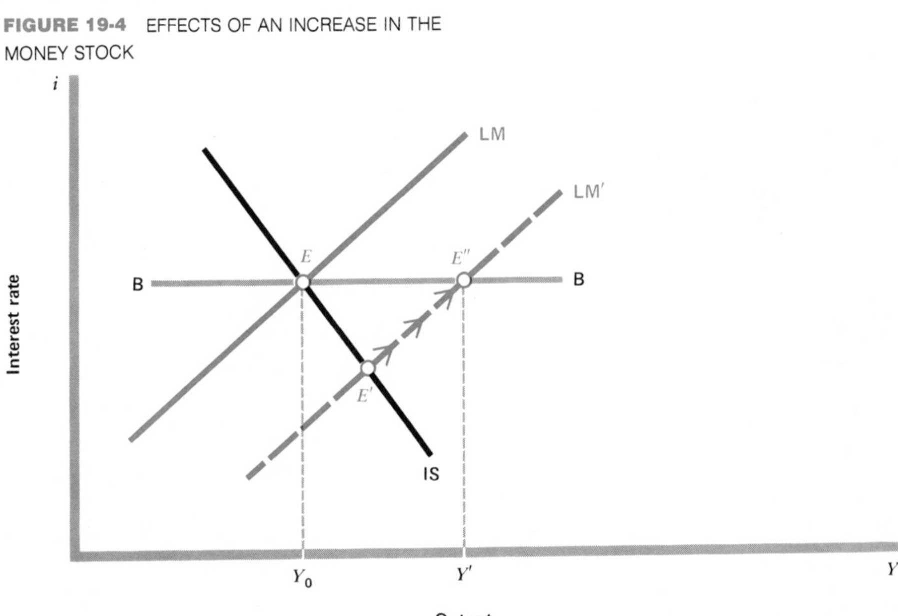

depreciation caused by the low level of interest rates implies that import prices increase, domestic goods become more competitive, and, as a result, demand for our output expands. The exchange depreciation therefore shifts the IS curve out and to the right. As the arrows indicate, exchange depreciation continues until the relative price of domestic goods has fallen enough to raise demand and output to the level indicated by point E''. Only at E'' do we have goods and money market equilibrium compatible with the world rate of interest. Consequently, there is no further tendency for exchange rates, relative prices, and hence demand, to change.[5]

We have now shown that a monetary expansion leads to an increase in output and a depreciation of the exchange rate under flexible rates. One way of thinking about this result is that with P fixed, an increase in M increases M/P. The demand for real balances is, from Equation (4), equal to $L(i, Y)$. Since i cannot differ from the world rate of interest, Y has to rise to equate the demand for money to the supply. The exchange depreciation raises net exports, and that increase in net exports in turn sustains the higher level of output and employment. One interesting implication of our analysis, then, is the proposition that monetary expansion improves the current account through the induced depreciation.

How do our results compare with those of a fixed exchange rate world? We argued in Chapter 18 that under fixed rates, the monetary authorities cannot control the nominal money stock and that an attempt to expand money will merely lead to a reserve loss as the central bank attempts to prevent the tendency for the exchange rate to depreciate in response to declining interest rates. Under flexible rates, by contrast, the central bank does not intervene and so the money stock increase is *not* reversed in the foreign exchange market. The depreciation and expansion in output actually do take place, given the assumed sticky prices. The fact that the central bank *can* control the money stock under flexible rates is one of the most important aspects of that exchange rate system.

Beggar-Thy-Neighbor Policy and Competitive Depreciation

We extend the analysis of the fixed price variable employment model with a brief discussion of the international implications of exchange depreciation and changes in net exports. We showed that a monetary expansion in the home country leads to exchange depreciation, an increase in net exports, and therefore an increase in output and employment. But our increased net exports correspond to a deterioration in the trade balance abroad. The domestic depreciation shifts demand from foreign goods toward domestic

[5] In the problem set at the end of this chapter we ask you to show that the current account improves between E and E'', even though the increased level of income increases imports.

goods. Abroad, output and employment therefore decline. It is for this reason that the depreciation-induced change in the trade balance has been called a *beggar-thy-neighbor policy*—it is a way of exporting unemployment or of creating domestic employment at the expense of the rest of the world.

The recognition that exchange depreciation is mainly a way of shifting demand from one country to another, rather than changing the level of world demand, is important. It implies that exchange rate adjustment can be a useful policy when countries find themselves in different stages of a business cycle—for example, one in a boom (with overemployment) and the other in a recession. In that event, a depreciation by the country experiencing a recession would shift world demand in that direction and thus work to reduce divergences from full employment in each country.

By contrast, when countries' business cycles are highly synchronized, such as in the 1930s or in the aftermath of the oil shock, exchange rate movements will not contribute much toward world full employment. The problem is then one of the level of total world spending being deficient or excessive while exchange rate movements affect only the allocation of a given world demand between countries. Nevertheless, from the point of view of an individual country, exchange depreciation works to attract world demand and raise domestic output. If every country tried to depreciate to attract world demand, we would have *competitive depreciation* and a shifting around of world demand rather than an increase in the world level of spending. Coordinated monetary and/or fiscal policies are needed to increase demand and output in each country.

*Imperfect Capital Mobility

The case of perfect capital mobility is extreme, and it probably overstates the speed with which capital moves internationally in response to interest rate differentials. It is therefore important to consider the effects of more moderate capital mobility, or *imperfect capital mobility*. In this case, the rate of capital flows increases as the international interest differential increases, but it remains finite. In equilibrium, interest rate differentials are possible. The larger the equilibrium differential, the larger the associated capital flow and therefore the current account imbalance.

How would monetary and fiscal policy work in a world of imperfect capital mobility? We leave as an exercise at the end of the chapter the demonstration of the following results: First, a fiscal expansion at home raises our interest rate and increases our income. With the higher interest rate, there will be an increased inflow of capital. This implies a deterioration in the current account, since the sum of the current and capital accounts is zero. However, the current account deteriorates by less than the fiscal expansion. There is less than full crowding out, and hence, income rises.

In the case of a monetary expansion, our interest rate falls, income rises, and the current account must improve. We know that the current account must improve since the lower interest rate implies increased capital outflows which, for payments balance, must be offset by an improvement in the current account.

The case of imperfect capital mobility clearly qualifies our earlier results. Now both monetary and fiscal policies are effective and the extent to which fiscal policy can affect income depends on the extent to which changes in interest differentials affect capital flows.

Summary

We have now taken a first look at exchange rate determination under flexible exchange rates. So far, we have studied the role of exchange rates in a world of fixed prices. In this setting, movements in exchange rates change the relative prices of foreign versus domestic goods. An exchange depreciation both raises foreign demand for our goods and moves our own demand away from imports toward domestic goods. The exchange rate thus plays a central role in the determination of macroeconomic equilibrium.

An examination of real and monetary disturbances under flexible exchange rates, fixed prices, and perfect capital mobility gave us the following results:

1 A fiscal expansion leaves output unchanged. The fiscal expansion tends to increase income and raise interest rates. The tendency for interest rates to rise leads to appreciation of the exchange rate as capital is attracted from abroad. The appreciation, by lowering import prices, shifts demand away from our goods and thus offsets the expansionary effect of fiscal policy.

2 This result is the opposite of that derived under fixed exchange rates. The difference results from the fact that under flexible rates, the money stock is exogenous and is kept fixed when fiscal policy changes, while under fixed rates, exchange rate stabilization makes money endogenous and thus accommodates the fiscal expansion.

3 For a monetary expansion, conclusions were also opposite to those for fixed rates. A monetary expansion leads to an increase in income and to exchange depreciation. The tendency for interest rates to fall as a consequence of monetary expansion leads to a capital outflow that causes the exchange rate to depreciate and thereby to raise demand for domestic output.

4 In the case of a fiscal expansion, the induced appreciation of the

exchange rate leads to a reduction in net exports, offsetting the increased domestic spending. With a monetary expansion, the depreciation that ensues leads to an improvement in net exports. The trade balance effects of the two policies are thus quite different.

5 With imperfect capital mobility, interest rates can differ internationally and both monetary and fiscal policies can affect the level of output.

The fixed price assumption of this section cannot be expected to hold over long periods. We would not expect wages and prices to stay fixed if there was substantial unemployment or if demand increased when the economy was already at full employment. Therefore we have to expand the model of this section to incorporate the flexibility of prices as well as exchange rates. Still, as in earlier chapters, the analysis of the fixed price case will be needed in understanding the flexible price situation, to which we now turn.

19-2 EXCHANGE RATES, PRICES, AND OUTPUT ADJUSTMENT

In this section we take into account the implications of price flexibility. In particular, we study the effects of price level and exchange rate adjustments on the level of output and the interest rate. To do so, we will have to ask what factors cause the exchange rate and the price level to change.

In the short run, given the exchange rate and the price level, income and the interest rate continue to be determined by the interaction of the IS and LM curves, as shown in Figure 19-5. We also show in Figure 19-5 the BB curve along which the balance of payments balances in the short run. The BB curve is not horizontal, since we do not assume now that capital is instantaneously perfectly mobile. Rather, we assume that the rate of capital inflow increases when our interest rate rises and falls when our interest rate falls. However, we assume that in the long run, capital *is* perfectly mobile. Capital will flow out as long as our interest rate is below the world level and flow in as our interest rate is above the world level.

Point E in Figure 19-5 is a position of both short-run and long-run equilibrium. Because the IS and LM curves intersect at that point, we have short-run equilibrium. Because the interest rate is (by assumption) equal to the world level and output is at its potential level, it is also a point of long-run equilibrium, given that the IS, LM, and BB curves pass through that point.

There is one more characteristic of the long-run equilibrium that is not obvious from the diagram. At point E, we assume also that the current account is balanced and there are no net capital flows. The reason this condition is needed for full long-run equilibrium is that if there were capital flows, we would either be increasingly in debt to foreigners or becoming

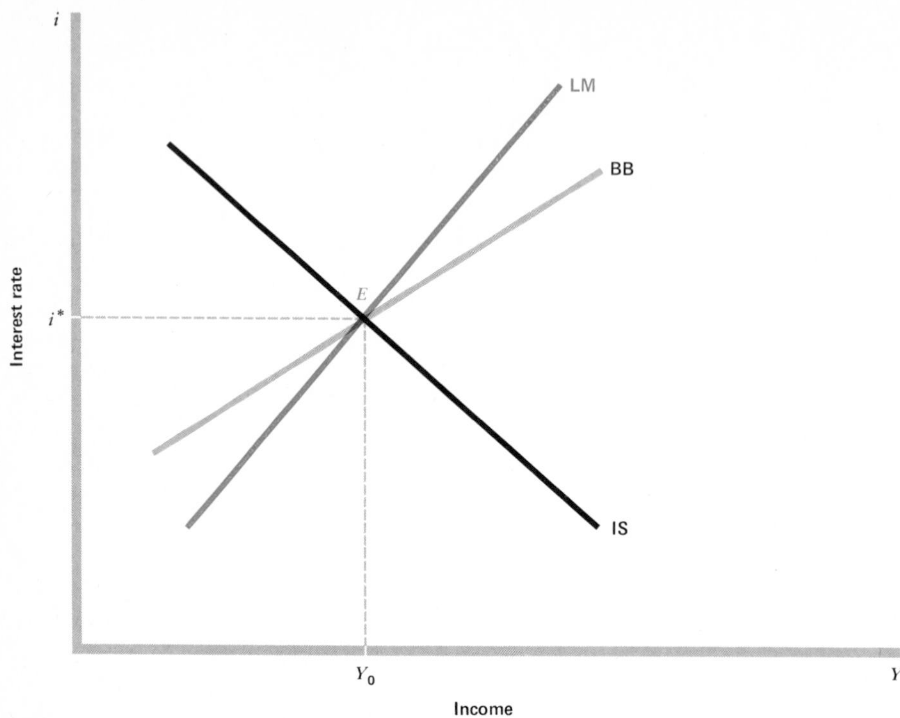

FIGURE 19-5 DETERMINATION OF EQUILIBRIUM, GIVEN THE PRICE LEVEL AND EXCHANGE RATE

increasingly wealthy by owning more and more foreign assets, and we could not then expect the economy to stay in equilibrium at E. If there was a capital inflow, we would effectively be borrowing from foreigners, becoming poorer over time and thus reducing our consumption. This cannot be a steady state. Similarly, if we were lending to foreigners, our consumption would be increasing over time and the economy would not stay at point E. Thus, in the long run, an economy that is not growing will be in steady state only if the current account balances.

Figure 19-5 shows how the short-run equilibrium of the economy is determined. But if we are not at full employment, and if the interest rate is not at the world level, the price level and the exchange rate will be changing. How? We make two particularly simple assumptions. First, we assume that prices rise when output is above potential and decline when output is below potential. Second, we assume that the exchange rate depreciates if the interest rate is below the world level and appreciates if the interest rate is above the world level.

These assumptions are shown in Figure 19-6. The direction of

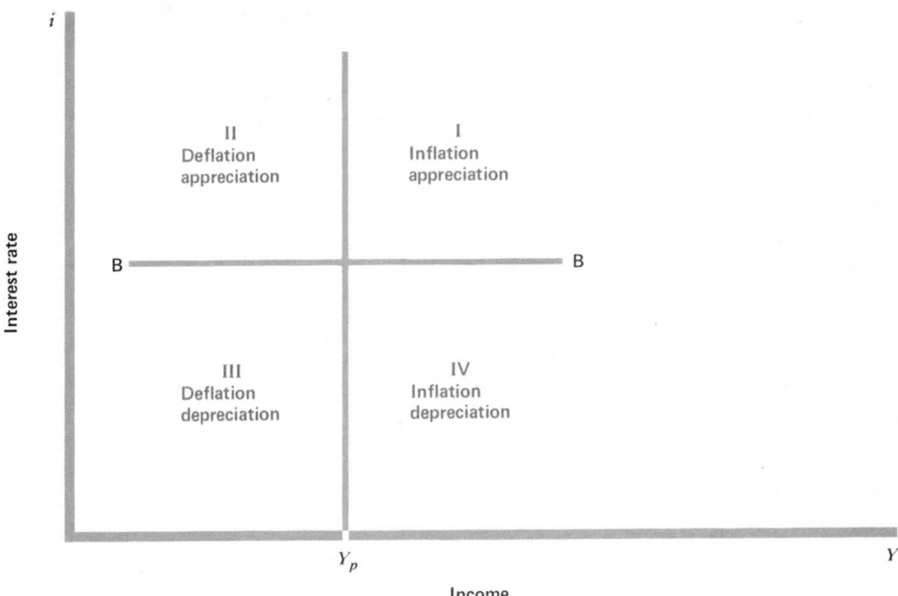

FIGURE 19-6 DYNAMIC ADJUSTMENT OF PRICES AND THE EXCHANGE RATE

movement of the exchange rate and the price level is shown for each of the four regions in the diagram.

The Adjustment Process

Consider, for example, region I, where we have interest rates above the world level and output above normal. The high interest rate would attract capital, leading to a balance of payments surplus and appreciation. The overemployment in turn leads to rising wages and prices. What adjustments would we expect from the movements in prices and exchange rates?

There are two channels through which changing prices and exchange rates affect interest rates and output. The first channel is the effect of changing prices on the real money stock. With nominal money given, the real money stock, M/P, depends on the price level. Falling prices imply a rising real money stock and rising prices imply a falling real money stock. A falling real money stock, of course, implies rising interest rates and thereby a contractionary effect on aggregate demand.

The second channel is that of relative prices or the terms of trade. Exchange appreciation lowers import prices and thus lowers the relative price of imports. Domestic inflation also raises our prices relative to those

TABLE 19-1 The Adjustment of Real Balances and Relative Prices

	Regions			
	I	II	III	IV
M/P	↓	↑	↑	↓
eP^*/P	↓	?	↑	?

of imports. Thus, both appreciation and inflation make us less competitive and therefore reduce the demand for domestic output.

In Table 19-1 we show the direction in which real balances and relative prices move in each of the regions of Figure 19-6. Thus, for example, in region I, inflation lowers the real value of the money stock, and inflation and appreciation both contribute to lowering the relative price of imports. Regions II and IV show a question mark for relative prices (the terms of trade). In region II, the appreciation lowers import prices, but at the same time we have domestic deflation. The movement of relative prices depends on the comparison of the rate at which the exchange rate appreciates and domestic prices fall and is thus ambiguous. We will introduce a further assumption below that will remove this ambiguity.

The next step is to go from the changes in real money balances and relative prices shown in Table 19-1 to the adjustments that they bring about in the goods and money markets. Our discussion uses Figure 19-7, which reproduces Figure 19-6 with a minor change. Consider first region I, with its inflation and appreciation and thus falling real balances and a falling relative price of imports. The inflation reduces the real money stock and thus raises interest rates. The falling relative price of imports implied by appreciation and inflation reduces the demand for domestic goods and thus, together with increasing interest rates, reduces output. Therefore, in region I we have rising interest rates and falling output, as indicated by the arrows. We leave it to you to demonstrate that exactly the opposite arguments apply in region III.

Consider next region II. We have already noted that with deflation we have rising real balances and therefore falling interest rates. There is an ambiguity, however, with respect to relative prices. With deflation and appreciation, both our prices and import prices are falling, and hence the behavior of relative prices, eP^*/P, depends on which one falls faster. We resolve that question by the plausible assumption that our prices fall faster, the larger the GNP gap (the further we are to the left of Y_p), and that the exchange rate appreciates faster, the higher our interest rate.

With this assumption in mind, we return to Figure 19-7 to study output adjustment in region II. With a large GNP gap, we have, as noted, very rapidly falling prices and therefore an improvement in competitiveness.

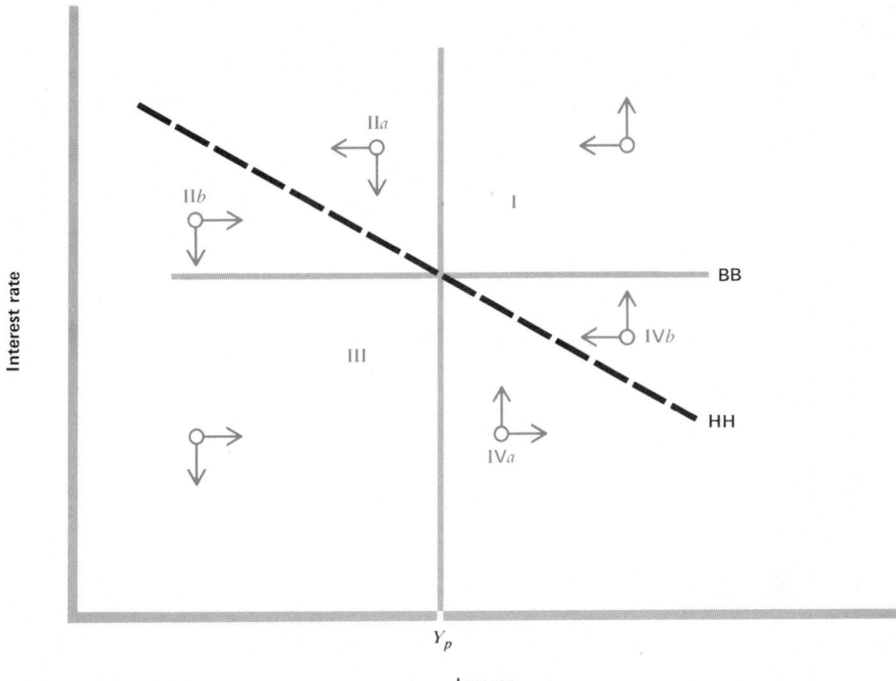

FIGURE 19-7 DYNAMIC ADJUSTMENT OF OUTPUT AND THE INTEREST RATE

The gain in competitiveness, together with falling interest rates, will increase demand and output. Region II*b* corresponds to this case. By contrast, when the GNP gap is quite small, as is the case in region II*a*, we are still losing competitiveness and the falling interest rates are not sufficient to raise demand, so that output is still falling. The broken line HH shows the borderline along which output remains constant by a continuing loss in competitiveness. Again we leave it to you to establish the symmetry of the argument for region IV and to provide the argument for the arrows we have drawn.

An Increase in Exports

We can now use our model to study the effects of an increase in exports. We will use the dynamic assumptions shown in Figure 19-7 to see how the adjustment process works.

Suppose that we start at point *E*, in Figure 19-8, in full equilibrium and that an increase in exports occurs. For a given price level and exchange rate, the LM schedule stays put and the IS curve shifts outward because of

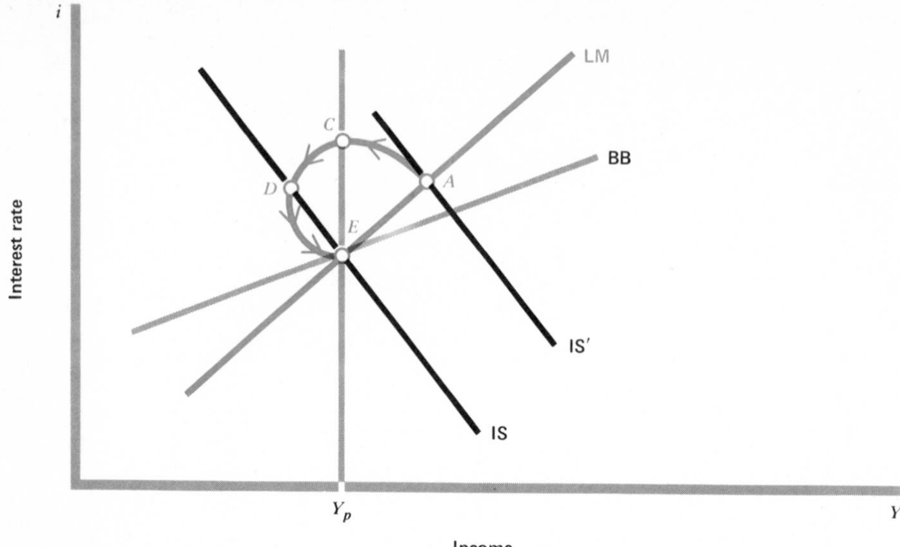

FIGURE 19-8 ADJUSTMENT TO AN INCREASE IN EXPORTS

the expansion in demand for our goods. We thus move to a point like A. At A the overemployment leads to inflation, reducing real balances and shifting the LM schedule up and to the left. The appreciation and inflation at A lower the relative price of imports, reducing demand, thus shifting the IS schedule down and to the left.

The successive intersections of the IS and LM schedules, as they shift in response to changes in relative prices and real money, are shown by the adjustment path from A to E. The arrows show the directions in which interest rates and output move.[6]

Starting from point A, with the interest rate rising and output falling, we come to full employment at point C at the border regions I and II. But at C the interest rate is above that compatible with external balance. Full employment implies constant prices and therefore constant real money, but the continuing appreciation keeps lowering the relative price of imports, thus reducing demand and lowering output. We therefore must move into region II. From here the process continues with falling interest rates and output that still declines beyond point C because appreciation runs ahead of domestic deflation. Only when output has fallen far enough and interest rates have declined sufficiently does the path of output turn around at point

[6] The path we have drawn is one plausible pattern of adjustment. The exact details of the dynamics, including the question of whether the adjustment is oscillatory, are not of interest here.

D, with a recovery accompanied by still falling interest rates. This phase takes us all the way to point *E*.

The adjustment process ends when we have returned to point *E* with the initial stock of real balances and thus the initial LM schedule, and when we are back with the initial IS schedule and an unchanged current account. The increase in autonomous exports has been offset by the effect of a lower relative price of imports that shifts demand away from domestic goods. The long-run effect of increased exports is thus to bring about an offsetting change in the terms of trade. Furthermore, that change is brought about entirely, in the long run, through an appreciation of the exchange rate.

A Monetary Disturbance

We complete the analysis of the adjustment process by studying a money supply increase. In the very short run, the effect of increased nominal money is to lower interest rates. The decline in interest rates and the induced depreciation serve to expand output immediately and thus, in terms of Figure 19-6, move us to region IV.[7] Inflation starts because of the overemployment, and depreciation continues because of the lowering of interest rates. Throughout, real balances are falling and the LM schedule is shifting back up toward its initial position. Output might initially expand further under the impact of depreciation, but soon the level of output has gone far above normal, so that inflation outstrips depreciation and demand starts declining. With declining demand and rising interest rates, the economy moves back to its initial equilibrium.

What is the long-run effect of the monetary expansion? In the long run, the economy returns to full employment and a monetary expansion has no lasting *real* effects. With prices fully flexible in the long run, a monetary expansion leads to an offsetting increase in prices, so that real balances ultimately remain unchanged.

But if prices rise, do we not lose competitiveness in that our goods become more expensive relative to foreign goods? In other words, would we not expect the terms of trade, eP^*/P, to improve as a result of the increase in P? Here the flexibility of exchange rates comes in. The exchange rate depreciates in precisely the same proportion as the price level rises, so that the terms of trade are unchanged and the competitive position of our goods relative to foreign goods is unaffected. Similarly, money and prices have changed in the same proportion, so that real balances, M/P, are unchanged. In the long run, then, *money is entirely neutral* and monetary changes are offset by internal inflation and external depreciation.

But note that in the process of adjustment, the monetary expansion does have real effects. During the process of adjustment, output is above

[7] You will find it easier to follow this discussion if you draw your own diagram like Fig. 19-8.

its full-employment level, the interest rate is below its equilibrium level, and the balance of payments is in deficit. These real effects of the monetary expansion are a consequence of the less than perfect flexibility of prices in the short run.

Purchasing Power Parity

The long-run neutrality of money discussed above illustrates the potential role of exchange rates in offsetting the effects of changes in the price level at home and abroad on the terms of trade. In the preceding analysis, the exchange rate rose by precisely the right amount to offset the effects of domestic inflation on the terms of trade. That is, the exchange depreciation maintained the *purchasing power* of our goods in terms of foreign goods between the initial and the final equilibrium positions.[8]

An important view of the determinants of the behavior of the exchange rate is the theory that exchange rates move primarily in response to differences in price level behavior between the two countries in such a way as to maintain the terms of trade constant. This is the *purchasing power parity* (PPP) theory. The theory argues that exchange rate movements primarily reflect divergent rates of inflation. Examining the terms of trade, eP^*/P, the theory maintains that when P^* and/or P change, e changes in such a way as to maintain eP^*/P constant.

PPP is a plausible description of the trend behavior of exchange rates, especially when inflation differentials between countries are large. In particular, we have seen that the PPP relationship does hold in the face of an increase in the money stock. If price level movements are caused by monetary changes—as they are likely to be if the inflation rate is high—then we should expect PPP relationships to hold in the long term.[9]

But qualifications are necessary. First, even a monetary disturbance affects the terms of trade in the short run. Exchange rates tend to move quite rapidly relative to prices and thus, in the short term of a quarter or a year, we should not be at all surprised to see substantial deviations of exchange rates from the rates implied by PPP. And indeed, the terms of trade do move in the short run, as we shall see in Section 19-3.

The second important qualification concerns the role of nonmonetary disturbances in affecting exchange rates. For example, we saw that an increase in exports improves our terms of trade or leads to currency appreciation at unchanged domestic prices. Or, if we look at an increase in potential output as another example, we will find that the equilibrium terms of trade worsen. To absorb the increased output, demand must rise, implying a decline in the relative price of our goods. Thus, it is apparent

[8] Of course, the terms of trade were not constant along the adjustment path.

[9] See "Purchasing Power Parity: A Symposium," *Journal of International Economics*, May 1978, for a review of the historical record on PPP.

that, over time, adjustments to *real* disturbances will affect the *equilibrium* terms of trade. Thus in the longer run, exchange rates and prices do *not* necessarily move together, as they do in a world where all disturbances are monetary. On the contrary, we may have important changes in relative prices. Such changes run counter to the purchasing power parity view of exchange rates.

As an empirical matter, then, PPP views of exchange rates will work well when, as frequently happens, monetary disturbances predominate. Thus PPP is an important explanation of some large exchange rate movements, particularly in hyperinflations. But not all exchange rate changes are caused by monetary disturbances, and PPP does not provide a good explanation for the short-run behavior of exchange rates.

Summary

In this section we allowed for price flexibility as well as exchange rate flexibility. We assumed that the price level increases when output is above the full-employment level and that the exchange rate appreciates when the interest rate is above the world level and there is therefore a capital inflow. The examination of real and monetary disturbances under flexible prices and exchange rates gave us the following results:

1 The price level and exchange rate adjustments affect the level of income and the interest rate. An increasing price level reduces real balances, tending to increase the interest rate. Changes in the price level and the exchange rate also affect the terms of trade and thus influence the demand for our goods.
2 An analysis of the dynamic process induced by these effects shows that the economy responds over time to disturbances, such as an increase in export demand or an increase in the money stock.
3 An increase in exports is ultimately totally offset in its effects on real income and the interest rate. However, both income and the interest rate differ from their long-run values during the adjustment process. The increase in exports leads in the long run to an appreciation of the exchange rate just sufficient to maintain net exports constant.
4 A monetary expansion in the long run increases the price level and the exchange rate, keeping real balances and the terms of trade constant. In the short run, though, the monetary expansion increases the level of output and reduces the interest rate, depreciating the exchange rate.
5 Purchasing power parity (PPP) theory argues that exchange rate changes are, in practice, caused by divergences in inflation rates between countries, with the exchange rate changing in a way that maintains the terms of trade constant. This theory is a good predictor of the behavior of the exchange rate over long periods when disturbances are caused mainly by monetary factors, such as in hyperinflations. But in the short

run, monetary disturbances are not neutral, and even in the long run, the exchange rate can change because there are real disturbances. Examples include changes in technology in different countries, shifts in export demand, and shifts in potential output.

We have now completed the core of this chapter. The remaining sections take up a number of issues that extend the basic analysis.

19-3 EXCHANGE RATE CONCEPTS

In this section we discuss two frequently used measures of exchange rates, the *effective exchange rate*, and the *real exchange rate*. These concepts are needed to provide a measure of exchange rate movements in a multiple currency world and to take account of the impact of inflation differentials on exchange rates respectively.

Effective Exchange Rates

The most conventional concept of an exchange rate is a *bilateral* exchange rate, such as the dollar price of yen or of Deutsche marks, or of sterling. In each case we talk about the dollar price of a particular foreigh currency, figures we can find in the daily press. If we looked at these rates over any period, we would find, for example, that the dollar had depreciated relative to the Deutsche mark, appreciated relative to the yen, and remained unchanged relative to sterling. How would we summarize such a situation by a simple statement about "the" exchange rate? The concept that has been developed to cope with this problem is the *effective exchange rate index*. This is an index for the dollar price of a "basket" of foreign currencies, each currency being given a particular weight, which we shall discuss. Table 19-2 gives an example of how effective rates are calculated.

In Table 19-2, we assume three foreign currencies: yen, (Y), Deutsche marks (DM), and pounds sterling (£). We assume that the weights attached to these currencies, respectively, are 0.3, 0.2, and 0.5, and thus sum to 1. Suppose now that our base year is 1970. In the base year we set the dollar price of each foreign currency equal to 100, and thus the index equals 100 ($= 0.3 \times 100 + 0.2 \times 100 + 0.5 \times 100$). Next consider the year 1980 where

TABLE 19-2 BILATERAL AND EFFECTIVE EXCHANGE RATE INDEXES: AN EXAMPLE

	Bilateral rates and indexes			Effective rate index
	Y	DM	£	
1970	\$0.0025 = 100	\$0.25 = 100	\$2.4 = 100	100
1980	\$0.0050 = 200	\$0.75 = 300	\$1.8 = 75	157.5

our hypothetical exchange rates have moved, with the dollar price of the yen rising by 100 percent and that of the Deutsche mark by 200 percent, while the dollar price of sterling has declined by 25 percent. In the second row, we show an index for each of the bilateral exchange rates (200, 300, 75) and the effective exchange rate as the weighted sum of these bilateral indexes. The effective exchange rate in our example has risen from the base year level of 100 to 157.5 ($= 0.3 \times 200 + 0.2 \times 300 + 0.5 \times 75$).

The effective exchange rate index thus serves as a summary measure of the "average" cost of foreign exchange where the nature of the average is determined by two considerations: First, the number of foreign currencies we choose in our basket and second, the weights given to each particular currency. In practice, the commonly used effective exchange rate indexes are based on a basket containing fifteen to twenty of the major currencies. The exact dividing line, as will become clear presently, is not really very important. The important issue is that of weights. We would want an effective exchange rate index to represent a relevant measure of the cost of foreign exchange. Accordingly, currencies of countries which are relatively unimportant in our external trade should receive a small weight and currencies of important trading partners should receive a more substantial weight. This perspective leads to a weighting system that uses bilateral trade flows as a basis. For example, if Canada accounts for 30 percent of our exports and imports, the Canadian dollar receives a weight of 0.3, while Germany is much less important in our trade and may receive a weight of only 0.1 or less.

An alternative weighting system uses *multilateral* trade weights as a basis. Here we assign to each country, as its weight, the share which that country has in world trade. This means, of course, that the large, industrialized countries account for most of the currency basket and that smaller countries are relatively unimportant in the effective exchange rate measure. The numbers which we report below are based on the multilateral trade weight basis.[10]

In Table 19-3, we show the effective exchange rate index for a number

[10] For the United States, the two series diverge quite substantially because Canada is an important bilateral trading partner but has only a small share in world trade.

TABLE 19-3 EFFECTIVE EXCHANGE RATE INDEXES (1970 = 100)

	United States	Canada	Germany	Japan	United Kingdom
1970	100.0	100.0	100.0	100.0	100.0
1973	121.5	97.8	83.8	81.2	114.3
1979	129.9	118.0	61.7	67.5	145.7

Source: International Monetary Fund, *International Financial Statistics.*

of countries. The table reveals that the U.S. dollar has undergone a substantial depreciation since 1970; the same is true for the pound sterling. The yen and the Deutsche mark, by contrast, have appreciated considerably relative to a trade-weighted basket of foreign currencies.[11]

Real Effective Exchange Rates

We have now found a simple summary measure of "the" exchange rate in the form of an effective exchange rate index. The next step is to find a corresponding simple measure of changes in competitiveness, that is, the costs of our goods *relative* to those produced by countries that compete with us in international trade. Such a measure must recognize two important facts: First, we are dealing with a multicountry situation and thus have to use an average measure that is representative of our position relative to our most important trading partners. Second, we must recognize that exchange rate movements do not signal one-for-one changes in competitiveness because they may merely be the counterpart of differing national price level trends. We saw this point in the discussion of purchasing power parity in Section 19-2.

The concept we are looking for is an effective price-adjusted exchange rate index. Such a measure would compare the domestic price of our goods with the "average" price of goods of our competitors measured in our currency. It thus corresponds to a many-country version of the relative price concept, or the terms of trade.

Price-adjusted or *real* effective exchange rates are constructed with the same weighting system as nominal effective rates. The novel point concerns the price adjustment, as we show in Table 19-4.

The first column of Table 19-4 shows the hypothetical development of the United States price level as measured by an index such as the CPI. Next, we look abroad. Here P^* shows the development of the foreign price level in foreign currency. Foreign prices in our example rise by 50 percent. The dollar price of foreign exchange, e, rises by 70 percent; thus, the index

[11] In official practice, effective exchange rates are quoted not as in Table 19-3 but rather as their reciprocal. This is just convention, much as driving on the opposite side of the road is a convention in some countries.

TABLE 19-4 REAL EXCHANGE RATE INDEX: AN EXAMPLE

	United States	Abroad			Real rate
	P	P^*	e	$eP^*/100$	eP^*/P
1970	100	100	100	100	100
1980	200	150	170	255	127.5

of the domestic currency price of foreign goods, $eP^*/100$, rises from 100 to 255, reflecting partially foreign infation and partially the depreciation of our currency. Now what happens to relative prices? The last column shows the ratio eP^*/P. From the base year level of 100, the relative price of foreign goods rises, since the index for 1980 is 127.5. The real rate index shows a gain in competitiveness by the home country.

Where does the gain in competitiveness in our example come from? It derives from the fact that the exchange depreciation of 70 percent exceeds the inflation differential of 50 percent. Thus the exchange depreciation *more than offsets* the inflation differential and leaves the home country with a gain in competitiveness.

We turn next from our hypothetical example to the actual evolution of real exchange rates. These rates are based on wholesale or producer price indexes.[12] Table 19-5 shows a gain in competitiveness of nearly 20 percent for the United States. By contrast, Germany and Japan show a loss in competitiveness since 1970, while for the United Kingdom, a transitory gain in competitiveness from 1970 to 1973 was wiped out by 1977.

Compare, now, the real exchange rate indexes in Table 19-5 with the behavior of nominal rates in Table 19-3. For the United States and Canada, we have a depreciation of the nominal rate and a gain in competitiveness. For Germany and Japan, the opposite is true. For Britain, finally, there is nominal depreciation and a loss in competitiveness between 1973 and 1978.

In Chart 19-2, we look in more detail at the United States real effective exchange rate over the period since the 1960s. We note that during the fixed rate period, with inflation rates rather close together, the real effective rate index moved very little. Until 1965, the nation gained slightly in competitiveness and then lost somewhat in the second half of the 1960s. The big change came with the large nominal depreciation of the dollar in the early seventies. The chart shows a corresponding change in the real exchange rate and accordingly a gain in United States competitiveness. That gain has been roughly maintained since then.

[12] The International Monetary Fund reports monthly a variety of real exchange rate series using GNP deflators, wholesale prices, and wages for the price adjustment. The series are published in *International Financial Statistics.*

TABLE 19-5 REAL EFFECTIVE EXCHANGE RATE INDEXES (1970 = 100)

	United States	Canada	Germany	Japan	United Kingdom
1970	100.0	100.0	100.0	100.0	100.0
1973	120.7	99.5	87.5	90.0	111.6
1979	120.1	112.5	85.1	92.5	91.2

Source: International Monetary Fund, *International Financial Statistics.*

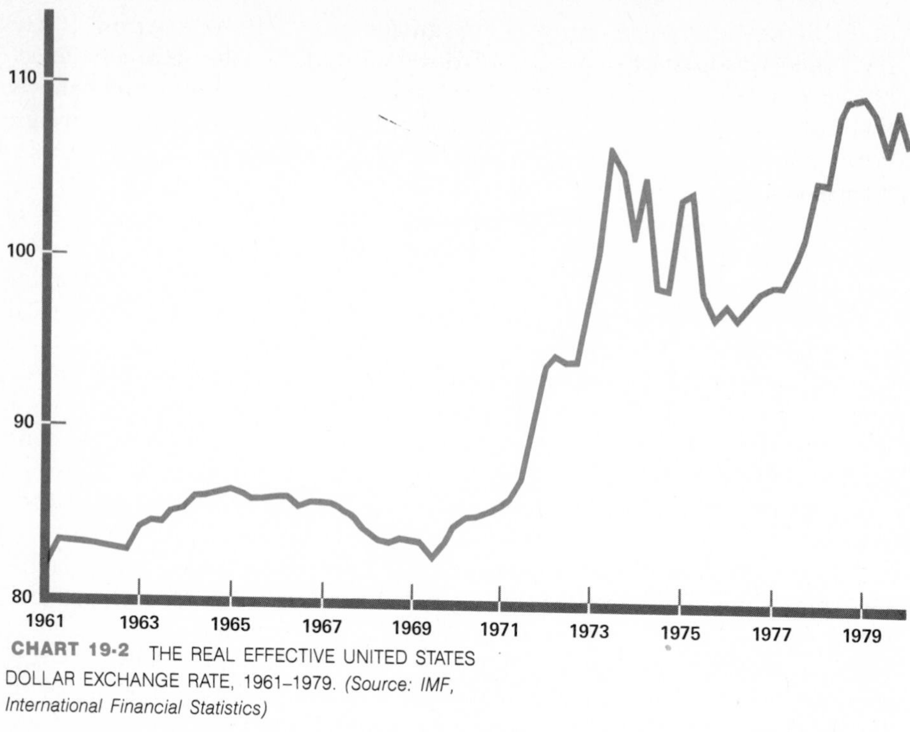

CHART 19-2 THE REAL EFFECTIVE UNITED STATES DOLLAR EXCHANGE RATE, 1961–1979. *(Source: IMF, International Financial Statistics)*

The real depreciation of the dollar shown in Chart 19-2 of course has an effect on trade flows and macroeconomic equilibrium. Given income in the United States and abroad and some adjustment time, the change in relative price shifts demand toward United States goods and away from goods produced by competitors. This shift in demand in turn implies an improvement in the United States current account or a reduction in the deficit that would otherwise occur.

Chart 19-2 is of interest also with respect to our discussion of purchasing power parity. The chart shows both long-term changes in real exchange rates, such as the change from 1969 to 1973, and considerable short-term variation in real exchange rates. On neither count is the purchasing power parity relationship strong.

19-4 INTEREST DIFFERENTIALS AND EXCHANGE RATE EXPECTATIONS

A cornerstone of our theoretical model of exchange rate determination in Sections 19-1 and 19-2 was international capital mobility. In particular, we argued that with capital markets sufficiently integrated, we would expect interest rates to be equated across countries. How does this assumption stand up to the facts? In Chart 19-3, we show the United States interest rates on certificates of deposit (CDs) and an average of interest rates in major industrialized countries.[13] It is quite apparent from the chart that these rates are certainly not equalized. Thus, in early 1979, the interest differential ranged between two and four percentage points. How do we square these facts with our theory?

Exchange Rate Expectations

Our theoretical analysis in Sections 19-1 and 19-2 was based on the assumption that capital flows internationally in response to nominal interest differentials. For example, if domestic interest rates were 10 percent and foreign rates 6 percent, we would, according to the earlier sections, expect a capital inflow.

However, such a theory is incomplete in a world where exchange rates

[13] Recall from Chap. 7 that CDs are interest bearing, short-term negotiable liabilities of banks.

CHART 19-3 THE INTEREST RATE ON UNITED STATES CERTIFICATES OF DEPOSIT AND FOREIGN INTEREST RATES. *(Source: Board of Governors of the Federal Reserve, Selected Interest Rates and Exchange Rates)*

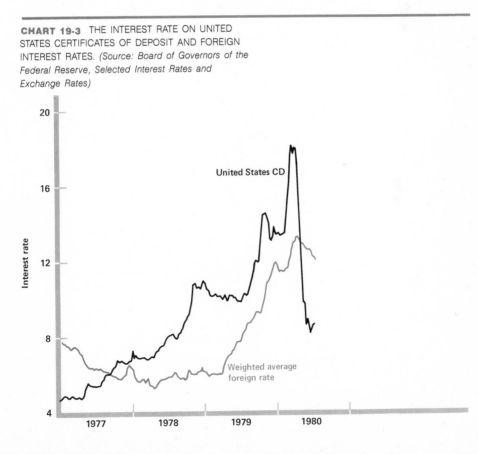

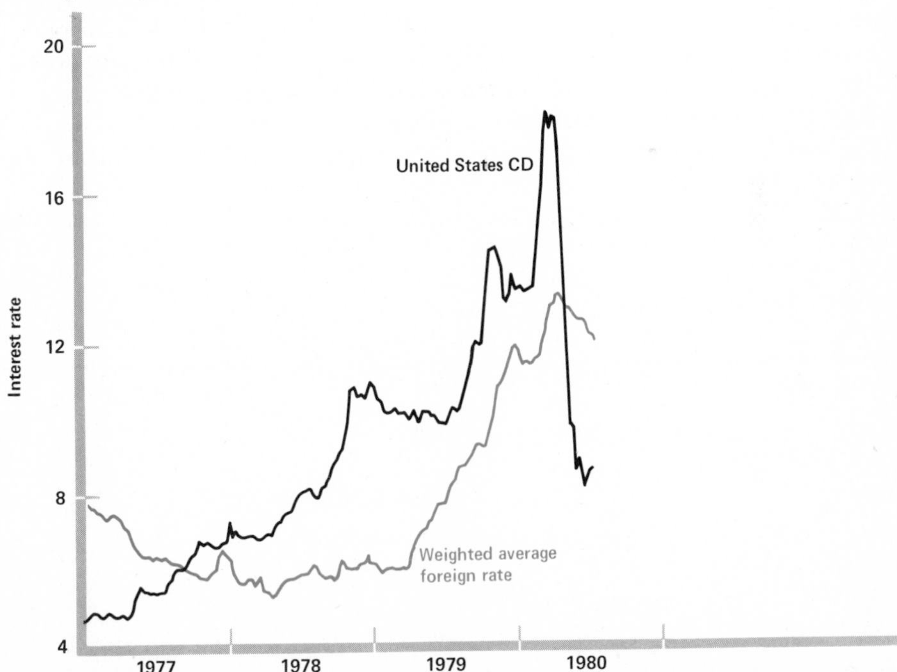

can, do, and are expected to, change. For example, consider a situation where the Deutsche mark is expected to appreciate by 5 percent over the next year relative to the dollar. Suppose the interest rate in Germany is 6 percent. Then anyone buying German bonds will earn a return in Deutsche marks of 6 percent. Suppose now that the United States interest rate is 10 percent. A German investing in the United States for a year will, at the beginning of the year, exchange his Deutsche marks for dollars, and then earn 10 percent on his dollars. At the end of the year, he will want to change his dollars back into Deutsche marks to spend in Germany. But he expects that by the end of the year, each dollar will be worth 5 percent less in terms of Deutsche marks, as a result of the expected depreciation. Therefore, in terms of marks, he will expect to earn only 5 percent (10 percent minus 5 percent) by investing in American bonds, whereas he earns 6 percent by investing in German bonds. He will naturally prefer to invest in German bonds.[14]

It is clear, therefore, that we must extend our discussion of interest rate equalization to incorporate expectations of exchange rate changes. Table 19-6 gives some combinations of the domestic interest rate, i, the foreign interest rate, i^*, and exchange rate changes $\Delta e/e$. Suppose we want to know the return, in terms of domestic currency, of investments here compared with those abroad. For domestic investments we just look at the interest rate, i. For foreign investments, we look at the interest rate, i^*, *and* at the exchange depreciation. Suppose foreign interest rates were 5 percent and exchange rates did not change. This is the case of row 1, and the *adjusted* interest differential ($i - i^* - \Delta e/e$) is 5 percent in favor of the home country. Row 2 considers the case where interest rates abroad are high (15 percent), but where our currency appreciates at the rate of 5 percent or the foreign currency depreciates by that amount. Here the depreciation exactly offsets the higher foreign interest rates and the

[14] You should confirm that an American who expects the dollar to depreciate by 5 percent would, given the 6 percent and 10 percent interest rates, also prefer to buy German bonds.

TABLE 19-6 INTEREST RATES AND EXCHANGE DEPRECIATION *(in percentages)*

	Domestic interest rate, i	Foreign interest rate, i^*	Depreciation, $\Delta e/e$	Adjusted interest differential, $i - i^* - \Delta e/e$
1.	10	5	0	5
2.	10	15	−5	0
3.	10	15	−2	−3
4.	10	15	−10	5

adjusted differential is zero—what would be gained in interest is lost through the foreign depreciation. Cases 3 and 4 show circumstances where the foreign depreciation falls short of, and exceeds, the interest differential, respectively. Clearly, in cases 1 and 4, we would want to invest in the home country; in case 2 we are indifferent; and case 3 favors the foreign country.

The trouble, of course, is that we do not know ahead of time how the exchange rate will move. We know the interest rates on, say, 3-month Treasury bills in the United States and the United Kingdom, so that we can compute the interest differential, but we do not know whether the pound will appreciate or depreciate over the next 3 months. Even if we somehow knew the direction, we would certainly not know the precise amount.

Investors then have to form *expectations* about the behavior of the exchange rate; that is, in deciding whether to invest at home or abroad, they have to make forecasts of the future behavior of the exchange rate. Given these forecasts, we would expect that in a world of high capital mobility, the interest differentials, adjusted for expected depreciation, should be negligible. That means that, a country that is certain to depreciate will have interest rates above the world level, and conversely, a country that is expected to appreciate will have interest rates below the world level. On this argument, Chart 19-3 would reflect the expectation of a depreciation of the dollar relative to other currencies, as indeed happened in 1978-1979.

The adjustment for exchange rate expectations thus accounts for international differences in interest rates. These differences are by and large due to differences in inflation rates and are reflected in trend movements of the exchange rate. High-inflation countries have high interest rates and depreciating currencies. We thus have an international extension of the Fisher effect discussed in Chapter 13. The international extension relies on PPP to argue that inflation differentials internationally are matched by depreciation. Our long-term relation then is

$$\text{Inflation differential} \simeq \text{interest differential} \simeq \text{depreciation rate}$$

The relation is only approximate because, as we have seen, exchange rates can move independently of prices and also because obstacles to capital flows may create long-term interest differentials.

There is another respect in which the introduction of exchange rate expectations is important and that concerns speculative capital flows and their impact on macroeconomic equilibrium. The point is easily made with the help of Figure 19-9. Here the BB schedule is drawn for a given foreign interest rate *and* a given expected rate of change for the exchange rate, say zero for simplicity. Suppose that we start in full equilibrium at point E and that the market develops the expectation that the home currency will appreciate. This implies that even with a lower home interest rate, domestic assets are attractive and so the BB schedule shifts down by the

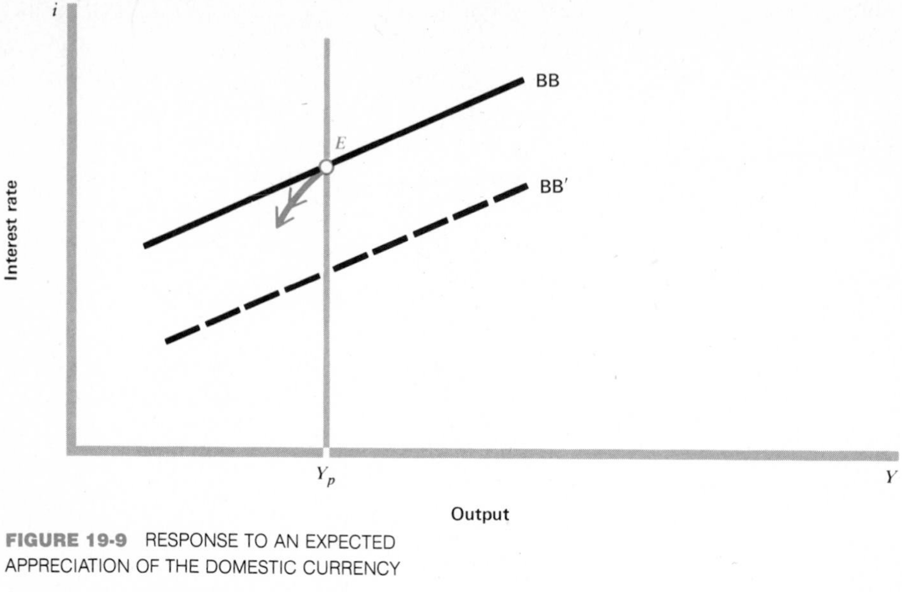

FIGURE 19-9 RESPONSE TO AN EXPECTED APPRECIATION OF THE DOMESTIC CURRENCY

amount of expected appreciation. Clearly, point *E* is no longer an equilibrium, given the shift of the BB schedule to BB′, but rather a position of surplus with large-scale capital inflows motivated by the anticipation of appreciation. (This might well describe the case of the United Kingdom after awareness of British oil discoveries spread in the market.) The surplus causes the exchange rate to start appreciating, and we move in a southwesterly direction, as indicated by the arrow. The speculative attack causes appreciation, a loss in competitiveness, and consequently, falling output and employment.

This analysis shows that exchange rate expectations, through their impact on capital flows and thus on actual exchange rates, are a potential source of disturbance to macroeconomic equilibrium.

*19-5 EXCHANGE RATE CHANGES AND TRADE ADJUSTMENT: TWO EMPIRICAL ISSUES

In this section we complete our analysis by taking up two important empirical issues related to the scope for current account adjustment through exchange rate changes. In our theoretical model of Section 19-1, we assumed that prices here and abroad were fixed, so that exchange rate changes affected relative prices one for one. In Section 19-2, by contrast, we explored a world where prices (and wages) are flexible and full employment is maintained in the long run. In this section, we consider the alternative possibility that wages and prices are flexible but that they may respond to movements in the exchange rate in a way that makes it impossible or at least difficult to change relative prices through exchange rate changes. This issue is particularly important if formal wage indexation arrangements link wage behavior to import prices and thus to the exchange rate.

The second issue we consider is whether changes in relative prices, assuming that they are possible, will affect the current account in the direction we have so far assumed. The assumption, so far, has been that a decline in the relative price of our goods improves the current account. But the possibility arises that at least in the short run there might be a perverse reaction. With import prices rising, for example, import demand may not decline sufficiently to compensate for higher prices, and thus total import spending (price times quantity) may actually increase. We turn now to these two issues.

Exchange Rates and Relative Price Adjustment

In studying the flexible wage-price model of Section 19-2, we assumed that wages and prices adjust to achieve full employment. Now we consider as an alternative the possibility that prices are based on labor cost or wages and that wages are inflexible in real terms. Suppose that labor wants to maintain the purchasing power of wages or to keep real wages constant. In such a world, changes in the cost of living would lead to changes in money wages, in labor cost, and therefore in prices, which in turn feed back into wages. Two points emerge from this description. The first is that in such a world, we may not be able to get to full employment. Labor may set the real wage too high and, at least in the intermediate run, the full-employment level of output cannot be sustained. The second point is that a process in which changes in prices feed back into wages and from there into prices is one of a *wage-price spiral* that may produce considerable volatility in the price level. Small disturbances can set off quite large changes in the price level.

Suppose, first, that the real wage is fixed in terms of the consumer price index that includes both domestic goods and imports. Let us assume, second, that changes in the consumer price index are fully passed on into wages, and, third, that changes in wages are fully passed on into increased domestic prices. Now assume that starting from an initial equilibrium, there is an exchange depreciation brought about by some short-term, reversible disturbance. The depreciation raises import prices and thereby has a direct effect on consumer prices and wages. To maintain the purchasing power of their wages, workers increase money wages and firms pass on the wage increase into higher prices. Where are we after the process ends? Real wages are constant, which means wages and the price level (a weighted average of the prices of domestic and imported goods) have risen in the same proportion; wage increases have been fully passed on, which means that real wages *in terms of domestic output* are also unchanged. The two results imply that relative prices are unchanged, or that the exchange depreciation is fully matched by domestic inflation.

Of course, this is not really the end because we have to ask how the higher price level affects the macroeconomic equilibrium. To the extent that lower real balances lower aggregate demand, we would have a reduction in employment. To round out our story, we can imagine that the central bank steps in to prevent unemployment by raising the money stock. If nominal money rises in proportion to the price increase, then the full-employment equilibrium, at the same terms of trade, is reestablished but, of course, at a higher level of wages and prices. This is an economy where there is very little stability in the price level because the slightest change in exchange rate expectations leads to actual exchange rate movements that are fully *validated* by domestic wage, price, and monetary developments.

A second context in which the idea of sticky real wages is important is that of real disturbances. Suppose our export demand declines permanently because of, say, the introduction of superior technology abroad. To return to full employment, we saw in Section 19-2 that the relative price of our goods must fall so as to encourage foreign demand. But how can the relative price fall? In Section 19-2, we argued that the exchange rate will depreciate, thereby raising import prices relative to domestic prices and restoring our competitiveness. In the present context we have to recognize that import price increases would be immediately matched by wage increases and that these wage increases would be fully passed on into price increases. Relative prices cannot change. The consequence would, of course, be protracted unemployment. Unemployment would continue until the *real* wage declines.

The empirical question, then, is, How flexible are real wages? This is, to an important extent, a question of institutional arrangements. In small open economies with substantial cost-of-living indexation in wage agreements, it may indeed be very difficult to change real wages and relative prices through exchange rate changes.

Relative Prices and the Trade Balance: The J Curve

We come now to the second issue, the effect of changes in relative prices on the trade balance and the possibility that a depreciation worsens the trade balance. To make this point, we write out the trade balance, measured in terms of domestic goods, as

$$NX = X - \frac{eP^*}{P} \cdot Q \tag{6}$$

where X denotes the foreign demand for our goods or exports and Q denotes our own import quantity. The term $(eP^*/P)Q$ thus measures the *value* of our imports in terms of domestic goods.

Suppose that we now have an exchange depreciation and that in the first instance, domestic and foreign prices, P and P^*, are unchanged. Then the relative price of imports, eP^*/P, rises. This leads to two effects. First, if the physical *volume* of imports does not change, their value measured in domestic currency unambiguously increases because of the higher price. With unchanged physical import volume, Q, higher prices mean increased import spending and thus a worsening of the trade balance. This is the source for the potentially perverse response of the trade balance to exchange depreciation. However, there is an adjustment that runs in the opposite direction. The increased relative price of imports makes us more competitive and shifts demand in volume terms toward domestic goods. This *volume effect* of substitution in response to changed relative prices shows up in Equation (6) in the form of increased export volume, X, and reduced import volume, Q. The volume effects thus unambiguously improve the trade balance.

The question, then, is whether the volume effects on imports and exports are sufficiently strong to outweigh the price effect, that is, whether depreciation raises or lowers net exports. The empirical evidence on this question is quite strong and shows the following result: The short-term volume effects, say within a year, are quite small and thus do not outweigh the price effect.[15] The long-term volume effects, by contrast, are quite substantial, and certainly enough to make the trade balance respond in the normal fashion to a relative price change.

Where does this asymmetry come from and what does it imply about trade adjustment to relative prices? First, the low short-term and high longer-term volume effects result from the time consumers and producers take to adjust to changes in relative prices. Some of these adjustments may be instantaneous, but it is clear that tourism patterns, for example, may take 6 months to a year to adjust and that relocation of production internationally, in response to changes in relative costs and prices, may

[15] See Michael C. Deppler and Duncan M. Ripley, "The World Trade Model: Merchandise Trade," *IMF Staff Papers*, March 1978.

take years. A case in point is increased foreign direct investment in the United States—say, Volkswagen moving from Germany to Pennsylvania. In the long term, such direct investment leads to reduced Volkswagen imports by the United States, and thus to an improved trade balance, but such an adjustment takes years, not weeks or months.

The lag in the adjustment of trade flows to changes in relative prices is thus quite plausible. The next question is, What do these lags imply about the impact of relative price changes on the trade balance? Suppose that at a particular time, starting with a deficit, we have a depreciation that raises the relative price of imports. The short-term effects results primarily from increased import prices with very little offsetting volume effects. Therefore, the trade balance initially worsens. Over time, as trade volume adjusts to the changed relative prices, exports rise and import volume progressively declines. The volume effects come to dominate, and in the long run, the trade balance shows an improvement. This pattern of adjustment is referred to as the *J-curve effect*, because diagrammatically the response of the trade balance looks like a *J*.

The medium-term problem of sticky real wages and the J-curve effect are important qualifications to the macroeconomics of flexible rates as spelled out in Sections 19-1 and 19-2. They imply that flexible exchange rates do not provide for instant, costless flexibility of relative prices and trade flows. At the same time, these considerations provide important clues for the interpretation of macroeconomic experiences across countries, particularly in showing why depreciations typically do not lead to improvements in the current account in the short term.

19-6 EXCHANGE RATE FLUCTUATIONS

We asked at the start of the chapter why exchange rates have fluctuated so much in the period since 1973, why central banks have intervened to affect exchange rates, and whether such dirty floating is desirable. The material covered in the preceding sections helps provide answers to these questions.

Before we briefly examine the volatility of exchange rates since the flexible rate system emerged, we should warn you that the discerning eye appears to detect cycles where statistical techniques cannot. It is difficult to establish, from the short experience we have had with flexible rates, that exchange rates under a flexible rate system will indeed cycle in the future. All we can say is that in the past few years, exchange rates have made large movements that were subsequently reversed.

The trend changes in exchange rates observed in Table 19-3 can be largely attributed to divergent inflation rates among the United States and other countries. In addition, as Table 19-5 shows, there have been changes in real exchange rates, which probably result from divergent productivity trends in the United States and other countries. However, there remains the big issue of short-term fluctuations.

We showed in Section 19-4 that the mere expectation of a change in exchange rates can lead to an actual change. Some of the movements in rates seen in Chart 19-1 result from expectations of exchange rate changes that reversed themselves. Such reversals are not necessarily a sign that the original expectations were unreasonable. For instance, it appeared during 1978 that the United States wanted the dollar to continue depreciating against other major currencies, particularly the yen and the Deutsch mark. Then, in November 1978, after substantial depreciation had taken place, the United States announced a package of measures designed to reverse the depreciation. The dollar exchange rate actually appreciated in response. Clearly, the new policy reversed expectations about the behavior of the dollar exchange rate—but that reversal was fully justified by the new information the change in policy provided.

Central banks intervene to affect exchange rates for several reasons. Probably the main reason is the belief that many capital flows merely represent unstable expectations, and that the induced movements in exchange rates move production in the economy in an unnecessarily erratic fashion. The second reason for the intervention is a central bank's attempt to move the real exchange rate in order to affect trade flows. The third reason arises from the effects of the exchange rate on domestic inflation, which we mentioned in Section 19-4. Central banks sometimes intervene in the exchange market to prevent the exchange rate from depreciating, with the aim of preventing a depreciation-induced increase in the inflation rate.

Should central banks intervene in the exchange market? The basic argument for such intevention is that it is possible for intervention to smooth out fluctuations in exchange rates. At one extreme, the argument would assert that any movements in exchange rates produce unnecessary fluctuations in the domestic economy and that exchange rates therefore ought to be fixed. This is the basic argument for dirty floating. The only—and overwhelming—objection to the argument that the central bank should smooth out fluctuations is that there is no simple way of telling an erratic movement from a trend movement. How can we tell whether a current appreciation in the exchange rate is merely the result of a disturbance which will soon reverse itself, rather than the beginning of a trend movement in the exchange rate? There is no way of telling at the time a change occurs, although with the benefit of hindsight, one can easily look at diagrams like Chart 19-1 to see which exchange rate movements were later reversed.

There is one circumstance under which central bank intervention might be desirable. It is clear from our earlier analysis that one of the key determinants of exchange rate behavior consists of expectations of economic policy. It may sometimes be possible to make it clear that there has been a change in policy only by intervening in the foreign exchange market. This is a case of putting your money where your mouth is.

19-7 SUMMARY

1 Under flexible exchange rates, without government intervention, the exchange rate adjusts to ensure equilibrium in the overall balance of payments. The sum of the current and capital account deficits is zero with floating rates and no intervention.
2 The demand for our goods depends on the exchange rate which, given foreign and domestic prices, affects the relative price of imports versus exports. An increase in the exchange rate—a depreciation—increases the demand for domestically produced goods by reducing imports and increasing exports.
3 When capital is very mobile, so that the interest rate essentially cannot differ from the world rate, fiscal policy becomes totally ineffective in changing the level of income. An increase in government spending merely reduces net exports, with the trade deficit being financed by a capital inflow.
4 Monetary policy—given prices—retains its effectiveness when capital is very mobile. An increase in the money stock leads to a depreciation of the exchange rate and an improved foreign balance, which increases demand for domestic output.
5 If an economy finds itself with unemployment, the central bank can intervene to depreciate the exchange rate and increase net exports and thus aggregate demand. Such policies are known as beggar-thy-neighbor policies, because the increase in demand for domestic output comes at the expense of demand for foreign output.
6 In the long run, exchange rate movements in the absence of real disturbances reflect changes in the price levels in the two countries concerned. A country with a more rapid rate of inflation will find its exchange rate depreciating against the currency of a country which is inflating less rapidly. The exchange rate movements induced by the price level changes merely keep the relative prices of goods produced in the two countries constant.
7 The effective exchange rate is an index of the domestic currency price of foreign exchange. The weights of the different currencies in the basket reflect their relative importance in trade.
8 Real effective exchange rates are an index of competitiveness. The real effective exchange rate index measures the extent to which the prices of foreign goods, adjusted for exchange rate changes, move relative to the prices of our goods.
9 Exchange rate expectations introduce divergences among nominal interest rates internationally. The international interest differential

equals the anticipated rate of depreciation when capital is highly mobile. A country that is expected to have a depreciating currency will have higher nominal interest rates than the rest of the world.

10 A currency depreciation can, in the short run, lead to a worsening of the trade balance. This occurs when the effect of changes in relative prices on the volume of trade is small because adjustments take time. Over time, trade adjusts and the depreciation improves the trade balance. This is called the J-curve effect.

11 Because it raises important prices, depreciation of the exchange rate raises the cost of living and may spill over into increased wage demands. If such spillovers are substantial, then a flexible rate system will have large movements in nominal prices and exchange rate movements may perform poorly in bringing about relative price changes.

12 Since the 1973 beginning of the flexible rate system, there have been substantial fluctuations in exchange rates. These movements are hard to explain. They affect the allocation of resources. A central bank which wants to intervene to smooth out the fluctuations has to know when an exchange rate change is going to be reversed and when it is permanent. For this reason, foreign exchange intervention to smooth out exchange rate fluctuations is extremely difficult.

PROBLEMS

1 Explain why the belief that a devaluation is imminent makes a devaluation more likely in a fixed exchange rate system.

2 Why do you think countries were reluctant to move away from the system of fixed exchange rates during the late sixties and early seventies, even though it was by then not operating very well? Also explain what "not operating very well" means.

3 Explain why an expansionary fiscal policy "beggars our neighbors" less than direct intervention by the central bank in the foreign exchange markets to depreciate the exchange rate.

4 Assuming there are no capital flows, explain how an increase in the domestic interest rate (which we have assumed fixed, so far) affects the level of income and the exchange rate. How could the domestic interest rate be changed?

5 *(a)* What are the terms of trade?
(b) Why does expansionary policy affect the terms of trade in a floating exchange rate system?

6 Assume that capital is perfectly mobile, the price level is fixed, and the exchange rate is flexible. Now let the government increase purchases. Explain first why the equilibrium levels of output and the interest rate are unaffected. Then show whether the current account improves or worsens as a result of the increased government purchases of goods and services.

7 Assume that there is perfect mobility of capital. How does the imposition of a tariff affect the exchange rate, output, and the current account? (*Hint:* Given the exchange rate, the tariff reduces our demand for imports.)

8 Explain how and why monetary policy retains its effectiveness when there is perfect mobility of capital.

9 Consult the *Wall Street Journal* or some other newspaper which has foreign exchange rates listed on its financial pages. For some countries, such as Britain and Germany, you should find future prices listed. This is the price to be paid today to receive one unit of the foreign currency in the future. A 30-day future price for the pound sterling, say, is the price paid today to receive £1 30 days from now. Explain why the future prices are not generally equal to the spot prices—the price paid today to receive the foreign currency today. See whether you can explain the difference between the relationship of spot and future prices for the pound and Deutsche mark, respectively.

10 Assume you expect the pound to depreciate by 6 percent over the next year. Assume that the United States interest rate is 4 percent. What interest rate would be needed on pound securities—such as government bonds—for you to be willing to buy those securities with your dollars today, and then sell them in a year in exchange for dollars? Can you relate your answer to this question to your answer to problem 9?

11 What considerations are relevant for a country deciding whether to borrow abroad to finance a balance of trade deficit, or to adjust?

12 Explain the purchasing-power-parity theory of the long-run behavior of the exchange rate. Indicate whether there are any circumstances under which you would not expect the PPP relationship to hold.

13 This problem deals with the current account effect of an expansion in the money stock, given prices, perfect capital mobility, and flexible exchange rates.

(*a*) Given the interest rate, i^*, the real money stock, M/P, and the money market equilibrium condition

$$\frac{M}{P} = kY - hi$$

solve for the equilibrium level of income, Y_0, that is compatible with monetary equilibrium.

(*b*) Consider next the goods market equilibrium condition:

$$Y = A(Y, i) + NX$$

Let $A = \overline{A} + cY - bi$. Substitute for $i = i^*$ and the equilibrium level of income from 13(*a*). What is the equilibrium value of the trade balance, NX?

14 Suppose capital is imperfectly mobile, so that the higher the interest rate at home, the higher the rate of capital inflow, but that the flows remain finite. Then we can write the balance of payments as

$$BoP = NX\left(\frac{eP^*}{P}, Y\right) + K(i, i^*)$$

where K denotes the net rate of capital inflow and i^* is the given foreign interest rate.

(*a*) Suppose the exchange rate adjusts to maintain payments equilibrium. Then $BoP = 0$ and the current account surplus equals the capital account deficit:

$$NX\left(\frac{eP^*}{P}, Y\right) = -K(i,i^*)$$

Suppose the goods market is *also* in equilibrium so that

$$Y = A(i,Y) + NX\left(\frac{eP^*}{P}, Y\right)$$

Substituting for the current account in the goods market equilibrium condition yields

$$Y = A(i,Y) - K(i,i^*)$$

Show this equation graphically in i,Y space and interpret it.

(*b*) Also draw an LM schedule in the same space and interpret the intersection point.

(*c*) Show now the effect of a fiscal expansion in the home country on interest rates, income, and the current account.

(*d*) Show the effect of a monetary expansion on income, interest rates, and the current account.

(*e*) What can you say about the exchange rate in cases 13(*b*) and (*c*)?

15 Suppose in year 1 we have price levels $P = 100$ and $P^* = 100$. Suppose next that in year 2 the respective price levels are $P_2 = 180$ and $P_2^* = 130$. Let the exchange rate initially be $2/£.

(*a*) If there were no real disturbances between year 1 and year 2, what would be the equilibrium exchange rate in year 2?

(*b*) If the terms of trade eP^*/P had deteriorated between year 1 and 2 by 50 percent, what would the exchange rate be in year 2?

16 This problem draws on the discussion of stabilization policy and beggar-thy-neighbor policy in Section 19-1. Suppose we have two countries with full-employment output levels of Y_p and Y_p^* at home and abroad, respectively.

(*a*) Draw a diagram with actual output levels, Y and Y^*, on the axes. Draw also lines corresponding to potential output levels. Label the resulting four quadrants I, II, III, and IV.

(*b*) Identify for each of the quadrants the state of demand in each country as boom or recession.

(*c*) Which policies can be pursued when output exceeds potential in each country? When output exceeds potential in one but falls short of potential in another?

(*d*) In which quadrants are beggar-thy-neighbor policies particularly dangerous? Where is coordination of policies essential?

INDEX

INDEX